Front Cover: "Virūpa Arresting the Sun," Tibet, first half of the thirteenth century; ink, opaque watercolor, and gold on cloth.

The mahāsiddha Virūpa is the seventh-century progenitor of the Path with Its Result (*lam-dre*) teachings, on which *The Three Levels of Spiritual Perception*, Deshung Rinpoche's commentary on *The Three Visions*, is based. He is shown here in the famous episode where he arrested the movement of the sun in the sky after being granted drinking privileges until noon at a tavern. Previously an abbot of royal birth at Nālandā University, the greatest seat of learning in India at the time, he resigned after beginning to act in an extremely unconventional manner. Actually, he had achieved the highest attainments in tantric meditation, and his acts were an expression of his pure vision. Removing his monk's robes, he donned a flower garland and roamed India as a "mad" yogi; the tales of his enlightened exploits are many. Surrounding the main scene are vignettes depicting the other eighty-three of the Eighty-Four Mahāsiddhas. The inscription on the verso of the painting includes the Buddhist creed of interdependent origination and a historic statement that the tangka was consecrated by the great Tibetan sage Sakya Pandita (1182–1251).

Photograph by John Bigelow Taylor, courtesy of the Kronos Collection.

THE THREE LEVELS OF SPIRITUAL PERCEPTION

The Venerable Deshung Rinpoche III

The Three Levels of
Spiritual Perception

An Oral Commentary on
The Three Visions (Nang Sum) of Ngorchen Könchog Lhündrub

by

His Eminence Deshung Rinpoche,
Kunga Tenpay Nyima

TRANSLATED *by* JARED RHOTON

Edited, with an Introduction, by Victoria R. M. Scott

WISDOM PUBLICATIONS • BOSTON

in association with the Vikramaśīla Foundation

WISDOM PUBLICATIONS
361 Newbury Street
Boston, Massachusetts 02115

Library of Congress Cataloging-in-Publication Data

Kunga Tenpay Nyima, Deshung Rinpoche, 1906–1987.
  The three levels of spiritual perception : an oral commentary on The three visions (nang sum) of
Ngorchen Konchog Lhundrub / Kunga Tenpay Nyima ; translated by Jared Rhoton ; edited by Victoria R.M.
Scott.
      p.   cm.
  Translated from Tibetan.
  Includes bibliographical references and index.
  ISBN 0-86171-101-7. — ISBN 0-86171-069-X (pbk.)
  1. Dkon-mchog-lhun-grub, Ṅor-chen, 1497–1557. Lam 'bras sṅon 'gro'i khrid yig snaṅ gsum mdzes rgyan.
2. Lam-'bras (Sa-skya-pa) I. Rhoton, Jared, 1941–1993. II. Scott, Victoria R. M. III. Dkon-mchog-lhun-
grub, Ṅor-chen, 1497–1557. Lam 'bras sṅon 'gro'i khrid yig snaṅ gsum mdzes rgyan. English.
BQ7672.4.D55535   1995
294.3'44—dc20   95–1490

ISBN 0 86171 069 X (pbk)
ISBN 0 86171 101 7 (cloth)

00   99   98   97   96
 6   5   4   3   2

Photographs: Cover courtesy of the Kronos Collection; frontispiece by Richard Barron;
other photos courtesy of Dagmo Kusho, Moke Mokotoff,
Jim and Meg Smart, and the Sapan Fund.

Typeset in Truesdell and Diacritical Garamond font families by LJ·SAWLiť, Boston.

Designed and produced by: LJ·SAWLiť

Wisdom Publications' books are printed on acid-free paper and meet the guidelines for permanence and durability of
the Committee on Production Guidelines for Book Longevity of the Council on Library Resources.

Printed in the United States of America.

This volume is dedicated
to the memory of the Venerable Deshung Rinpoche,
and with great respect to His Holiness Sakya Trizin.

It is also dedicated with gratitude to Jared Rhoton,
translator and interpreter extraordinaire.

೮ఎ ⚜ ೮ఎ

Photograph courtesy of *Victoria Scott*

Jared Rhoton

JARED RHOTON

JARED DOUGLAS RHOTON (Dharma name, Sönam Tenzin) was born on June 21, 1941 in Shiro, a small town in east Texas whose name is said to be of Japanese provenance, perhaps foreshadowing his future role as an interpreter of Asian culture for the West.

Raised a Mormon, Sönam, as most of his friends came to call him, devoted his adult life to the welfare of the Sakya school of Tibetan Buddhism, its teachers, texts, and students. In India in the early 1960s, he was one of His Holiness Sakya Trizin's first Western students and English teachers; over the next three decades, he traveled extensively to interpret for Deshung Rinpoche, Chobgyay Trichen Rinpoche, Jetsün Chimey Luding, and others, establishing and maintaining Buddhist centers at their request in several American cities.

In many ways, Sönam complemented Deshung Rinpoche's personality and style. Both were noted scholars, and Sönam earned advanced degrees on two continents—a master's degree in philosophy from Sanskrit University, Benares in 1975, a M.Phil. in comparative religion from Columbia University in 1981, and a Ph.D. in Indic studies from Columbia in 1985. Like Deshung Rinpoche, Sönam was noted for his humility and took jobs considerably below his scholarly abilities in order to devote the bulk of his time to the welfare of others. This humility, combined with his great facility as an interpreter and translator, made his voice *the* voice of Deshung Rinpoche for hundreds of Americans during the 1970s and 1980s. Like Deshung Rinpoche, Sönam pursued a monastic vocation, receiving the novice monk (*dge 'dun*) ordination in the 1970s.

Yet it is in his differences from Deshung Rinpoche that we see in relief key issues of the transition of Buddhism to the West. Sönam lived in a country and time when monks were looked down upon with suspicion and, in some cases, hostility. His own scholarly and somewhat introverted personality made working in fledgling Buddhist centers problematic at times, but he persisted because it was the wish of the Sakya lamas who were his mentors and spiritual friends. Bravely working through the final English version of Deshung Rinpoche's *Nang Sum* teachings and his own lyrical translation of works by Sakya Pandita (see bibliography), Sönam Tenzin passed from this life on May 9, 1993, six years almost to the day after the death of Deshung Rinpoche.

Sönam partook of two worlds, neither of which had an established place for him, and attempted to share what was best in each with the other. It is perhaps fitting that the work of this gentle scholar should be posthumous. Though oral translation is often an evanescent art, the pages that follow prove that it can be an exalted one.

Michael Roche

ఴ ⚡ ఴ

May all beings in the ten directions be happy,
May they ever be free from pain;
May they live in accord with the spirit of Dharma
And find all their hopes fulfilled.

The Guru Yoga of Sakya Pandita
by Gatön Ngawang Legpa Rinpoche
translated by Jared Rhoton

CONTENTS

List of Photographs   xv
Foreword   xvii
Acknowledgments   xix
Note to the Reader   xxiii
Introduction: The Tradition, the Teachings, and the Teacher   xxvii

1   A Priceless Jewel in a Garbage Heap   *3*
2   Reveling in the Wine of Bliss   *11*
3   First Things First and Last Things Last   *25*
4   Climbing a Steep Ladder without Hands   *31*
5   The Umbrella of Refuge   *45*
6   Holding Fast until Enlightenment Is Won   *53*
7   Suppose You Own a Fine Horse   *61*
8   The Needle Point of Worldly Existence   *69*
9   Sheer Pain   *75*
10   The Forest of Swords   *83*
11   Ignoble Stinginess   *93*
12   From Celestial Mansions to Murky Depths   *101*
13   No Rest from the Dance   *109*
14   A Fish Cast Up on Hot, Dry Sand   *119*
15   Careless Craving   *127*
16   Ceaseless Roaming   *135*
17   Imagine a Blind Tortoise   *143*
18   A Lump of Charcoal and a White Conch   *151*
19   Just Somebody Dressed in Red   *159*
20   The Great Fisher, Death   *169*
21   Discarded in Some Dark Hole   *175*
22   A Protector, an Island, a Great, Friendly Host   *185*
23   Deeds, Like a Shadow, Will Follow   *197*
24   A Great Vessel Filled by Drops of Water   *211*
25   Black Pebbles and White Pebbles   *223*
26   As Helpless As a Worm   *233*

27 Giving Our Parents a Piggyback Ride *247*

28 A Mind Like an Overturned Pot *257*

29 The Flavor of Compassion *261*

30 Rudderless on the Sea of Life *269*

31 A Coiled Rope in the Gloom of Night *277*

32 "Beloved Daughter" Kicks His Mother *285*

33 The Hand Must Help the Foot *293*

34 A Cloud of White Light or a Sudden Dawn *303*

35 Turning the Wheel of the Rat Race *313*

36 Doing What Bodhisattvas Do *321*

37 A Protector of the Protectorless *327*

38 Seeing Things Exactly as They Are *337*

39 Insight Yoked with Calm *345*

40 Pouring Water into a Vase with a Hole in It *351*

41 A Four-Petaled Blue Flower *359*

42 The Monkeys Were Perplexed *367*

43 The Flame of a Lamp in a Windless Place *375*

44 A Storm of Thought Processes *379*

45 Ten Million Blind Men *389*

46 Rebirth as a Woodchuck *397*

47 Saṃsāra Falls Apart Like a Tattered Rag *407*

48 If You Think of Yourself as a Tiger *417*

49 It Is "Natural" Not to Be Natural *423*

50 Paying the Tax of Compulsiveness *429*

51 Awakening Certitude *435*

52 Tasting Sugarcane for the First Time *441*

53 A Chamberpot, an Offering Bowl, a Buddha *453*

54 The Dreaming Mind Deludes Itself *465*

55 Tuning the Violin of Meditation *475*

56 The Sharpness of a Thorn, the Roundness of a Pea *483*

Outline of the Text *493*

Notes *497*

Bibliography *511*

Glossary of Tibetan Names and Terms *523*

Index *529*

PHOTOGRAPHS

Page

v   The Venerable Deshung Rinpoche III

x   Jared Rhoton

xvi   His Holiness the Forty-First Sakya Trizin

lxv   *Plate 1.* Gatön Ngawang Legpa Rinpoche

lxvi   *Plate 2.* Dagmo Kusho, Ani Chimey Drolma, Deshung Rinpoche, and Dr. Kunsang Nyima

lxvii   *Plate 3.* Dsongsar Khyentse Rinpoche II

lxviii   *Plate 4.* His Holiness Jigdal Dagchen Rinpoche and Deshung Rinpoche

lxix   *Plate 5.* Deshung Rinpoche and Jared Rhoton

lxx   *Plate 6.* Deshung Rinpoche and His Holiness Sakya Trizin

lxxi   *Plate 7.* Deshung Rinpoche IV, Ngawang Kunga Tegchen Chökyi Nyima

Photograph by Clive Arrowsmith

His Holiness the Forty-First Sakya Trizin

His Holiness
Sakya Trizin
HEAD OF THE SAKYAPA ORDER
OF TIBETAN BUDDHISM

192, RAJPUR ROAD
P. O. RAJPUR
DEHRA DUN, U.P., INDIA

11th February 1993

<u>F O R E W O R D</u>

"The Three levels of Spiritual Perception" will be extremely helpful for Dharma practitioners as a guide to their meditation and daily life. I am very happy that the Vikramashila Foundation is publishing this great commentary by the Venerable Dezhung Rinpoche. It is very important to practice in our daily life what knowledge we can gain through these great teachings. I wish everybody to have complete knowledge and also to be able to practice diligently.

H. H. SAKYA TRIZIN

Publisher's Acknowledgment

The publisher gratefully acknowledges the kind help of Miss L. B. Lim and Michael Hellbach in sponsoring the publication of this book.

ACKNOWLEDGMENTS

THE TEACHINGS CONTAINED in *The Three Levels of Spiritual Perception* were given by Deshung Rinpoche at Jetsün Sakya Centre, New York City, from September 7, 1977 to February 26, 1980, with Jared Rhoton interpreting. Many Jetsün Sakya students first transcribed the audio cassette tapes of these teachings in 1980; students at Palden Sakya Center in New York transferred those original four volumes of typescript to computer almost a decade later.

We are most appreciative of His Holiness Sakya Trizin, who has graciously supported both the Vikramaśila Foundation and the Sapan Fund since their inceptions.

And, of course, we will always be more than grateful to Deshung Rinpoche for "teaching the ABCs to Westerners" when he could instead have returned to India to teach the Dharma to learned monks, as His Holiness the Dalai Lama once suggested (see introduction).

Our heartfelt thanks, above all, to Jared Rhoton, for transmitting Deshung Rinpoche's discourses so thoroughly and faithfully, and for providing most of the information for the introduction. Without him, this book would not exist.

Special thanks to Helen Stendahl for her organizational work and interviews with many Sakya lamas. Sincere thanks are also extended to David Flood for providing the lion's share of the first transcription from audio cassettes, and to David Rich, Carolyn Cather, Carl Jossem, Tashi Drolma, Abby Petty Li, Cynthia Page, Marge Weinrich, Joan Remy, and Susan Mesinai for miscellaneous assistance on that initial version of the manuscript. Charles and Yvonne Byer generously did most of the word processing when the original transcript was transferred to computer; Patricia Honakar and family also provided substantial word-processing assistance.

To all the donors to the Sapan Fund, especially John Giorno and Tom Trabin, we are deeply indebted for financial aid. Our sincere thanks, too, to Sakya Thubten Dhargye Ling in Minneapolis, Steven Schoonmaker, and Paul Hagstrom for funding the first edited draft of the work. Many thanks also to Larry and Marsha Spiro of the Melia Foundation for taking the Sapan Fund under their wing.

We are most grateful to Dr. David Jackson for reviewing the introduction several times, thus rendering it more accurate, for invaluable reference to drafts of his "Biography of Dezhung Rinpoche," and for a last-minute review of the front and back matter that added to their overall accuracy.

Many thanks, also, to Dr. Mark Tatz for compiling the bibliography and standardizing Tibetan and Sanskrit names and terms throughout the text, and to Judy Robertson for use of her essay on the five founding masters of the Sakya school and for many helpful suggestions on the introduction.

Moke Mokotoff did us the invaluable service of arranging for the tangka of Virūpa to appear on the front cover, courtesy of the Kronos Collection, wrote the description of it, and provided the photo of Deshung Rinpoche IV as well.

We wish also to express our appreciation to Richard Farris for preliminary proofreading and secretarial acumen; to Barbara Ann Kipfer for partial copyediting; to Richard Barron for permission to cite his translation of Deshung Rinpoche's "A Lamp for the Path to Liberation" in notes to chapters 41 and 43, and for use of his photograph of Deshung Rinpoche as the frontispiece; and to Katherine Pfaff for supplying that photo.

James Sarzotti and Michal Bigger thoughtfully provided the translation of the eighth chapter of Shāntideva's *Bodhicharyāvatara* by Jared Rhoton and the Tibetan Classics Translators' Guild of New York, which is cited in the notes to chapter 39. Meg and Jim Smart kindly searched through their negatives for photos of Jared Rhoton. Nancy Cushing Jones generously read yet another book contract on our behalf, while Ingrid Mednis and Shirley Jowell were encouraging throughout.

We are very happy to have had the help and encouragement of Dagmo Kusho (Jamyang Sakya), Deshung Rinpoche's niece, and Ani Chimey Drolma, his sister. Dagmo Kusho generously loaned us several photographs from her family albums and provided welcome information about Deshung Rinpoche's reincarnation as well. Carolyn Dawa Drolma Lama, Deshung Rinpoche IV's mother, was quite helpful, too.

Thelma Rhoton, Jared's mother, and Judith and Jacqueline Rhoton, his sisters, were unfailingly supportive of the project, extending much-appreciated friendship and many kinds of assistance, both tangible and intangible.

At Wisdom Publications, Editorial Project Manager Connie Miller was most friendly and helpful from first to last; President Timothy McNeill contributed much to the process at crucial points; Jason Fairchild provided careful and welcome assistance; and Marketing Director Wendy Cook helped launch the finished barque.

Last but far from least, we would like to thank Lama Pema Wangdak, our teachers, families, and friends not already named, Abe Roche-Miessler, and Tony, Nina, and Lucia Misch for their great skill and kindness. Thanks, too, to John Bigelow Taylor, Clive Arrowsmith, and the unidentified photographers whose work so enhances these pages, and to everyone else who contributed in any way to *The Three Levels of Spiritual Perception.*

May this work benefit all beings without exception.

Victoria Scott and Michael Roche
The Sapan Fund

NOTE TO THE READER

DESHUNG RINPOCHE was a vastly learned but modest teacher who practiced constantly and who, beyond his mastery of Buddhist doctrine, had an encyclopedic knowledge of Tibetan people, places, anecdotes, teachings, history, and more. He used to speak extemporaneously for at least ten or twenty minutes before pausing to let his gifted interpreter, Jared Rhoton, speak.

In addition to being a luminary of the Sakya school, Deshung Rinpoche was a nonsectarian (*ris-med*) scholar who both sought teachings from and gave them to practitioners of all four traditions of Tibetan Buddhism; he taught at many different centers and never refused a request unless he was sick in bed. He was accompanied on his travels by his brother, Dr. Kunsang Nyima, a very playful, loyal sidekick and skilled physician who occasionally gave talks on Tibetan medicine and who granted medical consultations upon request.

I first encountered Tibetan Buddhism in 1970, through an introductory class at the University of Washington taught by Dr. Turrell Wylie, the scholar who brought Deshung Rinpoche and his family to Seattle from India in 1960. But I did not meet Deshung Rinpoche for another decade, and first saw the transcript of his oral commentary on *The Three Visions* when studying with him at the Sakya center in Los Angeles during the early 1980s.

As already noted, *The Three Levels of Spiritual Perception* was taught orally by Deshung Rinpoche at Jetsün Sakya Centre, New York City, from September 7, 1977 to February 26, 1980, with Jared Rhoton interpreting. There was a break from April 26, 1978 (chapter 27) to July 10, 1979 (chapter 28); during this time Deshung Rinpoche taught elsewhere and returned to his home in Seattle to welcome His Holiness Sakya Trizin (see introduction).

In 1991, at the request of Lama Pema Wangdak, director of the Vikramaśila Foundation, I edited the manuscript, which was by then on computer. In the summer of 1992, with invaluable help and information from Jared Rhoton, the introduction was written (characteristically, he insisted that his name not appear as coauthor of this work). Since then, I have fine-tuned the body of the text, provided chapter titles and notes, prepared the front and back matter, and shepherded the manuscript through the many steps of the publishing process. Much has also been done by many others to ready the book for publication (see acknowledgments).

The Three Levels of Spiritual Perception is a commentary on Ngorchen Könchog Lhündrub's *The Three Visions* (*Snang gsum*), which has been translated by Lobsang Dagpa, Ngawang Samten Chophel (Jay Goldberg), and Jared Rhoton as *The Beautiful Ornament of the Three Visions* (Singapore: Golden Vase Publications, 1987; reprinted Ithaca, N.Y.: Snow Lion, 1991). *The Three Visions* corresponds to the preparatory level of study and practice in the Sakya meditation system known as the Instruction on the Path with Its Result (*Lam 'bras bu dang bcas pa'i gdams ngag*, or *Lam 'bras* for short). The present volume, which is entitled *The Three Levels of Spiritual Perception* to distinguish it from the translation of the *Nang Sum* itself, also contains references to a second volume by Könchog Lhündrub, *The Three Continua* (*Rgyud gsum*), which corresponds to the advanced level of study and practice. No English translation of *The Three Continua* has yet appeared in print.

Lest we be tempted to undervalue the "preliminary" teachings of *The Three Visions* while awaiting a translation of the "advanced" teachings of *The Three Continua*, it is important to note that Deshung Rinpoche was at pains to emphasize, throughout the three years of teachings presented here, that *The Three Visions* is of crucial importance as the foundation that makes the advanced practices and principles "so significant, meaningful, and effective." As he puts it in chapter 13, "Only when we have established a very firm foundation of right attitude, genuine renunciation, and an uncontrived resolve to strive for the liberation of all living beings is it time to study and practice on the level of advanced tantra."

To cite just one more example, in chapter 19 Deshung Rinpoche states that "All the profound doctrines are given at the beginning; the advanced practices are just natural consequences of those profound insights and that reorientation of mental energies which occur at the preliminary stages. There is a saying that, 'Of the profound preliminary practices and the esoteric advanced practices, it is the deep teachings that are given first.' Without gaining the realizations and being truly affected through these preliminary practices, there cannot be any advanced realizations."

On a more mundane level, your reading of *The Three Levels of Spiritual Perception* will be enhanced by understanding the following points:

1.   Due to the general nature of much of the text, Tibetan and Sanskrit terms are few. A glossary of Tibetan names and terms has been compiled for those who know the language; there is, however, no corresponding list of Sanskrit words, which appear in phonetic form in the body of the text and in standard transliteration when in parentheses.

2.   Titles of works cited have been translated into English whenever possible, with the Sanskrit or Tibetan given in parentheses at the first occurrence in the text. The exceptions to this rule are the well-known *Abhidharmakosha, Bodhicharyāvatara, Dhammapada, Jātaka Tales*, and *Vinaya*, which appear as such, with English translations in parentheses at the first occurrence. The bibliography provides the Sanskrit and/or Tibetan title, author, and translation for each work, when available, and lists further reading as well.

3.   Notes are provided when possible, but without access to the great erudition of both Deshung Rinpoche and Jared Rhoton, every allusion and reference of interest could not, unfortunately, be pursued.

4.   No general glossary is provided because most terms are defined when they are first discussed in some detail. More extensive definitions and other basic information can be found in a number of the secondary sources cited in the bibliography, particularly *The Encyclopedia of Eastern Philosophy and Religion* and *A Handbook of Tibetan Culture*.

5.   Deshung Rinpoche's introductory remarks appear at the beginning of each chapter. He was wonderful at recapping not only the previous lesson, but also the proper motivation with which to approach the study and the point he had reached in the *lam-dre* teachings as a whole. This material has been retained both to preserve his particular teaching style and to remind us of the purpose of the teachings.

6.   Suggested practical meditations are extracted to facilitate use of the volume as the meditative manual it can so easily and fruitfully be.

7.   Quotations from the Buddhist canon are also extracted whenever they are more than two lines long. It is important to remember that this commentary was given orally in Tibetan and interpreted into English on the spot. Thus many of these citations are more in the nature of paraphrases

than exact, polished translations of scripture. Those who wish to can, in many cases, compare the off-the-cuff versions that appear here to the same lines as translated by Lobsang Dagpa, Jay Goldberg, and Jared Rhoton in Ngorchen Könchog Lhündrub's *Beautiful Ornament of the Three Visions* itself (see bibliography).

8. Deshung Rinpoche only occasionally used "he or she" and "his or her" when referring to "the teacher," "the meditator," and so forth. To convey as much as possible the flavor of his words, this style has generally been retained. However, the Sakya school is renowned for its women teachers and practitioners, and Deshung Rinpoche acknowledges the equality of women in several ways and places in these teachings (see, for example, chapter 45).

9. In a few cases, the original typescript noted that a cassette tape had been mislaid, so that parts of a lecture had to be reconstructed from students' notes. This material is now a seamless part of the whole, and I am confident that it accurately reflects the content of Deshung Rinpoche's commentary on the few occasions in question.

In composing the introduction and putting Jared Rhoton's oral interpretation of Deshung Rinpoche's words into published form, any errors and resultant lack of clarity are entirely mine. I hope that *The Three Levels of Spiritual Perception* is, nevertheless, a worthy tribute to them both.

Victoria Scott

INTRODUCTION

THE TRADITION, THE TEACHINGS, AND THE TEACHER

DESHUNG RINPOCHE OFTEN SAID that there are four levels of biography or autobiography: outer, inner, secret, and real. Outer biography would be a bare enumeration of everyday events, as in a curriculum vitae; inner, one's psychic history of dreams, visions, and thoughts, too personal to reveal to everyone; secret, one's tantric practices and their results; and real, the understanding that no biography is the true biography, since ultimately nothing has ever happened to oneself or anyone else. The biographical sketch that follows is a rudimentary outer biography at best.

Deshung Rinpoche (1906–1987) was among the last few Tibetan Buddhist masters, such as the Kagyu lama Kalu Rinpoche (1905–1989) and the Nyingma teacher Dilgo Khyentse Rinpoche (1910–1991), who studied, practiced, and taught in Tibet until full maturity, when the Chinese invasion of 1959 forced them into exile. Reading Deshung Rinpoche's life story, one is struck by the extraordinarily thorough training he received in his youth, by his willingness to be guided by his guru, and by his vast contributions to Tibetan Buddhism, both as a Sakya teacher and as a prime example of non-sectarianism at work.

Deshung Rinpoche was a truly pure lama, a model of and guide to how dedicated, scholarly, and spiritually accomplished a person can become. What he studied and how he practiced laid the foundation for the later activities that made him great.

THE SAKYA TRADITION

The historical record of the Sakya tradition that unfolds from Tibetan annals is a complex story woven from the three strands of mythology, royal lineage, and spiritual leadership.[1] Central to all of these is the genealogy of the ancient family of Khön. Although the earliest historical accounts of the Khön go back only twelve hundred years, almost all Tibetan histories trace its origin to the descent in prehistoric times of three sky gods from the "Realm of Clear Light." Entreated to become a ruler of men, the youngest of these gods remained on earth; his descendants were later said to have been born into "hostility" (*'khon*) because of the strife that ensued between the celestials and the fierce demons who then inhabited large areas of Tibet.

A member of the Khön family, Lü Wangpo Sungwa, became a disciple of the eighth-century Indian saint Padmasambhava. When the monastery of Samye was later built at Yarlung, he took ordination with the Indian abbot Shāntarakṣhita as one of the first seven Tibetan "monks on probation." Through the next thirteen generations (c. 750–1073), the Khön family was an acknowledged pillar of the "early propagation" (Nyingma) school in Tsang province.

By the middle of the eleventh century, however, the people of Tsang had become so lax in religious observances that the secret symbols and sacred dances of the Buddhist tantras were being featured as entertainments at town festivals in Dro and elsewhere. In dismay, the head of the Khön family decided that the time had come to seek out the new tantras from India that were just then beginning to appear. Thus he sent his younger brother, Könchog Gyalpo (1034–1102), to study with Drogmi the Translator (see next section). In 1073, Könchog Gyalpo built a monastery beneath an auspicious circle of white clay on the slopes of Mount Pönpori and named it Sakya ("white earth"). In this way the prophecies of both Padmasambhava (c. 750) and Atīsha (in 1040) that a great center of spiritual activity would arise in that place were fulfilled.

The master who gathered for the Sakya tradition its core of tantric initiations and prayers, as well as basic Mahāyāna doctrines, was Könchog Gyalpo's son, Sachen Kunga Nyingpo (1092–1158). When Sachen was twelve years old, Mañjushrī appeared as Sachen was meditating on him in a cave and transmitted the teaching known as *Parting from the Four Attachments*:

> If you have attachment to this life, you are not a religious person.
> If you have attachment to the round of rebirth, you have
> no renunciation.
> If you have attachment to your own interests, you haven't
> the resolve to attain enlightenment.
> If grasping ensues, you do not have the true view.

These teachings contain the essence of Mahāyāna doctrine. Through Sachen's efforts, hundreds of tantric works and transmissions were secured from eminent Tibetan masters, to become the basis of the Sakya canon.

Sachen left behind four sons. The eldest traveled to India as a young man and became a learned teacher there, but while returning to Tibet he was stricken with fever and died. Sachen's second son, Sönam Tsemo (1142–1182), obtained all the empowerments, explanations, and oral instructions from his father. He also studied for eleven years with Chapa Chökyi Sengay (1109–1169), one of the greatest logicians in Tibetan history and abbot at the seminary of Sangpu, located a short distance south of Lhasa. As a result, Sönam Tsemo was a master of the sūtras and tantras by the time he was in his twenties.

Sachen's third son, Dragpa Gyaltsen (1147–1216), also became a highly realized master, his most important teachers being his father and Sönam Tsemo, his brother. When he was thirteen years old, he dreamt that the three parts of the *Hevajra Tantra* entered his mouth and he swallowed them. After the dream it is said that he could effortlessly discourse on any aspect of the *Hevajra Tantra*. His students included great translators and accomplished yogis as well.

Kunga Gyaltsen Päl Zangpo (1182–1251), later called Sakya Pandita, was born to the fourth son of Sachen Kunga Nyingpo. Tutored by his uncle, Dragpa Gyaltsen, the boy was soon able to recite lengthy works of philosophy and tantra by heart. When he was seventeen, he dreamt that the master Vasubandhu appeared and conferred knowledge of the entire abhidharma system to him directly. At eighteen, he dreamt that he was given the key to all of Dignāga's teachings on logic, and when he awoke, it is said that he possessed a complete knowledge of that science. At the age of twenty-one, he came under the tutorship of several Buddhist pandits from India, including the great Kashmiri master Shākyashrī. After nearly ten years of further studies, Sapan, as he was known for short, was accomplished in medicine and all the known sciences, as well as in grammar, poetry, art, and music; he had also acquired full monastic ordination.

Through Sapan's efforts, a vigorous school of Dharmakīrti's logic took root in Tibet and a number of Indian sciences were introduced into Tibetan culture. Sapan composed numerous lucid philosophical treaties, and his skill in debate was unsurpassed. During one great debate in Kyirong, he defeated the Hindu scholar Harinanda, thus converting this master to Buddhism.

As Sakya Pandita's fame spread, Godan Khan, the Mongol emperor of China, sent messengers to Tibet to find the most outstanding lama there. According to Tibetan tradition, they reported that Sapan was the most learned in religion, the lama of the Drigung monastery was the most magnificent for wealth, and the lama of the Taklung monastery was the kindest and most sociable.[2] In 1244, Godan Khan invited Sakya Pandita to come to the Mongol court as his spiritual guide. Remembering his uncle Dragpa

Gyaltsen's counsel to accept without hesitation any future invitation to teach in a foreign land, Sapan journeyed to Mongolia at the age of sixty-five. The khan developed great faith in Sakya Pandita and received many important religious teachings from him.

Shortly before he died, Sakya Pandita named his nephew, Chögyal Phagpa (1235–1280), as his successor. As spiritual preceptor to Kublai Khan, Godan Khan's successor, Chögyal Phagpa was the first lama to unite religious and political authority in Tibet. At his request, the khan outlawed the practice of torturing and drowning political opponents throughout his realm and presented this to Phagpa as an offering for receiving special tantric teachings. But when Kublai Khan suggested that he decree that all Tibetans must practice only the Sakya tradition, Phagpa urged him not to do so, in order that all lineages of Buddhism might flourish.

Chögyal Phagpa spent most of his life in China, supervising the propagation of Buddhism there. He devised an alphabet for the Mongolian language, wrote over three hundred works on sūtras, tantras, and philosophy, and was instrumental in having the Tibetan Buddhist canon translated into Mongolian.

Although in the mid-1300s the political power of the Sakya order waned along with Mongol influence, many great Sakya monasteries and teaching schools continued to be established in the provinces of U-Tsang, Kham, and Amdo. In the fifteenth and sixteenth centuries, learned Sakya masters significantly enriched the intellectual and literary life of Tibet. Since the eighteenth century, however, the order has shown relatively little of its former vigor outside of Kham. There the work of Sakya masters and the nonsectarian movement of the Jamyang Khyentse reincarnations (see Deshung Rinpoche's biography below) continued to inspire monks of every order until the Chinese Communist army ravaged monasteries throughout the province beginning in 1959.

After 1806, the principality of Sakya was ruled alternately by the heads of two Khön palaces, the Drolma and Puntsog. According to the convention that evolved, succession to the throne rotates between the two. Thus the fortieth Sakya Trizin, Ngawang Thutop Wangchuk (1900–1950), who belonged to Puntsog Palace, was succeeded by Ngawang Kunga (b. 1945), the son of Ngawang Kunga Rinchen of Drolma Palace. Within months of the young Trizin's enthronement in 1959, however, Tibet lost her freedom and the forty-first Sakya Trizin was forced into exile in India, where he now lives and teaches.

THE LAM-DRE TEACHINGS

The Sakya order is the second oldest of the four principal traditions of Tibetan Buddhism.[3] At its heart is the lineal transmission of the Instruction on the Path with Its Result (*Lam 'bras bu dang bcas pa'i gdams ngag*, or *Lam 'bras*, for short), a system of knowledge and practice of the entire range of sutric and tantric teachings of the Buddha. The *Lam dre* was first enunciated by the Indian *mahāsiddha*[4] Virūpa (c. 650) and was brought to Tibet from India by Drogmi Shākya Yeshe (990–1074).

Following Langdarma's near-destruction of Buddhism in Tibet in the mid-ninth century and an ensuing "dark age" of political chaos, there began a second period of intense and active interchange between Indian and Tibetan spiritual centers in the late 900s. It was during this great revival that Drogmi the Translator, as he became known, set out for India. He studied the *Hevajra, Saṁvara, Guhyasamāja, Yamāntaka*, and *Mahāmāyā Tantras* for one year under Shāntibhadra (known as Shāntipa) in Nepal, then traveled to Vikramashīla Monastery, with a stopover in Bodhgaya for salutations to the Mahābodhi shrine.

For eighteen years, Drogmi studied monastic discipline, *prajñā-pāramitā*, and the *Saṁvara* and *Hevajra Tantras* with Shāntipa. He mastered the root, narrative, instructive, and supplemental fragment tantras, studying with many other teachers as well. Then the great master Vīravajra realized that Drogmi was a most able and worthy student and introduced him to the teachings of Virūpa, giving him the entire instruction on the triple tantras of the *Hevajra Root Tantra*, along with its exegesis. When the time approached for Drogmi's return to Tibet, Vīravajra instructed him in some eighty major tantras along with their exegetical commentaries, numerous meditative manuals with their rites, and about fifty mantras (*dhāraṇī*) connected with sūtras. As a parting gift, Drogmi received a *lam-dre* teaching (without the root text), its auxiliary instructions, and profound teachings on the transference of consciousness (*'pho-ba*). Vīravajra then told his pupil:

> Rejoice, for I have successfully transmitted all the teachings I have to give. Now go to Tibet and integrate your practice and teaching. I will come some time to help clear up your doubts. Since you are the holder of the teachings of Virūpa, there will come a master who will bring the entire teaching to your doorstep.

Drogmi returned to Tibet and taught many disciples, among them the great Marpa Lotsawa, Milarepa's guru. A thriving temple of ritual practice was established at Nyugulung, and students poured in from upper, central, and eastern Tibet. As Vīravajra had prophesied, early one morning the sound of a ram's horn was heard proclaiming the arrival of Pandit Gayādhara, who taught the entire *Lam dre*, including the root verses, for a period of three years. The initiations, instructions, and commentaries of the triple tantras were translated at the same time. Nyugulung was thus firmly established as the seat of lam-dre teachings and practices.

Although tantric and sutric teaching was well established in Tibet before Drogmi, the corpus of the lam-dre system was not known until he began to teach it. Twelve major schools of transmission of *Lam dre* arose in Tibet. Preeminent among these was that of the great Sachen Kunga Nyingpo (1092–1156), whose line of transmission is called the "direct line" because Virūpa, Dāmarūpa (an Indian master of *Lam dre* and the teacher of Gayādhara's teacher Avadhūtipa), and Gayādhara appeared to him in visions and gave a month-long transmission on seventy-two *anuttarayoga* tantras and the Four Profound Dharmas of Sakya. Later, Ngorchen Kunga Zangpo (1382–1456), the founder of the Ngor school of the Sakya order, caused *Lam dre* to become widespread through his lifelong career of transmitting its teaching.

Later still, in the time of Ngorchen's disciple Muchen Sempa Chenbo (1448–1530), the *Lam dre* developed into two major lines of transmission: the general presentation (*tshogs-bshad*) and the esoteric presentation (*slob-bshad*). They were first taught separately by Muchen. Tsarchen Lösal Gyatso (1502–1556), the founder of the Tsar school of the Sakya order, and his two foremost disciples, Khyentse Wangchuk and Lhündrub Gyatso, became prominent expounders of the esoteric *Lam dre*.

As the lam-dre teachings spread, gaining a few adherents even in Mongolia and China, they grew to comprise some thirty volumes. Through a succession of teachers, the system has been passed down to the present in an unbroken line of transmission. Among the eminent masters of this tradition are His Holiness Sakya Trizin (b. 1945), H. H. Dagchen Rinpoche (b. 1929), H. E. Chobgyay Trichen Rinpoche (b. 1920), H. E. Luding Khen Rinpoche (b. 1931), and the late Venerable Deshung Rinpoche (1906–1987), whose commentary on the lam-dre teachings of Ngorchen Könchog Lhündrub (1497–1557), entitled *The Three Visions* (*Nang Sum*), comprises the main body of this book.[5]

ભ ⚜ ભ

The lam-dre system is derived from the *Hevajra Root Tantra*. It presents the essence of the tripartite Buddhist canon: ethical discipline (*vinaya*), discourses of the Buddha (*sūtra*), and psychology/cosmology (*abhidharma*). The *Lam dre* is a complete and harmonious system of exoteric (sutric) and esoteric (tantric) methods. Its teachings have been passed down with special emphasis on the "four authenticities": authentic teachers, direct experiences, scriptures, and treatises. Central to the lam-dre system is its unique and profound view of "the nondifferentiation of saṃsāra and nirvāṇa" (*'khor-'das-dbyer-med*), within which perfect enlightenment, or buddhahood, is to be realized. There the nature of mind is explained as "the root of saṃsāra and nirvāṇa" and "the union of luminosity and emptiness." Deshung Rinpoche discusses these ideas at more length below.[6]

THE VENERABLE DESHUNG RINPOCHE III (1906–1987)

DESHUNG RINPOCHE I AND II

Deshung is the name of a large nomadic region in the Lithang district of the eastern Tibetan province of Kham, about a month's journey on horseback from Lhasa. Deshung Monastery was a branch of Nālandā, a more famous Sakya monastery named after Nālandā University and located one day's journey by foot to the north of Lhasa; all the monks of Deshung Monastery went to Nālandā for ordination. Deshung reincarnations, or tulkus (*sprul-sku*), are considered to be emanations of Maitreya, the buddha who is to appear on earth after Shākyamuni, the historical Buddha.

The first Deshung Rinpoche was a wandering yogi, Changchub Nyima by name, who attained the first level (*bhūmi*) of bodhisattvahood through meditating on the resolve to attain enlightenment (*bodhicitta*) for eighteen years while seated on stony ground (i.e., with no cushion at all). He meditated on Chenresi (Skt. Avalokiteśvara, the bodhisattva of compassion), Tārā (a savioress who embodies compassion and wisdom), Achala (the wrathful form of Mañjuśrī, the bodhisattva of wisdom), and others, saw visions of them, and became famous as a result. The people and the nomadic chieftain of Deshung invited him to stay there; he did so but had no definite residence of his own, preferring to travel about, especially to places of solitude and austerity. Deshung Rinpoche I was probably a Nyingma lama and was the author of six volumes of Buddhist studies. Before dying, he entrusted his personal hat and bowl to the chieftain of Deshung, saying, "I will come for these soon."

A son, Lungrik Nyima (1840s?–1898), was born to the chieftain the next year. The child had great love, compassion, sensitivity to animals, and a holy lifestyle. He was saddened by the sight of cruelty or pain and tried to protect life; when he was present, butchers and others could not kill or hurt animals. His father later understood him to be the reincarnation of the first Deshung Rinpoche and took him to Deshung Monastery, where he became a monk, studying logic and other subjects. Deshung Rinpoche II had a vision of Tushita (the buddha-realm of Maitreya, the buddha of the future) and foretold that he would go there upon his death. But on his deathbed he had a dream that he had ascended almost to Tushita when his special protector appeared in the form of a bearded brahmin and bade him return below.

CHILDHOOD

Deshung Rinpoche III's childhood name was Könchog Lhündrub.[7] His father was a doctor named Namgyal Dorje (c. mid-1880s–1922); his mother was Pema Chözom (1884–1950). They lived in the village of Tarlam. His mother came from a family of tantric practitioners; her grandfather had been a yogi known as a "weather man," who could stop hail and make rain.

When Könchog Lhündrub's mother was pregnant with him, she circumambulated Tarlam Monastery. She found a tangka (*thang-ka*, Buddhist scroll painting) depicting Jambhala, the god of wealth, wrapped in an offering scarf. She looked in all directions for the owner but saw no one; she then held it up in her hands so all could see and claim it. No one did, so when the child was born, she gave it to him.

A disciple of Deshung Rinpoche II, Drupthon Sangye Khaplen,[8] an adept who had been in Hevajra retreat eighteen times, came to Tarlam, placed the infant atop his head, and said, "This is my root guru!" As a result, rumors spread that Deshung Rinpoche II's reincarnation had been found.

Nevertheless, Könchog Lhündrub was not recognized as Deshung Rinpoche III until he was in his late teens (although he will be referred to simply as Deshung Rinpoche from this point on). Such delays sometimes occurred for religious, political, and/or familial reasons. In Deshung Rinpoche's case, since his previous incarnation had been born into the family of a Deshung princeling, no separate abbatial household had been established. When Deshung Rinpoche II died, family members did not expect to have another reincarnation in their midst, so they distributed all his belongings as offerings. Moreover, Gatön Ngawang Legpa Rinpoche (Pl. 1, p. lxv), who became Deshung Rinpoche's root guru, wanted him to remain under his own tutelage at Tarlam Monastery and to succeed him there, rather than going permanently to Deshung Monastery.

Deshung Rinpoche had five younger siblings: a sister, Nangdzin Wangmo (1908–1972); a brother who died in childhood; Puntsog Drolma (1913–1962/3), the mother of Dagmo Kusho;[9] Dr. Kunsang Nyima (1916–1990), a physician of Tibetan medicine and his elder brother's stalwart companion; and Ani Chimey Drolma (b. 1922), a nun who, after many years in Seattle, now lives at Tarlam Monastery in Nepal (Pl. 2, p. lxvi).

Deshung Rinpoche's paternal uncle, Ngawang Nyima, a monk of Tarlam Monastery, was in lifelong retreat. He had recited the *Om summa* (mantra of the goddess Vajrayoginī) a hundred million times and had performed all the preliminary practices (*sngon-'gro*) a million times each under the instruction of Deshung Rinpoche II. Ngawang Nyima was his nephew's first teacher. At his own request, Deshung Rinpoche stayed in his uncle's retreat house from age five to ten, walled off from his parents and the rest of the world except for a small window through which food was passed.

Like many Tibetan yogis of his time, Ngawang Nyima could read but did not write well enough to serve as a writing teacher, since there was little need for composition except among great scholars (even extensive practice did not require it). But Deshung Rinpoche practiced and learned the alphabet by himself. He could read by the age of six and write by eight. He studied Marpa Lotsawa's biography, Ngorchen Könchog Lhündrub's *The Three Visions* (*Nang Sum*), and other books recommended to Ngawang Nyima by Gatön Rinpoche.

Deshung Rinpoche recited so much that he memorized the *Songs of Milarepa* and various other texts. In fact, he read so well that he displeased his uncle by reading faster and better than he himself could. Deshung Rinpoche was capable of being mischievous, however: at the age of six, he snitched some food from Ngawang Nyima's Vajrayoginī feast-offering (*tshogs*). His uncle forbade him to eat it on the grounds that the boy had not yet received the appropriate initiation!

At the age of seven, Deshung Rinpoche wrote a twelve-verse poem in praise of the Buddha and presented it to his uncle, who was amazed at its eloquence. At that very instant there was a knock on the door of the retreat house: it was an official of the local ruler coming to offer a bowl of yogurt. Ngawang Nyima showed the poem to the official, who took it to Tarlam Monastery and showed it to everyone there. The official kept the poem himself, saying it was "a sign of greatness in the future."

ఴ ⚜ ఴ

Some time later, Deshung Rinpoche discussed doctrine with his uncle but disagreed with him on certain points. Ngawang Nyima sent a letter on the subject to Gatön Rinpoche, who replied that "The child is bright; he shows promise." He also recommended various practices and sent a Mañjushrī wisdom pill and a *mālā* (Buddhist rosary of 108 beads) for Deshung Rinpoche to wear around his neck. Thus Deshung Rinpoche was under Gatön Rinpoche's protection even before he actually met him.

When Deshung Rinpoche was ten, Gatön Rinpoche completed his own fifteen-year meditative retreat and returned to Tarlam Monastery, going straight to Ngawang Nyima's retreat house. (Ngawang Nyima broke his own retreat in order to meet him.) When the door was opened, Deshung Rinpoche met his guru for the first time. Gatön Rinpoche knew about Deshung Rinpoche's five years of meditation and good mind, but only asked Ngawang Nyima, "Is this your nephew?" "Yes." Gatön Rinpoche then looked at Deshung Rinpoche for a long time.

Deshung Rinpoche was delighted to see more distant places and to have the excitement of meeting Gatön Rinpoche and his attendants. His parents came and took him home; he played with his siblings and friends and was utterly happy to be in his mother's house. He thought he would spend the night there, but that evening his father gave him a package of yogurt and parched barley flour (*tsampa*) and told him to return to the retreat house. The boy was very disappointed to have to return so soon.

Shortly thereafter, Deshung Rinpoche came out of retreat to receive the *Anthology of Tantric Practices* (*Sgrub thabs kun btus*, a fourteen-volume compendium of sādhanas and initiations collected by Jamyang Khyentse Wangpo)[10] from Gatön Rinpoche, who became ill during the initiation. All the monks took a break and read the *Kangyur* (discourses of the Buddha) as a means of gathering merit for Gatön Rinpoche's health and longevity. Deshung Rinpoche finished his portion of the reading before the other monks had completed half of theirs. They suspected he might just be mumbling his way through without clarity or comprehension, so they tested him, thus proving that he really was the fastest and clearest in both enunciation and understanding.

When Deshung Rinpoche was twelve or thirteen, Gatön Rinpoche gave the esoteric lam-dre teachings at Tarlam Monastery, and Deshung Rinpoche received them for the first time. Afterward, Gatön Rinpoche summoned Deshung Rinpoche and bade him not waste his time but study hard, recommending that he begin with grammar under the tutelage of the Gelugpa yogi and scholar Chökyi Gawa. Deshung Rinpoche studied

Mahāyāna philosophy and doctrine with the learned scholar Dzogchen Shenga; he traveled to Jyekundo, a monastery of some five or six hundred monks located in Kyegu, the capital of the Ga district, to study with him for nine months when he was fourteen and fifteen. During this time his private tutor was Lama Gedün, a great *vinayadhāra* (strict observer of the vinaya, or monastic rules) and Deshung Rinpoche's maternal uncle.[11]

GATÖN NGAWANG LEGPA RINPOCHE

Gatön Ngawang Legpa Rinpoche (1864–1941) began his religious career as an ordinary monk at Tarlam Monastery. He loved books and meditation but was indifferent to worldly activities, and he was quite poor. As a young man he made a pilgrimage to Sakya and Ngor, as well as requesting teachings from many lamas of the four Tibetan Buddhist orders on both sutric and tantric subjects. At Dsongsar Monastery he tried to receive teachings from Jamyang Khyentse Wangpo Rinpoche (1820–1892), a founder of the nonsectarian (*ris-med*) movement, but he was so ragged that the master several times had him thrown out of the assembly hall. Eventually, Khyentse Wangpo Rinpoche recognized Gatön Rinpoche's intelligence and pure conduct, gave him teachings, and had his own secretary tutor him in grammar and literature, while other masters taught him Madhyamaka philosophy and other subjects. At this time, Gatön Rinpoche also met Jamgon Kongtrul Lodro Taye Rinpoche (1818–1899), another founder of nonsectarianism, from whom he received more than ninety-five teachings and empowerments.

Gatön Rinpoche's special practice was the *Lam dre*; his main lam-dre master was Khyentse Wangpo Rinpoche. At the age of thirty-seven he went into retreat for fifteen years, completing literally millions of prostrations, mantra recitations, prayers, and offerings; following this he became renowned throughout Tibet as one who had "seen the face" of Sakya Pandita. He then received and accepted numerous invitations to teach, and he subsequently completed many other retreats as well. He was very austere in his conduct, exhibiting a vinaya exterior while inwardly performing Hevajra and lam-dre practices. He was very thin, a strict vegetarian who lived on yogurt and tsampa, eating nothing after the midday meal but rock candy, which was allowed to monks who observed this vinaya rule (see Pl. 1, p. lxv).

Gatön Rinpoche recited the *Shejama* (*Shes bya ma*)—the invocation of Sapan's blessings of body, voice, and mind, found in Sapan's own *Treasure of Knowledge and Reasoning* (*Tshad ma rigs gter*)—for every occasion: for the dead, for the ill, as a blessing, and while doing prostrations. Upon returning from trips, he always went immediately to see Deshung Rinpoche; he was very fond but very strict. Deshung Rinpoche later said of Gatön Rinpoche:

> This master was endowed with oceanlike knowledge, self-discipline, and realization. Due to whatever karmic relation we had in previous lives, he watched over me with great loving kindness. Just about every teaching that he himself had obtained, I myself easily obtained from him. Until I am enlightened, I owe this teacher an unrepayable debt of gratitude, since whatever I know about sūtra, tantra, and the basic treatises on other fields of knowledge is due directly or indirectly to his kindness.

Gatön Rinpoche has been characterized as perhaps the greatest meditator of the Sakya lam-dre tradition during this century. Deshung Rinpoche showed a great willingness to be guided by him, following his advice not only until Gatön Rinpoche's death but until his own as well.

INVESTITURE AS DESHUNG RINPOCHE

When Deshung Rinpoche was fifteen, Gatön Rinpoche and Deshung Ajam Kunga Gyaltsen Rinpoche (1885–1952, hereafter Ajam Rinpoche), the nephew of Deshung Rinpoche II and throneholder of Deshung after his uncle's death, discussed whether or not the boy was to be recognized as the third Deshung Rinpoche. Gatön Rinpoche suggested asking the head of the Sakya order, the thirty-ninth Sakya Trizin, Dragshul Trinlay Rinchen (1871–1936). Ajam Rinpoche did so. After consulting Gyalpo Pehar, the guardian spirit of Nālandā (the mother monastery of Deshung), His Holiness Trinlay Rinchen wrote a letter stating that the child Könchog Lhündrub, son of Pema Chözom and Gonpo Namgyal, was the reincarnation of Lungrik Nyima (Deshung Rinpoche II).

When Deshung Rinpoche was sixteen, Gatön Rinpoche rebuilt the Tarlam temple and had the new structure painted. Over the door he ordered a painting of Ngorchen Kunga Zangpo, the fifteenth-century founder of the Ngor school, and other Sakya luminaries; below this Gatön Rinpoche had himself depicted, together with a likeness of Deshung Rinpoche holding a golden wheel. Deshung Rinpoche himself sponsored a painting of "Sapan in Abhirati" (the pure realm of Sapan's enlightenment), which was half of a mural depicting the life of Sapan that was located to the left and right of the temple door. He also sponsored and supervised a mural of the life story of Shākyamuni Buddha that was painted on both side walls of the monastery. First he studied the traditional details with Gatön Rinpoche; then he supervised the painters daily. This painting became famous in eastern Tibet.

In the same year, Gatön Rinpoche said that in a former life he himself had been a student of Ga Rabjampa Kunga Yeshe, a disciple of Ngorchen Kunga Zangpo, and recalled seeing Deshung Rinpoche there also. Deshung Rinpoche didn't dare ask which of Ga Rabjampa's students he had been.

At seventeen, Deshung Rinpoche underwent an investiture ceremony in recognition of his new status. Gatön Rinpoche was in retreat but sent a set of robes, saying he would perform another enthronement when he finished the new temple he was building. He told Ajam Rinpoche, "I know he is Deshung Rinpoche's reincarnation. You can give him the title, but he stays with me at Tarlam."

Like Deshung Rinpoche, Ajam Rinpoche regarded Gatön Rinpoche as his root guru. Thus he honored Gatön Rinpoche's decision, even though he himself was a tantric practitioner and had become a teacher at Gatön Rinpoche's request (his students included Deshung Rinpoche and Khenpo Appey Rinpoche, b. 1927, a brilliant student at Dsongsar seminary). Although of a noble family, Ajam Rinpoche never wanted to occupy the throne of a lama. A very strong renunciate, he spent most of his life either studying with the Sakya and Nyingma masters active in Kham at the time, or meditating in remote places. He spoke very little and, as a nomad, ate meat twice a day.

After his initial enthronement, Deshung Rinpoche spent several months studying and practicing Kunrig (Skt. Sarvavid-Vairocana, Tib. Kun-rig rnam-par snang-mdzad, the main deity in the *Elimination of Bad Rebirths*, Skt. *Durgati-parishodhana-tantra*), for rescuing beings who have fallen into unhappy states. He studied these and other rites with Deshung Chöphel, a learned monk from the Deshung regionwho was a close disciple of Gatön Rinpoche and who became the fifth abbot of the Dsongsar seminary.

When the new Tarlam temple was finished later that year, Gatön Rinpoche held the official investiture of Deshung Rinpoche III, regent and heir to the Tarlam throne. (There was no history of reincarnations per se at Tarlam Monastery; any monk of great sanctity and learning could rise to become its leader, as Gatön Rinpoche himself had.) During the ceremony, Gatön Rinpoche offered Deshung Rinpoche a statue of Mañjushri that was the most exquisite of all the images at Tarlam, a copy of the *Good Destiny Sūtra* (*Bhadrakalpika-sūtra*), Deshung Rinpoche II's personal bell, a scholar's slate upon which the opening lines of the Sarasvatī grammar were lightly written (to indicate his coming greatness as a scholar, including as a scholar of Sanskrit grammar), and a pen in the shape of a sword. He also presented a prayer for Deshung Rinpoche's long life that he had written himself:

> Long remain among us, O master of doctrines vast
> And illuminer of teachings that reveal the joy of transcendent wisdom!
> The second Maitreya, a loving sun among teachers,
> You are, for all beings, a protector endowed with wisdom, compassion, and power.
> Ever may your mind be adorned by the three codes of purest vows;
> Coursing to the end of all study, reflection, and meditation,
> May you increase in every way your holy works,
> Explaining, discussing, and showing to us the Way.
> May your Body of Illusion remain for hundreds of aeons
> And all your wishes spontaneously become fulfilled,
> That the sun of the teachings of Holy Sakya, and of its masters of wisdom,
> May shine throughout the worlds.
> Sun among speakers, live long to ripen the lotus fields
> Of teachings of Great Compassion,
> And pervade to the ends of every direction
> Your realizations, your knowledge, your holy deeds.

FURTHER STUDY AND PRACTICE

At eighteen, Deshung Rinpoche sat at Tarlam Monastery in a number of retreats in preparation for travel to Dsongsar Monastery for further study of various topics and practices. At nineteen, he accompanied Gatön Rinpoche from Tarlam to the retreat center of Derge Gonchen, where Gatön Rinpoche was to teach the lam-dre system of knowledge and practice.

On the way from Tarlam to Derge, Gatön Rinpoche and his party passed a place in Denma where there was a famous image of Tārā, the most prized in all Tibet due to its antiquity. That night, Deshung Rinpoche dreamt that he carried away the famous statue and was worried lest he be accused of thievery. Awake, he wondered if his dream were a bad sign, but Gatön Rinpoche said, "The biographies of many scholars show that they received the protection of Tārā in their labors. This shows that you, too, have a connection with her in your teachings, so you must practice her meditation regularly and diligently."

After Gatön Rinpoche had reached the retreat center and begun teaching, Deshung Rinpoche went on alone to meet Dsongsar Khyentse Rinpoche II, Jamyang Chökyi Lodro (1896–1959, hereafter Khyentse Rinpoche), the founder of the Dsongsar seminary and the "activity emanation" of the great nonsectarian practitioner Jamyang Khyentse Wangpo Rinpoche, Gatön Rinpoche's own teacher (see above). Khyentse Rinpoche (Pl. 3, p. lxvii) was in strict Hevajra retreat at the time, so Deshung Rinpoche didn't actually see him until later. Gatön Rinpoche instructed him, "Since Khyentse Rinpoche is truly Mañjushrī, when you first meet him you should request the reading empowerment of the *Song of the Names of Mañjushrī* (*Mañjuśrī-nāma-saṃgīti*)."

Khyentse Rinpoche spoke briefly and directly, without wasting time. He was the master of Dsongsar Monastery and many southern and northern branch monasteries; he had studied well and liked meditation. His own program was six months of study followed by six months of retreat, but he was too busy to follow it. He had both Nyingma and Sakya connections, and studied texts and did retreats of the Kagyu and Gelug traditions as well.

Gatön Rinpoche had written a letter for Deshung Rinpoche to give to Khyentse Rinpoche, requesting the latter's assistance in securing a Sanskrit tutor in the person of Palyul Lama Sherab Ozer. Khyentse Rinpoche was still in retreat, so the letter was not of immediate use, but Deshung Rinpoche obtained an introduction from the chaplain-monk of one of Gatön Rinpoche's sponsor families in Dsongsar. Hence he was accepted as a pupil, despite the fact that the Palyul Lama, then in his sixties, had given up normal teaching activities.

It was unusual for Tibetan monks to study Sanskrit. Gatön Rinpoche was eager that Deshung Rinpoche do so because, when he had consulted the *Song of the Names of Mañjushrī* for divination purposes at the time of Deshung Rinpoche's enthronement, he had opened the book to the words "immortal lord, teacher of the gods," a reference to an Indian deity of wisdom and eloquence whose particular domain was Sanskrit language and grammar. Gatön Rinpoche always insisted that Deshung Rinpoche study grammar and poetry in order to become skilled in composition and teaching: "Learn grammar before you study the *Bodhicharyāvatara*,"[12] he used to say. In Kham, skilled grammarians were rare.

Deshung Rinpoche studied these subjects throughout his twentieth year. In the years that followed, he received the *Anthology of Tantric Practices* teachings from Khyentse Rinpoche; studied many texts on Madhyamaka philosophy with Lama Jamyang Gyaltsen, his maternal uncle and a Tarlam monk; and received numerous other initiations (*dbang*), text transmissions (*lung*), and explanations and practical instructions (*khrid*) from various accomplished teachers. Lama Jamyang Gyaltsen was very disciplined; like Gatön Rinpoche, he was a vegetarian and did not eat after the midday meal. He spoke only when asked, and then spoke only about the Dharma; at farewells he always said, "Be mindful."

Hearing that Gatön Rinpoche was again giving lam-dre teachings in Horkog, Deshung Rinpoche gave his mule to Khyentse Rinpoche as a parting gift and walked for five days across many ridges in heavy snow and high winds, becoming snowblind from the glare and getting frostbite on his face from the fierce blasts of wind. Arriving at the teachings, he went to see Gatön Rinpoche, who asked, "Why are you here? Why aren't you studying grammar?"

Deshung Rinpoche asked, "Should I return?"

"Yes, go back and study," Gatön Rinpoche replied. "Later I will give the extensive *Lam dre* especially for you at Tarlam; at the present, learn grammar." But in the end, Ajam Rinpoche and others convinced him to let Deshung Rinpoche stay. During this period, Deshung Rinpoche performed his first initiation and gave a transmission of the Sakya canon to many yogis and practitioners.

When Deshung Rinpoche was twenty-three, Gatön Rinpoche took him to Deshung Monastery at Ajam Rinpoche's request. There he received full monastic ordination from Gatön Rinpoche, his name was changed to Kunga Tenpay Nyima, and he was formally introduced to—and recognized by—the monks and laypeople of Lithang as the new incarnation of Deshung Rinpoche II. But because Gatön Rinpoche felt that Deshung Rinpoche had wasted almost two years away from his studies, he arranged for him to study mornings and afternoons, perform initiation ceremonies during the noon hour, and be tested on his knowledge daily. It was a very busy, demanding time for Deshung Rinpoche. He then returned to Dsongsar Monastery and continued his Sanskrit studies with Kunu Lama Tenzin Gyaltsen.

When Deshung Rinpoche was twenty-six, Gatön Rinpoche wrote from Tarlam, "You have stayed in Derge seven years. Come back now." At the same time, Ajam Rinpoche wrote from Deshung Monastery, "Now you must return here." Deshung Rinpoche asked Khyentse Rinpoche what to do; the latter replied, "Gatön Rinpoche is your root guru. Best to do as he instructs."

ᥱᐩᥱ

Gatön Rinpoche told Deshung Rinpoche to master the Derge style of script before coming to Tarlam, so he went to the monastery of the eleventh Pälpung Situ Rinpoche, Pema Wangchok Gyalpo (1886–1952), and studied with his secretary. While there, Khenchen Samten Lodro of Derge Gonchen, a famous Yamāntaka adept, arrived to consecrate a huge new Maitreya statue. Khenchen had written a book on the "Meditation on the Master" entitled *Source of Jewels* (*Rin chen 'byung ldan*), which had never before been taught in full to any student. He offered to teach it to Deshung Rinpoche, saying, "Although I have given the transmission for this text to hundreds of monks, none has been able to teach it to others. Since you have studied with the great Khyentse Rinpoche, you should receive this teaching three times and then teach others, in order to continue the transmission."[13]

When Deshung Rinpoche finally arrived at Tarlam Monastery, Gatön Rinpoche inquired about his studies and said it would be good if he were to review all he had learned in a "study retreat." First, however, there was an eight-month course with Ajam Rinpoche on the *Chijönsum* (*Spyi ljon [brtag] gsum*), the three main Sakya exegetical texts on the *Hevajra Tantra*.[14] Ajam Rinpoche taught all the monks incessantly, but Deshung Rinpoche was his principal target of instruction, so he bade Deshung Rinpoche ask every question he might have.

Immediately thereafter, Deshung Rinpoche and Gatön Rinpoche did separate study retreats in adjoining rooms. Deshung Rinpoche was then twenty-eight years old; he spent the time chiefly reviewing questions on lam-dre topics, but he also performed thirty-five hundred prostrations daily because Gatön Rinpoche had completed that number during a previous retreat. Like his teacher before him, Deshung Rinpoche became ill from doing too many prostrations. Pain spread throughout his body, and his right leg became particularly sore. Arthritis developed in his right knee, which was badly swollen. He also developed digestive problems and was ill for a year in all. He then returned to Tarlam, where his paternal uncle Lama Josay Jamyang Gyaltsen was a doctor.[15] Deshung Rinpoche tried many remedies and was eventually able to walk with a cane, but the knee gave him trouble for the rest of his life.

Some time after this, several senior monks came to Tarlam to receive *Lam dre* from Gatön Rinpoche, and Deshung Rinpoche served as meditation instructor during the teachings. He then did a long Hevajra retreat, during which he was guided by Gatön Rinpoche, a Mahākāla retreat, and others.

He traveled to teach at the request of a Kagyu lama for three months; received the White Tārā empowerment from Gatön Rinpoche, following it up with a three-month retreat; and taught and studied with Tartse Shabdrung Rinpoche, Jampa Namkha Kunzang Tenpay Gyaltsen (1907–1940), and other eminent Sakya monks.

By this time Deshung Rinpoche was thirty-three years old. He went on a ten-day holiday in the mountains, enjoying picnics and songs with the nomads grazing their herds there. His brother, Dr. Nyima, who periodically accompanied him on his travels, arrived and offered Deshung Rinpoche a very fine ceremonial hat and robes. Deshung Rinpoche had not been able to make suitable offerings to Tartse Shabdrung Rinpoche, so now he offered the hat, robes, and a horse. Shabdrung Rinpoche asked, "Won't your brother be unhappy?"

But Deshung Rinpoche replied, "No, he already gave them to me." Shabdrung Rinpoche reciprocated by giving Deshung Rinpoche a Mahākāla statue, two Mahākāla texts, and a reliquary, as representations of the enlightened body, voice, and mind of Mahākāla.

RECOGNITION AS GATÖN RINPOCHE'S SUCCESSOR AT TARLAM

In the meantime, Gatön Rinpoche had been away teaching for twenty months. When he returned to Tarlam Monastery, he told Deshung Rinpoche, "Up to now, I haven't allowed you to travel or go away to teach but have kept you under my wing and controlled your career like a mother hen, until, like a fully developed fledgling with strong wings, you were able to fly without difficulty."

On an auspicious day, Deshung Rinpoche was officially coronated, on a great golden throne, as Gatön Rinpoche's personal successor. Gatön Rinpoche offered a table covered with every ritual instrument, fine clothes, dishes, and his own crown. He then announced to the assembly, "This is my successor at Tarlam."

Now it was time to teach, time to visit Lithang and Mi-nyak, and then Sakya and Ngor. Gatön Rinpoche wrote a letter addressed to all:

> Now I am old. I have accepted Deshung Rinpoche as my successor. There is no difference between us. Those who wish to meet me should meet Deshung Rinpoche. If they need teachings, ask him. Offerings to Deshung Rinpoche are the same as offerings to me; offerings made to him and merit dedicated will be accepted by me spiritually.

First, however, it was necessary for Deshung Rinpoche to receive the blessings and instruction of his tutors Khyentse Rinpoche and Lama Jamgyal (his maternal uncle Jamyang Gyaltsen). But on the road to Derge he met a messenger: Lama Jamgyal had died. Deshung Rinpoche stopped immediately and performed the "Veneration of the Master" rite for Lama Jamgyal. At Dsongsar he found that Khyentse Rinpoche was very ill, but Deshung Rinpoche did meet with him and give him an initiation that he requested. Proceeding to Deshung Monastery, he performed prayers there and did a six-month retreat on the bodhisattvas of wisdom, compassion, and power according to Ajam Rinpoche's instructions. (To be able to give the initiation for the *Anthology of Tantric Practices*, it is necessary to have done this retreat.) This was followed by a White Tārā retreat for long life and a Mahākāla retreat to dispel obstacles while traveling.

After this Deshung Rinpoche received numerous invitations to teach and gave many initiations and reading empowerments, especially to new monks who had yet to receive such teachings. He then went to Ri-khu, the original and chief Sakya monastery in Mi-nyak, and imparted the *Anthology of Tantric Practices*. Many Nyingma, Sakya, Kagyu, and Gelug geshes and tulkus attended; some seven hundred monks and five hundred laypeople were present for the four months of teaching.

Much traveling, teaching, and granting of empowerments followed, as well as bestowing novice and full monastic vows on all who qualified. When he met an eminent teacher—such as Kangkar Karma Drupgyüd Chökyi Sengay, the sixteenth Karmapa's tutor, whom the eleventh Situ Rinpoche called "the most learned man in all 180 Kagyu monasteries in U and Kham"—they exchanged many teachings and gave each other initiations upon request.

In 1941, when he was traveling and teaching among the people of Deshung, a messenger arrived from Tarlam to announce that Gatön Rinpoche had died. Deshung Rinpoche presided over the Deshung monks in recitation of the Sapan "Veneration of the Master" rite for seven days. From this time on, he was head of Tarlam in fact.

PILGRIMAGE TO SAKYA

When he was forty-one years old, Deshung Rinpoche returned to Tarlam Monastery and led the assembly for six months, then went on pilgrimage to Lhasa by way of Sakya and Ngor.

Deshung Rinpoche had been told repeatedly, from childhood, by both Gatön Rinpoche and Khyentse Rinpoche (see Pls. 1 and 3, pp. lxv and lxvii), that one's mother is very important on the spiritual path. Both teachers had often reminded him of the kindness of his mother, so he decided he would definitely take her along; his younger sister, Ani Chimey Drolma, a nun, also accompanied him. For six days, Dr. Nyima and other family members rode with them to see them off and to protect them from bandits. Four monks and a steward were in the party, while forty-two horses and mules carried the baggage. Following the nomads' trails, where the grass was good, they went first to Shigatse and stayed there for about a month.

From Shigatse they went to Sakya, where they lodged at the summer palace in the park. There they met the fortieth Sakya Trizin, Ngawang Thutop Wangchuk (1900–1950), as well as Ngawang Kunga (b. 1945), who was to become the forty-first Sakya Trizin but who was then just learning to walk. His Holiness Thutop Wangchuk was preparing to leave for Lhasa to perform the ancient Vajrakīlaya rite to avert obstacles to the Dalai Lama's government.[16] During his absence, Deshung Rinpoche was asked to perform the life-protecting rite in retreat for one month.

After doing so, he went on a six-month pilgrimage to the caves where the great yogi Milarepa had meditated, bestowing offerings and giving teachings wherever he went. At the spot where Milarepa had attained realization after twelve years of intense practice, Deshung Rinpoche stayed for over a month to perform many offering rites. His mother was very old, so she had remained at Sakya. Hearing that she was ill, Deshung Rinpoche returned, and she recovered quickly.

While at Sakya, Deshung Rinpoche performed many rituals for His Holiness Thutop Wangchuk of the Puntsog Palace and for Ngawang Kunga Rinchen (1902–1950), the Drolma Palace's prelate and future Sakya Trizin's father. He also received the Hevajra and other major initiations from Ngawang Kunga Rinchen, whom he regarded as one of his root gurus. Sadly, the latter's wife fell ill and died while he was there, so Deshung Rinpoche performed rites for her and supervised the appropriate offerings at more than a hundred Sakya temples in the region.

Deshung Rinpoche had long wanted to make a pilgrimage to Ngor Monastery to receive the *Lam dre* from a Ngor abbot—a necessity due to his position as the head lama of a branch monastery of Ngor. Early in 1949, he was finally able to do so. Following the lam-dre teachings, he made offerings to the assembled monks on four successive days.

In the meantime, his sister Puntsog Drolma and her daughter Sönam Tsedzon (Dagmo Kusho) came to Ngor with provisions. They all returned to Sakya together, where an important lama had arrived from Amdo to receive the Vajrakīlaya initiation from Ngawang Kunga Rinchen, who said, "This is the first time I am giving it to my son, so I will give the extensive version." The initiation had been requested by Deshung Rinpoche as the main patron.

Next, Deshung Rinpoche went to Kha'u Dagdzong, where Ngawang Kunga Rinchen's paternal aunt, Jetsünma Pema Trinlay, sister of His Holiness Dragshul Trinlay Rinchen (the thirty-ninth Sakya Trizin), lived in meditation. Her guru, Deshung Rinpoche II, had given the Vajrayoginī teaching to her, and through practice she had received the Vajrayoginī realizations (*siddhi*). She was a very famous nun, then seventy-eight years old, who could predict anyone's time of death. Deshung Rinpoche received the White Tārā, Vajrayoginī, and other initiations from her; when she requested one from him to cement their religious connection, he gave her the long-life empowerment of Tangtong Gyalpo (a great Tibetan saint of the fourteenth–fifteenth centuries) to ensure her longevity.

Back at Sakya, his niece Dagmo Kusho had become engaged to His Holiness Dagchen Rinpoche (Pl. 4, p. lxviii), the son of His Holiness Thutop Wangchuk. She had never had the Hevajra empowerment, and since all brides who marry into the Khön family need this, Deshung Rinpoche asked Ngawang Kunga Rinchen to perform the complete teaching for her.

Deshung Rinpoche and his family returned to Shigatse and traveled from there to Lhasa, where he made offerings at the Jowo shrine and elsewhere and went on pilgrimages to various holy spots in the area. Having given all he had in offerings, he had to borrow to buy gifts for friends back at Tarlam, where he also made many offerings in the temple upon his return.

TROUBLES BEGIN

When he was forty-four, Deshung Rinpoche went to teach among the nomads in the northern plains. Before leaving he gave a "death pill" to several relatives, saying, "While Gatön Rinpoche was at Dsongsar, his mother died. If my own mother suddenly falls ill, be sure to put this in her mouth."[17] Three months later, while he was away, his mother did become ill and die; soon thereafter, his uncle Ngawang Nyima performed a transference of consciousness (*'pho-ba*) ceremony for her. Deshung Rinpoche fasted and did other practices to help ensure his mother's good rebirth.

Ngawang Nyima, although not ill, died suddenly at Tarlam Monastery when Deshung Rinpoche was forty-five. For nineteen days his body remained in equipoise (*samādhi*). Deshung Rinpoche returned for the ceremonies and then went into retreat at Tarlam before returning to the northern plains to continue teaching.

A few months later, Deshung Rinpoche accompanied His Holiness Dagchen Rinpoche to Dsongsar, where they received both lam-dre teachings and teachings from the *Anthology of Tantric Practices* from Dsongsar Khyentse Rinpoche. Dilgo Khyentse Rinpoche (1910–1991), the "mind emanation" of the great nonsectarian teacher Jamyang Khyentse Wangpo, was also present. During the *Lam dre*, Deshung Rinpoche served as meditation instructor. Afterward, he received the Thirteen Golden Dharmas (a collection of sādhanas of the Tsarpa tradition of the Sakya school) and many other initiations and teachings from Dsongsar Khyentse Rinpoche.

In 1954, Dagchen Rinpoche accompanied His Holiness the Fourteenth Dalai Lama to Beijing as a representative of Sakya, while Dsongsar Khyentse Rinpoche, Deshung Rinpoche, and Dilgo Khyentse Rinpoche stayed together on the mountain of Ösel Lari Gang for ten days, discussing meditative experiences and realizations.

When Dagchen Rinpoche returned to Dsongsar, he reported that eastern Tibet was already being invaded by the Chinese and that he planned to leave. Dsongsar Khyentse Rinpoche replied, "I myself plan to go on pilgrimage to Lhasa and India." He told Deshung Rinpoche to stay with Dagchen Rinpoche, Dagmo Kusho, and their family. Deshung Rinpoche did so, although he wanted to return to Tarlam Monastery to fulfill his promise to Gatön Rinpoche to look after it. Deshung Rinpoche would never have disobeyed Khyentse Rinpoche, but he said, "I will remain and serve the family until they leave for Lhasa. At that time, I wish to be excused to return to Tarlam." In the meantime, he continued to teach and perform ceremonies as requested.

Returning to Tarlam, Deshung Rinpoche spent much of the next two years (1956–58) in retreat. His brother Dr. Nyima said that Deshung Rinpoche had a vision of Tārā during this retreat.

In the fall of 1958, Deshung Rinpoche began teaching the *Anthology of Tantric Practices* at Dsongsar Monastery, but only finished five volumes before his throat became so sore that he could not speak. He sent a Tarlam monk to Dr. Nyima at Kyegu Monastery (Jyekundo), asking him either to come or to send medicine. By that time, the Chinese had already taken control of the area around Kyegu and had decreed that all monastic officials needed a permit to travel; they gave Dr. Nyima permission for only five days. Three days later, they surrounded Kyegu and arrested all the officials of the monastery (Dr. Nyima was on their list). As forty-six Chinese army trucks approached the town, Tibetan resistance fighters ambushed the convoy; only one truck escaped to China. This started the war in that region.

Meanwhile, Deshung Rinpoche resumed bestowing initiations at Tarlam: the Tibetans thought that the defeat of the Chinese convoy had lessened the danger to Kyegu, so the teachings continued. A month later, ten thousand Chinese troops were reported to be on the way. On hearing this news, the people of nearby places began to flee, and Deshung Rinpoche had to stop teaching so the monks who wished to could escape. Meanwhile, Tibetan resistance fighters came to him requesting protection cords and death pills, since they were determined to fight and, if necessary, die. Deshung Rinpoche gave them what they asked for.

ESCAPE FROM KHAM

Deshung Rinpoche's escape from Kham took place in the autumn of 1958. First, he told all the Tarlam monks to leave. He and some of the monks traveled day and night to reach Goshung, where Rinchen Tsering, the Dra'u chieftain (ruler of the Ga district), and his followers had gathered. They stayed there for several weeks, but one day several Chinese military airplanes circled over the encampment and Rinchen Tsering's men managed to shoot one down.

The next day, Chinese foot soldiers attacked the camp from all directions. Deshung Rinpoche and Dr. Nyima became separated and took different routes to escape the fighting. Deshung Rinpoche, a large man in yellow on a white horse, was a prime target of the Chinese gunners' bullets. His sister, Ani Chimey Drolma, was with him (see Pl. 2, p. lxvi). He recited mantras and visualized six-colored light rays stopping the bullets. The Chinese troops chased them; they made it past one ridge but were still pursued; someone then shot one of the pursuers and the rest of the Chinese retreated. For the moment, they were safe. Deshung Rinpoche escaped with only his horse; he could take no personal belongings with him, not even books. Most of the others at Goshung were either killed or surrendered.

That night, some Tibetan resistance fighters came by and shared what they had with Deshung Rinpoche. He had no bowl to put food or tea in. While the Chinese were asleep, a few attendants returned to the camp and retrieved Deshung Rinpoche's box of religious articles and a little food and clothing. Only three or four Tarlam monks were still with Deshung Rinpoche at this point, and his whole party numbered only fourteen.

Deshung Rinpoche traveled circuitously for six months to Penpo, while

Dr. Nyima managed to go directly to Lhasa. Dagmo Kusho wrote to Deshung Rinpoche to come to Lhasa, too, where there was less danger just then. He arrived at the end of February 1959. On March 8, the party of thirty-eight or thirty-nine returned to Nālandā Monastery; it included Dr. Nyima, His Holiness Dagchen Rinpoche and his family, Ani Chimey Drolma, and a few Tarlam monks, the rest being scattered in Lhasa and elsewhere. On March 10, there was a general uprising in Lhasa. The Tarlam monks requested Deshung Rinpoche to go to India, since they had already traveled so far from Kham and still wished to save his life. Deshung Rinpoche decided to depart; when he told Dagmo Kusho, she and Dagchen Rinpoche decided to accompany him.

From Nālandā Monastery they went to Samye, then to Lodrag and on to Mayla Karchung, a pass on the border of Bhutan. Before leaving Nālandā, the Chinese planes strafed them, but from Samye on, two Kham guerillas guided them. It was a very difficult twenty-seven-day journey. The party had to learn where the Chinese were and travel around them, getting information from other travelers about roadblocks.

At the border, the Bhutanese did not allow them entry. There were seventeen hundred Tibetans waiting there, including many high lamas and nobles, such as Dorje Pagmo, the country's most famous female reincarnation. His Holiness the Sixteenth Karmapa had been admitted five days earlier. There was no food, so the refugees ate nettles. But some Bhutanese soldiers invited Dagchen Rinpoche to give a long-life initiation and offered him some rice; Tibetan soldiers also gave the party some food. Finally the order came: "Lamas and nobles have good reason to leave. Monks and the poor should go back. India can't help you, and life is different there. Bhutan is a small country. We can only accept three hundred at a time. Included in the first group is Sakya Dagchen." Thus Deshung Rinpoche gained entry into Bhutan because he was part of Dagchen Rinpoche's party.

Hadrungpa, the prime minister of Bhutan, who was at the border at the time, understood that Deshung Rinpoche was too ill to ride a horse, so he ordered relays of men to carry him. Many Tibetan aristocrats, pretending to be Dagchen Rinpoche's attendants, accompanied the original party. They were in Bhutan for about thirty days. From there, the larger group scattered, with Deshung Rinpoche and his family going to Siliguri, India, and thence to Kalimpong.

Deshung Rinpoche heard that Khyentse Rinpoche (see Pl. 3, p. lxvii) was ill in Gangtok. He wanted to visit him but could not do so, and a month later Khyentse Rinpoche died. Deshung Rinpoche and Dagchen Rinpoche then went to Gangtok. Deshung Rinpoche had received many teachings from Khyentse Rinpoche at Dsongsar Monastery, but felt he had not been able to make sufficient offerings compared to the inestimable value of the Dharma; therefore he had promised to offer more when he could. By traveling and teaching extensively, he had finally gathered thirty ounces of gold that he had brought with him to India. He now donated them toward the construction of Khyentse Rinpoche's memorial reliquary (*stūpa*), even though he and his family were destitute.

At Dsongsar, Khyentse Rinpoche had told Deshung Rinpoche, "Tulku, you and I are very close. When I die you definitely must come." Deshung Rinpoche had promised to do so. When he heard of Khyentse Rinpoche's death, he had immediately retired to make offerings and had forbidden others to enter his little room. In a dream or vision, he saw an amazing scene of Sukhāvatī (the pure land of Amitābha, the Buddha of Boundless Light). In Gangtok he was told that Khyentse Rinpoche had said, "Since Khyentse Loter Wangpo, Gatön Ngawang Legpa, Sachen, and others are in Sukhāvatī, I will go there also." This agreed with Deshung Rinpoche's dream.

In May 1959, Deshung Rinpoche and his family moved to Darjeeling. Dagchen Rinpoche and Dagmo Kusho had three sons by then—Minzu, Ānanda, and Mati. Deshung Rinpoche taught Minzu the Tibetan alphabet; the boy was very good at memorization and reading. Deshung Rinpoche also went on a three-month pilgrimage with Dagmo Kusho, her three sons, his sister Ani Chimey Drolma, and others. They went to Bodhgaya, Vulture's Peak, Nālandā, and Vārānasī. Deshung Rinpoche also met His Holiness the Dalai Lama at this time.

EMIGRATION TO THE UNITED STATES

In 1960, when Deshung Rinpoche had returned to Darjeeling, Professor Turrell Wylie of the University of Washington arrived, searching for a learned lama to bring back to the United States on a Rockefeller grant. Sandy and Ariane McDonald, Tibetologists working in Paris, told him, "In Tibet, Sapan was most learned. One of his descendants, Dagchen Rinpoche, is here." At the same time Deshung Rinpoche was offered a teaching job at Delhi University that included a salary and a house, as well as an invitation to teach in Bhutan for "more than whatever Westerners are offering, if you will accept."

Deshung Rinpoche did divinations and decided that Bhutan was best. However, a condition of the offer was that no more than three or four people could accompany him. Dagmo Kusho was very sad at this and begged

Deshung Rinpoche to come to the United States so that the family would not be separated. He agreed, and thus the family flew to Seattle in August of 1960.

The noble Surkhang and Yuthog families, who emigrated to Seattle in the mid-1960s, asked Deshung Rinpoche to give initiations. He refused, but he did teach the wisdom (*prajñā*) chapter of Shāntideva's *Bodhicharyāvatara* to former Tibetan cabinet minister Yutog and gave the Chenresi (Avalokiteśvara) initiation to Surkhang. These were his first teachings in America. Thubten Jigme Norbu, His Holiness the Dalai Lama's elder brother, and Robert B. Ekvall were translating a Tibetan play on which they consulted Deshung Rinpoche and Dagchen Rinpoche, who also contributed to other books by Professor Ekvall.[18]

At the University of Washington, Edward Conze and other professors said, "There are four Buddhist schools and four Tibetan orders, but their views are different. Please write a summary of their differences in theory and meditation." Hence Deshung Rinpoche wrote *Instruction for the Wise* (*Mkhas pa'i zhal lung*).

Until 1968, Deshung Rinpoche remained quietly in Seattle. He walked to the university but had to rest often, sitting down every day at one spot along the way. The family living there saw him and placed a chair on their lawn for him to use, so that he would not get wet from the damp ground.

In 1969, he had knee surgery. Dagmo Kusho had learned of a specialist at Swedish Hospital; Deshung Rinpoche was admitted and was there for more than forty days. Neither the first nor a second operation was successful, so he could no longer go to the university either on foot or by bus. Professor Wylie said, "Now stay at home. Students can come to study and ask questions." Several American students had over the years requested refuge and teachings, but Deshung Rinpoche sent them to India for refuge or to other Kagyu, Nyingma, Sakya, and Gelug teachers.

Deshung Rinpoche's daily practice included eleven meditative practices (*sādhana*). Every morning, from 2:00 to 4:00 a.m., he rose and meditated on Hevajra and Vajrayoginī, then slept again. At dawn he did the Black Mañjushrī and White Tārā meditations. At breakfast he recited prayers for the lamas of all four Tibetan Buddhist orders. In the morning he received visitors; if there were none, he studied texts. Lunch was from 11:30 to 12:00; in the afternoons he held audiences or meditated. He completed the long Chenresi practice once a day, and said the short version in the afternoon; in addition, he recited twenty thousand mantras of *Om mani padme hum* each day. He recited a praise to and took refuge in Shākyamuni Buddha 108 times daily, performed the Vajrasattva meditation, and did numerous other practices. The evening meal was around 7:00 p.m. He never missed making the water offering and completing the sādhana of Golden Jambhala (the god of wealth, a tangka of whom his mother had found shortly before his birth). He made short or long offerings to protectors (guardian deities of Buddhism) according to circumstances. He performed the sleep yoga by Sapan and always recited verses from the "Seven-Point Mind Training" before retiring, as had been the custom of both his uncle Ngawang Nyima and Ajam Rinpoche.

While in planes and cars, Deshung Rinpoche recited a memorized sūtra to remove confusion from the ten directions while traveling; he also recited a text by Padmasambhava, the twenty-one praises to Tārā, and some verses from chapter ten of Shāntideva's *Bodhicharyāvatara* on removing obstacles while traveling. He made offering prayers before each meal and always gave tea, food, and presents to visitors. To poor or disturbed visitors, he was especially kind; if they offered little, he gave back a hundredfold, citing his prajñāpāramitā and Hevajra pledges always to give gifts. He had no stinginess and was very kind and encouraging. Yet he always refused to give major initiations such as Hevajra, saying, "If I give these in the United States, there will be nothing to request from the great lamas when they arrive." His main later students included Their Holinesses Sakya Trizin and Dagchen Rinpoche, Luding Khen Rinpoche and Chobgyay Trichen Rinpoche, Kalu Rinpoche, Dilgo Khyentse Rinpoche, Tartse Kunga Rinpoche, Jetsün Chimey Luding (b. 1938, H. H. Sakya Trizin's older sister), and his niece, Puntsog Podrang Dagmo Kusho.

The essence of study is meditative practice, and through that Deshung Rinpoche attained a pure vision of faith in all lineages' systems and masters. Consequently, he developed impartial respect for all and became a true practitioner and teacher of nonsectarianism. He never asked his students for anything, never showed bias, and never encouraged attachment or opposition among them. He rejected all words of politics or criticism and never spoke unpleasantly about other people, let alone about other religious beliefs. When others spoke of politics he would only grunt in reply but not speak until the subject was religion.

On the future of Buddhism in the West, he said: "Whenever the Buddha's teachings appear, this religion spreads, because it addresses the problems of mind and people respond to its benefits. Educated people who examine it will accept it, just as a thoughtful person will search out the right medicine for an illness. Based on their own experience, they will appreciate it." On Westerners' faults, he said, "In meditation they can recognize the thought processes, but find it hard to get release from them."

TEACHING IN AMERICA

In 1971, Tartse Kunga Rinpoche (b. 1935, hereafter Lama Kunga) of Ewam Chöden Buddhist Center in Kensington, California, who had been a candidate for the abbacy of Ngor Monastery, and his students Janet Gyatso and Tom Trabin arrived in Seattle from Berkeley to request refuge and the Chenresi empowerment, but Deshung Rinpoche declined, telling them to ask Dagchen Rinpoche. Lama Kunga was unhappy and said, "We came to see you," so that it was difficult for Deshung Rinpoche to decide. At that moment a fruit vendor appeared at the door; Deshung Rinpoche said, "This is a good sign. Buy all the fruit." They did, and he agreed to give the teachings. This was one of the first times Deshung Rinpoche taught openly in the West, although he had quietly taught a few students, including Gene Smith, John Reynolds and Michal Abrams, during the early and mid-1960s.

In 1972, the Venerable Kalu Rinpoche (1905–1989) arrived in Vancouver, British Columbia, and started a center there. Lobsang Lhalungpa, Kalu Rinpoche's translator, and others at the center wanted to meet Deshung Rinpoche, so they arranged for a car to bring him to Vancouver in September. He stayed for ten days and conferred Chenresi and other teachings and empowerments.

In the summer of 1972, Lama Kunga had sent Janet Gyatso to study *The Three Visions* (*Nang Sum*) with Deshung Rinpoche. He also invited Deshung Rinpoche to Berkeley in June 1973; Deshung Rinpoche accepted, gave the Thousand-Armed Chenresi, and led a fasting retreat. After that Tarthang Tulku (b. 1935), a Nyingma lama living in Berkeley, invited Deshung Rinpoche to perform a ceremony for the purchase of a new house. Deshung Rinpoche knew him from Dsongsar Monastery, where both had received teachings from Khyentse Rinpoche. He gave a discourse on *Lam dre* to Tarthang Tulku only.

In 1974, Kalu Rinpoche returned to Vancouver and Deshung Rinpoche exchanged teachings with him. The same year, seven or eight students in Seattle requested the Chenresi commentary and the preliminary practices (*sngon-'gro*). They met weekly and gradually brought many others to the house. Then Dagchen Rinpoche said, "We must start a center officially," so Deshung Rinpoche inaugurated Sakya Tegchen Chöling that summer.

Seattle continued to be his home base, and he gave a vast number of teachings and initiations at Sakya Tegchen Chöling over the next twelve years, including *The Three Visions* in 1978–79.

Later in 1974, Deshung Rinpoche performed a four-month retreat at his residence in Seattle that is required in order to give initiations and teachings to Kagyu and Nyingma students.

In 1975 or 1976, Chögyam Trungpa Rinpoche (1939–1987), a young Kagyu lama teaching in the West, came to Dilgo Khyentse Rinpoche in New York and requested a teaching for fifty of his students who had completed the preliminary practices. Deshung Rinpoche had had some doubt about reports of Trungpa Rinpoche's system of teaching, but when Dilgo Khyentse Rinpoche told him that fifty of Trungpa Rinpoche's students had finished the preliminary practices, his doubts were dispelled and he rejoiced. Later he visited Trungpa's Dharmadhatu centers in various cities and on occasion recounted the lives of the previous Trungpas.

In 1977, Deshung Rinpoche established the Jetsün Sakya Centre in New York. On September 7 of that year, he began giving the *Three Visions* teachings that comprise the main body of this volume. Jared Rhoton was Deshung Rinpoche's interpreter for this and many other teachings (Pl. 5, p. lxix). He had learned Tibetan with the forty-first Sakya Trizin and others in India in 1964, while simultaneously tutoring His Holiness Sakya Trizin in English; later he received an āchārya degree from Benares Sanskrit University and a Ph.D. from Columbia University.

On October 29, 1977, His Holiness Sakya Trizin arrived in New York (Pl. 6, p. lxx), and despite a busy teaching schedule for both lamas, Deshung Rinpoche imparted to him the complete reading empowerment of the sixteen volumes of the *Sakya Kabum* (*Sa skya 'bka 'bum*, the collected works of the five Sakya founders). Later, in Vancouver, he also gave oral transmissions of the collected works (in thirteen volumes) of Gorampa Sönam Sengay (1429–1489), a commentator to the classics of the Sakya canon whose own works are accepted as canonical by Sakya scholars of later generations. In June 1978, Deshung Rinpoche returned to welcome His Holiness to Seattle, where they remained for three months. Deshung Rinpoche accompanied him to Vancouver and gave him the White Tārā initiation there. His Holiness then went to teach in Toronto and New York while Deshung Rinpoche returned to Seattle.

In 1977–78, Kalu Rinpoche visited Jetsün Sakya Centre, urged Deshung Rinpoche to establish a new Tarlam Monastery in Darjeeling, and promised that he would help. He told Deshung Rinpoche, "So far, practitioners of the Dharma are very rare. Some learn to read a little Tibetan, carry around a lot of books, and mix up a lot of doctrines and teachings from many systems. They confuse the sense and make it difficult to be understood. It may happen like that here. Thus I hope to establish a meditative retreat house so that clear-minded students can learn the Dharma thoroughly."

In early 1979, Lama Thubten Yeshe (1935–1984), a charismatic Gelugpa teacher, came to Seattle, received teachings from Deshung Rinpoche, and requested that Deshung Rinpoche teach his students at the Vajrapāṇi Institute in Boulder Creek, California. In June, Deshung Rinpoche went there for three weeks, accompanied by Dr. Nyima; David Jackson was his interpreter. He gave bodhisattva vows, foundation practices, and the Chenresi initiation, among others. With Lama Ganga, a Kagyu teacher, he visited a Kagyu nunnery established by Mrs. Freda Bedi, who had previously visited him in Seattle; he also gave teachings at Lama Lodu's Kagyu center in San Francisco and at Lama Kunga's Sakya center in Kensington. The latter included a White Mahākāla initiation given to more than a hundred people.

Later that year, Deshung Rinpoche established Sakya centers in Minneapolis and Boston. His Holiness the Dalai Lama visited all the Tibetan Buddhist centers in New York; Deshung Rinpoche presented the mandala offering to him at St. John the Divine's Synod House. His Holiness said to Deshung Rinpoche, "Rather than teaching the ABCs to Westerners, you should return to India and teach Dharma to learned monks. A nonsectarian lama is needed; you can teach to all four schools." This played a part in Deshung Rinpoche's deciding to reestablish Tarlam Monastery in Nepal a few years later.

After these visits, Deshung Rinpoche continued *Three Visions* lectures every week in New York until he finished his commentary on the text on February 26, 1980. He then returned to Seattle, where he gave several teachings and initiations at Sakya Tegchen Chöling.[19] He traveled to British Columbia many times, consecrating Kalu Rinpoche's retreat center on Salt Spring Island, giving teachings to the Tibetan residents, and so on. Also in 1980, Jetsün Sakya Centre offered $5,000 for the reconstruction of Tarlam Monastery.

REESTABLISHING TARLAM MONASTERY

In 1981, Deshung Rinpoche traveled to India and participated in the lamdre teachings at the Tibetan resettlement colony in Puruwala. At the river bank, his car was met by a large party of tulkus, officials, and well-wishers, who offered him tea. Horns announced his arrival, and he was met by His Holiness Sakya Trizin, His Eminence Chobgyay Trichen Rinpoche (head of the Tsarpa tradition within the Sakya school), His Eminence Luding Khen Rinpoche (head of the Ngorpa tradition), and many others.

Deshung Rinpoche stayed in Puruwala for more than a month. On the anniversary of Jetsün Dragpa Gyaltsen's death (his *parinirvāṇa* day), he gave the Chenresi initiation and expounded Dragpa's biography,[20] then offered money, tea, and food to the full assembly, which was fifteen hundred strong, since he had arrived during the closing part of lam-dre teachings. Western students gave a welcoming party for him, and Dsongsar Jamyang Khyentse Rinpoche (b. 1960/1)—the reincarnation of his own teacher Dsongsar Khyentse Rinpoche II, Jamyang Chökyi Lodro—requested a reading empowerment to establish a Dharma connection with Deshung Rinpoche, since this was their first meeting. The remaining four or five Tarlam monks in exile came from Mundgod, Bylakuppe, and Kamrao.

Deshung Rinpoche gave many initiations and teachings at the request of the monks, teachers, lay Tibetans, and Westerners who had gathered for the lam-dre teachings being given by His Holiness Sakya Trizin. His Holiness the Sixteenth Karmapa then asked him to come to Gangtok to teach. Kalu Rinpoche also asked him to come to Darjeeling to establish Tarlam Monastery wherever he wished, and again promised to help.

Before Tarik Tulku, a Sakya lama who had also been in the welcoming party, returned to Nepal, he told Deshung Rinpoche, "India is hot; please come to Nepal and we can take care of you. We can help you find a little plot of land and establish a monastery. Please come and have a look in Nepal." Deshung Rinpoche did so, and upon his arrival gave the reading empowerment of the collected works of the five founding Sakya masters (the *Sakya Kabum*) to seven tulkus at Tarik Tulku's monastery. After the first volume he fell ill for three weeks, but recovered and completed the oral transmission, which was attended by many Nyingma lamas as well. He also gave several other extensive teachings.

His Holiness Dudjom Rinpoche (1904–1987), the head of the Nyingma school, was in Kathmandu at the time. Deshung Rinpoche asked his advice on where to reestablish Tarlam, to which His Holiness replied, "Nepal is best." Dilgo Khyentse Rinpoche concurred, as did Deshung Rinpoche's own divinations and dreams, and so it was decided.

After the Tibetan New Year (*lo-gsar*) in 1982, Deshung Rinpoche spent four months teaching in Malaysia and at the Singapore Sakya center. He returned to Nepal, where he began to make preparations for the new Tarlam Monastery, then flew back to Seattle in September. Two weeks later he was invited to the newly formed Drogön Sakya Centre in Los Angeles. He stopped at Lama Kunga Rinpoche's center in Kensington, where he gave bodhisattva vows and the Chenresi initiation; Kalu Rinpoche was also in the Bay Area, so they were able to meet.

Deshung Rinpoche was in Los Angeles for a month, staying in the Hollywood hills and teaching at several centers (see Pl. 5, p. lxix). Jetsün Chimey Luding arrived from Vancouver to receive teachings from him. From there Deshung Rinpoche went to the Minneapolis Sakya center for ten days.

Returning to New York, Deshung Rinpoche moved to Jetsün Sakya Centre for a month of teaching. He taught at the Boston Sakya center, then returned to Seattle and, accompanied by Minzu Sakya (Dagmo Kusho and H. H. Dagchen Rinpoche's eldest son), left for a conference of all four Tibetan Buddhist orders in Taiwan. He was there for two and a half months, much of which was spent teaching and giving empowerments to groups of many hundreds of people.

Upon his return, Deshung Rinpoche was immediately invited to Los Angeles by Dr. Wei Chi Huang, the son of one of his sponsors in Taiwan. There he gave the initiations requested by the Chinese community, as well as teaching at Kalu Rinpoche's center, the Los Angeles Dharmadhatu (Trungpa Rinpoche's center), and Drogön Sakya.

Back in Seattle, he fulfilled Kalu Rinpoche's request to travel to Salt Spring Island, British Columbia, to give teachings and empowerments as needed by the students in retreat there. Deshung Rinpoche stayed for three months in retreat and giving teachings. He then traveled to Vancouver, Seattle, Boston, Santa Fe, Los Angeles, San Francisco, Eugene, Portland, and Honolulu, giving teachings, blessings, and empowerments.

Deshung Rinpoche's final teaching at Sakya Tegchen Chöling in Seattle was Sakya Pandita's *The Sage's Intent* (*Thub pa'i dgongs gsal*), which he taught from October 13, 1985 until late January 1986. He postponed what was to be his final journey to Nepal to do so, emphasizing to his students the importance, both for them and for himself, of completing this teaching in America before he left.

RETURN TO NEPAL

Deshung Rinpoche departed for Nepal after Losar in 1986. Before leaving he said, "I am now an old man. I don't know when I shall die. However, if it is up to me, it will be in Nepal. Why? The buddhas and bodhisattvas of the three times have appeared there; it is a place where all the ḍākinīs gather, a place where many masters and disciples have gathered. There are many monks and patrons to help accomplish Dharma works. My students and patrons have made large and small offerings in the hope of establishing a Tarlam Monastery there, and representations of the Buddha's body, voice, and mind are already assembled at the site."

He also said, "When I arrive in Nepal I want to recite Samantabhadra's 'Prayer for Good Actions,' because whatever virtues I have achieved through teaching and so forth in the United States, and whatever virtues my students and friends have achieved through study and practice and making offerings to Tarlam, must not be wasted but dedicated to the enlightenment of all."

When Deshung Rinpoche arrived in Kathmandu at the end of February 1986, H. E. Chobgyay Trichen Rinpoche, Tarik Tulku, and monks of all four orders were invited to Tarik Tulku's monastery to recite prayers for twenty-two days on behalf of the nascent Tarlam Monastery. Although the temple was not finished, Deshung Rinpoche was pleased that a beginning had been made. He then gave the explanation of the *Hevajra Tantra* in abbreviated form to the assembled monks. Dilgo Khyentse Rinpoche arrived and joined in the consecration of statues for the new monastery.

Deshung Rinpoche continued to give teachings and empowerments to all who requested them. In June, however, he fell ill, was in hospital for a week, and experienced death signs, but gradually he recovered. In October he gave several days of teachings to Tibetans and Westerners.

Then Tsechu Rinpoche, a Bhutanese by birth and the head of a Nepalese Buddhist organization, said he had received an emissary from Je Khenpo (the head of the Drukpa Kagyu order in Bhutan) requesting instruction on the *Sarasvatī Grammar* (Skt. *Sarasvatī-vyākarana-sūtra*; Tib. *Dbyangs can ma'i sgra mdo*), a treatise on Sanskrit grammar. Members of the organization had searched Bhutan, India, and Nepal but could not find anyone with the transmission to teach the material; it appeared that the lineage had been lost. Deshung Rinpoche said, "Gatön Rinpoche always made me study Sanskrit. He must have foreseen that in the future the lineage would fail. Thus it is his intent that I teach." On this basis he accepted the request, despite everyone in the monastery begging him not to jeopardize his health. "But it is my guru's intention," he replied. For two months he taught the text to six or seven Bhutanese. After finishing, Deshung Rinpoche gave each student a Sanskrit name, according to the Sanskrit custom, in addition to his own picture and one U.S. dollar.

Deshung Rinpoche started more teachings at Tarlam House (the lama's residence at Tarlam Monastery), but fell ill. In January 1987, on Sapan's parinirvāṇa day, there was an all-day assembly at which he gave the consecration. In March, he gave his penultimate teachings of the Ten Wrathful Ones (Gonpo Drocu) and the Ngorchen Chenresi explanation. His eyes failed, and he became weak.

In April, he fell very ill. The doctor's diagnosis was hepatitis, which worsened. Deshung Rinpoche fell into a coma for eight days. Dilgo Khyentse Rinpoche arrived with Dsongsar Jamyang Khyentse Rinpoche and conferred the Vajrasattva initiation, among others. Dagchen Rinpoche, who had arrived earlier, gave a long-life initiation to Deshung Rinpoche and told Dr. Nyima, Ani Chimey Drolma, and the monks to take him to the hospital. They refused, fearing he would die there, and Deshung Rinpoche himself nodded to indicate he did not want to go.

Thus Deshung Rinpoche was treated at home. Lama Pema Wangdak and Lama Kälsang Gyaltsen, as representatives of his Western students, along with Dawa, his faithful attendant and relative, saw to his needs. Dr. Nyima, Ani Chimey Drolma, Tarik Tulku, Geleg Rinpoche (an important Gelugpa lama from Lithang and longtime friend), and others all requested Deshung Rinpoche to remain, but also said, "If you must go, then please reincarnate soon." When he was most ill, Dr. Nyima gave him a "death pill" from the amulet box Deshung Rinpoche always wore, because Deshung Rinpoche had always instructed him to be sure to put one in his mouth when signs of death arose.

Deshung Rinpoche recovered from the coma but could not eat or speak. Then one morning, when it was still dark, he began to talk. The previous day, Dr. Nyima had given him some Tibetan medicine reported to help a patient recover speech. He had also received a visit from Chobgyay Trichen Rinpoche, which seemed to arouse him from his deep concentration. That morning, Deshung Rinpoche improved more and more. Dagmo Kusho arrived, and he was very glad to see her. Sogyal Rinpoche, a Nyingma lama and close disciple of Khyentse Rinpoche in Tibet, also came to pay his respects.

For a month thereafter, Deshung Rinpoche talked clearly and ate as usual. Everyone thought he was recovering, and long-delayed plans to teach in Taiwan were revised. The flight was confirmed for a May 21 departure, but then Deshung Rinpoche's condition worsened.

On May 13, Rinchen Tsering, the Dra'u chieftain of Ga, Deshung Rinpoche's native district in Kham, went to see him. Deshung Rinpoche was not receiving any visitors but made an exception for Rinchen Tsering, who found him very happy and relaxed in conversation. Rinchen Tsering asked him, "How is your health? Was it very painful when you were in the coma?" Deshung Rinpoche said, "I had no pain in any part of my body. I was aware of everything, especially what Dagchen Rinpoche, Tarik Tulku, Dilgo Khyentse, and other teachers did." He said that Dilgo Khyentse Rinpoche had given him instructions on what to think at the time of death, and added, "Now Dilgo Rinpoche has made me ready to go. These days, I'm recovering. Also, others are helping and taking care of me, so it's enjoyable. But while I was in the United States, I was invited to Taiwan by some people and I agreed to go there. They still are asking when I can come. If I say I can't go, it is breaking a pledge. If I say I will come, my strength won't allow it. Thus it is difficult to decide what to do."

Rinchen Tsering asked Deshung Rinpoche whether he had had any special dreams. Deshung Rinpoche replied:

> These days I have lots of dreams, and I can't decide whether or not they are good. But last night someone came and offered a mandala. Suddenly that mandala appeared underneath my body. I thought, "Why am I here in the middle of the mandala?" Simultaneously, the door to my private room was opened by a lady, and I sensed that the scene was real, not like in a dream. The lady wore lots of decorations, with turquoise on her head like a Khampa, and was very noble, dignified, and beautiful.
>
> Usually, when I dream of her, it is a good sign. In my whole life I have dreamt of her only three times. The first time was just before escaping from Tibet; after dreaming of her, I met difficulty in traveling. The second time was in America, several years later, and I had much success in teaching after that. But the first two times she was not as beautiful and dignified or as ornamented as last night, so I think it is a good sign for me.

Deshung Rinpoche then joked with Rinchen Tsering that the dream "must have been an indication of your visit to me today. We are relatives and I'm extremely happy that you came while I am able to talk." Nevertheless, he seems to have identified the lady of the dream as Maksorma, the personal deity of his family.[21]

On May 15, Deshung Rinpoche asked, "Is Dilgo Khyentse here?" Told that he had left Kathmandu, his condition deteriorated slightly. That day Deshung Rinpoche told Lama Pema and Geshe Jamyang Tsultrim, "Today some people came and requested a Dharma connection. Why don't we recite the Samantabhadra prayer together three times? I will listen carefully. You two recite it clearly and slowly." After this, Deshung Rinpoche said three times, "Sapan's blessings are truly great."

Lama Pema asked, "Is Rinpoche speaking about the guru yoga of Sapan or some part of his teachings?"

Deshung Rinpoche replied, "I am not referring to guru yoga but to Sapan himself. Sapan is no different from the Buddha." These were his last words. He left no letter and gave no other definite indication about his next rebirth.

Dilgo Khyentse Rinpoche returned about 8:00 a.m. on May 16 and touched Deshung Rinpoche's forehead with his own, bidding him keep his mind and bestowing the *Instruction of the Gnosis-Guru* (*Khrid yig ye shes bla ma*).[22] Deshung Rinpoche breathed heavily and exhaled; then his breathing stopped.

Tarik Tulku arrived and performed the "Inconceivable Meditation of Vajrayoginī." Dilgo Khyentse Rinpoche prepared the body in the samādhi position and said prayers. He told the others, "Now he is in meditation."

Deshung Rinpoche remained seated in samādhi position in his room, dressed in his robes, for three days. On the afternoon of the third day, he was bathed and dressed in new robes and a vajra and bell were placed in his crossed hands. Tarlam monks performed the "Veneration of the Remains." On the fourth day, at noon, in a stūpa built on the rooftop of Tarlam House, there was a cremation ceremony. Tarik Tulku and the monks of his monastery placed Chenresi, Kunrig, and Hevajra mandalas under the corpse; Tarik Tulku then recited Hevajra's funeral rite, and the Tarlam monks, led by Khenpo Jamyang Sherab, a teacher at Tarlam Monastery, recited the "Purification of the Lower Realms."

Earlier in the day, many monks and laypeople of all four schools had come to offer scarves and to pay their last respects. On behalf of Deshung Rinpoche's Western students, Lama Pema, Lama Kalsang, and several monks recited the Chenresi practice and meditated. Many Westerners were present as well.

When the stūpa was ignited, it burned fiercely, and seven vultures appeared high in the sky. Afterward, the whole stūpa was covered with mud and left until an auspicious date. When it was opened, a rainbow appeared clearly to the east of Tarlam house, and thereafter, every seven days, a gentle shower of rain fell. The bones were gathered by seven Hevajra retreat practitioners, according to the Kunrig tradition, then pulverized, mixed with clay, and molded into clay figurines of deities that were given to each disciple who requested one. All this was done during the forty-nine days following Deshung Rinpoche's death, during which all the monks recited the "Prayer for Good Actions" in assembly.

Two large memorial reliquaries have been built for Deshung Rinpoche: one on the grounds of Tarlam Monastery in Kathmandu, the other at Sakya Tegchen Chöling in Seattle, Washington. In a prayer composed in 1987 at the request of Dr. Nyima, His Holiness Sakya Trizin addressed Deshung Rinpoche thus:

> Compassion is the essence of your mind,
> and so we request you not to remain
> in the Realm of Reality for your own sake
> but, for others, to reappear
> in the Realm of Form for the sake
> of beings and the teachings.

Deshung Rinpoche's reincarnation, Sönam Wangdu, was born in Seattle, Washington, on November 12, 1991, to a Tibetan father, Tenzin Choepel Lama, and an American mother, Carolyn Dawa Drolma Lama. He was recognized by both H. H. Dagchen Rinpoche and H. H. Sakya Trizin. When he was almost two, his father died in an automobile accident. Sönam Wangdu was formally identified and enthroned at Tarlam Monastery on March 8, 1994 (Pl. 7, p. lxxid). His hair-cutting ceremony was performed by H. H. Sakya Trizin on April 6 of that year, at which time H. H. Dagchen Rinpoche gave him his formal name, Ngawang Kunga Tegchen Chökyi Nyima. He and his mother live at Tarlam House, where the young Deshung Rinpoche IV is learning Tibetan from the monks at Tarlam Monastery until he is old enough to begin his formal studies there.

Plate 1. Gatön Ngawang Legpa Rinpoche (1864-1941), Deshung Rinpoche's root guru, went into retreat for fifteen years at the age of thirty-seven. In this portrait he probably looks much as he did to the ten-year-old Deshung Rinpoche when, in 1916, they met for the first time. A strict vegetarian, Gatön Rinpoche lived on yogurt, *tsampa* (parched barley flour), and rock candy. (Photograph courtesy of the Sapan Fund.)

Plate 2. From left to right: Dagmo Kusho (Jamyang Sakya), Deshung Rinpoche's niece; Ani Chimey Drolma, his sister; Deshung Rinpoche; and Dr. Kunsang Nyima, his brother, at home in Seattle, Washington. Deshung Rinpoche emigrated to the United States in 1960, along with His Holiness Dagchen Rinpoche, Dagmo Kusho, and the couple's three young sons. Ani Chimey and Dr. Nyima followed. (Photograph courtesy of the Sapan Fund.)

Plate 3. Dsongsar Khyentse Rinpoche II, Jamyang Chökyi Lodro (1896-1959), in a playful mood. Khyentse Rinpoche was one of Deshung Rinpoche's two main teachers, the other being Gatön Rinpoche. A great nonsectarian master, his own program was six months of study followed by six months of retreat, but as the head of Dsongsar Monastery and many branch monasteries, he was too busy to follow it. (Photograph courtesy of the Sapan Fund.)

Plate 4. His Holiness Jigdal Dagchen Rinpoche and Deshung Rinpoche in Seattle, Washington, probably in the late 1960s or early 1970s. During their first years in America, both men acted as consultants to Western scholars of Tibet, including Turrell Wylie, Robert Ekvall, and Edward Conze. (Photograph courtesy of Dagmo Kusho.)

Plate 5. Deshung Rinpoche and his interpreter, Jared Rhoton, in Ananda Hall, International Buddhist Meditation Center, Los Angeles, California, 1982. Deshung Rinpoche had an encyclopedic knowledge of all things Tibetan and used to speak for ten or twenty minutes at a time before signaling to Jared that it was his turn. (Photograph courtesy of Jim and Meg Smart.)

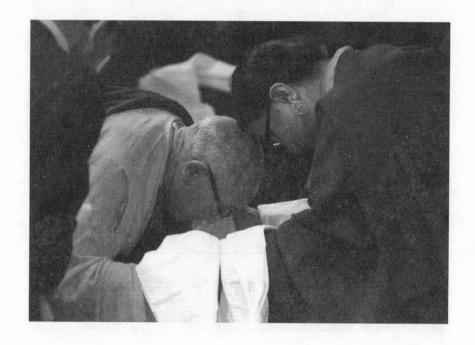

Plate 6. Deshung Rinpoche and His Holiness Sakya Trizin exchanging *kata* (offering scarves) in New York City in the fall of 1977, shortly after Deshung Rinpoche had begun giving the weekly commentary on *The Three Visions* that comprises the main body of this book. (Photograph courtesy of the Sapan Fund.)

Plate 7. Deshung Rinpoche IV, Ngawang Kunga Tegchen Chökyi Nyima, at Tarlam Monastery, Nepal, March 1994. Born in Seattle in 1991 to a Tibetan father and an American mother, "Tulku Rinpoche," as he is called, has been formally recognized as Deshung Rinpoche III's reincarnation. He is learning Tibetan from the monks at Tarlam until he is old enough to begin his formal studies there. (Photograph courtesy of Moke Mokotoff.)

PART I

THE PRELIMINARIES

I

A Priceless Jewel in a Garbage Heap

THERE ARE THREE WAYS, the sūtras say, of showing respect to your spiritual teachers or friends. The easiest way is by making offerings—either by repeating verses of praise, offering material goods, or giving other things that might please your teacher or that he or she might need. The second way is by spreading the Dharma, helping others, establishing monasteries, temples, and centers, accomplishing any other dharmic work, or helping in lesser ways.

Third, an alert student will try to show his or her reverence. This is the very best way of serving your teacher. Although teachers give the teachings to many, not every student takes their words to heart and endeavors to follow their instructions through actual performance, making the effort to study and learn the teachings rightly, helping others do so, and, having learned the instructions, teaching them to others. Actually putting the teachings of the Buddha into practice is said to constitute the highest form of respect for your teacher, and it is the very best way of offering homage to him or her. Your teacher embodies all the Buddhist teachings, which have been preserved in a very pure form since the time of Lord Buddha himself and which are now being transmitted to us.

PREFATORY REMARKS

In Tibet, when monks gathered with their particular teacher to study the Sakya text *The Three Visions: A Guide to the Meditation of the Lam-dre System*, a ceremony was conducted to prepare their minds to receive the teachings. This ceremony was designed both to remove all spiritual and psychic obstacles to the transmission of these instructions and to invoke blessings, so that the teachings might be understood with a clear mind and retained in the student's memory.

The ceremony consists, first, of the recitation of a long mantra called the *mahā-uṣṇīṣa-dhāraṇī*. Following that, there is a Vajrayāna song written by Sachen Kunga Nyingpo, the founder of the Sakya order, who composed it spontaneously when he had a vision of the mahāsiddha Virūpa, the spiritual fountainhead of this particular lam-dre teaching sacred to the Sakya order.

It is sung in a very melodic fashion. Unlike regular chanting, it is much like a Tibetan folk song, but the words are very profound. This is followed by a recitation of the *Heart Sūtra* (*Prajñāpāramitā-hṛdaya-sūtra*) and verses invoking the blessings of several masters of the Sakya order, particularly Jetsün Dragpa Gyaltsen,[23] a great yogi of the lam-dre system, and Ngorchen Kunga Zangpo, the founder of Ngor Monastery. The ceremony concludes with an invocation of one's own guru to teach this doctrine for one's own and others' benefit. Following that, the teacher expounds the teachings. He reads the text aloud—several pages, or whatever amount he has determined to teach at this particular session—and then explains it. Generally, in the course of a session, the complete day's teaching is heard at least three times. Following the teaching itself, the assembly of students recites verses dedicating any merit accrued to the enlightenment of all sentient beings. Thus there is a regular ceremony for participation in study that is almost a meditative session in itself.

To prepare your own mind for the proper reception of these teachings, reflect as follows on the difficulty of obtaining such an opportunity: (1) it is difficult to obtain human birth; (2) even after you have obtained it, it is difficult to be born in a time and place where the Buddhist teachings of enlightenment are available; (3) even in such a time and place, it is difficult to find a qualified teacher willing and able to guide you in the practice of those teachings; and (4) even if you meet such a teacher, it is rare to obtain all the necessary conditions for proper practice. For all these reasons, those who are endowed with the good qualities and conditions for study and practice are said to be the most fortunate of beings.

If you have somehow obtained such a rarely won opportunity, almost like a blind man who has somehow discovered a priceless jewel in a garbage heap, it doesn't augur well if you then waste it: your opportunity should be put to good use to benefit others and yourself. Now, since we are such fortunate beings, we are able to meet with the teachings of enlightenment and follow the path to buddhahood. Among the many Buddhist teachings available to us, the doctrine we are practicing is one that belongs to the Mahāyāna, or Great Way. This is the way of the great bodhisattvas, and among the many good religious teachings available to human beings, this one is most excellent. It is free from censure, free from all faults of being illogical, and free from all disputes about its veracity. It is a teaching that is excellent in its beginning, its middle, and its end, because at all these stages it promotes nothing but the well-being of all who come in contact with it.

ఴ ⚮ ఴ

The teachings of the Great Way can be divided into two categories: those of the exoteric Mahāyāna-pāramitā path, and those of the esoteric Vajrayāna path.[24] The first consists of practices based primarily on training the mind in various spiritual qualities that result in bodhisattvahood or buddhahood. These include, of course, both meditation and the intuitive perception of emptiness. In exoteric Mahāyāna, the emphasis is on the mind, relatively little use being made of the body and the voice. When one meditates on the exoteric Mahāyāna path, one is making efforts on the stage of causality to develop within oneself certain spiritual qualities that will eventually result in perfect buddhahood.

The Vajrayāna is esoteric Mahāyāna Buddhism. It has the same goals as exoteric Mahāyāna and the same motivation of great compassion for all beings, but differs in that it has a much wider range of more effective methods. Its practices are often performed on the result stage, so that one meditates and performs virtuous actions not as if they are causes that will someday ripen into buddhahood, but as if one is already on the stage of enlightenment. It also differs from exoteric Mahāyāna in that it makes full use of the body and voice as well as the mind. In the tantric meditations of the Vajrayāna path, much use is made of the breath and the various psychic channels and elements within the body. These and the vocal recitation of mantras are all used to bring about certain spiritual attainments. Because the body and voice are used in conjunction with the mind, and because these tantric methods are so much more direct and efficacious than exoteric Mahāyāna practices, buddhahood can be attained much more quickly. The system of meditation called the *Lam dre* (*Lam 'bras*, the Path with Its Result), which belongs to the Sakya order, comprises both the exoteric practice of the perfections (*pāramitā*) and the esoteric tantric practices. These are nondually combined, just as water and milk can be imperceptibly blended.

THE THREE STAGES OF PRACTICE

In every Buddhist meditation there are three stages: (1) the preliminary preparation, (2) the actual practice itself, and (3) the conclusion, which consists of the dedication of merit and prayers for the benefit of all beings. The lam-dre teachings also contain these three stages, even though they comprise a complete system of seeking and attaining enlightenment, not just a single session of meditation. Thus they include the stage of preparation, the stage of experiential practice, and the attainment of the result. We can see this same pattern not only in Buddhist meditation but in almost every worldly action. Even in taking your daily meals, you have the stage of preparing the food—it's not as if you suddenly sit down and the meal miraculously appears, cooked and ready to eat. First, someone has to take the trouble to prepare the food and cook it. Then you eat and, having finished the meal, you are aware that "I've eaten again" and have a sense of completion. In the same way, in meditation you have to go through stages of preparation, actual practice, and completion.

In the *Lam dre*, these three stages correspond to the texts whose study we are now undertaking. The stage of preparation corresponds to *The Three Visions (Nang Sum)*. Here are those basic meditations found in exoteric Mahāyāna Buddhism, so reference is made primarily to the sūtras spoken by Lord Buddha, to the abhidharma, and to other exoteric Buddhist literature. The stage of actual practice corresponds to the text called *The Three Continua (Gyu Sum)*. In this text, the practices belong to the Vajrayāna path and include detailed explanations of the most profound tantric meditations known to the Sakya order. These are expositions related primarily to meditation related to the *Hevajra Tantra*, and all the detailed instructions on making use of the breath and psychic channels, body and voice are fully described in this text. The stage of completion corresponds to the result of buddhahood, the attainment of the five bodies of a buddha.

These three stages also correspond to the three visions of the *Nang Sum*. The three visions are said to be (1) the impure vision of the ordinary experience of ordinary beings, (2) the vision of the path on which efforts are still being made to attain buddhahood, and (3) the pure vision of the perfectly enlightened ones.

THE AUTHENTICITY OF THE TEACHINGS

In undertaking to learn and to practice something as serious as a spiritual path, you should be concerned that the doctrines you are exposing yourself to are valid, beneficial, and authentic. You must have confidence in their truthfulness, in their beneficial qualities, and in their actually being able to lead you to the spiritual results that you seek and that they promise to provide. That is why Buddhist yogis and meditators have stressed that the lineages of teachings and of teachers must be pure and authentic. No matter how good a teaching may sound, no matter how profound or eloquent it may be, or how similar to other true teachings it may appear, it is wise to have reservations about any doctrine that promises to lead to this or that spiritual goal. Such a teaching should be examined carefully before you embark on its path.

First of all, a doctrine that is worthy of study and practice should be one that was taught by Lord Buddha himself. Of all teachers, Lord Buddha is the one who attained the highest possible spiritual enlightenment, and through his great compassion taught others the way to that same enlightenment. His words are undeceiving, so students can be sure the teachings they are receiving are truly the words taught by the Buddha himself. Second, students should make sure that the teachings spoken by Lord Buddha are among those that were collected by the great compilers such as Vajrapāni and Mañjushrī, the great bodhisattvas who bore the responsibility of preserving the direct teachings of Lord Buddha in written form. Third, students should ensure that the teachings in question are among those expounded by the great pandits such as Nāgārjuna, Asanga, and others. The instructions discussed here were elaborated and elucidated by those renowned scholars, the great pandits of India.

Fourth, the teachings should be among those that were meditated on by the great yogis and siddhas of India and Tibet. They should also be included among the texts that were translated by the great translators from their original Sanskrit into other languages. Finally, the teachings should be well known among great Buddhist scholars. They should not be recondite teachings of doubtful veracity, doubtful origin, or cryptic sense. When you have found teachings that meet all these criteria, you can be confident that you have found authentic teachings that are worthy of your time, effort, and study.

The various systems of meditation and study known in Tibet all had their source in Indian teachers who were disciples of Lord Buddha and his disciples. The Nyingma order venerates Vimalakīrti and Jñānagarbha; the Gelug order looks to the teachers (*ācārya*) Nāropa and Maitripa; and the Kagyu order looks to Nāropa, Kukuripa, and Maitripa. Many major tantric systems are included in the Sakya canon and practiced by its meditators. The principal part of Sakya literature, however, is the lam-dre system of meditation, which originated with the mahāsiddha Virūpa, who lived in India around 650 C.E. (Virūpa is spelled Birwapa in Prakrit, and appears in most books, and in Tibetan, in that form). The lam-dre teachings are modeled on the *Hevajra Tantra*; they were conferred upon Virūpa by Hevajra's consort Vajranairātmyā, passed down by Virūpa's disciples, and then transmitted to the founders of the Sakya order. Sakya practitioners also venerate Nāropa for the very special *Vajrayoginī Tantra*, which belongs uniquely to the Sakya school, and the Indian mahāsiddha Vararuchi for the *Mahākāla Tantra* and its very special teachings. These are three of the half-dozen or so major tantras, each of which has a complete canon of exegetical literature. The Sakya order is noted for its vast amount of tantric and philosophical literature and also for the authenticity of its tantras and philosophical views, which were transmitted directly from Indian masters to the founders of the Sakya school.

QUALIFICATIONS OF THE TEACHER

Not only must the teachings be authentic, but the person from whom you intend to learn them must also be a qualified teacher. In Buddhist teachings, any number of requisite qualifications are listed for the teacher, but to be brief, a proper teacher must have at least the following qualities. First, he must be endowed with pure, unblemished moral conduct and with self-discipline in his actions of body, voice, and mind. Second, he must be pure in his intentions. He must be motivated by a genuine desire to benefit his disciples, to further their spiritual well-being, and must sincerely wish to help them attain the spiritual goal of buddhahood. In short, he must be free from all selfishness. Third, he must be pure in wisdom. He must have a comprehensive knowledge of many diverse scriptures and an accurate, unerring understanding of their meaning. It won't do if he has only a partial knowledge of the sūtras, tantras, and other types of Buddhist literature. He must under no circumstances teach these erroneously. Also, he must have attained some realization, some insight into their true sense—not only of the words but of the spirit. If you have such a teacher, you can be confident that he or she is worthy of your utmost respect.

QUALIFICATIONS OF THE STUDENT

The student must also have certain qualities. Serious teachings of this sort are not to be taught to just anyone who asks for them. To abridge these into three principal qualities, we can say that a disciple must first of all be endowed with faith in his teacher. He must be receptive to the teacher's instructions and confident that they are valid teachings. Second, he must be diligent in study—in seeking to remove his own misunderstandings, in clearing up doubts, in asking questions, and in understanding the true sense of the teachings so that he will be able to practice them without mistakes. Third, the disciple should be clear-minded and intelligent, so that he won't remain indifferent to profound teachings or be discouraged by instructions that seem difficult or over his head. In other words, he must have the native intelligence to understand their importance, and hence the reason for making the effort to learn them properly. If a student is endowed with these three qualities—faith, diligence, and intelligence—he is the kind of student masters look for and hope for, and is certainly worthy of receiving the teachings of the *Lam dre*.

THE THREE STAGES OF THE PATH

Let us proceed to the teaching itself. *The Three Visions* is a practical guide for meditators who are following the lam-dre system of meditation. The title refers to the three stages on that path. The first stage is the impure vision of ordinary worldlings. On this stage, the instructions deal with reflections on death and impermanence, on the difficulty of obtaining the opportunity to practice, on the efficacy of the law of karma (cause and result), and on the natural sufferings of worldly existence in the six realms.

The second stage of meditation is called the vision of the path. This is experienced by students who have undertaken actual meditative practices. On this stage, the teachings are concerned with training the mind—with developing certain spiritual qualities such as great love, great compassion, the aspiration to attain enlightenment (*bodhicitta*), insight into the various stages of concentration, insight into wisdom or emptiness, and so forth.

Third is the pure vision of those who have attained the goal of buddhahood. On this stage, the teachings are concerned with the nature of enlightenment, the qualities and powers of buddhahood, and the nature and function of the bodies of buddhahood—according to various treatments of the subject, the five, four, or three bodies of a buddha.[25]

2

REVELING IN THE WINE OF BLISS

TO APPRECIATE THE PRESENT TEACHINGS, it is helpful to reflect on what is necessary to get even this far along on the spiritual path. First of all, it isn't easy to attain human birth. In comparison to other realms, such as the animal realm and other states of existence, humanity is quite rare. And even after one has obtained a human birth, it is difficult to be born in a time and place where the teachings on enlightenment are available. Even when one is fortunate enough to have gained birth in such a time and place, it is not easy to find a qualified teacher who is willing and able to guide one in gaining the understanding one needs to enter the path of practice. Finally, even if one has been able to find such a teacher, it is only seldom that a person finds the leisure, freedom from distraction, and freedom from personal problems that enable him to learn those teachings, take them to heart, put them into practice, and attain the result. For these reasons it is said that even a single opportunity to hear a teaching of the Dharma is a very rare event among human beings, let alone among the other beings in existence.

We should also be clear in our minds about the teachings' proper context. There are two systems within Buddhism. The first is that of the Hīnayāna path, or so-called Lesser Way, in which one strives for liberation for oneself alone: personal salvation is the motive there. However, we are going to be studying what is known as the Great Way of Mahāyāna Buddhism. A follower of the Mahāyāna path commits himself to striving for the liberation of others as well, which is why it is called the Great Way. Within Mahāyāna, there are the exoteric Prajñāpāramitā discourses and the esoteric Vajrayāna teachings. Although the goal, the motive, and the main factors on the spiritual path are the same in both, the Vajrayāna differs in its methods, which are said to be more efficient and speedier. The *Lam dre* combines both exoteric and esoteric instructions. Of course, these are presented in a graded system, starting with the exoteric teachings and working up to the esoteric teachings.

The liberation to which these instructions lead is identical to the perfect buddhahood of Shākyamuni Buddha. Although known by different names, it is taught by each of the four main traditions within Tibetan Buddhism. The Nyingmapa call it the Great Perfection or *dzog-chen* (*rdzogs-chen*); the Kagyupa dub it *mahāmudrā* or *chagya chenbo* (*phyag-rgya-chen-po*), the Great Symbol; the Gelugpa know it as the *lam-rim* teachings or "graded path to enlightenment"; and among the Sakyapa it is known as *khorde yerme* (*'khor-'das-dbyer-med*), "the nondifferentiation of worldly existence and liberation," or of saṃsāra and nirvāṇa.

Every Buddhist meditation consists of three stages. These are usually described as the preliminary stage, the actual meditation itself, and the conclusion. The *Lam dre* can also be subdivided into three stages: (1) the preparatory stage corresponds to the teachings called *The Three Visions*; (2) the next stage corresponds to the text called *The Three Continua*, which gives a comprehensive explanation of tantric meditation; and (3) the stage of conclusion corresponds to realizing the goal of buddhahood, in which one attains what are known as the five bodies of buddhahood and the five transcendental wisdoms of an enlightened being.[26]

THE ORIGIN OF THE *NANG SUM*

We should know the origin of this particular text. The first piece of basic literature that we know of was a brief set of instructions written by the great siddha Virūpa, with whom this philosophical and meditative system originated. Virūpa was abbot of the great Nālandā University around 650 C.E. He renounced his post and attained buddhahood during that very lifetime. He is known as one of the Eighty-Four Mahāsiddhas, or attainers of spiritual results. One of his Indian disciples wrote a commentary on Virūpa's instructions, and later another Indian disciple wrote a commentary to that commentary. This was repeated several more times over the centuries. In Tibet, the founder of the Sakya order not only received these written instructions and the initiations of the lam-dre system (which had been passed from one yogi to another and brought to Tibet by Gayādhara in the eleventh century), but also received them directly from Virūpa, who in a very nonhistorical fashion transmitted these same teachings to him personally. In these two forms of transmission, the entire set of meditative instructions was transmitted to the Sakya order in Tibet.

In later centuries, lengthy commentaries on these teachings were written by great masters such as A-Mye Shab, Kunga Sönam, Jamyang Khyentse Wangchuk, Könchog Lhündrub, Lhündrub Gyatso, and many others. The most famous of these commentaries, which has also come to be regarded as the most useful, was written in the fifteenth century by the great abbot of

Ngor Monastery, Ngorchen Könchog Lhündrub (1497–1557). He was both a realized yogi and an eclectic scholar who had mastered not only the literature of Indian Buddhism and the Sakya exegetical literature but the writings of the other Tibetan schools as well. He composed a set of two books called *The Three Visions* (*Snang gsum*) and *The Three Continua* (*Rgyud gsum*). These describe and provide teachings appropriate for a person from the very moment of becoming interested in Buddhist teachings to the actual accomplishment of buddhahood. This set of two books will be the basis for our discussions throughout this course of study.[27]

These teachings are presented in a traditional Tibetan style. You may find this style difficult to follow and the doctrines presented unclear. In that case, by all means seek clarification. If you can be patient and persevere in hearing the whole story, there is no doubt that you will derive considerable benefit from merely listening to the teachings. And whatever thought and reflection, let alone practice, they may stimulate will undoubtedly be of great benefit not only to you but to other beings.

There are various ways of studying the text. Traditionally, you would first read it to make sure you understood the words and the general sense. On a second reading, having the advantage of an overview of the entire text, you would try to understand each part in the context of the whole. Throughout, you would attempt to remove all confusion about the meaning, particularly of the instructions that are imparted.

THE PRELIMINARY VERSES

Those who are familiar with Tibetan or other types of Buddhist texts know that they begin with auspicious verses in which the author invokes the blessings of various holy beings in order that his work may be beneficial. He also sets forth, in brief, his purpose in writing the book. In our text, the very first words are *Om svasti siddham*, three Sanskrit words often found at the beginning of tantric texts. Roughly translated, they mean, "May the author's purpose be accomplished in an auspicious way."

Then the title of the text is given—*The Three Visions: A Guide to the Stages of Tibetan Buddhist Meditation*, or *A Guide to the Stages of the Lamdre System of Meditation*. This book is called a guide because it not only contains instructions introducing the various meditations in a systematic order, but supports those instructions with references to other teachings by Lord Buddha and by authoritative Buddhist saints, such as Nāgārjuna. It also makes reference both to Buddhist texts that are accepted as authoritative by all Buddhists and to various logical reasonings: that is, it establishes philosophical points by reference to certain forms of logic that were accepted as valid by the Buddhist teachers of India and Tibet. It refers as well to the tantras taught by Lord Buddha and explained by Indian and Tibetan saints of the past twenty-five hundred years. Hence it promises to be a true guide that you can rely on with confidence.

The three visions refer to three types or stages of perception. These are distinguished from one another with relation to the perceiver. The first type of vision is called the impure vision of ordinary worldly persons. It is impure because perception is filtered through subjective concepts of ego and also through concepts of a subject–object dichotomy and other very fundamental delusions. On top of that, this first type of vision is filtered through various passions, such as attachment, aversion, ignorance, and the rest. Since the mind is obscured by these factors, the first stage is said to be the impure vision of ordinary people.

The second stage is the vision of experience, in which one has ceased to see things as an ordinary deluded worldling and instead sees them as they appear to someone on the spiritual path. This is the vision of the meditator or yogi. Finally, there is the pure vision of those who have attained perfect buddhahood. This third type of vision is called pure because it directly intuits ultimate reality as it is, perceives the nature of all inner and outer phenomena as they are, and is not obscured by any veils of passion or ignorance.

The Three Visions is considered to be an ornament or a jewel because of its clear exposition of meditative instructions, backed up by useful references to various sūtras and tantras to reassure one at every stage that these instructions are authentic and worthy of being practiced. For all these reasons, it is said to be like a jewel that adorns the teachings of Mahāyāna and Vajrayāna Buddhism.

Next is the invocation, in which Ngorchen Könchog Lhündrub invokes the blessings of his preceptors before undertaking his work. He writes, "With devotion, I bow at the feet of the holy preceptors revered and endowed with great compassion." When he speaks of his holy preceptors, Könchog Lhündrub is referring not only to his own guru, from whom he received this particular teaching, but to all the lamas, yogis, and teachers who preceded him, from the time of Shākyamuni Buddha to that of his own guru. He salutes them and expresses his gratitude for having received the teachings from them through their great kindness.

These preceptors are called holy because they have devoted themselves in every lifetime to works of great unselfishness. Abandoning all inclination to act selfishly for their own benefit, they have devoted all their time and effort toward painstaking learning and practice of the teachings of Buddhist enlightenment. And having learned, practiced, and attained those teachings, they have unselfishly devoted themselves to guiding others, that they might gain the same benefit.

"Preceptor" is translated from the Tibetan word *lama* (*bla-ma*), a translation of the Sanskrit *guru*, which really means "a heavy," someone who is important for the student. The Tibetans weren't too happy about rendering the word literally, as it didn't convey exactly what they wanted, so they chose lama, which means "the highest."

These preceptors of Ngorchen Könchog Lhündrub are said to be "endowed with great compassion," and again he reflects on their great kindness in painstakingly learning and realizing the teachings and carefully transmitting them down through the centuries so that he and all others, like ourselves in this century, would be able to share in their great spiritual benefits. It is with their kindness in mind that he pays homage to them.

At this point, Könchog Lhündrub again follows Tibetan tradition by invoking the blessings of his particular lama, of the buddhas, and of the great yogi Virūpa, who was the fountainhead of this particular teaching. This is done in four verses of Tibetan poetry. The first verse is as follows:

> May the Master, that Jewel of the Sky who, mounting the chariot of virtue's twin heaps, ascends high into the vast sky of cognizable things, and who is skilled in diffusing the rays of his boundless deeds, keep watch over us.

"The Master" refers to the author's own kind preceptor, who is also likened to a "jewel of the sky"—a metaphor for the sun—because such a jewel is unique, bright, radiant, of great value, and so forth. "Mounting the chariot of virtue's twin heaps" is a poetic way of saying that the master moves though space—meaning the space of the realization of emptiness—by relying on the twin heaps of the accumulations of merit and wisdom, the requisites on the bodhisattva path. Every bodhisattva must make efforts to accumulate merit through kindly deeds and through training in generosity, patience, meditation, and the like, and must also accumulate wisdom through meditative insight. Thus the master has ascended into the sky of profound realizations by relying on his efforts in accumulating merit and transcendent wisdom.

Not only is the sky a place of deep realizations, it is "the vast sky of cognizable things," meaning that a bodhisattva must train not only in meditation and the other spiritual practices, but also in almost every other kind of science. He must learn medicine to benefit those who are ill; languages to be skilled in explaining the teachings, thus removing the misconceptions of human beings; logic to be quite clear about the true teachings of the Buddha and able to dispel wrong views; and philosophy and art to be able to communicate the teachings as a philosopher, painter, sculptor, and the like. The bodhisattva learns all these skills in his zeal to enable others to enter into the teachings that lead to liberation.

Again, in keeping with the metaphor of the teacher being like a sun, Ngorchen Könchog Lhündrub says that his master "is skilled in diffusing the rays of his boundless deeds," meaning that, throughout countless lifetimes, the teacher devotes his time and energy to helping others gain spiritual maturity, ripen in the realization of the various doctrines, and move toward liberation. He is very skilled at presenting the teachings in accord with the various capacities and karmic inclinations of his disciples. Hence his deeds of compassion performed among beings are said to be like the beneficial rays of the sun: not only do they remove darkness, they cause things to grow. Finally, a guru who is endowed with such benign qualities is certainly worthy of salutation, and is invoked with the words "keep watch over us." Although he has already accomplished so much, his continued kindness is again sought.

The second verse invokes the enlightened ones, the buddhas:

> May the Incomparable Victorious Ones, who, having cleansed all illusory impure visions through the vision of meditative experience, transcend time with all-pervading pure vision, keep watch over all these living beings.

This states in a nutshell what *The Three Visions* is concerned with and tells us that we are dealing with a matter of viewpoint. We start with the impure view of deluded worldly beings, which is filtered through the obscurations of egocentricity, extreme subjectivity, and the attendant mental stains of the passions—attachment, aversion, ignorance, and the rest. A person whose mind is governed by these basic erroneous views, such as belief in a real self, will not perceive things as they are in reality: rather, he will have a faulty perception of his experience. This impure vision is the ground that is to be purified.

The second line refers to "the vision of meditative experience." A yogi who has undertaken to train his mind in the various stages of meditation will find that he no longer perceives things as an ordinary, deluded worldly person. He will not only be able to see things more clearly but also much more accurately. For example, an ordinary person thinks of time as something quite real and abundant, and may also see it as a commodity, believing that there is some sort of real continuity there. He may even hold concepts of eternity and so forth. In contrast, a yogi sees time as discrete moments or flashes of instants. He perceives things much more finely, much more subtly, and may be able to see that there is no real continuity of time. He would view the idea of continuity as just a human conceptualization and would also see that instants of time are in themselves not only momentary but discrete. Thus he would be much closer to an accurate perception of time than an ordinary person would be. Moreover, he would perceive impermanence where a worldling would see permanence, impurity where a worldling would perceive purity. The yogi would have a much clearer perception of what is going on, of what his experience is. Although his is not an enlightened view, it is certainly no longer an ordinary worldling's view, for the yogi undergoes a change of perception—a change brought about by his meditative experience.

Finally, there is the third stage of perception, which is called the "all-pervading pure vision" of the victorious ones. The perception of an enlightened being is no longer obscured by defilements, by belief in subject and object, and hence is no longer governed by this basic dichotomy that separates ordinary beings from enlightened beings. The perception of the enlightened ones is purified of all those obscurations. It is free of all ignorance about the true nature of reality, the true nature of all internal and external phenomena. It is all-pervading because through the attainment of enlightenment one becomes endowed with omniscience, which is unlimited, unhindered, and unchecked. Hence the vision of the buddhas is the unhindered perception of things as they really are.

The verse says that the pure vision of the incomparable victorious ones transcends time. Not only does it transcend all human concepts of time, but when an enlightened person awakens to buddhahood, it is like our awakening from a dream state. Then we are no longer subject to all the experiences, emotions, and thoughts that held us enthralled during the dream. We can see it for what it was: only a dream in which the mind was projecting certain images, in which we were reacting in certain deluded ways, thinking the dream experience to be real. An awakened person is able to see that experience for what it really is. Similarly, an enlightened person sees the true nature of the round of birth and death and of all the experiences of pleasure and pain, happiness and unhappiness, bondage and liberation that beings undergo through their belief that things are real. He sees all that as it really is, and is thus freed. He is liberated from the round of birth and death, just as a person awakened from a dream is no longer bound by the dream experiences that were troubling him.

In the final line of this verse, the blessings of the buddhas are invoked, through their great compassion, to benefit all beings who remain unenlightened. For the sake of all beings without exception, who through their own delusions are unable to help themselves, unable to find their way to liberation, unable to see reality as it really is, and unable to deal with their situations effectively, Könchog Lhündrub invokes the compassion of the victorious ones and prays that they will keep watch over them all.

The third verse runs:

> Reverently I salute the feet of that Lord of Yogis, ever reveling in the wine of great bliss, who stopped the great flood of worldly existence defiled and held arrested in space the immaculate sun.

"Lord of Yogis" refers to Virūpa, because his achievements in teaching and meditation were unsurpassed. Virūpa was the abbot of the great Nālandā University, which was the center for almost every form of education in India during the seventh century C.E. Tens of thousands of young monk-students gathered there from all parts of India to study the five major and five minor sciences. Virūpa had been chosen as the most learned and accomplished of all those monks. Having written many books on philosophy and logic, he became known as the Venerable Dharmapāla, which means "Defender of the Faith."

During the day, Virūpa taught many classes in philosophy, logic, and other sciences. He only taught the pāramitās and other exoteric Mahāyāna teachings. Moreover, he was always very careful in his deportment, in his observance of the vinaya, the monastic code, and in setting a good example for the other monks at Nālandā. He was very popular. But secretly he spent most of every night in the practice of tantra, which, according to tradition, should be practiced at night and in secret in order to get the best results. Virūpa practiced in this way for about twenty-four years but garnered not even a glimmer of a sign of a result. Finally, he began to get a bit discouraged. What was worse, he started have bad dreams. He saw the hells, he saw the sun and moon falling from the sky, he had any number of inauspicious dreams, and each was worse than the last. It occurred to him that perhaps tantric meditation wasn't such a good idea. He decided not to practice any more, so he threw away his rosary, which he had been using all those years in meditation on the deity Chakrasamvara. Then he was very happy for a day.

The next evening, a funny-looking woman appeared who belonged to one of the lower castes. She was dark, almost blue-black in color, gaunt, and just a sight. She came up to him and said: "Son, you've done a very poor thing by throwing away your rosary. I am your deity. You should have been meditating on me all this while. Had you performed my meditation, you would have gained results. What I want you to do now is go get the rosary." (Virūpa had thrown it down the toilet, by the way.) She told him to wash his rosary very carefully, scent it with perfume, and resume his meditation, but meditate on her.

Virūpa realized that this woman was Vajranairātmyā, the Goddess of Non-Self, who is the consort of the great tantric deity Hevajra, so he did as she requested. He got his rosary, washed it off, perfumed it, and resumed his tantric meditation. Almost immediately after he sat down, Vajra-nairātmyā appeared with her retinue of attendant deities: her entire man-dala appeared to him, just as visible as we are to one another right now. It wasn't a dream, it wasn't just a vision. It was a clear appearance of this man-dala with its deities, who proceeded to bestow on him all the blessings and insights of this particular meditation. That very night, Virūpa attained tremendous insights and ascended to the first of the ten stages (*bhūmi*) the bodhisattva must traverse on his way to buddhahood. On each subsequent night thereafter, he progressed. After six nights he had reached the sixth bhūmi, which is the stage of irreversibility, after which it is only a very short time until one reaches the stage of buddhahood, which he did.

Things changed very radically for Virūpa. Instead of teaching, being very careful in his observance of the monastic vows, and setting a good example for his students, he started eating meat and drinking wine, and he didn't go to class. Not only that, but it seemed to the other monks that their abbot was having female visitors at night. What they were really seeing was the goddesses appearing in his meditation, but it seemed to them that he was determined to create a scandal for Nālandā, and they were quite upset about it. Finally, they told him that he was really disappointing everyone, setting a very bad example for the young monks, and becoming quite a bad yogi and a bad Buddhist. Virūpa replied, "Yes, you are quite right, and for the sake of Nālandā University, I think I should leave." They agreed, and so he left.

After leaving Nālandā, Virūpa roamed about and meditated in the jungles for a while. He got quite sunburned and became quite dark. He had also become quite heavy from eating meat. His hair and his beard were quite long, and he had taken to adorning himself with garlands of flowers, which was considered in very bad taste, particularly for Buddhist monks in India at that time. Everywhere he went, everyone said, "Look at that bad Buddhist beggar," and they didn't have any respect for him. In fact, he had changed so much that instead of calling him the Venerable Dharmapāla, people began calling him Virūpa, which means "The Ugly One."

One day Virūpa was on his way to Vārānasī (Benares) and came to the river Ganges, but the boatman refused to take him across because he had no money for the fare. Virūpa performed a certain gesture (*mudrā*), pointed his finger at the Ganges, and addressed the river, saying, "You're quite a holy river, I understand, and of course quite pure. I myself am an ugly Buddhist monk. I don't want to dirty you by swimming across, so I think you should back up." The Ganges did, and he walked across. This is the exoteric meaning of the line that refers to Virūpa as he "who stopped the great flood of worldly existence defiled." There is also an esoteric level of interpretation for this verse, which will be explained quite soon. But the historical story is that Virūpa was the yogi noted for causing the reversal of the Ganges in flood.

Once he had crossed the Ganges and reached Vārānasī, the first thing Virūpa did was go into a pub and order some wine. He started drinking, and after a while the barkeeper became a bit anxious that perhaps this customer was not going to settle the bill for his wine, so he asked Virūpa to pay up. Virūpa replied, "I definitely will. I intend to, but I am going to drink until noon, so until the sun's rays hit this particular mark"—which he proceeded to draw on the table—"I won't pay you, and keep the wine coming."

So it was agreed, and Virūpa kept on drinking. This went on for what seemed a very long time. In fact, it went on for seven days, and the sun's rays never got to that particular mark. In the meantime, after seven days of late morning sun, the rest of the world was really beginning to become upset. Finally, the people went to the king and told him that he had to do something. The king consulted with his cabinet and determined that somewhere some yogi must be showing off, and that something would have to be done about it. So they searched and found Virūpa—still drinking. When the king understood what was going on, he agreed to pay the bill. This is what is meant by the line, "held arrested in space the immaculate sun."[28]

It was with Virūpa that *The Three Visions* originated. Although the events in his biography that we have described seem quite miraculous and hard to believe, it is not really a great marvel, because when the verse calls him "that

Lord of Yogis, ever reveling in the wine of great bliss," we must remember that the wine Virūpa partook of as an enlightened being was really the nectar of perfect enlightenment. It is likened, in a simile, to wine, which is a cause of great joy for ordinary people, making them happy in a certain way. But for the yogi, wine is the ambrosia of perfect enlightenment.

Similarly, to check the flow of the Ganges means to check the flood of defilements. The mind is like a great rushing river that is impossible to turn back. The flood of desire, hatred, and delusion, of ignorance, pride, and selfishness is like a great river that is hard for any human to deal with, let alone to turn back. But as a great yogi who had attained mastery over both his own mind and all external phenomena, Virūpa could indeed check "the great flood of worldly existence." When he attained perfect buddhahood, he attained the nature of the *dharmakāya*, the Body of Reality, which is the transcendent wisdom of all the buddhas.

This source of knowledge and wisdom is likened to a sun that illumines all the darkness of space, of bodies, and of all forms. Thus the line which says that Virūpa "held arrested in space the immaculate sun" refers to what we have just discussed on an esoteric level. On the exoteric level, Virūpa was merely performing a miracle or two by checking the river's flow and by stopping the sun in space, and was quite a drunkard to boot. But on a spiritual level, he was accomplishing certain other feats that his attainment of buddhahood made possible.

The final verse is:

> Give heed, for this is the exposition of his words on the basic practices that are the essence of all sūtras and tantras, comprising the sole path which all the enlightened traverse and the method in which the holy sages of Sakya rejoice.

Here Ngorchen Könchog Lhündrub states his purpose and promises to accomplish it. He promises that the text he has written will be a true exposition of the words of Virūpa. Now, we have said that the lam-dre system of meditation consists of two sets of teachings: the basic practices and the advanced practices. Ngorchen Könchog Lhündrub expounded the former in *The Three Visions* and the latter in *The Three Continua*. He says that the instructions for practice given in these two books "are the essence of all sūtras and tantras." The sūtras are the authentic words of Lord Buddha himself. The tantras are also the words of the Buddha—they are the various tantric meditations he taught. Ngorchen Könchog Lhündrub's teachings are not a word-by-word repetition of the sūtras and tantras but are their essence, in much the same way that cream is the essence of milk. He has extracted those teachings that a serious meditator needs to know and has expounded them in a way that is easily understood. He has not omitted anything that is truly essential.

These teachings are quite special. They comprise, he says, "the sole path which all the enlightened traverse." Buddhahood is the result of certain conditions; like everything else, it is a result that arises from causes. If the causes are present—if a person trains in those spiritual factors and undertakes those spiritual practices which will lead to enlightenment—then the result will also arise. The causes of enlightenment are (1) great compassion, (2) wisdom (or realization of emptiness), and (3) the accumulation of great amounts of merit and insight. Ngorchen Könchog Lhündrub's instructions include all these prerequisite factors and, if practiced correctly, definitely will lead to buddhahood. Indeed, they are the only way one can attain buddhahood. Buddhahood is the result of certain causes, certain practices. This teaching sets forth those causes; it explains those practices which result in buddhahood. Thus it is the only path that all the enlightened traverse through all the stages of bodhisattvahood, from the state of an ordinary being to the final attainment of buddhahood.

Finally, the author calls this teaching "the method in which the holy sages of Sakya rejoice." Not only is it the sole path of all the buddhas, it is the system of philosophical view combined with meditative practice that has been taught by the great masters of the Sakya order from the time Sachen Kunga Nyingpo received these teachings from Virūpa up to the very present. The lam-dre system, to which *The Three Visions* belongs, forms a vast amount of Tibetan literature, all of it written by Sakya authors over the centuries. Because these teachings are complete, comprehensive, and extremely effective, they have led hundreds of thousands of meditators over the centuries to attain perfect enlightenment.

These four verses serve a very important function at the beginning of a teaching. If you have practiced Tibetan Buddhist meditations, you know that before you do the actual meditation or visualization, you must prepare by taking refuge in the Three Jewels—"I take refuge in the Buddha, Dharma, and Sangha." In Buddhist literature, such verses at the beginning of a text serve the purpose of taking refuge. They also remove obstacles, not only for the author, so that he will be able to accomplish his work for the true benefit of all beings, but also for us as students. To repeat these verses, to study them, and to be aware of their purpose invokes the blessings of the buddhas and bodhisattvas, who, as the second verse says, "keep watch over all living beings." Attention to the meaning of these verses will actually help us accomplish our goal of hearing this teaching through to the end and gaining some knowledge that will help us on the spiritual path.

3

First Things First and Last Things Last

THE LAM-DRE SYSTEM OF MEDITATION is said to constitute the unique way that has been traversed by all those who have attained enlightenment in the past, who are attaining it in the present, and who will attain it in the future. This is the sole way of all the buddhas. Now buddhahood, like everything else, comes about through causes and conditions. It is the result of right causes, meaning right practices in meditation, and it is the result of a particular right way of spiritual training. The lam-dre instructions are intended to let other meditators know, in some detail, all they need to know about the right way to meditate in order to attain their spiritual goal. Because the *Lam dre* omits no instruction that a serious meditator might need and doesn't include any extraneous material, it is said to be the quintessence of the true sense of all the Buddha's teachings, whether found in the sūtras or the tantras. In particular, it contains those precepts and instructions which were transmitted by the mahāsiddha Virūpa himself.

As already mentioned, Virūpa was the spiritual fountainhead of the meditational system of the *Lam dre*, and through it he attained perfect enlightenment in his lifetime. He transmitted these same teachings to his disciples, who also attained buddhahood. Thus *The Three Visions* contains those instructions that the great saint Virūpa taught to his own disciples many centuries ago in India.

The lam-dre teachings also promise to expound the method for realizing the true nature of emptiness, which in Mahāyāna Buddhism is a kind of code word for ultimate reality. Realization of the true nature of all internal and external phenomena is a prerequisite for the attainment of buddhahood, or perfect awakening. Whether on the pāramitā level of practice or on the tantric level, the realization of emptiness plays an essential role, not only in every type of meditative practice per se but in every other type of spiritual effort one might make on either level. It is said that, as a result of following these instructions, one gains unerring insight into the true state of emptiness. Emptiness is difficult, if not impossible, to understand for those who are not motivated by genuine compassion for all living beings and who have not trained in selflessly striving for the spiritual well-being of all sentient beings. But for those who are endowed with compassion and who are sincere in their striving, these instructions on the realization of emptiness are like a stairway that they can easily climb on their way to what is known as the "City of Liberation." To give other similes, these teachings are like a bridge for wise people, and also like a lamp that illumines the true sense of all the sūtras and tantras.

THE ELEVEN SPECIAL FEATURES OF THE *LAM DRE*

The *Lam dre* has eleven special features that make it unique as a meditative system. The first is that it contains instructions both for the meditator who is on the causal stage and for the meditator on the resultant stage. Generally, when you set out to attain a certain goal, spiritual or otherwise, you begin on the causal stage and make efforts that will eventually lead to the achievement of your aim. In meditation, also, feeling yourself to be something less than a perfectly enlightened buddha, you set out to attain buddhahood, train in certain practices, and try to develop certain spiritual qualities that are said to result in buddhahood. The *Lam dre* contains instructions on this causal level. It also contains instructions on the stage of the result, meaning that you can meditate and accomplish other spiritual practices as if you are already enlightened.

Now, this is a special tantric teaching. For example, to cultivate great compassion, in the exoteric meditation you think of all suffering sentient beings and direct thoughts of love and compassion to them. By training your mind in awakening these qualities, you expect eventually to have the great compassion that a buddha is said to have. But in the esoteric meditation, you can actually identify with the enlightened compassion of the Buddha in the form of the Bodhisattva of Great Compassion, Avalokiteshvara, meditating as if you are on the resultant stage and hence already endowed with the spiritual qualities of wisdom and compassion. There are instructions in the lam-dre system for both stages of practice.

The *Lam dre* also contains instructions through which, it is said, you can understand all teachings—that is, by understanding a single teaching, you can understand all teachings, and by attaining realization in one way, you can attain all realization. To give a practical example, the lam-dre system is based on the meditation of the *Hevajra Tantra*. As a major tantric cycle, *Hevajra* is meant for practice by anyone and everyone, unlike many other tantric meditations, which are designed to help people who have obstacles about one particular thing or another. Because it is an extremely powerful tantric meditation, the *Hevajra* offers all the most efficient methods for attaining perfect buddhahood. Thus, by practicing one meditation, you can obtain the result of all meditations.

Also, the *Lam dre* contains instructions for turning obstacles on the path into spiritual attainments (*siddhi*). Generally, an obstacle is sickness or any inner problem, where, say, your mind becomes overwhelmed by anger, desire, or distraction; obstacles also occur if you are attacked by malignant ghosts, hostile spiritual forces, or the like. The *Lam dre* includes instructions for turning obstacles, whether outer or inner, into progress on the path, so that instead of deflecting you from your practice, they become part of it. By realizing their true nature, obstacles become the source of insight and even of spiritual attainments.

In this system, everything that happens is made part of your practice. Whether external or internal, good or bad, everything serves to further the practice of the path and the attainment of buddhahood, so that however formidable your problems might appear to be, mentally or physically, you are shown ways of turning them into good results. As already mentioned, when you enter the stage of actual practice, you can experience a realm of perception radically different from the familiar scenes of ordinary, nonmeditative persons in this world. The sights and sounds you pick up on at this stage are not always auspicious; it is known in many religious traditions that spiritual practice is sometimes attended by obstacles. If you feel that you are up against all kinds of hostile forces and that you are really having a hard go of it, you may become discouraged, not knowing how to deal effectively with the problem. But in the *Lam dre*, you are instructed according to whatever you experience on the path. If it is very auspicious, you are guided and blessed by the gurus and the buddhas and bodhisattvas, attended by deities, and instructed on how to turn that into benefit for yourself and others on the path. Similarly, if you do run into obstacles, whether real or imagined, you are instructed on how to turn them into the path rather than allow them to deflect you from it.

Thus these instructions enable us to transform our experiences in this world and on the spiritual path into religious insight, so that any and all problems arising from ignorance, desire, and hatred are transformed into aspects of enlightenment itself. It is rather like alchemy, in which a particular substance, *rasāyana* (similar to the Western notion of the philosopher's stone), is supposed to transform base metals, like iron, into gold. To borrow this example, these instructions permit us to transform the deluded stuff of human experience into the experience of full, complete enlightenment.

Finally, these instructions provide a complete explanation of the secret tantric teachings taught by Virūpa in his *Vajra Verses on the Path with Its Result* (Skt. *Marga-phala vajra-gāthā*; Tib. *Lam 'bras rdo rje tshig rkang*).[29] This book was the result of his own experiences as a tantric yogi and of his attainment of enlightenment through these very methods. It is said to be like a wish-fulfilling jewel because it is of great value, extremely rare in the world, and, if possessed, able to fulfill all our wishes.

Because this is a tantric system of meditation, it is said to be secret, in that it is not made available to those who are unable to appreciate its value or who are not ready for its practice. For the sincere student whose intentions are pure, there is, of course, no bar. It is secret in that the instructions are not taught to just anyone. The state of enlightenment that it is directed toward is not known to everyone, and its practices are known only to those who have approached it properly. For these and other reasons, it is said to be a secret teaching.

THE FOUR KINDS OF VALID AUTHORITY

We need to know, also, how the *Lam dre* will be taught. For example, how will all the claims that will be made be supported? For what reasons will we be expected to accept them as valid statements, worthy of our attention and practice?

These instructions will be taught with reference to four kinds of valid authority: (1) the root text of the *Hevajra Tantra* and its most important commentaries—the extraordinary or more advanced commentary, the *Vajra Tent of the Ḍākiṇī Tantra* (*Ḍākiṇī-vajrapañjarā-tantra*),[30] and the ordinary one, the *Saṃpuṭa Tantra*; (2) the *Vajra Verses* by Virūpa; (3) the teachings and experiences of the Indian and Tibetan masters of the lam-dre lineage down through the ages, such as Virūpa and Gayādhara, who gained enlightenment through these very teachings; and (4) our own realization attained through the preliminary practices (*sngon-'gro*) and through our main practice of tantric meditation, through which we can directly perceive the validity of an instruction—i.e., whether or not it does indeed bring the result that it promises if practiced properly.

In the transmission of this type of teaching, certain factors must be present. There must be an authentic transmission, known as the uninterrupted transmission of the blessings of this lineage, meaning that this teaching originated with Lord Buddha and has been transmitted down through the generations to your teacher, who is now passing it on to you. Because there has been an uninterrupted transmission of this teaching and the realizations that it carries, and because it is still attended by the blessings of those great teachers who have attained enlightenment through it, and by the protectors of this particular teaching, we are able to receive the teaching in its entirety and undertake its practice without any doubt about its authenticity.

There must also be the right approach in transmitting the teaching. For example, first things should come first and last things last. We start out with the preliminary teaching and advance through the teaching in its proper order, rather than inverting the order or omitting or adding teachings where they don't belong. This is the responsibility of both the teacher and the student. In addition, there should be confidence not only that the teaching is authentic, but also that the teacher who is giving it is a qualified teacher, worthy of respect and attention. If your own motive is genuine, the teacher qualified, and the teaching valid, worthwhile, beneficial, and authentic, then the effort that you put into approaching a meditative system and a set of teachings like this one will be fruitful.

This completes the introduction to the teaching. Ngorchen Könchog Lhündrub has now given the background of the teaching, its origin, its benefit or value, how it should be studied, its contents, and how they will be approached.

4

CLIMBING A STEEP LADDER WITHOUT HANDS

AS EXPLAINED EARLIER, the lam-dre text we are studying is one of the principal teachings of the Sakya order. We should keep in mind the uniqueness of the situation and should think of ourselves as very fortunate in somehow becoming able to benefit from the conjunction of so many requisite conditions. It is difficult to obtain human birth, to hear the teachings, to find someone willing and able to teach, and to have the opportunity to learn those teachings properly and put them into effective practice. Anyone who is able to benefit from such a favorable conjunction of circumstances owes it to himself to recognize the situation as a rare one and make the utmost of the opportunity.

There are several ways a teaching of this sort can be given. It can be taught by explaining the most important features of the path; for example, the path can be subsumed under six main practices or features, and each of these can then be explained. It can also be taught with reference to the type of audience the teacher has—that is, modified to suit the faculties of his or her listeners. The main points can be simplified for those who have less developed spiritual faculties, or they can be extrapolated upon for those who have both experience and considerable insight. But we won't be studying this text in these ways. We will study the full system exactly as it was taught by the mahāsiddha Virūpa in his root text, on which *The Three Visions* is based. We will proceed step by step and consider fully each of the different steps in the meditative system, starting with faith and continuing to the final, most advanced tantric practices.

Sachen Kunga Nyingpo wrote in his *Summary of the Path with Its Result* (*Lam 'bras don bsdus ma*):

> The elements of this path can be compiled in seven topics. They are: fundamental meditations, advanced meditations, the removal of doubts, the ambits of the path, progress, dispelling of obstacles, and the view of the ultimate including the result.

Briefly speaking, "fundamental meditations" refers to all those meditations that are explained in *The Three Visions*. These meditations are said to be the foundation for the advanced tantric meditations that follow, such as the *Hevajra*. The "advanced meditations" consist of the twin tantric processes of creation, or the development stage (*bskyed-rim*), and completion, or the fulfillment stage (*rdzogs-rim*). "Removal of doubts" refers to instructions and explanations that remove all doubts both about the proper way to practice and about the results you can expect to achieve.

"Ambits of the path" means that we should also recognize those factors which can cause us to experience difficulties or to fall from the spiritual path. We should also be aware of those factors that will keep us on the path, ensuring eventual achievement of the spiritual results we are seeking. "Progress" refers to the clear explanation of the various stages of experience on the path, so that we will recognize each experience as it dawns. "Dispelling of obstacles" means that we should know those inner and outer conditions that create obstacles to our practice of the path. Not only should we be able to recognize potential obstacles, we should also know the remedy or antidote to each of them as it occurs.

Last is "the view of the ultimate, including the result," which refers to the unique philosophical view of the lam-dre system, and hence of the Sakya order itself. This view is known as "the nondifferentiation of saṃsāra and nirvāṇa" (*'khor-das-dbyer-med*) and coincides with the Madhyamaka view expounded by great teachers such as Nāgārjuna. It corresponds to the view of the ultimate held by the other orders of Tibetan Buddhism, although it is known by different names to adherents of the Nyingma, Kagyu, and Gelug schools. "The result" consists in the attainment of the five transcendental wisdoms with which the enlightened mind of a buddha is endowed, corresponding to what are known as the five bodies of buddhahood. This is a tantric concept that will be explained later.[31]

Jetsün Dragpa Gyaltsen, the fifth patriarch of the Sakya order, also stated that while the lam-dre system of meditation could indeed be expounded under these seven topics, it could be further subsumed under two main points or sections, namely, fundamental and advanced practices:

> If you wish to guide a faithful disciple, who heeds whatever his preceptor enjoins, according to the complete teachings of the lam-dre system, he should first be guided according to *The Three Visions* and then according to *The Three Continua*, because all the teachings of the system are therein compiled.

After Jetsün Dragpa Gyaltsen, the great Ngorchen Kunga Zangpo, the founder of Ngor Monastery, also expounded this same system of meditation with reference to two main topics. For our purposes, this is most convenient, so the teachings will be presented here in that way.

FAITH

We now enter our first main topic of discussion: faith. When we ask, "What sort of person should be taught *The Three Visions*?" the first essential requirement is that he or she be endowed with faith. As the sūtras say, "Even as green sprouts never spring forth from seeds that fire has scorched, so holy phenomena do not arise in people who have no faith."

Just as there is no possibility for a green sprout to spring from a scorched seed, so there is no way for someone who has no faith in the validity, benefit, and truth of the teachings to enter into proper practice and attain the result that is born of it. If you do not have faith, there is no foundation on which the wholesome factors of the spiritual path can be built. Nor will someone without faith be influenced by the idea of seeking liberation. Even the concept of buddhahood will not be a source of inspiration, precisely because of lack of faith. First, the door of actual experience and attainment of buddhahood will remain closed because you simply aren't inspired to seek it. Then, lacking faith in the need to develop the requisite qualities of spiritual training and meditation, you won't make efforts to develop those qualities and won't be able to experience the results that are gained from them. Finally, you won't seek or receive the blessings of experienced masters and teachers, nor rely on the blessings of the Three Jewels.

In short, a person who has no faith is not a very likely candidate for this path, because he has closed his mind to the development of all those essential factors that bring about the result of buddhahood, and has perhaps also closed it to the possibility of attaining such a result. In any case, he has cut himself off from helpful factors, such as the blessings and guidance of experienced masters and the blessings of the Buddha, Dharma, and Sangha. Hence faith is the first requirement for someone who wishes to follow this path.

The *Jeweled Lamp Sūtra* (*Ratnapradīpa-sūtra*) tells us this about faith:

> Faith goes before and, like a mother, gives birth; it causes all virtues
> to rise and grow, clearing away doubts and rescuing from floods;
> faith reveals the City of Happiness.

Faith goes before all the other experiences of the path—the awakening of love and compassion, the resolve to attain enlightenment for the benefit of all sentient beings, and insight into the true nature of phenomena—all essential factors that become possible only in one who has faith. Thus faith is like a mother because it gives birth to all other spiritual qualities and experiences of the path. Because of faith, one undertakes to listen to the teachings, understand them, reflect on them, and meditate on them. As a result, the various types of understanding that are acquired through reflection and meditation become possible. Faith causes all virtues—such as the six spiritual perfections (*pāramitā*) of generosity, moral conduct, patience, diligence, meditative insight, and wisdom—to arise in one's mind and to increase from one level of insight to another.

Faith also clears away doubts because, when confronted with problems of understanding the true sense of the teachings, a person with faith will be inclined to search for true answers. Either he will resort to a learned teacher who can remove doubts and explain the points of doctrine that he finds confusing, or he will make efforts to refer to the various teachings of the Buddha. And because of his faith, he will be inclined to credit the answers he finds as very likely true. But a person who doesn't have faith will probably not seek answers in those ways and, even if he is given correct answers, may be inclined to discredit them because of his lack of faith. Hence faith does clear away doubts and rescue us from the floods of birth, old age, disease, and death, as well as the other kinds of grief, illusion, confusion, and unhappiness that all living beings experience.

Faith makes possible the aspiration to freedom from those very forces that cause continued birth, death, and suffering. It causes us to make the correct efforts that lead to liberation from those forms of suffering. Finally, faith reveals the "City of Happiness." One who has faith in the teachings of Lord Buddha will credit the possibility of eventually attaining enlightenment and perfect happiness, whereas that possibility remains closed to those who have no faith in it.

The verse continues:

> Faith makes the mind unsullied and pure; it casts off pride and is devotion's root. Faith is like a treasure. It is wealth and peace unexcelled, and, like hands, is the chief means of gathering virtue.

Ordinarily, the mind is sullied not only by confusion about its true nature but also by emotional states of desire, aversion, indifference, pride, jealousy, and the rest. Thoughts that arise in such a mind are jangled by having arisen from basic delusion and the passions. However, when faith arises in your mind, your thoughts become tranquil and clear because they are directed toward objects of great value—for instance, reflections on the qualities of the buddhas and bodhisattvas, enlightenment, and love and compassion for all beings. As a result, your thoughts become focused not only on the Three Jewels and on cultivating virtue for the benefit of others, both of which are appropriate sources of support in your spiritual efforts, but also on the attainment of buddhahood itself. Faith makes all these ennobling thoughts possible. Your mind comes to reflect those qualities to one extent or another, and as a result you will feel constantly happy, uplifted, and purposeful. Thus the verse says that faith purifies the mind.

Faith also "casts off pride" because when we reflect on the great permanent values of the buddhas and bodhisattvas, who strive unselfishly for the greatest good of all beings, we see our own efforts and motives in proper perspective. It becomes difficult to remain conceited and proud about our accomplishments in comparison. Thus faith is "devotion's root" because it causes us to open our minds in appreciation of the spiritual qualities of the buddhas, bodhisattvas, and other religious persons. Thoughts of devotion, respect, and appreciation arise in us toward those beings, so that we forget our own lesser qualities.

This is illustrated by the story of Drugpa Kunleg, who was known as a sort of crazy lama in Tibet. He was quite famous for his jokes and tricks at the expense of other lamas, and often showed up the pride of other lamas in very telling ways. But when he himself went on a pilgrimage to Lhasa, he entered the Jowo Lhakhang, the great "cathedral" of Lhasa, which contains a very exquisite statue of Lord Buddha, for the first time. He stood looking at the statue for some time, reflecting on the Buddha, and finally he addressed the statue, saying,

> You and I started out alike, as ordinary sentient beings, but through your greater diligence, you have now become a perfectly enlightened being, endowed with all the qualities of a buddha, and are able to help countless sentient beings. I, through my laziness, am still roaming about from one place to another here on earth; thinking of this great difference that your diligence has made between the two of us, I offer my salutations.

Then he bowed down before the image three times.

Like buried treasure, the extraordinary experiences of insight and spiritual attainment that are achieved by a bodhisattva remain hidden to us. They are not part of our present experience, but faith makes them possible. It reveals where that hidden treasure lies and the way to acquire it. Faith is like wealth or property, in that when you have money you are able to acquire the various things you need. In the same way, if you have faith, it is no problem to attain other spiritual qualities such as bodhichitta, insight into the true nature of all phenomena, the spiritual perfections, and the different stages of meditation.

Faith is an excellent pair of feet because it can carry you along the spiritual path that leads from worldly existence and bondage to the "City of Liberation." It can lead you through the door of Dharma along the path of the bodhisattvas. Faith is also like a pair of hands, in that it is the chief means of gathering virtues. Those who wish to attain buddhahood must accumulate a tremendous store of spiritual merit by meditating and by performing good deeds, plus a great store of insight into the nature of mind, phenomena, and so forth. Faith is the best and quickest way of accumulating these requisites. Without faith, the practice of the path would be like climbing a steep ladder without hands. With faith, our ascent is very steady and sure.

THE THREE KINDS OF FAITH

We have said that faith is extremely important. You may be willing to accept that this is so, but what do we mean by "faith"? Is it just blind faith in whatever the Buddha says? Should whatever a Buddhist teacher tells us be accepted just because it is spoken? The abhidharma literature tells us:

> Faith is full confidence in the efficacy of deeds and their result, in the Truths, and in the Three Jewels. It is also aspiration for spiritual attainment and a clear-minded appreciation of the truth.

Thus there are three kinds of faith: (1) full confidence in the efficacy of deeds and their results, in the Four Noble Truths, and in the Three Jewels, (2) aspiration to attain spiritual results, and (3) clear-minded appreciation of the truth.

The first kind of faith has three parts, the first of which consists of confidence in the efficacy of the law of karma. If we understand that there is a connection between actions—mental, vocal, and physical—and the experience of pleasure or pain, then we can be said to have accepted the law of karma. We need to know that there is a direct connection between wholesome and unwholesome actions of body, voice, and mind and pleasant and unpleasant experiences, respectively. The *Bodhicharyāvatara*, a famous

Mahāyāna text by Shāntideva,[32] teaches that all suffering is the result of unwholesome deeds, all happiness the result of wholesome ones. When we accept that, we have a certain confidence in the connection between actions and results and thus will be seriously inclined to avoid the ten unwholesome actions of body, voice, and mind. In practical terms, we will be inclined to give up killing, stealing, and so forth and to practice virtues, such as protecting the lives of others and giving to those in need.

Next, we should attain some degree of confidence in the Four Noble Truths—the first exposition of the Dharma given by Lord Buddha. In a sermon at Deer Park in Sarnath, he explained the first truth, that the nature of worldly existence is suffering. In the second truth, he taught that craving is the cause of suffering. Craving includes attachment to selfish patterns of behavior and entails basic ignorance, belief in a self, and the attendant self-cherishing passions of desire, anger, delusion, pride, envy, and the rest. Third, the Buddha taught the truth of cessation—namely, that we can put an end to this unsatisfactory state of worldly existence and attain an alternative mode of being, known as nirvāṇa. Finally, he taught the truth of the way to put an end to suffering and attain liberation; the methods he taught constitute the path to enlightenment. When we hear and reflect on the teaching of the four basic truths expressed by the Buddha and agree that they all seem worthy of consideration and practice, then we are endowed with confidence in the Four Truths.

Last, we need confidence in the Three Jewels, a collective term used to denote the enlightened teacher, the Buddha; his teachings or doctrine, the Dharma; and the assembly, or Sangha, of bodhisattvas who are his followers on the path. These three are called jewels because a jewel has great intrinsic value and is quite rare in this world. If you consider the qualities represented by the Buddha, his teaching, and the assembly of bodhisattvas, you can appreciate these three as a truly great store of spiritual qualities that are valuable for mankind. By reflecting on them, you can gain confidence in the Three Jewels as a valid source of inspiration, guidance, and support.

The second kind of faith is aspiration. If you reflect on the Buddha, the bodhisattvas, the great teachers, such as Guru Padmasambhava, and the great saints of the past, and aspire to become equal to them in your own efforts and accomplishments, this is said to be the faith of aspiration, or faith that arises from a desire for spiritual attainments.

ೞ ‡ ೞ

The third kind of faith is clear-minded appreciation of, or confidence in, the truth of the Buddhist path. The Buddha, Dharma, and Sangha represent spiritual qualities that have been achieved time and time again by countless beings. They are possible because Lord Buddha, out of a pure desire to remove the sufferings of all beings, attained buddhahood and unselfishly shared it with all other beings who might be inclined to benefit from this teaching. His insight is valid both because it corresponds to ultimate reality and because his motives were pure, being born of great compassion, as were those of all the other teachers since him who have transmitted these teachings. The teachings, the Three Jewels, and all the practices were born of a genuine desire to free beings from suffering and to promote, in every way possible, the well-being of every being. Thus the teachings are undeceivingly true and reliable. When you fully understand that a wonderful doctrine of liberation such as this issues from great compassion, without the slightest chance of misrepresentation, guile, or deceptiveness on the part of its promulgators, then the faith of belief arises in your mind. You can see that it would be impossible for those truly endowed with great compassion to inflict some hoax upon beings.

How can we know who is endowed with these three kinds of faith? If a student remains steadily interested in the Dharma and is persistent in his efforts toward attaining buddhahood, then he is endowed with these three kinds of faith. Steadiness on the way is a sign of being endowed with the faith of clear-minded appreciation, aspiration, and confidence. A person who is unsteady in his practice is weak in faith. Faith is essential to keep a person on the path. A person who has faith will not be separated from striving toward buddhahood.

The Four Causes of Abandoning the Path

There are four main causes of leaving the path: (1) desire, (2) anger, (3) fear, and (4) ignorance. One whose mind becomes governed by one of these four is likely to give up the Dharma; it is said that his mind of faith has been breached by the forces of delusion. In contrast, one whose mind remains steady in the three kinds of faith will remain on the path in all circumstances and situations.

The first of these causes is desire. One who has steady faith will not give up his efforts on the path even if, by doing so, he would gain a very substantial reward in this life. He will not give up his practice even for the sake of a kingdom, great wealth, fame, or any other achievement, because he knows the faults of attachment—namely, that worldly pleasures are ultimately unsatisfactory because they are impermanent. Moreover, they separate you from attainment of the complete and long-lasting happiness of liberation. The great bodhisattva Maitreya taught in the *Adornment of the Mahāyāna Sūtras* (*Mahāyānasūtra-ālaṅkāra*):

> Though they win them not, the greatly deluded seek worldlings' ephemeral pleasures, while steadfast seekers of liberation renounce them, yet gain the riches of an ideal kingdom.

Worldly people run after ephemeral pleasure without regard to the cost involved, in the hope of obtaining some degree of enjoyment. They are "greatly deluded" because their search often leads them into great suffering. They may well be thwarted in finding even a limited amount of temporary pleasure, and even if they do attain it, there is no way they can actually retain it. This inevitably leads to suffering, because sooner or later they must be parted from such pleasure by death or some other cause.

Bodhisattvas, who remain steadfast in seeking liberation, give up worldly aims of fame, wealth, power, dominion, and so forth. Even if they have obtained them, they renounce them. Lord Buddha himself was a prince, and had he chosen not to renounce the world and enter the path of Dharma, it was foretold at his birth that he would attain the rank of a universal emperor. He also had at his fingertips all the pleasures that money and his father's position as king of the Shākya clan could provide. He had entertainment, wealth, and attendants, yet went into the forest to undergo six years of diligent meditation. Those who are wise will follow his example in not giving themselves over to extreme attachment to worldly pleasures; rather, they will remain steadfast in seeking a greater good for themselves and others.

The second cause for a possible lapse in your practice of religion is anger. In the *Bodhicharyāvatara*, Shāntideva wrote,

> A single instant of anger annuls all the merits of thousands of aeons gathered through good deeds and generosity, through worshiping the buddhas, and through other practices.

Shāntideva also says,

> There is no sin like anger, nor is there any penance like patience; strive, therefore, to become practiced in forbearance.

Even if you have trained your mind in moral conduct, generosity, and the stages of meditation and have accumulated great stores of merit, a situation can arise in which you react with great rage. If that occurs, it will not only destroy your accumulated merit but separate you from your spiritual path. Hence you should try to exercise forbearance even in extreme circumstances in which you feel you are being abused. This can be done first by reflecting on the harm that anger causes you. Not only does it burn your mind and destroy merit, it also harms other beings whom you are trying to benefit through your practice. Thus for their sake, at least, try to avoid giving up Dharma practice through anger.

The third way you can relinquish your Buddhist path is through fear. Should you encounter extremely fearful situations, either externally or internally, so that you fear for your health, life, or sanity, the only way to escape might seem to be to give up your commitment to the Dharma. But when you are steady in faith, having first become convinced not only of the possibility of enlightenment but of the potentially great value your practice holds for yourself and all others, you will not give up your commitment to the Dharma even under these circumstances.

In 1040 C.E., when the great Indian pandit Atīsha was living in Tibet, he was visited by several of his disciples from northern India. The big news in those days was the Muslim invasion of northern India and the destruction of Nālandā and other Buddhist monasteries. When Atīsha asked his students about the most recent developments, he was told of an instance when Muslim soldiers had threatened a Buddhist monk at Nālandā University. They had given him a choice: either give up his commitment to enlightenment, in which case he would be very nicely rewarded, or face death. He replied that even though he feared for his life and hated the prospect of a violent death, he was convinced not only of the truth of Buddhism but also that giving up his vows, and thereby so much potential good for beings, would cause him much anguish in future births. Hence, under no circumstances could he consider giving up his refuge in the Three Jewels and his commitment to enlightenment. The soldiers did indeed kill him.

When Pandit Atīsha heard this, he was very moved. He often spoke of this particular monk as a very good example of the kind of steady faith we need, so that even in the most dire circumstances we remain firm in our commitment to the path. Even though the option of giving up your practice might save your life, there are other considerations. Not only would you suffer a great loss of morale and merit, but there would be an inconceivably great loss to other beings whom you had promised to benefit as well. Giving up something as valuable as the Dharma can easily lead to very unhappy karmic results. To substantiate this, there is another verse from the *Bodhicharyāvatara*, in which Shāntideva writes,

> Were all gods and men my foes, they could not lead me into Avīci's flames, united with which not even the ashes of Mount Sumeru would remain; yet there am I hurled in a moment by these mighty foes, the defilements.

The defilements are, for example, fear. Out of fear for ourselves, we might react foolishly and thereby bring upon ourselves a very unhappy karmic result.

The fourth of the causes for leaving the Dharma is ignorance. The *Bodhicharyāvatara* says:

> Even as a man afflicted by illness is helpless in all his actions, so, too, a mind afflicted by ignorance is powerless in all its works.

If a person engages in the practice of religion or seeks to train in a spiritual path, he won't get very far if he isn't clear about what should be practiced and what should not be. If, for example, he engages in animal sacrifice, thinking to accumulate virtue, he will just be accumulating the sin of taking life. Thus you should not be ignorant either of actions that bring about wholesome results and that should thus be practiced, or of actions that should be avoided because they bring about counterproductive results. It is your responsibility to gain a comprehensive understanding of what should be practiced and what should be avoided on the path.

To avoid downfall through ignorance, make efforts to learn all there is to know about the practices of the path: what they are, how they are to be pursued, the stages of experience, and the results obtained through them. You can do this by attending to others who are experienced in meditation and familiar with the teachings of the Buddha. Also you should study the biographies of great masters, the story of the Indian youth Shrī Saṁbhava and the young Indian girl Shrīmatī, and that of the bodhisattva Sudhana. You can follow their example in avoiding these four causes of downfall. In this regard, the *Bodhicharyāvatara* states:

> One should learn how to attend preceptors according to the story of Shrī Saṁbhava; the way is to be known after reading this and other discourses of the Enlightened One.

If your mind is agitated or influenced by ignorance, you will not be able to make effective efforts on the path. You need to be able to recognize clearly, "This is what I should do, and this is what I should not do." For example, if you undertake to follow certain rules, whether the lay precepts, the bodhisattva vows, or the tantric vows, you must (1) understand thoroughly what you have assumed, (2) know how to preserve your vows, and (3) know how to purify vows should you violate them.

To accomplish right meditation, you need to (a) know how to awaken right motives within yourself, (b) know how to undergo meditative experiences, (c) know how to remove unexpected obstacles and other adversities, should they arise, and (d) know how the result of the meditation is to be obtained. To succeed in all of these, you must make many efforts in study, reflection, and meditation.

The alternative is to make mistakes that will become compounded and increase your delusion. To remove ignorance and gain understanding of the right ways to practice, study the stories of Shrī Saṁbhava and the maiden Shrīmatī, which are related in the *Array of Stalks Sūtra* (*Gaṇḍavyūha-sūtra*). This sūtra is found in the Avataṁsaka literature. You may also consult the story of the youth Sudhana to see how he sought out and served his preceptors, and the numerous biographies of masters who trained in giving, patience, meditation, and the other perfections. Through relying on the examples found in the sūtras and in the lives of eminent Indian and Tibetan adepts, you will gain a clear comprehension both of how to practice and how to avoid errors.

A person who does not relinquish the practice he has undertaken, despite his desire, anger, fear, or ignorance, is a fit vessel for the teaching of the Buddha. As Ārya Nāgārjuna stated in his *Precious Garland* (*Ratnāvalī*),

> "Faithful" is he called and a "vessel of the teaching of emancipation" who does not relinquish religion through fear, anger, desire, or ignorance.

If you have a steady faith and are able to avoid forsaking the Dharma, you will receive the blessings of the preceptors and the Three Jewels, your practice will flourish, and you will surely win through to liberation.

The resolve to remain firm in practice can be nurtured by reading the sūtras and by abandoning companions who tend to lead you away from practice. In their place, associate with friends who encourage you in study and practice of the Dharma. Also, persevere in training your mind in those methods that cause faith to grow and your practice of the path to become strengthened. As Shāntideva taught in his *Compendium of Trainings* (*Śikṣāsamuccaya*):

> He who longs to put an end to sorrow and to reach the sublimity of happiness must firmly plant the root of faith and steady his mind in enlightenment's quest.

5

THE UMBRELLA OF REFUGE

WE HAVE OFTEN SAID that it is salutary to reflect on the difficulty of finding an opportunity such as that of studying the *Lam dre*. It is difficult, first of all, because human birth is difficult to obtain. Even among humans, it is difficult to find the right time and place, the right teacher who is willing and able to teach, and to have your affairs arranged so that you can practice the teachings received. It is even more difficult to receive the tantric teachings, which were only very seldom taught by the buddhas of past aeons and which will seldom be taught by buddhas in future aeons. Indeed, little is known, even now, of the tantras because of the great care tantric masters have taken to preserve their efficacy by transmitting them only to the most intelligent, capable, and spiritually advanced of disciples. Hence it is important to take these teachings seriously, to listen to them with an undistracted mind, to glean whatever understanding you can from them, and to follow up with questions, answers, further studies, and with practice itself.

In the last lesson, we discussed faith as the first prerequisite on the bodhisattva's path and likened faith to a seed, saying that lack of faith is like a seed that has been burnt. Just as a scorched seed will not grow, so your practice of various meditations and spiritual exercises will be fruitless if you do not enter into them with faith.

We also must consider the ground that will be helpful if we wish to grow in the Dharma and increase our faith. We know that we must avoid the four obstacles, such as anger and fear, that are inimical to the growth of our faith. But what conditions are favorable to its growth? First of all, if you feel you are weak in the three kinds of faith, if you feel doubts about the possibility of liberation from worldly existence, or if you feel that you don't understand the doctrine of cause and effect, there are certain things that can be done.

HOW TO CULTIVATE FAITH

To begin with, you can rely on the Three Jewels. You should pray for their blessings, pray that your mind will be strengthened in right understanding, and also pray that, through right understanding, faith will arise. Also, you can study biographies of great bodhisattvas of the path. By learning of their spiritual qualities and activities, and the efforts they made to attain them, you can awaken the faith of desire—the desire to attain such spiritual qualities yourself. For this, as mentioned in the last lesson, you can refer to the *Jeweled Lamp Sūtra* and the stories of the youthful bodhisattva Shrī Saṁbhava and the young maiden Shrīmatī.

It is also very helpful to associate with people who are more advanced on the path. They have already gone through these stages and have become steady in their confidence in the validity of the teachings. You can benefit from their knowledge of the Dharma and thus dispel your own doubts and insecurities. It is also a good idea to disassociate yourself from friends and acquaintances who are inclined to turn you away from study or practice of the Dharma, whether through their lack of appreciation of it or through a wish to involve you in nondharmic activities.

The great Indian master Shāntideva wrote in his *Compendium of Trainings*:

> One who wishes to put an end to all forms of unhappiness and to attain the farthest limit of well-being should steady his mind in faith and direct his mind toward enlightenment.

The abhidharma literature also tells us that faith is one of the five most important faculties that help a person attain buddhahood. These five essential mental states are: (1) steady faith, (2) great compassion, (3) intense diligence, (4) pure wisdom, and (5) pure conduct. Of these, faith is the forerunner of the remaining four. We have suggested several ways in which you can awaken, increase, and reinforce faith.

THE REQUISITES FOR MEDITATION

Since *The Three Visions* is a guide to the stages of meditation, we have considered faith in that context. A person who is a worthy disciple, who has faith in the veracity of the teachings and a desire to attain spiritual qualities, should undertake to put that faith into practice, reinforcing it, after study, through an experience of meditation. Here we will take up our second topic, which is the requisites for meditation. The aspiring meditator should choose a place that has all the right conditions for practice.

As the bodhisattva Maitreya taught in the *Adornment of the Mahāyāna Sūtras*, you should practice in an auspicious place where only helpful persons are found, plus all the other requisites for successful practice. An auspicious place is one that is not under the control of persons or forces likely to interrupt meditation or cause an obstacle to practice. For example, it should not be in a country controlled by a dictator who might interfere with or be inimical to your spiritual activities. Nor should it be inhabited by nonhuman spirits that would create obstacles to practice. Finally, if you are meditating in the wilderness, it should not be in a place where your life is endangered by flesh-eating animals, such as tigers or bears.

The place you choose should be one where water, food, peace and quiet, and all the other factors that further good meditation are available. It shouldn't be a place where you have to associate with people who are not interested in the Dharma or who might dislike your efforts to learn and practice meditation. It should be free from persons who are noisy, careless, and thoughtless and who, through their carelessness, might create obstacles to your practice. It should be a place where your neighbors are either sympathetic or at least disposed to respect your privacy and willing to help you avoid disturbances to your practice. All the requisites you might need should be considered so that, once you have undertaken meditation, it will not have to be interrupted, abandoned, or otherwise impaired due to logistical problems.

Once you have found such a favorable place for practice, how should you dwell there? First of all, arrange your meditation cushion facing an image of the Buddha. The cushion itself should be quite comfortable, so that you can remain in meditation as long as possible.

Next, take care to learn the correct posture of meditation. There are seven points involved: (1) You should be seated, preferably in the *vajra* posture, which is the meditative posture associated with the Buddha Vairochana—that is, the full cross-legged lotus posture. If this isn't possible, try to approximate the half-lotus posture (*ardhaparyanka-āsana*). (2) Most important, the spine should be kept straight at all times. (3) The shoulders should be balanced evenly. (4) The neck should be kept almost straight but very slightly bent forward. (5) The eyes should be either closed or half open, and focused on a spot at arm's length in front of you or on the tip of your nose. (6) The mouth should be slightly open and the tongue slightly curled upward, with the breath very moderate and gentle. (7) The hands should be folded in your lap with the thumbs touching each other.

REFUGE

Now we approach our third topic, which is: "How should we enter into this practice of meditation?" Meditation consists of three stages: (1) the preliminary stage of taking refuge in the Buddha, his teaching, and the assembly of bodhisattvas; (2) the main meditation, i.e., your own experience in meditation; and (3) the concluding stage, in which you turn over the merit acquired through meditation to the enlightenment of all sentient beings. Not only in meditation but in every dharmic action, no matter how spontaneous, these three stages should be remembered and observed. For example, in making a gift to a needy person, remember to invoke the blessings of the Three Jewels as you make the gift, and then dedicate the merit to the enlightenment of all beings.

To return to the practice of meditation itself, first be seated, put aside all distracting thoughts, and, directing your mind toward the Buddha, Dharma, and Sangha, take refuge three times. It might be helpful to consider taking refuge through a division into these same three stages. Since refuge is the first practice we undertake in sitting down to meditate, we need to understand quite fully what it involves. We can examine refuge thoroughly via an understanding of its five main features: (1) our motive in seeking refuge, (2) the object of refuge, (3) the manner of taking refuge, (4) the benefits of taking refuge, and (5) the instructions for practice that attend the taking of refuge.

Our motive in taking refuge in the Buddha, Dharma, and Sangha may be fear, faith, or compassion. Fear is often the motive for those who, having become aware of the nature of worldly existence as suffering, respond by wishing to become free from both present suffering and potential suffering in the future. Or people may take refuge in the Three Jewels out of faith, having heard about the possibility of buddhahood and the spiritual qualities that are attainable. Finally, for Mahāyānists, compassion is the prime motivation, in that our sensitivity to the sufferings of all beings impels us to follow the path to enlightenment in order to remove those sufferings.

The object of refuge consists of the Three Jewels: namely, the teacher or enlightened one, the teaching of enlightenment, and the assembly of bodhisattvas who have undertaken to strive toward buddhahood. We have taken refuge in the Three Jewels if we have sincerely and formally resolved to rely on them as guides on the path.

We consider the Buddha our teacher or guide; his teachings as the instructions we will follow, the experience we hope for, and the realization we aspire to attain through right practice; and the Sangha as those spiritual friends who can help us move forward on the path. Regarding the Three Jewels as the source of inspiration and support in our practice, the manner of taking refuge is formally to recite the refuge formula three times.

The benefits of taking refuge are both that we receive directly the blessings of the buddhas and bodhisattvas in removing obstacles to spiritual attainments and that we are protected from all malignant beings (both human and nonhuman), untimely diseases, accidents, and the like. Additional benefits are knowing that we are on the right path and being receptive to the guidance of the Three Jewels.

Finally, there are certain instructions that attend the taking of refuge. Taking refuge in the Buddha means that you resolve and commit yourself to striving for buddhahood. This becomes your spiritual ideal, so it follows that your actions and spiritual efforts and practices will be directed toward that goal and not elsewhere. By taking refuge in the Dharma, you automatically undertake to give up harming others, since the essence of the doctrine is to promote the well-being of all living beings. By taking refuge in the Sangha, you undertake to disassociate yourself from beings whose actions are thoughtless, cruel, and harmful either to themselves or others. As a corollary, you undertake to associate as much as possible with spiritual friends who will promote your own and others' progress on the path.

Let us consider each of the five features of taking refuge in a bit more detail. To return to the first of these, the motive for taking refuge in the Three Jewels can be one of three things: fear, faith, or compassion.

"Fear" is not a very good word for what we mean here, which is a kind of anxiety that results from an awareness that worldly, egocentric existence is, by its very nature, a source of past, present, and future unhappiness. Worldly existence comes about as a result of ignorance, including ignorance about our own nature. This ignorance expresses itself in egocentricity and in the attendant belief that we should act for ourselves rather than for others—i.e., in a selfish or self-cherishing attitude. This kind of belief is the basic cause of suffering in saṃsāra; it is extremely common and is at the root of both the unending cycle of birth and death and all the truly terrible extremes of pain that beings sometimes experience, whether in the human realm, in the hells, among animals, or wherever.

Knowing this, it is healthy to react to our awareness of the all-pervasiveness of pain with something like alarm or anxiety. Our circumstances are not ones in which we can remain complacent. A clear appreciation of the fact that we are subject to certain forms of natural suffering—and may face even worse suffering—should make us pause and give thought to our situation. When we have reflected on the truth of suffering in all the realms of existence, we may well be motivated to turn to the teachings of the Buddha and to his example as the best way of learning the causes of suffering, removing them, and eventually attaining liberation from the various kinds of unhappiness.

If you have faith that the Buddha, Dharma, and Sangha not only offer the prospect of liberation from suffering but can actually help you gain liberation, either by example or by direct blessings and guidance, then you have what is called "the faith of confidence." And if you accept the law of karma—that there is a causal relationship between good actions and states of well-being, and, similarly, between wrong actions and states of mental or physical unhappiness—then you have achieved a certain amount of what is called "the faith of clear appreciation." If you aspire to attain the qualities of enlightenment based on your knowledge of the examples of the Buddha and other great masters, you have also achieved a certain amount of "the faith of desire."

When you feel some alarm about the suffering of worldly existence but also have faith that the Three Jewels can guide and support your practices in seeking liberation from it, all that remains is to awaken within yourself compassion for others. This notion of compassion as a cause of taking refuge is a unique feature of Mahāyāna Buddhism. Although arhats and followers of the pratyekabuddha path are far from devoid of compassion, they are more likely to seek refuge out of the fear and faith that we have just described. In the Mahāyāna system, while the bodhisattva certainly is not without the same anxiety about future pain and the same faith in the Three Jewels found among Hīnayānists, his primary motive in seeking refuge is great compassion. Knowing that beings are subject to all the sufferings of worldly existence and that the Three Jewels are able to help them, he takes refuge to help himself and others move toward enlightenment. His primary aim is to become able to remove their sufferings as quickly as possible.

When we take refuge in the Three Jewels, we should try to have these three factors in mind. But it is not enough merely to recite the formula "I take refuge in the Buddha, Dharma, and Sangha" three times and then feel assured that we have indeed taken refuge. It is never enough to do things merely by rote. What is required is genuine motivation and mental concentration— i.e., an undistracted mind filled with sincerity. To give an example, if you are caught in a rainstorm and are in need of an umbrella, reciting the words "Shelter! Shelter!" or "Umbrella! Umbrella!" really doesn't protect you at all; similarly, you cannot expect much from just mouthing the words of the refuge formula. But when you take refuge with a sincere mind, you can definitely expect to receive the blessings and guidance of the Three Jewels.

છ ✳ છ

Let us consider in detail the object of refuge. We said that the Three Jewels consist of the Buddha, Dharma, and Sangha. We need to know that the Buddha is to be considered a worthy object of refuge because of his spiritual accomplishments. Through his painstaking training in the spiritual practices of the bodhisattva, he not only attained enlightenment but became endowed with the wisdom of insight into things as they really are. Coupled with his wisdom is great compassion for all beings, so that his response to all beings who remain unenlightened is very spontaneous and intense great compassion and great love. Finally, he is endowed with great power. Wisdom and compassion alone are not enough to extricate others from painful karmic situations, but because of his spiritual power the Buddha actually rescues beings from suffering and, by showing them the path to liberation, helps them gain freedom from all kinds of sorrow.

The Buddha is a being who, through his meditation, has attained the *dharmakāya*, or realization of reality, and yet, as a manifestation of his compassion for others, also manifests a Body of Illusion (*nirmāṇakāya*), in order to show the way to liberation. He has mastered all that needed to be discarded: all ignorance and selfishness. For these and many other reasons, the Buddha is a true source of refuge for unenlightened beings.

The Dharma is the teaching, or doctrine. This also has two aspects: (1) the scriptural Dharma, which consists of the words of the Buddha, the teachings and instructions he has given on the Hīnayāna, Mahāyāna, and Vajrayāna levels; and (2) the Dharma of realizations, which consists of the realization of the emptiness of all dharmas (phenomena)—i.e., the true nature of things—and the other insights on the path of enlightenment.

The Sangha consists of the great bodhisattvas who have followed Lord Buddha on his spiritual path, such as Ārya Mañjushrī, Avalokiteshvara, Maitreya, and others. It includes all those bodhisattvas who have attained at least the first bhūmi, or spiritual stage, of a bodhisattva.

This is what we have in mind when we turn to the Three Jewels as a source of refuge. Because they resemble the Three Jewels themselves, we should also show respect to images of the Buddha, to collections of scriptures, and to monks who wear yellow or red robes and who are training in the manner of bodhisattvas.

Since we have undertaken to study *The Three Visions*, which is part of a tantric system of meditation, we should also point out that the Vajrayāna has a special feature in which the Three Jewels are considered to be embodied in your own lama, because he or she introduces you to the teachings of the Buddha. Our particular teacher shows us the practices, points out the way, and does everything that a buddha would do for us were he present. He does this because, through his own efforts and attainments, he has gained knowledge of the scriptures and has experienced the realizations that he teaches us. Since your teacher is also the representative of the activity of the bodhisattvas and of all who follow the bodhisattva's path, he or she embodies the essence of the Buddha, Dharma, and Sangha. Thus, when tantric practitioners take refuge, they usually recite a four-part formula that begins with taking refuge in the guru and goes on to taking refuge in the Three Jewels.

The important thing to remember is to be single-pointed in taking refuge. Direct your mind sincerely and undistractedly toward the Three Jewels and recite the formula. If you have an image of the Buddha, position your cushion so that you are directly in front of it and then take refuge in the Three Jewels. You can also just visualize the Buddha in front of you and take refuge along with all other beings. In either case, visualize that on your right is your father, on your left is your mother; in front of you are all those beings who you dislike or who are giving you a bad time. Surrounding you, visualize all other beings in existence. But don't think of them as animals, hungry ghosts, or hell beings (which is very distracting): think of them as having human form and as joining with you in taking refuge.

6

HOLDING FAST UNTIL ENLIGHTENMENT IS WON

IN THE LAST LESSON, we began to discuss the five salient features of taking refuge: its cause, its object, its procedure, its benefit, and its attendant instructions.

THE REFUGE PRAYER

When taking refuge in actual practice, visualize yourself surrounded by your parents, friends, enemies, and all other sentient beings; then, directing a mind of single-pointed sincerity to the Buddha, Dharma, and Sangha, recite the refuge formula twenty-one, one hundred, or one thousand times, or as many times as you wish. The formula is:

> I take refuge in my guru.
> I take refuge in the Buddha.
> I take refuge in the Dharma.
> I take refuge in the Sangha.

After you have recited these four lines, again direct your mind toward the Three Jewels and request their blessings for yourself and all other beings. This request can be expressed in words such as these:

> To the Preceptors and Three Precious Jewels, we pay homage and take refuge. Please bestow your blessings on us in all our lifetimes. Bless us that our minds might become attuned to the teachings, that we might move forward on the path, and that errors on the path might be allayed and illusions appear to us as transcendent wisdom. Bless us that unreligious thoughts might not spring up even for a single moment, and that genuine love, compassion, and aspiration to enlightenment might arise. By your blessings may we quickly attain the stage of perfect enlightenment.

This can also be expressed by reciting certain verses composed by Ngorchen Könchog Lhündrub. I will not explain them in detail but will give you some general idea of their sense. The verses are:

Holding fast from this time until the essence of enlightenment is won, I and all living beings spread to the bounds of space itself seek refuge in the Holy Preceptor. Of the Ten Tathāgatas of the three times and ten directions, he is the quintessence of their qualities and deeds, their body, voice, and mind: he is the source of the eighty-four thousand teachings of doctrine and the master of all the noble assemblies of saints.

With great devotion of body, voice, and mind, we take refuge in the Holy Root and Lineal Preceptors; with great devotion of body, voice, and mind, we take refuge in the Enlightened One, who has reached the end of renunciation and realization; with great devotion of body, voice, and mind, we take refuge in the Holy Teaching, which reveals the nature of his precepts and discourses; with great devotion of body, voice, and mind, we take refuge in the Noble Assembly of holy beings, upholders of the teachings, and bodhisattvas.

Note that in taking refuge on the Mahāyāna path, you do not seek enlightenment for yourself alone but include all other beings in your spiritual efforts. This is indicated by the words "all living beings spread to the bounds of space itself." Space is boundless, so all beings who inhabit space are always included in all your own spiritual efforts, as well as in taking refuge itself.

THE OBJECTS OF REFUGE

The first verse also says "seek refuge in the Holy Preceptor." As already mentioned, in the Sakya system of *Lam dre*, monks and laymen recite a four-line formula in which the first line refers to taking refuge in one's spiritual teacher, followed by refuge in the Buddha, Dharma, and Sangha. This differs from the exoteric Buddhist practice of taking refuge only in the Three Jewels. The reason for the addition is explained in the next line: "Of the Ten Tathāgatas of the three times and ten directions, the guru is the quintessence of their qualities and deeds, their body, voice, and mind."

In Vajrayāna Buddhism, the various aspects of buddhahood are described in terms of five buddha races, or families, each of which manifests a certain aspect of buddhahood. More specifically, Vairochana is associated with the Buddha's body; the Buddha's voice corresponds to Amitābha; his mind corresponds to Akshobhya; his spiritual qualities are represented by Ratnasambhava; and his activities on behalf of sentient beings correspond to Amoghasiddhi. When we say that the spiritual preceptor is the quintessence of the qualities and deeds, body, voice, and mind of all the tathāgatas, this means that he personifies all aspects of buddhahood. Through his presence, he embodies all the spiritual aid we might hope to receive from the five tathāgatas just named, so he is said to be the quintessence of these five aspects of buddhahood. He manifests them to us, he reveals the path to us, he shows us the way and guides us, doing everything for us that the Buddha himself would do if he were present. He leads us to the attainment of those five transcendent wisdoms to which the five buddhas correspond.

The teacher is "the source of the eighty-four thousand teachings of doctrine." This refers to the legend that there were a total of 84,000 teachings taught by Lord Buddha for the benefit of beings. These were divided into four kinds:

(1) To counter the mental poison of desire, Lord Buddha taught 21,000 instructions relating to attachment. These are compiled in what is known as the *Vinaya*, the code of discipline for laypeople and Buddhist clergy.

(2) The second 21,000 discourses were taught to counter the mental poison of anger. In other words, the sūtras were the Buddha's teachings explaining the role of a bodhisattva, the way a bodhisattva should behave, the view of a bodhisattva, and the spiritual training a bodhisattva should undertake. The main thrust of these teachings was to overcome the inclination to feel different from or averse to others, and to help spiritual practitioners overcome patterns of behavior that could be typified as aversion or hatred.

(3) Third, he taught 21,000 doctrines to counter ignorance, found in the abhidharma collection of teachings. Here the teachings of Lord Buddha about the nature of phenomena, the nature of mind, the mental constituents that lead to enlightenment, the categories of external and internal phenomena, and so forth were classified and explained.

(4) Finally, to counter desire, anger, and ignorance together, the Buddha taught the 21,000 doctrines of the tantric path.

This teacher of ours, it is said, is "the master of all the noble assemblies of saints." This means that, through his presence, he manifests the quintessence of all the assemblies of bodhisattvas. In Mahāyāna Buddhism, when we say, "We take refuge in the Sangha," this means we take refuge in the assembly of great bodhisattvas, those beings on the spiritual path who have attained the first bhūmi or any of the subsequent nine stages of bodhisattvahood.

In reciting the verses of refuge, we first utter the words, "With great devotion of body, voice, and mind, we take refuge in the Holy Root and Lineal Preceptors." Devotion is expressed bodily, by clasping the palms of your hands together in the direction of the shrine; vocally, by reciting the words of the refuge formula; and mentally, by single-pointedly focusing on the Buddha, Dharma, and Sangha and taking refuge from the heart. The "root preceptor" means your own immediate teacher from whom you have received the transmission of the teachings; he is considered to be your root, primary, or cardinal teacher. The term "lineal preceptors" refers to those who preceded your root teacher, through whom he received the transmission of the teachings, all the way back to Lord Buddha himself. They are called your lineal preceptors because they belong to the lineage through which the teachings have been transmitted to you.

The second line of the refuge formula runs "With great devotion of body, voice, and mind, we take refuge in the Enlightened One, who has reached the end of renunciation and realization." Lord Buddha, it is said, has discarded everything that ought to be discarded, renounced everything that ought to be renounced, and attained everything that ought to be attained by any sincere, intelligent seeker of truth. He has achieved perfection in his efforts to reach the spiritual goal of buddhahood for the sake of others. For this reason, you can take refuge in him with confidence.

The third line is "With great devotion of body, voice, and mind, we take refuge in the Holy Teaching, which reveals the nature of his precepts and discourses." The Dharma is said to consist of two aspects: (1) the scriptural teaching, which consists of all those discourses, precepts, and instructions taught by Lord Buddha and later elaborated on by great disciples of his, and (2) the realizations to which those scriptural teachings refer. For example, a teaching on the doctrine of emptiness might be found in one of the sūtras, and you might also have the direct experience of it in your meditation on emptiness. This realization, or direct experience, is also said to be an aspect of the holy Dharma. It corresponds to the realizations achieved by putting into practice the Buddha's teachings on moral conduct, meditation, and wisdom (Skt. *prajñā*; Tib. *shes-rab*).

The final line is "With great devotion of body, voice, and mind, we take refuge in the Noble Assembly of holy beings, upholders of the teachings, and bodhisattvas." These are all the same: the holy beings and upholders of the teachings *are* the bodhisattvas. In Tibetan, bodhisattvas are called "Sons of the Conquerors." The conquerors are the buddhas, who have overcome the forces of delusion and attained self-mastery. The bodhisattvas are intent on treading the same path the buddhas followed to enlightenment. In everyday usage, a teacher acquires a spiritual "son" whenever a disciple understands the significance of the teachings he or she is giving, takes them to heart, puts them into practice, and attains that same dharmic experience. Their relationship then becomes that of a spiritual father or mother to a spiritual son or daughter.

The bodhisattvas are called "sons" in this sense, just as the founders of the Sakya order, Sachen Kunga Nyingpo and others, could be said to be the spiritual fathers of later masters, such as Ngorchen Könchog Lhündrub and Ngorchen Kunga Zangpo, the founder of Ngor Monastery. These great masters were, of course, not descendants of the same Tibetan family, but they were spiritual descendants of the Five Great Jetsüns and are called their sons because, through their own sincere efforts, they achieved the status of spiritual sons in relation to those teachers.

Invoking Blessings

The four lines of refuge should be recited three times or as many times as you wish. Following that, you may recite a further prayer to request the blessings of the Three Jewels:

> With great devotion of body, voice, and mind, we take refuge in you, most excellent Preceptor and Three Precious Jewels! Please bestow your blessings upon the body, voice, and mind of myself and all livings beings. Bless us that our minds might be attuned to the Dharma and move forward on the path of religion: may the way be cleared of all errors, may illusory visions appear as transcendent wisdom and unreligious thoughts never rise. Bless us in the awakening of love and compassion; may we tomorrow learn the two kinds of enlightenment thought and quickly attain enlightened buddhahood.

Through these verses, the blessings of the Buddha, Dharma, Sangha, and preceptors are invoked so that the minds of all living beings might be turned away from the distractions of daily life and toward the spiritual path.

When our minds become attuned to the Dharma, we pray that we might actually begin to move forward on the path of religion, that we might undertake those efforts of study, reflection, and practice which will launch us on that spiritual path. We pray also that, through the blessings of the gurus and the Three Jewels, our efforts might not be thwarted by mistakes on our part or unpropitious events, that all errors and obstacles might be cleared from our spiritual path. We also invoke their blessings that the illusory, impure visions of this world might appear to us as manifestations of transcendent wisdom itself, and that our spiritual state of mind might not be disturbed by selfishness or by the mental poisons of desire, hatred, and delusion. Finally, we pray for the blessings of the Three Jewels and the teachers that we might succeed in arousing within ourselves great love and great compassion for all living beings, along with the two kinds of bodhichitta: (1) the intention to strive for the eventual liberation of all living beings, and (2) the understanding that enlightenment ultimately consists in the recognition of the true nature of mind, that is, its nondual clarity and emptiness. Since love, compassion, and this enlightenment-oriented attitude are the causes of the attainment of buddhahood, we also pray that we may quickly succeed in actually attaining that exalted state.

After reciting these verses once, thrice, or as many times as you wish, Ngorchen Könchog Lhündrub suggests that you sit in silent meditation. In front of you, visualize the assembly of your teacher, the lineal preceptors, and the Buddha, Dharma, and Sangha. Think that, through their transcendent wisdom, they see you. Visualize that they are aware of your prayers invoking their blessings for you and other beings, and that, through their great compassion, they respond by bestowing blessings of empowerment, sharing with you their own power of spiritual activity and enriching your mind with their ability to act for the benefit of beings. Imagine that they protect you with their great spiritual power, which removes inner and outer problems that might arise at various stages of your spiritual path. Through their great power they do protect you, bless you, and keep watch over you, so that you will be able to reach the noble goal that you have undertaken for the benefit of all beings.

When you have completed this meditation and want to end the session on refuge, dedicate the merit you have acquired to the enlightenment of all living beings. Then, undertake to reinforce your refuge through the practice of mindfulness. Whenever you arise from your session of meditation, pause for a moment to reflect:

> Through the merit I have acquired in this way, may my parents and all others attain the stage of the enlightened ones who have succeeded in accomplishing the well-being of themselves and others.

This dedication of merit can also be expressed by reciting a verse written by the great philosopher Nāgārjuna:

Through this virtue, may all beings fulfill the accumulations of merit and wisdom; may they attain the two Holy Bodies that arise from wisdom and merit.

The two holy bodies referred to here are the nirmāṇakāya and the dharma-kāya. The latter is the Body of Reality, which corresponds to the transcendental wisdom of the mind of the buddhas; the former is the Manifestation Body of a buddha, which appears in order to communicate the realizations of buddhahood to unenlightened beings.

After you have arisen from meditation, bring to mind the excellent qualities of the Buddha, Dharma, and Sangha time and time again, and try, in your spare moments, to reflect on what you have learned of the qualities of the Buddha, such as his compassion and his activities on behalf of all beings; reflect, too, on the nature of the doctrine contained in his teachings and the qualities of the bodhisattvas who comprise the Sangha. Try to imbue your mind with a certain amount of recollection and mindfulness, so that you not only occasionally recall the Three Jewels but also aspire to train in accord with the practices of the buddhas and bodhisattvas, such as not harming others and the like.

7

SUPPOSE YOU OWN A FINE HORSE

THERE ARE THREE WAYS of making an offering to your guru. The best way is actually performing the Dharma instructions your teacher has given you. This is the highest way of making an offering and serving your guru. The second way is to offer material goods, things that are valuable in the sense that they are helpful to your teacher in his own religious efforts. The third and most inferior way is the offering of praises, recitations of hymns, and the like. We should try to make the very best offering we can. Here I will offer my efforts to teach and explain the profound doctrine of the *Lam dre*. On your part, you can offer a sincere desire to study carefully and take the teaching to heart, carrying it into your own practice of the path.

To give an example from the lam-dre teaching that we are studying, it can be said that the text known as *The Three Visions* is like the foundation, walls, and roof of a house, whereas the advanced teachings, known as *The Three Continua*, are like the inhabitants of the house. Thus you have the foundation and the path. The path, of course, consists of the advanced meditations found on the levels of *The Three Continua*.

HEEDFULNESS, RECOLLECTION, AND MINDFULNESS

In the last lesson, we concluded with the instruction on taking refuge. It follows that we should not only take refuge in the Three Jewels sincerely, but also protect that observance and the attendant practices of the path with three things: (1) heedfulness, (2) recollection, and (3) mindfulness.

It is taught that all the virtues we might accumulate through religious efforts are futile if they aren't sustained by these three factors. Since this is so, it is extremely important that we always keep them in mind. As it is taught in the *Bodhicharyāvatara*:

> The robbers of nonmindfulness always seek to enter the mind of one who is making efforts on the path. When his carelessness allows them an opening, they snatch away his mindfulness, his virtues, and as a result he winds up in a wretched state.

Hence we should always be alert, protecting the virtues we have accumulated for the benefit of others. We should be aware of our actions of body, voice, and mind at all times. Through introspection, we should be alert to what is going on in our minds, which situations are propitious to practice and which are likely to lead to trouble. Also, we should recall that we are engaged in practice and recollect what should be practiced and what should be avoided. As a rule of thumb, the ten virtuous deeds of body, voice, and mind should be observed, whereas the reverse of those ten should be avoided as obstacles to the path.

Recollection of what should and should not be practiced is of great importance in protecting our spiritual efforts. We should exercise this mindfulness at all times and in every situation by watching the doors of body, voice, and mind, keeping an eye on the actions we might be committing mentally, physically, or vocally, and trying to restrain the mind from actions that will cause our practice to be impaired. We should always strive to reinforce wholesome inclinations.

If you sincerely want to undertake the practices of the path, training according to the instructions given in this and similar teachings, you must, of course, remember these factors of mindfulness, heedfulness, and recollection. The *Bodhicharyāvatara* teaches that one who wishes to sustain spiritual training should first of all protect the mind. This training consists of the three efforts in which a Buddhist practitioner strives for mastery: (1) moral conduct, (2) meditative practices, and (3) insight. Success depends on the effort you make to guard the mind, restrain it from unwholesome ways, and sustain it in wholesome actions.

For example, suppose you own a fine horse. To get the best use out of this horse, you would naturally take care to feed it properly and give it the water, grass, straw, and whatever else might be required to keep the horse in good health. Toward that end, you would tether the horse where there was the best grass you could find, plus abundant water and shelter when it needed them. You would also need to keep checking the horse to make sure that it hadn't broken tether and become lost. (I suppose it might ruin the example if we changed it to a car for New Yorkers. We'll stick with the Tibetan example of a horse that you tether on the mountainside.) Being the owner of a fine horse requires you to make all these efforts just to preserve your property.

The mind is like a horse, except that you need to accomplish spiritual rather than material aims and must have a well-trained mind able to accomplish the great good that you have undertaken to achieve. Tethering the horse in a suitable place is similar to restraining the mind from wayward inclinations and putting it in an optimum situation for the practice of virtues. Remembering that "I've got my horse tethered on the mountainside" is very much like the constant recollection that "I've got my mind in training; I shouldn't forget what my mind is up to; I have to keep checking on it." This kind of reminding yourself of what you are about is said to constitute the practice of recollection.

Checking on the horse again and again is very much like constantly examining the mind: "Where is my mind now? What is it up to? Is it still engaged in virtue, or has it become scattered and distracted by useless activities and inclinations?" The practices of recollection and mindfulness are a natural part of the spiritual path. You must develop these resources just to sustain the efforts that you have undertaken.

The Benefits of Taking Refuge

Taking refuge in the Three Jewels is said to be the source of infinite benefits for those who do so sincerely. As the sūtras put it, if the merit of seeking refuge had a form, the whole of space would not be large enough to contain it.

Why is there so much merit in taking refuge? Briefly stated, it leads us to awaken within ourselves all the spiritual vows of the bodhisattva, which result in so much benefit for ourselves and others once enlightenment is attained. Moreover, as a result of entering the path to enlightenment and taking refuge in the Three Jewels, we become protected by the buddhas, bodhisattvas, protectors of the Dharma, and gods who love the Dharma. Through their truly tremendous powers, our spiritual way is freed from obstacles. Also, through the simple act of taking refuge, all the gross obstacles and countless sins collected through ignorance from beginningless time are said to be purified.

For these and other reasons, once we have taken refuge we ought to strengthen that act. We should awaken a mind of rejoicing in refuge, thinking, "Today my life has become worthwhile and significant. I have accomplished something truly good for myself and for others."

Just as good citizens conform to secular laws, so a practitioner of the Dharma should keep the injunctions laid down by enlightened masters for the infinitely great benefit of all beings. Generally speaking, this means training in refuge and the attendant practices, associating primarily with spiritual persons, and respecting the Three Jewels. Of course, you should feel and show respect for images of the Buddha as well as for renunciate followers of the path. We are also taught that, in the last days of the Dharma, the only place Buddhism will be found will be in books. Therefore it is especially important to respect and care for holy books, elevating them rather than leaving them on the floor.

In addition, you should never take refuge in worldly deities or unenlightened beings still bound to the wheel of saṃsāra. They can in no way help you. This pertains to taking refuge in the Buddha. As you take refuge in the Dharma, give up all thoughts, inclinations, and actions that bring harm to yourself or others. And as you become firm in taking refuge in the Sangha, give up associating with people who oppose your practice, avoid inferior teachings, and don't become involved with philosophical views of a lower sort that might conflict with your understanding and practice of the Dharma.

You should show respect for the Three Jewels by taking refuge upon arising and retiring, by making prostrations or salutations. Pandit Atīsha advised us to approach our meals as offerings, too, by dividing the food into four parts. Offer the pure, untouched portion to the Three Jewels, the second part to the guardians of the teachings, and the remnants of your meal to the unhappy spirits, the protectorless, animals who can't hunt, ghosts, destitute humans, and those who practice religious austerities. Sanctify your food with a grace offering of *Om Ah Hum* or a prayer in which you make offerings to your personal deity (*yidam*), wealth deities, teachers, and special spirits. Eat to nourish the body, not just for sensual pleasure. Pray that it will give you strength to practice. There is great benefit to be gained if you pray that these daily actions may benefit all beings.

In all activities, great and small, wholeheartedly rely on the Three Jewels. Even when things go badly, don't abandon hope, feel ignored, or think that you are not getting the help you need. Remember that the Buddha understands the true nature of all beings and that his great power and compassion will be manifested in help along the path in answer to your refuge prayers. Think in this way:

> The Three Jewels are able surely to protect and sustain a sincere practitioner. The Buddha knows us in our deepest nature and will recognize our sincerity. In his great compassion he only desires our progress on the path. There is no doubt he will respond. Furthermore, it is my own fault I'm not yet enlightened, not the fault of the Triple Gem. Things go wrong not

because of the elements of refuge, but because I am somehow out of phase. Even though I have lived countless lives and passed aeons in saṃsāra, somehow I have missed the most important thing of all: enlightenment. It follows that I must become very diligent and rely totally on the Three Jewels rather than on my own ideas and fancies. Thus far, my record is quite poor, or I would be awakened by now.

Part II

The Main Teaching

8

THE NEEDLE POINT OF WORLDLY EXISTENCE

WE HAVE NOW COMPLETED our discussion of taking refuge and are entering the main topic—instructions on the three visions themselves. First are the instructions on the impure vision, which produce a spirit of renunciation. Second are those on the vision of experience, intended to awaken within us a spirit of noble resolve. Third are the instructions on the pure vision, intended to engender enthusiasm for the result.

THE IMPURE VISION

The first set of instructions corresponds to the level of impure vision, by which we mean the perception of ordinary, worldly folk. These instructions are designed to awaken a spirit of growing detachment from the ordinary pursuits of worldly people, whether for gain, pleasure, power, or what have you. They are concerned mainly with pointing out the unsatisfactory nature of worldly existence in order to awaken within us an awareness of its true nature and of the unworthiness, at least in the long run, of acting with attachment toward transient, insubstantial objects of worldly desire.

The instructions on the vision of experience concern the awakening of faith in the Buddhadharma, an attitude of great love and great compassion that encompasses all living beings, and a firm resolve to strive only for their benefit, and hence for perfect enlightenment on their behalf.

The instructions on the pure vision are intended to awaken enthusiasm within the practitioner by pointing out the excellent qualities acquired through the attainment of buddhahood and the tremendous benefits for oneself and others that result from striving for such an exalted goal. These instructions are not known directly by unenlightened people. But by giving some description of the result, namely, the three bodies of buddhahood, we can become clearer about the nature of the goal for which we are striving.

THE UNSATISFACTORY NATURE OF WORLDLY EXISTENCE

Let us turn to the first of these sets of instructions, which are given to awaken within us a feeling of apprehension about the true nature of worldly existence. "Apprehension" is used in a dual sense here: (1) in the sense of perception, because by becoming aware of the true nature of worldly existence, we apprehend that it is by nature unsatisfactory, no matter what we like to think about it; and (2) in the sense of anxiety, because if the true nature of worldly existence is suffering, we might well question whether worldly existence is really worth clinging to.

Second are instructions on the rarity of this opportunity to learn and practice the teachings of enlightenment. These are supposed to evoke a spirit of keen diligence, a desire not to waste another moment but to make the best of the opportunity that we now realize we have, rather than squandering it as we have done repeatedly in the past.

Third are instructions on karma—wholesome and unwholesome actions and their results. These are designed to help us discern which sorts of behavior are helpful to ourselves and others and which should be avoided as unhelpful or unwholesome.

In the *Vajra Verses*, the root text for this teaching, Virūpa uses the phrase "for living beings," meaning that, if we examine the modes of existence of all living beings, we can clearly see that no matter where, when, or how they exist, they never get beyond the pale of worldly suffering. For that reason, those who are spiritually aware strive to check the causes that lead farther into suffering and to attain spiritual liberation from all pain. That is why religious masters of almost every tradition teach that we should abandon attachment to worldly existence.

In the Buddhist system of practice it is taught that, to be able to keep in mind the unsatisfactoriness of worldly existence, we should become familiar with worldly existence and understand quite clearly that it indeed has a nature of suffering. It was with this in mind that Sachen's third son, the great Dragpa Gyaltsen, wrote in one of his songs that we should seek to abandon attachment to the three realms of existence, and that to do so we need to remember the faults of worldly existence itself. (It will become clear as we proceed what is meant by worldly existence.)

In the *Stations of Mindfulness of the True Dharma Sūtra* (*Saddharma-smṛti-upasthāna-sūtra*), it is written:

> The realm of desire is faulty by nature, the realm of form is also faulty by its nature, and the formless realm likewise is faulty. The state of liberation alone is seen to be faultless.

As you may know from your studies of Buddhist cosmogony, beings are said to be found in three realms of existence. The first is the realm of desire (*kāmadhātu*). This includes all beings from the lowest level of hell, Avīci

Hell, on up through the six levels of celestials within the desire realm. The second of these realms, the realm of form (*rūpadhātu*), includes those gods and ascetics who exist in the four worldly states of meditative absorption (or four *dhyāna;* Tib. *bsam-gtan-bzhi*), which, qualitatively at least, are higher than the desire realm. Finally, there is the realm of formlessness (*arūpadhātu*), in which certain yogis and other beings dwell in meditative absorption on formlessness. This state may be achieved by Hīnayānists who meditate that there is nothing but space, or even by meditators in that tradition who concentrate on the fact that there is nothing that exists. These three realms have been described as faulty or unsatisfactory in nature. We will explore in later lessons what makes them so.

Moreover, the great bodhisattva Maitreya related in his *Adornment of the Mahāyāna Sūtras* that even as ordure lacks fragrance, so the five modes of existence lack happiness. The nature of worldly existence is ever one of suffering, just as the touch of fire and weapons and the taste of sal ammoniac are painful by nature. We don't expect perfume from ordure because, by its very nature, it does not have such a characteristic. In the same way, it is a mistake to look for bliss, ecstasy, and happiness in the five modes of worldly existence. Generally we speak of six modes, or realms, of existence—or six kinds of living beings—but in this case the gods and the demigods (also called titans, or asuras) are subsumed into one category. Thus we have the hell beings, hungry ghosts, animals, humans, and gods, and none has a nature of happiness. A nature of happiness is not to be expected within worldly existence, any more than pleasure is to be expected from contact with fire, sharp weapons, or the taste of sal ammoniac.

What exactly are the faults found in the various state of worldly existence that make them so undesirable? The *Stations of Mindfulness Sūtra* tells us:

> The beings of the hells are afflicted by the torments of extremes of cold and heat; the ghosts are tortured by the pains of hunger and thirst; the animals are oppressed by darkness, constant fear, and the agony of being devoured by each other; the humans are short-lived; and the gods live so carelessly that they become undone by their carelessness.

The sufferings of the hells, as they have been described, are hard to credit. Faced with descriptions of such inconceivably great pain, to be endured over such great lengths of time, our first reaction is to discount them as mere warnings of symbolic value alone. Yet they do represent the experience of beings whose existence, while not absolutely real, is as real to them as our human existence now appears to be to us. In those states of existence, even the idea of a moment of peace or good feeling is out of the question.

The same is true of the unhappy ghosts, who are constantly afflicted by great hunger and thirst and always looking for the sustenance that is denied them. The animals are afflicted by darkness of intelligence, so that they are not always able to cope with their situation. As a result they are constantly in fear of losing their lives and are in mortal fear of one another. This we can judge, from our own experience, to be the case with most animals.

Human life is like a dream; if we're lucky, the longest we can hope to live is about a hundred years, and even that amount of time passes terribly quickly. One event follows another and, almost before we know it, we are at the brink of death. Our human life is insubstantial; it is a mixed bag of pleasure and pain.

The gods, who seem to be free from suffering for very long periods of time, are, by their very conceit and carelessness about liberation, unprepared for the exhaustion of those causes which brought about their godlike existence in the first place. When the merits that caused their rebirth on the celestial plane are exhausted, they are not ready for their descent to the meritless realms. Seeing the true nature of what is experienced in these five states of existence, Lord Buddha taught, "There is indeed no happiness to be found on the needle point of worldly existence."

THE THREE KINDS OF SUFFERING

When we begin to reflect on the different states of existence in which beings find themselves, we understand their experience to be primarily one of unsatisfactoriness. With further reflection, we can discern three different kinds of suffering.

The first and most obvious is the suffering of pain per se, in the sense of physical pain, mental pain, and all the gross and subtle experiences of unhappiness, including disease, impairment of the senses, growing old, dying, being separated from those you love, being deprived of things to which you are attached, being forced to spend time with people you dislike, and so forth. Reflecting on the myriad types of such pain that beings experience, a feeling of sadness arises that this should be the sum of experience for beings in all these states of existence. Everyone desires happiness just as we ourselves do; thus we feel sad that they should have to undergo endless types of unsatisfactoriness and even very painful degrees of suffering.

The second kind of suffering is that of change or impermanence. By reflecting on this characteristic, which pervades the three realms and five modes of existence, we learn to relinquish our attachment to the round of worldly existence by seeing that it is insubstantial. It is easy to point to countless examples of the constant flux that our own experience in this life is and becomes. We ourselves constantly undergo change, and we can expect this to be the case for the foreseeable future. For humans this involves growing up, becoming middle-aged, growing old, dying, and leaving everyone and everything to go we know not where. Change also separates people and brings them together: where there were many people before, there may later be one or none remaining; where once there were no people, there may be many. This dance of beings from place to place, from rebirth to rebirth occurs constantly throughout space. Also, there is what might be called vertical change. A person who begins in an exalted position in life, enjoying excellent health, wealth, and reputation, can later find himself plunged to the lowest rungs of society, without any resources at all. This applies to the other realms of existence as well. Even the highest of gods can suddenly find himself hurtled from that state. We can see from human history how often the very powerful have been brought low. These are examples of the constant impermanence to which all beings are subject. Impermanence is the very nature of worldly existence—nothing but change is to be expected from it.

The third kind of suffering is that of conditioned existence. This is a bit subtler and requires some explanation, because it involves regarding beings and events not as real, individual entities but from the dharmic perspective of someone on the spiritual path. The very constituent of existence is, by nature, suffering. From a Buddhist viewpoint, beings are not substantial, solid beings in themselves but are brought about by causes and conditions, like everything else, animate or inanimate. At least for animate beings, these causes and conditions result in the five aggregates (*skandha*): form, feeling, perceptions, impulses, and consciousness. Since these aggregates arise from an ignorance of reality, by the very nature of their causes and conditions they arise in a state of unsatisfactoriness. By reflecting on the suffering of conditioned existence, we become interested in striving for liberation, as opposed to perpetuating our blind craving for continued existence regardless of the cost in terms of delusion, pain, and so forth.

To repeat these three, we reflect on the suffering of pain to awaken sadness for beings, on the suffering of impermanence to relinquish attachment to worldly existence, and on the suffering of conditioned existence to awaken within ourselves the desire for liberation.

9

SHEER PAIN

REFLECTING ON THE DIFFICULTY of obtaining human birth in the first place and of finding propitious situations where the teaching, a teacher, and the opportunity to practice are available, we should all try to be mindful of our extreme good fortune. That good fortune is manifested in the opportunity to hear and reflect on authentic teachings of enlightenment, which, if we put them into practice, can bring about perfect buddhahood in this very lifetime, provided we are among the more intelligent of beings. If we are among the mediocre or middling class of beings in our intellectual and spiritual capacities, we are still within reach of attaining buddhahood during the intermediate state between successive lives (*bardo*). And even if we are among those of weaker spiritual faculties, we have the assurance of reaching it within the next few lifetimes. Considering not only the odds against our good fortune but also the boundless good results that can ensue from such an opportunity, it behooves us all to keep these points in mind.

We are beginning a reflection on the suffering in the realm of worldly existence. We have already noted that worldly existence is characterized by (1) the suffering of sheer pain, (2) the suffering of impermanence, and (3) the suffering of conditioned existence, that is, the realization that all phenomena which arise through causes and conditions are involved in a process that is painful by its very nature. This realization of the true nature of all phenomena helps us form the resolve to strive instead for the happiness of the unconditioned, namely, the happiness of true liberation.

THE SUFFERING OF SUFFERING IN THE THREE LOWER REALMS

By reflecting on the suffering that characterizes the round of worldly existence, we try to awaken within ourselves a feeling of sorrow and grief that this is indeed the lot of beings wherever they may be reborn. As the great Jetsün Dragpa Gyaltsen, the fifth patriarch of the Sakya order, wrote in his *Parting from the Four Attachments* (*Zhen pa bzhi bral*):

> The suffering of sheer pain is found in the three lower realms. If we think seriously of those unbearable pains which beings must undergo

there, we humans could in no way bear even the thought of such pain, let alone the experience of the pain itself. And yet humans, ignoring the opportunity to accumulate the virtues of renunciation, spend all their time accumulating useless actions that lead to rebirth there. This great delusion of beings everywhere is a cause of great sadness, of great pity.

To repeat: the suffering of suffering is found in the three lower realms, which we could in no way bear, and yet we strive only to accumulate the causes of rebirth there. What a pity this is.

In his reply to the teacher Tratön, Dragpa Gyaltsen further states:

> The suffering of suffering is found in the abode of the three lower realms of existence. Like the wounds of leprosy on top of a blister, if it be properly reflected on, how could anyone possibly bear it? And so, one should diligently refrain from unvirtuous ways.

The three lower realms, those of the hell beings, ghosts, and animals, are characterized by extremes of both mental and physical suffering. The type of suffering experienced there is gross, sheer pain, as opposed to the subtler sufferings of impermanence and of conditioned existence itself. The suffering found in the three lower realms is likened to the wounds of leprosy breaking out on top of blisters caused by great heat or fire. Thus, on top of the general suffering of worldly existence itself, we find a fresh suffering, a greater, stronger, more intense and unbearable suffering—the suffering of the lower realms.

Thinking carefully about the possibility of such long-lasting extremes of pain, no one in his right mind would consider undergoing them himself. When we reflect on how tender we are in experiencing a little burn, the prick of a needle, or slight heat and cold, how could we possibly bear the suffering of the lower realms? It follows that we should at least be careful to avoid those unvirtuous deeds which are described as the causes of such suffering.

In our reflection we will consider the pains of (1) the hells, (2) the ghost realms, and (3) the animal world. In the first of these, we will discuss the sufferings found in the eighteen hells: (a) the eight cold hells, (b) the eight hot hells, (c) the neighboring hells, which are adjacent to the great hot and cold hells, and (d) the temporary hells, where the location and duration of sufferings are not fixed (generally, they are of shorter duration and the extremes of suffering are somewhat less).

The Sufferings of the Hell Realms

In Buddhist cosmogony, the hells are said to exist some 20,000 leagues (*yojana*) beneath the human world. A yojana is a unit of measure a good bit longer than a mile—perhaps a league in length. The neighboring hells are on the periphery of the great hells. Temporary hells can be located at different points on the round of existence, even in the human realm.

The Eight Cold Hells. We will consider the extreme pain experienced by those beings so unfortunate as to be reborn in the eight cold hells. These eight hells, whose Tibetan names I will be giving you, are translated from the Sanskrit. I will try to indicate the general significance of each name. The first cold hell is the hell of cold blisters (Skt. *arbuda*; Tib. *chubu*);[33] the second is the hell of bursting blisters (Skt. *nirarbuda*; Tib. *chubu dolba*); the third is the "achoo" hell (Skt. *atata*; Tib. *achu serba*), named for a cry of pain. Beings in this hell cry out constantly due to the extreme cold. The fourth hell is known as the "ky-hoot" hell (Skt. *hahava*; Tib. *kyihud serba*), another cry of extreme grief and agony due to the touch of even greater cold. In English, it corresponds to "Alas!"

The fifth hell is called the hell of clenched teeth (Skt. *huhuva*; Tib. *sotham*). Here the pain is so unbearable that beings are no longer able to cry out but remain with teeth clenched. Next is the blue flower hell (Skt. *utpala*; Tib. *utpala tar-gepa*), in which the skin turns blue and cracks open. Seventh is the lotus flower hell (Skt. *padma*; Tib. *pema tar-gepa*), in which the skin itself is carried away by fierce winds and the raw, red flesh cracks open, looking like the petals of a lotus flower. Finally, there is the great lotus hell (Skt. *mahāpadma* or *puṇḍarīka*; Tib. *pema chen-po tar-gepa*), in which sufferings like those of the seventh hell are experienced with even greater ferocity.

Now we will examine the sufferings undergone by beings born in the first of these eight cold hells, the hell of cold blisters. As a result of one's former unwholesome deeds, which have now ripened into rebirth in such a place, one is born in an instant through what is called the process of miraculous birth—in other words, without undergoing gestation and birth from a womb or another type of birth. One finds oneself endowed with a very large body, naked, on an icy plain encircled by rows of great snow mountains, and on this icy plain one's body is stricken by the touch of unbearable blizzards. One is denied the sight of the sun anywhere on the horizon; there is not even the glimmer of a single star to be seen, let alone the prospect of finding shelter from the terrible blizzards. One hasn't even the fortune to rest on a patch of cloth. There is no source of warmth to which one might turn for comfort. As one roams about, driven by the snowstorms, masses of blisters begin to appear on one's body due to the intense cold.

The touch of cold in the second hell, the hell of bursting blisters, is twenty times greater than that in the hell of cold blisters. In this second cold hell, one's blisters begin to burst open, and blood and watery fluid pour out, freezing on one's body and turning into ice.

The third hell, the hell of wailing, is twenty times colder than the second. Due to the extremity of pain there, beings roam about alone, emitting wailing sounds due to the cold.

In the fourth hell, the cold is again twenty times greater. The beings who are roaming about roar with pain and scream out, "Alas, alas!"

In the fifth hell, the hell of clenched teeth, the pain is so great that the beings there cannot even cry out in agony. Due to the cold, twenty times greater than in the fourth hell, the skin of one's body turns blue and begins to crack into pieces.

In the sixth hell, the utpala hell, one experiences cold twenty times greater than in the hell of clenched teeth, the skin of one's body turns blue, and it cracks open so that the wounds and burst blisters resemble the petals of the blue utpala flower.

In the seventh hell, that of lotuslike wounds, the cold is twenty times greater still. One's skin is carried away by gusts of wind from blizzards and gales, and the raw, frozen surface of one's body turns red and begins to crack into pieces.

In the great lotus hell, characterized by even greater cracking of one's flesh, on top of all the foregoing pains, one's body also begins to crack into thousands of pieces, one's entrails flow out, and they too freeze and burst open.

These eight hells are characterized not only by cold but also by other types of suffering experienced therein. Some of these were described by the great Indian pandit Āchārya Chandragomin, who wrote:

> Due to an unrivaled wind that, sinking to the bone, carries away the dry body's shaking flesh, one hangs on, ready to die, while insects spring forth from the hundreds of bursting blisters and afflict one with weapons, so that blood, watery fluid, and marrow flow out.

According to this very graphic description, a wind, so terrible that nothing in human experience or imagination can exemplify it, arises and pierces one straight to the bone. One is absolutely defenseless. It is so fierce that it carries one's flesh from the bone, yet one is unable to die. On top of that, terrible insects spring forth from one's wounds and afflict one with their beaks and hellish weapons.

The span of one's lifetime in such a place is described in the *Abhidharma-kosha* (*Treasury of Advanced Doctrines*), where Lord Buddha stated the duration of such pain in these words:

> The life span of the beings reborn in the first of these eight hells is equal to the length of human time that would be exhausted if one were to extract a single sesame seed once every hundred years from a very large barrel of sesame. The life span in the remaining seven hells is progressively twentyfold.

Let us examine this verse in some detail, using a system of measurement employed in Magadha, the kingdom in northern India in which Lord Buddha lived. According to this system of measurement, a *tiljong* was a very large vessel used for sesame. For our purposes, we can visualize a vessel large enough to hold a ton of sesame seed. The simile says that, assuming you were to remove a single sesame seed from a tilong once every hundred years, the length of time required to empty it would equal the life span of those beings born in the first of the eight cold hells. In the second cold hell, the life span is twenty times longer than in the first—in other words, it would equal the time required to empty 20 tiljongs in the manner just described. For the third hell, 400 such vessels would have to be emptied; for the fourth hell, 8,000 vessels of sesame; for the fifth hell, 160,000 vessels; for the sixth hell, 3.2 million; for the seventh cold hell, 64 million vessels; and for the eighth hell, one would have to empty 1.28 billion of these large vessels at the rate of one seed each century.

The life spans described in this example from the *Abhidharmakosha* should be understood to be only approximate. It is very hard to grasp such extreme lengths of time, let alone the idea of spending them in such unbearable pain. Actually, the Buddha said that the length of time beings remain in those states is even greater:

> If, for example, O monks, someone were to extract a single sesame seed every hundred years from a tiljong vessel of the Magadha country, which contains 80 kals (*kal*) and is brimful with sesame, the exhaustion of all those 80 kals through this process

would be relatively quick. But I do not say that the life span of those beings born in the first of the eight cold hells would come to an end so quickly.

In other texts we have quotations such as:

> One life span of the second hell is equal to twenty of the life spans of the first hell, and so on, until we get to the life span of the eighth cold hell, which is equal to twenty of those in the seventh hell.

We should learn how to meditate on these states of existence known as the cold hells, reflecting on their significance to us and on the possibility of such suffering. To do this, be seated in the posture of meditation and take refuge in the Three Jewels, invoking their blessings that your meditation may be accomplished successfully for the benefit of yourself and others. Then reflect in your own words, or use the words we give here as a kind of model. You might reflect in this way:

> Alas, through countless aeons I have been afflicted by innumerable floods of suffering due to roaming in the various birthplaces in the round of worldly existence. If, on top of all the manifold kinds of distress I have experienced up to this point, I should no longer have to experience other sufferings, how good that would be. But until this mechanism of subject–object dichotomy is destroyed, I shall continue to be reborn helplessly in the birthplaces of the three realms and five modes of existence. If yet again I should be afflicted by countless feelings of pain, whatever shall I do? Even before tomorrow comes, I might be reborn in those cold hells where the place is [such and such], the natural conditions are [such], and the life span is [of such and such a length].

Here you should stop and reflect on the descriptions for each of these eight hells, visualizing their sufferings almost as if you were there, undergoing them yourself. Then proceed:

> If I were born in such a place, how could I possibly bear it? If I cannot bear even a slight touch of cold, as experienced in the human realm, even for a single day, how could I bear it if the agony of the cold hells should befall me? And yet I have no assurance that it will not. Every day, anger, which is the cause of the

experience of those hells, arises within me countless times and governs my mind. If those sufferings befall me and I have no way at all to bear them, what shall I do? Therefore, I must rightly practice the holy teachings, which are the antidote to those sufferings.

Next, you can think in this way:

> Furthermore, the practice of the holy teachings that I am to do must not be mere artifice, mere pretense, but true practice attuned with the teachings of the Enlightened Ones. The practice I shall engage in must be derived from an uninterrupted line of transmission. I shall definitely engage in and experience the practice of these instructions of the *Lam dre*, the jewel among teachings. May the Three Jewels and the compassionate preceptors please help me that I might be able to do this.

These instructions are for the regular meditation in which you sit and meditate on the cold hells. Generally speaking, in nonmeditative times, you might also be mindful of acting in accord with the instructions given by the great master Nāgārjuna in his *Precious Garland*:

> The practice of religion consists, in brief, of refraining from alcoholic beverages, right livelihood, thoroughgoing nonviolence toward others, gifts offered with devotion, reverence to the excellent, and love toward the lowly.

Finally, always try to govern your behavior in daily life by acting in harmony with the teachings of enlightenment. As a result, great merit for yourself and others will ensue; remember, also, always to dedicate all merit to the enlightenment and benefit of all sentient beings. Try at all times to remain endowed with recollection and mindfulness of what you have learned, and strive to maintain a feeling of awareness that

> Now I understand the nature of worldly existence for what it is, and it is right that I should keep that awareness constantly in mind, turning away from further involvement in this process of birth and death, which leads beings to such unbearable pains.

For that reason also, try to be mindful in watching your conduct, making certain that it accords with the teachings of enlightenment.

10

The Forest of Swords

The profound instructions of the *Lam dre* belong to the Vajrayāna class of teachings, the jewel of all the doctrines of enlightenment. Therefore, it behooves us to respond rightly to this rare opportunity to receive them. We can do so by recalling their rarity, directing our minds with single-pointed attention to the teaching that follows, and placing that teaching in the context of the topics we have already discussed.

The Three Visions treats the various experiences that correspond to the impure vision of unenlightened beings, the vision of experience encountered by meditators on the spiritual path, and the pure vision of enlightened beings who have attained the direct perception of ultimate reality. At the moment we are studying the instructions that correspond to the level of impure vision. We need first to become acquainted with the teachings on the faultiness of worldly existence in order to awaken within ourselves sincere renunciation of clinging to and craving for worldly existence. Toward that end, we are considering in detail the negative aspects of the six realms of existence. In the last lesson, we discussed the pains experienced by those beings unfortunate enough to have been reborn in the cold hells. We continue by looking at the hot hells.

The Eight Hot Hells. These are the reviving hell, the black-thread hell, the crushing hell, the wailing hell, the great wailing hell, the ordinary hot hell, the very hot hell, and the interminable hell.

The first of these hot hells is the reviving hell (Skt. *samjiva*; Tib. *yang-so*). Due to the accumulation of evil karma through unwholesome actions of body, voice, and mind, a person finds himself miraculously born in the reviving hell, a region where the ground is of burning iron swept by raging, blazing fires. He is born with a very large, sensitive body, unable to bear the slightest bit of heat or fear. As soon as he is born there, he is naturally unhappy about the prospects. The minute he looks about, he thinks something like "Alas, I am born into such a place as this." The only hope is that perhaps no one will bother him. But the very moment he thinks "I hope no one hurts me here," from all directions there suddenly appear terrible, fearful-looking demons. Carrying all kinds of cruel weapons, they chase him down as a hunter would chase a deer. When they catch him, they treat him in much the same way a butcher would handle an animal that had been sent to him for slaughter. With the roughest, rudest sort of treatment they join in tormenting him by beating and cutting his body and piercing it with sharp weapons. Finally, he can take it no longer and falls into a swoon due to the intense pain. It is almost as if he had died. He loses consciousness but is revived by a voice from the sky that says "Revive," and is touched by a cold wind that brings him to life again.

This process is repeated over and over again for unendurably long periods of time. The sūtras say that a being reborn in this hell has to experience this suffering ten thousand times before he is freed. The *Bodhicharyāvatara* tells us that, due to their many evil deeds, beings fall into a state where they must experience the intense fear and pain brought about by fierce beings who attack them with weapons, flay their skin, and cut their flesh into hundreds of pieces. It is also taught in other texts that beings in the hot hells are hypersensitive to pain. In each part of their bodies, the experience of pain is unbearable.

The second hell is the black-thread hell (Skt. *kālasūtra*; Tib. *thig-nag*). Here everything is just as before: the experience of being born in such a place, the pain and the fear are just as in the reviving hell. However, when the hell beings have chased you down, they treat you just as carpenters treat wood: they draw eight, sixteen, or thirty-two intersecting black lines on your body and then saw along those lines with sharp, blazing saws. The person who is reborn there is unable to escape. As Ārya Nāgārjuna wrote in his *Letter from a Friend* (*Suhṛllekha*), "Some are sawed by saws while others are split by terrible, sharp axes."

The third hell is called the crushing hell (Skt. *samghat*; Tib. *du-jom*). Here a being is born onto a ground of burning iron, even though he is unable to bear the touch of heat. His only thought is to flee. As he seeks escape, he looks about him and on all sides sees great fearful mountains that resemble the faces of yaks and water buffalos. These mountains begin to converge until he is caught between them and crushed, just as a sesame seed is ground between rocks. His body is pulverized and an endless stream of blood pours out of it. Finally, he loses consciousness, only to be revived as the entire process is repeated endlessly. It is said that he goes through this experience ten thousand times every day and night. As Nāgārjuna wrote in his *Letter from a Friend,* "Some are squeezed like sesame and others are pulverized like fine powder."

The fourth hell is the wailing hell (Skt. *raurava*; Tib. *ngu-bod*). Here the environment is much the same as before. A person reborn in such a place immediately looks for a way out. He spies a house in the distance and runs there, all the while experiencing unbearable heat because the ground is burning iron with flames bursting forth from it. Finally, he arrives at the house, which is also made of iron, and dashes inside; the doors close behind him, and he is unable to escape. Inside, he finds he cannot distinguish between the flames and his own body, or the flames and his own mind. There is nothing he can do except wail. He remains there for an unbearably long time, crying as if the sobs were being pulled out of his very heart.

The fifth hell is called the great wailing hell (Skt. *mahāraurava*; Tib. *ngu-bod chen-po*). Here things are very much as before, except that inside the first house he finds a second house, which he enters. There the heat is twice as intense and the pain so much greater than before that his screams and wails are twice as loud.

The sixth hell is the ordinary hot hell (Skt. *tapana*; Tib. *tsha-ba*). Here the being is chased down and caught by the guardians of hell, who impale him very roughly on a blazing iron spike that is pushed through his anus to the crown of his head. Due to the great heat of the spike, his innards catch fire and flames flutter out of his mouth.

Next is the very hot hell (Skt. *pratapana*; Tib. *rab-tu tsha-ba*). Here a being is run through from top to bottom with a blazing three-pronged spike. From the wounds in his body, blood and melting fat emerge, and flames pour out of his mouth and ears. As the *Letter from a Friend* states, "Some are wholly threaded through by greatly blazing, thorned iron spikes."

Finally, there is the interminable hell (Skt. *avīci*; Tib. *mnar-med*). It is called interminable because the sufferings there are constant and of the greatest duration of all the hells. Avīci Hell resembles a great stove of blazing iron about 20,000 leagues long. Here a being is subject to the uninterrupted torment of measureless agonies that are just impossible to bear. The sufferings of this particular hell are said to be the worst in worldly existence. As Nāgārjuna wrote:

> Just as, among all pleasures, the joy of the extinction of craving is foremost, so, among all kinds of sufferings, the painful flames of the Avīci Hell are most terrible.

In this hell one finds oneself like so much fuel in a great raging cauldron of fire. One's entire body burns as if it were flame itself. One is so caught up in intensely raging flames that one's body and mind seem to become nondual with the fire.

Now we should consider the life spans of beings so unfortunate as to have been reborn in the hot hells. The *Abhidharmakosha* tells us:

> Fifty years of human life is a single day in the life of the lowest kāmadevas, and the life span of those deities is five hundred of their years. The life spans of the gods in the two higher god realms are successively twofold. So a single day in the reviving hell is equal to the life span of a kāmadeva.[34]

We will now explain this in detail.

Fifty human years equals one day in the life of the gods who inhabit the Heaven of the Four Great Kings (the Chaturmahārājikā gods). Thirty of their days constitutes one of their months, and twelve of their months makes one of their years. In Chaturmahārājikā, gods live five hundred of their years. Counting a lifetime of those gods as a single day, the life span in the reviving hell is five hundred years.

A hundred human years equals a single day in the life span of the gods who inhabit the Heaven of the Thirty-Three (the Trāyātriṁśa gods),[35] and those gods live one thousand of their own years. One life span of those gods equals a single day in the black-thread hell, and a person must remain in the black-thread hell for a thousand black-thread years.

Two hundred human years equals one day in the life of the gods of the Heaven without Fighting (the Yāma realm), who live two thousand of their own years. One life span of those gods equals a single day in the crushing hell, and a person must remain in that hell for two thousand crushing-hell years.

Four hundred human years equals one day in the life of the gods of the Joyful Heaven (Tuṣita), who live four thousand of their own years. The life span of the Tushita gods equals one day in the wailing hell, and a being in the wailing hell must remain there for four thousand wailing-hell years.

Eight hundred human years equals a single day in the life of the gods who inhabit the Heaven of Delighting in Emanations (the Nirmāṇarati realm). Their life span consists of eight thousand of their own years. The life span of those gods equals a single day in the great wailing hell, and a person must remain in that hell for eight thousand great-wailing-hell years.

Sixteen hundred human years equals a single day in the life of the gods who inhabit the Heaven of Ruling the Creations of Others (the Paranirmita-vasavartin gods).[36] Those gods live sixteen hundred of their own years. The full life span of those gods equals a single day in the ordinary hot hell, and a being must remain there for sixteen hundred ordinary-hot-hell years.

The life span of a being in the very hot hell lasts for half an aeon, and the life span of a being reborn in the interminable hell is a full aeon. To summarize: 500, 1,000, 2,000, 4,000, 8,000, and 16,000 celestial years, a half aeon, and a full aeon are the life spans in the eight hot hells.

How are we to reflect on the meaning of these teachings on the hells? Obviously, such descriptions are intended to strengthen a sense of renunciation of worldly existence by helping us become aware of the possibilities for extreme unhappiness and suffering, thus making us careful to avoid the causes of such possible sufferings. To bring about this sort of wholesome reaction to such teachings, we are instructed to meditate on the sufferings of the hot hells.

To do this, proceed as described with reference to the cold hells, by sitting in the posture of meditation and performing the preliminaries of taking refuge and invoking the blessings of the Three Jewels. Then reflect in this way:

> Alas, the round of worldly existence is greatly burning, intensely blazing. On that round of worldly existence are such places as the hot hells, where conditions are [such and such], the life spans are [such], and the pains are [such].

Here reflect on the particulars of the descriptions that were given, and then proceed:

> If, even now, I can't bear the slightest feeling of pain caused by the touch of a tiny weapon such as a needle, or a small flame such as a match, how could I possibly bear it if such agonies as those found in the hot hells were to befall me?

Continue as with the cold hells, turning your reflection into a resolve to practice the Dharma sincerely, diligently, and devotedly, without any kind of artifice. Affirm that the particular practice you have undertaken is the lam-dre system of meditation. You may refer to the previous instructions as a model for this reflection.

The Neighboring Hells. There are six neighboring hells, four of which are explicitly stated in the text and two of which are implied. They are called neighboring hells because they are on the periphery of the eight hot hells. The *Abhidharmakosha* says:

> There are, in all, sixteen hells, hot and cold, and on their four sides are found the neighboring hells, called fire trench, putrid corpse, razor-blade lane, and the river. Even when one finally has become free from the intense sufferings of the eight hot hells through the exhaustion of one's bad karma, still one must experience, once each, the sufferings of those four neighboring hells that lie in the four directions.

When a being finds himself finally released from the cold and hot hells, his first thought is "I must escape to some better place." Hence he strikes off in any direction and encounters, first of all, a fearful pit filled with embers; but due to his delusion—and his anxiety about finding a better place—he thinks he sees a very pleasant plain. Without hesitating, he sets out across it, but his body begins to sink in up to the top of his head. His skin and flesh are seared by the embers, and he experiences terrible agony that penetrates to his very bones.

Upon being released from that neighboring hell, he sees something in the distance that looks like dirty water. Since he has just been freed from the terrible afflictions of great heat, he runs to the water and enters it in hopes of finding some refreshment. But there, too, he sinks, and the water turns into terribly bad-smelling, putrid mud inhabited by worms. These worms, which have yellow bodies and black heads, pierce his body straight to the marrow and cause him great pain.

When he emerges from that, he sees something like a green pasture in the distance, but when he gets there he discovers that it has been transformed into a great path filled with razorlike blades. Wherever he places his feet, they are sliced into bits, so that he loses his balance and falls onto the terribly sharp blades, experiencing the countless pains of having his entire body cut and sliced.

When he is finally released from that part of razor-blade lane, he spies a dense forest in the distance. Again, his only thought is "I should escape from here, and perhaps I can stay there for a while." He strikes out toward the forest, but when he arrives, a great wind arises. It shakes the trees so fiercely that the leaves snap off and fall on him like a rain of swords. He thus experiences once more the great pain of having his body sliced into pieces.

Before concluding our discussion, I hasten to reassure you that it is necessary to cover all the details of the neighboring hells, even though we are doing it in a very hurried fashion here. These descriptions are very much a part of our study of the impure vision, as examples of what is experienced by beings who are deluded through their lack of perception of reality. I do hope that, at the very least, as a result of your studies of this section of *The Three Visions*, you will have a working outline of the teachings of the hells.

There was a particular Tibetan geshe who fancied himself quite well read in Buddhist literature, but when he visited another lama who questioned him about his learning, he didn't seem to do so well. The other lama asked him, "What are the eighteen hells?" He should, of course, have replied, "There are the eight cold hells, eight hot hells, and the neighboring and temporary hells." The geshe did all right with the eight cold hells and eight hot hells, but he forgot the neighboring and temporary hells, so he said, "There are the red hat hells and black hat hells." In Tibetan, this is a play on the titles of the Shamar, or Red Hat, and the Karmapa, or Black Hat, lamas. In English, one might obtain the same humorous effect by referring to "the Protestant and Catholic hells."

Let us return to our lesson. When a being finally escapes from the forest of swords, he spies a great mountain in the distance and sets out toward it. When he arrives at its foot, he is set upon by fearful brindle-colored, hellish dogs. Though he screams for help, there is no one to protect him. The dogs drag him down and tear him to pieces.

When he recovers consciousness, he hears from the top of the mountain some person, either male or female, whom he has been fond of in his former life as a human. Upon hearing this person's voice, he immediately sets off, with great joy, to meet him or her. He climbs up the mountain, even though the flesh is torn from his body by the sharp iron thorns of the *shamali* trees that grow on its slopes. As he tries to reach the top, the iron thorns point downward and rip his flesh. Finally, he arrives in agony at the summit but doesn't see anyone at all. Instead, fearful birds of hell attack him. They pluck out his eyes, drink his brain, and rip open his belly. When he recovers consciousness, he hears the same beloved person calling his name from the foot of the mountain, so he sets off for the bottom, but this time the iron thorns point upward against him and rend his body in that way. It is written in the *Letter from a Friend,*

Some, raising their arms to the skies, are scratched by fierce iron-toothed dogs, while other helpless ones are carried off by crows with sharp iron beaks and terrible claws.

Again the being's body becomes as before, and he is still motivated only by the wish to escape. He takes off running. He comes to a great river, an unfordable river of hot ashes, but he doesn't hesitate: he tries to cross it to get away from the hells he has already experienced, diving in even though he is afflicted by the intense heat. The water of this river of hot ashes is caustic like the touch of acid.

When he finally makes it to the opposite shore, he finds that it is guarded by the wardens of hell, who carry various cruel weapons. They prevent him from emerging onto the shore, turning him back again and again. Finally, he has no choice but to turn back, finding himself again in the hot and cold hells.

When he sees that he has been wandering in a circle, he can't stand it. He remembers the terrible pain he has already experienced in all those hells. Unable to bear that pain again, he takes off in yet another direction. He quickly flees, say, to the southern direction, but the same cycle reoccurs—first the ember pit, then the putrid mud, and so on. He returns to the river, crosses it, is turned back, and once more finds himself in the main hells. He attempts to flee to the north, to the west, to the center, and in each of those directions he has to go through the entire cycle of the neighboring hells again.

What is the proper manner of meditating on the hells? Should we take refuge, meditate on all eighteen hells, and then dedicate the merit, or should we take refuge, meditate on the first hell, dedicate the merit, then take refuge again, meditate on the second hell, dedicate the merit, and so on?

You can do it either way, depending on the amount of time you have. In each session of meditation on the faults of worldly existence, begin by taking refuge and invoking blessings, then proceed to your main meditation and conclude by dedicating the merit. If you have time only for reflection on, say, the cold hells, then they are your object of meditation. If you have more time and desire to do so, there is nothing wrong with including reflections on both the cold and the hot hells in one meditative session. But each formal meditation session should consist of three parts: the preliminaries of taking of refuge and so forth, the main meditation, however long or short, and the dedication of merit.

If you are in tune with the sufferings of the hells, you might wonder how you could smile anymore. Even hearing about the possibility of such sufferings for anyone, whether yourself or someone else, should awaken feelings of great compassion and pity for all beings who might experience them. Any compassionate thoughts or prayers that these reflections evoke in you are very much in keeping with the spirit of this meditation.

11

IGNOBLE STINGINESS

THERE ARE MANY DOORS to the Mahāyānist doctrine. The one we have entered is the system of meditation known as the *Lam dre*. Whenever we study this particular system, the very first reflection we are enjoined to practice is that on the difficulty of obtaining an opportunity to hear a doctrine such as this one. This is because, as in meditation itself, study must be guided by the right motivation. To approach this teaching of the *Lam dre* rightly, we need to bring consciously to mind the reflection that an opportunity such as this is only rarely won in the realm of human beings. Due to the exigencies of their various states of existence, most beings are handicapped to such an extent that human birth itself is beyond their reach. Even among those who have obtained human birth, it is rare to be born when and where teachings of enlightenment are being taught on this globe, and to find a teacher willing, able, and qualified to expound those teachings to you. Finally, the opportunity to undertake serious study, reflection, and meditation on these doctrines is, by its nature, rarely obtained by human beings. Therefore, when we find ourselves once again enjoying such an opportunity, we do not want to treat it lightly or waste it through inattention.

The Temporary Hells. In Tibetan, these are called, literally, "the day-long hells," because their duration is much less than that of the great hells and the neighboring hells. The pains experienced here are less intense as well. The Buddhist literature summarizes the experience of certain of these hells in the following verse:

> Beings there experience the pains of being cooked in great vessels,
> of eating hammers, of drinking molten bronze, of having their
> tongues furrowed by plows, of being wrapped in iron sheets,
> bound by iron chains, and roasted in burning iron powder.

Someone who finds himself in one of the temporary hells must undergo the pains of being cooked in molten bronze in various vessels. The wardens of that hell force-feed him with blazing metal hammers, and he has no choice but to swallow them. They also force him to drink molten bronze;

or his tongue is stretched out for several miles and very roughly furrowed with plows of burning iron; or his body is bound with chains of burning iron, and he is roasted in burning iron powder.

The temporary hells are not limited to certain places but are found even in the human realm, where beings, due to their poor karma, might find themselves born in stone pillars, beneath rows of seats, in brooms, or the like, experiencing the tremendous pains of being cramped and disregarded by the human beings who are making use of these objects. There are other places where they experience some feelings of pleasure during the day but unmitigated suffering at night, or vice versa. All these are categorized as temporary hells.

There is a story in early Buddhist literature about an arhat named Droshi Kai who, during his travels, arrived at the Indian coast. Remaining on the seashore for some time in meditation, he noticed that a lady as beautiful and happy as a goddess seemed to pass each night enjoying a great feast and a lot of entertainment. But when the sun rose each morning, she was transformed into a fearsome crocodile and was tortured by heat and parasites. Each day seemed to bring nothing but agony, and this was repeated over and over again. Droshi Kai became intrigued and sought the karmic reason for such a circumstance. He learned that, in a former lifetime, this particular being had been a butcher who, for reasons of caste and birth, had had no recourse to any other means of livelihood for supporting his family.

However, the butcher had once encountered the Buddha Katyāyana, listened to his teachings, served him, and made offerings to him. Due to the respect the butcher had shown, and due to hearing Katyāyana's advice to cease killing living beings (despite not having been not able to follow it), he had accumulated merit. As a result of this mixed bag of good and bad karma, the butcher had been reborn in this way. Thus he experienced the pleasures of the gods at night, which is when he had ceased his labors as a butcher and devoted himself to meditation and reflection on the Buddha Katyāyana's teachings, whereas during the day he had to be a lowly, tormented being as a result of his own cruel behavior as a butcher. This story illustrates the type of karma that leads to rebirth in one of the temporary hells.

Even the most intense, longest-lasting pains we can imagine in no way approach the agonies experienced by beings in these so-called temporary hells. Even our worst human experiences cannot serve as examples for that kind of suffering. As Nāgārjuna wrote in his *Letter from a Friend,*

Whatever the pain of being fiercely struck by three hundred spears in a single day, even that great pain will not serve as an example for the least pain of hell. Nor can it be considered equivalent to even the smallest amount of pain in the hells.

If you are wondering about the cause of experiencing such unbearable pains, the answer is very clear. All those experiences of pain in the temporary hells are the ripened result of actions of great anger, expressed through body, voice, and mind, that have brought harm to yourself and others. Thus any intelligent person who wishes future well-being for himself should, at the very least, train in relinquishing anger and try to the best of his ability to cultivate forbearance, tolerance, and patience. As Shāntideva wrote in his *Bodhicharyāvatara*, "If I am in no way able to bear those pains of the hells, why, then, don't I give up anger, which is the cause of all that pain?"

Finally, we have the instructions on how to reflect on the meaning of these descriptions of the hells. As in your previous meditations on the plight of beings in the cold and hot hells, remember to preface your meditation by taking refuge in and invoking the blessings of the Three Jewels. Then reflect somewhat in this manner:

> The painful feelings of the temporary hells are extremely fearful. If I cannot bring myself even to look upon such sufferings of other beings, how could I possibly bear the suffering of the greater hells myself? The temporary hells are [such and such], their sufferings are [such], their life spans are [such], and their duration is [such].

Here recall the descriptions that have been given, and reflect on the details of each one. Then think:

> Since those places are so terrible, how could I possibly bear it if such sufferings of the temporary hells should befall me? If, here and now, I cannot bear even the prick of a thorn or the slightest touch of a small flame, how could I possibly bear all that suffering?

Again, continue your reflection, as described in earlier lessons with reference to the cold and hot hells.

You should use these reflections to develop a sense of awareness that such terrible states of existence are possible and that there is potential for experiencing them through your own negative actions performed with anger and ill will. These reflections should help you resolve to refrain from such actions and devote yourself diligently to the practice of Dharma. Again, recall that the particular method you are going to employ in your efforts to win liberation is the lam-dre system. Then invoke your own line of gurus and the Buddha, Dharma, and Sangha, that through their blessings your meditation may be successful. Conclude by dedicating the merit of your reflection to the enlightenment of all living beings.

The Sufferings of the Preta Realm

The realm of the hungry ghosts (*preta*) is also a place of extreme mental and physical pain. As Nāgārjuna stated in his *Letter from a Friend*, "The ghosts also have to experience constant, incurable pains due to their being afflicted by craving, hunger, thirst, heat, cold, and fear."

The basic experience among the ghosts is one of deprivation. In almost every way, the pretas are frustrated in their efforts to obtain the objects of their craving. And if they are able to obtain them, these very objects of craving become the cause of even greater suffering. All this mental and physical pain is due to the mental poison of miserliness and avarice. When humans spend their lives refusing to share their property with those who are in need, and in inordinate attachment either to their own or others' property or to other beings, then they accumulate causes for rebirth among the pretas.

In general, pretas can be divided into three categories, although it is explained in the *Stations of Mindfulness Sūtra* that there are actually thirty-six categories of ghosts. These three broad categories are known as (1) those who are afflicted by outer defilements, or obscurations, (2) those who are afflicted by inner defilements, and (3) those who are afflicted by "defiled defilements."

Just as we find ourselves reborn together in the human realm because, as individual beings, we have accumulated similar karmic propensities, so other beings accumulate similar karmic causes for rebirth as pretas. Beings who in former lifetimes practiced possessiveness toward beings and property to such an extent that they accumulated causes for rebirth as pretas are, in due course, born in a place that resembles a tawny-colored desert of pebbles totally lacking in water. The bodies that they acquire there are described by Nāgārjuna in his *Letter from a Friend*:

> Some have mouths the size of a needle's eye, while their bellies are
> of mountainous size. Though they are tormented by hunger, they

are unable to obtain even the tiniest bit of filth for food. Some of them are naked, their bodies just skin and bones. They resemble the dried fronds of palm trees.

This verse describes ghosts who belong to the first category. To elaborate on that description: their mouths are the size of a needle's eye, their throats are the diameter of a horse's hair, their limbs are as thin as large stalks of grass, their bellies are as large as mountains, their hair is shaggy, the whole of their skin and body is utterly dry, and their bones are sunken and hollow. In their general appearance these pretas resemble the fronds of dead palm trees. They never have an opportunity to remain in any one place at leisure because they are compelled to roam about endlessly due to their intense hunger and thirst. Their bodies give out groans and cracking sounds like the pulling of old carts, and as they move about, their joints clack loudly. They brush against one another and cause one another intense pains that feel as though flames were breaking out in their bodies.

Along with the endless pains of roaming about, they experience great mental weariness and despair because, no matter how much they search for it, they find no food or drink. Even if, once in a very, very long while, a preta should find a small morsel, it is always guarded by others who drive him away with weapons or beat him and pelt him with clods and pebbles, preventing him from obtaining the morsel he has discovered. Totally bereft of the possibility of any feelings of satisfaction and enjoyment, the preta roams about, experiencing great agony of body and mind.

Thus the first category of ghosts experiences pain from an external source. Most of their pain comes from searching for external objects that, even if found, are denied them. In contrast, those who belong to the second category experience internal pains when they consume food or drink. In his *Letter to a Student* (*Śiṣyalekha*), the Indian master Chandragomin wrote the following description of the pretas who belong to this class:

> While their mouths are about the size of a needle's eye, their distended bellies are many miles in girth. Even though they drink the waters of a great ocean, not even a single drop of water enters their throats because it is dried up by the poison of their breath.

Through an intensive, long-lasting search, these pretas finally find a small morsel of sustenance, but due to the ripened result of their former habit of denying needed objects to other beings, they are unable to consume what they have found. When they try to eat the food, it won't enter their mouths; or, if they are able to get it into their mouths, they are unable to swallow it. And if eventually they are able to swallow it, it only arouses even greater pangs of hunger and thirst than before. In this way, ghosts who belong to the second category experience constant agony because of their inability to gain a satisfactory meal.

Third are those pretas who are afflicted in every way. Ārya Nāgārjuna described them with these words:

> Some, with fire blazing from their mouths at night, eat as food the
> sands that fall into their burning mouths. They beat each other on
> the face and drink the pus of ripened goiters on their throats.

These pretas discover that as soon as they have swallowed a morsel of food, it blazes up, and tongues of flame flutter out of their nostrils and mouths. They utter terrible cries and make horrible noises of pain. They also experience terrible suffering through trying to eat burning sand and quarreling with one another over food. They even beat one another. Due to their delusions, they come to look upon the pus in the abscesses on their own bodies as food, and try to eat and drink that.

Moreover, it is common to all pretas that even the light of the summer moon makes them hot, and even the light of the winter sun makes them cold. Whenever they approach a great river or a fruit-bearing tree, or merely look at them with the faint hope of perhaps enjoying a drink of water or a taste of real food, those visions immediately vanish. Thus tantalized, their mental anguish and physical suffering are inexpressible. The *Letter from a Friend* summarizes their sufferings:

> For the ghosts, in summertime even the moon is hot and in winter
> even the sun is cold. Trees turn fruitless and rivers dry up whenever
> they merely gaze on them.

We will now explain the life span of beings in the preta world. The *Abhidharmakosha* states that they live "five hundred years, whereof a day is equal to one month." This is explained as meaning that they live for five hundred of their own years. One human month equals a single day for the pretas. If calculated like human years, their life span would be fifteen hundred years.

ଏଓ ❧ ଏଓ

In summary, Nāgārjuna wrote:

> The Enlightened One taught that the cause of those manifold sufferings encountered by pretas is the human propensity for avarice and ignoble stinginess.

We should know how to reflect on the significance of these teachings. As always, preface your meditation by taking refuge and invoking the blessings of the preceptors and Three Jewels. Then ponder in the following manner:

> If the birthplaces of those beings born in the preta world are [such and such], if their misery is [such], and if their life span is [such], how could I possibly bear such sufferings were I to be reborn there? Here and now I cannot bear the slightest hunger and thirst even for a single day. Yet I have no confidence that such suffering will not befall me. Countless times every day attachment to objects and miserliness arise in my mind, and these are the causes for rebirth among the pretas. Since I have no way at all to bear those sufferings should they ever befall me, I must diligently practice the holy Dharma, which will surely prevent rebirth there.

Conclude by reinforcing the thought in your mind that the true Dharma is none other than this system of meditation known as the *Lam dre*. Also invoke the guidance and blessings of the preceptors and Three Jewels so that your practice will be successful and of benefit to yourself and others, remembering to dedicate the merit of your meditation to the benefit and enlightenment of all beings.

FROM CELESTIAL MANSIONS TO MURKY DEPTHS

WHEN WE SAY THAT IT IS RARE to hear the teachings of the holy lam-dre system of meditation, we have only to reflect on our own experience to see that this is in fact the case. It is only seldom in our own past that we can recall an occasion such as this, and we have no guarantee that we will ever have such an opportunity to hear the Dharma in the future. This makes the present situation all the more significant. For that reason alone, we owe it to ourselves—and to the beings whom we have undertaken to help—not to waste this opportunity through idle thought and distraction.

To return to our topic: We are engaged in describing the first of the three types of suffering that characterize worldly existence as a whole—namely, the suffering of mental and physical pain. Thus far, we have described the types of pain experienced by beings in the various hells and in the ghost realm. We will complete our discussion by describing the sufferings of animals.

The Sufferings of the Animal Realm
When the sufferings of animals are compared with those of hell beings and ghosts, they appear to represent something of an improvement. However, the plight of beings who are reborn among the animals is an extremely sad and most unbearable one. Ārya Nāgārjuna wrote, in his *Letter from a Friend*:

> Those who forsake calming virtues also undergo extremely terrible sufferings in the realms of animals, through slaughter, bondage, beatings, and devouring each other.

For the purpose of Buddhist meditation, the animal kingdom is divided into three categories: (1) animals who dwell in the oceans, (2) animals who dwell in dark places, and (3) animals who are scattered throughout the human and celestial realms. Most animals belong to the first category.

There is an almost infinite number of aquatic creatures. They are found in a great variety of sizes and types, but suffering is common to all of them. They are afflicted by a great veil of stupidity and delusion that causes them to experience much pain, as if they were being pressed down by a great mountain. This great ignorance prevents them from dealing with their karmic situation intelligently. The most obvious sort of suffering common to animals is that they are, by their karmic circumstances, forced to feed on one another. Most of their time is spent searching for food, devouring one another, or trying to escape being devoured themselves. They live in fear of being eaten and never have mental security about their survival.

A few examples of the sufferings experienced by aquatic beings shows that, whether large or small, none is exempt from being devoured. Crocodiles and other such creatures constantly prey on the fishes. Over and over again, larger creatures devour the smaller; again and again, smaller creatures devour the larger. The crocodile, though not threatened by river fish, is yet undone by the conch, which bores into the crocodile's body and causes him tremendous pain. The serpent spirits (*nāga*) also fall into this category and experience much suffering. Their natural enemies, eaglelike birds (*garuda*), prey on the nāgas, who are also afflicted by showers of hot sand that cause them great pain.

Common to all these animals is the suffering of being cramped. Even in places of relative safety, they are constantly suffocated and spend their lives surrounded by fetid smells. They are never certain of their habitat or companions. The fear of meeting foes and natural enemies is constant. The tremendous agony of being caught and devoured by those foes is a common experience. On top of that, they undergo the suffering of intense cold in winter and intense heat in summer. By day they experience extremes of heat, and by night they experience extremes of cold. In short, the suffering experienced by animals is constant and terrible.

Second are those animals that dwell in dark places. In Buddhist cosmology there are four continents, of which our earth, Jambudvīpa, is in the south. In the east is Videha, in the west is Godanīya, and in the north is Uttarakuru. In the dark spaces between these continents, according to the *Abhidharmakosha*, there are any number of beings.[37] On top of the sufferings already described for aquatic animals, these animals also experience special sufferings due to the absence of light. They never even see their own limbs, and despite being impelled by great hunger and thirst, they are seldom able to find anything to eat except whatever appears right in front of them.

The animals with which we are familiar are those of the third class. They are found scattered about in the regions of space inhabited by gods and humans. For the sake of meditation, we can divide these animals into wild and domestic. Even those that are wild are slaughtered not only by one another but also by humans, for their fur, flesh, hides, bones, pearls, and so forth. Domestic animals also undergo great pain, being used as slaves by humans who tie them up, beat them, and finally slaughter them. The more we think about it, the more we will understand that their suffering is constant and on a much greater scale than we like to admit. As Nāgārjuna wrote,

> Some die for the sake of their pearls, wool, flesh, bones, and hides; other helpless animals are made to serve after being abused by kicks, slapped, and prodded by iron hooks.

Even in Tibet, you can find many Tibetans who are very fond of animals and always treat them with great kindness, but you will also find many who don't think twice about eating animals, as well as those who raise animals, treat them very lovingly, and in the end slaughter them. However humans generally respond to animals, the point is that, as Buddhists, we need to be very clear about how we relate to animals and all other beings, but especially to animals, who are karmically in a very unfortunate state. Compared to us, they are very handicapped. At the very least, we cannot countenance causing harm to other living creatures. As Buddhists, we know that it is admirable and desirable that we develop compassion for all beings, including animals, to the utmost of our abilities. This is at the very heart of Buddhist practice. However other beings may or may not relate to one another, we should be very clear in the way we ourselves do so.

It is your spiritual development that determines how you relate to other beings, human or nonhuman. Looking at a Buddhist society, such as Tibet, we can see that there are great living bodhisattvas who spend their entire lives in meditation and doing all kinds of pious deeds, with the one thought of alleviating the sufferings of those very animals that other Tibetans are slaughtering and eating every day. We can also find Tibetans who formerly treated animals badly but who have undertaken to purify that bad karma.

Now let us consider the life span of beings in the animal realm. As the *Abhidharmakosha* tells us, the longest life span among animals is one aeon. The kings of the nāgas are said to live the longest because of the great merit they have acquired through devotion to the Buddhist teachings.

Other animals are not so fortunate. An elephant is considered to be an animal of some merit and usually lives to be about fifty years old. Yet the life span of most animals is not certain; most meet with a violent, untimely death. Even by nature, there are countless animals that live only a very short time—a day or a few moments only.

The cause of the sufferings experienced by all kinds of animals is, quite simply, not knowing which principles are to be accepted and which are to be rejected. Through ignorance of the law of karma—which entails lack of skill in avoiding unwholesome karma and in accumulating sufficient merit for higher rebirths—beings are reborn among the animals. Realizing this, we should be extremely diligent in acquiring a right understanding of the teachings of enlightenment, which are a light able to dispel the kind of darkness experienced by animals.

Finally, we should learn how to reflect on the meaning of these teachings. As before, be seated in the posture of meditation, take refuge, generate the enlightenment thought, and then reflect in this manner:

> Alas, the habitat of those beings born into the birthplace of animals is [of such and such a nature], their sufferings are [of such a nature], their life span is [of such and such a length]. Since the sufferings of the animal realm are [such], how could I possibly bear them if were I ever reborn among the animals due to the ripening of my own karma and mental defilements?
>
> Even now, I can't bear physical pains such as having to work diligently for my living even for a full day. That being so, how could I possibly bear the slavery that animals experience? I have no confidence that those sufferings will not happen to me, because I have accumulated, and am even now accumulating, countless unwholesome karmic acts brought on by delusion. These karmic acts and their delusions are none other than the cause of being reborn in the animal realm. Thus, no matter what happens, I must practice the holy teachings, which are able to prevent rebirth among the animals.

Again, remind yourself that the practice you have undertaken is the lam-dre system of meditation, and conclude by invoking the blessings of your preceptors and the Three Jewels, that by their blessings true realization and diligence in avoiding the causes of rebirth among animals may arise within you. Then dedicate the merit of your meditation to the enlightenment of all sentient beings.

We have now completed our first topic, the suffering of sheer pain, both mental and physical, as experienced by beings in the lower realms.

THE SUFFERING OF CHANGE IN THE THREE HIGHER REALMS

After hearing the description of the sufferings of beings in the lower states of existence, you might think, "Even though beings may actually experience such pains in the lower realms of existence, those in the three higher realms of humans, asuras, and gods can be characterized as happy." But when these realms are examined carefully, this is found not to be the case. Lord Buddha taught in his *Extended Play Sūtra* (*Lalitavistara-sūtra*):

> In those realms, also, all objects of desire are impermanent. They are unsteady, inconstant, changing like dreams, like mirages, like cities of illusion, like lightning, and like bubbles.

Because all phenomena, even in the relatively happier realms, are subject to the law of impermanence and are constantly undergoing change, decay, cessation, and the rest, there is no steady feeling of happiness to be obtained by relying on such objects. All appearances, including those that seem to be objects of pleasure, are impermanent and unsteady by nature. Because they are transient and ephemeral, they are called "deceptive phenomena," for they cannot provide the type of true, lasting happiness that beings in the three higher realms expect from them.

To reflect on the sufferings that beings experience due to the law of impermanence, we have four topics: (1) general aspects of the suffering of change, (2) sufferings of the human realm, (3) sufferings of the asura realm, and (4) sufferings of the gods' realm.

General Aspects of the Suffering of Change

First, let us examine change as it is experienced in general. It follows from the very impermanent nature of beings that they are never assured of complete security, no matter what efforts they make or what status they achieve. Just as all beings who are born are fated by their very nature to experience death, so there is not a single being in the round of worldly existence who is able, through his own worldly accomplishments, to avoid the suffering of change. Even if you become a universal monarch, your status is not permanently assured. There are many accounts of universal monarchs who have fallen into rebirth as the lowliest of servants. There are any number of stories about Shakra, the king of the devas, who, after obtaining sovereignty over all the celestials, again fell to rebirth on earth.

You cannot have any confidence in your status even if you have attained the stage of the great deity Brahmā, for there is still the possibility of falling all the way to Avīci Hell even from that exalted state. Nor is it of any benefit to be reborn as a celestial inhabiting the sun or the moon. (According to Indic mythology, there are certain types of gods who inhabit the sun and the moon, which appear to them as their own luminous celestial mansions.) Even from those places you can fall into the darkness that exists between the planets or continents.

Hence the higher realms that you might experience are limited on all sides by impermanence. As Nāgārjuna wrote in his *Letter from a Friend*,

> Having become Shakra and worthy of the world's worship, one again falls down to earth due to one's karma. And even though one becomes the universal emperor himself, one may become just a slave on the round of existence.

He also wrote, in the same book:

> Though one attains very great bliss, the fulfillment of one's desires in the realms of the gods, and the unattached bliss of Brahmā himself, again one may fall, to become Avīci's fuel and undergo unceasing torment. Having illumined the whole world through the light of one's body and having dwelt on the sun and moon, again one may fall into the murky depths of darkness where one cannot even see one's own hands and feet.

And Jetsün Dragpa Gyaltsen, the fifth patriarch of the Sakya order, wrote in his *Parting from the Four Attachments*:

> When you reflect on the suffering of change, remember the stories of Shakra, the sun and moon, and the universal monarchs who fell from their exalted states. Even though the teaching of impermanence can be credited if you rely on the scriptures, still ordinary folk cannot understand it. Therefore, they should look at the changes experienced by humans themselves.

There is not actually much interaction between realms. Hell beings and pretas are bound by the very nature of their existence, by the karmic limitations of the suffering they have to experience, and so forth. They are quite limited: there is, quite simply, no way out of these realms until you have purified the karma that brought you there. But some animals are found in the realms of gods and humans, and you can judge for yourself what kind of interactions there are between animals and humans. It is true that gods have great mobility and do, on occasion, appear in the human realm. But to be honest, they don't come very often because humans smell awful to the gods, who have pure, radiant bodies and a wonderful fragrance all their own, whereas humans have a very coarse, smelly sort of existence. The asuras also occasionally come to the human realm, but we never see them.

It is possible that some beings experience rebirth in a graduated sort of progress through the higher realms. Thus a being might first be born in one realm of the gods and then work his way up to another. But it doesn't usually happen that way because rebirth in any state of existence, including that of the gods, is due to the particular propensities of one's karma in getting that far. For ordinary worldlings, it's not really an orderly progression, and certainly not a matter of inevitably working one's way to the top, as in a theosophical scheme.

What does happen is that there is an orderly progression on the spiritual path. This can easily be confused with a bodhisattva's progression from the first through the tenth stages, until he or she arrives at buddhahood. That is where conscious, guided karmic effects bring a particular result. In contrast, ordinary worldlings are reborn in the human or gods' realms only when they have accumulated enough good karma. But there is no methodical, evolutionary scheme involved in their rebirth in those places. In fact, if you do pass your human life accumulating virtue by practicing wholesome actions of body, voice, and mind, you needn't go through any intermediary state at all. And if you are going to be reborn as a god, it is like the transition from human life to rebirth in the buddha-realm of Tushita, where Maitreya Buddha dwells, or the transition between a dream state and awakening: you leave off your human dream and awaken in the realm of Maitreya Buddha. If you spend your life in the accumulation of virtues and right practices, it's easy to be reborn in the very highest realms, but there's no fixed scheme at work.

A true story: Perhaps you have heard of the great Patrul Rinpoche, a famous Tibetan lama who was from my part of Tibet.[38] He was meditating in a cave near a river at one time, and it happened that an old man drowned near the place of his meditation. Patrul Rinpoche's disciples had been unable to rescue him, but they quickly retrieved the corpse, brought it to Patrul Rinpoche, and asked him whether he could do something for the old man whom it was too late to save. Would he do a transference of consciousness (*'pho-ba*) ceremony for him?

Patrul Rinpoche was willing, but when they started to do the ceremony, he broke out laughing. His disciples were a bit taken aback. They asked why he was laughing all of a sudden, and Patrul Rinpoche said, "Here I was, thinking to help the old man and alleviate his karma. But this poor old man has just been reborn as a god in Tushita, and in fact, here he is now." The erstwhile old man, now a god, was laughing, too, because things had turned out so well for him, whereas Patrul Rinpoche's disciples were still feeling sorry for him.

13

NO REST FROM THE DANCE

WE SHOULD NEVER BE UNAWARE of our extreme good fortune in having gained human birth and met qualified Dharma teachers. We should be thankful that our physical and mental faculties are intact and that no external circumstances prevent our receiving teachings or putting them into practice. It would be a pity to waste this life's precious opportunity to attain buddhahood.

These instructions are intended to turn us away from further involvement in worldly delusion and toward the path to liberation. This essential turning is to be achieved through study of (1) the difficulty of attaining human birth, (2) the impermanence of that brief life once attained, and (3) the unsatisfactory nature of worldly existence. We have already covered the unsatisfactory nature of worldly existence in terms of the suffering of mental and physical pain, the suffering of change, and the suffering of conditioned existence.

It would be especially sad, and extreme folly, if, having acquired this opportunity to hear the teachings of enlightenment, we were to let it slip away by not appreciating it properly. Another sign of our good fortune is that, without any great effort on our part, such profound teachings of enlightenment as the *Lam dre*, which has been the great treasure of many generations of enlightened masters, arrive at our doorstep and are made available to us. It is salutary to be joyful in having such an easy opportunity to hear these teachings and to develop within ourselves a determination not to take them for granted or let the opportunity slip away through carelessness or folly on our part.

The *Lam dre* is a complete system of meditation that takes the spiritual aspirant all the way from the first awakening of the slightest desire, interest, or faith in the Mahāyāna teachings of Lord Buddha right up to the attainment of buddhahood itself. Jetsün Dragpa Gyaltsen, the great Sakya patriarch, wrote that, for purposes of study and practice, it is convenient to consider the system on two levels: (a) preparation, or foundational study and practice, and (b) advanced study and practice. Corresponding to the first level is the text we are presently studying, *The Three Visions*; corresponding to the second level is that called *The Three Continua.*

Only when we have established a very firm foundation of right attitude, genuine renunciation, and an uncontrived resolve to strive for the liberation of all living beings is it time to study and practice on the level of advanced tantra. However, once we have developed these qualities, it is possible to attain buddhahood in this very lifetime, provided we learn the instructions in *The Three Continua*, receive tantric initiation into the great *Hevajra Tantra*, and practice that meditation rightly.

Thus these two levels are complementary. Needless to say, *The Three Visions* is of crucial importance as the foundation of the advanced tantric instructions and practices. It is this foundation that makes the later practices and principles so significant, meaningful, and effective.

The Sufferings of the Human Realm

Change is a state common to all realms; it is a cause of unhappiness. Let us consider change among humans. When we honestly appraise human existence, we recognize it as unsatisfactory by its very nature. Worldlings are so involved in affairs of this life, this world of delusion, that they seldom examine existence accurately. Their view is distorted by many factors. However, the buddhas and bodhisattvas, with their enlightened view, see the faults of worldliness, are actually more sensitive than we ourselves to our pains, and see clearly that even our pleasures are really sufferings or potential causes of suffering. Their sensitivity is expressed in the following example: If you put a grain of sand on the palm of your hand, it doesn't hurt, but put that grain in your eye and you won't be able to stand it. So it is with the enlightened ones' perception of our human sufferings.

Nāgārjuna tells us that worldly existence is the source of the many sufferings that afflict beings when they are deprived—by death, illness, and old age—of all that they cling to. One can only feel sad on hearing the recitation of life's faults.

Next, we have an example which shows that there is no certainty in the continuity of human existence. An arhat walked on the beach one day and saw a fisherman sitting on a doorstep holding his baby son and feeding him some fish. A hungry dog tried to snatch away the fish, but the man threw a rock and drove the dog away. The arhat just laughed sadly because he saw, with clear vision, the karma of these beings. The last time around the cycle of rebirth, the fish had been the fisherman's father, the dog, his mother, and the child, his worst enemy. Here they were, reunited, but in a different pattern, now blind to their previous connections. This illustrates that there is nothing at all to cling to in relationships. There is no rest from the dance, short of buddhahood.

Parting from the Four Attachments states that human suffering due to change is inconceivably vast. The proud are humbled, the wealthy made poor, foes become friends, kin turn into foes. Our families and neighbors scatter, and who among them has escaped impermanence? It is all so because we cling. Clinging is the root of all this painful suffering.

The baby suffers at birth. Old age is experienced as the wretched destruction of youth and health. Disease impairs mental and physical faculties. And death is the inevitable end to this life's body. Where, in all this, can you find something through which you really profit by "virtue" of clinging to it?

Birth, Old Age, Disease, and Death. However pleasant human existence may seem at times, we don't have a balanced view of human life if we don't include the negative aspects as well. It is undeniable that human existence does involve, for every human being, the processes of birth, old age, disease, and death.

Birth is the source of all the other kinds of human suffering simply because it precedes them. In this light even death can be said to be the result of birth, since it is experienced only because birth has preceded it. The main point is that birth, like the other three types of human suffering, is by its very nature painful, because the process of birth has as its cause the mental poisons of desire, hatred, and delusion. Governed by these poisons, we are forced to take rebirth in one or another of the various states of existence. Thus birth itself comes out of negative mental states; its nature is involved in suffering. Just as we can say that the nature of fire is hot and involved with heat, while water is involved with wetness, so birth must be construed as involved with mental and physical pain.

Let us start when the disembodied being in the intermediate state between death and rebirth first sees the apparition of his future parents in cohabitation. Driven, so he thinks, by the apparitions of the bardo and the compulsions of his own karmic inclinations, he is in a hurry to take rebirth in a womb. (Rebirth can take place in four other ways as well: via the miraculous birth that occurs for hell beings, who suddenly find themselves in a terrible situation; via the miraculous birth that occurs for gods, who suddenly find themselves in the gods' realm; via birth due to the presence of warmth, which occurs for certain types of insectlike beings; and via birth from eggs, which occurs for some animals and other beings.)

Since we are talking about womb-born humans, we shall describe the processes that a consciousness has to undergo on its way to becoming a human being. To begin with, there are the fears of the bardo, which it is seeking to escape. After rushing into the womb of its future mother, it finds itself trapped there. During the nine months when the fetus is growing, its consciousness is confined in a very dark and constricted place, subject to all kinds of changes in position every time the mother rises or sits. The fetus is jarred, it seems that it suddenly is being plunged over a precipice, and so forth. Whenever the mother partakes of hot or cold foods, it experiences the extremes of sudden hot or cold. Throughout, there is the sensation of being on the verge of suffocation, and at the time of delivery there is the feeling of falling into a chasm or being drawn out forcibly, as if through a tiny hole made in leather, then flung into a pit of thorns. To the newborn, all these sensations are intensely painful.

In describing this experience, Chandragomin, in his *Letter to a Student,* compared the nine months spent in the womb to a type of hell, due to the constriction there and to never knowing what is really happening. Because it has absolutely no control over its existence, the baby is constantly hurt by one sudden extreme after another. Chandragomin wrote:

> Having entered the womb is like a hell of being strangled by heaps
> of fetid smells and dwelling in the gloomy darkness of a narrow
> place; the being endures suffering that is almost like death itself.

As for old age, in the *Extended Play Sūtra* the Buddha taught:

> Old age turns a beautiful form ugly,
> Old age vitiates strength and brilliance,
> Old age snatches away radiance and causes death,
> Old age snatches away happiness and generates sorrow.

To examine these effects of aging, we need only repeat that old age snatches away the beauty you had in your youth, then changes your form so that you become an object of ridicule or, at best, disinterest. Where once you had a fine form, healthy color, good features, and shining hair, you becomes wrinkled and lose teeth; your features change and become care-worn. Hair becomes dull, turns white, or falls out altogether. Your figure also is lost, so that all pleasure in having a fine form and enjoying your youthful beauty is snatched away for good. Along with the physical process of aging and becoming weaker, there is the mental anguish of realizing that, despite all your wishes to cling to youth, there is no way to prevent your body from growing old.

Your faculties are impaired by old age so that you are no longer able to do the things you used to. Where once you could get around with ease and work all day if necessary, it becomes difficult even to make small efforts. You easily grow tired. Things that were quite easy become impossible; you have little strength. In the advanced stages of old age, you can't even stand or sit without leaning on someone. In rising and sitting, coming and going, you are unable even to carry your own body properly, as you could before. Your voice grows weak, and your words are indistinct and faltering.

Your mental powers also begin to grow dim. You find it hard to work up any enthusiasm for activities, whereas in earlier years you always had time and zeal for projects and undertakings. You begin to forget everything you hear as soon as it has been said. You make one mistake after another and find that you are helpless to do anything about the decline of your mental and physical faculties.

Your status is also impaired. Whereas in your prime you might have occupied a position of some esteem, in which you were able to have your way through eloquence, strength of character, or ability, you now find that you are shunted off to the side. No one feels obligated to pay attention to anything you might have to contribute. You become the object of ridicule even for children, even for babies. Your own children secretly deplore your feebleness. Behind your back they may despise you or resent your being around. There is little you can do to alter this change in your status.

Meanwhile, your body continues to grow colder, and your senses continue to fail. You never seem to be warm enough. When you eat, it is hard to distinguish flavors. When people tell you something, it is hard to understand the true sense of what they are trying to say. Finally, you are reduced to praying for death to come. Losing its former luster, your body turns greyish or bluish, and you realize that you are definitely caught by the exigencies of old age, which are relentlessly pushing you toward separation from everything you enjoy and love and leading you closer to one fatal illness or another. You are prey to all the other kinds of suffering common to old age and what it leads to—namely, death.

When you are old, you often find it difficult to digest the food you eat. You find it difficult even to breathe; with each inhalation you wheeze and gasp. Even if you're not stricken by any disease, the general decline in your faculties and the constant weakening of your physical components are such that you eventually die of old age.

Old age is highly prized by the worldly, who pray that they will live to a ripe old age, but only a deluded person would make the sufferings of old age an object of desire. Wise people recognize that old age is just one more state in the process of human existence, which is rightly described as painful. In preparing for the decline in your faculties and strength in old age, you should be diligent in remembering the buddhas and bodhisattvas, and especially in directing your mind toward the Buddha of Boundless Light, Amitābha, whose meditation is particularly helpful for the elderly and those on the verge of death.

Disease is obviously a form of suffering. While it is possible for deluded people to think that birth and old age may be pleasant, there is no way anyone can imagine that disease is enjoyable. We needn't describe the various types of disease and the extremes of mental and physical pain those diseases cause, except to say that it is extremely unlikely that you could find a person who has not experienced disease during his or her lifetime. The human experience of disease is so pervasive that Chandragomin, in his *Letter to a Student*, very aptly described humans as like another class of pretas, because the diseases among them are so pervasive, so terrible, and so endlessly recurring that those who suffer them are almost as unfortunate as ghosts.

A person who has fallen ill must first deal with the pangs of his disease. If he is stricken by a serious illness, there are the debilitating effects of fever or whatever is troubling him. Those pains can be quite intolerable. He has also to undergo the unwanted therapy prescribed for the disease, going to great trouble to find the right remedy and the right doctor and sticking to a regimen that he hopes will cure him. Certain foods, activities, and unpleasant treatments are prescribed for him. He has no choice; he has to undergo them.

Now when he eats food or takes drink, it doesn't benefit him, for it is not possible to counterbalance the general weakness of his physical body. It is also difficult to pass the time. If he manages to make it through the night, he can't get through the day; if he manages to pass a single day through the diversionary efforts of his friends or whatever imagination he can bring to the situation, he may find himself growing desperate through the night, unable to sleep. His fears and apprehensions grow. The longer he remains ill, the worse his fears become. He becomes concerned that he might not recover, and that leads him to contemplate death—another terrible experience very much unwanted. He begins to worry about his family and property and wonders what will happen to them. Finally, he becomes fearful that his doctors and nurses are going to abandon him. The sick person becomes prey to an endless succession of worries and anxieties.

As long as things are going fairly well, we don't give too much thought to parting from human existence. Generally, it is only when we are on the verge of death that we begin to deal with the prospect. However, death is imminent throughout life; every moment since leaving the womb is a progression toward that inevitable moment. Everything that happens, every instant that passes is leading you inevitably closer to parting from this world. But most of us assure ourselves that we will have long lives and that there is plenty of time to prepare for the experience of death.

Our plans notwithstanding, it often does happen that a sudden illness seizes us that prayers, rituals, and blessings are unable to check. Operations and medicines are also unable to turn its course. If all these frantic efforts to cure ourselves do not succeed, we are forced to face death itself. Now we know that we are sure to die, even though we can hardly bear to imagine what it might entail. Further, it is extremely painful to think of leaving this world and all our experiences and loved ones that comprise our familiar situation. It is terrible to feel that we are being forced to leave them in a way that we definitely don't wish to.

Finally, at the advent of the death experience, we are faced with the frightful apparition of the Lord of Death, Yama (Lord of Death). Black in color, holding a noose and a hook in his hands, he comes to drag the consciousness into that unknown experience. The Lord of Death appears to the ordinary, deluded mind as a very fearful, terrifying apparition. The messengers or attendants of death are frightful, too, because over and beyond your acute experience of pain—the pain of your disease or of your fear of death—there also arises at this moment the remembrance of your own evil deeds, shortcomings, faults, and wrong actions throughout your lifetime. For sinful people, the death experience is usually one of great remorse and anxiety about having to face not only death but the results of their own misdeeds also.

It comes to this: You are finally brought to lie on your last bed, surrounded for the last time by kinsmen and friends. You speak your last words, you sip your last spoonful of water, you take your last morsel of food. You are powerless to remain any longer in your house, which you might have built yourself. You are powerless to take with you anything you have accumulated in this lifetime. You can't stay a moment longer with your friends or loved ones, and you have no idea where you are headed.

Thus you have the anguish of being completely alone, unable to find any help, source of security, or reassurance in any quarter. None of your friends or family can aid you in the least. There is no way you can change the inevitable arrival of death. There is no way you can undo the misdeeds of body, voice, and mind that you have accumulated through ignorance, delusion, and selfishness during your lifetime. At this last moment there is no way you can help yourself, and you are quite alone in facing this experience. It cannot be shared. Alone you have to go through the anguish of parting from everything that is familiar and strike out in an unknown, empty direction.

All this is inevitable for each of us. Through the very fact of being born, each human being is faced with the inevitable experience of his or her own death.

There is no one who has lived on this globe who has been able to avoid these four experiences of birth, old age, disease, and death. They are, as Lord Buddha said, like four great rivers that carry away all living beings in their flood. As the Buddha declared in the *Mahākāshyapa Chapter Sūtra* (*Mahākāśyapa-parivarta-sūtra*):

> For humans, disease approaches, grinding out health. Old age approaches, grinding out youth; adversity approaches, grinding out good fortune. Finally, death approaches, grinding out life itself.

Birth, old age, disease, and death are an integral part of human existence. We can doubt the descriptions of the sufferings experienced by the beings in the cold and hot hells, or by the ghosts and animals, simply because they are not obvious to our own observation right now. We can doubt that there really is such suffering or that there are beings experiencing it. Yet there is not one of us who can deny what has been said about human existence itself. We can see people right now who are experiencing one or another of these four states. Therefore, if you merely agree that these experiences are a part of the human situation, that should serve as an incentive to diligent practice of the Dharma.

It is said that a thoroughbred horse needs only the slightest tap to send it racing. A sensitive, intelligent person only needs to be told once that human existence is transient and that it involves great suffering to become diligent and determined to devote his or her life to right practice while not prevented from doing so by old age, disease, or death. The time to practice is definitely *now*, while you are able to. When you have been struck down by some terrible disease or find yourelf on your deathbed, you may not be able to meditate. An intelligent person looks ahead to the inevitable, prepares for it well in advance, and puts to good use his youth, health, physical vigor, mental clarity, and opportunity to practice, not assuming he will have them forever.

Other Sufferings of the Human Realm. On top of these four general kinds of human suffering, there are infinite possibilities for other kinds of suffering during a human life span. For example, most human effort is directed toward accumulating property. This means that most humans are unhappy due to lack of property and hence try to acquire it, by good or bad means. There is discomfort even when you have accumulated wealth and property, because you must then protect it. You have to be on guard so that you won't be deprived of it by enemies, governments, thieves, or the like. If you do lose it, you are forced to work for others just to stay alive, but if you keep it, others always seem to be after it. Governments and members of your own family are the worst. Whether by trickery or by force, it seems that there is a conspiracy to take away your wealth. Just having wealth can become the cause of meeting your death. Someone may kill you for it. The suffering that rich people experience is endless.

For those who are destitute there is no happiness, because they too are driven by their thoughts of wealth and the desire to accumulate it. They roam about, taking a job here, a job there, hoping for a lucky break. They often are unable to find breakfast for themselves in the morning or any place to sleep at night. The stars are their hat, frost is their shoes, their own legs are their horse. They travel about giving the flesh of their legs to strangers' dogs and the smiles on their faces to prospective employers. By day they find little to eat, even though they search diligently, and at night they find nothing to shelter them from the cold. Even if a poor man is able to acquire a little through great hardship and labor, he does not get to enjoy it because it is taken away by taxes, debts, or whatever. Thus the poor man is constantly driven by lack of money. For him, human existence can become unhappy simply because of this one extra source of suffering: the desire for wealth and prosperity.

For both rich and poor, there are the additional possibilities of losing those they are fond of, losing what they are attached to, being forced into the company of those they dislike, meeting an enemy, or being defeated by an enemy. Whether or not you lose your loved ones or meet enemies, there is always the apprehension that these things will occur. Throughout human life, there is an almost endless array of worries and sources of mental unhappiness in addition to the four great inevitable types of suffering.

It is only the deluded who think of human existence as a totally happy experience. Anyone with eyes can see that human existence involves a great deal of involuntary suffering. For sensitive creatures like ourselves, just the prospects of disease, parting, and death are hard to cope with, let alone the actual experiences themselves. Yet we are all faced with them constantly; they are very much part of the warp and woof of human life, even though, compared to hell beings, pretas, and animals, we are in a fortunate state.

Human existence is not a state of unmitigated mental or physical pain: for beings who are very much attached to it, it does have its enjoyments. Yet for all humans there are facts that make life a state of suffering by and large. A wise person will become thoughtful and not allow himself to waste this human life or become prey to the great adversaries of death, disease, and old age. He will use his energy in the right practice of Dharma while he is able, so that his human existence will become the cause of genuine happiness for himself and others.

14

A Fish Cast Up on Hot, Dry Sand

In the last lesson, we discussed birth, old age, disease, death, and the other sufferings of the human realm. We will now consider the sufferings endured by beings who are born as asuras and as gods.

The Sufferings of the Asura Realm

Although the realm of the titans (*asura*) is included among the three higher realms, it is nonetheless devoid of happiness because, as Ārya Nāgārjuna put it in his *Letter from a Friend*:

> Inasmuch as the asuras by their very nature experience hatred for the splendor of the gods, they endure great mental suffering. And though endowed with intelligence, they are unable to perceive the truth because of their minds' natural obscurations.

By their very nature, the titans are said to spend their entire life span consumed with envy for the superior state of the gods. Although titans are endowed with considerable merit, intelligence, natural powers, and long life, they are inferior in all these respects to the devas, or gods. The gods are the natural adversaries of the asuras, who are also known as "antigods" (*sura* means god, and *a*- forms the negative). Just as there is natural enmity between cats and dogs, the mentality of the titans is governed by this consuming hostility, and as a result they devote themselves to a futile attempt to defeat the gods in battle. They spend their energies in fashioning more and more weapons, devising new types of armor, and laying different kinds of battle plans. They never for a single moment enjoy mental or physical leisure. Even though they devote their time solely to war, they are never able to achieve their great aim: the power of their merit is not equal to that of the gods, so the outcome of every battle is defeat. Whereas the gods are not destroyed in battle, the titans do experience the pain of being mangled and slain on the battlefield. And because they are doomed to experience defeat, their minds are contracted with grief.

Since they spend their lifetimes in war and attendant nonvirtuous behavior, the asuras accumulate very strong negative karma arising through the passions of envy, jealousy, hatred, and anger. Dying on the battlefield, they are generally reborn in the hells and other lower realms. Even though they are naturally endowed with great intelligence, anger characterizes their existence, so they are never able to pay attention to the Dharma. If they did, they would be able to understand it, but as it is, they derive no benefit from their rebirth in the realm of the titans.

The Sufferings of the Gods' Realm

Gods of the Desire Realm. It is generally thoughtrealm of desire (*kāmadhātu*) that in the realm of the gods beings get to experience happiness, but the celestials, too, are not free from the possibility of mental and physical pain. Even though the gods of the realm of desire do experience much longer lives than other beings in the round of existence, have more leisure, are free from many vexations that elsewhere limit the possibilities for happiness, and experience much greater aesthetic pleasures, their happiness is not true, pure, or unalloyed. It is what is known as "defiled pleasure" because it arises through delusion about the nature of existence; it is conditioned by ignorance. The happiness of the gods seems considerable only in contrast to that experienced in the lower realms.

Every god will, sooner or later, undergo suffering said to be the greatest experienced in any realm, including the hells. Because of their greater sensitivity to suffering when it does arise, and because they have become accustomed to pleasurable mental states over a very long period of time, the gods are the least prepared for suffering when it appears, as it inevitably does. As Ārya Nāgārjuna wrote in his *Letter from a Friend*:

> Even in the higher realms, the suffering of change that is experienced by those beings endowed with great happiness is still greater than that of the hells. Reflecting thus, virtuous men should not long to be reborn in those higher realms, which also inevitably come to an end.

After living for a very long time, a god one day finds himself confronted by five signs of death. These signs were described by Ārya Nāgārjuna in this way:

> The body's color turns ugly, a god no longer likes the throne on which he is seated, his flower garlands wither, odors cling to his garments, and sweat appears on his body where none appeared before. These are the five signs that indicate death in the higher realms.

Although these signs do not appear terribly severe to humans like ourselves, they are a great cause for alarm to a god because his friends and associates begin to shun him. Whereas formerly they treated him with great esteem and affection, now they only toss flowers and speak to him from a distance. It comes as a great shock suddenly to find his radiant body losing its luster. He no longer finds joy in taking his throne in the midst of the gods' assembly. The flowers he wears begin to wither on his body, and unpleasant odors begin to cling to his garments. He begins to sweat, and other signs of mortality arise. Unprepared as he is for the onslaught of these signs, they are the source of unbearable anguish.

Just as, when a human approaches death, certain signs become apparent to him and to others, so it becomes clear that a god is approaching the moment of death when five other signs arise on his person. According to the *Question of the Sage Vyasa Sūtra* (*Ṛṣivyasa-paripṛcchā-sūtra*), these five signs are: the body's luster grows dim; when he bathes, particles of water stick to his body; his garments and ornaments give out unpleasant sounds; his eyelids begin to blink; and he finds himself becoming mentally attached to one object at a time, even though this is not the nature of a god's mind.

To elaborate on these signs, it is said that gods' bodies are characterized by great luster—that they are radiant to a distance of 1 yojana (i.e., some 5 to 8 miles)—but that when death approaches, the color of a god's body becomes quite ugly to him and to other gods. As a result he is shunned by his relatives and even by his close friends; whereas formerly they honored him with garlands placed at his feet or around his neck, now they toss a single flower in his direction from a great distance and are unable to draw close to him to give him any comfort at all, so that he finds himself isolated from the celestial assembly.

When this happens, the god knows that death is approaching rapidly, and with his divine prescience, which enables him to survey all the lower realms of existence, he searches about to ascertain where he will be reborn. At that moment he realizes that because he has spent his life as a celestial indulging in careless attachment, enjoyment of sensual objects, and aesthetic pleasures, he has not accumulated an iota of merit that would help him gain a good rebirth or sustain the good rebirth that he presently enjoys. He sees very clearly that he will be reborn in the hells, and this foresight afflicts him with the greatest suffering known to any being in all the six realms of existence. The knowledge of the future sufferings that await him causes him to act very much like a fish that is suddenly cast up on dry, hot sand. He is plunged into such turmoil because he knows that, at this late date, there is no way he can avoid falling into such great mental and physical suffering.

The death of gods is different from that of beings like ourselves who are endowed with physical forms. The gods have a much more subtle, mental type of body, so they simply grow dimmer and fade away until they vanish, like a rainbow disappearing into the sky. But because of their advanced, supernormal mental powers, the anguish they experience upon suddenly finding themselves fading away from the delights of godly existence, combined with their knowledge of what awaits them in the hells, makes this an excruciating time. As the *Stations of Mindfulness Sūtra* says, "They fall downward, lamenting, 'Alas, O chariots and groves. Alas, O lakes and rivers. Alas, O beloved gods of the realm of consciousness.'"

The same sūtra tells us that all the physical pain experienced by sinful beings in the flames of Avīci Hell does not equal even a sixteenth of the mental anguish experienced by a god when he approaches death.

Gods of the Form and Formless Realms. In one of our earlier lessons, when we were describing Buddhist cosmology, we said there were three classes of celestials: (1) the gods of the realm of desire, (2) the gods of the realm of form, and (3) the gods of the formless realm.[39] We have just described the sufferings of the gods in the realm of desire. The devas in the remaining two realms do not experience the same sufferings. Beings reborn in these two realms of existence have achieved those states as a result of certain types of meditation. Through meditation on formlessness and the like, they achieve a state of meditative absorption characterized, as long as it lasts, by complete absence of mental and physical pain. These states last for very long periods of time but, just as birds flying in the sky sooner or later must return to the ground, so, when that meditative absorption begins to wane, beings in these states find that their consciousness begins to descend into the other states of existence.

When the thrust of their meditation is no longer able to sustain them, they start to come out of their absorption; it loses its power. They become alarmed and begin to doubt the very premises on which their whole meditative existence was founded, for they thought that this exalted, painless state was liberation itself. When they find themselves being slowly but inexorably dragged downward into grosser states of existence, they believe that the whole concept of attaining liberation through meditation is nothing but a lie. The intensity of their doubt brings them crashing down into a very painful rebirth, usually in the lower realms of existence. All the merit they have accumulated and all the mental stability they have achieved are exhausted by these grave doubts. As Ārya Nāgārjuna put it in the *Letter from a Friend*:

> When they quit the gods' realms, they helplessly proceed to rebirth
> in one of the lower realms of the animals, the ghosts, and the hell
> beings because they have utterly exhausted their virtues.

We need to make it clear that the gods of these realms are reborn in the lower states as a result of the tremendous self-doubt that arises in their minds. Because they spend such a long time peacefully enjoying the rarified, subtle pleasures of the meditative states of absorption, they come to think that they are immune to the suffering experienced by other beings. When meditative force begins to run out, worldly apparitions arise, and they realize that they are still very much involved in the round of birth and death. In their anxiety, they produce great wrong views. Again the great delusion of "self" grips them, and they feel that they have been utterly deceived by the teachings of liberation, the results of meditation, and so forth. Due to the intensity of the wrong views that are now causing them to plummet downward, they are utterly consumed by self-doubt and fall into states of terrible suffering. As Nāgārjuna explained it, "The fully ripening results are terrible for a person who practices well with the wrong views."

In other words, they felt that this was liberation when it actually wasn't. Because they aimed all their spiritual efforts at attaining skill in meditative absorptionrather than at realizing the truth of selflessness and uprooting the sense of a personal self, which alone is the door to liberation from the round of birth and death, they are unable to escape rebirth in the lower realms of suffering.

Now for how to reflect on the significance of these descriptions of the gods' realms. As we said earlier, seat yourself formally on a cushion; then take refuge in the Three Jewels, invoking their blessings and resolving to win enlightenment for the sake of all living beings. Next, reflect on the various types of unhappiness encountered by beings in the three higher realms of existence:

> It seems that we are greatly deluded when we think that we beings
> in the three higher realms of humans, asuras, and gods are
> endowed with happiness; it is only because we don't examine
> them carefully that we could possibly think in this way. For the
> same reason, it is only because of being deluded and careless in

our estimation of these three higher realms that we could possibly make rebirth in those three realms the object of all our hopes and prayers.

We always hope and pray that we will be reborn as humans or among the gods, but if we carefully examine these states, which seem to offer happiness and pleasure, we see that they are merely collections of insubstantial, essenceless phenomena that are deceptive by their very nature. Where they seem to be long-lasting, permanent, and a source of happiness, they are discovered to be quite insubstantial, lacking in any inherent nature of their own, fleeting, and a source of suffering. Yet we become attached to the mere appearance of brief flashes of happiness and devote all our thoughts and energies to achieving just those brief patches of what could appear as happiness only to deluded people like ourselves.

Actually, we are much madder than mad men to devote all our energies and efforts, including our religious ones, to attaining these appearances of happiness in the three higher realms. When we consider what happens even to the most fortunate, well-endowed beings in each of these realms, whether he be Brahmā, Indra, or a universal monarch, we see that each of them, without exception, is by his very nature bound to lose all that good fortune and exaltation. Here, among humans, the various kings are thought to be fortunate, majestic, and endowed with great fame and power, yet they will certainly experience the pains of old age, disease, death, and the decline of all their fortunes just as much as the humblest beggar will. Even the most fortunate humans are fated to undergo the unexpected pain of meeting with what they dislike and parting from what they love.

At this point, reflect in great detail on the various kinds of suffering undergone by humans; then reflect on the sufferings of the asuras as they have been described, and finally on the mental suffering experienced by the three classes of gods. Continue by trying to develop a sense of renunciation for the whole of worldly existence—and, in particular, a strong resolve not to direct your spiritual efforts toward being reborn in any of the three higher realms. Toward that end, reflect in this way:

Who that is wise would become attached to the mere appearance of happiness in worldly existence? When they are looked at honestly, these three higher realms of existence—those of the humans, asuras, and gods—resemble an island of demons that, however attractive it may appear, only leads to the destruction of those who enter and become attached there. Just as a person who becomes attached to existence on an isle of demons is sure to meet destruction, so beings who grow attached to worldly existence in the realms of humans and gods are certain to meet it.

Like birds who seek to escape a burning forest or swans who fear to light upon a frozen lake lest they be trapped there, we should diligently reach a decision about the round of worldly existence and resolve that we will no longer allow ourselves to become further involved in the machine of delusion that is the round of existence and that can only lead to more suffering for ourselves and others.

Now, no matter what happens, I must practice from my very heart the holy teachings of Lord Buddha, which will surely lead to liberation from this round of worldly existence, and undertake those practices and instructions that belong to the lam-dre system of meditation, which offers the most excellent and unerring guide to liberation.

15

CARELESS CRAVING

EACH OF US IS ENDOWED with buddha-nature. It is only due to our ignorance of our true nature that we find ourselves in a worldly situation in which we are confused not only about the true nature of our minds but about our state of existence itself. Through holding deluded, erroneous views about our nature, we become involved in the problem of ego-centered states of mind and the attendant poisons of desire, hatred, delusion, and the like. With minds governed by these negative mental states, we are impelled to take action based on delusion, which further involves us in the round of becoming. That round of becoming is described by holy men as a round of suffering.

Having attained human birth, those of us here have somehow also acquired an opportunity to receive instructions on the remedy to these sufferings and their causes. Having obtained such teachings—and a teacher able to explain them to us—we have a chance to understand and practice them. The result that can ensue from their practice is happiness even while we remain within the round of worldly existence. We will avoid states of suffering and attain states of relative happiness. Further, we will draw closer to the great ultimate happiness of liberation itself. Please keep these reflections in mind as we begin our next studies.

It has often been stated by enlightened teachers and by Lord Buddha himself that worldly existence is, by its very nature, an unsatisfactory state. Whether a being finds himself in the highest heaven or the lowest hell, there is not a single place on the round of existence where he is free from the certainty of suffering. In the most general terms, beings are subject to three different kinds of suffering. First is the experience of pain itself, mental and physical. In its grossest forms, this typifies the experience of beings in the three lower realms of existence. The three higher realms of existence are characterized by another kind of suffering, namely, impermanence. For beings in these three states, who are strongly oriented toward the acquisition and experience of pleasure, the absence of pleasure is a constant source of unhappiness.

THE SUFFERING OF CONDITIONED EXISTENCE

The third type of suffering is that of conditioned existence. This is a subtler but nonetheless all-pervading form of suffering. The mere fact of our existence involves us in a set of conditioned circumstances. For example, being endowed with form, feeling, perception, impulses, and consciousness (the five aggregates, or skandhas) involves us in a whole process that can only be described as painful. The acquisition of these five components of conditioned existence results from developing thought-patterns centered on the notion of an ego, rather than cognizing our own true buddha-nature instead.

Merely to possess the five skandhas is to be involved in an unsatisfactory state of being. Why is it that ordinary beings do not recognize this fact? Most people would not agree that existence is, by its very nature, a state where true happiness cannot be found. Worldly people are likely to ignore an insight of this sort because they are concerned solely with the acquisition of pleasure and the avoidance of specific instances of pain. They are preoccupied with gross manifestations of suffering such as disease and death, and while they try to avoid such obvious types of pain, it doesn't occur to them to reconsider the nature of existence itself. They are not inclined to take a long look at the whole round of existence; instead, they seek short-term solutions to individual pains. Yet this doesn't mean that teachings which point out the negative aspects of conditioned existence are false or unduly pessimistic.

These teachings issue from the insight of holy beings, such as the bodhisattvas and buddhas, who have, unlike worldlings, overcome the mental inclinations of attachment to ordinary pleasures. These holy beings are not afraid to look beyond the particular manifestations of unhappiness and survey existence as a whole. What they see there is the source of their strong spirit of renunciation of all worldly attachments. As the commentary on the *Abhidharmakosha* tells us by way of example:

> If a single hair is placed upon the palm, one feels no discomfort or pain, but if that same hair is inserted in the eye, it causes extreme pain and discomfort.

Foolish people are like the palm of the hand to a single hair. When a hair is placed on the palm of your hand, it causes very little distress, but if that same hair gets into your eye, it will be the source of much pain until it is removed. Holy people like the bodhisattvas and buddhas are endowed with such sensitivity because they are much more honest about the situation we call existence; they are prepared to face up to its negative aspects and recognize them for what they are. They no longer try to deceive themselves that what is actually pain is some kind of pleasure or source of happiness.

For our purposes of learning to recognize and reflect on this subtler kind of suffering, we will discuss three manifestations of the suffering of conditioned existence: the pain involved in (1) ceaseless human activities, (2) never being satisfied by the objects of desire, and (3) never learning to renounce the round of birth and death. In other words, we never grow weary of the experience of birth and death, and in this way our options are severely limited.

Ceaseless Human Activities

With regard to the pain involved in ceaseless human activity, the great teacher Āryadeva wrote in his *Four Hundred Verses* (*Catuḥśataka*):

> It takes efforts to accomplish a work which, once done, is effortlessly destroyed. But even though you see this to be so, why do you remain attached to the idea of work?

Human beings are characterized by their attachment to activity. Their lives are spent planning one project after another, attempting to accomplish their plans, and then seeing their plans either accomplished or thwarted. Almost from infancy to the time of death, people are not loath to take up new projects and busy themselves in one sort of work or another. They fill their time and expend their energy in works both good and bad. Thus we see farmers who don't hesitate to smear the blood of their feet on stones, woodsmen who routinely shed the blood of their hands on wood, and tradesmen who don't question the necessity of undertaking long, often dangerous journeys, settling in foreign countries, associating with all kinds of strangers, and abandoning their families, perhaps forever—all because of their attachment to the idea of work itself. As the *Bodhicharyāvatara* relates:

> Many are the base-minded people who have given themselves over to their desires for worldly gain and advantage and who never hesitate to labor all day, so that when they return home at night, utterly exhausted, their bodies already resemble corpses.
>
> Other foolish people who are deluded by the idea of selfish gain don't hesitate to undertake long journeys abroad and arrange their lives so that they are separated for many years from their loved ones, for whose sake they claim to be seeking profit.

To give yourself over to the idea of work for the sake of selfish profit is merely the way of fools, who don't hesitate to expend their precious human energies in such pointless, dangerous, and painful undertakings. Yet it is typical of people who deceive themselves that they consider these labors to be the source of great happiness. They hope to gain a reward from their accomplishments—to obtain some security in their old age, some social advantage, or additional status and comfort. But the limited types of happiness they hope for are just so many other manifestations of pain, and are certainly never happiness itself.

It doesn't often occur to worldly people to question the necessity of all these endless efforts, or the desirability of expending so much of their lives in attachment to work. They would probably not see attachment to work as a source of unhappiness. As the *Exhortation to Higher Aspiration Sūtra* (*Adhyāśaya-saṃcodana-sūtra*) tells us:

> Such people give themselves over completely, day and night, to thinking about worldly affairs, to thoughts of food and drink. They never even aspire to accumulate virtues. These are the faults of those who delight in works.
>
> They produce great attachment to the objects of their deluded desires and never hesitate to indulge themselves in their attachment; and yet they are never satisfied by the gratification they obtain. These are the faults of those who delight in works.
>
> They also delight in surrounding themselves with many friends and associates, and become distressed if they find themselves separated from their attendants.

People who have an undue attachment to activities like to involve their friends and associates in a similar waste of time. They are so attached to how they are spending their lives that they fail to recognize that those to whom they become attached are subject to change, old age, and death. When their friends die, move away, or are separated from them by karma, they are never prepared for it, are always distressed by it, and feel somehow let down by the inconstancy of their friends and of circumstances.

These people wallow about in painful situations like asses on the ground; they foolishly delight in worldly activities. If they stopped to reflect, they would realize that most of their energy is expended on pointless, insubstantial activities that are like so many ripples on the surface of a pond. Involvement in such activities leads the mind on endlessly from one project to another, until it has exhausted its energy in deluded, essenceless accomplishments that actually prevent the accumulation of virtue, which is the true cause of happiness in this and future lives.

Never Being Satisfied by the Objects of Desire

Now we will reflect on the pain incurred through not being satisfied by the objects of desire. Generally speaking, we can describe desire as a source of suffering by quoting from the Buddha's words in the *Extended Play Sūtra*:

> Desire is the root of suffering; it impairs meditative practice. Desire is like a drink of salty water, which only causes thirst to grow more intense.

It seldom occurs to ordinary people to think of sense objects—and attachment to sense objects—as a source of pain. We are so attached to the idea of sense objects bringing satisfaction that we don't like to think of them as mere cogs in a painful process. However, upon examination it becomes apparent that the uncontrolled desire of our sense organs for sense objects involves us in painful situations. Indulging the desire of the eye for sights, of the ear for sounds, of the nose for fragrances, of the tongue for tastes, and of the body for sensations causes us to search outside ourselves for sense objects and then attempt to acquire them. The result is either frustration in that attempt or, if we do acquire them, a failure to derive genuine satisfaction from their acquisition; in both cases this causes us mental and physical pain. Worse, the unchecked propensity to indulge our desire for sense objects only increases our thirst for more and more of them.

The Tibetan teacher Patrul Rinpoche[40] offered very apt similes for this kind of pain. He said that the desire of the eye-consciousness for sights is like a moth that plunges into a flame; the desire of the ear-consciousness for sounds is like a wild animal that is attracted by the artificial mating-calls of hunters; the desire of the nose-consciousness for fragrant smells is like a honeybee that gets trapped within a blossom; the desire of the tongue-consciousness for tastes is like a fish duped by bait; and the desire of the body for pleasant sensations is like an elephant that, distressed by the heat of summer, plunges into a deep lake and drowns.

In this and former lifetimes, there is not a single pleasure that you have not experienced. In countless lifetimes through beginningless time, you have obtained every conceivable object of desire, have been attached countless times to such objects, and have felt the inclination to seek them out again and again. Despite all that experience, you are still no closer to satisfaction. The only result is that your mental inclination to be attached to those sense objects has grown stronger. Thus it is correct to say that all beings continue to roam from one state of existence to another simply because of their carelessness in relating to sense objects.

Never hesitating to indulge in sense desires, we also never hesitate to act in ways that bind us further to the limiting conditions of worldly existence. As a result we experience one kind of suffering after another, time and again undergoing every type of pain available in the hells and other lower realms.

Thus, in former lifetimes, you have drunk limitless amounts of molten bronze in the hells, consumed measureless amounts of blood and pus among the ghosts, and devoured innumerable heaps of flesh as an animal—all as a result of your careless attachment to, and inclination to act on, the desire for sense objects. There is not a single type of suffering you have not experienced as a result of your own careless craving. As an outcome of all that indulgence, is there anything good to which you can point?

Worst of all, this process continues: the same attachments and inclinations as before are still very much present. This constant craving is sure to cause further pain and bondage unless dealt with properly now. The *Extended Play Sūtra* again tells us:

> Even if a man were to gain all the objects of his desires, he would still be discontent and continue the search. Acquiring all the objects of desire only causes craving to increase. The final result for such slaves of desire is the experience of being cut and split open in this life and the next.

People who give way to inordinate desires for sense objects find themselves tortured, even in this life, first by craving and then by the course of action through which they seek to satisfy those desires. It is very common to see thieves arrested, beaten, executed, or imprisoned for long periods of time merely as a result of their inordinate desire for sense objects. If they suffer so much even in this lifetime as a result of their indulgence in craving, what possible good result can they hope for in the lower realms of existence, where such actions inevitably lead them?

The point of this reflection is to help us see the weariness of indulging our desire for sense experiences and learn to direct our minds toward wholesome objects that do not increase suffering but lead to extrication from it. Not only is attachment to sense objects a cause of much suffering, recognized or unrecognized, for ordinary folk; it is also a special obstacle for those following a spiritual path. For meditators on Buddhist teachings such as these, the first prerequisite is mental tranquillity, the ability to direct the mind with some degree of concentration toward spiritual goals and virtuous objects.

The first obstacle that you will face as a meditator is the problem of attachment to worldly objects. Although this attachment can take many forms, the two most common (and most difficult to overcome) are attachment to inanimate objects such as property, wealth, and the like, and attachment to other beings. As the *Bodhicharyāvatara* tells us:

> Those who give themselves over to attachment to material goods have very little likelihood of experiencing happiness, much less attaining liberation, in this lifetime. They devote their mental energies to the acquisition of property, and even when they have gained it, their thoughts are concerned primarily with protecting what they've got.

Such people are preoccupied with separation from the property they have gained, which is taken away from them either by guile, force, taxes, friends, or enemies, or by the advent of old age and death. Hence, at all stages of their careers, they are concerned only with getting, guarding, and finally losing their property.

There is something inherently ignoble about people who think and act from such motives. Shāntideva likens them to cart-pulling beasts that spend their lives performing arduous tasks and yet receive only a bit of dried grass tossed into their stables at night. People who seek wealth slave for pitiful, trifling, insubstantial rewards. Even if obtained, these objects can in no way recompense them for the happiness-destroying efforts they have invested in obtaining them. Shāntideva concludes that,

> For the sake of an object of desire no less common than a morsel of grass—a relish that is not rare even among beasts—men of ill fortune blight even the opportunity of birth in the human realm, which is so hard to win.

For the sake of obtaining a small amount of gold, several acres of property, or a certain number of valued goods, you blight your chances for happiness in this lifetime, let alone future lifetimes. It is a mark of folly to devote your energies in such a way, wasting the very real and very precious opportunity offered by this human existence.

The second type of attachment that a meditator must overcome is attachment to other beings. The strongest manifestation of this is experienced in the sexual desire of a male for a female, or vice versa. As the *Stations of Mindfulness Sūtra* tells us:

> Women are in every way the source of destruction, because, first of all, they destroy your wealth and cause you to fall into the lower realms. How could there possibly be any happiness for men who desire women?

Since men and women bring about destruction for each other, you should totally renounce the opposite sex for your own well-being in this world and the next. Unchecked sexual desire will lead you to waste much of your energy earning money in order to be able to remain near the person you love, while your thoughts will be misdirected toward achieving and maintaining your attachment to that object of desire. Finally, sexual desire will lead you into grief when the relationship comes to an end. Thus this kind of relationship with another transient being can, by its very nature, openly involve you in distraction and unhappiness.

To attain tranquillity and concentration in your meditation, you must learn to direct your energies away from attachment to sense objects and other people. Recognize them as a source of distraction and pain; train your mind, instead, to seek out virtuous objects and holy phenomena, which lead to genuine well-being for yourself and others.

16

Ceaseless Roaming

WE ARE BEINGS WHO ARE ENDOWED with the foundation of enlightenment, which is our own essential buddha-nature. We are further endowed with the basis for striving for that enlightenment, i.e., the human body, which is so difficult to obtain. We also have qualified teachers willing and able to expound the teachings of liberation. Through our good fortune and their kindness, we have encountered the most excellent of methods known to the Mahāyāna path.

Through the practice of these instructions, it is possible for any diligent, intelligent student to attain perfect enlightenment within a single lifetime. Even those of mediocre spiritual faculties and diligence will obtain liberation during the post-death state, and a practitioner of inferior diligence and faculties will succeed no more than sixteen lifetimes after he has entered this course of practice. With these considerations in mind, we can see that our present situation, in which we have gathered to learn something of those teachings, epitomizes not only our own good karma but also our prospects for liberation. Thus anyone who is mindful of the significance of the situation will pay close attention to what is being discussed now.

Even though I am here as a teacher of the Dharma and you are here as students of the same Dharma, it is probably only fair to say that few of us appreciate the situation fully. Very few of us are motivated by an awareness of the impermanence of all phenomena, including ourselves. Very few of us are motivated to come here out of a recollection of the uncertainty of the time of our own death, let alone out of an altruistic desire to benefit others, however slightly. It is not often that we stop to think carefully about undertaking an action of this sort, even for our own benefit in this life and in the long run. This is understandable because, due to the way the human mind gets caught up in other affairs, it is hard to be clear about spiritual efforts and why they should take precedence over all our other concerns. In this modest effort we are making to teach and to study a system of practice that promises such an inconceivably wonderful result as buddhahood, it is hard to do justice to the situation in a few words or through a momentary reflection.

It makes no difference whether you undertake practice according to the

Sakya school or one of the other Tibetan orders—you will find identical teachings in them all. One of the first factors of practice is the distinction among types of practitioners. Whether you are studying the *Parting from the Four Attachments* of the Sakya order or the corresponding teachings found in the Nyingma, Gelug, and Kagyu orders, everywhere it is stated that "the doctrine is the same." What differ are the spiritual capacities, degrees of diligence, and levels of motivation among practitioners.

There are three broad categories of practitioners, distinguished by the motive that leads them to practice Buddhist meditation. First are those known as meditators of inferior motivation. They have learned to relinquish undue attachment to the affairs of this world and have given up gross ambition for worldly attainments; however, since their motive is to avoid suffering in this or future lifetimes, it is basically selfish. They are eager to avoid the manifold kinds of pain in the lower realms of existence, but are keen to experience the more pleasurable conditions of rebirth in the human or higher realms.

The second category consists of those whose motive is mediocre. These are Buddhists who have come to recognize the faults of all forms of worldly existence, whether in the lower realms or the higher states. They understand that the whole of worldly existence is characterized by one form of suffering or another. Through this realization, they have learned to direct their energies toward the attainment of liberation and away from activities that involve them further in the round of birth and death. However, because their efforts are directed toward liberation for themselves alone, their practice is characterized by spiritual selfishness.

This practitioner is inferior to the third category of meditator, who is motivated by a completely unselfish resolve to bring about the ultimate liberation of all living beings without exception. These Buddhists are determined to include all living beings in the benefits of their own spiritual efforts and to share with them the results of their accomplishments. The teachings we have undertaken to study belong to the instructions practiced by this third category of Buddhists. In common jargon, this type of Buddhist is known as one who follows the bodhisattva's way.

The teachings of the *Lam dre* are considered to be the jewel in the treasure house of Sakya doctrine and practice. The *Lam dre* is a complete set of instructions meant to guide the Buddhist from the initial stages of entering the path to the attainment of his or her final goal. We have discussed the teachings of *The Three Visions*, which are meant to inculcate renunciation in ordinary worldlings by pointing out the faults of worldly existence and all its manifestations. To that end, we have described the three kinds of suffering experienced by all sentient beings: (1) mental and physical pain, (2) the pain incurred due to transformation and change, i.e., impermanence, and (3) the suffering that all beings experience by virtue of being born among conditioned phenomena and as conditioned phenomena themselves. We are presently describing the last of these three.

The Inability to Renounce the Round of Existence

Now we will reflect on the endless sufferings that beings undergo through their inability or refusal to relinquish their craving for the round of worldly existence. This is primarily a teaching on the ceaseless round of birth and death. Once you have become involved in the process of birth and death and the operation of karma, there is no way—short of liberation—that you can avoid further birth and death. The process is quite ceaseless. As long as the causes for it are present, there is no way to avoid further roaming about in one state of existence or another; when viewed with some objectivity, this ceaseless roaming is seen by the pure-minded as a very wearisome, sad state of affairs. Chandragomin's *Letter to a Student* tells us:

> There is no region in which I have not dwelt, nor any womb in which I have not lain through aeons of time. From beginningless time right up to the present, I have never ceased roaming from one place of birth to another. All this is due to the power of my own karma and the deluding power of my passions.

To give some sense of the feeling this teaching is supposed to engender, Nāgārjuna says in his *Letter from a Friend*:

> My own bones that I have acquired in each rebirth among beings would, if piled up, surpass the height of Mount Sumeru itself. And if the number of my mothers in the past could be measured in the same way, there would not be enough room on earth.

And Jetsün Dragpa Gyaltsen wrote in his *Parting from the Four Attachments*,

> When we reflect on the unsatisfactoriness of conditioned existence, we see that there is no end to the worldly works of men. No matter whether there are many people gathered together or just a few, they are prone to experience one form of suffering or another. No matter whether a person is rich or poor, he is not immune to the experience of suffering.

In surveying human life, we see that most people die while still in the process of getting ready for something, whatever that may be. Throughout their lives they prepare for the accomplishment of this or that worldly undertaking. At the time of death they are still involved in such projects. Even in death there is no end to the process of preparation because, whether they like it or not, they are preparing for their next rebirth. There is very little in worldly existence to commend attachment to it. Only those who are deluded or bad-hearted by nature would continue to be attached to such a round of wretchedness after looking at the prospects carefully.

Worldly existence is said to be like a patient who never recovers, a prisoner who is never released, or a traveler who never reaches his destination. No matter what you do, where you dwell, with whom you associate, or what pleasures you enjoy, there is never anything but suffering. All these experiences are inextricably bound up, by their very nature, with suffering. They are either manifest suffering or the source of other forms of pain.

Once this has been pointed out, an intelligent person will not, upon examination, be able to find any countervailing reasoning to deny it, and will hence undertake to develop within himself great vigor. His diligence will be single-pointed and highly motivated, like the actions of someone whose clothes have caught on fire and whose one thought is to separate himself from the flames as quickly as possible. Similarly, a person who clearly understands the painful aspects of worldly existence grows diligent in his efforts to avoid further involvement in the process of endless birth and death, and instead directs wholehearted efforts toward liberation from that cycle. As Nāgārjuna pointed out in his *Letter from a Friend,* there is nothing in the world more important for a human to accomplish, and no project that should take priority over it:

> Inasmuch as worldly existence has a nature of this sort, there is in fact no good birth at all among gods, nor among men or hell beings, ghosts or animals. Know, therefore, that birth is a source of many afflictions. Just as, if fire were suddenly to blaze forth on your head or body, you would abandon all other activities to check the flames, so you should strive diligently to avoid further rebirth. There is no higher necessity than this.

It is most important that we try to turn our minds away from further involvement in worldly activities and direct our energies to the best of our abilities toward the attainment of liberation. To that end, it is necessary to remind ourselves again and again to recognize the deluded, painful aspects of human existence and to generate diligence in practice. Only in this way is there any hope of obtaining liberation as an alternative to further suffering. As the great teacher Shāntideva wrote in his *Bodhicharyāvatara*:

> I experience such a wretched state of affairs right now because, not only in this lifetime but throughout former lifetimes, I have never bothered to develop any enthusiasm for the practice of virtue. Who but the most deluded of people would forsake the benefits of virtuous practice for further involvement in deluded suffering?

It is not enough just to listen to teachings on the unsatisfactory nature of worldly existence. Merely listening has benefits, but does not in itself help liberate you from further suffering. What is required is that you actually think in this way—not merely mentally acquiescing that perhaps the round of existence is not such a good idea, but actually reflecting on its suffering as part of your own practice. Thus you need to make a concerted effort to develop within yourself a strong feeling of renunciation and desire to relinquish all forms of attachment. You might want to reflect in this manner:

> For many lifetimes now, I have always thought that the aggregates of my own phenomenal existence were something to be cherished. I have never questioned the desirability of the kind of conditioned existence I have experienced, or dreamt that, as a result of all my toil in this and former lifetimes, I was only accumulating further suffering for myself. The efforts I have made toward achieving worldly aims and obtaining some degree of worldly happiness are like so many ripples on a pond. I have carelessly sought to enjoy the various objects of desire. But not only has my attachment to sense objects impaired my intelligence and spiritual faculties, it has caused my attachments and desires to increase unabated. It is this very kind of attachment and desire that has always been the cause of my suffering in one state of existence or another. My indulging in sense objects is just like putting more wood on the fire of suffering, or trying to quench my thirst by drinking saltwater.
>
> Though I have undergone countless rebirths in the six states of existence, I have not yet even approached the fringe of liberation. My situation right now is equally precarious. Based on my efforts so far, in my former lives and even in this lifetime, how can I hope to avoid further states of suffering? Yet this plight has not been

inflicted on me by anyone else. It is I who have fashioned my own bondage, I who have deceived and cheated myself all this while.

The sufferings that I have experienced and now experience are simply the result of my own actions. I have held worldly existence to be a source of pleasure and have not recognized it as having a nature of suffering. Nor have I believed in the teachers of Dharma and the Three Jewels. Moreover, I have always held the impermanent happiness of the human and higher realms to be permanent. Throughout, I have been carried along by attachment to deceptive objects of desire, which are like so many deceiving devils. And during all the suffering I have experienced and have known others to experience, I have felt little remorse about, or sadness for, this "contraption" of birth and death.

Now, however, I am resolved to discard all insubstantial worldly works and all those activities that are usually performed merely for the gratification of this temporary body. I am determined to cast off these attachments like spittle and direct my mind solely toward the teachers and the Three Jewels. I am determined to take the first step on the path of liberation by relying on the instructions of spiritual friends. I am determined to practice from the heart the infallible teachings that alone are able to extinguish the fires of suffering. The teaching that I am determined to follow is the *Lam dre*, which is the sole path traversed by all the buddhas of the past, present, and future.

Continue to ponder the plight of beings who, by their very nature, are involved in these many kinds of ceaseless sufferings, until this kind of reflection comes to mind very naturally. Persevere until it becomes your spontaneous response to their plight, and until your own resolve to seek liberation comes, in the Tibetan phrase, "from the very marrow of your bones."

When the whole of your energy is turned sincerely toward liberation, your meditations and reflections have been fruitful. At this stage your attitude toward worldly existence should be like that of a prisoner whose only thought is of freedom. The point is to keep meditating until you have accomplished the purpose of this particular type of reflection—namely, a strong determination not to become further involved in worldly affairs, but rather to direct your efforts toward liberation.

In conclusion, pray with great faith and devotion that the line of preceptors, your own teacher, and the Three Jewels may bless you and help you move along the path of liberation. Then dedicate any merit you may have accrued to the benefit and enlightenment of all living beings. This is, of course, in keeping with the instruction that this sort of reflection be treated as a meditative session, prefaced by taking refuge and motivated by the aspiration to attain buddhahood for the sake of all beings.

17

IMAGINE A BLIND TORTOISE

IN REFLECTING ON THE GOOD FORTUNE of attaining human birth and encountering the teachings of enlightenment, we are readily able to see that if these are rightly used, we will develop right practice. We will have all the motivation we need to develop bodhichitta, the resolve to attain liberation for the sake of all sentient beings. Our right practice will progress through the six pāramitās, or perfections, of the bodhisattva. We should clearly appreciate the difficulty of gaining all the advantages we possess in being here with these favorable conditions, and understand that, with true diligence, we can expect the finest result of any effort: perfect buddhahood.

All religious systems have been organized with the intention of relieving the sufferings of humans; all seek to promote happiness. The religion of the Buddha has a position of preeminence among them all, both because it has devoted itself to a thorough analysis of the causes and modes of the suffering and happiness of all beings and because it is dedicated to establishing effective methods for removing the causes, manifestations, and results of suffering.

The Buddha's teachings were given to all beings, in all realms of existence, without exception. They benefited India for many centuries before a decline that resulted from historic and karmic causes. In Tibet, also, Buddhism flourished long and was a source of great psychological and cultural benefit until the Chinese military incursion there caused an abrupt decline in the teachings. Now history is repeating this pattern in the West, where the words of the Buddha were formerly unknown. At last the four main Tibetan lineages (Nyingma, Gelug, Kagyu, and Sakya) are represented here. There is no real difference among these schools in terms of philosophy, systems of practice, conduct, or ultimate result. All teach the Middle Way to ultimate enlightenment, cognition of the ultimate reality of all phenomena, and the state away from all extremes of existence and nonexistence.

All four of these schools train the mind in three stages of meditative practice: (1) concentration, to bring the mind to the stage where it can be focused single-pointedly, at will, for long periods of time; (2) insight, in which the mind contemplates the ultimate nature of mind itself; and

(3) the combination of these two disciplines. And all four subscribe to the accumulation of spiritual merit and transcendent wisdom through practicing the six perfections.

The goal of all this activity is perfect enlightenment. This consists of attaining the three bodies (*trikāya*) of buddhahood: the Body of Reality (*dharmakāya*), the Body of Bliss (*sambhogakāya*), and the Transformation Body (*nirmāṇakāya*).

The four orders of Tibetan Buddhism are alike in all essential respects, with only minor variations in emphasis due to the tradition and history of their arising. As practitioners, we are concerned with the authenticity of these teachings, wanting to be sure that those we receive actually go back in an unbroken transmission to the historic Buddha (or to Vajradhara, his tantric form—shown with blue skin, silks, and jewels in his sambhogakāya form; all four schools hold to the vision of tantric Vajradhara, although his form may differ slightly). The teachings we are studying now were transmitted to the sage Virūpa, who passed them down, through a succession of masters, to us. They are to be respected as authentic and are the foundation of our own spiritual efforts. These teachings are exoteric, with Shākyamuni Buddha accepted as their true source. The lam-dre teachings we are studying epitomize the Sakya tradition of instructions from the beginning of the path to its ultimate conclusion in buddhahood, and include, in *The Three Visions* and *The Three Continua*, everything the diligent practitioner needs to know for the journey.

THE DIFFICULTY OF OBTAINING THE OPPORTUNITY TO PRACTICE DHARMA

We have now finished reflecting on the unsatisfactory nature of worldly existence itself and can turn to the second theme in our system of instruction, which is designed to develop the right attitude in our own practice. The first set of instructions pointed out the need for practice; next, we are going to develop the right approach toward practice. This is accomplished through reflecting on the difficulty of obtaining the opportunity to practice the teachings that lead to enlightenment. As our root text, the *Vajra Verses*, written by the great yogi Virūpa, points out, "This teaching is meant for deluded beings."

The operative words here are "for deluded beings." This is a reference to the basic cause for the existence of living beings. Buddhist sages identify the root cause of existence itself as delusion—i.e., ignorance and karma.

This topic will be discussed with reference to the three requisite conditions for practice, namely (1) the absence of the eight unpropitious situations that must be avoided to achieve the opportunity to practice, (2) the five conditions that we must achieve through our own positive karma, and (3) the five additional positive conditions derived from other sources. Taken together, these factors are called "the conjuncture of the eighteen auspicious conditions."

In describing the eight negative conditions that must be avoided, we have a quotation from Shāntideva's *Bodhicharyāvatara*:

> It is extremely difficult to obtain human birth, and the acquisition of the totality of auspicious conditions is also extremely rare. It is rarer still that an Enlightened One such as the Buddha would appear among beings.

Given the great benefit that ensues from a genuine encounter with such teachings—namely, great happiness in this life and all future lives, and eventual liberation from mental and physical suffering for ourselves and all others—this situation is ripe with tremendous potential for everyone. Yet such a conjuncture is so rarely achieved and so fragile that it may be lost at any moment. We may be separated from the Dharma, from this life, or from the opportunity to study and practice. Moreover, if this rare conjuncture of auspicious conditions is lost after having been found, due to not making full use of the opportunity when it is presented to us, there is very little likelihood that we will meet with it again.

THE RARITY OF HUMAN BIRTH

Even the attainment of human life is said to be extremely rare. We can establish its rarity by considering it from three angles: (1) its cause, (2) its frequency, and (3) its nature.

The cause of human birth is said to be the observance of moral conduct. If your karmic pattern is dominated by observance of wholesome conduct—specifically, by refraining from the ten unwholesome actions of body, voice, and mind and observing the corresponding ten wholesome actions—then human birth is assured. Indeed, it can be said that beings are reborn among humans due to the ripened result of whatever wholesome conduct they have managed to practice in former lifetimes. However, your humanity can easily be lost through failure to maintain moral conduct. As Shāntideva wrote in the *Bodhicharyāvatara*,

> Humanity is lost through making few efforts to maintain ethical behavior and indulging instead in unwholesome acts. Having lost

humanity, one cannot even count on hearing the word "liberation" for hundreds of aeons.

Taken as a whole, most beings fail to maintain moral behavior, which alone is the cause of human rebirth, because of their ignorance and the weakness of their karmic propensities. Hence most beings fail to be reborn among humans. As it is said, "If one's leg of moral conduct has been shattered, one is unable to stand."

Without moral conduct, there is no way to progress toward higher realms and liberation. Other good traits, such as generosity, are unable to help us toward higher rebirth and liberation if they are not based on and supported by "legs of moral conduct." Moral conduct is the requisite for human rebirth. Lacking it, we receive the results of our other good actions in lower states of existence rather than in the human realm.

Second, let us consider how humanity is quantitatively rare. Although we might think that there are humans enough on this globe, in the context of all living beings, the number is really very small. Unfortunately, most beings are not virtuous. Because of their failure to accumulate enough wholesome karma, they are unable to gain human rebirth and are reborn in the lower realms of existence. It is said that most beings on the round of existence are found in the hells, and that the number of ghosts and beings caught in the bardo is simply countless. In this context, humanity is said to be almost out of reach for most beings. The number of beings who fail to attain human birth is beyond the power of mind to imagine. Quantitatively, beings are karmically situated in a pyramid that has a very broad base of those born in restless states of existence characterized by great suffering. The number of fortunate beings who have managed to be reborn among humans and celestials is, in contrast, exceedingly small.

Indeed, the number of beings who have attained humanity could be likened to a particle of dust under your thumbnail. The number of beings in the hells would then be like all the dust on earth; those in the realms of the ghosts, like the grains of dust in a sandstorm; and those reborn as animals, like the dregs left in the bottom of a wine barrel. In these terms, the attainment of humanity is nothing more than the glimmer of a possibility on the whole round of existence—just the faintest gleam of an opportunity that could happen, but one that, in practical terms, simply doesn't occur.

One example of the rarity of human birth is given by Lord Buddha himself in the *Ordination of Nanda Sūtra* (*Nanda-pravrajyā-sūtra*). Imagine a blind tortoise living at the bottom of the ocean, and imagine also that once every hundred years he swims upward in an effort to place his neck through a wooden yoke floating on the surface of the ocean. The chances of that tortoise succeeding in his efforts are better than those of most beings in their efforts to obtain human rebirth. This example is also quoted by Ārya Nāgārjuna in his *Letter from a Friend.*

Third, we consider how humanity is rare by its very nature. Here we are talking about members of humankind who are endowed with the conjuncture of the eighteen favorable conditions.

THE EIGHTEEN FAVORABLE CONDITIONS FOR PRACTICE

Freedom from the Eight Negative Conditions

Rebirth in any of eight restless states prevents us from encountering the teachings of liberation. These are: (1) the hell realms, (2) the realm of the ghosts, (3) the realm of the animals, (4) the realm of the long-lived deities, (5) existence as a human barbarian, (6) existence as someone endowed with wrong views, (7) existence as someone living where no buddha has ever appeared, and (8) existence as someone with impaired mental faculties. Thus there are four states of nonhuman existence in which we have no opportunity for entering the path of enlightenment, and four human states where this is also not possible.

If you are reborn as a hell being, you are so oppressed by constant mental and physical agony that there is no opportunity to consider the practice of Dharma. Pretas, too, are so mentally afflicted by hunger and thirst that they are unable to think about the practice of religion. Animals are so weighed down by their lack of intelligence that they cannot understand the Dharma even if they encounter it. And the long-lived gods are prevented from appreciating the Dharma both by their freedom from immediate problems and by their false belief that their status is permanent and due to their own natures. Not seeing their position as the temporary result of their own karma, they dwell in conceit throughout their lives and make no effort to practice.

Barbarians are bereft of any appreciation of the law of karma, and their conduct is not guided by proper consideration of what is fitting, wholesome behavior conducive to their own spiritual welfare. They do not distinguish between good and evil in this sense. Among barbarians, there are unthinkable customs, such as a son taking his own mother for a bride. Also, one very seldom meets holy men among them, so it is difficult for them to encounter the right teachings.

Those beings who have wrong views do not accept wholesome actions as the cause either of rebirth in the higher realms of existence or of liberation itself. They do not accept the Three Jewels as true, authentic sources of spiritual benefit, nor do they accept the doctrine of cause and effect as it applies to their own moral conduct.

Also, there are many humans born in places in this world that are devoid of any teachings of enlightenment. Beings born in such times and places are, of course, cut off from the possibility of practicing these teachings.

Finally, people who are impaired in their mental faculties find it difficult to encounter or understand the teachings and to receive instructions so that they can practice what should be practiced and avoid what should be avoided.

All these eight states of existence are characterized by a lack of opportunity to receive and put into practice the teachings that lead to liberation.

The Ten Auspicious Conditions

Attainment of humanity is further characterized by ten conditions that are due to our own karmic efforts or to the results of our former karmic deeds. The first of these is human birth itself. When you obtain human birth, you move significantly closer to the possibility of encountering the Dharma. Second, you must be born in a central place, which is traditionally defined as a place where fully ordained Buddhist monks and nuns are found. Third, your mental faculties must be unimpaired, so that you will not be handicapped in encountering or practicing the teachings. Fourth, you must have the inclination to receive the Dharma and the propensity to awaken faith in the teachings of liberation. Most humans disregard such teachings, considering them to be of no interest or importance. Thus they don't awaken the desire to learn more about the spiritual goal toward which these teachings are oriented. Fifth, you must not be karmically hindered by inclinations to practice actions harmful to yourself and others, which could prevent you from receiving the teachings or entering very far into their practice. This is particularly true if you have somehow managed to perform a terrible deed such as matricide, patricide, or the like.

Next, we have the five conditions that are due not to our own karma but to other circumstances. First, a buddha must appear in the world during an aeon when you are born as a human. Since this is an extremely rare event, we can appreciate with what difficulty we ourselves have managed to encounter the teachings of Shākyamuni Buddha, who appeared in India some twenty-five hundred years ago. Of the last 360 aeons, there have been only four in which buddhas appeared. The remaining 356 are called dark or empty aeons.

Second, the buddha who appears must actually give the teachings of enlightenment. You may have heard that it was only after some hesitation that Shākyamuni decided to teach others about the enlightened state of mind he had discovered through arduous meditation. According to tradition, Lord Buddha remained in meditative absorption for seven days after his enlightenment at Bodhgaya. It was only after Brahmā, the king of the gods, appeared, made an offering of the Dharma wheel (*dharmacakra*), and requested him three times to teach others about the subtle enlightenment he had attained that Lord Buddha agreed to do so out of compassion for other beings who remained in ignorance. As a result he embarked on his ministry, wandering throughout India for the rest of his life and expounding the path of enlightenment to his disciples.

Third, there must be an uninterrupted succession of those teachings which the buddha of a given aeon sets in motion by turning of the Wheel of Dharma. In our case, authentic teachings were communicated to Lord Buddha's disciples on several occasions, so the possibility of their being made known to others did occur. Through the uninterrupted succession of his disciples, who made painstaking efforts to understand and attain the realizations to which the teachings referred, the Buddha's doctrines and teachings remain in this world.

Fourth, there must still be disciples of the buddha in question who uphold the teachings and embody the principles of his doctrine in their own lives, through the insights and spiritual qualities they have arduously developed.

Fifth, there must be sustenance for the teaching and its adherents—monasteries where teachers can teach, retreat centers where meditators can practice, patrons to support the religious efforts made by renunciates and other ascetics, and so forth. All these conditions must be present for the transmission of these doctrines down through history to the present time.

Only as a result of all these conditions is it possible for you to be among the fortunate few among all living beings who are in a position to receive and benefit from teachings such as these. In my eyes, all of you are endowed with all the requisites for a spiritual career that we have just described, and each of you is motivated by a very real interest in, and respect for, the teachings. This is why you continue to listen to, reflect on, and learn more about these teachings. This is a cause of great happiness for me, and I rejoice in your good fortune and good karmic inclinations. As your teacher, I would like to encourage you to carry your efforts one step farther by undertaking more practice to enrich the teachings to which you are listening. As Jetsün Milarepa repeatedly exhorted his disciples, it is not enough merely to listen to the teachings. The teachings are meant to be practiced. The realizations to which the scriptures and teachings such as the *Lam dre* refer are very real. They are very available states of mind, but they are accessible only through right practice.

I am confident that you would be able to recognize these teachings if you heard them again, and that you would be able to explain their basic structure to some degree. Most people have the intellectual ability to understand, remember, and reflect on these teachings in a discursive way. To that very real accomplishment, I can only add that I hope you will also make efforts to enrich your understanding through personal experience of each of these lam-dre teachings. For instance, it would be very salutary if you were to spend some time reflecting on those that are meant to awaken renunciation and diligence in practice by contemplating the sufferings of worldly existence, the doctrine of impermanence, and so forth.

To give an example: one of my own teachers, Gatön Ngawang Legpa Rinpoche,[41] spent fifteen years meditating on this very text, *The Three Visions*. He locked himself up in a room and cut only a small hole in the wall through which to receive food. The first three years he spent reflecting on the unsatisfactoriness of worldly existence. He spent twelve months meditating on impermanence and so forth. He practiced continuously, taking refuge millions of times, and likewise reciting the hundred-syllable mantra of Vajrasattva, making mandala offerings, and doing prostrations millions of times.

Although it is not possible for us to devote years to the actual practice of this text, we may be able to find some time to try to experience these teachings in our own minds, instead of merely listening to them. If, by so doing, we develop a sense of sadness and fellow-feeling for the many unfortunate beings who experience great unhappiness due to their ignorance of such teachings, then future efforts that we make in study and practice will be much richer and more meaningful.

18

A LUMP OF CHARCOAL AND A WHITE CONCH

WHY DO WE, as so-called living beings, think that it is possible for us to attain buddhahood? Most beings are overcome by delusions, their minds sullied by ignorance, passion, and constant involvement in one kind of unhappy destiny or another: What makes us believe that an exalted state of total spiritual perfection is possible for beings in such a plight? If beings are lowly and buddhas are perfect, the distance between them is immense. Isn't our aspiration like the attempt to find something in common between a lump of charcoal and a white conch? They seem to be of a completely different nature.

The crucial point, however, lies in our definition of a being. A living being is someone who doesn't recognize that his true nature is precisely that of a buddha. Since the true nature of all phenomena, and all beings, is simply buddha-nature, buddhahood is always just an insight away from everyone. It is within the reach of all beings who are able to perceive, with certain realization, their true nature. Through relying on the teachings and practices that enable us first to see through the erroneous belief in a subject and an object, and then to purify our minds of unwholesome inclinations, we, too, are certain to gain the realization of our own minds' true nature. This true nature transcends duality to consist of the nonduality of emptiness and clarity, or cognition. This recognition of buddha-nature, which is possible for all living beings, is certainly within our reach, also. For this reason it is not only possible but quite appropriate that we concern ourselves with efforts to attain the state of buddhahood.

From time to time, we need remember what we are about, recall our goal, and bring to mind once again that it is the attainment of buddhahood (i.e., recognition of our own true buddha-nature) which is the object of all our endeavors. We must, of course, make the necessary efforts to reach that goal. Realizing that it *is* attainable and is of great benefit to both ourselves and others is reason enough to learn how to make those right efforts.

There are many paths of practice that lead to the goal of buddhahood. We are studying one such path, known as the lam-dre system of meditation.

This system incorporates the profound philosophical views of the Sakya order of Tibetan Buddhism. The entire system can be conveniently divided into three stages of study and practice: (1) the stage of foundational practice, (2) the stage of advanced practice, and (3) the result. We are now discussing the first stage. The instructions that we are concerned with here are taken from the root text known as *The Three Visions*. In the preceding lessons, we have progressively examined the painful aspects of unspiritual, or worldly, existence. At the second level within that first stage, at which we now find ourselves, we are concerned with developing the right attitude of renunciation and diligence in undertaking the practices described.

At this point, we are concerned with three topics: (a) the difficulty and rarity of obtaining human existence and an opportunity to undertake spiritual practices such as these, (b) the great benefit to be obtained through a human birth and right practice of the Dharma, and (c) the impermanence of such an opportunity to practice, for the chance that a human birth offers is fleeting and, once lost, is very seldom recovered. We have discussed the eighteen prerequisite conditions to an encounter with the teachings of enlightenment. Now we will take up the great benefits to be obtained through practice of the Dharma.

THE BENEFITS OF HUMAN BIRTH AND RIGHT PRACTICE

We have explained how extremely difficult it is for other living beings ever to achieve the status of humanity. Many examples were given of how very rarely a being attains human existence and whatever measure of happiness, or at least freedom from suffering, it provides. We also discussed how it is even rarer for a being, once human, to be endowed with a conjuncture of all the conditions necessary to encounter the teachings that lead to liberation from the round of worldly existence. Despite this, humanity is not always rightly prized by human beings. It is thrown away by many, and even we ourselves can't honestly claim that we always fully appreciate the spiritual opportunity that our birth as human beings has granted us.

It is not surprising that some people fail to realize that human birth really offers such a great opportunity. Yet we would assert, first of all, that human existence is of much greater value and benefit than a wish-fulfilling jewel. If we had a gem that could grant our every wish, we would rightly consider ourselves very fortunate. Such jewels are very rare in this world, but humanity itself is an even more precious jewel and is only rarely obtained by beings. And if, as humans, we undertake to practice religion, then happiness and gain are ensured in this life, in future lives, and on the ultimate level as well.

There is no better result than this: that, through attaining humanity, forever after we would have the causes for ever-increasing joy and, eventually, the ability to benefit others as well. It is hard to conceive of anything more valuable or beneficial than this. There is nothing higher than buddhahood, and this highest result is available only through the efforts made by religious-minded human beings. As the great master Chandragomin wrote in his *Letter to a Student*:

> What kind of person would waste and make fruitless that human
> life which is of greater value than a wish-fulfilling jewel, and which
> enables us to cross over the ocean of birth and death through the
> practice of virtues?

Shāntideva also wrote that the achievement of spiritual benefit for oneself and other beings is the essential goal of humanity. It is for this very purpose that human existence is obtained. If we waste the opportunity that it provides, how can it possibly be regained?

When we examine the Sanskrit word for "human," which is *purusha* (*puruṣa*), we can see etymologically that a spiritual sense is observed, for *purusha* has the sense of "potentiality." From this it is easy to understand the teaching that the acquisition of a human body endowed with the eighteen requisite conditions for practice of the Dharma does indeed contain the potential for attaining transcendent states of being. For the most inferior type of Buddhist practitioner, who practices not to attain liberation but to avoid rebirth in unhappy states of existence, rebirth in higher, happier states of existence is ensured. For the mediocre practitioner, who seeks only to gain liberation from any possibility of suffering, liberation as an arhat is assured, provided he makes the right efforts. The aspiration of a superior person to effect liberation from suffering for all beings as well as himself is also certain if the right efforts are made. Thus the state of humanity contains the potential for transformation from lower to higher spiritual states.

At this point, you might wonder whether or not other beings have the same opportunity as humans. The answer is that they don't. Humans alone are capable of encountering the right spiritual path and making the right spiritual efforts to bring about such transcendent results. The actions of human beings are generally much more effective than those of other beings. When a human commits wholesome or unwholesome actions, they are usually accompanied by just the right amount of self-awareness to produce karmically clear effects. Thus, if you consciously commit unwholesome actions, those actions (because they are supported by human intelligence) will bring about very definite unwholesome results, often within the same lifetime. Likewise, if virtuous efforts are made (supported by human intelligence and aspirations), they will in a very short time begin to bear fruit.

This is not usually the case with other forms of living beings. They have no choice between virtue and nonvirtue, either because they can't conceive of a spiritually wholesome course of action or because the circumstances that govern their existence prevent them from making such efforts. It is said that, even among the different kinds of beings who inhabit the four great continents of this universe according to Buddhist cosmology, those who are endowed with human bodies are the most powerful, in that their mental and physical faculties give them a wider range of choice and a great ability to bring about good or bad effects. In his *Letter to a Student*, Chandra-gomin relates:

> Neither gods nor nāgas nor yakshas nor garudas nor vidyādharas nor other spirits have ever obtained the spiritual path which is uniquely available to those human beings who rely on the doctrines of the Enlightened Ones.

Among the six realms of living beings, humans are most fortunate from the spiritual point of view. And among humans, the most fortunate are those who are endowed with the eighteen requisite conditions for practice of the Dharma, since they have the power to shape their karmic destiny and bring about the highest possible well-being for themselves and others. It is of the utmost importance that we frequently remind ourselves of this and avoid the temptation to waste, disregard, or undervalue the opportunity granted us by our human existence. If this good fortune is not rightly used while it is available, there is no certainty that we will ever again find such a happy meeting of good conditions for right practice.

Those of you who have read Shāntideva's *Bodhicharyāvatara* will probably remember his exhortation to think of the human body as a boat on which one can cross the ocean of sufferings that is worldly existence. With this image in mind, he urges us not to think of this as a time for slumber. Yet many who come to accept the teaching that human existence is rarely obtained and a source of great potential benefit nonetheless decline to make diligent efforts just now, reasoning that "as long as I don't do anything very bad, I'll avoid rebirth in the lower realms, be reborn as a human again, and carry on slowly, wending my way to enlightenment in a leisurely fashion. Since I'm very busy in this lifetime with a number of other affairs, I don't have time for diligent practice, but I'll be sure to practice a lot more next time around."

There is no guarantee for any of us that it is going to happen like this. First of all, your next rebirth is not determined solely by the effects of your karmic actions (good or bad) in this lifetime. Nor is your present life solely the result of your actions in the lifetime just preceding it. You never know which of your karmic inclinations is going to surface and govern your lot in any given lifetime. Unwholesome actions committed long ago may be approaching the time when they will mature, involving you in a karmically impossible situation, such as birth in a place where Dharma teachings do not exist or where you are truly prevented from practicing them.

Even worse, you can't trust your karmic pattern based on what you know of it from this present lifetime. You can have no confidence that, merely by avoiding extremes of bad behavior now, you will not be reborn in the lower realms in your next life. Nor will you automatically be reborn in the human or gods' realm simply because you have managed to accumulate a certain amount of virtue in this life. As Shāntideva reminds us, "As a result of a single moment of unwholesome behavior, one may find oneself spending a full aeon in the deepest hell." Since there is no telling what harmful deeds we may have committed in past lifetimes that have not yet ripened for us, it is better not to take a sanguine approach to future lives.

The thoughtful person who understands the sense of these teachings will practice diligently as long as he or she is able. By "practicing religion" we don't mean just altering our external patterns of behavior, saying the right words, or showing ourselves to be a practitioner while inwardly retaining attachments and hypocritically indulging ourselves in them. Practice is not simply a matter of engaging in formal religion, professing our intentions and philosophical views, and managing to keep the letter of the precepts and rules.

The *Parting from the Four Attachments* warns us that such pretensions to religious practice only cause increased suffering in this life and the next. The outward appearance of virtuous practice will not help you avoid the least bit of suffering in your next life, nor will it further your progress on the spiritual path. What intelligent person would delude himself with the hope that the requisite conditions for practicing Dharma in the future could be obtained by a mere semblance of religious behavior now? The rare conjuncture of the eighteen essential conditions that enable us to practice is definitely not to be obtained by such means. Even rebirth as a human would be quite difficult to achieve thereby, let alone a human birth that provides all the requisite conditions for effective practice.

Moreover, if you do not attain humanity in your next life, you will experience only suffering, since that is the very nature of nonhuman forms of existence. The karmic forces which govern life in those states are such that you are prevented from practicing Dharma and can only accumulate further demerits. Having once fallen, it is said to be extremely difficult to make it back to the human realm. As Shāntideva put it,

> Since my character is what it is in this life, it is not very likely that
> I will be able to reattain human birth, and if I do not, only sins
> and not virtues will ensue.

And again, in his chapter on wisdom:

> The leisure to study and practice the Dharma is extremely difficult
> to find, and in this world the advent of a buddha to teach us is
> rare. It is so hard for beings to check the flood of delusions; for
> most, life is truly a succession of one sorrow after another.

What would you think of a person who traveled to an island where priceless jewels were available for the taking, and who nonetheless returned empty-handed? If you fail to take advantage of the rare opportunity offered by human existence, you are just as foolish, just as blighted as such a person. When these profound doctrines, practical instructions, and an opportunity to practice them are available, as Shāntideva wrote in his *Bodhicharyāvatara*, "If I don't practice virtue now, after obtaining this opportunity of humanity, surely there is no greater delusion nor any greater deception than this."

The purpose of all these teachings on the rarity of both human existence and the opportunity to practice is to help us develop a better appreciation not only of humanity but of the importance of making diligent efforts while we are unhindered. We are instructed to reflect on these teachings as follows.

After seating yourself as in a regular session of meditation, begin by taking refuge three times in the Three Jewels and reciting three times the resolve to attain enlightenment for the benefit of all living beings. Then reflect in this way:

> Throughout beginningless time, I have experienced one birth after
> another, so that my karmic career thus far resembles a great chain

in which one link leads to the next. All this time, I have had to experience so many unsatisfactory situations and so much pain simply because I was unable to avoid them. Even now, I am still carried away by the processes that govern worldly existence and am almost inextricably involved in the floods of birth, old age, disease, and death. If, in this lifetime, I am not able to make the right efforts that will enable me to get out of this vast machine of birth and death, or cross the ocean of suffering which is worldly existence, then I honestly can't foresee when I shall ever obtain release.

When shall I ever become free from the jaws of the passions—hatred, attachment, lust, pride, ignorance, and the rest? Existence is a great ocean of suffering where passions and delusions are like so many terrible water monsters and crocodiles that afflict helpless beings.

Now that I have obtained the boat of humanity, which, properly used, will enable me to cross this fierce ocean, I must be diligent in making the right efforts. Having obtained humanity, there could be no greater self-deception than mine were I to throw away that boat or lose it through carelessness. From now on, no matter what happens, I must direct all my efforts toward the attainment of liberation. Throughout these efforts, I must consciously make full use of this human existence with which I am endowed.

Now do a step-by-step review of the teaching that human existence can be endowed with the eighteen requisite conditions for practice of the Dharma, which are obtained through the causes of virtue and observance of moral conduct. Next, review the teaching that this human existence is very rare by way of the number of human beings compared to the number of other beings, and by way of its nature. Reflect on all these points to fix in your mind the idea that human existence and the opportunity to practice the Dharma are only rarely obtained.

Next, reflect on the teaching that human existence has the potential for beneficial results, and as such is likened to the discovery of a wish-fulfilling jewel. Then remind yourself that, because of its rarity and the great benefit that the practice of virtue during human life may yield, you resolve not to deceive yourself in throwing away such an opportunity.

Resolve that your practice of religion will be from the heart, without artifice, and effective. You have already resolved to alter your karmic pattern for the better and to rely on right efforts to bring you closer to that exalted state in which you can remove the sufferings of other beings as well. Here, in your practice, become very specific and think:

The practice that I have undertaken to bring about this result is the practice of the lam-dre system of meditation. From now on, I will diligently study and put into practice all the progressive instructions I receive concerning this system. May my teacher, the lineage of gurus through whom these teachings have been transmitted, and the buddhas and bodhisattvas, all of whom are endowed with great compassion, please bestow upon me their blessings, that I may do this sincerely and from the heart. Through their blessings, may my study and practice become effective and a cause of joy and benefit to all beings.

19

JUST SOMEBODY DRESSED IN RED

THE VERY ESSENCE of human existence is said to be the spiritual opportunity to obtain liberation. Hence it is of utmost importance that we who are endowed with humanity and all its favorable conditions apply our minds diligently to right efforts to understand and practice these teachings, which, if followed, surely lead to liberation and spiritual benefit for ourselves and others.

Undertaking the quest for buddhahood is a very important matter in anyone's existence, so it is crucial to rely on trustworthy, authentic instructions for practice. Now, to attain all the results of Mahāyāna Buddhism, we look to the guidance given by the Buddha after he had attained enlightenment himself and, through compassion for the world, explained it to others. His instructions were recorded by his foremost disciples, the arhats, who were present during his lifetime. These teachings were meditated on by the great saints and attainers of spiritual goals, proclaimed and commented on by the greatest Buddhist pandits and philosophers, and translated by the great translators. Whenever you have a teaching that was spoken by the Buddha and compiled by the arhats, bodhisattvas, and translators, you can be sure it is an authentic Mahāyāna doctrine that has been found to be reliable for practice by the greatest minds of Asia for more than two thousand years.

In Tibet, such doctrines were preserved in their entirety by each of the four great traditions, the Gelug, Nyingma, Kagyu, and Sakya. The question of one school or another having more profound doctrines or special, unique doctrines not known to the others does not arise. All are equally profound, and insofar as they are the same teachings, they are equally authentic. About the only difference is the individual traditions or lineages that have been entrusted with the transmission of these doctrines. Therefore, today we have these identical doctrines and instructions preserved for us by four great traditions. The doctrines are the same, and the result of buddhahood to which each points is the same. You can say that, temporarily, there are some differences, but they are mostly conceptual ones. You can also ascribe a name to a particular lineage and say that you are associated with it rather than with another one. But that is really about as far as it goes, and these differences are all on the conventional level of truth only, where people make such distinctions. Ultimately, the goal is the same.

Indeed, when you have attained enlightenment by practicing the teachings of any of these four orders, you will understand that the results obtainable through each are identical. It is very much like buying an airplane ticket to India. There are any number of routes you can take: one of you might go west through Hawaii and Hong Kong to Delhi, another might go through Europe and Bombay, and there are many other routes as well. But the destination is the same. Every one of the planes will land at the airport, and that is exactly the case with these four different schools. They are all talking about the same enlightenment, and all their instructions are aimed at the same spiritual goal.

The teachings that are entrusted to our Sakya order originated with the Primordial Buddha Vajradhara and were transmitted first to the great Indian saint Virūpa, who more than a thousand years ago was the most learned abbot of the great Nālandā University of India. Through his own practice of these instructions, he attained the sixth bhūmi, or stage of bodhisattvahood, and reached perfect buddhahood in one lifetime. He transmitted these teachings to a number of his disciples, such as Krishnapāda and others, and they, in turn, through assiduous practice, also gained enlightenment and transmitted the teachings to the next generation.

In Tibet, these teachings were first conferred upon the great translator Drogmi Shākya Yeshe, who entrusted them to the five founders of the Sakya order, the Five Great Jetsüns. Not only they but a large number of their disciples attained the highest spiritual results through the practice of these same instructions. Many attained buddhahood in one lifetime, while others ascended to the Pure Lands without giving up their physical forms. Ever since that time, in generation after generation, there have been numerous meditators who concentrated on putting these instructions into practice and, as a result, attained spiritual insights. Thus these instructions have been fruitful for more than thirteen hundred years. For many generations of practice, meditators have been attaining the same exalted results of bodhisattvahood and buddhahood.

For the sake of students of this lineage, the instructions have been conveniently divided into two volumes; the first of these consists of the foundational instructions found in our text, *The Three Visions*. We are discussing the first of the three visions, the impure vision of ordinary worldly experience.

DEATH AND IMPERMANENCE

Now we will consider the reflection on impermanence. This reflection is salutary because it (1) teaches us to be alert and mindful in making right efforts, and (2) helps us see our present opportunity to study the Dharma and experience religious practice as the most worthwhile and beneficial work we can possibly do. As Lord Buddha instructed an assembly of monks:

> Monks, one who ponders on impermanence worships the Enlightened Ones; one who ponders on impermanence is prophesied by the Enlightened Ones; one who ponders on impermanence is blessed by the Enlightened Ones. Monks, the footprint of an elephant is chief among footprints, and the perception of impermanence is chief among perceptions.

Reflections on Death and Impermanence

The enlightened ones are made happier by one who reflects on impermanence because they know that his meditation and his efforts to achieve virtue will become diligent and honest rather than self-deluded, self-conceited, or beside the point of religious practice. One who reflects on impermanence is not interested in deceiving himself any more or in merely pretending to be pious in order to deceive others. He knows that impermanence is the nature of all conditioned existence and definitely a part of his own conditioned existence. Thus he is no longer inclined to play at religious practice. Because reflection on impermanence inspires this kind of sincerity, buddhas consider it to be the best kind of worship.

The best way to show respect to the buddhas is to recollect their teachings on the impermanence of all phenomena, which they consider to be the most profound of all doctrines, because it alone can instill in human minds the requisite degree of renunciation to allow all subsequent states of the spiritual path to unfold. Unless you have learned to disentangle your mind from preoccupation with worldly affairs, you will not be able to attune it to the holy phenomena that arise through right practice of the path. When you have developed this spirit of renunciation through remembering impermanence, you will be well established on the path. Finally, a mind influenced by these reflections will be oriented toward beneficial, wholesome matters. Because this is the case, this kind of thinking is said to be the best of all thoughts.

Whether or not you keep in mind this reflection on impermanence determines whether or not you are a religious person. A monk who is not mindful of impermanence is just somebody dressed in red. Anyone who is genuinely religious is first of all aware of impermanence. As *Parting from the Four Attachments* tells us in its very first line, "If you desire this life, you are not a religious person." It is precisely reflection on impermanence that is able to wean the mind from overwhelming attachment to things of this world.

When you seriously admit to consciousness the recognition that you are destined to live only a short while, that human life is by its nature very brief, that the minutes and hours, months and years are passing by at a very rapid rate, that everything you do and every minute that passes only bring you closer to that inevitable time when you will have to leave the affairs of this world, and that this is the nature of all conditioned phenomena—then you can appreciate that some things are a waste of time. People who have set their minds solely on the affairs of this world don't think about whether or not these affairs are really worth such valuable time. But someone who recollects the teachings on impermanence can very quickly decide what is worthwhile and what is not, and will soon become discriminating about his actions. He will be interested in developing wholesome ways of conduct that will sustain him not only in this life but in future lifetimes, and will not be inclined to act blindly or immorally simply to achieve some short-range advantage. In other words, he won't jeopardize his karmic destiny just to gain some selfish advantage or promotion.

To develop the desired state of detachment from deluded affairs of this kind, it is necessary to call to mind the doctrine of impermanence. The teaching of impermanence is likened to a goad or whip that, if applied to an intelligent person, will spur him on to diligent right efforts. The idea of impermanence is beneficial to anyone who brings it to mind. It makes a superior practitioner even more diligent in perfecting himself in right efforts; it makes a mediocre practitioner strive even harder to make progress on the path; and it makes the inferior type of person very keen to find out what the Dharma is all about, causing him to think very seriously about entering some sort of practice.

To sum up, the reflection on impermanence yields inconceivable benefits: (1) it checks desires for things, (2) it becomes a good that stimulates vigor, (3) it is an antidote to sufferings, and (4) it is a helper in realizing ultimate emptiness.

ભ ❧ ભ

Ordinary worldlings like to think that things are more permanent than they are. Rather than wishing to see things as transitory, they want to hold on to the things they are attached to, such as their own existence. Hence they like to promise themselves long lives and a lot of time in which to make their dreams come true. They are not honestly interested in thinking that there is no length of time at all that is guaranteed to them. If people were willing to see the transitoriness of all phenomena, including their own existence, their value systems would be radically altered.

The belief in permanence is the very first wrong view that Buddhism seeks to overturn, and the reflection on death and impermanence is the tool for accomplishing that change in perception. This reflection is effective because it corresponds to the true facts, whereas the belief in permanence cannot be supported by any honest examination of human existence. By reflecting on impermanence, you will recognize that human life really is brief and that it is folly to throw it away on pointless, energy-wasting, even harmful activities.

To give one example, my own root guru, Gatön Ngawang Legpa Rinpoche,[42] started out as an ordinary Buddhist monk in Kham, the eastern province of Tibet. He wasn't recognized as a reincarnated lama; he was just an ordinary monk. He happened to go to Ngor Monastery, and there he heard the complete lam-dre teaching from two different masters. He heard the exoteric explanation from Ngawang Lodro Nyingpo and the esoteric instructions from Jamyang Rinchen Dorje. He returned to his homeland in the district of Ga, and there he built a small retreat in the mountains, not too far from his village of birth, and sealed himself inside. He made a small window, through which water from the nearby stream and food brought to him from his relatives could be handed to him, and went into retreat for fifteen years. The first three years he meditated solely on *The Three Visions*. The first year he devoted to reflection on impermanence; then he meditated on the whole of *The Three Visions* for the next two years. For the remaining twelve years he meditated on the advanced practices of *The Three Continua*. He attained the spiritual results and, at the end of the fifteen years, was recognized throughout Tibet as the great teacher Ngawang Legpa Rinpoche. He was famed as one of Tibet's greatest masters of modern times, and his fame continues to the present day. We ourselves are benefiting from the diligence with which he meditated those many years ago.

This is a concrete example of the results that can ensue from reflecting on impermanence. It is said that it is the preliminary practices—namely, the taking of refuge and reflection on impermanence—that are the profound doctrines. All the profound doctrines are given at the beginning; the advanced practices are just natural consequences of those profound insights and that reorientation of mental energies which occur at the preliminary stages. There is a saying that, "Of the profound preliminary practices and the esoteric advanced practices, it is the deep teachings that are given first." Without gaining the realizations and being truly affected through these preliminary practices, there cannot be any advanced realizations.

Thus Gatön Rinpoche did not merely perform the requisite quotas of a hundred thousand prostrations, a hundred thousand recitations of the refuge formula, an equal number of recitations of the hundred-syllable mantra of Vajrasattva, and so forth. He recited the refuge formula 2.7 million times. He performed the mandala ceremony 1.8 million times, and so forth and so on. He wasn't concerned with merely establishing his right to enter advanced practices or with filling a standard quota. He realized that it is only through a solid foundation of preliminary practices that we can hope to achieve the exalted results of advanced practices.

That he was quite right is evidenced by his career after he emerged from retreat. In his biography, it is said that he went about the preliminary practices in a very patient, mindful way. Every morning, without fail, he performed the meditation of great compassion and recited five thousand mantras. In this way he recited *Om mani padme hum* more than a hundred million times in his lifetime. He recited the *Shejama* (*Shes bya ma*), the well-known verse of praise to Sakya Pandita, more than 6.5 million times. This verse is an invocation of the great wisdom, compassion, and spiritual power that Sakya Pandita attained in his lifetime through much the same practices. To give a quick translation of that verse, it runs something like:

> All cognizable things, his wide eyes perceive;
> Merciful one who achieves the weal of all living beings,
> Having the power to perform activities transcending thought,
> At the foot of that guru who is Mañjushrī, I reverently bow.

In this and other practices, we can see that Gatön Rinpoche wasn't impatient to skim over the preliminaries. Instead, he concentrated on each in its proper context and mastered it, without any hurry to move ahead to "heavier" practice. As a result, he did more advanced practices and attained the most excellent results there, also; and he gained the ability to spread the benefits of his attainments on a much wider scale, geographically and through time, than most other teachers. That he did attain the highest results is evidenced by the fact that very often the great founders of the Sakya order—Virūpa, Jetsūn Dragpa Gyaltsen, and others—appeared to him openly and expounded the doctrine. The great Sakya Pandita also appeared to him frequently, and it is said that he was always attended, visibly, by the protector Mahākāla. At the age of sixty-eight, Gatön Rinpoche had established all his disciples on the path, founded a great monastery, and performed great work for the Dharma. At that time, he told me and others that he had decided to leave the world, that he would ascend to the Pure Land of Sukhāvatī, and that he did not intend to reincarnate.

The Certainty of Death

The reflection on impermanence also leads us to face up to our own mortality and recognize that death is the fate of all conditioned phenomena. By "conditioned phenomena" we mean anything that arises through causes and that is dependent on other causes and conditions. Any animate or inanimate phenomenon whose existence is brought about through other conditions or causes is a conditioned phenomenon; human beings also qualify for that status.

Death Is the Fate of All Conditioned Phenomena. When you recognize that everything that is brought into existence inevitably has death lying in store for it, you realize that you yourself are not exempt from this natural process; indeed, from the very moment of conception everyone proceeds toward death, and every second that passes leads inexorably toward that moment.

This is the case not only with us, but with all living beings: whoever they are, wherever they are, they are all involved in this same process; by having been born, they are on their way to death. Of all the countless millions of beings who have lived in former generations, not one remains alive on the surface of this earth. All around us, every day and at all times, young, old, and middle-aged people are dying or are on the verge of death; at a not too distant time in the future, everyone living today will have passed away as a result of being involved in this same process.

Have you heard of anyone who is exempt from old age and death, and do you have any reason for thinking that somehow you will escape this same fate? It is quite certain that you will die, so it is better to face up to this aspect of your situation, especially when it can serve you in a very salutary way. By remembering that death is certain and that the time of death is uncertain, you can make the best possible use of the time, life, and energies you now have.

The following quotation from the *Jātaka Tales* (*Garland of Past-Life Tales*) is relevant:

> Beginning from the night when they first entered the womb, all these people are swiftly, inexorably drawing nearer to the Lord of Death. This is the path on which they have embarked, and they do not swerve elsewhere.

Even arhats, bodhisattvas, and buddhas relinquish their bodies. Although the buddhas and bodhisattvas have gained mastery over birth and death, in keeping with the natural process of death, they pretend to pass away. Lord Shākyamuni himself, to inspire his disciples to more diligent efforts, gave up his own aggregates and passed over into nirvāṇa. Thus even the purified bodies of these great saints are not exempt from death. As for ordinary folk like ourselves, our existence is governed from beginning to end by desire, hatred, and delusion, and birth and death are part of the warp and woof of these forces of ignorance.

Therefore, there is no place at all where you might hope to be born in order to become exempt from death. Death travels everywhere. He is not barred from any locale, whether in the heavens or the lowest regions. There is no place beyond his reach. As it says in Ashvaghosha's *Dispelling Sorrow* (*Śoka-vinodana*):

> The great sages endowed with the five kinds of prescient knowledge traveled far into space, and yet were unable to reach any place where death did not occur.

And in the *Dhammapada* we are told that:

> No matter where you might dwell, there is no place to which death does not penetrate—neither in the sky nor in the oceans' depths, nor in the crevasses of a mountain.

Death Is Certain Because the Human Body Is Insubstantial. Now we will focus on these human bodies of ours and try to see how, by their very nature, they are inextricably involved in dying. In the *Exalted Utterance* (*Udāna-varga*) there is a verse that runs:

> Compounds, alas, are impermanent. Things that arise also perish. Having been born, they come to destruction. It is well, therefore, to bring them to conclusions.

Generally speaking, all compounded phenomena (i.e., anything that has arisen through a concatenation of causes and conditions, such as our own human bodies) are by their very nature nothing more than perishable and momentary. As such, they are not really fit receptacles for our confidence. In other words, we cannot rely on such transitory, insubstantial phenomena as sources of our own well-being, much less of our mental and spiritual good.

Even external phenomena, things which seem truly huge—colossal, very firm, solid, endurable—are not immune to decay and destruction, no matter how gigantic they might be. Even objects the size of a planet or a world system are not finally exempt from the process of destruction. Natural phenomena—oceans, mountains, worlds, planets—are all fashioned out of the collective karma of human beings. It is said in Buddhist literature that even these world systems are destroyed at the end of an aeon, and that there will come a time when space will be completely empty of planets and other bodies. If destruction occurs on such a vast scale as that, what real hope can we cling to that our own frail human bodies, which are quite tender by their very nature, will somehow endure and avoid death, simply because we very much want it to be like that? As Ārya Nāgārjuna wrote in his *Letter from a Friend*:

> If even ashes will not remain of the great masses of earth, of the great Mount Sumeru and all the oceans—if all these will eventually be burned up by the blaze of seven suns, what, then, to say of we frail human beings?

Among animate beings, we have only to look at the enlightened ones. The body of the Buddha was compounded not of defilements (as are those of ordinary beings) but of the great merit he had acquired, yet even his pure body was impermanent. What to say, then, of our own insubstantial bodies, born as a result of karmic propensity and delusion? In *Dispelling Sorrow* it is written:

> If even the Vajra bodies, adorned by the marks and signs of perfection, are nonetheless impermanent, what to say, then, of these bubblelike bodies of ours, which, like plantain trees, are utterly devoid of essence?

The point is that we should give up the fond delusion that our bodies, to which we are so attached and on which we lavish so much tender loving care, are going to endure. No matter how much we love them, they will not last long, and because they are transitory by their very nature, they are deceitful. In other words, these bodies deceive us in that, through our attachment to them, we spend an immoderate amount of energy caring for their comfort, indulging in sense gratification, and so forth. In short, because of them we are accumulating unwholesome karma that is not in our own best interests.

In the final analysis, a human body is something that will eventually be turned into ashes, thrown into the water, or devoured by insects. Perhaps it will be dried up by the heat of the sun, become food for worms, or be carried away by the winds. It will be scattered and dissolved. Nāgārjuna summarizes this line of thought in his *Letter from a Friend*:

> The body at last becomes ashes. At last it sinks down into water, or at last it dries up. At last it turns into filth devoid of essence, or at last it is completely destroyed and rots.

Death Is Certain Because Human Life Is Impermanent. This is the third reason for being absolutely convinced that death is inevitable for us as individuals. If, in general, you understand that all conditioned phenomena are impermanent because they are momentary by nature and consist only of discrete, consecutive moments of existence, then it is easy to realize that the life of a human being is also impermanent. And among all conditioned phenomena, there is said to be nothing more rapid than the exhaustion of human life. To give an example, if a very agile archer were to shoot an arrow in each of the four directions, and a very fast runner were able to chase down and catch each of those four arrows before it fell to the ground, that would be pretty fast. But the hungry ghosts are said to move even more swiftly than that; the progressions of the sun and moon in their orbits are said to be even swifter than the speed of those pretas; even faster than the sun and moon are the gods; and even faster than the movement of the gods is the exhaustion of human life.

If life is decreased by each single moment that occurs, and each moment is seen in this light, then how else are we to view the passing of whole minutes, hours, days, weeks, months, and years? From the moment of birth right up to this present moment, your life has been inexorably decreasing. Even since yesterday, your life span has shortened. As Shāntideva wrote, "Day and night, this life decreases, and in no way does it increase."

20

THE GREAT FISHER, DEATH

IT IS SALUTARY to begin our session of study with the reflection that we are extremely fortunate in having obtained human birth in a time and place that enable us to encounter the teachings of liberation. Further, we are fortunate in having met qualified teachers willing and able to help us understand those instructions correctly and undertake their right practice. Indeed, we are among the most fortunate of living beings.

Realizing this, we should not for a moment become inclined to waste such a rare opportunity. On the contrary, we must remain diligent and mindful and, above all, concerned to make progress in actual practice as long as we have the opportunity to do so. As Mahāyānists, there are two sets of teachings available to us: the exoteric teachings of the pāramitā path and the esoteric teachings of the Vajrayāna path. These are preserved in their entirety in the four great traditions of Tibetan Buddhism (the Nyingma, Kagyu, Gelug, and Sakya). We are studying the teachings of the Sakyapa, where the Mahāyāna and Vajrayāna teachings are expounded in two stages: the preliminary, or preparatory, stage of practice and the advanced stage. Our studies are concentrated on two texts, the first of which is known as *The Three Visions*, on which our present discourse is based.

The instructions of the three visions do not differ in any essential way from similar instructions found in the teachings of the other Tibetan schools, whether the four reflections for turning the mind of the Nyingma and Kagyu orders, or the graduated path of the three types of practitioners of the Gelug order. All serve the same purpose of turning the mind away from overweening involvement in worldly activities and reorienting it toward spiritual goals. When this has been accomplished, it is fruitful to practice the preliminary exercises, such as taking refuge, awakening the resolve to win enlightenment, meditating on great love and great compassion, and so on. All these are paramount at the first stages of entering the actual path of spiritual experience. All the sets of instructions found in each of the four schools are identical in their substance and in their effect. It is foolishness to prize one set over the others or to accept one and reject the others. There is no way to distinguish superiority or inferiority either among these sets of teachings or among the four traditions themselves.

We will now continue our study of the topics of death and impermanence, with the intention of stimulating diligent, sincere practice by pointing out the dangers of continued carelessness, laziness, and procrastination. The topic of impermanence is discussed to help us awaken within ourselves a sense of the transitoriness of human life itself. In Buddhist literature, four examples are given to describe the fleeting nature of human life. Far from seeing the human life span as a considerable length of time in which we will have ample opportunity to accomplish all our aims, we are asked to see human life as a commodity that is, by its very nature, hard to come by and hard to retain. Moment by moment, it is quickly passing out of our grasp.

The four examples are these: human life is like (1) a mountain waterfall, (2) a prisoner being led to the place of execution, (3) fish that have swum into a fisherman's net, and (4) animals that have been led into the pens of a slaughterhouse.

First, the human life span is likened to a mountain waterfall that plunges over a precipice and, having begun its descent, can in no way be turned back until it has reached the bottom of the slope. Just as water falling from a mountain rushes downward faster and faster, with more and more momentum as it goes along, never reversing its downward course, so human life passes quickly away and never swerves from its destination. Once born, a human does nothing but proceed toward the moment of death. Every action he performs, every breath he breathes, every moment he lives only brings him closer to that inevitable moment when he leaves this world, his body, and the human state that he temporarily enjoys.

Next, human life is likened to the situation of fish that have swum into a fisherman's net from which no escape is possible.[43] Nothing happens except that, one by one, fish are plucked out of the net and perish in the dry air, until not a single fish remains. Humans are like fish in that they are all caught in a situation where they are highly vulnerable to death; indeed, not a single one will escape. As the *Bodhicharyāvatara* says:

> We have been chased into the net of birth by the fishers that are the defilements; greed, hatred, and delusion have herded us into this net of birth. Having entered, there is no way we can escape being caught by the Great Fisher, Death.

Finally, human beings are like so many animals that have been driven into the pens of a slaughterhouse where, one by one, they are hauled off and killed. Without fully appreciating that they are in such imminent danger, they wait in the pens, still drinking water, eating, sleeping, and playing about. There the sheep and lambs gambol without any thought for their fate, although it is staring them in the face. We, too, have been herded into the pens of birth. Death is eyeing us right now, with only one intention for each of us: our destruction. Yet we don't feel any sense of alarm, even though every day, all around us, we see first one person and then another being plucked away by death. We somehow manage to ignore that and content ourselves with food, drink, and entertainment, passing the time in sleep and idle activities. We don't see that all the escape routes have been closed. Like a water buffalo slumbering in a butcher's yard, we give no thought to the real facts of our situation and fail to take action until the butcher is ready for us.

Reflect for a moment on whether or not the human situation is correctly described here. Of all the past generations of humans who have lived on the face of this earth, how many remain? Of all the millions of people in each human generation, didn't all of them—men, women, and children—meet with death? In the present, aren't people dying left, right, and center? Isn't it a fact that every day we hear of people who have died? Haven't you lost friends, relatives, and parents? Haven't you heard of people, both strangers and relatives, who have suddenly died? Aren't you convinced that everyone who is living today, in this generation and this time, will sooner or later meet his or her demise? Isn't it likely that the lot of future generations will be similar to our own in this respect?

All these reflections help us face the fact that human life is not to be taken for granted. We should not make the mistake of promising ourselves longevity and much time for future practice. Though painful, the reflection on death is also healthy, in that it helps us to become honest about our human life span and inclines us to value more highly our present opportunity for beneficial practice.

Now we have the more detailed instructions for how to reflect on human impermanence. As always, be seated for a regular session of meditation. Begin with taking refuge and awakening the aspiration to attain enlightenment for the sake of all beings; then proceed in this way:

> Human existence is hard to obtain and, once obtained, quickly
> passes away. Human life passes like a mountain waterfall; human

existence is like the death wait of a condemned animal. It is like the plight of a fish caught in a fisherman's net, like that of an animal waiting to be slaughtered in the butcher's pit.

All the generations of human beings who lived in the past have died, without exception. Even now, all around me, humans have died, are dying, or are growing nearer to their inevitable deaths. In the future, the human situation with regard to death will remain the same. Since death is the lot of all who have been born, and since even the buddhas and bodhisattvas are not exempt from this process, I have no reason to expect that I can somehow evade my own death.

Since I have neither assurance that my life will be a long one nor any guarantee that my death will not occur suddenly, at any moment, it is only fitting that I should face up to my situation and make the most of the opportunity that my human existence affords. I must reflect on death and impermanence diligently and repeatedly, in order to stimulate my mind to sincere, persistent practice now, while I am able. I must not allow myself to procrastinate in the practice of religion, nor to practice lazily or insincerely. In the lam-dre system of meditation that I have undertaken, may my teacher and the teachers of that lineage bestow upon me their blessings, that I might practice diligently and without self-deception.

The human body is frail; it is born of causes and conditions, fashioned by karma and mental defilements such as attachment, aversion, and delusion. Though to us the human body, which we cherish so much, is everything, its true nature is not only impermanent but insubstantial. It is changing every instant. The tender human body, which can't stand even slight extremes of heat or cold, pain or abuse, actually seems intended for destruction rather than endurance.

According to Indian mythology, Mount Sumeru is the epitome of firmness, steadiness, and endurance. Yet even Sumeru, the sun, the moon, the planets, the great mountain ranges and oceans are destined to be destroyed at the end of the aeon. It is said that seven great suns will arise simultaneously in the sky to dry up the oceans and reduce Mount Sumeru to particles of dust, so that it vanishes and not an atom remains. If that kind of destruction occurs for these great physical bodies, what hope have we that our delicate human organisms will somehow evade the process of destruction?

Think in this way sincerely, from your heart; again and again bring to mind the resolve that you are going to practice diligently. Conclude by dedicating the merit. By thus reflecting on the insubstantiality of this human body with which you are temporarily endowed, you will strengthen your resolve to put it to the best possible use while you do have it, unencumbered by obstacles and uninterrupted by death.

21

DISCARDED IN SOME DARK HOLE

AT THIS STAGE in our study of *The Three Visions*, it is good to keep each session of study in its proper context. It will suffice to remind you that *The Three Visions* is divided into three sets of instructions. The first corresponds to the impure vision of ordinary, worldly experience. The instructions on this level are intended to awaken within us a sense of detachment from the things of this life. The second set corresponds to the vision of the path. The instructions on this level are designed to help us awaken a special spiritual attitude toward ourselves, others, and the practices in which we are engaged. This means that we are trained to develop a broader interpretation of the spiritual life, so that our efforts are directed toward achieving the highest spiritual benefit for both ourselves and others, rather than for ourselves alone. The third set of instructions concerns the pure perception of enlightened beings. These are designed so that we can develop an accurate conception of that toward which we are striving. These last instructions, as contained in this book, are primarily to awaken a sense of enthusiasm for the attainment of that result.[44]

We are presently engaged in learning the instructions for the first stage of perception, the impure vision. Here the major teachings concern (1) recognition of the nature of worldly existence as a whole, (2) reflection on the difficulty of obtaining human birth and the opportunity to practice the Dharma, (3) recollection of the imminence of death and the all-pervasiveness of impermanence, and (4) the operation of the law of karma, which conditions our present and future states of existence. We have fairly thoroughly discussed the first two of these and are now considering the reflection on death and impermanence.

As we have said, reflecting on impermanence is salutary, in that an appreciation of the brevity of human life and the certainty of death inspires us to take seriously the instructions for practice and helps us to awaken a sincere attitude toward practice. That is, it goads us into making the best use of our present opportunity and prevents us from deceiving ourselves or others by merely playing around at practice rather than doing it properly.

Unless we have some perception of impermanence as it affects human life, it is very difficult to awaken a genuine interest in the teachings of renunciation and diligent practice that we encounter in Mahāyāna Buddhism. Thus we can understand why most people don't become interested in the teachings of Buddhism. Even when they encounter these teachings, they don't feel motivated to take any special interest in them, simply because their attention is preoccupied elsewhere. The teachings don't strike them with the same force that they do more clear-minded folk. But when you are inclined to take seriously the teachings on impermanence, you will find that your practice on any level and of any type of Mahāyāna meditation becomes enriched through your increased awareness of the uniqueness of the situation. Your meditational practice becomes much more effective because of your increased sincerity and diligence.

We have said that diligence is the key to success in following the spiritual path. Unless you are able to sustain your practice through diligent effort, there is no way you can experience the stages of the path as they are known to other practitioners. This diligence, which is the sine qua non for advanced experience, cannot be feigned or forced; it can only be stimulated through right thinking about impermanence. Impermanence is the most helpful of all reflections because it forces us to lay aside all self-deception, pretension, and inclination to be lazy and, in a word, insincere.

We have already explained how to reflect on the certainty of death and the uncertainty of the time of death. If, even after doing so, you still don't have a keen sense of death's imminence and your own impermanence—if your life span still seems to be a fairly reliable stretch of time, and you feel no anxiety about the prospect of death—again sit in meditation and reflect in this way:

> Right now I am quite free from disease, am not unhappy, have all the requisites for continued life, and seem likely to continue to live for a good while; moreover, I enjoy food, clothing, and comfortable furniture, and am surrounded by relatives and friends, while my time is being passed in an interesting and, on the whole, quite pleasant way. Yet precisely because this is my present experience, I must be very careful not to lose sight of the prospect of death. Though it is natural that I should want to settle down in the present, enjoying these experiences and hoping to live a long time, it doesn't take too much foresight to see that eventually my situation will change and I will be separated from all this.

There will come a time when I will have to set out on a long journey and will no longer see any of the people and places I now enjoy. At that time I will have to travel alone, in unknown and possibly fearful regions. Since that time is approaching with every moment that passes, and it is certain that I must one day face it, it is better for me to keep it in mind now, in order to become mentally prepared for what is to follow by practicing, to the best of my ability, the teachings of enlightenment. Though I am weak in motivation and inclination to practice, I pray that my teachers and the Three Jewels will compassionately bestow upon me their blessings, that I may become mindful of my own impermanence and better prepared for the advent of my own death.

Think in roughly this fashion, and reflect again and again until this mood "takes," so that you are praying sincerely from the heart. Coupled with the descriptions and teachings that we have already covered, this should be all you need to awaken the recollection of death.

In the *Advice to a King Sūtra* (*Rāja-avavādaka-sūtra*), further instructions are given for timely reflections on our subjection to death and impermanence. To paraphrase that sūtra, it is said that you should make a special effort to bring to mind your own imminent death at the very times when you are most preoccupied with worldly affairs. For example, when you are engaged in a pleasant conversation, consciously bring to mind the teachings of impermanence and remind yourself,

> Though now I am enjoying pleasing conversation with my friends, the time will definitely come when I shall be totally separated from them.

When eating, no matter how pleasant the situation or how delicious the food itself might be, deliberately bring to mind the thought,

> Even though I am enjoying a pleasant meal now, on my deathbed I will not have any interest whatsoever in food or drink. Even if I have an opportunity to eat there, it won't benefit me at all.

When putting on your best clothes, think,

> Now I am wearing fine clothes, but the time will surely come when I will be wrapped up in stiff clothing and thrown away.

When riding in a comfortable automobile, remind yourself,

> Now I am riding in a fine car, but that time will surely come when
> I will be carried away by the pallbearers.

And when seated on a comfortable chair or sofa, reflect,

> Now I am seated on a fine seat, but that time will surely come
> when I shall be discarded in some dark hole in the ground.

Even with these rather gloomy reflections, try to impress on your mind
the sense that they will really come to pass. It is quite true that, though you
are now experiencing all the enjoyments of an active life, there will come a
time when you will be forcibly separated from all this. By very consciously
trying to bring these reflections to mind, even in the midst of your normal
moments of pleasure, you will find that your remembrance of death and
impermanence is gradually strengthened and reinforced.

This reflection serves to awaken within us a sense of the brevity of the
present opportunity we now have for serious practice. Rather than promising ourselves a long life, we learn to shorten our time range so that we no
longer think in terms of many years or many decades in which to accomplish everything as we hope; instead, we learn not to take the future for
granted. This heightens our appreciation for the present opportunity and
reinforces the sincerity with which we make present efforts.

The Uncertainty of the Time of Death

There is no certainty about the time of death because (1) there is no fixed
limit to the human life span, (2) the causes of death are manifold, and (3)
the causes for uninterrupted life are few.

The first of these subtopics is discussed in this way: Generally, a person who
is contemplating whether or not to make religious efforts or take up some
system of meditation will be inclined to find reasons for procrastinating.
Even though, intellectually, he agrees that death is certain, he likes to think
that "At present I'm in good health, and it's most likely that I will continue
to enjoy good health for quite some time. There is still time to practice.
Although I should definitely make efforts before the time of death, I feel
justified in waiting until the situation is just right for practice. In the meantime I am really not ready to renounce pleasures, so I think I'll enjoy them
for a few more years; when I'm a bit older I'll find myself naturally ready to
give them up. Starting then, I will be serious about my practice."

He might also think, "I really should practice right away, I can see that, but my circumstances are such that I should work for another year, save some money, and make the optimum arrangement for all that diligent practice I'm going to do, so I'll start those things next year."

This kind of thinking is just so much self-deception. First of all, there is no guarantee of being able to practice in the future. If you think you do have such a guarantee, who was it who gave you his word that it will happen as you wish? If you plan to practice next year, perhaps, or in the last half of your life, what guarantee have you that it will really happen that way? What certainty have you that you will live that long?

If you are honest, you will have to admit that you don't know whether you will be here next year or already in your next life. You can't even be sure that you will be here next month, or next week. When you come right down to it, you really don't know whether you are going to be alive or in the bardo tomorrow morning. As it is said in the *Exalted Utterance*,

> Since there is no certainty whether tomorrow or the next life will come first, it is certainly right to make efforts now for the sake of the next life, instead of for the sake of tomorrow.

The *Abhidharmakosha* also explains the reasons for this:

> In this world, the end of human life is uncertain, even though the life span of humans on the other three continents is fixed, and ranges from ten years up to a very large number of years. On this continent of Jambudvīpa, human life is of no fixed duration. Also, there is no collective karma that might determine some common length of the human life.

To return to the *Exalted Utterance*:

> Some people die while still in the womb, some upon being born; some die while still crawling about, some while learning to walk. Some die when they are old, and some die when they are young. Some die while still in the prime of life, and others like the fading of ripened fruit. But, one by one, they all go.

Thus there is not the least reason for our unexamined confidence that our lives will not come to a close this very day. We have no assurance at all that we will not die before the day is over. As the *Bodhicharyāvatara* tells us:

> It is not intelligent to think that "Even though I am going to die, it is not going to happen today." We have no assurance whatsoever

for continued life, whereas it is certain that death could come at any moment.

Second, we don't know when death will strike us down because the causes of death are manifold. Even when we try to reassure ourselves of a long life span by means of reasoning, we find no cause for comfort. In fact, we can give three very good reasons for positing a shorter, rather than a longer, lifetime:

(a) The body and the life force are very easily separated. The body is a delicate machine; human life is a very subtle, very fragile force. It doesn't take much to separate a body from life.

(b) Death comes to everyone. Death is absolutely unkind. There is no way that death can be avoided. The usual human stratagems to avoid pain or unpleasant situations are of no use whatsoever when dealing with death.

(c) The hostile forces that rob us of human life are innumerable—disease, malignant spirits, dangerous situations, adversity, deprivation of the requirements for life, such as air and water, and so on. There are any number of diseases to which we can fall prey, and any number of life-destroying situations into which we could tumble at any moment.

With regard to the first of these, it may seem that a certain additional portion of time is likely to come our way and that we still have a bit of living to do, but in fact there is no way to know whether or not that time will suddenly be interrupted by an unfortunate concatenation of forces. Consider a lamp that is extinguished by a sudden gust of wind, even though its wick is still in working order and there is plenty of oil in its container. Although some conditions for its continuing to burn remain present, it is roughly extinguished. In the same way, our lives can be extinguished suddenly by any one of a number of forces, despite other conditions that make us think they will continue. As Ārya Nāgārjuna phrased it in his *Letter from a Friend*, "Like the flame of a lamp shaken by a strong wind, there is no confidence that this life will endure for even a single moment more."

Nāgārjuna gives further counsel on how to reflect on this. He says that we should recognize that the body and mind are very easily separated. It is a wonder that one inhalation follows another; it is a cause for surprise every time we wake up in the morning; it is a miracle that we continue to endure despite the many causes for death and the few for our continued existence. As he also wrote in the *Letter from a Friend*,

There are many adversities in this life, and, as with a lamp caught in a strong wind, the duration of human life is uncertain. Human life is more fleeting than a water bubble. It is truly a great wonder that inhalation follows exhalation and that, after falling asleep, one nonetheless awakens.

Next, there is no certainty about the time of death because death cannot be moved or evaded. Death is cruel. Death has no other thought, no other intent than to take away your life. There's not the slightest chance that Death is going to take a look at you and say, "What a nice, friendly, good-hearted fellow this is. I think we'll let him carry on for a little while longer." Death is in no way interested in letting you off the hook. Like a hunter chasing down a deer, his only thought being to catch it and kill it, when Death draws near you, he never swerves from his single thought of killing you. As Shāntideva wrote in his *Bodhicharyāvatara*, "No reliance can be placed upon the Lord of Death."

Finally, there is no certainty about the time of death because the hostile forces of illness and malignant spirits are many. Let's consider in some detail the various causes of death. Death can occur when either the outer or inner elements are disturbed. When the outer elements of earth, air, fire, and water become imbalanced or agitated, you can lose your life as a result. And inwardly, either through extremes of heat or cold or a disturbance of the natural balance of elements within your body, you might very easily die. Death can occur if you are afflicted by evil spirits who, for one reason or another, cause you to grow ill or even to commit suicide. You can also be buried in a landslide, carried away by a flood, caught in a burning building, whirled away by a tornado, and the like; all these things could kill you as well, and they happen all the time to other humans.

If, internally, the element of earth becomes disturbed, you might die of some convulsive disorder. If the element of water is disturbed, you might get one of the heart diseases that would do you in. If the fire element is thrown into imbalance, you might die of fever. Also, it doesn't take too much imagination to think of the various ways you could die just going about your daily affairs. Even the very food you eat could become a cause of death. People lose their lives to other beings, whether malignant spirits or murderers. You might be killed by strangers, friends, or even relatives; practially anyone could suddenly decide to kill you.

There are hundreds and hundreds of different kinds of diseases that affect other humans all the time. People are dying all around you because of them. You can't be immune to all of these illnesses, and it is conceivable that you might suddenly contract one that could kill you. Political situations can also develop in such a way that you might be killed in a war, through social disturbances, and so forth.

Third, the time of death is uncertain because the causes of uninterrupted life are few. What does it take to maintain human life? You need the sustenance of food and drink, you need warmth to protect you from the cold, and you need shelter to protect you from the elements. All these sustain life, but they are very few in number, whereas the things that deprive you of life number in the thousands and are encountered every day. Moreover, even something that ordinarily sustains life can become a cause of death: food cooked improperly can turn into poison; shelter built to protect you from the elements can collapse or catch on fire, trapping you inside; even your relatives and friends can turn against you in an instant and deprive you of your life.

Nor is it only the diseased who fade away and die; death often strikes people in the prime of health. As we said, young children and people in their youth, with no thought of death and no indication of its approach, can be struck down, while those who are bedridden and weakened by disease may live on for many more years. Mere health at present is no reason to take long life for granted.

To summarize: human life is a delicate, fragile situation that is sustained by a very narrow range of causes and conditions. Only optimum causes and conditions sustain further life. Life is beset on all sides by many unfavorable conditions and hostile forces that can very easily bring death at any moment, even when you are young and in good health. As Āryadeva's *Four Hundred Verses* describes it, "Human life is so frail and beset by such powerful adversities that you humans seem to be designed for dying, meant to die, or not meant to live."

In conclusion, reflect on the uncertainty of the time of your death by reflecting in this way:

> Though at present I enjoy good health and am fortunate in having the conditions for continued life, it would be a grave mistake were I to take for granted the prospect of a long life span. My continued existence is dependent on conditions that are very easily thrown into imbalance and that can very easily turn into the causes of my

death. The causes of death are many, and, like other humans, I am liable to fall prey to any one of them, whether external or internal. Whether I am set upon by disease, hostile beings, or any other cause, I am at all times vulnerable to sudden death.

Since this is so, I should be honest with myself and give up the habit of thinking that I will have a long life in which to practice the Dharma rightly. With this in mind, I must value more highly my present opportunity to put into practice the teachings I have received. I must strive to develop the spiritual qualities within myself now, while I am living and not experiencing obstacles or interruptions. The teaching that I must practice is this teaching of the *Lam dre*. May my teacher and the Three Jewels bestow upon me their blessings, that without any further delay I might be able to do this.

Even though reflecting in this way may not seem a very appealing pastime, or even a profound one, its effects are remarkable. For example, there was a wealthy Tibetan merchant who lived not very far from Sakya. I myself visited this merchant, whose name was Lhatsa Kargyal, in his very beautiful palace; I knew the man. Lhatsa Kargyal was one of the richest men in Tibet, he was the Rockefeller of Sakya, so he was, of course, well known for being a successful businessman. But at one point in his life he decided to start practicing, and he began by meditating on death and impermanence. Although he wasn't a particularly well-educated or even a very bright person (despite his great success in business), he took the teachings to heart and really reflected on them. As a result, he was deeply impressed by the facts that he himself really would die and that it was not intelligent to cling too much to the affairs of this life or to act selfishly just for evanescent gains.

After meditating for a while on death and impermanence, Lhatsa Kargyal became very generous. He went down to the great monastery of Tashilhunpo and offered barrels of grain to each of the four thousand-odd monks there, giving them provisions to see them through many months of study and meditation. He became a great supporter of other monasteries as well, and used his wealth very liberally in promoting the study and practice of Buddhism. He built stūpas for circumambulation and *mani* wheels[45] for the use of devout villagers; he turned his palace into a virtual monastery by inviting eight monks to live there full time, saying many prayers.

Next, he himself became a monk. Not only that, but his wife became a nun, and all his children became monks and nuns. They all renounced lay life as a result of the influence that reflecting on impermanence had on this one man.

Finally, Lhatsa Kargyal fell ill and was no longer able to practice. Despite the prayers that were said and the medicine that the doctors prescribed, he continued to weaken and found himself on his deathbed. His family and attendants were very grief-stricken, but he called them all to his side and told them:

> There is really no point in taking it this way. In fact, I have been prepared for this moment for a very long time, knowing that sooner or later I would have to die and that it would probably be very much like this. Now that death is here, I don't feel unprepared. Knowing that I've used my wealth and time to meditate and to help others meditate, I certainly have no remorse about any of the good things I have managed to do. I don't have any real anxiety about my future, either. I really don't feel any unhappiness, even though I am on my deathbed. I am concerned for you all and do want to urge that you spend the rest of your lives in devoted practice of the Dharma. Learn all you can and help others, also, to practice. So please be careful yourselves.

This is one example of how radically an ordinary life can be changed simply by giving some thought to these teachings on death and impermanence.

22

A PROTECTOR, AN ISLAND, A GREAT FRIENDLY HOST

AMONG THE MANY DOORS of Mahāyāna doctrine through which practitioners can gain entrance to the insights that are the special feature of this spiritual path, we are concerned with one of the most illustrious, the lamdre system of meditative theory and practice. This system has rightly been called the jewel of the Sakya order. As we have explained, the *Lam dre* is divided, for the sake of convenience, into fundamental and advanced teachings. *The Three Visions* and *The Three Continua* are the two texts that correspond to these two sets of teachings. We are presently concerned with the first of these. The three visions refer to three stages of perception to be discerned on the Mahāyāna path.

The first of the three is called the impure vision. This alludes to the uncritical perception of ordinary worldly folk, whose mental grasp of the objects of perception is governed or influenced by mental poisons such as desire, hatred, delusion, and the like. Because their perception is said to be uncritical and sullied by passions, it is called "impure." Our text first presents a set of instructions that are to be studied and practiced as a remedy for the errors of this impure point of view.

The second stage is called the vision of experience, or of the path. Here a person's perception of phenomena—internal and external—is shaped by the meditative experiences undergone in Mahāyāna training.

The third level of is called the pure vision, or the perception of enlightened beings. Although there is no longer anything to be practiced at this stage, unenlightened practitioners can benefit from a description of the spiritual qualities and characteristics of the enlightened state.

To reiterate, we are presently engaged in a discussion of those teachings which correspond to the first level of perception. There are three major topics to be discussed here: (1) the reflection on the unsatisfactoriness of worldly existence as a whole, that is, on the painful characteristics of unenlightened existence; (2) the difficulty of obtaining the opportunity to undertake spiritual practices such as these, which includes the reflection on impermanence and death; and (3) the reflection on the law of karma (i.e., cause and effect), through which we can develop an awareness of those mental, physical, and vocal deeds that are to be engaged in because they are wholesome, as distinguished from actions of body, voice, and mind that should be avoided because they bring about unwholesome karmic results. Following these teachings are practical instructions that tell us exactly how to (a) distinguish wholesome from unwholesome actions, and (b) avoid unwholesome actions while nurturing wholesome ones.

THE LAW OF KARMA

In beginning our discussion of this topic, we would do well to note that both the fifth patriarch of Sakya, Jetsün Dragpa Gyaltsen, and another illustrious Sakyapa saint, Kunga Yeshe, emphasized, in their writings, teachings, and practice, the necessity of great care in the study and observance of Lord Buddha's teachings on karma.

The gist of the teachings on karma is that you must learn to develop a sense of awareness about your mental, physical, and vocal activities. First, you must be aware of what you are doing and be able at any given moment to distinguish between wholesome and unwholesome activities. As a rule of thumb, wholesome actions are those that do not bring harm to anyone, including yourself, and that promote your own and others' well-being. Unwholesome deeds are the opposite.

We should therefore cultivate a sense of mindfulness rather than allowing our minds to remain governed by thoughts that are careless. We should not allow ourselves to be so preoccupied by trains of thought and daily affairs that we are constantly thinking, "Now I must do this, now I must do that, tomorrow I'll have to see to this, and next year I shall be involved in that." We tend to get carried away by schemes about present, past, and future courses of action. We need to learn to moderate this kind of rash, unexamined activity, in order to make sure that our undertakings are worthwhile and, if so, that they are performed in a wholesome manner.

There should be a constant check upon our actions. That is to say, you should be able to ask yourself at any given moment:

> If I were to die this very day, would this action that I'm engaged in be really worthwhile? Would it be karmically beneficial? Is it really an action that I can afford to die while doing? Can I afford to leave this world on this particular note? Is it really that useful, that helpful, or even good for myself and others? Does this type of activity incline me toward more virtuous actions? Whether I am still alive

tomorrow or whether I'm dead, does it incline me in a virtuous direction, or otherwise?

We develop an interest in the practice of Dharma or some other sort of spiritual undertaking as a result of sincere reflection on the uselessness of irreligious conduct. Briefly stated, we might say that Dharma, or religion, should be practiced for three reasons: (1) worldly affairs and worldly objects of desire are ultimately useless, (2) worldly friends and associates are ultimately useless, and (3) personal power, prestige, charm, and charisma are ultimately useless. This is so because, at the time of death, your personal possessions and accomplishments—such as money, property, friends, prestige, eloquence, and the rest—cannot be taken with you. At that very critical moment they are, in more cases than not, obstacles rather than any help. They are not a source of true succor when you need it most of all.

First of all, fortune, wealth, and property obviously cannot be taken with you, nor will you be in any position to rely on the advantages that might have been derived from them in this life. You are certainly not going to get any better treatment by trying to bribe Death, sweet-talk him, or somehow to worm your way out of this particular spot. Death cannot be moved by your power, prestige, charisma, or good appearance. Nor will any tricks you may have used in this world, either to get your way or to get out of difficult situations, be of any help. Just as someone will casually remove a hair from a butter lamp, so your consciousness will be plucked out of this familiar world of ours. You will have to leave quite alone and quite empty-handed. As the poet Shāntideva wrote in the *Bodhicharyāvatara*:

> Having spent your life acquiring many belongings, having enjoyed various pleasures for all this while, eventually you will find yourself destitute, as if you had suddenly been robbed by thieves.

Hence these various attributes, which are considered advantageous by worldly folk, not only don't help at the moment of death but actually cause more harm than not. Over the course of your life, you tend to build up a very large amount of strong attachment to these things. To be quite suddenly and irrevocably separated from all of them is a shock and a trauma—much as if a lame person were suddenly deprived of the crutches on which he had been leaning for so long. Shāntideva said, on this very topic:

In this way, those very things to which that pleasure-beguiled mind grows attached rise up again, not as objects of pleasure but as objects of suffering, and this time magnified a thousandfold. Therefore the wise will not desire them, since from attachment fear arises.

Second, at the time of death you will find that, of the many friends and relatives, associates and servants you have accumulated throughout a long life, none is of any help to you. They certainly can't prevent the onslaught of your death, nor can they go along with you in your most difficult moment. A person's hopelessness at that moment is evoked in the *Bodhicharyāvatara*, where the dying person is described as lying on his deathbed surrounded by kin whose tear-swollen eyes are red with grief. But none of them is of any use, and he must experience alone the pangs of death:

> When one has been seized by the fearful minions of Death, of what benefit are kinsmen? At the time of death, only virtue is a friend. And that, alas, you have not acquired.

Thus it is that at the time of death, friends and relatives are are unable to help you, even though you long for any sort of friendly gesture, anything to separate you from the hideous fears of leaving this world and heading out in some empty, unknown direction. When you most need a friend, there are none.

At the time of death, only the wholesome karma that you have accumulated is of any use to you. A virtuous person can face death unafraid, without any great anxieties about his next destination. He hasn't a guilty conscience at that critical moment, nor any evil karma that threatens to drag him downward. At that time virtue is the sole friend on which he can rely.

Unfortunately, most worldly people devote very little time or attention to the accumulation of virtue. Through delusion and ignorance, they spend much of their lives in self-centered, fruitless, or karmically unwholesome activities. Indeed, those very friends, relatives, and loved ones who we bank on for help at the critical moment of death have, more likely than not, been the source of real injury to us. For their sake we have often acted selfishly, passionately, or even sinfully. For the sake of winning affection, of wooing this person or keeping the friendship or love of that one—not to mention for the sake of looking after our own—we may have engaged in all kinds of harmful activities. We may have spoken angry words or even committed criminal actions, thereby accumulating bad karma for the sake of those we cherish most.

But at the time of death, not one of your friends or loved ones will take a single step into death with you. You can count on it. The unwholesome karma you have accumulated for their sake will definitely go with you, however, and will influence your good or bad fortune in the hereafter. It pays, then, to be aware of all this before the moment of death. What is the use of developing a mind of intense remorse when it is too late? The timely moment is now, when you can influence not only the mental state with which you confront death but the course your karmic destiny takes. This is why it is important to practice a spiritual discipline seriously in this life.

Third, it doesn't matter how eloquent you are or how much prestige and power you may have had in life: at the time of death, these faculties and advantages will also desert you. During your life, you may have been in a position of power from which you could easily command others and force them to do your bidding. With skills of persuasion and eloquent speech, you may have been able to influence others and have many people hanging on your words and following your guidance. Yet all that skill and power, as well as the pride, arrogance, and conceit that come in their wake, will be of no use to you when you are on your deathbed.

To give an example, the lion is rightly called the king of beasts. If he really wishes to, he can bring down mighty elephants and by a single roar send all the other animals in the forest scurrying away. But even for the king of the beasts, death comes eventually. None of his physical power, none of his great roars can stay death. In the end, he lies down tamely and submits.

By extrapolation, consider the case among humans. Great rulers with unchecked power—able to control the lives and minds of others—are in positions in which their every word and deed are of great importance to everyone else. Dictators can even extend their power over a long period of time and gather more and more people under their sway. But when those like Mao Tse-tung and others grow old and face death, they are quite helpless to forestall it: very tamely they, too, must submit. As a verse in the *Jātaka Tales* tells us:

> Even lions, who subdue giant elephants with their sharp nails, ripping open their heads and baring their brains, and terrifying the

minds of other animals by their roars—even those mighty lions lose their power and arrogance when death comes, and meekly they, too, lie down to sleep.

Not only do power and eloquence fail to be of any help at the time of death, they also work injury because, through exercising them, your mind becomes poisoned with delusion about yourself and others. It becomes filled with pride, arrogance, and conceit, not to mention with the effects of all the unwholesome actions that pride and arrogance themselves can lead you to commit. As the *Bodhicharyāvatara* tells us:

> "I am esteemed by many people, I have many friends and followers."
> Ah, but fears rise up at death for the man who harbors such conceits
> as these.

To summarize: as we have said before, there are only a limited number of causes and conditions that sustain life, such as food, shelter, health, and so on, whereas the causes and conditions that deprive us of life are manifold. Hence life is very fragile, and death is certain to befall every person who has already experienced birth.

When death approaches, it is not prevented by your worldly goods, no matter how many you have accumulated. It is not prevented by the recitation of mantras and spells. Nor can you evade death by feats of valor; even a hero, with all his strength and dignity, cannot manage to escape it. A rich man with his wealth cannot evade it, nor can a learned man with his knowledge and skill in conduct. An eloquent person cannot talk his way out of death. A nimble person cannot sidestep it. A swift person cannot outrun it, and a magician cannot trick his way out. As the sūtras tell us, "Though a magician may manage to deceive the eyes of many people assembled before him, there is one, Death, who he will not deceive."

The point is that, following your reflections on impermanence, the certainty of death, and the uncertainty of the time of death, it is good to develop, right now, a spirit of detachment toward the things of this life that you might subconsciously still be banking on. Even though you are convinced intellectually that, "Yes, I shall die eventually, and I am going to have to experience that," you might still be clinging to some last-minute game plan, or might have the notion that the things which work for you in this life will be helpful to you when death does come.

Thus our lesson here is to loosen our attachment to these various thoughts through the realization that they will not support us when death comes, and to pinpoint our attention on what will really be of some use at that time. We will then see that what is of use is meritorious action, or wholesome karma. As the Buddha said to an Indian king in one of the sūtras:

> O great king, when the time of death befalls you, when you are pierced by the spear of the Lord of Death, you will part from pride and—without a protector and without a refuge, without kinsmen and hosts, afflicted by disease, dry-mouthed, your face altered, your hands and feet trembling, your teeth gnashing, unable to rise, giving out a wheezing sound, your body smeared with urine, ordure, and vile vomit, unable to resort to food and medicine—sleep in your last bed, sinking into the waters of worldly existence. Frightened by the minions of Death, the movement of your breath will cease, your mouth and nostrils open.
>
> At that time you will relinquish this world, go into the other world, embark on the great journey, enter that great darkness, fall into the great abyss, be tossed by the great ocean, be carried by the river of karma, travel in a stationless region, and no longer have any part in the sharing of your wealth. Crying "Alas, my father; alas, my mother; alas, my son," you will go.
>
> At that time, O great king, there is no other protector except Dharma, there is no other refuge and no other kinsman. At that time Dharma alone becomes a protector, a refuge, a base on which to rely, an island, and a great friendly host.

WHY VIRTUE IS THE ONLY HELP WHEN DEATH COMES

What, other than virtue, can be a friend at the time of death? If the mere description of the experience of death inspires us to reflection and to an interest in avoiding such a painful situation, where we are at an obvious disadvantage, then it should also persuade us to grow diligent in the practice of Dharma. This is why the teachings on death and impermanence are taught. They inspire us to many salutary actions and spiritual efforts. It is quite right that, while we are healthy and whole, we should remind ourselves:

> Just now, my organs and faculties are clear and my body and mind are able to practice the Dharma. If I don't practice any Dharma

now, while I am endowed with clear faculties, health, and leisure, what do I really plan to do when I have grown old, when my faculties are dim, my body weakened, and I move around like a breathing corpse just on the point of death? Will that really suffice to prepare me for what follows?

As Dropu Lotsawa Jampay Päl (d. 1250s), one of Tibet's greatest masters, wrote:

> If one doesn't develop the three kinds of vigor right now, while one is able, then their practice on the verge of death is very much like a soldier who puts on his armor after he has already been mortally wounded and then stands there, beating his chest.

Granted that neither wealth, power, nor friends are of much use to a dying person, or able to prevent death, don't people who practice the Dharma also die? Religion doesn't prevent the onslaught of death any more than anything else does. However, no two deaths are quite alike. There are differences between the death of a virtuous man and that of a man who has lived carelessly, selfishly, and sinfully. Among religious people, a person who has attained some degree of spiritual maturity, insight, and merit will die happily. His death will not be fearful or attended by pain and anxiety. Instead, he will embark on the experience of death much as a bee or butterfly will desert one flower to move on to another. A mediocre practitioner of Dharma will also die without fear about what is coming next or grief for the things he leaves behind. And even an inferior practitioner, who has not been able to practice wholeheartedly or who has failed as yet to attain any profound insights, will die without regrets, untormented by recollections of many misdeeds in the life he is being forced to abandon. As the *Adornment of the Mahāyāna Sūtras* says:

> A religious person, who has realized that all things are illusions and that people come and go like the leaves of a tree, is not frightened by the sufferings of the defilements in times of his own increase or decline.

The *Bodhicharyāvatara* says:

> Having mounted the chariot of the enlightenment thought, he proceeds from one joy to the next. How is it possible that such a person would experience grief and anxiety? [46]

In contrast, consider the death of a person who has not practiced the Dharma. First of all, he is stricken with remorse for the selfish, mean, sinful deeds that he has committed, and feels regret that he did not devote himself to virtuous ways. Second, he is attacked by the natural process of death and is wracked by agonies, as if his very vitals were being torn apart. Finally, he dies while confronted by the terrible dread of death. As Shāntideva wrote:

> Just as a criminal who is being led to the execution block no longer has any interest in food and is unaware of what is going on around him, but searchs wildly in every direction for something that at the last moment might save him, so he is led step by step onward. He seems altogether different from his former appearance.

When we are seized by Death, we will become utterly frenzied by the hideous apparitions of his minions, terrified at the recollection of all of the misdeeds we have accumulated, full of remorse for all our missed opportunities for virtue, and frantic because we don't know in which direction we are headed. Or we will search the empty directions for a helper and see no one. What need to say that at that time we are going to be drastically changed?

To make this topic a subject of formal meditation, first be seated in the proper posture on a comfortable cushion. Precede your reflection with taking refuge and awakening within yourself the resolve to attain buddhahood to promote the benefit and enlightenment of all living beings. Then recollect the teachings about the need for Dharma at the time of death:

> Well, it is true that death will surely come for me, and it is also true that I don't know when it will come. But if I have not yet developed any virtuous patterns of thought and behavior that will be of use at the time of death, and have become overly attached to the things of this life, striving mainly for worldly objectives and advantages; if my mind has for the most part remained agitated and distracted by worldly concerns, and I have been guilty of acting as if the insubstantial were really substantial; if I have acted in a very deluded way about sense objects and their acquisition, and have not even come up with a religious practice that will serve me at the time of my death—if all this is the case, what am I going to do when I die?

Sit and think about this for a long time, until you have absolutely faced up to the facts that you are not really prepared for death and don't know what you are going to do when it comes. When this meditation begins to "take," you will experience some feeling of sadness, not only about your own plight but also about the fact that this is the common condition of so many others who are afflicted in very much the same way. When you have a feeling of unbearable sadness for their plight as well as your own, plus a sense of revulsion at acting in such a self-indulgent, perpetually deluded way, without even looking after your own best interest in this life or the next, then this meditation is indeed taking hold.

Now proceed with these thoughts, in which you try to achieve some degree of assessment of your present situation:

> I have become more and more attached to worldly aims, ambitions, and affairs. But if I don't really practice these teachings sincerely from my heart, I will be just as foolish as if I left an island of jewels empty-handed. There is no greater self-deception than mine if I don't make good use of this human existence while I have it. Now, at any rate, no matter what happens, I must definitely undertake to practice the Dharma. And I must choose for practice a religious path that I can definitely rely on at the time of death.
>
> Moreover, I should start practicing right now. I must not allow myself to fall under the sway of laziness and procrastination. My efforts must be vigorous, as if I were trying to put out a fire that had blazed forth on my own head or clothes. I must be just as diligent and as direct as that. Since I now understand that food, wealth, property, loved ones, relatives, and all the other sources of support that I rely on in this life are not going to be able to help me at the time of my death, I must discard my weak-minded clinging to them. I must get rid of this deluded attitude as if it were just so much spittle. I should no longer exhaust my energy in getting and guarding things such as food, wealth, friends, relatives, property, and power.
>
> Directing my mind to the truly worthwhile sources of support—to my teacher and the Buddha, Dharma, and Sangha—from now on I have nothing else to perform except Dharma. May my teacher and the Three Jewels please help me, that this resolve of mine to practice will be truly accomplished and become successful.

Think in this way from your heart, again and again. When you know that your longing to practice is unfeigned, when it is an authentic wish that you be able put aside this kind of distraction, then you have performed this reflection correctly. You should reflect in this way again and again, with really intense fervor and longing. You should be able to pray sincerely, not just repeating the words and approximating their meaning.

Conclude your formal session of meditation by dedicating the merit of your reflections to the enlightenment of others. Even in the intervals between practice sessions, repeatedly bring to mind and retain this reflection about death, reminding yourself very clearly:

> I will surely die, and I don't know when. At the time of death, nothing but the Dharma—nothing but my own religious practice of virtues—will be of any help.

Also, as you go about your daily affairs, if you see someone die, hear of others' deaths, or see a corpse or bones, remind yourself:

> I, too, am no different from this. I am a being who has a nature just like this, and I am subject to experiencing death just as this person has.

By reflecting in this way, try to weaken your overinvolvement in the affairs of this life and your overindulgence in the pursuit of sense objects, prestige, and other concerns that are obviously good only for this life. Whenever you find yourself overwhelmed by present situations and attachments, very forcibly and clearly remind yourself of what is truly important. Try to distinguish between the things of this life and those things that will be of some help to you at the time of death and in your next life. Try not to associate with friends who are greatly attached to worldly activity and who indulge overmuch in the pursuit of objects of desire. Try to develop a sense of wise detachment and go about your own life with only as much involvement as necessary. Try, also, to be content with whatever you have, even if it is only temporary. Learn to make do with only a sufficient amount of food, clothing, decent shelter, and the other necessities of life, without indulging in unneeded luxuries that might become a source of weak-minded attachment.

In all your practice of the Dharma and all your efforts, remind yourself first of all that human life is brief, and death certain:

> I, too, am an impermanent being, by my very nature destined to experience one day a separation from the things of this life and to go elsewhere.

Keep this sort of reminder always at hand. Whatever practice of Dharma you might be engaged in, whether study of religious teachings, contemplation of them, or meditation on them, always precede it with the reflection on death and impermanence. Goad yourself into diligence and mindfulness through this reflection.

If you practice in this way, your meditation will obviously be sincere, and its fruition will be speeded up. You will find that you make real progress in following the path and in attaining those virtues and spiritual insights that will be of true benefit to you, not only in this life and at the time of death, but in all your future existences right up until liberation. It is for this reason that this teaching on death is given, and that those who long for liberation should always keep in mind this reflection on impermanence.

23

DEEDS, LIKE A SHADOW, WILL FOLLOW

AMONG THE MANY SPIRITUAL PATHS, we are concerned with the lam-dre system, the most valuable jewel within the treasure house of the Sakya order of Tibetan Buddhism. The teachings in this system are divided into the foundational level and the advanced level. At present we are concerned with the first of these, as explained in *The Three Visions*.

The three visions are the impure vision of ordinary people, the vision of experience on the spiritual path, and the pure vision of enlightened beings. These instructions are provided to remedy the deluded type of perception characteristic of unenlightened, worldly people. They are intended to help an ordinary person become more aware of the dangers of worldly existence. Through awakening this sense of alertness, coupled with a feeling of sadness when we do recognize the often unbearable forms of suffering to which unenlightened beings like ourselves are subject, the teachings inspire a spirit of renunciation and a willingness to become less attached to worldly experience.

A readiness to relinquish the harmful things of this world is also kindled, and a spirit of diligence encouraged through the teachings that follow. The student is taught that human existence itself is only rarely obtained, and that the opportunity which humans have to receive and put into practice the necessary teachings that lead to enlightenment is also very rare and, once obtained, quite fleeting. The reflections on the difficulty of obtaining the opportunity to practice Dharma, the certainty of death, the uncertainty of the time of death, and the all-pervasive nature of impermanence that all phenomena share are all designed to encourage diligence in our practice.

After developing renunciation and a sense of readiness to practice, a willingness to persevere in our efforts follows. Next to emerge is a sense of carefulness, or heedfulness, in making right efforts. Toward that end, we are now discussing the teaching on karma, which is our third great topic on the level of the impure vision.

Through awareness of the efforts that need to be made and the actions that must be avoided, we can rightly proceed on the Mahāyāna path. When we speak of an impure level of perception, we are referring to everything that unenlightened beings perceive—everything that we cognize as being internal or external, as having form, shape, or color. Whatever appearances we perceive are called "impure" first of all because our perception of them is filtered through our subjectivity, i.e., through our deluded notions about ourselves as the center of the universe, as the ultimate perceivers. Second, our perception of phenomena is conditioned by our mental impressions of desire, hatred, delusion, and the other emotional states, and is sullied by these negative mental conditions. In other words, the impure vision is a deluded, erroneous vision; it is not a true, accurate, valid perception of what is really there. All the appearances that we perceive on this level and all our experience on this level arise as the manifestation of karmic results. Our own karma produces these perceptible appearances.

ILLUSORY APPEARANCE AND KARMIC APPEARANCE

We can distinguish between two kinds of phenomenal appearance: illusory appearance and karmic appearance. By "illusory appearance" we mean the automatic distinction that all unenlightened beings make between subject and object. Always there is the unquestioned notion that "In this situation I am the subject who is perceiving, and over there is the object being perceived by me." This seemingly real division into subject and object is shared by all beings on the round of existence. On the level of ultimate reality (that is, on that level of truth perceived by the buddhas), no difference between subject and object is found to exist.

By "karmic appearance" we mean a certain special aspect of general illusory appearance—that particular aspect which we know as the arising of personal phenomena that pertain to our own individual karmic patterns. This is the personal experience of happiness or unhappiness, long or short life, much or little wealth, and the like. All these conditions arise due to the wholesome or unwholesome nature of our individual karmic patterns.

The illusory appearance of the sun, moon, stars, cities, and other things that are experienced collectively is also due to our individual karmic patterns. Although these "objects" are shared to the extent that they are called the result of collective karma, their appearance is also due to our individual karmic patterns: it just so happens that the latter are similar enough that we find ourselves reborn in the same place, at the same time, experiencing the same sort of phenomena with the same type of sense faculties. Thus it is collective karma that brings about this appearance of the human realm, or world.

That all these appearances of the world are produced by karma is substantiated by the words of Lord Buddha himself and also by those of Vasubandhu, who states, in his commentary to the *Abhidharmakosha*, that

"All these worlds arise as a result of karma" and "Karma is the cause of the manifestation of all these worlds."

Let us make it clear that we are speaking of illusory appearance and karmic appearance. Illusory appearance is the perception of all phenomena by unenlightened minds. Karmic appearance is the individual experience of varied conditions, such as a long or short life, happiness and suffering, and so forth. This particular experience is a result of individual karma, rather than some extrapolated, generalized sort of human karma.

HOW OUR DEEDS FOLLOW US INTO DEATH

The appearances and experiences that unenlightened persons encounter are the results of either virtuous or nonvirtuous karmas, or actions. In connection with our discussion about the importance of virtue at the time of death, we may wonder whether our accumulation of wholesome and unwholesome karma will follow us when we die. Previously, we said that none of the pleasures and pains of our present life, none of our relatives, friends, associates, or property, go with us into death. Might it not be the case that our wholesome and unwholesome karmas also stay behind? From the Buddhist point of view, it is not true that our karma does not go with us. As Lord Buddha taught in the *Advice to a King Sūtra*:

> Afflicted by time, O king, at the time of your death, neither property nor loved ones, neither kinsmen nor friends will follow you. But wherever a person goes, his deeds, like a shadow, will follow.

In the *Hundred Verses on Karma* (*Karmaśataka*) it is said that:

> Karmic actions do not ripen in the soil,
> They do not ripen in stone,
> But they ripen in the skandhas alone.

The skandhas, you will recall, are the aggregates of embodied existence: form, feelings, perception, impulses, and consciousness. These five aggregates are the result obtained through karmic action. The difference between having the tortured body (or skandhas) of a hell being and the blissful body of a celestial is determined by the ripening of your own karmic propensities.

Deeds do follow you into death; they do determine the nature of your rebirth, whether good or bad. Deeds do not remain behind, nor do they follow some other person, nor are they canceled. Like the shadow that follows a bird flying in the sky, they follow the doer and are not exhausted even by the passage of an aeon or more. In the *Vinaya* (*Discipline Scripture*) it is taught:

> Not even in a hundred aeons do the deeds of an embodied being disappear. Yet they end in a ripened result only when the conditions and time for ripening are right.

There is only one thing that will happen to a karmic propensity once it has been formed through your perpetration of it: it will ripen in some karmic result, whether good or bad. There is no way you can escape its inevitable ripening.

Let's become a bit more specific about karma. There are three kinds that should be recognized: (1) wholesome karma, (2) unwholesome karma, and (3) neutral karma. Our discussion of karma will be built around these three. First, we will reflect on the results of unwholesome karma, in order to generate a desire to reject them; next, we will reflect on the results of wholesome karma, in order to awaken a desire to perform wholesome actions; and finally, we will reflect on the nature of neutral karma, in order to learn how to transform neutral actions into positive, wholesome karma.

UNWHOLESOME KARMA

Turning to the first of these, we have three subtopics to cover: (a) recognition of unwholesome karma, (b) recognition of the results of the various kinds of unwholesome karma, and (c) reflection on their renunciation. Through recognizing them for what they are—unwholesome—and through acknowledging their harmful results, we can make efforts to discard such patently harmful ways.

Let us turn to the first of these subtopics, the recognition of bad karma. Ārya Nāgārjuna said in his *Precious Garland,* "Actions that are produced through attachment, aversion, and delusion are unwholesome." These include all actions motivated or conditioned by any sense of attachment to yourself, to your own side, or to the desire to acquire things or people and bring them over to your side. Aversion toward the other side—the desire to get rid of or avoid anything that you identify as not-self or as not belonging to your side—is a manifestation of anger, hatred, and aversion, in the sense that you are trying to expel something. In addition, all actions that spring from a sense of delusion, or ignorance, about their results are unwholesome, because you are not aware of, neglect, or fail to believe the fact that actions do have results, and that those results are either beneficial or harmful as a result of their good or bad causes. Any disbelief in this fact of existence is bound to produce unwholesome karma.

If the leaves, flowers, and fruit of a tree are poisonous, the roots are, too. Similarly, all actions perpetrated by a mind that is governed by attachment, aversion, and delusion are bound to be unwholesome by definition.

The Ten Kinds of Unwholesome Action

For the sake of convenience, we can analyze the various kinds of unwholesome actions into three types perpetrated by the body, four by the voice, and three by the mind. The three unwholesome bodily actions are (1) taking life, (2) taking what is not given, and (3) sexual misconduct; the four unwholesome actions perpetrated by voice are (4) lying, (5) slander, (6) harsh speech, and (7) idle speech; and the three unwholesome actions committed by mind are (8) covetousness, or envy, (9) ill will, and (10) clinging to wrong views.

We should first learn to recognize these ten kinds of actions, which are called unwholesome simply because their result is harmful to living beings (or simply to oneself, if not to others also). Whatever truly works harm for a being—whatever karmic patterns bring about pain, unhappiness, or situations and conditions that are harmful to him, physically or mentally—all these are said to be unwholesome. The first step is to be very clear about what kinds of physical, vocal, and mental actions bring about such painful results.

Let us examine in some detail each of the ten kinds of unwholesome action, beginning with the three kinds perpetrated by your body. By killing, we mean taking the life of any other living being with the intention of doing so. If you take the life of another being in this way, regardless of whether the being in question is human or nonhuman, you have committed the unwholesome karma of killing. It doesn't matter whether it is a god you kill or a flea. If you have the intent to kill and make the effort to do the deed, either by yourself or through someone else who is at your command, then you are guilty of killing. It doesn't matter what method you use, whether poison, fire, weapons, or any other means; as long as you have the intent to deprive another living being of its life, your action is karmically unwholesome.

The second physical action that must be avoided is theft, stealing, or taking what is not given. If you make any effort to appropriate any item whatsoever belonging to another, whether large or small, by force, stealth, or guile, then you are guilty of stealing.

The third type of physical bad karma is sexual misconduct—i.e., sexual intercourse with anyone who is not your own spouse, anyone for whom you do not have the clear conception that "this person is my spouse, my wife or husband." It also includes having sexual relations with anyone closely related to you by blood. A person who is not your spouse or who is a blood relative is not considered a proper partner or "object," so in those two cases, sexual relations incur the fault of "improper object." Even with your own wife or husband, sexual misconduct can be incurred if engaged in at the wrong time. If sexual relations occur while the wife is pregnant or when she is performing a religious fast, that constitutes sexual misconduct because of impropriety in time. There are also considerations due to improper place. You should avoid having sex in a temple or other sanctified location, or in the presence of your parents or your religious teacher. Sexual misconduct can also be incurred through impropriety in technique. Anal or oral intercourse, even with your spouse, is considered misconduct. Thus there are four considerations: (a) impropriety of object (i.e., your choice of partner), (b) impropriety in time, (c) impropriety in place, and (d) impropriety in technique. All must be taken into account in determining whether or not your sexual behavior will result in unwholesome karma.

Nāgārjuna summarized these three kinds of physical misdeeds in his *Precious Garland*:

> Killing is taking another being's life with the intention of doing so, whether it is perpetrated by oneself or by giving a command to others. Stealing is making the property of another one's own, whether by force or stealth. Sexual misconduct is intercourse with an improper partner, at an improper time, in an improper place, or through an improper technique.

We turn now to the four kinds of unwholesome karma perpetrated by voice. First is lying—namely, speaking untrue words with the intent to deceive others. If you utter anything with the idea of misleading, misinforming, or beguiling any other person, and he or she understands your words, then you have perpetrated a lie.

Second is slander, which is incurred whenever you say anything at all with the intent of creating a schism between other people. It doesn't matter whether the words are truth or falsehood. Nor does it matter whether the people concerned are on friendly terms or already at odds; if the words you speak contribute to a split, you are guilty of slander.

Third is the fault of harsh speech. If you speak words, whether true or false, to or about another person that wound his or her feelings, causing mental pain, anguish, unhappiness, or injury of any sort, then you are guilty of harsh speech. Abusive words are definitely a kind of bad karma.

Fourth is idle speech—silly prattle, gossip, talk about wars and presidents and armies and plays and the rest. Meaningless discussions, much talk about matters that we know aren't spiritually helpful or meaningful, the discussion of wrong philosophical notions of other schools—all these constitute idle speech. When you talk merely to be erudite or to kill time, knowing that the topics discussed aren't really helpful, either to yourself or others, this is also idle speech and a form of unwholesome behavior.

Nāgārjuna summarized these four in the *Precious Garland*:

> Lying is speaking untrue words intentionally, with the thought of deceiving others. Slander is speaking various kinds of defiled words in order to create schisms among others. Harsh speech is uttering unpleasant words that pierce another's heart. Idle speech is talking of wrong scriptures and indulging in flattery, songs, talk about dramas, and the like.

The first of the three kinds of unwholesome karma accumulated through misuse of the mind is covetousness, or envy, which is the wish, whether expressed or not, to acquire another person's property, whatever it might be. If you wish it were yours rather than his or hers, then you are guilty of envy, which is a negative state of mind.

Second, ill will, or malice, is production of the thought that another being should be unhappy. If you ever hope that another living being will suffer any form of unhappiness, then you are guilty of ill will.

Third, the tenth kind of unwholesome karma is accumulated through clinging to wrong views. There are many kinds of wrongs views, but the principal one is to disbelieve in the efficacy of cause and effect (i.e., the law of karma). If you refuse to accept the idea that good actions bring about good results, just as bad actions bring about bad results, this constitutes a wrong view. Similarly, after hearing the teachings on the qualities of the Three Jewels, you may choose to disbelieve them. Perhaps you say, "I don't believe that the Buddha really has the spiritual qualities with which he is credited, that his teaching is necessarily a true one, or that evil actions will lead to rebirth in the hells and good actions to happier states of existence." If you reject these teachings, even though they are true, and act as though you have no responsibility for your good and bad actions, you have committed the error of clinging to wrong views. Of all the ten kinds of unwholesome karma, this is the worst. It is the source of the most unhappiness and yields the greatest unhappy result, for, based on this wrong view about karma and truth, nothing but blind, deluded, harmful actions are likely to ensue.

The Results of the Ten Unwholesome Actions

In the most general of terms, we have the words of Nāgārjuna in his *Precious Garland*: "From unwholesome actions arise sufferings and every unhappy state of existence." Each of the ten kinds of unwholesome action has a threefold result: (a) the fully ripened result, (b) the result that is similar to its cause, and (c) the owner's, or proprietor's, result.

First, carried to their logical or karmic conclusion, each of these ten unwholesome deeds has the potential to bring about the fully ripened result of our experiencing the mental and physical sufferings of the three lower realms of existence. As Nāgārjuna wrote in the *Precious Garland*, "The first result of these deeds is that one goes to realms of ill." For example, if you commit actions through great anger, it is possible that you will go to hell; through desire, you may be reborn among the tantalized ghosts; through delusion, as an animal. Again, Nāgārjuna wrote, "Through anger one is reborn in hell; through desire one is reborn among the pretas; through delusion most go to the animal world."

Thus rebirth in one of the three lower realms of existence could be the fully ripened result of any of the ten unwholesome actions, depending on the frequency and intensity with which you commit them. For example, if you perform unwholesome actions to a great extent, the result will be rebirth in the hells; to a middling extent, rebirth among the ghosts; and if you commit them only a little, you will be reborn among the animals.

Second, we will consider karmic results that are similar to their causes. Here we have two types of karma: (1) the experience of karmic *results* that are similar to their causes, and (2) the experience of further karmic *actions* that are similar to their causes. The first of these two subtopics states that, as a result of unwholesome actions in this life, a person will eventually experience unhappy results: either he will experience the fully ripened results and be reborn in one of the lower realms of existence, or—even after having experienced that fully ripened result in the hells, among the ghosts, or what have you—he will still have some residual karmic results of his previous unwholesome actions that will influence his subsequent experience in the higher realms.

For example, say you commit murder. In this life, you may very well experience certain karmic results: as the ripening result of your murdering karma, you may suffer illness, find your own life endangered, or have it cut short through execution, or through being murdered in retaliation for your own misdeed. You will also be reborn in a hell, and even after having attained release from the hells and a higher rebirth—say, among humans again—you may again experience illness, a short life, and so on, due to your karmic pattern having been conditioned by your former action of killing.

To give another example: even after you have regained one of the higher realms of existence, human or otherwise, as a result of theft in a former lifetime, you may very well find yourself destitute or, if you do own a little property, you may lack the power to use it as you wish.

As a result of sexual misconduct in the past, you may find yourself with few lovers and many enemies in this life, or your wife or husband may be very rude.

As a result of lying, you will find yourself frequently slandered in this life, spoken harshly to, abused by others, and easily deceived.

As the result of your own past slanders, you will have few dear friends of your own. And even when you find a friend, you will be easily separated from him or her.

As a result of harsh speech, you will hear unpleasant speech from others, and whatever others say to you will be disagreeable, while everything you say will become the cause of their wanting to quarrel with you.

As a result of your own idle speech, you will find that other people don't believe you, even when you tell them the truth.

Through coveting the property of others, your own envy will ripen into failing to attain the object of your wishes or, should you attain it, into not being content with it.

As a result of malice, you will always be fearful that others might cause you injury.

Finally, as a result of holding wrong views, you will come into contact with other wrong views and will be endowed with little wisdom. Even if you gain some degree of insight, you will find that it is easily impaired.

To summarize, in the words of Nāgārjuna:

Through killing, your own life will be short. As a result of stealing, you will be destitute of property. As a result of sexual misconduct, you will have enemies. As a result of lying speech, you will often be slandered. As a result of slander, you will be separated from your friends. As a result of harsh speech, you will hear unpleasant things. As a result of idle speech, your own words will not be credited. As a result of coveting, your own hopes will be blighted. As a result of malice, you will experience fear. As a result of wrong views, you will incur even more wrong views.

Let us turn to the second type of karmic results that are similar to their causes: the experience of further karmic actions that are similar to their causes. By committing nonvirtuous actions at present, you will find that, throughout your future career, you will have the karmic pattern to repeat unwholesome actions through force of habit alone. For example, if you take the life of another being now, your perpetration of the inclination to kill will become the cause for future killing on your part, whether of human or nonhuman beings. Thus actions beget like actions; karma begets like karma. Criminal actions are often repeated simply because the mind becomes habituated to certain unwholesome actions, whether in this life or future lifetimes. This is true not only of killing but of the other nine kinds of unwholesome karma as well.

The third type of result of unwholesome karma is called the "owner's result." By this awkwardly translated term we mean that the wholesome and unwholesome karma that a person accumulates serves to condition the environment in which he finds himself in the future, whether in this life or future lifetimes. To give one scriptural reference for this: it is said that, as a result of perpetrating the ten kinds of unwholesome action, one will be reborn in nondescript places of little splendor, with lots of rain or many dust storms, where it smells bad or the ground is rocky and uneven, where the fields are saline, or where the seasons are perverse and the crops no good. We can elaborate on this by paraphrasing Nāgārjuna's *Precious Garland*:

> As result of killing, one will be reborn in a region of little splendor. As a result of taking what is not given, one will be reborn in a region afflicted by hailstorms. As a result of sexual misconduct, one will be reborn in a place of many dust storms. As a result of lying,

one will be reborn in a dirty, foul-smelling place. As a result of slandering others, one will be reborn in a very uneven region, where the topography is very rough. As a result of harsh speech, one will be reborn in a place where the earth is salty. As a result of idle speech, one will be reborn in a place where the seasons are perverse. As a result of envy, one will be reborn in a place where the crops are scanty and the fruit small. As a result of ill will, one will be reborn where the fruit tastes sour. Finally, as a result of wrong views, one will be reborn in a place where there is no fruit at all.

This is not to say that these are the only results that will be experienced, just that these are some possible side effects; the main result is to be reborn in some terrible situation that you don't like.

In conclusion, you should recognize and understand very clearly that no matter where you might be, no matter what you might experience, the particular unpleasant conditions of your time, place, and environment are the results of your own unwholesome karma. As the *Bodhicharyāvatara* tells us:

> Wherever the doer of unwholesome karma goes, then and there he finds only unhappiness, although his single thought is to find happiness.

Renunciation of Unwholesome Action

We have learned to recognize the ten kinds of unwholesome behavior and have been taught something about the possible negative results that ensue from perpetrating them. It follows that we should learn how to wean ourselves from such patently undesirable actions. Still, there might be a bit of quibbling on our part; we might like to tell ourselves that, whereas it may be true that we might be reborn in the hells through committing terribly angry actions, such as murder, it is not terribly likely that we will reap such a bad result as a consequence of lesser acts of anger. But there is no assurance that this is true. It is sure that we will eventually experience the ripening of all those karmic actions, although certainly the more intense ones may bring us more quickly into the hells or other painful states. However, there is no assurance at all that less serious karmic actions will not bring about terrible results.

For example, it is said that there was one particular Buddhist nun who got angry at her companions and called them "a lot of bitches." As a result, she was reborn five hundred times as just that, a dog. Also, a particular king had many attendants, among whom were certain pratyekabuddhas. One of these Buddhist saints was crippled, his body bent over with gout. One day, at an assembly in court, that particular pratyekabuddha was absent. One of the king's daughters imitated the old man's limp just to get a laugh, and said, "The old cripple isn't here today." As a result, she herself spent many rebirths as a crippled woman. Indeed, we have it from the sūtras that:

> If you were guilty of plucking out the eyes of all the people on this earth, and plundering all their property, your bad karma would still be less than that you would incur if you merely stared disrespectfully at a bodhisattva.

Moreover, it is said:

> If you direct a thought of ill will and anger toward a bodhisattva, even once, you will have to experience the sufferings of hell for as many aeons as the number of seconds your anger lasted toward that being.

This is supported by Shāntideva in his *Bodhicharyāvatāra*. You never know who is a bodhisattva and who is not. For this reason alone, you should learn to be careful in treating—or mistreating—other people.

But these are just random misdeeds—a moment of anger, a single gesture of ill will, and the like. If we can go to hell for aeons for a single misdeed, what can be said about our chances for a happy rebirth if we repeatedly commit all these ten unwholesome acts? Idle speech, envy, ill will, wrong views, killing insects, and so forth are very commonly practiced by human beings, so what will the result be if they are all practiced frequently?

Our chances of getting off scot-free are not so good. This is not to say that it is a cut and dried affair, and that if you do this, you are going to get that bad result, but it *is* a warning. An intelligent person should, upon hearing these teachings, take cognizance of them and discipline himself accordingly. He or she should exercise some restraint in actions such as killing and stealing, which, even for non-Buddhists, are considered to bring about harmful results.

The main point is that we understand, thoroughly and very clearly, that the commission of nonvirtuous deeds results in future suffering: it is the source of past, present, and future unhappiness for oneself and others. Therefore, think:

Now that I really can think clearly about it, no matter what happens, I must not indulge in these unwholesome ways again.

From now on, as Shāntideva says,

My uppermost thought should be just this: from unwholesome actions sufferings arise. How am I going to get free from them?

What, then, are we to claim for our own intelligence, as thoughtful human beings? Here we have obtained human existence and a human body equipped to understand and practice virtuous ways that bring about happiness for ourselves and others. We have the opportunity to use this human life for meaningful, helpful actions. Having obtained such an opportunity, what greater folly could there be than to misuse the human body to perform harmful, mean actions that only result in increased suffering for ourselves and others? This is just as stupid as if we were to use a very precious vessel, fashioned of pure gold and adorned with costly jewels, to vomit in or as a chamberpot. It would be just about as intelligent and as fitting as this example, which Nāgārjuna himself cited.

We must learn to be reflective about the efficacy of these unwholesome karmic actions, which are very easily practiced through mere habit. We should learn to recognize them for what they are, because they bring future unhappiness to ourselves and others. Great sins should certainly be avoided at all costs, but smaller indulgences and lesser misdeeds should also be avoided. In the *Vinaya*, the code of discipline for Buddhist monks, it is said:

You should not despise even little misdeeds, thinking, "They won't hurt," because, even by tiny sparks of fire, a mountain-high heap of grass can be burned.

To summarize, we should develop the awareness that, through carelessness and ignorance throughout beginningless lifetimes right up to the present moment, we have accumulated unwholesome karmic patterns of activity, thinking as follows:

Even now, not a single day passes without my accumulating one or another of the ten kinds of unwholesome karma. Since it is quite sure that the result of all this karmic accumulation is not going to ripen to anyone but me, it would be intelligent if I were to learn to be careful in watching my actions and diligent in practicing the right methods for avoiding the acquisition of bad karma. Further, I should learn methods of purifying my past acquisition of bad karma. If, despite my best efforts, I still find myself perpetrating any of these ten, I should learn how to purify that by confessing my failure with very genuine and intense remorse; then, with renewed diligence, I should keep my precepts and commitments and not perpetrate these actions henceforth.

As the sūtras tell us:

> There are two kinds of religious people: those who remain unstained by vices, and those who confess whenever they arise. In other words, there are those who somehow manage to remain free from misdeed, and there are those who sometimes slip but are careful to purify their failure immediately.

The logical question then is, "Can karmic misdeeds be purified merely by confession?" Yes, they can be purified by confession, provided it is accompanied by genuine, heartfelt remorse. As Nāgārjuna wrote in his *Letter from a Friend*, "He who formerly was careless and afterward becomes careful rules in beauty like the unclouded moon or like Ānanda, Angulimāla, and Ajātasatru."

This verse refers to three well-known figures in Buddhist history. Ānanda was the younger brother or cousin of Lord Buddha himself, and was, of all his disciples, most noted for his lusty propensities. He came to epitomize monks whose minds are controlled by the desire for sex. Angulimāla was a murderer who even attempted to kill his own mother, and hence the foremost example of a disciple who began his career overwhelmed by the passions of anger and hatred. Finally, there was Ajātasatru, who, through his delusion about right and wrong, didn't hesitate to kill his own father and mother to acquire the rule of their kingdom. All three were able to give up their karmic patterns of terrible misdeeds of desire, hatred, and delusion by making diligent, sincere efforts to enter the holy life taught by the Buddha, and as a result of their practice, in their very lifetimes they attained the liberation of arhatship.

If it is possible for greatly deluded people such as these to purify their sins by relying on the teachings of enlightenment, how much more likely is it that people such as we ourselves, who at least have not committed such terrible sins as they, can purify our karmic patterns?

24

A GREAT VESSEL FILLED BY DROPS OF WATER

FIRST OF ALL, let us remind ourselves of the great difficulty with which we have attained humanity and an opportunity to receive these valuable teachings that lead to enlightenment. Let us make our minds firm in the resolution not to waste the opportunity that these contacts with the Dharma provide, and resolve to use our span of life effectively, by engaging in the practice of virtue and making the right efforts that bring about spiritual liberation for ourselves and others.

Among the many doors of Dharma, we have entered the one known as the lam-dre system of meditation. This authentic teaching is the special treasure of the Sakya order of Tibetan Buddhism. It is divided into the preparatory and advanced stages of practice. At present, we are studying the instructions for the preparatory stage, which are arranged to correspond to three levels of perception: the impure vision of worldlings, the experiential vision of meditators, and the pure vision of enlightened beings.

At this stage, we are examining the level of impure perception. We have already discussed the negative aspects of worldly existence and the all-pervasiveness of death and impermanence, and are now studying the distinction between wholesome and unwholesome karmic activities. Previously, we discussed the ten unwholesome actions of body, voice, and mind, their possible results, and how they are to be avoided. Now we will discuss the ten wholesome actions of body, voice, and mind.

WHOLESOME KARMA

To stimulate ourselves to take an interest in the performance of wholesome actions, there are three reflections that we should know and practice: (1) reflection on the nature of wholesome, or virtuous, deeds, (2) reflection on their results, and (3) reflection on the way to accomplish them.

First, let us define virtue, good karma, or wholesome actions. In his *Letter from a Friend*, Nāgārjuna put it this way: "All actions that are produced free from attachment, aversion, and delusion are wholesome and virtuous." To elaborate, whatever mental, physical, or vocal efforts we make when our minds are not governed by attachment to our own side or aversion to the other side, and that are produced by a mind that is not confused about good and bad actions and their results, are automatically classified as virtuous and wholesome. Just as all the leaves, flowers, and fruit that spring from a medicinal root are medicinal, so all actions produced by a mind that is free from the mental poisons automatically bring about good results.

The Ten Kinds of Wholesome Action

Briefly put, the so-called wholesome actions are the opposite of the ten unwholesome types of behavior. If, for example, you refrain from all acts of taking life, that in itself is a virtuous action. The three wholesome actions of the body thus consist of refraining from taking life, refraining from taking what is not given, and refraining from sexual misconduct. If you refrain from the four unwholesome actions of voice (lying, slander, harsh speech, and idle speech), you acquire virtue through that restraint. Finally, you acquire virtue through refraining from the three unwholesome actions of mind (envy, ill will, and holding wrong views).

By their nature, these ten virtuous actions are opposites of the ten non-virtues, or unwholesome ways of acting. They consist of the mental commitment, resolve, and promise to renounce killing, stealing, and so forth. If you exercise restraint concerning the ten unwholesome kinds of action and further strengthen that attitude by positive actions—not merely passively refraining from unwholesome acts but, for example, protecting the lives of others instead of killing, making generous gifts to those in need instead of stealing, and so forth—then you will gain a very good idea of the nature of these ten wholesome actions.

The Results of the Ten Wholesome Actions

Each of these ten wholesome actions has a threefold aspect with regard to its result: (1) a fully ripened result, (2) a result is similar to its cause, and (3) what is known as the "ownership result."

A fully ripened result means that each one, or any combination, of the ten wholesome types of behavior can produce the relative happiness of the higher realms of existence (that is, rebirth among the humans, asuras, or gods). As Ārya Nāgārjuna wrote in his *Precious Garland*:

> These wholesome deeds release beings from the hells, from among
> the ghost and animals realms, and cause them to attain happiness,
> splendor, and vast dominion among the gods and humans.

Whereas, generally speaking, practice of the ten unwholesome actions leads a being to rebirth in the lower realms of existence, refraining from them assures rebirth in the three higher realms. Moreover, the degree to which you practice this renunciation of evil ways determines the place of your rebirth. For example, if you perform the ten wholesome actions a great deal during your human life, you will be reborn among the gods; if you practice virtue only a middling amount, you will be reborn among the titans; and by relatively smaller amounts, you will be reborn as a human.

You might be inclined to question this statement, remembering that we taught earlier that the human body is the most valuable acquisition on the round of existence. If it is so valuable, why does it require so much less merit than rebirth among the gods and titans? We should explain that, when we asserted the relative value of human rebirth, we were discussing the difficulty of obtaining it from the point of view that it is only through possession of a human body that one can acquire the best possible foundation for achieving buddhahood. Now, however, we are discussing the variants among the good and bad results of karmic action. In any case, the fully ripened result of performing wholesome actions is rebirth among the three higher realms.

Next, there are two kinds of result that are similar to their causes. First, we will enjoy *results* that are similar to their causes. For example, through renouncing killing, you will enjoy long life, by renouncing stealing, you will enjoy great wealth, and so on. We have described the results incurred through unwholesome actions of body, voice, and mind, and the various opposites of those painful results can simply be substituted here. As Nāgārjuna wrote in the *Precious Garland*, "Just the opposite of whatever was pronounced as the result of the so-called nonvirtues will occur as the result of all their opposing virtues."

Second, as a result of your wholesome actions, you will experience future *actions* that are similar to their causes. That is, as a result of refraining from killing in this life, in future lifetimes you will have no interest in taking the lives of others; by refraining from stealing in this life, you will have no mental propensities to steal in future rebirths; and so on for the other eight wholesome actions. These are called "resultant actions similar to their causes."

Finally, we must explain the "ownership result" of these virtues. We have said that this term refers to the nature of your environment in future rebirths. Generally speaking, as a result of refraining from the ten types of unwholesome actions, you will be reborn in an environment that is just the opposite of the various unpleasant situations we described before. For example, we said that as a result of much desire, you would be reborn in a desert; in contrast, by successfully restraining your desire, you will be reborn in a very pleasant and beautiful country. As the *Bodhicharyāvatara* tells us, "Wherever a virtuous man goes, there he encounters the results of his virtuous deeds." Thus your virtue (as well as any vice) goes with you and conditions the environment of your future existence.

If the practice of these ten wholesome deeds is conjoined with the special Mahāyāna practices of bodhichitta (the bodhisattva's resolve to win enlightenment for the benefit of all beings), it will become not only a cause of higher rebirth but a cause of attaining perfect enlightenment as well. Similarly, if the practice of these virtuous deeds is conjoined with meditation on emptiness, which sees the true nature of dharmas, so that you perform such deeds with insight into the empty nature of all phenomena, then you will accumulate transcendent merit, which becomes a cause not merely of rebirth in the higher realms but of buddhahood itself. Thus you would refrain from killing, for example, while realizing that there is neither anyone who refrains from killing, nor any beings who have been spared from slaughter, nor any restraint from killing; if you have this wisdom through your realization of emptiness, tremendous merit is accumulated that leads directly to perfect buddhahood. Finally, if you perform these ten wholesome actions with a desire to accumulate merit for the benefit of beings and then dedicate that merit toward the enlightenment of all, your practice will also become the cause of liberation.

To summarize, mere restraint from the ten unwholesome patterns of behavior is enough to ensure rebirth in the higher realms of existence. If your renunciation is conjoined with (1) the preliminary practice of bodhichitta, (2) the main practice of insight into emptiness, and (3) the concluding practice of dedication of merit, then those ten practices become not only the cause of higher rebirths but also the cause of liberation and perfect omniscience.

Cultivation of Wholesome Action

Having heard about the good results that ensue from practice of the ten wholesome patterns of behavior, and having contrasted them with the terrible results of their opposites, we should become interested in learning how to successfully cultivate virtues and avoid nonvirtues. Shāntideva was speaking of this when he wrote, "One should start with the *Vajra Flag Sūtra* and learn diligence in the practice of virtue." The *Vajra Flag Sūtra* (*Vajradhvaja-sūtra*) is concerned with the purification of karmic patterns accumulated in the past.

We should begin by making firm the ground for our practice of virtue and avoidance of nonvirtue. In purifying our past karmic inclinations, we should make a firm, clear-minded start in learning wholesome patterns of behavior and develop a sense of pride in thinking:

> It is for me to learn how to avoid the repetition of harmful actions,
> and it is for me to accumulate merit through the practice of virtue.
> Whether or not others make effort, I must not fail.

Nor should we disdain even trifling amounts of merit and virtue. Even the smallest virtuous action should not be ignored simply because we are looking for more glamorous ways to practice virtue. Even a trivial wholesome action is definitely able to yield a result. As it is written in the monks' code of discipline, the *Vinaya*,

> Do not despise even little virtuous deeds, thinking, "They will not
> be of much benefit," for even a great vessel is gradually filled by
> accumulating drops of water.

Next, we need to know how large and small virtues and nonvirtues are to be distinguished. How are they to be determined? What constitutes a great sin and what is a great virtue? What makes one sin greater and another lesser, or one virtue greater than another? These are determined by a number of factors, including (1) time, (2) intention, (3) object, (4) the number of doers, (5) place, (6) occasion, and (7) monastic status.

First of all, a sin or a virtue is made great or small by consideration of *time*, for if you practice one of the unwholesome deeds repeatedly or continuously, then it becomes a great sin. Likewise, if you promise always to refrain from killing or stealing and succeed in doing so over a long period of time, then that wholesome action becomes much more powerful and is considered to be a great virtue, whereas if you only occasionally or temporarily commit a sin out of sudden passion or through a fluke of circumstances—such as taking a life all of a sudden and then never again—then the unwholesome action is of less karmic strength than if it is a repeated practice. By the same token, if you practice virtue just temporarily or by accident, it is of lesser strength than virtue practiced repeatedly over a long period of time.

Second, *intention* determines whether a sin or virtue is considered great or small. In committing any deed, there must be three steps: (a) preparation, (b) performance, and (c) conclusion. Let us say that you have the conscious intention to perpetrate either a virtuous or nonvirtuous deed, that your intention is then conjoined with making the efforts to accomplish that deed, and finally, that the action is completed. If the deed has been committed—regardless of whether it consists, for example, of refraining from taking life or of taking it—then karmically efficient action has taken place. If you have a strong sense of these three steps—if you have the intention to do good or bad, make deliberate efforts to do it, and actually accomplish that good or bad deed—then the resulting karma is much greater than if the action is unintentional, and that karma creates a much greater virtue or sin.

What you are forced to do against your will—as, for example, when a king, dictator, or someone else gains control over your actions—is much less powerful than what you do on purpose. The same is true if you are requested, ordered, or begged to do something by your family or close relatives and associates. If you are coerced or persuaded to act against your will, the resulting deeds will have less karmic efficiency than intentional ones. However, if you perform good or bad actions through holding wrong views, that efficiency will be stronger: for example, sacrificing animals in order to attain liberation will result in strong adverse karma. But you may also perpetrate good or bad actions out of careless ignorance (just as children, in play, not really knowing what they are about, might do), without understanding the consequences, circumstances, or moral considerations involved. Whenever a person acts in this state of ignorance, his actions are less powerful and have less effect than do intentional ones, whether for better or for worse.

Regardless of whether you commit an unwholesome or a wholesome action, it will be much more powerful if, after acting, you do not regret but rejoice in whatever bad or good you have done. For instance, if you kill someone and refuse to feel any remorse about it but rejoice in your action, the sin of killing becomes much stronger. The same is true of virtues: if you rejoice after you commit an action of benefit to others and don't wish that you hadn't made the effort, and if you continue to rejoice in it, that magnifies the power of the virtue that you accomplished. Similarly, if you do experience regret and no longer rejoice in what you did, then a given sin or virtue is lessened.

It is important to note that if you do perpetrate an unwholesome action of body, voice, or mind, you should be very quick to awaken remorse within your mind and confess your deed to many people with an attitude of genuine regret. But if you have done a good deed, keep it to yourself—it grows in strength if you don't share it. Avoid any sense of conceit or pride, and by all means avoid boasting to others about your virtuous efforts.

Third, the relative strength of good and bad actions is also determined through a consideration of the *object* toward which those actions are directed. For example, among beings, we can speak of three different fields or types of recipients of our actions. The first is the "field of virtues," which means that when you direct virtuous and nonvirtuous deeds toward the buddhas and bodhisattvas, toward your teacher or lineage of teachers, toward the Three Jewels, and in general toward all those who expound the Dharma, the results are intensified much more than if those same actions had been directed toward ordinary, secular people.

The same is true when our good or bad actions are directed toward the "field of elders"—namely, our parents and those who have been our benefactors and shown us kindness. Actions toward them will be intensified because of our own strong karmic rapport with them. The same actions will be less effective, for better or for worse, when directed toward strangers and others.

Finally, we have the "field of mercy." When we direct either benefit or injury toward the sick, the protectorless, the suffering, and those who trust us, our actions will be magnified greatly, whether for better or worse, and those same actions will be less potent when directed toward beings who do not belong to these categories.

To summarize, the most important factors are your intent in undertaking good or bad actions and the object, or field, toward which a given action is directed. As it is said in the *Abhidharmakosha*, "Actions become endowed with physical result through the categories of field and intent."

You will not necessarily experience the karmic result of an action if the three steps of intent, perpetration, and completion are not accomplished, however. For example, you might accidentally step on a bug in the street. This would constitute taking life, but since you had no intention to do so, there would be no conscious conclusion to your action. Hence the karmic result would be correspondingly weaker than if you had seen the bug ahead of time and deliberately squashed it.

However, you *can* reap the karmic result of a deed you yourself don't commit due solely to your intention or conclusion. For example, if you mentally ponder taking someone's life or rejoice when, by some circumstance that is not your own direct action, that person dies, you may accumulate and share in the bad karma of having killed him. The same is true of virtues: if you have the intention to perform virtuous actions, even though you are not able to do so, or if you rejoice in the virtuous deeds of others, these good intentions collect results despite the fact that you yourself haven't completed them. Thus your mere intent or participation in the concluding step of an action is enough to be karmically effective, and it is quite certain that you will receive the corresponding result, whether good or bad.

There is also a fourth consideration: the *number of doers*. If many people perform a good or bad action in accord with one another, it is much more powerful than the same action done separately or individually. For example, if many members of the Sangha join in reciting a sūtra, the merit is multiplied by the number of monks and nuns and is much more meritorious and beneficial than if one person were to recite it alone. Similarly, if many people consult together about taking another person's life, the sin of that single killing will be multiplied—say a hundred times over, if one hundred people had consulted together, because each of the hundred will incur the sin of killing a human being. Conversely, if one man kills another without consulting anyone else, there will be relatively less sin because it will be confined to one perpetrator alone.

The fifth consideration that determines whether an action is karmically more or less powerful is *place*. Any virtuous or nonvirtuous action of body, voice, or mind will be magnified if it is committed in a temple, in front of a shrine, or in a place where preceptors, teachers, or members of the Sangha reside.

There is yet another consideration, which is *occasion*. Whatever virtue or sin you might commit becomes much more powerful if it is done on an occasion such as the four auspicious dates that correspond to the waxing and waning moon, the full moon day, the festivals in commemoration of Lord Buddha, or the parinirvāṇa days of great teachers such the Five Great Jetsüns, Tsong-kha-pa and his two chief disciples, Marpa, Milarepa, and the like. Virtues and nonvirtues are of comparatively less strength when they are performed at times other than these.

တ ⚜ တ

Consider, too, the difference that is effected by the *monastic status* of the doer. Virtue or nonvirtue is much more powerful when done by someone who has renounced the world and entered the monastic life. Those who have consciously taken upon themselves the bodhisattva vows, the lay precepts, or the various stages of ordination will find that their good and bad actions are greatly magnified and that the results are much greater, for better or for worse, than those experienced by a householder who has not undertaken these trainings. To lend authority to this, we have a quotation from Lord Buddha:

> If a householder bodhisattva were to offer to the buddhas an oil-filled lamp as large as three thousand world systems, his merit would not be so great as that of a renunciate bodhisattva who might merely light a twig dipped in oil at the doorstep of a temple.

Karmic results also ripen much more quickly and strongly when the perpetrator is a renunciate.

There are three groups of four types of actions that concern such a renunciate. First, there are four deeds that will cause a renunciate Buddhist to go to the hell realms like a shot: (1) if, wearing robes, he should accept alms from the faithful while not maintaining his vows and moral conduct; (2) if he consciously ignores the injunctions of Lord Buddha concerning the code of discipline and ethical behavior; (3) if he fails to confess and purify any infraction of his vows immediately, thus causing the sin of those infractions to continue to increase; and (4) if he develops a bad case of jealousy toward others who are endowed with good qualities and spiritual accomplishments.

Second, there are four conceits that will make a renunciate Buddhist leave very quickly for hell: (1) conceit about his accouterments, such as his religious equipment, or about the fact that he can receive alms—all the favors, all the respect, all the attention that he wants and things he needs—simply because he is wearing robes; (2) conceit about his spiritual accomplishments—thinking that he is very well versed in doctrine or skilled in meditation; (3) conceit about his popularity—thoughts of himself as a person who is entitled to great respect and admiration, as someone who requires a great retinue, and so forth; and (4) conceit about his observance of moral discipline—fancying himself to be an upright, honest, and staunch upholder of the moral code, whereas other monks or Buddhists are immoral or unethical. In short, the second group of four is concerned with the dangers of conceit in practice.

Finally, there are four actions that will make a renunciate go straight to a hell from which he will never get out: (1) having contempt for the sets of rules enjoined by Lord Buddha for householders, novice monks, and fully ordained monks and refusing to be bound by them, even though he has undertaken the commitment to them—including not believing that infractions of these rules must be purified and avoided, and having the idea that if he breaks these rules, it is not really true that something bad will happen; (2) disparaging bodhisattvas and teachers of the Dharma, and showing dislike for their work or actively creating obstacles for them so that they cannot teach, such as interrupting the spiritual work they have undertaken on behalf of beings; (3) disparaging and creating obstacles to the holy teaching, such as interfering with plans to start a school or center for the study of Dharma; and (4) harboring wrong views about the veracity of the Three Jewels—such as, after hearing about the benefits of the Buddha's teachings, nonetheless developing a spirit of dislike toward them and refusing to recognize any good qualities in them, maintaining that "It's all a pack of lies and of no use to the world."

We should be very clear about these considerations of good and bad karma. Our intention is paramount: it is the most important thing involved. Thus it is important to remember that angry thoughts, aversion, and ill will are, on balance, even stronger than thoughts of attachment. It is said that a bodhisattva will suffer more from having a single thought of anger toward living beings than if he were to commit acts of attachment and desire for a hundred thousand aeons. Anger toward living beings on the part of a bodhisattva who has pledged his entire life to promoting their happiness is much more terrible in its karmic consequence than all thoughts of attachment to beings. Also, actions performed for the sake of others are stronger than those performed for the sake of oneself.

Throughout all this, intention is the most important factor. Even actions that would normally be classified as unwholesome can be meritorious if performed with good intentions. To give one example, there is a story in the *Jātaka Tales* of one of the earlier lives of the Buddha as a bodhisattva. In that rebirth he was a sailor. While crossing a river in a ferry, through his bodhisattva's prescience he realized that one of the passengers was planning to kill all five hundred people aboard the ship. Quick as a wink, he killed the person with the evil intention. By doing so, he saved not only the other passengers but also the person who was planning to kill them, preventing him from committing such a terrible sin. Even though he did this at the price of killing a living being himself, because his intention was so good and was motivated by compassion, both for the other passengers and for the would-be killer, it was, on balance, a meritorious action.

Conversely, there are deeds that might appear to be virtuous but that are nonvirtuous when accompanied by wrong intentions. For example, if a lama practices his religion merely for the sake of receiving offerings, that practice becomes nothing but a way of accumulating sin. Hence intention is of the utmost importance. As Shāntideva enjoins in his *Bodhicharyāvatara*, "One should understand that the mind is foremost."

If you wish to make progress in spiritual training, you must first of all guard the mind. When the mind is guarded, you will be able to observe and maintain the training and make progress on the path. If the mind remains unguarded, you will not be able to maintain the training, and all your efforts will come to naught.

This concludes our discussion of wholesome actions. Next we will finish our instructions on the impure vision by considering the third class of karma, which consists of actions that bring neither a good nor a bad result. We must learn how to transform such neutral actions into good karma. Thereafter, we will take up the instructions on the vision of experience, namely, the instructions for meditators.

25

BLACK PEBBLES AND WHITE PEBBLES

WE SHOULD SOMETIMES be kind to ourselves and remind ourselves of the great difficulties through which we have come so far. We have attained not only humanity but an opportunity to hear and put into practice teachings that will bring us nothing but benefit and happiness for all time. Having encountered something of such priceless value in this life, we should not do ourselves the disservice of throwing it away or neglecting it through carelessness, laziness, or procrastination. With all this in mind, we should apply ourselves diligently to study of, reflection on, and practice of the holy doctrines taught by Lord Buddha.

There are many doors to the Dharma. The one we have entered is the lam-dre system of meditation. These teachings of the Sakya order are comprised of foundational practices and advanced practices. Our studies thus far have been of the first of these two stages. The text that is serving as our guide is *The Three Visions*. In this lesson, we will conclude our discussion of the instructions that have to do with the impure vision. We have been discussing the topic of karma, learning something of wholesome and unwholesome actions and the results that each bring. We will continue with an explanation of the characteristics of karmically neutral actions.

NEUTRAL KARMA

In defining virtuous and nonvirtuous actions of body, voice, and mind, we said that unwholesome, sinful karma includes every action that ensues from a mind governed by any or all of the three mental poisons, namely, desire/attachment, anger/aversion, and delusion/ignorance. Any action produced by such a mind is unwholesome because it causes a correspondingly undesirable, unhelpful result. A virtuous action of body, voice, and mind was explained as any action issuing from a mind not governed by the three poisons.

There are also other actions, which we perform every day, that cannot be included in either category. They are not unwholesome because they don't produce karmically negative results, and they are not wholesome because they don't cause what can be regarded as good or happy results. Examples include walking from one place to another, eating, sleeping, sitting, standing, and the like. You can think of many more. All are neutral activities that sustain our lives. But they don't produce good or bad results, so we call them karmically neutral.

For example, if a seed is poisonous by nature, then the root, stem, branches, leaves, and fruit will all be poisonous. Conversely, if a seed is medicinal, the entire plant will be medicinal. But not all plants are either poisonous or medicinal. Similarly, there are actions that are all negative because their source is negative and they bring ill effects, and there are other actions that are helpful and productive of happiness for the person who performs them because they spring from a mind that is free from desire, hatred, and delusion. Finally, there are actions that are neither negative nor positive and that produce neither unhappiness nor happiness. We must learn to identify these neutral actions and transform them into wholesome acts, since as religious persons we want to make use of all possible ways to produce beneficial results for ourselves and others.

It is probably fair to say that, although we don't think of ourselves as evil people, most of our actions are nonvirtuous. Very few of our actions really spring from undefiled states of mind. They are usually performed on the spur of the moment, prompted by our desires, egotistic needs, or selfish motives. Our deeds may be based on delusion, they may be fueled by craving, strong attachment, and desire, or they may be motivated by aversion, ill will, anger, and spite. If we are honest, we have to say that almost all our ordinary actions spring from these unwholesome states of mind.

It is only occasionally that our actions spring from great faith in the Buddha and his teachings, positive convictions, a spirit of renunciation, feelings of love and compassion, and a mind endowed with insight into what is really going on—what we could call the opposite of confusion and delusion. Very seldom do we come up with this sort of action, so it is quite right to say that most of the time our actions are karmically unwholesome. If they aren't prompted by desire and attachment to one thing or another, they are caused by anger or resentment about something else. In the absence of either of these, we are absolutely lazy, deluded about our own nature, confused about what's going on in this samsaric situation, unmindful of the operation of karma, or forgetful of the teachings.

An example is the story of a very good monk who, after hearing the teachings on good and bad karma and the importance of the states of mind from which they arise, became curious to learn just how virtuous his actions were, so he set up a very simple test. Every time he had a thought that arose out of faith, wisdom, unselfish love and compassion, or a desire to benefit others, he would put down a white pebble, and every time he found himself producing an unwholesome thought or action of any sort, he would put down a black pebble. After he had done this for two or three months, being very honest with himself in recognizing his intent and the nature of his actions, he found that he hadn't been able to lay down a single white pebble but did have a huge mound of black stones. This inspired him to be more careful about his thoughts and actions, to think more about the Dharma, and to be much more watchful of his motivations and impulses, both good and bad. After a few more months he found that, while he still had many more black pebbles, there were also some white ones. As time went on, he had more and more white pebbles, and finally, he had nothing but white ones piled up. By then he had attained spiritual results—the special siddhis—and was well on his way to becoming a great bodhisattva.

This is a very graphic description of the true nature of ordinary actions, their origin and karmic significance. It also illustrates the great difference that being truly careful about our actions can make, no matter how insignificant they might seem at the time.

Now, this third category of actions is called "neutral" because such actions do not produce good or bad karmic results. In a sense, you might say that neutral actions are all right as is, simply because they don't produce suffering. But that is not good enough for followers of a spiritual discipline. Since so many of our actions do belong to this category, they should not be ignored or allowed to waste energy that could better be used for our own and others' spiritual uplift.

The point is that neutral actions should be transformed into virtuous actions, by entering into them with a mind directed toward the spiritual benefit of all living beings. By intending to perform even neutral actions so as to bring about some benefit for other living beings, karmically neutral actions are transformed into virtuous ones. We have a number of classic examples for doing this, and you can come up with your own as well. For example, when at home or in the homes of other people, think:

May all living beings dwell in the City of Liberation.

When seated, think:

May all living beings be established on the throne of enlightenment.

When falling asleep, think:
> May all beings attain the Body of Reality, the dharmakāya.

When you wake up in the morning, think:
> May all beings attain the Form Bodies of the Buddha, the nir-mānakāya and sambhogakāya.

When dressing think:
> May all beings be robed in restraint from bad actions.

When bathing and washing, think:
> May all beings be purified from the moral and mental defilements.

When leaving the house, think:
> May all beings leave behind the City of Saṃsāra.

When partaking of food, think:
> May all beings secure the sustenance of meditation.

When traveling, think:
> May all beings enter the path of the bodhisattva.

When meeting other people, think:
> May all beings meet Lord Buddha.

When performing any physical action, any sort of work, think:
> May all beings accomplish their own and others' spiritual aims.

When returning home, think:
> May all beings enter the City of Liberation.

When arriving home, think:
> May all beings attain buddhahood.

And so forth and so on. You can use your own imagination. The point is not to let the actions remain karmically neutral, but to transform them into virtue through the power of your conscious intent that they in some way be linked to the achievement of ultimate spiritual benefit for all other living beings.

Next are the instructions for formal sitting meditation on this topic. Assume the correct posture and begin by taking refuge three times, reciting preliminary prayers, cultivating bodhichitta, and so forth. Then reflect in this way:

When I die, all the food, clothes, wealth, property, servants, and relatives that I possess will not accompany me. But all the virtuous and nonvirtuous karma that I have accumulated during this lifetime will definitely go with me. All the actions that were produced through my body, voice, and mind will ripen into karmic results. The fully ripened result of unwholesome deeds is rebirth in the three lower realms of existence, from which there is no escape. And since, generally, the karmic result is similar to its cause, I will have to experience the painful results of my misdeeds even in the higher realms of existence. I will suffer according to the suffering I have created for others. Moreover, the harmful karmic propensities and habits I have acquired through misdeeds of body, voice, and mind will continue to influence my future rebirths. My future environment will be similarly influenced by the ripening results of the misdeeds for which I must claim ownership.

No matter what happens, it is quite sure that unwholesome actions always result in suffering, so if I am at all intelligent, I will regard my unwholesome actions and karmic propensities as my true enemies. It is certain that no one and nothing else will ever work greater harm on me than these. In the past, I was either ignorant of this fact, didn't recognize it, or disregarded it and neglected to act accordingly. Even in this present life, I can't begin to count the many major and minor misdeeds I have perpetrated through body, voice, and mind. They are indeed countless, and very likely there are also countless wrongs that I have induced others to commit in this life.

Also, I have surely rejoiced in the misdeeds of others or have supported them mentally in their bad karma. In my past lives, I have probably accumulated much more bad karma than good. I have no idea what terrible misdeeds I might have committed in the past or what karmic patterns I might have developed then. It is likely that the results of those processes are either ripening now or are still to ripen for me. Considering my predilection for unwholesome karma in this life and in past lives, I really don't see how I shall avoid rebirth in the lower worlds.

Why have I acted in this way? Why have I done all these harmful things? Either my mind was absolutely deluded, wrapped in spiritual darkness or controlled by demons, or I simply don't have any mind at all. Henceforth, I make a firm resolve not to commit the slightest misdeed of body, voice, or mind, not to accumulate the slightest bit of negative karma again. But if, despite my best efforts, I should lapse and again create bad karma, I resolve that, however slight it might be, I will not let that karmic habit stay with me for even a single day. I will stop it and purify it.

After you have meditated on unwholesome karma in this manner, reflect on what you are going to do about it:

From virtuous acts, too, I will get the same three results: fully ripened results, results similar to their causes, and the ownership result. The fully ripened result of virtuous actions is rebirth in the higher realms. For instance, the result of refraining from taking life is that I will have longer life and freedom from illness. There will also be the karmic results of virtue. Those virtuous habits that I cultivate now, or have cultivated in the past, will continue to influence my good fortune and good environment in future lifetimes. Through the ownership result, I will be born in auspicious places.

To summarize: virtuous habits and deeds of body, voice, and mind are really beneficial. They are the best friend that I could possibly have. The good I have managed to perform in the past, the good I now do, and the support I give others in their practice of virtue—all this is sure to be of great help to me not only in this life but in future lives as well.

Realizing this, I should throw off laziness and procrastination so as to use every day to accumulate habits that are possessed of virtue, performing beneficial deeds of body, voice, and mind. As quickly as I can, I should also train in the practice of transforming my neutral actions, such as sleeping and walking, into good deeds by performing them for the spiritual benefit of all beings.

I have remained in one state of suffering or another for so long. I know that all the unhappiness, illness, and other problems I have experienced are simply the ripening result of my own bad karma, for which no one but myself is responsible. Now I understand my situation with regard to my own actions and assume responsibility for those actions.

From now on I must, during every moment, in all my conscious efforts, avoid evil actions and develop good habits. I must be diligent, also, in the transformation of neutral actions into good ones.

I pray that the Buddha, Dharma, Sangha, and all the bodhisattvas will help me practice in this way.

At the conclusion of this kind of meditation, dedicate the merit of the meditation itself to the enlightenment of all beings. In your nonsessional practice, also, when going about your daily affairs, always try to keep an eye on your own behavior. Watch what your mind is up to. If you are acting according to the Dharma, in ways that bring about real benefit for yourself and others, be thankful to the Three Jewels for the virtuous inclinations with which you are endowed, and rejoice in your good intentions and actions. In this way you will strengthen and reinforce them.

Resolve to continue acting in this same way in life after life. But if you find that you are slipping, or that you are about to practice—or are actually practicing—unwholesome or neutral actions, remind yourself very quickly as follows:

From beginningless time I have been stuck in saṃsāra, precisely through the performance of wrong deeds like these. If I continue to act in this way, it is quite sure that I will never get through saṃsāra, let alone attain buddhahood. Even in this life I will only create enemies, despair, neuroses, and other suffering for myself.

By reminding yourself of their negative results, try to eschew unwholesome actions.

It is well known that some so-called fine people practice religion. They have heard all the rules of religious conduct, but their intent is only to win the respect, praise, and goodwill of other people. If your actions flow from this kind of intention, even if you fool other people, those actions have as their source a defiled state of mind and will not serve as an antidote to the three mental poisons. Although it is enjoyable to please your associates and win their goodwill, it really doesn't matter how you look or whether or not they are contemptuous of you: as long as your practice is truly effective in purifying your mind of desire, hatred, and delusion, your actions will yield excellent results. And by purifying your actions, you will create karmic patterns that flow naturally from doing so.

Unless you are really working on the eradication of these negative states of mind, it doesn't matter what your religious practice is: it will not be effective, and it is not the Dharma. You may fool ordinary people, convincing them that you are practicing the Dharma when you are not, but you cannot fool the buddhas and bodhisattvas. There is no way you can conceal your actions from them. This in itself should give you pause and awaken some sense of shame about wrong actions or hypocritical religious practice.

But mostly it is a matter of being intelligent. If you perform wrong actions now, you may very well remain in saṃsāra forever. Right now is the crucial time for deciding whether you are going to move up or down on the karmic scale. It is entirely up to you.

Even in ordinary life, when you have the flu or a toothache, you follow your doctor's advice very carefully because you want to get well. And if you are hospitalized due to some physical or mental problem, you want to understand the nature of your disease, so you consult doctors and take the medicine they prescribe. But here we are suffering from the disease of karma and the defilements; we are in the sick ward of saṃsāra; we are wracked with the pains of karmic results. Fortunately for us, the very best doctor there is, Lord Buddha himself, has come along. If we are at all interested in our own recovery, we really should follow his advice. The stupidest thing we could possibly do would be to disregard his instructions on how to gain our own spiritual health, happiness, and genuine well-being.

To sum up: any and all suffering we experience in this life and in all future lifetimes depends on our own misdeeds of body, voice, and mind committed right now. Hence we should, at the very least, learn to be careful.

THE PROBLEM OF EVIL AND THE LAW OF KARMA

At this point we need to consider whether or not all these teachings on actions and their results are true. How is it that we often see people who are quite nonvirtuous, and not at all religious, yet who appear happy? Why do people who do not practice virtue often seem to be endowed with all the good things associated with the life of the just? The answer is that their present happiness is not the result of their present karmic activity; rather, it is the fully ripened result of their good actions in previous lifetimes, whereas the result of their present nonvirtuous behavior has not yet ripened but will do so sometime in the future.

Why does it also seem that people who are quite wicked often have better jobs and are happier than people who are sincerely committed to the path of virtue? The answer to this one is that the force of their present bad actions has upset their karmic pattern so that the happy results of their former good actions have been quickened into ripening right now, all at once. After these good results have been exhausted, these people will have nothing but bad karma and painful results to fall back on.

Then there are people who are deeply devoted to the Dharma, always doing the right thing, and virtuous in every way. Many such people suffer very much indeed. Sometimes very grievous and tragic circumstances befall them. How can this be so? The answer is that their present suffering is not the result of their present virtuous actions but of unwholesome actions committed in past lives. The very power of their present virtuous activities causes the evil results of their former bad karma to ripen quickly now, so that they experience these painful results all at once. After their bad results have ripened, these people will have nothing left but good karma and very extraordinary, fortunate good results.

A person who is interested in practicing the Dharma needs to be able to recognize the operation of the law of good and bad karma even when it seems to contradict the straightforward teaching that wholesome actions yield wholesome results and unwholesome actions yield unwholesome results. Through realizing what is happening karmically in the long run, no matter what appears to be the case in the short run, you can maintain your calm and experience happiness without feeling overwhelmed by any of forces in your present situation. This will prevent your envying apparently happy sinners or being discouraged by any adversity that seems to dog your efforts to follow a spiritual life of service, seeing this, too, as the ripening and purifying of your own bad karma, which is an obstacle to your liberation.

You can even try to be happy that adversity is happening right now and not later, when you may be less prepared to deal with it. If you were condemned to death and, at the last moment, had your hand cut off instead, you would probably think it a good bargain. Similarly, if you realize that you may be avoiding having your past and present bad karma ripen into rebirth in the hell realms by undergoing a little pain and unhappiness in this life, you can actually appreciate any present hardship as a good thing.

Let us summarize the whole section on karma. In order to succeed in the spiritual life, you need to recognize which actions are beneficial and which are harmful to yourself and others. By acting in accordance with what you know of the law of karma, you will make every effort to practice the Dharma properly and will sincerely pursue virtue. If you do so, you can be confident that in the future you will definitely experience the happy results of your present good efforts. With this we conclude the instructions on the three kinds of karma, and also the set of instructions that belongs to the first of the three visions.

26

AS HELPLESS AS A WORM

THROUGH OUR STUDIES of the lam-dre system, we have learned that humanity is not something that can be taken for granted but is, rather, of great value, both because of its rarity in the context of existence as a whole and because of the unique opportunity for spiritual progress that it provides. When we reflect on worldly existence as a whole, we come to recognize that it is by nature imbued with certain pervasive forms of suffering, just as fire is, by its nature, hot. Then we learn to appreciate detachment from the things of this life and to direct our minds toward nonworldly goals—in a word, buddhahood, or spiritual liberation.

We develop diligence in reorienting our minds in this way by contemplating the various forms of suffering in worldly existence. These include the sufferings experienced not only by humans but by animals and other forms of life, as well as the sufferings of death and impermanence, the certainty that death will befall each one of us, and the uncertainty of the time of death. Through mindfulness of the brevity of human life, we learn to make the most of what we have while we have it, and thus to become sincere and actually persevere in making right efforts in meditation and other religious practices. This is necessary because, at the time of death, only the wholesome actions that we have been able to accumulate in this life will be of any benefit in determining the conditions under which we are reborn.

THE VISION OF EXPERIENCE

With all these reflections in mind, we approach the second stage of the lam-dre system of meditation. Let us say that we now have the right attitude toward practice. We have some idea of where we are going and what our spiritual orientation should be, and we see how it is to be achieved. What is lacking is real practice: practical experience in meditation and in other Buddhist techniques. But if we do undertake practice with the right attitude, right orientation, and right degree of diligence and mindfulness, then we can expect to achieve, one after another, the various stages of yogic experience.

In our study of the lam-dre system of meditation, we are basing our practice on a particular Tibetan text known as *The Three Visions*. The title refers to three levels of perception on the Mahāyāna Buddhist path—the impure vision of ordinary worldlings, the vision of experience of meditators, and the pure vision of enlightened beings. We have completed all the instructions for study, reflection, and practice that correspond to the impure level of perception. We will now discuss the teachings, doctrines, and practical instruction given in this text for the meditator's vision of experience.

The purpose of this second level of instructions as a whole is to help the Buddhist meditator develop a universal, or all-inclusive, ideal toward the various practices in which he will engage. On the first level of instructions, he has learned to recognize the faults of remaining indifferent to the spiritual life, along with the value of undertaking such a spiritual career on his own. On the second stage, he must learn to undertake practices that are designed not for his liberation alone but to enable him to accomplish the spiritual benefit and ultimate liberation of other beings as well. Thus he has to learn to develop a universal commitment and sense of all-inclusiveness about his practice.

These instructions belong to the exoteric branch of Mahāyāna Buddhism. They consist of three major topics: the development of (1) all-inclusive love for living beings, (2) all-inclusive compassion for other beings, and (3) a resolve to accomplish the highest spiritual good of those beings. Let us begin with a few brief definitions.

First, the kind of love that is meant here is a completely unselfish concern for the well-being and happiness of all other living beings, without exception. When your practices are motivated by this spirit, you can be said to be endowed with *great love*.

Second, compassion here means the completely unselfish resolve to remove the sufferings and causes of unhappiness for all living beings without exception. When you achieve this spirit, you can be said to be endowed with *great compassion*.

Third, bodhichitta, the resolve to attain buddhahood for the sake of others, has two aspects. The first is the conventional resolve to attain enlightenment, which is simply a formalized, conscious commitment to strive for such a spiritual goal. Here you eschew all thought of seeking liberation for yourself alone and resolve to work for the benefit of other beings instead. The practices that correspond to this *conventional bodhichitta* are the bodhisattva's training in the six spiritual perfections of giving, moral conduct, patience, vigor, meditation, and insight. Second is the ultimate resolution, which consists of performing all actions through insight into the true nature of all phenomena—i.e., while realizing that there is no personal ego, or self, within which the agent acts, no recipient of your act, and no act itself. When you perform actions through such an insight into the ultimate nature of all dharmas, or phenomena, you are said to be acting from the standpoint of *ultimate bodhichitta*. The practical effort associated with this ultimate aspiration to attain enlightenment consists of training in the two stages of meditation: concentration and insight.

We have just said that there are two kinds of bodhichitta, or resolve to win enlightenment. One is conventional, and for that you practice the six perfections of the bodhisattva. The other is ultimate bodhichitta. Thus we are dealing with two levels. The first is the level of *conventional reality*, which is reality as it is perceived by unenlightened beings like ourselves; the second is *ultimate reality*, which is reality as it is perceived by enlightened beings, or buddhas—indeed, a buddha is, by definition, one who sees the true nature of phenomena. Now, since conventional reality is reality as it is perceived by unenlightened beings, the practices that are described for such beings are the six spiritual perfections of the bodhisattva. You must first of all train in these.

Ultimate reality is reality as it is perceived by buddhas. A buddha perceives things as they are. Where we see a real self as the agent, someone else as the recipient of that agent's action, and something as the object ("I'm doing this, this is what I'm doing, and this is the recipient of my action"), an enlightened being sees their true nature. He realizes that there is no really existent personal ego, as we deludedly believe. He sees that there is no recipient, nor is there is an object. (For example, you give a gift, but there is no giver, no recipient, and no gift.) This is true because phenomena are, by their very nature, ultimately devoid of inherent, independent being. This is not to say that everything is empty like so much space or sky. Enlightened beings see the true nature of things—namely, that they don't exist as substantial entities in the way that unenlightened beings like to believe. The bodhichitta practices on this ultimate level consist of training in the two stages of meditation: concentration (*śamatha*) (Skt. *śamatha*; Tib. *zhi-gnas*) and insight (*vipaśyanā*) (Skt. *vipaśyanā*; Tib. *lhag-mthong*).

Love, compassion, and bodhichitta are called the ordinary, or common, meditations of Mahāyāna Buddhism, in contrast to the extraordinary, or uncommon, practices encountered in tantric Mahāyāna Buddhism. The ordinary meditations and instructions are intended for meditators who are weak in love, compassion, and the resolve to win enlightenment. As the sūtras say, "For the common meditator, there are common meditations; for the uncommon meditator, uncommon meditations." An uncommon meditator is one whose mind is very much imbued with the three qualities of love, compassion, and bodhichitta, and who is really ready for advanced yogic techniques. But these three meditations are common Mahāyāna practices for practitioners who are still struggling not to be selfish about their spiritual careers.

We have said that great love is the desire for all beings' happiness, that great compassion is the desire to remove the unhappiness of all beings, and that bodhichitta is the resolve to seek the highest spiritual good of all beings, rather than your own benefit alone. These three are essential in Mahāyāna meditation. Without them, you cannot claim to be a follower of the Great Way, nor can you hope to achieve any of the common, let alone the uncommon, yogic experiences that belong to the Mahāyāna system of meditation.

In other words, if your practice is not motivated by great love, great compassion, and the resolve to win buddhahood for the sake of all beings, then you are, at best, a person who is seeking your own liberation alone. From the Mahāyāna point of view, this kind of practice is inferior because its benefits are limited. It prevents you from experiencing the total liberation of buddhahood and from acquiring the ability to help a great number of beings, over a vast area, for a long time. That is why the common meditator on the Mahāyāna path must take care to develop these qualities within his mind before advancing to the esoteric levels of practice.

There are three questions we should consider at this point. Earlier, we described three kinds of Buddhist liberation. We said that there were arhats, who meditate on the Four Noble Truths and, by eradicating the causes of rebirth (namely, craving, attachment, and karmically efficient propensities), attain the static nirvāṇa of arhatship. Then we said that pratyekabuddhas, meditating on the doctrine of interdependent origination and trying to eradicate the causes of rebirth, can also attain a state of liberation in which they are freed of the possibility of being reborn in worldly existence. Finally, we described the perfect buddhahood attained by a bodhisattva, who trains in the six pāramitās with the resolve to win that state of buddhahood for the benefit of others.

Since we have granted that arhats and pratyekabuddhas also attain a nirvāṇa that is free from ever being reborn into the suffering of worldly existence, why shouldn't we, too, make that our spiritual goal? What is wrong with striving for an arhat's liberation? It is wrong because there is something mean about striving for such a goal. When we realize our basic identity—or similarity, at least—with respect to all other living beings, we see that, since we ourselves wish only to attain happiness and to avoid unhappiness and its causes, we are really no different from other beings. They all seem to be motivated by these same basic instincts.

Moreover, we must recall the various kindnesses that other beings have done us even in this life. For example, our parents gave us life and cared for us when we were helpless, our friends have sustained us in one way or another when we most needed it, and so forth. We must also recall the various kindnesses we have received from all beings in countless former lifetimes. Knowing all this, it is really an act of ingratitude and insensitivity to turn our backs on them—deciding, in essence, to abandon those who have been our kind parents and friends, those who have helped us, who are very much like ourselves, and who are still subject to suffering. Knowing that they are unable to help themselves, it is a mark of meanness to disregard their kindness, striking out on our own for the shore of nirvāṇa and our own personal salvation.

What would you think of a son who rescued himself from a river, pulled himself onto the dry bank, and watched his own mother drown, when he could very easily have made the effort to save her? He would be condemned by others as a selfish, cowardly, and mean sort of person, and rightly so. This is how those religious people appear who pursue their own spiritual salvation alone. It is not that they are incapable of helping others. Thus, as followers of the Mahāyāna path, we are enjoined to avoid making such an inferior decision. As the great Jetsün Dragpa Gyaltsen, the fifth patriarch of Sakya, wrote in his *Parting from the Four Attachments*,

> There is no good in seeking liberation for oneself alone, because all beings in existence are truly like one's fathers and mothers. To leave one's parents in suffering while seeking happiness for oneself alone would be cruel-hearted.

Nevertheless, you may still be thinking, "Even though it's true that all beings have been kind to me and are, in a sense, like mothers, this human life is very brief, and the time of death quite uncertain. I haven't any assurance of a long time in which to practice the Dharma, so wouldn't it be best to concentrate on trying to save myself, rather than spending a lot of time thinking about this great universalist ideal of saving all beings? Wouldn't it be wiser just to make really effective efforts toward reaching the goal of liberation for myself alone, rather than taking on such a colossal burden?"

Here, too, the answer is no, for we must consider the quality of the goal itself. Not only is your motivation inferior when it is confined to seeking your own liberation alone, but the goal is an inferior one, also. The highest goal is the liberation of all sentient beings, precisely through developing those spiritual qualities—of great love, great compassion, insight into emptiness, and the bodhisattva's training—which alone enable a person to become fully enlightened. Self-liberation by itself is an inferior spiritual goal, and hence is to be avoided.

Now, you might have a final doubt, which runs like this: "It is true that I should not seek liberation for myself alone, and it may also be true that I should not seek an inferior goal such as that kind of limited liberation. But the Mahāyāna path is much more difficult than these other paths to liberation. On the Mahāyāna path, I must develop all the spiritual qualities of a bodhisattva, learn to give away my organs to beings that need them, devote myself to the service of others for countless aeons of time, and even go to hell on their behalf, undertaking tremendous suffering myself in order to remove their sufferings. It requires extraordinary heroism even to contemplate embarking on such a spiritual path."

But this not true. Mahāyāna is far from being the most difficult of paths: indeed, it is really the easiest of all, because you have much more help on it. In fact, all other beings are helping you, wittingly or unwittingly. Whenever you see an unhappy person, the mere sight of him helps you develop great compassion, and should you wish that he might instead experience happiness, that person is helping you develop great love. Every time you think, "I must really try to do something good to promote another's well-being" (however modest your ambition might be, and regardless of whether or not you follow through with efforts of any kind), that being is helping you develop bodhichitta. Moreover, when people are rude, unkind, or even do you great injury, to whatever extent you can refrain from retaliating with anger, ill will, or the desire for revenge, you are training in the bodhisattva's perfection of patience. And every time you respond in any positive way to a request for your assistance, you are accomplishing the bodhisattva's training in giving.

Hence every other living being helps you cultivate within yourself the causes for your own liberation. Without other beings, you could not develop the love and compassion that are truly causes of attaining buddha-hood. Not only are other beings helping you, but the buddhas are helping you as well; as enlightened beings endowed with unhindered wisdom, compassion, and spiritual power, they exist solely to help those who are unenlightened go on to achieve enlightenment. From every angle, you have much more help on the Mahāyāna path. The buddhas, with their unhindered power and compassion, will actively assist you, and other beings are at all times existing simply to help you develop—on their behalf—the spiritual qualities of love and compassion that you need for your own liberation.

We have already said how kind other beings have been to you in this life or in the past. They are very deserving of your own kindness, thoughtful consideration, and refusal to abandon them in their difficult straits. Considering how very positively they are helping you achieve your own spiritual goal of highest liberation, you should be loving toward them, always striving to develop in your mind a very real devotion toward, and active love for, all beings. Just as parents have profound love for their children and an active interest in their well-being, so you should strive to awaken within yourself a similar interest in the happiness of all beings and a sincere desire to benefit them. You will achieve much more spiritual merit by meditating on love for all beings than by making innumerable offerings of valuable goods to the buddhas. There is more merit in a single thought of love for other beings than in showing all kinds of reverence for, and doing prostrations in front of a shrine to, the buddhas.

The buddhas themselves are endowed with great love for all living beings. If you want to show your appreciation to the buddhas, be loving toward other living beings. Whoever promotes the happiness of beings pleases the buddhas, for the buddhas' sole thought and motivation is to achieve the highest possible good of all living beings. Conversely, whoever hurts beings hurts the buddhas, and whoever causes any harm to the buddhas displeases them. Thus, if you have any desire for rapport with the enlightened ones, for that reason, if no other, you should be loving toward beings and avoid injuring them.

As a final argument, you should know that beings are, by their very nature, endowed with buddha-nature. Whether or not they know it, all beings are buddhas, just as you yourself are one. For this reason alone they are worthy of being treated with respect, kindness, and thoughts of love.

To summarize, there are three very good reasons why you should give up all thoughts of seeking a self-oriented form of salvation: (1) it is an inferior attitude, or motivation, (2) it is a limited state of liberation, handicapped by certain limitations, and (3) the bodhisattva's way, the Mahāyāna path to liberation, is the easiest path, since you have help from the buddhas and all other beings along the way.

GREAT LOVE

Because all living beings are endowed with buddha-nature, to hurt them is to hurt the buddhas, and to make them happy is to please the buddhas. There are quotations from Shāntideva and Āryadeva, the essence of which is that great love for all living beings is the first prerequisite to entering Mahāyāna Buddhist meditation. When you have set your heart on the happiness of other beings, excluding none, you are endowed with the great love we are talking about here.

In certain forms of meditation on love taught by the Buddha, you encompass the entire universe by directing your mind in every direction and then wishing and praying that all beings might always enjoy happiness and the cause of happiness, which is the result of wholesome actions or virtue. If this quality of love is so essential on the Mahāyāna path, how is it to be developed within yourself? We will give some practical instructions on the way to thus meditate.

To do this, we break down our meditation by focusing on three or more categories of beings, and start with whatever love we already have in our minds. Most of us have a certain amount of affection or fondness for the people we relate to through family or friendship, so we start with these. We can build on the love we are already in the habit of feeling by meditating first on our kinsmen, then on love for our enemies, and finally on love for all living beings.

Now, in most cases, your own mother is easiest to love. From your very birth onward, her kindnesses to you and her claim on your affections are most obvious. Hence, modeling other meditations on the following meditation of love for your mother, first separate your meditation into four subtopics: (1) recognition of your mother; (2) recognition of her kindness to you, (3) recognition that you should repay her kindness, and (4) meditation on how to accomplish that repayment.

RECOGNITION OF YOUR MOTHER

Be seated on your meditation cushion and complete your regular preliminaries of taking refuge and awakening the enlightenment thought, as always. Then visualize your mother, whether living or dead, as you remember her best. Visualize her very clearly in front of you. Think of her sitting there, gazing at you with loving eyes and smiling. See her very clearly and just focus on her. Allow the very clear, conscious recognition that "this is truly my own mother." Now begin the reflection to awaken a recognition of her kindness to you.

RECOGNITION OF YOUR MOTHER'S KINDNESS

To begin with, your mother carried you in her womb for nine months, during which she was constantly concerned for your safety. She avoided actions, foods, and circumstances that might have endangered your health or welfare. Even before you were born, she was thinking about your benefit and making efforts to remove your sufferings. It is actually through her efforts on your behalf that you now have an opportunity to hear the Dharma and the rare chance for enlightenment in this life or in future lifetimes. These auspicious conditions are the result of her kindness in giving you a human body and molding you in such a way that you value an encounter with the Dharma such as this one.

Even in your infancy, when you were incapable of talking and as helpless as a worm, your mother kept you warm and fed you. At that time you were absolutely helpless and would certainly have died had you been left to fend for yourself. Your mother didn't let you die but nourished you with great love. She carried you in her arms, fed you from her breasts or from her own mouth, and cleaned and bathed you with her own hands. She protected you from diseases and dangers. She held you up between her ten fingers and sang to you. She called you sweet names and gazed on you with loving eyes.

Throughout your childhood, your mother couldn't be separated from you even for a single moment. If she was separated from you, it was as if part of her own heart had been taken from her. Her every concern was for your well-being: What were you doing? Were you okay? You were never far from her thoughts even when you were physically separated. When you had grown a little, it was she who taught you how to eat, drink, walk, and sit. She taught you how to communicate; later, she began to teach you to discriminate between what was helpful and what was harmful. In this way she was like a teacher to you. She helped instill a moral sense within you, a code of behavior that is of spiritual benefit years later.

At all times, your mother remained concerned for your well-being. If you grew even slightly ill, she became alarmed and called doctors, worried that you might die. She said prayers for you and worried that you wouldn't be as successful as the other kids. She had lamas perform ceremonies for you, had fortunetellers make predictions for you; she went to psychiatrists on your behalf. She was always concerned for you. In fact, it was really for your sake that she grew old; she never allowed herself a free moment or thought to call her own as long as she felt responsible for your well-being. She often went without sleep at night and worked until her bones grew tired. Her feet and hands would ache from working on your behalf, but this she was willing to do. She never begrudged all those long and ceaseless labors as long as you were well provided for and she could feel that you were all right.

For your sake, also, your mother became almost like a miser. She denied herself food and clothing when necessary, and passed up luxuries and comforts for herself that you might have them. The things that she thought too good for herself—or wasted on others—were all right for you. Had she had the power, she definitely would have made you a universal emperor, placing you at the very apex of happiness and power. By always thinking of you, she thought less and less of her own benefit. Your life and your advantage, your comfort, happiness, and well-being were of more concern to her than her own. Had she spent her life thinking of her own liberation from worldly existence, she might have acquired real happiness for herself. Ungrudgingly, she thought instead of your worldly gain, your advantage, your spiritual progress, your benefit.

How can we forget such kindness? No matter what our relationships with our mothers, how can we deny that they have been, in this basic way, so kind? Let us consider other kindnesses that we have received through our mothers' love. On the round of worldly existence, it is extremely rare to hear the name of the Buddha even in passing. But if you do have an opportunity to practice, thanks to good karma, that practice becomes the cause of happiness not only in this life and in the bardo but throughout future lives. Thus you have the possibility of obtaining the highest good available to living beings, and that opportunity arises only through your mother's kindness, since she gave you human birth and a human form, and reared you in such a way, time, and place that you are able to profit from an encounter with the Dharma.

Not only in this lifetime has your mother been of benefit to you, but in many prior lifetimes as well. Again and again she has served as your kind mother. Through countless lifetimes she has been as kind as in your present life. Countless times, she has had to beg to feed you. Countless times, she has been born among fishermen and hunters and has committed sinful actions to save your life and promote your happiness. Countless times, she has had to live among the animals and die to save you from the attacks of others. If you were to collect all the milk that you have drunk just from this one kind mother over the countless aeons of time, it would be more than all the water in the oceans.

In other lifetimes, she has been not only your mother but your father, and has done much for you. She has been your kinsmen, your best friends, your lovers. If you collected all the tears she has shed for you throughout time, they would more than overflow the oceans. In fact, were we to make a list detailing the various kindnesses that this one mother has done for you throughout time, it would take an aeon to compile. There is no evading the fact that this present mother of yours has benefited you in countless ways. You should, therefore, recognize that kindness.

RECOGNITION OF THE NEED TO REPAY YOUR MOTHER'S KINDNESS

Having recognized your mother's kindness, you should also recognize your responsibility to repay it. Having received so much benefit and love from another being, what kind of person would simply reap the advantages of it and not have the thought that "I, too, have some responsibility here and should repay this kind of kindness. I have received great kindness from this being, and it deserves to be repaid"?

It would be a very cruel-hearted child who would forget all about his mother's kindness, or take it for granted and say it was "just her tough luck" or "so much wasted energy on her part," not feeling any obligation to repay her. From a Buddhist point of view, this kind of neglect and avoidance is an indication of a very base, mean sort of human character. Thus, when you set about to recognize your obligation to repay your mother's kindness, reflect in this way:

> Even after benefiting from my mother's kindnesses one after the other, lifetime after lifetime, year after year, I haven't yet started to repay her. What have I really done to help my mother so far? How have I done anything that has truly promoted her happiness? I really haven't repaid her, and yet, if I don't make efforts to do so, I don't deserve any self-respect, nor am I worthy of any respect from others. It is just too cruel-hearted to forget all about it. It is quite obvious that I should repay her kindness, and I will. I will consider this kind mother of mine and her present situation, and reflect,

"How can I repay that kindness? How can I really benefit this mother of mine? What would be most beneficial for her?"

Reflecting in this way, you will realize that helping your mother achieve material comfort or financial stability—a holiday in the Caribbean, or whatever—won't really repay the kindness you have received from her. What she really wants and needs, and what would be most beneficial to her, is happiness. If she were truly happy and had happiness's cause, that would be the very best thing you could wish for her. If you could achieve your mother's true well-being, you could be sure that you had repaid her in the best possible way. Having understood this, you may reflect:

> When I look at this mother, I see that she is not very happy. She doesn't even have the causes for present and future happiness. Through her concern for me and through ignorance of the Dharma, she hasn't accumulated those virtues and spiritual qualities that would truly make her happy.

MEDITATION ON REPAYING YOUR MOTHER'S KINDNESS

Meditate on your mother: just focus on her and think about her, with a feeling of sadness about the plight she is in and her inability to achieve the happiness she longs for. Then, directing your mind toward her with real love and a genuine desire for her happiness, think:

> I pray that this kind mother might have happiness. May she always have happiness and its cause, which is virtue. May this mother of mine truly have happiness and its causes.

Think in this way again and again, sincerely wishing for her happiness. This is called "meditation that is linked to one's intention or wish." Then reflect:

> It is not just enough to sit here and think, "May she be happy, may she be happy." I must do something for my mother. I really must achieve her happiness somehow.

This is called "meditation that is linked to bodhichitta, the enlightenment thought." After reflecting on her in this way, think:

> Thoughts alone really don't achieve my mother's happiness; I must actually do something. What am I going to do? Right now, I am

unable to help her. I just don't have the brains, the spiritual qualities, the wisdom, or the power to establish her in the kind of happiness I know she wants, needs, and deserves. The only way I can help is by achieving buddhahood and the ability to remove her sufferings, establishing her in that kind of happiness. For her sake, I will strive for buddhahood. I'm going to practice the Dharma rightly, just the way it has been taught, in order to achieve buddhahood and the ability to remove her from her present suffering and establish her in the highest happiness.

Do these three types of meditation. If you are stronger in one of them, start with that one and gradually build on it. Switch from one to the other in your meditative sessions: they are all meditations on love. Just play them back and forth, lengthening and shortening the time of meditation according to your state of mind—whatever is best for your own meditation. Practice in this way for a long time, and repeat your efforts regularly. Every day, set aside some time for this meditation on your mother, so that it becomes very easy, very natural, and not a hard exercise. Finally, you should think:

At present, I don't have the power to help my mother attain happiness. Who does have this power? The Buddha, Dharma, and Sangha have the wisdom, compassion, and power to help my mother right now. They are endowed with that kind of spiritual power.

Pray to the Three Jewels, your teacher, and the lineage of teachers from your heart on your mother's behalf. Call on them to bless and protect your mother, remove her sufferings, establish her in happiness, and do all that you are presently unable to do for her.

It is very much as if a mother who lacked arms were to see her baby being carried off in a torrent. Knowing that she is unable to rescue her child from drowning, all she can do is call for help. This she does, running along the bank, calling for other people to come quickly and rescue her child. Lacking the ability to establish your mother in real happiness at present, all you can do is call on the buddhas and bodhisattvas to help.

You will soon find that, by building on your existing affection, love flows easily from your heart. When you have used this image of your mother with some success, move on to lovingly visualizing your father, by simply adjusting the details. From there, work on your kin, your friends, and on strangers for whom you have no feelings. Next, meditate on your enemies, who arouse anger every time you think of them. Recall that they have all been your own kind mother in past lives, but that they are unable to recognize this because you and they are so changed; in their deluded states, they cannot see that reality. And until such time as you can really see these enemies as your mother, remember the harm to yourself of vengeance and anger.

27

GIVING OUR PARENTS A PIGGYBACK RIDE

WE WHO HAVE BEEN FORTUNATE enough to acquire human birth, come into contact with the teachings of liberation, and find a teacher willing to teach us also have an excellent opportunity to achieve a stage of irreversibility on the path of practice, provided we put our minds to it. We have the opportunity to attain the highest Body of Reality—the dharmakāya, or enlightened mind of the Buddha—if we wish it. Thus it would be well if we were to think carefully and reflect, "Why shouldn't I undertake something in this life that will promote my well-being in future lifetimes?" If we practice properly, there is no reason we can't achieve such results.

In undertaking a path of practice, we find that there are many doors to the Dharma. The particular door we have entered is the lam-dre system of meditation, which contains the most cherished doctrines of the Sakya order. Our studies are based on the text known as *The Three Visions*.

Before resuming our discussion, it might be helpful to consider *The Three Visions* as a whole. What is it all about? As we have explained before, the title refers to three levels of perception: the impure level, that of experience, and that of perfect enlightenment. *The Three Visions* is designed to help us enter the path of practice rightly, and thereby prepare our minds for the advanced stages of meditation.

The Three Visions is concerned, first of all, to awaken within us a spirit of renunciation. This comes about when we have learned to recognize the negative aspects of worldly existence—when we see its nature as conditioned, faulty, inclined to pain, and insubstantial, not to mention impermanent. Then it becomes possible to reorient ourselves toward a transmundane spiritual goal. The reflections discussed in our study of the impure vision help bring about such a spirit of renunciation. The reflections on the particular sufferings of each of the realms of existence, on death and impermanence, and on the operation of the law of karma were all designed to stimulate both an awareness of the flaws inherent in worldly existence and a desire to do something about them.

Second, *The Three Visions* is concerned to awaken within us sincere love and compassion and the heartfelt wish to attain enlightenment for the sake of all beings. Thus our forthcoming discussion of the vision of experience will cover three main topics: (1) the meditation on great love, (2) the meditation on great compassion, and (3) the meditation on bodhichitta. The intent of these instructions is to help us develop spiritual and mental qualities, as well as an attitude toward practice, that will remove the obstacles inherent in a self-centered perception of our practice and goal.

When we have developed great love and great compassion, our efforts in meditation (and everything else we do) will be motivated not merely by the desire for spiritual reward but by the very altruistic desire to achieve the benefit of others. When our perception of other beings is tempered by the thought of love, and our hearts' wish is that those beings should experience happiness and all the virtuous causes of happiness, now and for all time, then our minds are truly endowed with the spirit of love. And that great love, which doesn't exclude any being from the wish for happiness, leads naturally to the awakening within ourselves of great compassion.

Great compassion is a mental attitude toward other beings that is not merely content with wishing their happiness but, perceiving their unhappiness, cannot bear it. When we have great compassion, we would give anything to be able to remove the unhappiness of others.

Only when our minds are endowed with these two great qualities of love and compassion, which become the impetus for attaining the spiritual goal of liberation, can we begin to experience the various stages of the Mahāyāna path. At this point our wish for the happiness of others, and that they be free from unhappiness, is translated into concrete action. Activity becomes crystallized in what is known as bodhichitta, or the resolve to win enlightenment for the sake of all beings. We no longer think of seeking buddhahood simply because it is the highest spiritual goal available, because it is a reward, or out of desire for our own personal liberation. In fact, we now regard attainment of buddhahood only as a means of best accomplishing our good wishes toward suffering beings.

Bodhichitta, or resolve, has two forms. First, there is the formal resolution, which is simply the thought or verbalization of the resolve in our hearts to strive for buddhahood on behalf of beings. Later, this resolve becomes translated into positive action, as we undertake to train in all those practices that will bring about the attainment of buddhahood for their sakes. On the level of conventional reality, these practices are the "deeds of the bodhisattva"—generosity, moral conduct, patience, diligence in making right efforts—in short, all those wholesome efforts that promote the happiness of beings, remove their sufferings, and bring us closer to buddhahood.

On the level of ultimate reality (that perception of reality attained by enlightened beings), our resolve to work for beings is expressed through insight into the ultimate nature of those beings, ourselves, and all phenomena. Thus we no longer cling to coarse conceptions of independent individuals or real things, but see them as they really are: devoid of any ultimate, absolute, inherent nature of their own. We perform all beneficial actions—the accumulation of merit through kindly deeds and the two stages of meditation (concentration and insight)—without clinging to any unenlightened preconceptions about what constitutes the object of our good actions or their goal. We no longer think of the spiritual goal as a real thing that we will attain as real egos, or agents, nor do we see others as real beings. Rather, our actions are performed through a state of insight. When actions are performed on this level of ultimate insight, they are said to be expressions of bodhichitta on the level of ultimate reality.

Finally, *The Three Visions* is concerned with the third level of perception, the pure vision of enlightened beings. We need to be confident that, by making all these efforts and undertaking the various stages of practice, the goal is attainable and worthwhile. We need to know the benefit of striving for and obtaining the goal of the Mahāyāna path. The explanation of the pure vision is intended to strengthen our resolve to strive for the goal of buddhahood by describing its nature, qualities, and benefits.

These three sections of the *Lam dre* have been so divided to make it convenient for a meditator to (1) understand the stages of the exoteric Mahāyāna path, (2) comprehend the full path, and (3) relate to the various practices and experiences within the context of the path as a whole. All the other Buddhist teachings that you may hear from other teachers or encounter in books can be related to these three stages of perception. This is of great help to a meditator who needs to know where he or she is on the path to enlightenment, what the appropriate practices are, and which remedies and instructions are to be applied at each stage. Once you have gained some familiarity with these three levels of perception, you won't be caught by surprise; you will have some reference to enable you to place your meditative experience in its proper context. Moreover, teachings that belong to other systems of meditation (though they may be described under different names or in a different sequence) can easily be recognized as identical to the stages on this path.

Let us return to the discussion of love, compassion, and bodhichitta. We have described how love is to be developed gradually, through meditating first on those for whom you feel natural or habitual affection, next on strangers and people toward whom you have neutral feelings, then on enemies or people you dislike, and finally on all beings without exception. This is to be done by visualizing your mother. Through reflecting on her many acts of kindness toward you in this life and in past lives, you will develop a feeling for her kindnesses and an awakening of love toward her, and then, gradually, a powerful wish for her to experience the benefits of happiness. After you have developed these strong feelings of love toward your mother, you should meditate on your father, other members of your family, close friends, and other people of whom you are especially fond.

It is very easy to extend wishes for happiness and feelings of love to people who are close to you. By identifying strangers as having been in much the same relationships to you in past lives as your own mother, relatives, and close friends are to you now, you will develop the same feelings of closeness toward them, accompanied by a strong desire for their genuine, lasting happiness. After meditating in this way for as long as it takes to awaken a feeling of love for all beings, you will experience a spontaneous wish for their happiness and desire for their well-being whenever you see or even think of them. This is an outflowing of goodwill, real love, and affection for others, no matter who they are. When you feel this, you can be said to have achieved great love on the Mahāyāna path.

In a mind moved by great love, it is very easy for compassion to arise. Wishing only the well-being and happiness of others, you will not be able to bear their unhappiness. The perception of their grief, pain, and unhappiness will be a source of great personal grief and sorrow. This feeling of sadness, and the wish that other beings might not have to endure such suffering, will awaken within your mind a very strong sense of empathy. Whereas through love you wished only for beings' happiness, through compassion your only thought is that all beings somehow be freed from suffering.

This thought of compassion is to be developed, as we said, through meditating first on your mother, father, and those who are closest to you. Through the natural empathy you have with those beings, you will develop thoughts of compassion and the desire to see them become free from suffering. As before, gradually extend that compassionate empathy to strangers, enemies, and then to all beings without exception. When your response to all beings, or merely the thought of them, is a natural outflow of empathy and a strong feeling of sadness and regret to see them subject to pain or unhappiness—mental, physical, or karmic—then you are endowed with great compassion for beings.

Out of great love and great compassion that don't exclude any being, there arises a very strong determination and spiritual resolution to do something about their predicament. Thoughts of love and compassion, though very noble, do not in themselves establish other beings in happiness or remove them from the prospects of suffering. Now your attitude toward beings becomes transformed into action. You become motivated by the desire to achieve their true well-being and to remove them from all their sufferings. The accomplishment of the path to buddhahood takes on significance: it achieves its true meaning as a way of reaching your real goal, which is to perfect the well-being of all beings and remove all their causes of unhappiness.

Through the actual practice of love, the egocentric limitations of mind are gradually overcome, as are the negative mental states of anger, ill will, and all other thoughts of aversion to beings. That is why you begin by visualizing your mother. From the time of your birth, your mother has been most kind in giving you human form and caring for you when you were helpless. You will seldom, if ever, meet a person more concerned for your well-being, success, and happiness than your mother. Through recognizing her kindness, a natural feeling of reciprocity arises.

When this kindness is extended into past lives as well, you can see how very indebted you are to your mother and how you owe her your present state, which has become a basis for potential liberation. If you achieve buddhahood now, it will be due to your mother's kindness in giving you human birth and caring for you in such a way that you have been able to come into contact with practices that lead to your liberation. That in itself is an inestimably great kindness. Hence, when you remember her many kindnesses on your behalf, a feeling of indebtedness and a desire to repay her kindness should arise. This will be true for any right-thinking person.

How can you repay your mother's kindness? Merely making thoughtful gifts or helping in temporary or material ways will not really repay her. The best thing you can possibly do is ensure her true happiness. If you could achieve genuine well-being and happiness for your mother, free from suffering and the prospect of suffering, then you could say that you had done something truly beneficial for her.

Reflecting again and again on this wish for her happiness, repeatedly direct your mind to your mother and unceasingly pray for her happiness, even though you yourself do not yet have the ability to effect it. But through relying on your teachers and the bodhisattvas and buddhas, you do have the power and compassion to work for her happiness and pray for her benefit. Over and over again, direct your mind to your mother from the very bottom of your heart; come to long for her true happiness and well-being.

At last, when a strong feeling of love comes spontaneously to mind whenever you think of your mother, start meditating on your father also. Although he didn't carry you in the womb or give you milk during your infancy, he gave you life, love, and protection and always sought to promote your own welfare in all his actions. Thus it is very easy to extend to your father those same reflections. Continue to build on this natural empathy and extend it to all beings.

If you discover mental obstacles that your ego creates, or experience reluctance to extend genuine love to a given being, recognize this as the residue of past anger or general obscurations that you may have accumulated in the past. Then, before undertaking the meditation on great love, try to overcome such obstacles by thinking of the good qualities of the loving mind: how open one feels, how unrestricting the compassionate mind is, and how happy and free from the pain of harboring anger, ill will, and malice. Consider how much good is achieved, even in the present situation, both for yourself and for the recipient of a loving state of mind. Reflect on how this love also leads you closer to your spiritual goal and to freedom from any possibility of experiencing the evil states of existence that result from selfish and unkind thoughts toward others.

If your reluctance still doesn't go away, think about the faults of anger itself, how it is truly your greatest enemy. There is no other fault that burns the mind like anger. If you really have an enemy, it is not that deluded person who spoke unkindly or treated you poorly. You should be angry at yourself for harboring your own greatest enemy in your own mind. If there is one thing that will cause you the greatest harm you could ever experience in saṃsāra, it is the anger within your own mind. Hence it is crucial to persevere in trying to overcome any obstacles you might experience, such as a reluctance to be loving toward others. Think as follows:

> Just by meditating in this way—whether or not I really mean it, whether or not I am really achieving a state of all-out love by meditating on these thoughts of love—I am accumulating merit and benefiting myself. I don't know whether directing thoughts of

love to him will benefit my enemy, but I can be sure that it will benefit me. Thus, if I really am self-interested, if I prize myself over this goal of mine, I should continue with my meditations of love.

If I can't bear even a few days of mental or physical pain, how will I bear the long-lasting suffering that I will experience in the lower realms of existence—the hells and elsewhere? That is all I am doing: by clinging to and cherishing these thoughts of ill will and malice, I am simply preparing the causes for rebirth in some lower state of existence.

Actually, there is no one more foolish that I am. I am really quite stupid if I claim to be following the Mahāyāna path and still harbor anger and ill will in my mind. The essence of the Mahāyāna path is love and compassion for all beings, excluding none. This is the Great Way.

Reflect again and again on the faults of harboring anger. Try to realize that, if you succeed in getting rid of these thoughts within your own mind, you will also have vanquished your external enemy. When you no longer have the concept of "enemy" or a feeling of anger toward anyone, you have removed all your enemies at once, just by uprooting anger from your own mind. Reflect repeatedly on the dangers of anger and ill will and on the virtues and benefits of love and compassion. Your aversion will gradually weaken, the hold of anger will loosen, and the impulse toward love will grow, because your mind will be freed from the bonds of self-centeredness and malice toward others.

The mind experiences joy through this all-embracing outflow of love and compassion. Having once experienced this all-encompassing, pure state of love and joy, your mind will see for itself the great difference between the narrow, constricted confines of anger, ill will, and self-centeredness and that vast, joyful state which wishes only for your own and others' true benefit.

If your mind is filled with thoughts of love for others and a sincere wish only for their well-being, you will, as the sūtras say, find happiness wherever you go. This is because wherever the loving person moves, no matter what the situation, he will encounter no enemies and meet only friends and helpers on his spiritual path. As it is said in the *Bodhicharyāvatara*,

It is clearly impossible to upholster the whole surface of this globe with leather merely to avoid stepping on sharp stones and thorns, but if you cover the soles of your feet with leather, it is as good as if the whole world had been covered over.

In the same way, it is not possible for us to change the actions and states of mind of other people. If they act rudely or violently through anger and delusion, we can't help it. However, we need not let our own minds become poisoned or hurt by their delusions. If our own minds have been purified of any impulse to retaliate with anger and ill will, that is as good as if the whole world were treating us with love.[47]

In your practice, persevere in developing the thought of love for all beings in all situations. Gradually try to extend the range of these feelings of love and goodwill. If you find it difficult to think of all beings at once in every direction, take it step by step. Think, for example, of the beings in each of the six realms of existence, starting with the hell beings and working up through the ghosts, animals, humans, titans, and gods. Direct your thoughts of goodwill toward them, and break up the meditation in whatever way you find convenient or helpful.

The main technique is to develop thoughts of love toward at least one being and then, through identification, to extend those thoughts to others until all beings are included. When you feel that your mind is wholly concerned with the well-being of others, that it is sincerely interested only in their mental and physical well-being and does not exclude anyone, you can rest assured that you have a loving mind. Just as a mother has a strong feeling of love, affection, and concern for the happiness of her only child, so you should come think of all beings with that kind of active concern for their well-being and constant wish for their ultimate benefit.

Now, let us analyze this state of love toward beings. The formal practice of meditation that we described previously consists of visualizing your mother (whether living or dead) looking at you with very loving eyes. You then enter the meditation with recognition of her as your kind mother who has benefited you in so many ways, and experience a feeling of indebtedness toward her, saying to yourself:

> It would really be a poor show, truly a bad reflection on my character, if I simply accepted all these kindnesses and never expended the least effort to repay her.

Next, out of your desire to repay her kindness, reflect on the best way to do it. As the sūtras say, merely giving her gifts or trying to make her comfortable in her old age does not repay your mother's kindness. Even if we were to carry our parents around on our shoulders day and night, all over the globe, or were to make offerings of whole universes filled with riches, it really wouldn't repay the kindness we have received from them. Through many lifetimes they have sacrificed their own chances for happiness and liberation merely to promote our own interests. The fact that we now have an opportunity to gain liberation from the round of suffering is due solely to them.

By now, this feeling that your parents' kindness should not be ignored or allowed to slip by should be very strong. Through reflection, you will come to realize that the best way to repay that kindness is through achieving your parents' true happiness. If they were experiencing physical and mental well-being—if they truly felt happy, without any source of present suffering or prospect of future suffering; if they experienced nothing but one joy after another, of the sort derived from virtuous actions—then you could feel good about your parents. And if you yourself could bring about such a state for them, then you could think, "Yes, I have really done something to repay the kindness of my parents." Hence this becomes the ground of your meditation.

The meditation on great love consists of three stages. First is the concern for your mother's well-being and a wish that she might truly be as happy as you want her to be.

Second, there should be a formalization of this thought, as you verbalize (either out loud or to yourself, mentally), "May this kind mother be happy. May she always be established in good actions." By now, you know that true happiness is the result of wholesome deeds (right actions of body, voice, and mind) and that every mental and physical suffering is the result of unwholesome actions. Therefore, wishing her always to have joy and virtue, you should pray very hard.

The third element is prayer. Pray to the guru, buddhas, and bodhisattvas from your heart, again and again, that through their compassion and power they may bestow upon your kind mother a blessing of happiness and all that you wish for her. At this stage you should develop the resolve to win enlightenment on her behalf, thinking:

> Right now, I don't have the power to help this kind mother as I
> would like. To achieve the ability to establish her in the kind of joy

and happiness that she needs so badly, I will strive for and attain buddhahood for her sake.

Pray that your teacher and the Three Jewels will help you succeed in this. Then meditate in this same way toward your father, strangers, enemies, and all beings without exception.

Even in your nonsessional practice (after you have left off your formal practice of great love), continue to develop this attitude toward all beings while going about your daily affairs. Make efforts to save the lives of insects and other animals, no matter how small. Protect them with thoughts of concern for their well-being. Give food, clothing, and shelter to the homeless and others who are needy. Extend your loving protection to those who are without protection, and your love to those who are in need of love and have no friend or guardian.

In your speech, also, try always to speak only kind and loving words that encourage the minds of others and remove their suffering. Encourage them with the thought that someone does care for them, that you are concerned for their well-being. By speaking always in this kind and loving way, try to promote their own prospects for feeling happy.

You can also try to teach the Dharma in appropriate ways, thus helping other beings come closer to true happiness and free themselves from the causes of suffering. Even for animals, you can at least recite the name of the Buddha. You can actually plant the seeds of future happiness by speaking aloud to them the names of the buddhas and bodhisattvas and reciting a mantra, such as *Om mani padme hum*, while sincerely wishing for their eventual liberation.

Thus the real root of the Mahāyāna religion is love for other beings. Without it, there is no prospect for any progress on the path. Without it, buddhahood and the spiritual goals could never be attained. But with love, both compassion and bodhichitta arise spontaneously.[48]

28

A MIND LIKE AN OVERTURNED POT

DHARMA DISCOURSES have two major parts: in the first, the teacher talks about the background and special instructions needed to receive the teaching; in the second, he expounds the topic itself, which in this case is the lam-dre teachings and, specifically, the meditation on great compassion. But first there are some preparatory instructions that we have not yet discussed concerning what we may expect of ourselves as lam-dre students.

It is important that we learn to recognize and avoid the three faults that impair the capacity of a practitioner. The first is lack of attention. No matter how great the teaching or the teacher, a student with this fault allows his mind to run and wander; such a mind is like an overturned pot, which cannot contain milk. The teaching, so to speak poured into him, is thus wasted.

The second fault is that of not retaining the teachings. Even though this type of student is attentive during the presentation of the teachings, he is unable to retain them intact but inevitably garbles them, mixing them up with his own distorted fantasies. This student is likened to a pot with holes in its side, through which milk runs out and is wasted on the ground.

The third impairment concerns giving teachings whose aim is to decrease egotism and defilements to a mind that is still ruled by greed, lust, pride, envy, ill will, despondency, and anger. All the beneficial lessons memorized by a student subject to this fault come to nothing, strangled by these defilements. This situation is like pouring milk into a pot that already contains poison; only death or illness can result.

In addition to these three faults, there are six further obstacles on the path:

1. *Pride.* If you approach a Dharma center for teachings but carry in your heart and mind self-centered thoughts about your own importance, capacity, superior education, background, good looks, status, wealth, family, or occupation, you have a good block right there. The Dharma is directed toward lessening all of these—toward selflessness. There is no room for ego, or pride, on the path.

2. *Lack of confidence, or faithlessness.* Suppose you arrive to take teachings with an attitude critical of the teacher, his attainments, qualifications, or skill in teaching. Here is another obstacle to beneficial teachings. If you are not receptive to the Dharma and your guru, the prospects for your growth on the path are poor. Sprouts don't come from scorched seeds; so, too, a mind lacking in faith can hardly sprout. Keep your mind open, test and prove what you are taught. Practice, and give the teachings a chance. Don't block them.

3. *Treating the Dharma, the guru, or the occasion too lightly.* Here, you permit yourself to think the situation banal, boring, or of no value, the teachings repetitious or not worth your effort ("Perhaps I should have stayed home"). Thus you allow an attitude of neglect to overpower you. But what does it matter if you have heard all this before? These are still profound teachings that lead to buddhahood, and you are still a student much in need of them.

4. *Distraction.* In this case you may be present, but only physically: your mind wanders to daily affairs, and your other senses draw the mind away. The eyes wander to pictures on the walls, examine others in the room, and gaze out the windows.

5. *Forcing the mind.* In your zeal to avoid all of the above, especially distraction, you may force your mind to concentrate too much on every word. Don't force your mind to be more attentive than needed. Find the median. Be alert and natural.

6. *Discouragement.* Having taken up study, you may find yourself with some of the obstacles just mentioned, or with personal or family illnesses or other circumstances that make attendance difficult. Alternatively, doubts may assail you; you may even doubt your own ability to attain enlightenment and talk yourself out of trying. Counter such times of despair with reflections that encourage you to persevere. It is crucial to recognize such situations as obstacles when they arise, overcoming them with proper reflections on the teachings, their supreme value, and the great benefit they offer you and all sentient beings. Make your heart strong. Sakya Pandita[49] said that when we bestow gifts on others, we can feel the good that it does us—and them as well. If you fully grasp this, you will also be convinced, on a gut level, of the good that ensues for both yourself and others when you receive teachings.

୧ ⚜ ୨

It may also be useful here to see yourself as the patient and your guru as the doctor. If you have ever been ill, you know that the ideal relationship between patient and physician is one of confidence, or faith, in the physician's skill and in his medicine; then, if all goes well, health will be recovered. Now, we are all, by nature, afflicted with ignorance. Ignorance arises due to the erroneous belief in an a substantial, truly existing self. The guru knows all about this illness of ignorance, its cure, the potions to prescribe, and their dosages. The words of the Buddha are the remedy for ignorance: they bring insight into the true nature of reality by showing that there is no real ego, and they purify mental states through realization of wisdom. Just as you hope to recover from ordinary illnesses, so you can have every confidence that the teachings of enlightenment constitute the remedy for your spiritual disease. Recovery and liberation are one.

By now, you know that the opportunity to hear the Dharma is only rarely met by beings. Such teachings are of great power in and of themselves, because through them you can attain perfect enlightenment; coupled with a sincere and dedicated mind, they can bring about wondrous transformations. Thus we should not take them lightly.

Two stories illustrate this point. There was a frog who was squatting on the road when an old, blind Buddhist monk came by, chanting as he walked along. Although the frog heard the monk, the monk couldn't see the frog and accidentally squashed him with his cane. Having made this curious connection with the Dharma, the frog was reborn in the gods' realm. Much amazed, he wondered how he had gotten there. With his new powers, he was able to discover the reason, and so went back to make the monk an offering of flowers.

Vasubandhu, the third- or fourth-century Indian sage, wrote much of the Buddhist canon and was a great memorizer and reciter of scripture. He shared his cave with a pigeon, who thus went to sleep and awoke hearing sūtras. When the bird died, he was reborn in a fine family and pestered his parents to reunite him with the sage. The parents sought out Vasubandhu and found him at Nālandā University. The child recognized him and became his disciple Sthiramati.

If such things are possible for mere animals, how much more might we (and our cockroaches) hope for if we practice diligently? Always remember that the human body and human intelligence are endowed with great power and potential. We *can* attain buddhahood in a single lifetime. We must integrate the teachings into our daily experience and keep these words of advice always in mind, so as to benefit from them.

29

THE FLAVOR OF COMPASSION

IT IS OF GREAT SIGNIFICANCE that we have obtained human birth and the other requisites for receiving and putting into practice the teachings of enlightenment. If we have confidence in those teachings and are diligent in their application, we can attain the highest level of spiritual attainment available to any being: perfect enlightenment, or buddhahood. If we make only moderate efforts, we may attain the stages of bodhisattvahood, from the first bhūmi through the tenth. And even with the least amount of effort, it is possible to achieve, as a result of our efforts in this lifetime, the stage of arhatship. If such exalted, far-reaching, and truly wondrous results depend on the amount of effort we put into study and practice here in this life (where we are so fortunate as to encounter these teachings of enlightenment), it certainly behooves each of us to take very seriously this present opportunity and recognize in it the need to become diligent.

In its doctrine of perfect enlightenment and its method for gaining that highest of all stages of spiritual attainment, the Buddhist religion is truly unique among the great religions of the world. Its teachings of enlightenment, and techniques for attaining it, are categorized as belonging to either the exoteric or esoteric systems of meditation. The lam-dre teachings belong to the latter, which are, essentially, tantric practices for attaining enlightenment. In essence, the *Lam dre* doesn't differ at all from the other meditation systems that were practiced in Tibet, such as the Great Perfection doctrine of the Nyingma school and the mahāmudrā doctrines of the Kagyu and Gelug.

All these doctrines and techniques of the tantric path are authentic. They are truly the words uttered by the Buddha and compiled, preserved, and transmitted by the great bodhisattva compilers—Vajrapāṇi, Mañjushrī, and the rest. These same teachings were unerringly commented upon by the great sages of India, meditated upon by the great siddhas, translated by the great translators, and then introduced into the religious life of Tibet. Because these teachings were so carefully safeguarded by these great beings, their authenticity is ensured.

The lam-dre system that we are studying is worthy of our confidence as one such authentic teaching. It is one of the essential systems of practices prized by the sages of the Sakya order, so we should certainly be diligent in learning it.

The lam-dre system originated with the great Indian yogi Virūpa, who received it directly from the yoginī Nairātmya when she appeared to him, revealed her mandala, and instantly transmitted this teaching to him. At that very moment, he attained the first stage (*bhūmi*). During subsequent teachings from the goddess on the following six nights, he ascended progressively up to the sixth stage of bodhisattvahood, and then on to perfect enlightenment. He transmitted this teaching to his chief disciple, who in turn transmitted it to a succession of illustrious sages. Finally, the Indian saint Gayādhara brought it to Tibet and transmitted it to Tibetan Buddhist meditators.

It was from Gayādhara that this teaching was transmitted to the founders of the Sakya tradition. It is through their reliance on this great system of practice that innumerable meditators of the Sakya order have, throughout the succeeding centuries, attained extraordinary insights and even the highest spiritual attainment possible. This teaching, then, is of inestimable value because of its proven results, as experienced by great teachers in both India and Tibet, and because of the efficacy of its methods for awakening in oneself both the experience of the path and its result. It has rightly been treasured by holy persons throughout the centuries as a thing of great value.

Lam (*lam*) means "the path" and *dre* (*'bras*) means "the result." What does this imply? When Buddhists speak of the path, they are generally referring to the means that enable us to arrive at, or achieve, the result of buddhahood. Thus the path begins when we take refuge, awaken the resolve to attain enlightenment, and train in the progressive practices and experiences of the Five Paths that the bodhisattva must traverse to reach his goal: (1) the path of accumulation, (2) the path of application, (3) the path of perception, (4) the path of meditation, and (5) the path of no more training (the stage immediately preceding buddhahood, and the point after which you don't have to study or practice anymore).

Progressing through these five, the bodhisattva arrives at the result of buddhahood. This consists of what are called the the five bodies of buddhahood, or the five transcendent wisdoms, in tantric terminology. They can also be enumerated as three bodies or as four, but in this system, five bodies are distinguished. Thus there is a distinction in Mahāyāna Buddhism between the path of practice and the result of buddhahood.

The unique thing about the lam-dre system is that, while it does incorporate these two categories of path and result, it also contains a special doctrine of the path that contains within it the result. Hence, even when you are on the causal path, your practice, or experience, is that of the result. Technically, this is called "the Path as the Result." And when the *Lam dre* speaks of the result of buddhahood, it recognizes that the result also contains within it the causal stage. This is expressed by the saying that "The cause is the result, and the result is the cause."

At this stage, however, the path of meditation not only distinguishes between the two but also teaches that, while on the path, one can practice on the resultant stage, and while on the resultant stage, one also retains some elements of the path. This particular system of meditation is distinguished by eleven special factors, such as the instructions for practicing on the resultant stage even while one is still on the path, and vice versa. It also has special techniques for transmuting the experiences of the path, such as obstacles, into corresponding attainments (*siddhi*) on the resultant stage. For example, what would appear as an obstacle to an ordinary yogi would be transmuted for a lam-dre practitioner into a special attainment or insight. This is one of the special aspects of this path.

The basis of our study of the lam-dre system is *The Three Visions*, which contains an exposition of the foundational practices of meditation that must be mastered before one can proceed to tantric practices. These instructions are elaborated with reference to the three levels of perception indicated by the title. The first set of instructions refers to the impure vision of ordinary people and includes reflections on the unsatisfactory nature of worldly existence, death and impermanence, the law of karma, and so forth. These reflections are designed to awaken a resolve to turn away from worldly involvements and toward the spiritual life.

The second set of instructions refers to the vision of experience and includes the meditation of great love, the meditation of great compassion, the awakening of bodhichitta, and the instructions on concentration and insight meditation. All these are elaborated to help us arouse within ourselves something like great-heartedness. This is an extraordinarily noble resolve about one's practice. One doesn't allow one's mind to be selfish any longer, but takes on arduous tasks for the sake of others and produces a truly noble resolve to bear the sufferings of others in order to accomplish their good. This is the intent of these meditations: to break through the sense of self-orientation in one's spiritual life and produce a sense of nobility about one's spiritual practices.

The third set of instructions refers to the pure vision of enlightened beings. These teachings describe the major characteristics of buddhahood and are intended (1) to dispel misconceptions about our goal, and (2) to awaken within us a sense of confirmation in our own efforts. The goal is attainable; it is worth making efforts for. Its qualities are such that every other aim in life pales by comparison. In short, this set of instructions is meant to awaken within us a sense of encouragement about, and identification with, the goal of buddhahood.

We have already completed the set of instructions for awakening renunciation. In the second set of instructions, we have completed those for cultivating great love. We will now take up the instructions for awakening great compassion.

GREAT COMPASSION

We must begin by recognizing the nature of what Mahāyāna Buddhism terms great love and great compassion. The words "love," "pity," and "compassion" are often used in an ordinary sense—i.e., with the understanding that their scope is restricted. An ordinary person may very well love others, but not all others. An ordinary person loves someone else, or several other beings, but this does not constitute great love. An ordinary person may feel pity for others, but only for a few, not all.

Whenever a limit is set on the feeling of pity or compassion, there is no great compassion. In Mahāyāna practice, love and compassion are called "great" when they are extended to all beings, whether near or far, good or bad, dear or disliked. Because these feelings are truly all-inclusive, they are called "great" or "boundless." What is the object of great compassion? It is, obviously, all other beings.

What is the nature of feelings of great compassion? After you have awakened all-inclusive love and concern for all beings, and have the sincere desire to progress on the path for their sake, you cannot harbor ill feeling. When you contrast what you wish for beings with the nature of their real existence, you desire only to free them from their suffering and its causes.

Of what use is compassion? In the *Compendium of Doctrines Sūtra* (*Dharmasaṃgīti-sūtra*), Avalokiteshvara says to Lord Buddha that one who wants enlightenment should train not in many doctrines but in one only: compassion. The analogy is made that, wherever a universal monarch goes, his retinue follows him. All the qualities of enlightenment follow upon compassion. If compassion is absent from your mind, you will have neither the path nor the result. Thus compassion is the foundation of the Mahāyāna path.

In the *Adornment of the Mahāyāna Sūtras*, compassion is likened to a great tree that has for its roots compassion, for its trunk compassion, and as its fruit (or result) compassion. In other words, for the whole of the Mahāyāna path, compassion is foremost: it is the principal factor, and it flavors the whole experience of Mahāyāna Buddhism, right up to the result. The sūtra also says that if compassion is lacking in a practitioner, he will not be able to endure the rigors of other practices. For example, even if you persevere in trying to awaken wisdom through the practice of concentration and insight, or train in the other pāramitās, without being motivated and guided by great compassion, practice will be difficult.

For the meditator who first awakens within himself the motive of compassion, not only do all the experiences of the path come naturally, but even the suffering that is feared by those who hesitate to awaken compassion is, for him, transformed into happiness. For the bodhisattva, whose only happiness is the removal of others' suffering, every experience, even that of the hells, is transformed into a cause of joy. In all situations he rejoices in his ability to remove others from their suffering, to share their suffering with them, and to take it away from them. As the *Adornment of the Mahāyāna Sūtras* continues:

> Who, then, would not aspire to arouse within himself compassion
> for beings, which is the source of all spiritual qualities, and from
> which, for him who has this compassion, not suffering but bound-
> less joys ensue?

Three types of great compassion are distinguished: (1) compassion directed toward beings, (2) compassion directed toward the elements, or dharmas, and (3) objectless compassion.

The first of these consists of becoming aware of the plight of other beings, feeling pity for them, and wishing to remove their sufferings. Through our practice of insight meditation, we come to recognize that the sufferings they experience (as well as our own) all arise from the erroneous belief in a real self, and that it is this ignorant attachment to the notion of a self which causes beings to accumulate sources of suffering and to experience the results of their own deluded actions.

Second, we recognize within us our own selfishness and how the cause of all suffering is this ignorant attachment to the notion of a self. We realize that actually there is no self within other beings or within ourselves. Here we have as our object not beings as such but their components. We see beneath the surface to the source of beings' suffering, which is their false belief about themselves. Unenlightened beings cling to the belief that there is a real self within their component parts—i.e., form, feeling, perception, impulses, and consciousness (the so-called five aggregates, or skandhas). Thus we generate compassion through a ripe understanding of beings' ignorance about themselves.

The third type of compassion is objectless compassion. This arises when we see that there are no such things as beings. In ultimate reality, there are no beings and there is no perception of beings. Hence there are no components—no form, feeling, and so forth—no aggregates which, in unenlightened beings, become the source of their erroneous attachment to the notion of a self. Nonetheless, we realize that, from a conventional point of view, those unenlightened beings who are still deluded about the reality of their true nature remain subject to the experience of suffering. Thus we don't abandon those beings or leave them in ignorance about reality; rather, we feel unceasing great compassion for them and hope that they will become enlightened about their true nature.

COMPASSION TOWARD BEINGS

We will outline the instructions for cultivating each of these three kinds of great compassion, beginning with the first. Awakening compassion directed toward beings consists primarily of generating the wish that all beings, without exception, may become free from suffering and its causes.

As Chandrakīrti said, great compassion is, in essence, an attitude of protectiveness toward suffering beings. As with the meditation of great love, the way to practice this is to generate compassion first toward your own mother. Making her the object of your meditation, recall her many kindnesses to you and reflect that she may very well have been your own kind mother in many other lifetimes as well. Then remind yourself that,

> Rather than seeking her own liberation or her own benefit, this kind mother of mine has spent much time in this life—and, very likely, in other lifetimes as well—looking after me and caring for my welfare instead of her own. As a result, she has roamed about in worldly existence for a very long time. Out of concern for me and lack of concern for herself, she has accumulated causes that may

very well keep her in saṃsāra. She is likely to experience many painful experiences against her wishes.

Next, remind yourself that you have a responsibility to repay your mother's kindness. In seeking to do so, you will come to understand that there is very little you can do for her that would truly be of any help. Nothing would be commensurate with her kindness, short of removing her altogether from her suffering and her prospects of suffering. It does not suffice merely to see to her comfort in old age or provide her with money, kind words, and kind thoughts. As long as she remains subject to suffering, you have not really acquitted yourself with regard to your responsibility toward her.

Hence you should be willing to accept the responsibility to remove this kind mother directly from her sufferings and prospects for suffering. Indirectly, you must remove her from the causes of her sufferings, which are her own unwholesome actions accumulated through ignorance. She has acquired the experience of mental and physical pain and remains subject to the prospects of further pain. Your job is to free her from this plight.

Reflect on her situation, seeing that she is subject to the natural pains of old age, disease, and death, of being forced to part from all that she holds dear, of undergoing the fearful experiences of rebirth, and of encountering many painful, frightening situations that she may not be able to understand. Reflect, also, that she will continue to experience these painful circumstances without cessation as long as she is not free from their causes. When you see your mother in this unhappy state, and faced with the prospect of future unhappiness as well, you will have a feeling of unbearable pity for her plight and a great longing to see her free from all these present and prospective states of suffering. You will also have a single-pointed wish to do anything within your power to so free her.

When you have gotten to this state of mind, begin to connect these feelings of commiseration with, and alarm about, your mother's plight with a resolve to do something about it, starting with prayers to the gurus and buddhas to help her by taking immediate action on her behalf. Recognize that you yourself are not yet able to help her as you wish, but that the buddhas and gurus do have that power. Invoke their blessings on her behalf; this will also strengthen your own resolve to become truly able to help her.

After you have meditated in these stages with regard to your mother, turn your mind toward your father, going through the same steps of (1) recognition, (2) awareness of his kindness, (3) recognition of his state, (4) resolve to free him from suffering, and (5) invocation of the buddhas on his behalf. Then direct your mind toward other beings who are suffering: those who are crazy, ill, afflicted, or distressed in one way or another.

In other words, begin by meditating wherever it's easiest—toward someone with whom you naturally identify and empathize; then include those toward whom compassion doesn't come very easily, such as to people who are far away or toward whom you usually feel indifferent.

Finally, learn to include even your worst enemies in your meditation, recognizing that, by hurting you, they are only acting out of their own delusions and ignorantly accumulating further causes of suffering for themselves. When you feel unbearable compassion for your enemies even when they are doing you injury, when you have an impulse to shield them from their own bad karma, and when you recognize in them your own kind mother, then you can be sure that you have this feeling of great compassion.

To do this, think that your enemy is that kind mother of yours who in the past was very good to you, but who, through ignorance and mental delusions, no longer recognizes you and therefore throws up obstacles on your spiritual path. If, through this reflection, you feel even greater compassion and resolve to help that being, you have achieved the desired stage of compassion.

30

RUDDERLESS ON THE SEA OF LIFE

To PURIFY THE GROUND for this effort you are making in learning the Dharma, think of your present circumstances and environment as those of the Pure Land, rather than as an ordinary situation and location. The teacher should be regarded as Shākyamuni Buddha himself, in person, who is teaching you. He is seated on a lion's throne, his body emitting radiant light, every word he utters imbued with the teachings of voidness. Think of yourself as Mañjushrī, intent on learning the Dharma for the good of all beings.

The teachings of the *Lam dre* originated with the great Indian pandit and siddha Virūpa, who received them directly from the goddess Vajranairātmyā, through whose blessings he instantly attained the first bhūmi and then proceeded through the remaining stages of bodhisattvahood. Virūpa transmitted these teachings to his disciples, who in turn passed them down to the founders of the Sakya order. Since that time, this system of meditation has been the principal source of guidance for masters of the Sakya tradition.

This teaching, like any other meditation, consists of two parts: the preliminary stage and the main body of the teaching itself. The text we are studying, *The Three Visions*, relates to the preliminary stage of practice; its instructions are preparatory to the advanced stages of insight described in *The Three Continua*.

The Three Visions distinguishes three stages of spiritual perception. We have completed our instructions on the impure vision, the first of the three. The second level is that of the meditator's vision, which goes beyond worldly experience. These instructions are designed to awaken a strong resolve to follow the path and seek the goal of buddhahood. Within the vision of experience, we have completed the instructions for awakening great love toward all living beings, and have begun those for awakening great compassion. The instructions for arousing this latter quality are treated in three topics: (1) compassion toward beings, (2) compassion toward the elements/components/phenomena (dharmas), and (3) objectless compassion. Here we continue with the study of compassion for dharmas.

COMPASSION TOWARD PHENOMENA

Chandrakīrti defined great compassion as the wish to protect all beings from pain and suffering. When Buddhists classify suffering, they recognize three types: (1) the suffering of suffering, (2) the suffering of change, and (3) the suffering of conditional existence. The first of these, the suffering of gross pain, is often observed either in our own experience or in that of other beings (whether animals or beings in the other lower realms), and consists of the various pains to which we are heir—those of birth, old age, disease, grief, and the like. These are easily understood, and it is simple to awaken within ourselves feelings of pity for any being who experiences them.

However, those we regard with pity are often oblivious to their own pain, danger, or unhappy plight. We see humans whose desire for great pleasure leads them to seek sense gratification, wealth, and the other causes of what they consider to be happiness. In the process, they burn up their lives and energies, destroying whatever prospects they might have for genuine happiness. Yet they do not recognize their course of action as involving present and future sufferings. It is like eating food that disagrees with you: thinking that you are consuming something pleasurable, you disregard the fact that it will lead only to pain when you are unable to digest it. Similarly, worldly activities in the pursuit of pleasure are really the causes of considerable pain.

Thus beings are often unaware of their own sufferings or unwilling to recognize them as painful. But their plight is apparent to the great bodhisattvas and buddhas, who, with their overview of human existence, see those pleasures for what they really are. They also see ordinary beings' ignorance about their true state, and when they observe this, they experience tremendous, almost unbearable compassion.

What we mean by compassion directed toward dharmas, as distinguished from compassion directed toward beings, is as follows: When we recognize that beings are endowed with both suffering and the cause of suffering, which is ignorance, then we feel compassion for them and have realized the cause of their suffering. When we have awakened within ourselves a wish that they be free from that suffering and its cause, then we have compassion toward dharmas.

It is necessary to develop this sense of awareness along with our compassion for beings and their plight. If we cannot get rid of the cause of suffering, we cannot get rid of the suffering that results. To help beings, it is necessary to assist them in dispelling their ignorance, which is the cause of their experience of pain. We must go beyond merely describing or removing their experience of pain and dig at the roots of suffering itself. As Dharmakīrti wrote, "The root of all unhappiness is ignorance, and that ignorance itself consists of false views about the self." And Shāntideva wrote in his *Bodhicharyāvatara*:

> Even though beings wish to avoid suffering, they run straight toward suffering alone. Even though they desire only happiness, they destroy happiness as if it were their own enemy.

All beings are motivated by abhorrence of pain and desire for pleasure, but because of their ignorance, they somehow manage to acquire only suffering. As long as beings are ignorant about their own nature, they will not be able to see clearly their own true aims of avoiding suffering and achieving happiness. This ignorance is rooted in the belief in a self. The perception of self where there is none is very much like our mistaken perception of a coiled rope: believing it to be a snake, we experience great fear and alarm. Similarly, beings such as ourselves misperceive the five skandhas as constituting a real, existent self and take action based on that ignorant misbelief. This leads only to sorrow and pain.

At this stage of your meditation, reflect on such beings and think of them with great compassion in light of the difficulties under which they are laboring. They are endowed with basic ignorance about their own nature, which is the source of their unwholesome actions and negative mental states, which in turn result in their great suffering.

OBJECTLESS COMPASSION

After you have meditated on compassion toward dharmas, meditate on objectless compassion. Look at beings from an ultimate point of view and understand that actually there are no beings—that in ultimate reality, no beings exist per se. Yet as long as those beings remain unenlightened about ultimate reality, they are bound tightly by the shackle of belief in a self. This belief, as we have said, is the source of all their many woes.

The purpose of this meditation is to awaken within yourself the wish to remove all beings from the belief in a self, which is the cause of all their suffering. As the *Bodhicharyāvatara* says, "Living beings are like a dream; they are like the plantain tree." In Indian literature, the plantain or banana tree is a simile for the insubstantial, for that which is lacking an inherent nature of its own. Like an onion, the plantain tree can be stripped down to its parts, but when you have exhausted all its leaves, bark, and so on, there is no pit or central core. Similarly, when you strip away one skandha after another, searching for the being itself, no being is found.

Shāntideva proceeds to ask: "If no beings exist, toward whom, then, should we have compassion?" He then answers:

> To attain the result of buddhahood, which is to be achieved only through the awakening of great compassion, one should direct one's compassion toward whatever it is that unenlightened beings call "beings."

On the conventional level of reality, beings do exist as they are perceived to by other unenlightened beings. The bodhisattva realizes that, in ultimate reality, there are no beings who exist as unenlightened beings think, but that on the conventional level, those beings do experience suffering. Hence he directs his mind toward those beings as they perceive themselves. On the ultimate level, he sees no beings, but he realizes that, on the conventional level, beings think they exist and do experience suffering. dOut of objectless compassion, therefore, he directs his mind toward them.

The purpose of the meditation on objectless compassion is to awaken within your mind a sense of pity and great compassion for unenlightened beings, who do not ultimately exist as they think they do. While we are not saying that they are nonexistent, we are saying that neither they nor their sufferings exist as they like to think they do. The bodhisattva perceives such beings as they really are; he knows that, although they do not exist in ultimate reality, they are nonetheless bound tightly by the false belief in an ego. This belief in an ego causes unwholesome karmic actions and negative mental states, which give rise to rebirth and thus keep unenlightened beings on the wheel of worldly existence. As it is written,

> As long as there is the apprehension of the skandhas, as long as there is belief in a self and the apprehension of a self, karmic actions will proceed. From those karmic actions there will ensue birth and death.

MEDITATION ON GREAT COMPASSION

Finally, we have the instructions for how to meditate on these three types of compassion. This should be done in the proper posture, preceded by taking refuge and so forth. Regarding all beings as your own kind mothers, direct your mind toward them, and think, "Alas, these kind mothers of mine have benefited me so often, so much, and in so many ways."

Here you should reflect on the many kind benefits you have received from your present mother in this life. Without thinking of her own happiness, she always strove to benefit you and protect you from all harm; without seeking her own liberation, she unhesitatingly sacrificed her present and future prospects of happiness that you might have a chance at true well-being. For your sake she accumulated unwholesome karmic patterns and neglected her own prospects for liberation. As a result, she remains subject to suffering and faces the prospect of endless suffering in the future.

Thinking about her in this manner should awaken a sense of great compassion toward your mother and, by extrapolation, toward all other beings. Recognize her situation: that this kind mother is subjected to the experience of pain even though she does not wish it. See that she is not skilled in discovering the ways to rid herself of suffering and the causes of her suffering. She hasn't the knowledge or leisure to deal with this problem of suffering, nor does she understand how to uproot the cause of her suffering.

After reflecting very intensely for a long time about her plight, you will reach the stage where you feel, from the very marrow of your bones, that you would give anything at all if only she might be free from suffering and the causes of suffering. When you have this intense longing in your heart, try to strengthen your mind in a resolve to free her from that unhappy state; awaken within yourself the resolve to do something for her.

Conclude with a prayer to the buddhas, bodhisattvas, and gurus for their protection and blessings, that you might become able, with their help, to free your mother from her plight. You should feel so intensely about her painful situation that you are willing to take upon yourself all the suffering that she bears now or may bear in the future. No matter how unbearable it is, be willing to take it upon yourself that she might be spared.

Reflect again on your mother's state, realizing that she not only has suffered much in the past but even now carries with her the cause of future suffering—namely, unwholesome karma and negative mental states, which arise from the erroneous belief in a self. Thus she still has that same cause of suffering which has tormented her for so long. Recognize that she is deluded about her existence, herself, and her condition, and is truly an object of pity for these reasons. Then think:

> Even though I must free her from suffering and its cause, I am still unable to do so. Right now, only the guru and the Three Jewels have the power to help her. May they, in compassion, please take heed of this mother of mine and free her from suffering and its cause.

Pray again and again in this way, entreating the buddhas and bodhisattvas to help her.

After you have meditated on your mother in this way and attained a feeling of intense compassion for her, direct your mind toward your father, toward relatives and friends, and then toward those strangers to whom you are ordinarily indifferent. Finally and especially, meditate on your enemies for a very long time in this way. When you have gotten to the point of thinking of your worst enemy as if he were your own dearest, kindest mother, extend this meditation toward all beings in the six states of existence: meditate on the beings in the hells, reflect on the terrible facts of heat and cold and other tortures to which they are subject, and so forth. Meditate until you are willing to take upon yourself all that terrible suffering of theirs.

When you have a strong awareness of their suffering and a genuine, unfeigned will to remove them from it, inject into this feeling the realization that their suffering arises from unwholesome karma and negative mental states. Realize that karma and negativity spring from basic ignorance, and that, as long as all these beings are endowed with these causes of suffering, they are truly objects of pity. Reflect on this basic source of suffering of theirs, and awaken a great feeling of compassion for them. Meditate again and again that these beings may be freed from suffering.

Once again, reflect that the basic ignorance with which they are afflicted is none other than the false belief in a self, and that although beings do not have an inherent nature of their own, they do not recognize this. Consequently, they are bound tightly by the mistaken apprehension of a self. For this reason, too, they are objects of great pity. Again meditate with the wish that these beings might become free from suffering and the cause of suffering, which is the mistaken apprehension of a self.

After you have risen from your meditation sessions on this subject, continue to meditate unceasingly on compassion toward your enemies and toward those for whom it is difficult to arouse feelings of pity—malignant spirits, evil people, harmdoers, people who are absolutely under the control their delusions, butchers, fishermen, others who kill for their livelihood, and so on. Next, cultivate great compassion toward those who are destitute, afflicted by diseases, and without a protector or champion—in other words, those who are rudderless on the sea of life. Constantly direct your mind toward them in compassion, even when not in meditative retreat.

Do everything in your power to help remove the suffering of beings you encounter. If you are able to help them overcome their suffering, you must do it; if you are not able, at least resolve that you will become able to help them as soon as possible. To do this is to follow the example of the great Sakya Pandita,[50] who was endowed with great compassion for all beings, especially those who had fallen into the long-lasting hells. In meditation, he always prayed that, if he were not able to help them, he might join them in order to share their suffering; he hoped that he could experience hell beings' immense suffering himself rather than abandon them to their fate. You, too, should try to think in this way about the sufferings of others and consider how beings might be freed from their plight and established in liberation. Apply yourself unceasingly in training to become able to remove them from their suffering.

These instructions are crucial to your practice, for if you don't develop this kind of compassion for beings, you don't really belong on the Mahāyāna path, but elsewhere. When you have this kind of compassion for beings, then you are truly a follower of the Great Way.

31

A COILED ROPE IN THE GLOOM OF NIGHT

IN THIS LESSON, we will explain how the Buddhist meditator seeks to awaken within his mind the noble resolve to attain buddhahood for the benefit of all living beings.

CONVENTIONAL BODHICHITTA

By the term *bodhichitta*, Mahāyāna Buddhists mean that the mind of the practitioner has become imbued with, and impelled by, a strong desire to accomplish the highest possible good for all other living beings without exception. That is a very tall order, and it takes a lot of practice to awaken this kind of great-heartedness, which doesn't exclude any living being from your own spiritual efforts and attainments. However, this wish to accomplish the highest possible good for all other beings is a natural outcome of the preceding meditations on great love and great compassion. After you have trained the mind in great love (the desire that all beings have genuine happiness), you meditate on great compassion (the desire that all beings be removed from suffering and the cause of suffering). Your mind is then imbued with these two qualities of all-embracing love and compassion for beings, and becomes acutely aware of your inability to achieve what you wish for them.

Due to that sense of helplessness, you feel impelled to make efforts that will equip you with the power actually to help all those beings. Out of this strong sense of wishing to do something for others, there arises what Buddhists call bodhichitta—the resolve to win buddhahood for the benefit of all other living beings.

The awareness of your present limitations makes you fully appreciate the fact that only when you have attained the qualities of buddhahood will you be able to accomplish the good of all beings. When your mind is truly imbued with this sense of urgency, this acute sensitivity to the sufferings of beings and intense desire to remove them from suffering, bodhichitta arises quite naturally and easily. Therefore, the meditation on bodhichitta follows logically after the two meditations on love and compassion.

It is also essential that you make the effort to awaken bodhichitta because it is a requisite of enlightenment. Attainment of buddhahood is the result of having awakened this resolve to help all beings. You might be inclined to think, "As a good Buddhist, isn't it enough merely to avoid the ten unwholesome patterns of karmic activity and train in the ten wholesome kinds of karmic activity? Isn't it enough to awaken in the mind a sense of love for beings and a sense of compassion and sympathy for their sufferings? Aren't these enough to enable me to win enlightenment?"

The answer must be that, although all these factors are essential as auxiliaries to the spiritual path, they are not enough in themselves to enable you to attain buddhahood. It is as if you tried to get rid of a tree by lopping off this limb and that limb, or these leaves and those; you could not be sure that the tree would not sprout again as long as you had not dug it up at the root. In the same way, you cannot have any certainty of attaining true liberation as long as there is any vestige of self-clinging, self-centeredness, or belief in a self still within your mental continuum.

The root of our being in worldly existence is none other than this sense of egocentricity. Until this belief in a self is excavated, there is no way enlightenment can be obtained. The sufferings of worldly existence all spring from unwholesome karmic actions, and karmic actions themselves issue from negative emotive states such as desire, anger, and ignorance, which all have their origin in none other than the belief in a self. Thus the belief in a self is at once the root of the great tree of suffering—i.e., worldly existence—and the stake that keeps us tethered and bound in suffering.

Buddhist scriptures such as the *Bodhicharyāvatara* very clearly identify this belief in a self as the real villain. They include verses such as:

> Whatever injury exists in the world and whatever suffering is found there all ensue from the belief in a self. Since this is so, why do we harbor or cherish a harmdoer such as the ego? Just as one will never get free from the pain of burning as long as one doesn't throw away the flame, so one will never be free from suffering as long as one clings to the belief in a self.

You may ask, "Exactly how do all these faults and negative mental states arise from the belief in a self?" It happens this way. The mind falls into the false belief in a self where there is none by misapprehending its own true nature—that is, by falling into the habit of apprehending a self within what are known as the five skandhas. These five aggregates—form, feeling, perception, impulses, and consciousness—are the components of our total existence. For the sake of convenience, and to orient itself within raw reality, the mind falls into the habit of identifying with these components and mistaking them, as a whole, for a real self, a real identity, a real person. On that basis, it then proceeds to make a distinction between self and other.

The mind thus falls into thinking in terms of "I" and "mine" as distinguished from everything else. All else is not I or mine; it is other. Due to this dichotomy between self and other, the mind begins to react to all that it perceives as "other" with emotions such as attraction, desire, attachment, lust, aversion, anger, and hatred. Alternatively, the mind reacts indifferently to the other; it is neither attracted nor repelled by it, and so ignores it. Through this ignorance, the other negative mental states also have occasion to arise. When they govern the mind, they cause one to take deluded actions based on them. These actions then begin to shape the way we live our lives and the way our minds operate. They form patterns of habit that begin to condition and limit both our present existence and our prospects for future existence. That is why we say that the basic error of belief in a self is at the root of all the sufferings of saṃsāra, and that it binds beings in worldly existence.

It is like mistaking a rope for a snake. One happens to spot a coiled rope in the gloom of night and, without examining it, thinks one sees a snake. One feels alarm, anxiety, fear, and a wish to be elsewhere. If, upon examination, one recognizes that what one thought was a snake was never anything but a harmless piece of rope, one realizes that one's emotional responses were quite inappropriate to the reality of the situation. In the same way, as long as the mind is not taught to recognize its true nature, it continues to assume that, as we have been habitually taught, there is an ego, a self, that is quite real. As a result, we think that there is no other way to live except by acting for the self and in the context of the duality of self, as distinguished from not-self.

But when we examine the mind to learn its true nature, we search for the self and realize that there is nothing that corresponds to that notion. Then we see that all the negative mental states that we have been expending our energies on are quite inappropriate, since they are based on a premise of self that has never existed. From this point on, we can no longer justify them. There is no longer any basis for their arising, let alone for their governing our actions.

When you are under the sway of the belief in a self, you have attachment to your own side and aversion to all that is not-self. You remain ignorant of your own true nature and experience the presence of the three mental poisons—desire, hatred, and delusion. These are like three links of a chain that are intertwined one with the other: they keep the mind bound in suffering. As long as you are controlled by the belief in a self, you experience the arising of the passions and the results of the mental, physical, and vocal actions that proceed from them. As it is written in the *Treatise on Valid Sources of Knowledge* (*Pramāṇa-vārttika*):

> Where there is a notion of a self, there is also a notion of other. And from this dichotomy of self and other arises attachment and aversion. And from the interaction of self and other, all faults arise.

This establishes our case that the root of all the sufferings of saṃsāra, which we have described in graphic detail, is precisely this mistaken belief in a self where there is none. Therefore, any intelligent, thoughtful person who wishes his own good, let alone the good of others, will regard this mistaken belief in a self as the true spiritual enemy, the true source of obstacles, suffering, bondage, and all ill. If he perceives this belief as the real villain in life, he won't hesitate to take action that will counteract the mistaken belief in a self—namely, meditation. There are two types of bodhichitta meditation aimed at attaining buddhahood for the sake of all beings: conventional bodhichitta and ultimate bodhichitta.

In conventional bodhichitta meditation, you develop, or awaken, a strong sense of love and compassion for all beings. Then, as a result of your desire to remove their sufferings and establish them in happiness, you meditate on the exchange of self and others. When you have recognized that there is no real self to be distinguished from others and that the belief in a self is only a habit of mind, it becomes easy to exchange self for others—in meditation, at least. In this process you meditate on exchanging the sufferings of others for your own merit, happiness, and benefit; you exchange your own good fortune for the ill fortune of others.

This meditation counteracts the habitual ego-centered state of mind in that, instead of making the self foremost, you make others foremost. It is a good way of training the mind, for it subdues and humbles the pride of ego and all selfish impulses. But conventional bodhichitta meditation doesn't suffice to excavate the sense of self from the very root of the mind; for that, you must proceed to meditation on ultimate bodhichitta. There, through training in the two stages of meditation, concentration (*śamatha*) and insight (*vipaśyanā*), you directly intuit the true nature of mind, recognizing the void nature of all things. Through this insight, the belief in a self is finally and totally uprooted from the mind.

Why does it take ultimate bodhichitta to counteract the belief in a self? The reason is that, on the conventional level, where you love and have compassion for beings, you still believe that beings and a self actually exist. And in any case, love and compassion are not the antidotes, not the direct opposite of this belief in a self. Just as you need water to extinguish fire, so you need insight to extinguish the belief in a self. Wisdom, or insight, is the direct antidote to ignorance, and the belief in a self can be dispelled only by its true antidote. Thus practicing the meditation of ultimate bodhichitta is the only way you can deal with the root cause of suffering.

THE BENEFITS OF AWAKENING BODHICHITTA

What is the benefit of undertaking this meditation? The benefits are immeasurable because, as the sūtras tell us, if the merit of awakening this bodhichitta within one's mind had a form, there would not be enough room in the whole of space to contain it. The *Bodhicharyāvatara* says,

> Even a miserable, wretched criminal in a prison becomes transformed merely by awakening this bodhichitta within his mind. In that very instant he becomes worthy of worship by all gods and men. He becomes a son of the Enlightened Ones.[51]

Thus the moment you awaken within your mind a genuine wish to win buddhahood for the sake of others, you undergo a transformation in name, for you are no longer an ordinary being but the spiritual offspring of the buddhas. Your nature, too, is no longer ordinary but endowed with this great purpose, and therefore becomes that of a great being, a bodhisattva. The *Bodhicharyāvatara* puts it thus:

> Just as a philosopher's stone can turn base metal into gold, so an impure, even worthless human life can be transformed instantly into an exalted bodhisattva's if this enlightenment thought is awakened.

The buddhas have pondered for aeons on the wheel of life, considering the cause of good for unhappy beings. They have not seen anything more beneficial than this single thought of enlightenment. It alone is the best way to help those beings; it alone offers the best prospect of present happiness and future liberation for those beings caught up in delusion.

The benefits are also long-lasting. If you are generous and do kind deeds, there will be a result from those actions, yet once your deeds have come to fruition, you will experience the good result and then it will be over. But the benefits of awakening bodhichitta are endless. Having once awakened the genuine thought of attaining buddhahood for the benefit of others, there is no end to the good results that ensue. It is like the difference between the fruit of a plantain tree and that of a wish-fulfilling tree. The plantain tree produces its fruit and then dies, but the wish-fulfilling tree constantly bestows on all petitioners the fulfillment of all their wishes. The results of bodhichitta are like the fruit of the wish-fulfilling tree—they are constant and unceasing.

Also, bodhichitta is the best kind of friend, the best refuge, the best spiritual strength you could possibly have. It is stronger than all the virtues. Although patience, generosity, and the other virtues are excellent, they haven't the strength to deal with ignorance in the same way bodhichitta can. Just as a frightened man surrounded by powerful enemies might take heart only if a fearless and mighty warrior suddenly appeared to protect him, so we who are weak in virtue and afflicted by powerful impulses for nonvirtue, carrying around a great bagful of unripened negative karma, can find a friend, or place of security, only in bodhichitta. It alone has the strength to deal with powerful, dreadful, terrible sins. Its power is such that, just as the entire universe will be destroyed in an instant at the end of an aeon, so even a heavy and fearsome burden of great sins can be destroyed in an instant simply by awakening the genuine resolve to win buddhahood. Needless to say, then, bodhichitta is an attitude worth developing by intelligent people who desire their own and others' good.

SPECIAL CHARACTERISTICS OF BODHICHITTA

In conclusion, we will briefly describe some of the special characteristics of bodhichitta. First, it is oriented toward the attainment of perfect enlightenment—full and complete buddhahood—and not toward any other spiritual goal, no matter how worthy. It is the direct opposite of the ordinary worldly mind, which is synonymous with ignorance and selfishness. Although, in Buddhist parlance, liberation is synonymous with nirvāṇa, bodhichitta is not directed toward the nirvāṇa of the arhats (that is, the liberated state of an arhat who has sought nirvāṇa for the sake of self alone); rather, it is oriented toward, and is a factor in, the attainment of the nonabiding nirvāṇa (*apratistita nirvāṇa*) of the fully enlightened buddhas. The full liberation of the buddhas is called "nonabiding" to distinguish it from the fixed nirvāṇa of the arhat, who has won liberation from the round of birth and death and can no longer be reborn. Because the arhat doesn't realize the phenomenon of non-self, he still believes that his nirvāṇa is real and does not have the nonabiding mobility of those who attain enlightenment as a buddha and henceforth remain neither in nirvāṇa nor in saṃsāra.

Bodhichitta can be awakened in two ways: formally or spontaneously. The first is accomplished by participating in a formal ceremony, in front of teachers and in the company of other like-minded aspirants to buddhahood, in which you formally repeat vows to strive for buddhahood for the sake of all beings. You then undertake constant training of the mind to avoid the factors hostile to maintaining this attitude of bodhichitta, learning what mental states and actions impair your enlightened attitude toward other beings, as well as how to avoid them. This is the bodhisattva's training.

Second, you can attain bodhichitta directly from the absolute, or ultimate. Here you realize bodhichitta through the force of your own meditative insight into the suffering of beings, the source of their suffering, and what has to be done to free them from that suffering. Through clear insight into the true nature of beings and how they can best be helped, you receive a kind of inspiration, in meditation, that is a reflex of your own buddha-nature. You simply know what must be done, and bodhichitta then arises spontaneously in the mind. This spontaneous bodhichitta is not something acquired from another person; rather, it develops in your mind through the force of meditation.

There are other ways bodhichitta can be discussed as well. For example, it can be categorized with reference to its objects, in which case we have two types of bodhichitta, the conventional and the ultimate (also known as the practical and the final). Bodhichitta can also be categorized by way of its two kinds of applications, known as the bodhichitta of aspiration and the bodhichitta of application itself. In the former, you simply have a resolve, thinking that you must attain enlightenment for the sake of all living beings. This is the bodhichitta of aspiration, or the "wishing enlightenment thought." You may not follow up with effective actions, so it remains just a wish, an aspiration, a prayer. In the latter, you undertake training in those steps that lead to attainment of buddhahood and thus acquire the bodhichitta of application, or the "entering enlightenment thought."

We can also distinguish four stages of bodhichitta. First is the bodhichitta that is acquired through devotion. This is what you obtain until you reach the first stage of bodhisattvahood, or first bhūmi. As long as you are an ordinary being striving to attain the first bhūmi, your bodhichitta is derived from this sense of yearning and orientation toward attaining bodhisattvahood. The second stage of bodhichitta is called "pure resolve" and is acquired on the first stage of bodhisattvahood. The third is called "fully ripened" and is acquired when, as a bodhisattva, you reach the seventh, eighth, ninth, or tenth bhūmi. Here you have almost reached the goal. The final stage of bodhichitta is called "that which is free from obscuration." This is the bodhichitta of a fully enlightened buddha.

32

"Beloved Daughter" Kicks His Mother

As the title of our Tibetan text, *The Three Visions*, indicates, it consists of three sets of instructions for the Buddhist meditator. The first corresponds to the impure perception of worldlings and contains instructions designed to wean the mind away from the world and reorient it toward a spiritual goal. The second is called the vision of experience. It corresponds to the view of a person who is engaged in the actual practice of the bodhisattva path and includes instructions for developing great love, great compassion, and bodhichitta. These meditations are intended primarily to awaken within our minds a sense of great-heartedness about our spiritual efforts; in other words, they are designed to eradicate any clinging to selfishness with regard to our spirituality. The third level of perception is called the pure vision. Here the instructions are designed to acquaint us with the characteristics of the result of the Buddhist path—namely, the nature of buddhahood, its qualities, attributes, powers, and so forth—in order to inform, and generate zeal in, our minds.

We have completed all the instructions for the first of the three visions, and we have also completed the instructions on great love and great compassion. We are in the midst of discussing how to awaken bodhichitta, the resolve to attain buddhahood for the sake of other beings.

We have said that bodhichitta can be categorized from various angles—by way of example, motive, cause, and so forth. We also said that bodhichitta can be awakened either formally, through participation in a ceremony in which one takes the bodhisattva vows, or through direct encounter, as it were, with the Buddha's Body of Reality (*dharmakāya*). In the latter case, the meditator receives some inspiration from the Buddha's mind while in a state of meditation and, through the force of his own meditative insight, awakens bodhichitta spontaneously.

Bodhichitta can also be classified as conventional or ultimate. These terms relate to two different stages of practice. Conventional bodhichitta refers to the time when you are just a lowly meditator, still very much in the world but meditating and making all the right efforts. Here the main practice consists of developing a sense of sameness about self and others—learning not to distinguish the self from others and to make others' interests paramount over your own. Ultimate bodhichitta is developed through continued practice of concentration and insight meditation. There are also two other ways bodhichitta can be categorized—by aspiration and by application.

THE BODHICHITTA OF ASPIRATION

The aspiration to attain buddhahood is a manifestation of bodhichitta. From the moment you formulate within your mind a conception of your spiritual goal of attaining buddhahood in order to accomplish the highest good for other beings, your spiritual path has a direction. Thus the bodhichitta of aspiration is the first step in becoming a bodhisattva. When you study the careers of the great bodhisattvas, you will see that they always began by resolving to strive for the highest good of all other beings. Indeed, the great bodhisattva Maitreya defined the bodhichitta of aspiration as the wish to attain perfect enlightenment for the sake of other beings.

Aspiration to buddhahood is likened to the *idea* of setting out to reach a given destination. When you plan to go somewhere on a journey, you must first have a goal; only then can you undertake to travel until you reach that destination. The two aspects of bodhichitta can be understood in the same way. In the first stage, the bodhichitta of aspiration, you define your goal, and the nature of that goal defines the efforts that you make to attain it. The second stage, the bodhichitta of application, is like actually traveling to your destination.

Now, there are several subtopics to the bodhichitta of aspiration. The first is a description of the benefits of thinking of attaining enlightenment. Tremendous merit ensues merely from formulating a sincere wish to attain buddhahood for the sake of others. The *Bodhicharyāvatara* makes this comparison: If a person becomes meritorious in this world merely by wishing to become a doctor in order to remove the illnesses of other beings, how much more meritorious is someone who sincerely plans to attain buddhahood in order to become able to help all beings?

Obviously, this kind of aspiration carries with it a great power of merit. Thus bodhichitta is not only the single true, real, and effective source of long-lasting benefit for living beings but also a rarity in this world, for seldom does anyone form the sincere thought that he will strive for buddhahood. Since bodhichitta is extremely rare and extremely beneficial once it has been awakened, its benefits are boundless.

ल ❖ ल

To illustrate this, there is the story of a bodhisattva named Beloved Daughter. He was given this name by his parents, out of a superstitious wish to lengthen his life. Even though he was born a male, and a healthy one at that, his parents had some reason to fear that his life might be short, so they tried to sidestep fate by pretending that he was female.

Beloved Daughter was the son of a very wealthy and virtuous Indian merchant whose business was to sail to the islands of Southeast Asia to collect pearls and other jewels. But when Beloved Daughter was just an infant, his father drowned in a shipwreck, and the bodhisattva was raised by his mother, who from that time on had a great fear of losing him, too, at sea. Thus, despite the fact that, according to the Indian caste system, a son must only do the job that his father did before him, she refused to tell Beloved Daughter what his father's occupation had been.

When the boy was in his teens, he began pressing his mother to let him take over the leadership of the family and provide for her. But when he asked her about his father's vocation, she told him that his father had been a grain merchant, so he took a job in the market selling grain, and whatever small profit he made he dutifully turned over to his mother. After a while, however, some acquaintances told him that his father couldn't possibly have been a grain merchant, so he returned to his mother, who told him that his father had actually been a cloth salesman. He took up that job and, like a good son, again gave all the profits to his mother. Once more he was disillusioned by his friends, whereupon his mother told him that his father had been a jeweler; he took up the new business and continued to give the profits to his mother. It wasn't long before someone told Beloved Daughter that he had known his father, who had been a seagoing captain in search of jewels. Beloved Daughter returned to his mother and confronted her with his knowledge. She confessed that she had tried to prevent him from knowing about his father for fear of losing him, also.

As soon as Beloved Daughter learned what his true vocation was, there was no stopping him. Immediately he made plans with friends to go off to sea in search of jewels. One evening, he told his mother that they were leaving the next morning, whereupon she begged him not to go and told him of the many relatives, including his father, who had been lost at sea. As her only son, she wanted to keep him alive. He wouldn't listen to her, so his mother fell asleep at his door, in order to be able to reason with him in the morning. Beloved Daughter, however, slipped out at dawn over her sleeping body. As he stepped over her, he accidentally kicked her in the head. He did collect a lot of jewels, but on the way home a storm arose and everyone was killed.

Beloved Daughter found himself floating on the ocean. He floated for a long time, until he reached a very beautiful island inhabited by several beautiful maidens who invited him to stay, which he did. He enjoyed his visit very much, all the tropical delights and so forth. But after some time he heard a voice from the sky say, "Go farther south." Despite the maidens' warning him of danger in that direction, he went south until he came to a larger island with a beautiful mansion inhabited by a great number of beautiful maidens. He stayed there as their ruler for a long time. Then, again, the voice called to him, and he followed its urgings to travel farther south.

This time, Beloved Daughter approached a strange-looking, eerie island on which an iron building stood. As he went inside, he saw a man whose brain was being crushed by a spinning wheel of iron. The man was obviously in excruciating pain. When Beloved Daughter asked him the meaning of this, the man told him it was the karmic result of his having kicked his mother in the head. At that moment the bodhisattva remembered that he, too, had accidentally kicked his mother's head, and he became very anxious about what might happen to him. He began to see the drift of things.

All the good that Beloved Daughter had done for his mother, in giving her his profits and so on, had led him to experience one happy situation after another, but finally his bad karma was catching up with him. Disobeying and mistreating his mother had led him to a terrible place like this. The moment he began to grow anxious, a voice from the sky said, "Now it's your turn." The iron wheel spun off the other fellow's head, crashed onto his own, and he was seized by unbearable pain. His head was being crushed and split, there was no end to the thing, and it only grew worse.

Since there was no escape, the thought occurred to him, "It is finally happening to me that I can't get out of this suffering, but there may be others like me and this fellow who make the mistake of mistreating their mothers. Since I have to suffer, let all their pains also be experienced by me alone, and let them be spared this unbearable pain." The minute Beloved Daughter thought that, the wheel stopped rotating and he was reborn into the realm known as Tushita, where he became a great bodhisattva.

This story illustrates the results of merely wishing to remove the physical or mental pains of others, wishing to take on their trials and spare them pain. How much more beneficial, meritorious, and powerful is the sincere thought to win buddhahood in order to remove all the sufferings of all beings for all time, establishing them in the highest possible good! This is what we mean when we say that the merit of sincere bodhichitta is truly boundless. We need only reflect on how seldom beings aspire to the highest good for themselves, let alone for others' sake. Even loving parents, who wish for the well-being and happiness of their children, seldom if ever think of wishing this highest good for them. Even the luminaries of the human race don't come up with this idea for the good of mankind. Even the great god Brahmā never managed to think in this manner.

All these parents, sages, and gods never even dream of achieving this highest good for the sake of those in need of help or those they love. No matter how much a parent loves his children, it is very seldom that he thinks of winning enlightenment to accomplish the maximum good for them. Only rarely does this aspiration to enlightenment arise within anyone's mind, but when it does, it is like a jewel of tremendous value.

This bodhichitta of aspiration, which is of such rare value, arises directly out of compassion. As the sūtras say, great compassion is the precursor of the bodhisattva's resolve to attain buddhahood. Great compassion is its source, its spring, its cause. Without great compassion, bodhichitta will never arise. Now, great compassion, as we established earlier, has as its cause great love. Thus we must first cultivate within our minds great love and great compassion for beings—the nonexclusive wish that all beings might have genuine happiness and its cause, and the authentic wish that all beings without exception might be free from suffering and its cause.

THE BODHICHITTA OF APPLICATION

Only when you are endowed with the two qualities of great love and great compassion will the genuine thought of winning enlightenment arise within your mind. But it doesn't stop there. When it does arise, that aspiration to win enlightenment will naturally prompt you to make the right efforts on behalf of beings. First of all, you will become keenly aware of the great disparity between what you wish for beings and what you are actually able to offer them. In other words, you will become aware of your own weakness and limitations. Hence, after you have sincerely promised to win enlightenment for the sake of others, you are brought back to earth when you recognize that,

> As things are now, not only am I unable to make others happy and to remove their suffering, I cannot even do this for myself. I don't know how to accomplish my own good and avoid my own pains, let alone how to do so for others.

This great gulf between your aspirations and your present abilities causes you to ponder just who is able to benefit the beings you have promised to help. If you look around at other beings, you see that they are very much like yourself—all of them struggling for happiness and seeking to avoid pain, but failing more often than not. When you consider the great leaders of the world or the great gods, you see that, in the long run, even they are not able to protect beings from the boundless suffering of worldly existence or establish them in buddhahood. Thus the situation boils down to recognition that only a buddha has the requisite compassion, wisdom, and power to achieve the ultimate good of these beings.

Because the Buddha's spiritual efforts were motivated at all times by great compassion, because his enlightenment was the outcome of his compassionate efforts to help beings, and because he attained unerring insight into the true nature of beings, the cause of their problems, and how to solve their problems, he gained the saving knowledge of the way to help them. He is endowed not only with compassion and wisdom but also with great power. As a result of his painstaking effort, meditation, and training in the six perfections, the Buddha is able to respond effectively and spontaneously to all beings who are in need of help, not only establishing their well-being in this life but also helping them achieve the ultimate good of liberation. Because only the enlightened ones are endowed with the compassion, wisdom, and power required to benefit all beings, a person who genuinely wishes to achieve the highest good of all beings should make efforts to become a buddha. There is no other possible spiritual goal for one who sincerely wishes the highest good for all.

The formulation of the resolve toward enlightenment naturally impels us into making the necessary efforts to bridge the gap between our present abilities and our ideal of attaining the Buddha's capabilities. Part of that aspiration also entails an awareness of the skill and means that will be required of us as bodhisattvas. Just as the skillful captain of a ship might keep up the spirits of his crew by telling them of the wonders of the various ports they will be visiting en route to their destination, so the bodhisattva learns to recognize the spiritual inclinations and capacities of the various beings whom he helps attain the stage of ultimate liberation. Some of these, because they lack merit and insight, are unable to conceive of making spiritual efforts without reference to a selfish goal, such as salvation for the sake of oneself alone. These he teaches the prospect of attaining the arhat's nirvāṇa for their own sakes. For those who are able to recognize the essential oneness of all beings, and who are big-hearted enough to include others in their own spiritual path, he teaches the path that leads to the perfect enlightenment of the Buddha. But all this is done with the understanding that all beings will eventually be led to the attainment of perfect buddhahood.

We now have the instructions on how to meditate on the bodhichitta of application. As always, begin with taking refuge, awakening the thought of enlightenment, praying for the blessings of the buddhas, bodhisattvas, and masters of your tradition to bless your meditation, and the like. Then think of the lives of the people you know and of other beings in the world, and reflect:

> These beings are all striving only for happiness, and yet they are so unskilled in achieving what they want that many of them experience instead much pain and suffering. Others are in the process of accumulating nonvirtues that become the causes of really fearsome suffering. These beings are blinded by their own ignorance. They have no real prospects of striving for or achieving liberation. They have not been taken in hand by spiritual friends and, far from being headed toward liberation and the joys of the spiritual life, are instead headed toward the fearful precipice of the lower realms of rebirth.
>
> For these reasons, all these beings are true objects of pity. But merely thinking of them with pity and compassion is not going to help them at all. If I really have compassion for these beings, and if I really want to see them happy, the only way to help is to make real efforts to free them from their sufferings and establish them in true happiness. Right now, I don't have that kind of ability, that power. Right now, only the Buddha has that kind of power, through being endowed with the Body of Reality and Body of Illusion. He is able to work unceasingly and effectively with his every action to help countless living beings.

33

THE HAND MUST HELP THE FOOT

WE ARE STUDYING the foundational instructions of *The Three Visions*. We have already discussed how to develop a sense of renunciation about the world, and are now discussing how to develop a great-hearted attitude about our spiritual experience. This consists of three main topics: (1) development of great love for all beings, (2) development of great compassion for all beings, and (3) development of the enlightenment attitude, or bodhichitta. We have discussed the first two of these and are now concerned with the instructions for awakening the enlightenment thought.

Previously, we said there are two aspects of bodhichitta: (a) conventional bodhichitta, which corresponds to ordinary experience and the mundane conceptualizations of unenlightened beings, and (b) ultimate bodhichitta, which is experienced by holy beings, such as the great bodhisattvas, yogis, and buddhas themselves. Conventional bodhichitta is so called because it corresponds to conventional reality as it is perceived by unenlightened beings. It is further discussed under two headings: (i) the bodhichitta of aspiration, the awakening of a resolve to strive for enlightenment for the general well-being of all living beings, and (ii) the bodhichitta of application, in which we actually undertake the appropriate efforts to accomplish that resolve. We are in the midst of discussing the bodhichitta of application.

It is necessary to distinguish between the mere aspiration to achieve enlightenment and the actual effort put forth toward fulfillment of your resolve. Whenever your actions are motivated and guided by your intent to win enlightenment for the sake of all beings, those actions constitute the bodhichitta of application. It is like first making up your mind to make a journey to India and then taking the steps to get there: you buy the ticket, board the plane, undergo the experience of traveling, and finally arrive at your destination. In the same way, the bodhisattva first makes up his mind to strive solely for buddhahood and then undertakes to train in the six pāramitās and so forth.

What makes this resolve and these actions a manifestation of your bodhichitta is the presence in your mind of great love and great compassion, especially the latter. With a true sense of the limitless sufferings with which beings are faced—a sense that you cannot bear to be indifferent to their sufferings, nor to have them remain in their sufferings—you feel impelled to make any effort in your power to remove them from those sufferings. When you have this sense of compassion, and when it is so intense that you feel it to be almost unbearable, then you can be said to be motivated by true great compassion, and whatever action you take to attain buddhahood automatically becomes bodhichitta because it is genuine.

The same is true of your aspiration: it is not merely a verbal promise or an intention that sooner or later you will get around to doing something for beings. It becomes true bodhichitta of aspiration only when you feel it from the heart and follow up by performing right actions. As the bodhisattva Maitreya said:

> It doesn't look good if an intelligent person who is carrying on his head the great burden of all living beings dallies along the way. One who has resolved to liberate himself and others from the bonds of worldly existence should exert himself in efforts that are a hundredfold greater than usual.

When you really feel for beings and take on the responsibility of acting according to your promise to remove them from suffering, you will feel compelled to develop energy and diligence on their behalf and not waste time before training in the bodhisattva's practice.

Bodhichitta leads to the highest enlightenment, that of buddhahood. What methods are there for obtaining such an exalted state? The method consists of relinquishing all selfish interest and striving for the good of others rather than for your own good alone. It is this resolve and willingness to act for the good of others that distinguishes a follower of the Great Way from ordinary worldlings. This is the deep secret of the Mahāyāna path, that one acts for others instead of oneself. As Shāntideva wrote in his *Bodhicharyāvatara*:

> Whatever joy and good exist in the world arise from the wish for others' well-being. And whatever suffering exists in the world arises from the wish for one's own selfish happiness.

Selfishness and selfish actions are the source of all suffering in the world, and unselfishness and unselfish actions are the source of all true joy in the world. As Shāntideva put it,

There is really no point in marshaling many arguments to convince you of the relative merits of selfishness and unselfishness. Merely take a look at the difference between ordinary folk, who put their own interests before those of others, and the sages, who put others' interests before their own.

People who put their own interests first remain childish, immature, enmeshed in problems, worries, and sufferings, and unable to accomplish their own worldly aims, let alone the benefit of others. In contrast, people who have learned to make others' interests paramount experience true joy in this life and increasing joy in the future. They are easily able to accomplish their own and others' aims in this world and on the spiritual path as well. We needn't marshall many arguments to prove that it's better to be unselfish than selfish. We have only to look at the difference between holy sages who act for others' good and worldlings who act for their own selfish interests.

Let us look at selfishness in this light. From beginningless time right up to the present, we have indulged in selfishness; we have made the interest of the self paramount. But what have we accomplished in all those aeons of effort? We have only come this far, and in doing so we have experienced countless sufferings, accumulated a heavy burden of karma that is ripening or still to ripen, perpetuated countless errors, and harmed both ourselves and others. All this time, we have disregarded the interests of others even though they have been our kind mothers; we have put our own gain and pleasure above those of beings who have been helpful to us. We have indulged in all kinds of delusion in the name of self. We have clung to the notion of an independently existing ego where there is none; we have cherished the notion of a self where there is no self.

By pampering this notion of self and acting always to gratify our sense of ego, we have managed to work great injury on others as well as on ourselves. We have managed to accumulate much unwholesome karma through misuse of body, voice, and mind. As a result, we have experienced pain in the past, experience it the present, and face the prospect of future pain. This is the experience we have had throughout countless lifetimes, and it is all the outcome of our selfishness alone. As the *Bodhicharyāvatara* says:

> O mind, due to your urge to act only for the sake of self, you have passed countless aeons of time, yet as a result of that great labor of yours, you have reaped only suffering.

Hence one who wants to put an end to this cycle of rebirth and death, winning freedom from the forces that bind him to delusion, should rightly regard this apprehension of self, this belief in a self, this selfishness as the true enemy. He should mindfully accomplish every action of body, voice, and mind for the benefit of others rather than the benefit of self alone.

It isn't easy to change our mental habits. The inclination to put our own interests above those of others has been with us for aeons. Thus we need a practical way to bring about the transition to an unselfish state of mind. According to *The Three Visions*, there are three steps in this process of transforming the mind from self-centeredness to other-directedness: (1) the meditation on the sameness of self and others, (2) the meditation on the exchange of self and others, and (3) the training in these two types of meditation, which will be subsumed in the discussion of the first two.

The Sameness of Self and Others

It is necessary first to train the mind in accepting the concept of the sameness of self and others. It would be difficult to proceed immediately to the meditation of exchanging self for others because, in the ordinary state of mind, there is such a disparity between the two: one's own interests seem so vital, so near, so much more important, and of such greater interest to the ordinary mind. It is very hard to make the leap of identification to the side of others and go directly into a point of view that stresses others' interests rather than one's own.

Therefore, it is a matter of skillful means on the part of the meditator to first train the mind in accepting the sameness of self and others. Once we recognize that there is really no great difference between our own existence and others' existence, our own problems and aims and other beings' problems and aims, it is very easy to bring the mind to an acceptance of the interests of others as just as vital as our own. As Shāntideva wrote:

> At the beginning, one should diligently meditate on the sameness
> of self and others, because beings are like oneself in wishing only
> for happiness and to avoid pain. Therefore, they should be treated
> as one treats oneself.

It does not take great inference to recognize that other beings are very similar to ourselves in wishing to experience pleasure, happiness, and well-being. They are like us in wishing to be free of pain when they are experiencing it, and wishing to avoid the prospects of pain as well. The actions of other beings are very much like our own, in that they are directed toward these two purposes: attainment of pleasure and happiness, and avoidance of pain and unhappiness.

Just this much serves as the foundation for accepting the sameness of self and others. The bodhisattva makes this observation about beings the basis for his decision to be a helper in their search for well-being and their efforts to avoid pain. Knowing that beings are like himself in not wishing to experience pain, he takes it upon himself to be their friend. He stands between them and their pain and works on their behalf in their efforts to avoid the experience of pain. As the *Bodhicharyāvatara* tells us:

> When I and all others are alike in wishing for happiness, why strive for my own happiness alone? And when I and all others are alike in fearing pain, what distinguishes my self, that I protect it and not others?[52]

The question is how to justify the wish to protect ourselves from pain to the exclusion of so protecting others. Why should we not also wish to protect them? It is the usual worldly idea that each being should look after his own interests and take care of himself. Worldly people say, "Another person's pain or pleasure is not my business, nor is it my business to protect others from suffering. I look after myself; let the other fellow look after himself."

If we stress the separateness of beings, this self-centeredness with regard to the suffering of others is justified. But Ngorchen Könchog Lhündrub says that this argument is specious. It is like arguing that the hand shouldn't come to the protection of the foot if the foot happens to step on a thorn. The pain is experienced only in the foot, so why does the hand have to remove the thorn and apply ointment to a wounded foot? Könchog Lhündrub's answer is that help is given in the interests of the organism as a whole. The hand should come to the aid of the foot because they both belong to the same body, and the body belongs to the self. Still, worldly folk say, "Other beings are distinct, they are quite different from me; therefore I have no obligation to come to their rescue."

Actually, even this body doesn't necessarily belong to the self. The body was formed out of the combination of the sperm and ovum of one's parents. It was fashioned out of elements contained in the body. It is only through habit that the mind has any notion of a self. This concept, which identifies with this particular body, is merely a matter of habitual thinking. Just because the mind chooses to identify solely with this particular organism doesn't mean that that body necessarily is the self or belongs to the self.

It is simply a matter of mental habit; it is only that you want to identify with this body and this notion of a self to the exclusion of others. This is selfishness. You could very easily learn to identify with other beings if you chose to do so. For example, you are able to think in terms of "my family," "my community," "my country," and "my people." If you want to, you can also extend the notion of a self to include all other beings. If you must identify with others in order to justify being concerned for their welfare, why not think in terms of "my sentient beings," "my living beings"? Why restrict identification to your immediate person?

To summarize, all beings are very similar in their desire for happiness and wish to be free from pain. Having understood this, it should be obvious that it is only a mean sort of person who creates obstacles to the happiness of others, or who deliberately brings them unhappiness.

The second thing that a Buddhist has to do is train in great-heartedness, or magnanimity of spirit, which stems from a resolve to do everything possible to increase the happiness of others and reduce their unhappiness. Toward that goal, you then exert every effort. As the *Bodhicharyāvatara* continues:

> I must remove the sufferings of others simply because they suffer. And I must bring about the well-being of others simply because they are living beings like myself.

The bodhisattva is ready to identify with other living beings and with their search for happiness and efforts to avoid pain. The only argument that he needs as a basis for his efforts is that they are beings like himself. If they want happiness, then he also wishes for their happiness. And he is their friend in their wish to avoid pain.

For the beginner, this may seem problematic, because beginners are notoriously aware of their own limitations and do not yet have confidence in their spiritual efforts. They tend to think, "I would like to increase others' happiness and be able to remove their sufferings, but I am not yet able, so what to do?" Our instructions say that, even if you really don't have the ability to bring about the happiness of others, you can grow in intent and accomplishment. As Nāgārjuna wrote:

> Even though one lacks the ability to act for the well-being of others, nonetheless, one should constantly harbor that intent within one's mind, for a person's actions come to manifest whatever he intends within.

In other words, your actions are reflections of the intent you have within your mind.

We now have the instructions for how to reflect on this topic of identification of self with others. To make this a regular meditation practice, begin by taking refuge and praying for the blessings of the guru, lineage of gurus, and Triple Gem. Then awaken the thought of enlightenment by reciting appropriate verses, such as:

> To free all beings from worldly existence, I must attain perfect enlightenment, and for that purpose I shall practice this profound meditation, which is the path of all the Enlightened Ones.

After reciting this prayer three times, proceed to reflect in this way:

> Even though I aspire to attain the perfection of buddhahood for the sake of all living beings, I will not be able to do so as long as any of my actions of body, voice, and mind are committed not for the benefit of others but for myself. Nor will I be able to attain enlightenment as long as I have not controlled my belief in a separate individuality. This is the issue, and I really want to attain buddhahood. For that reason, starting now, I am going to give up pampering and cherishing this notion of a self, which is nothing more than the cause of so much wretchedness. From now on, all my actions of body, voice, and mind will be performed for the benefit of others.
>
>   In this way, I will be coursing in the meditation of the sameness of self and others, which is the sole path to buddhahood followed by all the buddhas and bodhisattvas. There has never been a bodhisattva or buddha who has not undertaken to perceive the sameness of self and others among living beings; therefore this is the path that I, too, will follow. Just as I want only to experience happiness, so all beings want to experience happiness; hence I will be their friend and helper in the attainment of happiness. And just as I do not wish to experience pain, so other beings also wish only to avoid pain; hence from now on I will be their friend and helper in the avoidance of pain.

Reflect in this way for a very long time, again and again. If, after a while, your mind starts to take on the flavor of these reflections, and you begin to have spontaneous impulses to identify with beings and with their happiness and pain, reinforce that impulse by meditating joyfully on your accomplishment and thinking that this positive state of mind is the cause of great good for others and for yourself. Whenever such positive states of mind arise, always reinforce them by rejoicing in your accomplishment of awakening a new state of mind. In that way it will become part of your personality.

With this we conclude our discussion of the sameness of self and others, which constitutes one part of the bodhichitta of application.

When we talk about positive states of mind and the like, you should understand that Buddhists do not ascribe any real location to mind, because it is not viewed as having any shape, color, form, or other property that would make it an object about which we could say, "It is to be found here and not there, it has location here and not elsewhere." Having understood that, you will see that your mind is empty of being an independent entity that has a location.

Nonetheless, generally speaking, Buddhists do say that mind, or the faculty of consciousness, is located in the region of the heart. But they also say, especially in the tantric doctrine, that there is an aspect of mind located in the brain. This is elaborated on in the Nyingma dzog-chen doctrine, which also makes a distinction in its tantric meditations between peaceful and wrathful deities. The peaceful deities are supposed to have their abode in the region of the heart, and the wrathful, in the brain. That is to say, the faculty of consciousness is more or less centered in the region of the heart but also resides in the region of the brain. It is mainly in tantra that the brain aspect of consciousness is mentioned. For this reason the tantras accord more with the Western notion that consciousness is located in the brain rather than the heart.

Another question that may arise is what to do when you are not able to give someone what he wants, or find that he does not want what you are able to give. In those cases, it will suffice merely to have the intention to help and the resolve to become able to accomplish the true well-being of that person. Suppose you are unable, either through your faults, others' faults, or limitations of circumstance, to accomplish some beneficial action. In this case, you must merely strengthen your intention to become able to help the beings in question. Couple this intent with the resolve to win buddhahood in order to become able to help these beings, whom you must now regretfully pass by.

You must remember that mind is the most important thing. It is mind that attains enlightenment. Enlightenment occurs through mental actions, through training in buddhalike qualities and impulses. As you continue to train your mind in these, it becomes easier to manifest them through outer actions. Eventually, you will become endowed with clairvoyance, the ability to read others' minds, and the knowledge of where they stand karmically. This is the best way to help others and to see the results of your own actions on their behalf.

In the meantime, it is difficult to know exactly how to help others, so you must do the best you can to the utmost of your ability. If you are absolutely unable to do anything directly, then help indirectly, by strengthening your resolve to gain buddhahood on their behalf. Develop a wish to become able to help them.

34

A CLOUD OF WHITE LIGHT OR A SUDDEN DAWN

OUR INSTRUCTIONS CONSIST of three topics: the meditation of great love, the meditation of great compassion, and the awakening of bodhichitta, or the resolve to attain enlightenment for the sake of others. We have completed the first two topics and are now discussing bodhichitta. This, again, has two subtopics: the meditation on the sameness of self and others, and the meditation on the exchange of self and others. We have already described the first of these two.

The Exchange of Self and Others

One who wishes to attain enlightenment quickly must definitely undertake this practice of the exchange of self and others. Rather than spending many lifetimes—or even aeons—in the pursuit of buddhahood, it becomes possible to attain it in a very short period of time merely by emphasizing this meditation. As Āchārya Shāntideva wrote:

> One who wishes quickly to remove his own and others' sufferings and establish them in happiness should diligently practice this holiest secret of the Buddha's religion, this meditation of exchanging self for others.

But, you might wonder, isn't it possible to attain buddhahood if one merely practices the meditation of the sameness of self and others? Here the answer is no, because, as Shāntideva also says, "Unless one exchanges self for others, one cannot attain buddhahood."

The point of these verses is that unless you are willing to exchange your own happiness for the sufferings of others, it is not possible to attain total enlightenment. The reason is that developing the qualities of the state of enlightenment depends to a great extent on your relationship with other beings. It is only through reflecting, concentrating, and focusing on our sense of relationship with beings such as parents, relatives, friends, loved ones, and so forth that we are able to cultivate any of the mental states of love, compassion, and empathy out of which bodhichitta can then arise.

Also, beings are one of the two objectified fields whereby we can develop the insights and spiritual qualities that will enable us to attain enlightenment. First, we can accrue merit by promoting a relationship between ourselves and pure objects—namely, the buddhas and bodhisattvas. By making offerings to the enlightened ones, whether they need them or not—by showing respect for them, following their instructions, and accomplishing their works—we can accrue merit. The second way to accrue merit is by relying on ordinary beings who are in need of help, protection, giving, and the like.

Relying on beings, we can accrue a vast store of merit that will enable us to attain enlightenment, and thereby the Body of Buddhahood (*sambho-gakāya*). Hence, whether we act in reference to enlightened ones or unenlightened beings, the merit that we acquire is equally valid and becomes a cause of attaining buddhahood. The same is true of the qualities of compassion: we cannot attain buddhahood without having first developed great compassion, and this can only be done in terms of other beings.

Further, we must keep in mind the teachings that all beings without exception have at one time or another been as close to us as our own parents. This means that all beings (whether born from a womb, miraculously born, born from an egg, or born from sweat) must be considered to be just as close to us in intimate, personal relationship as if they were still our own kindly mother. It is very important that you have such an intimate sense of relationship to all beings and recognize all the kindnesses they have bestowed upon you since beginningless time. With a very sincere, whole-hearted mind, you should visualize, wish, and pray that all the unhappiness, suffering, illness, and causes of illness that they face ripen to you alone.

In exchange, turn over whatever present or future happiness you may have accumulated, however temporary or slight, unreservedly to all beings who are suffering. Visualize this exchange. Wish and pray, with a mind filled with great longing, that those beings might truly experience your happiness, well-being, and prospects of future well-being, and that they might become totally free from the suffering, causes of suffering, and prospects of suffering with which they are now encumbered. It is very important that you perform this exchange of your happiness for others' suffering with a mind filled with longing that other beings might really be free from suffering and established in happiness.

If you are not willing to exchange your own sense of well-being and good karma for suffering and unhappiness, it will not be possible for you to attain buddhahood. You simply cannot attain enlightenment without being willing to sacrifice your happiness in order to remove the sufferings of others. The alternative is to cling to you own well-being, in effect wishing for your own happiness and permitting the prospect of suffering for others. With this kind of self-centeredness, you will not attain happiness on the samsaric level, let alone an exalted state like perfect enlightenment. Therefore, knowing that beings are close to us and that their happiness can be achieved, and realizing that our own enlightenment depends on our willingness to exchange self and others, we should definitely undertake to practice this meditation.

Reflect how, from beginningless time, we have accumulated only wretchedness as a result of our unwillingness to wish happiness for others. By our insistence on seeking our own happiness alone, we have achieved only the countless accumulations of bad karma that are still with us. As a result, we haven't been able to achieve happiness in worldly existence, let alone move any closer to liberation. Since the nature of saṃsāra is one of suffering, worldly existence is constantly linked to the experience of mental and physical pain. It will definitely be impossible for us to achieve real joy or well-being in the world as long as we insist on making our own interests and happiness paramount. As Shāntideva wrote:

> By wishing for one's own exaltation, one reaps humiliation instead, but by wishing for exaltation for others, one becomes exalted as a result.

Indeed, as the verse says:

> If one misuses others for the sake of one's own interests, one will consequently experience the pains of the lower realms in future births.

Instead of achieving one's aims of self-exaltation, one will be reborn either as a servant to others or, depending on one's misdeeds, in the midst of the hell realms, ghost realms, or animal realms. Even if one is reborn in the human realm, one will be handicapped by afflictions, such as deafness and the like.

However, if one serves others, seeking their exaltation rather than one's own, one will be reborn as a king, as a ruler or leader of men, or even in the gods' realms. Again, as Shāntideva tells us:

> Through using others as servants one reaps servitude, but through serving others one reaps mastery over others.

If one exploits other beings, putting them to work to further one's own selfish aims, then in the next life one will be reborn as a lowly servant, forced to execute the will of other beings. But if one puts aside one's own interest and serves others, one will be reborn in a situation where one is honored and exalted as a leader of beings.

The *Bodhicharyāvatara* continues:

> If all the unhappiness of this world arises from this great demon of egotism, why, then, do we cling fast to it?

As this verse tells us, the belief in a self is truly at the root of all worldly sufferings. All mental and physical pains have their origins in this deluded belief in an independently existing ego. When the mind fails to perceive its true nature and develops habitual attachment to the five skandhas, it proceeds to apprehend its experience in terms of self and other. As a result of this dualistic perception of experience, negative mental states of desire, aversion, and indifference are spawned. All actions that proceed from these states must by their very nature be negative, and their consequences painful. In this way the whole of samsaric existence is said to be painful by its very nature.

Thus the deluded belief in a self is rightly said to be the source of all unhappiness in this world. Accordingly, there can be no more harmful being, no more malevolent demon, no greater enemy than this very belief in a self. How is it that we still cherish, nourish, indulge, and act upon egotism, despite realizing that it is always the source of misery?

As long as you cling to the belief in a self, you will necessarily undergo suffering and be unable to achieve happiness in this life or any future life, much less be able to attain any kind of liberation. There is no way to attain liberation from worldly existence as long as that goal is sought for the self or through methods that merely reinforce the belief in a self. Nor is there any way to achieve the happiness that everyone seeks as long as the belief in a self is not relinquished, because when you interact with other beings from the standpoint of "I," or self, you inevitably come into conflict with them. Through attachment to your own interests—your sense of identity and attachment to your own circle of family and friends—you will experience only pain.

As a result of cherishing and acting on the premise of a truly existent self, the world as a whole spends its time in useless quarrels, attachments, relationships, and efforts that only increase the unhappiness of everyone involved. In contrast, through mindfulness of the true relationship between yourself and other beings, you will obtain both temporary and final benefits. In this very life, you will obtain the ripening results of happiness, good fortune, good health, and long life, while ultimately you will obtain the joy and bliss of liberation as an arhat, a pratyekabuddha, or a perfectly enlightened buddha.

When you do recognize all beings as your own dear parents, realizing that it is through your relationship to them that you are able to develop the enlightening qualities of a bodhisattva (i.e., great love, great compassion, and bodhichitta), then you have the right attitude toward, and insight about, beings. With those changes truly made in your mind, the quality of your actions will be superior, whatever you may undertake—whether study, reflection, or meditation. (Here "study" includes all attempts to comprehend both the sūtras and tantras, whether this understanding is acquired through asking a qualified teacher or through personal efforts at reading.)

We will also acquire merit through the practice of moral conduct—abandoning the ten kinds of unwholesome actions and practicing their opposites. Such virtues include those derived by sincerely pondering the doctrines, principles, and precepts that we have studied and understood, thereby integrating them into our own perspective on ourselves and the world. Whatever virtues we might accrue through meditative practice are enhanced as well.

Thus any and all virtues acquired through moral conduct, study, reflection, and meditation are directed toward, and effectively ripen in, the attainment of enlightenment, provided they are practiced with a mind filled with this exchange of self for others. Actions performed without this antidote to belief in a self only become the cause of increased egotism, for they are devoid of virtue and cannot become a cause either of happiness or of the cessation of suffering. Rather, they become a cause for increasing pride in our own cleverness, learning, virtue, ability in meditation, and so on—and even a cause of envy toward others who have developed these qualities. Although such actions may appear to be quite virtuous, if they are devoid of this spirit of exchanging self for others, they do not become a cause of enlightenment.

The *Bodhicharyāvatara* continues to speak of how important exchanging self and others is for those who rightly undertake and accomplish efforts in moral conduct, study, contemplation, and meditation. When this exchange is present we are able to attain liberation, whereas when it is absent we cannot.

You may wonder whether you will be able to practice this exchange of self and others, for fear of not being able to bear the sufferings of other beings. There is no reason to worry about this. It may be true that you would not be able to bear the sufferings of all other beings if that mass of suffering were suddenly to befall you as a result of meditating in this way. But this is not the way it happens. You need not fear that the sufferings of other beings can actually be transferred to you simply by your wishing it so. Karma is not transferable in this way. However, by praying, meditating, and wishing for the exchange of self and others, your mind does become able to identify with the sufferings of others, their happiness and joys, their wish for happiness and desire to be free from pain.

When this occurs, you are ready to make the switch from being concerned only with your own selfish interests to becoming concerned with the interests of others instead. Then, out of your concern for others, it does gradually become possible for you to give up your life, happiness, and belongings to promote their well-being and enlightenment. In this very gradual manner, your mind learns to care for others and, finally, to make their well-being more important than your own. You have, in a sense, exchanged self for others—at the very least, you have certainly exchanged self-interest for others' interests.

Through training in the exchange of self and others, you become able to undertake the bodhisattva practices, training in the six perfections. Here, too, your ability develops gradually. In the beginning, as the *Bodhicharyāvatara* tells us, one is only able to give away vegetables and small gifts, whereas later one is able to give away that which is held most dear: one's children, one's wife or husband, even one's own limbs and life. Through training in the small, easier steps, you become able to perform great moral and spiritual deeds. The result is that you eventually attain buddhahood.

As the *Bodhicharyāvatara* also tells us, even if you cannot believe this to be true, you should still undertake these practices. By the undeceiving words of the Enlightened One, you will see for yourself the truly great result of practicing this simple exchange of self and others. You should definitely undertake to exchange self and others, and also train in giving and the other perfections while keeping in mind the spirit of exchange. By doing so, you will experience truly wondrous spiritual results, both in this world and in the next. As surety for this, we have the undeceiving words of Lord Buddha himself, who was endowed with omniscience of things as they really are and who, through his great compassion, could not possibly think of harming beings by misrepresenting the truth. The Buddha's own enlightened words assure us that the results of this exchange of self and others are truly extraordinary and worthwhile.

❧ ✦ ❧

Furthermore, as we have already mentioned, the sages act only for others' benefit, whereas ordinary folk act only for their own. And look at the difference: worldlings seek their own gain and act against the benefit of others, only to accumulate suffering and the causes of continued wandering on the round of birth and death, whereas sages act for the good of others and enjoy the great bliss of liberation and the perfection of the enlightened ones. Reflecting on this, you should develop enthusiasm toward, and diligence in, practicing the meditation of exchanging self and others.

The power of this exchange is illustrated in a story from the *Tales of the Wise and the Foolish* (*Damamūka-sūtra*),[53] which tells of a former incarnation of the bodhisattva who was to become Shākyamuni Buddha. In that life, the bodhisattva had been reborn as a hell being as a result of the ripening of former evil actions. He was yoked with a companion and forced to pull wagons, goaded on by fierce and heartless guardians of hell. Both he and his companion, Kāmarūpa, were experiencing intense, unbearable pains both mentally and physically. Even though they were unable to bear the pain or perform the work, they were forced on constantly by their heartless driver. When the bodhisattva saw that his companion was even weaker than he and was receiving most of their driver's blows, he felt pity and said to the driver, "Please leave him alone; he is unable to pull the cart any farther. I will pull it for him."

The guardian of hell became enraged and began to beat the bodhisattva fiercely, saying that every being must experience the ripening of his own karma and that no one could experience it for him. He picked up a huge club and beat the bodhisattva about the head so fiercely that he died on the spot, only to be instantly reborn in a gods' realm, among bodhisattvas and deities devoted to the holy Dharma.

This tale was recounted by the Buddha as an example of the great power of pity and the resolve to take upon oneself the burdens of others.

Having established that there is great benefit in the thought of exchanging self for others, we are led to inquire about the method for practicing this exchange. This is to be done through meditation. After taking refuge and developing the meditations of great love and great compassion, focus on your own mother, since she has been most kind to you both in this life and in the past, and you naturally have great feelings of affection for her and great concern for her happiness.

Visualize your mother as if she were clearly before you and meditate that all her suffering and causes of suffering might not be experienced by her.

Instead, pray that they might be experienced by you alone in her place. As you pray sincerely from the heart, visualize that all her pain lifts from her like a dark cloud and is absorbed into your own heart, so that she is instantly and totally free from all suffering. As you meditate, rejoice that your mother has become freed from such pain.

Then visualize and pray that all your own happiness and causes of happiness are turned over to this kind mother of yours. Think that all your virtue and happiness are transferred to her in the form of a cloud of white light. As it is absorbed into her heart, she is filled in both body and mind with great, pure happiness and well-being. Then meditate with a sense of joy that you have been able to establish her in happiness.

After you have practiced with your mother until the meditation has become easy and natural, meditate in the same way toward your father, toward friends and relatives, toward strangers, and finally toward enemies and all beings without exception. Meditating on them all in the same way, you will develop a mind willing to take away their sufferings in exchange for your own happiness.

Next are the actual instructions for what you should be thinking in this meditation itself. As before, focus your mind on your own dear mother and think as follows:

> Alas![54] This is my kind mother, who has so often in this life protected me from discomfort, pain, fear, and danger. She would have given her own life for me. In so many ways she has nourished me, promoted my interests and well-being, and done all that she could to bring about my happiness and advantage. Yet this poor mother of mine has not achieved happiness for herself. Being subject to belief in the self, which is like a demon, and to the negative mental states of desire, hatred, and delusion that afflict us all, she experiences many kinds of unhappiness in body and mind. She also has the cause of future suffering. If only she were free from this suffering and prospect of suffering.
>
> To free her from that suffering, I would do anything. I will definitely strive for and attain enlightenment in order to gain the ability to free her from all these sufferings and causes of suffering.
>
> Thus far in this life, I have only acted selfishly, for my own pleasure and happiness, disregarding the sufferings of my mother. But from now on, I resolve to overcome the demon of the self and meditate, strive for enlightenment, and attain it in order to free this

kind mother from her sufferings and establish her in happiness.

May the sufferings and causes of suffering that afflict this kind mother of mine truly ripen to me, including all negative mental states, the mistaken belief in a self, all the wrong actions she has accumulated through ignorance, and all the other negative states and possibilities of negative, painful experiences. May she never experience them, but may I instead experience them for her.

Pray very intensely, again and again, in this manner. Then visualize that the mass of ignorance, delusion, suffering, and causes of suffering that afflicts your kind mother rises from her in the form of black light and descends to become absorbed into your own heart and consciousness. Think that she is now totally free from all those pains and causes of pain and that, as they are absorbed into your consciousness, your own mind becomes free of all clinging, self-centeredness, and selfish desire to act only for your own happiness.

The belief in a self is, as we have stressed, always the root of all ignorance itself, and consequently the root of all suffering and the causes of suffering. The notion of a self is the demon, the villain, the enemy of happiness, and it must definitely be overcome through insight. It can be overcome by insight when we perceive that there is no object that corresponds to our notion of a self. The notion of a self where there is no self is like that of a snake where there is no snake but only a coiled piece of rope. There never was a snake but only a misapprehension that caused us to act erroneously; so, too, there never was a self, although belief in a self causes us to act in harmful ways that create suffering for ourselves and others.

When we search for the self, we cannot find it. If there is such a thing as a personal identity, it must correspond to our personal name, body, or consciousness. Yet when we examine each of these, we see that it does not exist in any of them. Name is not our personal identity because it is merely a sound, a label given us by our parents. The body is not the self because if it were, and we should die tomorrow, the self would have been destroyed, yet those who believe in a self believe that it continues after death. Consciousness or mind is also not the self because consciousness is momentary, as the *Bodhicharyāvatara* tells us, and changes from instant to instant: our thoughts of this morning are not the same as they were at noon, nor are those at noon the same as they are in the evening. Because consciousness constantly arises and passes away, we cannot say that it constitutes a self; if this were so, there would be many selves arising and passing away in each instant.

You may ask, how does the self exist? The answer is that it doesn't exist at all. There is no existent object that corresponds to our notion of self, just as there was no snake there when we thought one existed.

Realizing this, meditate on removing the sufferings of your mother and establishing her in happiness. Visualize yourself giving her all the happiness and causes of happiness that you yourself have accumulated, may presently enjoy, or hope to enjoy in the future. Without any reluctance whatsoever, freely turn them all over to this kind mother of yours. As you do this, visualize that all your virtue and happiness arise from your heart like a cloud of white light or like a sudden dawn, when the rays of the sun first appear and bring instant joy to the beholder. This cloud of white light is then absorbed into your mother's consciousness, whereupon she immediately experiences total happiness in body and mind, freedom from all suffering and its causes, and pure joy.

Your intention is to establish your mother in happiness in every way—both temporary happiness, so long as she is in saṃsāra, and ultimate happiness, the perfect joy of total enlightenment. Therefore visualize that, in exchange for her sorrows, you are turning over to her all the happiness, virtue, wisdom, compassion, and bodhisattva qualities that will bring her the great bliss of buddhahood.

35

TURNING THE WHEEL OF THE RAT RACE

ALL OF US HAVE BEEN BORN with fairly sound bodies and all the right conditions for meeting with the Buddha's teachings. Because we realize that this is a good opportunity to benefit all sentient beings, we have decided to practice the Dharma and improve ourselves in this way. This is the basic motivation for what we are doing.

You may be wondering what is meant by "the Dharma." Here, what we are talking about is the religion that was taught in the snow lands of Tibet. In this religion there are several different traditions—the Nyingma, Kagyu, Sakya, and Kadam, which is similar to the Gelug. All are Buddhist teachings and have their origin in India in the teachings of Lord Buddha. The differences among the traditions are mainly ones of (1) lineage, that is, which particular teachers transmitted the teachings that have come down to us, and (2) methods of meditation. But all the basic practices of all the traditions are exactly the same. For example, they all begin with cultivating bodhichitta, and their goal of attaining buddhahood is exactly the same. If you were to say that they are not the same, you would be implying that one is better than another. That is not the case; they are all equally good.

The particular Dharma that you are practicing is the result of your previous karma and your particular tendencies. These get you into a particular school. For example, I myself, due to my own karma, am a student of the Sakya school.

The teaching of the Sakya lineage is called *Lam dre*, which means "path with the fruit" or "the path with its result." The *Lam dre* is a Vajrayāna teaching that originated with the Indian siddha Virūpa, who received it from the ḍākinī Vajranairātmyā, who is no different from Hevajra himself. Nairātmyā and Hevajra are basically the same, but the particular form manifested to Virūpa was Nairātmyā. The lam-dre teachings were passed on through Indian teachers like Gayādhara and then transmitted to Tibet with Drogmi Lotsawa and other teachers, down to the main teachers of the Sakya school, which also includes the Ngorpa and Tsarpa sects. Thus there are three basic lineages in the Sakya school, and they all transmit this lam-dre teaching.[55]

Within the lam-dre teachings, *The Three Visions* (*Nang Sum*) consists of preliminary practices to prepare yourself for actual entrance onto the path. It touches on subjects such as the six pāramitās, basic techniques of meditation, and appreciating the fact that we have the right opportunities and leisure to practice the Dharma. *Nang Sum* actually means "three visions," or three ways of experiencing reality. The first is the impure appearance, or vision, of reality, which is the worldly view of ordinary beings. The instructions here look at the fact that all sentient beings are confused; they also examine the problems we know the world has. The second vision is the appearance of meditative experiences, or the way of seeing life when you are meditating. This refers to all the different practices and experiences you encounter once you have entered the path: for example, you give rise to bodhichitta and then proceed through the stages of a bodhisattva's training. The third vision is that of pure appearance, which is the worldview of someone who has become enlightened. When you actually attain buddhahood, everything you see is in the form of a buddha or of the particular deity you have meditated on, everything you hear sounds like mantras, and everything you think is complete enlightenment.

After you have understood the three appearances discussed in *The Three Visions*, you can enter the Vajrayāna path, which is discussed in *The Three Continua* (*Gyu Sum*), and receive the Hevajra initiation and other empowerments. You can then practice the creation stage (*bskyed-rim*) and the completion stage (*rdzogs-rim*) according to the teachings of this system. *The Three Visions* is based on the teachings of the sūtras, although there is some Vajrayāna mixed in with it.

We have completed our studies of the impure vision, which is all about cause and effect, or karma, the unsatisfactory condition of saṃsāra, and appreciating the fact that we have all the right opportunities for practicing the Dharma. Now we are studying the teachings on the meditational experiences. We have covered those on compassion and are discussing giving all your benefits and merits to other sentient beings and taking on their problems. We have covered the quotes from the sūtras and other classical sources and have come to the point of actually meditating on this particular teaching.

You may well want to know how actually to assume this way of thinking. The *Bodhicharyāvatara* states:

> Thus, to make my own suffering and also the suffering of others subside, I put myself in the place of others and hold in my mind the thought of others.

In other words, you give up thinking only of yourself and your own desires because that leads you farther into saṃsāra. Instead, you try to think constantly of other sentient beings rather than yourself. You think in this manner no matter what you do or how you do it. This is the teaching that will help you develop the compassion and good-heartedness of a bodhisattva.

We all know how difficult it seems to be to have great compassion and great love for all sentient beings. Indeed, this perceived difficulty is nothing new. A long time ago, there was a lama called Pupalo, who was not only a great lama but the incarnation of other great bodhisattvas as well. In trying to teach compassion to his students, he realized that it was very difficult for them really to comprehend it. A woman who was his student was having trouble understanding exactly how to develop compassion, so Pupalo suggested that she think about her son. Obviously, she was always trying to help her son, protect him from any kind of danger, and give him whatever she could. Pupalo told her, "First, concentrate on your son. Recognize your own compassion for him, then take that same feeling and transfer it to other beings. Slowly you will become able to understand the meaning of compassion." The woman was, of course, able to relate to that idea. Pupalo thought that was good, because if she truly understood the exchange of self and others, she would be able to attain buddhahood quickly.

Similarly, it is easy for us to have a great deal of affection for our mothers. We know everything they have gone through for us and love them very much. When practicing the meditation of exchanging self and others, first visualize your mother. When you can understand compassion in that context, think about your father and then your friends, gradually expanding your thoughts to include all sentient beings.

We care very much for our mothers because they gave us the bodies we have. If you didn't have this body and this particular situation, how could you be practicing Dharma or doing anything at all? You really owe your mother quite a lot. Thus you want to get rid of all her problems, troubles, and sufferings and help her as much as possible.

First of all, while you are meditating, make the very firm resolve that you are definitely going to do something to help your mother dispel her problems and receive great benefits. Once you have done this, the first question is, What are your mother's problems?

Basically, the very essence of the Buddhist teachings is the Four Noble Truths: the truth of suffering, the truth of the cause of suffering, the truth of the path, and the truth of cessation. The first two state the basic problems that we have. The first, the truth of suffering, is evident both in mental pain, which results from our constantly grasping at things and attaching desire or aversion to them, and in physical pain, which we all experience when we fall ill or have physical problems of one sort or another. This manifest suffering of body and mind is what is known as the truth of suffering.

The second truth, which is more subtle, is the source of suffering. This consists, basically, of two things: (1) karma, or actions, that you perform—specifically, your wrong actions, and (2) your emotions and passions, which are constantly getting you into trouble. These two situations cause a continuum of suffering to arise.

While you are meditating, think about all this manifest suffering and about the causes of suffering that your mother has to endure, and wish that they may all fall upon you instead of your mother. Then visualize that you are experiencing all your mother's problems and taking all their causes on yourself. If you are able to experience that feeling, you should be pleased, because it is the purpose of this meditation to accomplish just that.

Keep thinking, over and over again, that all these problems are coming to you alone. In other words, give up all care for your own welfare, which has only caused you to remain in saṃsāra anyway; and think only in terms of your mother, not in terms of your own benefit at all.

After you have visualized that for a while, think about what could possibly help your mother. What would help in terms of manifest feelings? If she felt bliss or happiness, would that be beneficial? In terms of cause, it would be very good if she were to engage only in meritorious actions, thoughts, and speech instead of producing bad karma and emotional problems. Now imagine that all this bliss and all these meritorious actions actually do come to your mother: imagine whatever happiness and merit you have accumulated being sent to her, that her body and mind are very, very happy, that she is blissful and possesses a great store of merit. If all this were really to occur, you yourself would be very happy, so if you can visualize it happening, you will have a feeling of happiness and satisfaction at the end.

Once you have done this for your mother, you can slowly start to do the same for your father, friends, enemies, and all sentient beings.

What we have just studied is the rationale behind the whole meditation on the exchange of self for others. Now we will explain what you should be thinking to yourself when you actually meditate. First, clearly visualize what your mother looks like—her face, her coloring, and so forth. Then say to yourself:

Kena.[56] I really love my mother very much; she is the person who gave me this body capable of accomplishing enlightenment, which is a very precious thing. I must protect her from any kind of danger, fear, or problem. If I could somehow accomplish immeasurable benefit and happiness for her, it would be extremely good. Ever since I have been wandering in samsāra, my mother has been protecting me with limitless great compassion. By doing so much for me, she herself has had to go through samsāra, which is very unfortunate.

Now, in order to help my mother, I must attain the stage of total enlightenment. Everything I have done only for myself has been a great error on my part. My life is very short and everything is uncertain, but I must control the demon of caring only for self, holding onto the notion of a self, and always thinking selfishly about everything. I must discard all these selfish thoughts and practice the Dharma for the benefit of my very kind mother.

What is it that is bothering my mother? It is suffering and the causes of suffering. I will now try to take upon myself all these sufferings of my kind mother, that they may ripen for me instead.

When you are able to meditate in this way, you can be very pleased with yourself.

Next, think that the very notion of yourself as an individual ego is an illusion. Like realizing that what you thought was a snake lying in the shadows is merely a coil of rope, recognize that you are not a real, solid, individual ego that stands by itself but just an illusion caused by your own bad karma and ignorance. Wake up and see that your self and all of this "reality" are without basis. Rid yourself of that illusory frame of mind. Again think:

What would help my mother? If she were to have happiness and the causes of happiness, that would help her. Therefore, may she have all my own happiness and causes of happiness. Everything that I have, may she have it. May all my own bliss and causes of happiness, all my own merit, ripen for my mother instead of me.

Actually say this out loud to yourself. Visualize that light as radiant as the sun's is shining forth from your heart and that all your merit, which is in the form of light, instantly travels from your heart into your mother's. As a result, your mother makes use of all this merit, becomes very happy, and has all the right circumstances for practicing the Dharma—such as a teacher, a good place to meditate, good health, and enough to eat—so that she is able to do something worthwhile. Then visualize that all her bad karma, unhappiness, and misdeeds travel from her in the form of black light and merge into you. Visualize this as much as you can.

Thus this exchange has two parts: (a) the sending, or giving away, of your own merit, and (b) the taking in of your mother's misdeeds and unhappiness. Your meditation cannot be casual; you must do it with all your might, putting your whole heart into it. Sit for a while, and visualize and experience what we have just described.

After you have done this for some time, expand the meditation to include your father, friends, enemies, and all sentient beings. Visualize the six classes of sentient beings and think about all their great sufferings. Eventually, you will have tremendous compassion for all their problems, and will decide for all their sakes that you are definitely going to reach the stage of buddhahood. Practice this twofold meditation for all sentient beings.

Also, remember that there are two types of bodhichitta, relative and absolute. In this practice, relative bodhichitta is generated on behalf of all sentient beings, your mother, yourself, and all the states of mind we have been discussing. This bodhichitta is called relative because in reality none of these factors actually exists—neither the beings whose sufferings you want to exchange for your own happiness, nor the person who is helping them (you), nor the "actual" sufferings themselves, nor your own happiness, merit, or any of the rest. It is not easy for us to understand this truth, so, in the relative sense, we nevertheless generate tremendous compassion for beings and vow to attain buddhahood for their sakes.

After thinking all this, share all the merit that you have accumulated in doing so.

This is the actual visualization and meditation of the exchange of self and others, which is now complete. Afterward, continue this practice in all your daily activities; to do so is to follow what is called "the path of activity." Always keep in mind your basic viewpoint of compassion toward all sentient beings. You can say these two lines to yourself:

> May all the suffering of all sentient beings fall upon me, and may all sentient beings have any good points or merit that I might possess.

By saying this to yourself, you will constantly be making great efforts to help sentient beings through what are called the Three Doors—i.e., the three ways of manifesting whatever you are doing through body, speech, and mind. With your body, you can do religious practices, like prostrations, or physically help sentient beings. With your speech, you can pray or say good things, like the two lines just mentioned. And with your mind, you can think constantly about all sentient beings in the universe.

If at any point you again become very attached to yourself, falling in love with yourself and thinking only about yourself, try to realize that this has happened hundreds of thousands of times before, and that it is the whole reason you have been in saṃsāra from beginningless time, constantly turning the wheel of the rat race. As the *Bodhicharyāvatara* says:

> You must realize this to be your basic enemy. Therefore you should totally destroy all selfish, egotistical, one-pointed thinking.

36

Doing What Bodhisattvas Do

THE EFFORT YOU ARE MAKING to study the lam-dre teaching can become a direct cause of attaining enlightenment. If you undertake to learn the Dharma with the proper intention, it can be just as effective as diligent effort put into meditative practice. Here the proper spirit is the resolve that your efforts to understand and recall the teachings be directed toward the attainment of buddhahood for the sake of all living beings—in other words, bodhichitta. If you do not keep this resolve in mind, then your efforts will lack the proper motivation and do nothing to enhance your orientation toward buddhahood.

When receiving teachings, think of your teacher as Shākyamuni Buddha himself and relate to him as if you were in the Buddha's presence. Think of yourself as the great bodhisattva Mañjushrī, who spares no effort to seek out the teachings of enlightenment and the insights to which the words refer. Receive the teachings as if they were the Buddha's own words spoken to you for the benefit of all living beings. And while thinking of yourself as Mañjushrī and your teacher as Shākyamuni Buddha, try to attune yourself to ultimate reality by refraining from reifying this present situation. In other words, don't sink down by thinking of it—and your own efforts—as too real, in the way that ordinary people think of their present experience. See the effort you are making as a manifestation of nondual appearance and voidness; regard the words you hear as the nonduality of sound and void. Keep in mind that the ultimate reality of the present situation is away from all extremes and conceptualizations of existence and nonexistence, positive and negative, and the like.

Having reminded ourselves about our intentions in undertaking this course of study, we should also consider our present course. In the context of the lam-dre system as a whole, Lord Buddha taught some eighty-four thousand doctrines of enlightenment. All these can be subsumed in two categories: those belonging to Hīnayāna systems, and those belonging to Mahāyāna systems. Mahāyāna itself also contains two categories: exoteric pāramitā teachings, and esoteric tantric teachings.

As you know, the lam-dre system originated with the Indian mahāsiddha

Virūpa when he received initiation from the ḍākinī Nairātmya and shortly thereafter attained the sixth bhūmi, or stage of bodhisattvahood. This teaching has been transmitted down through the generations by a series of Indian and Tibetan masters. The system as a whole consists of sets of instructions which are to be practiced on two different levels, corresponding to the exoteric pāramitāyana and esoteric Vajrayāna paths. The pāramitā teachings are considered to be the foundation for the advanced Vajrayāna practices.

Ideally, a practitioner of the lam-dre system will first learn the system as a whole and then undertake the fundamental, or foundational, practices. Next, he will learn the advanced tantric practices. Finally, through initiation into the mandala and practice of the meditation of Shrī Hevajra, there will arise within his mind the ultimate view of reality, which is called "the non-differentiation of saṃsāra and nirvāṇa" ('khor-'das-dbyer-med). When this view arises, he will attain buddhahood.

The foundational instructions, which are given in *The Three Visions*, are essential to the graduated states of meditation expected of a practitioner on the bodhisattva path. By their accomplishment, we are brought to sufficient maturity and stability to undertake with some hope of success the more advanced training on the tantric level. These fundamental teachings consist of the reflections on death, impermanence, karma, and so on, in order to wean the mind away from worldly attachments. They also include training in great love, great compassion, and bodhichitta, in order to ennoble our minds with the universal impulse and extend our spiritual efforts to include all beings.

In our last few sessions, we completed the discussions of great love, great compassion, bodhichitta, and the training in awakening bodhichitta by first recognizing the sameness of self and others and then exchanging self for others.

THE SIX PĀRAMITĀS

Although there are many sets of instructions related to the bodhisattva's spiritual training, all of them, without exception, can be condensed into these two: (1) teachings on the awakening of bodhichitta, and (2) teachings on the bodhisattva's training in the six transcendent virtues, or pāramitās. Thus far, we have received only the instructions on the former, so we will now begin our discussion of the latter, describing just how the bodhisattva trains in these six qualities in order to bring his mind to spiritual maturity. We will also learn how he trains in the four social means in order to bring other beings to spiritual maturity. Actually, there are three topics: (a) general training in the bodhisattva's conduct; (b) specific training in the six perfections, in order to bring oneself to spiritual maturity, and (c) training in the four social means, in order to bring others to spiritual maturity.

General Training in Bodhisattva Conduct

Speaking of the task of the bodhisattva, Shāntideva says that one who follows this way must be prepared to give away without reserve his body, wealth, virtue, and any merit collected in the past, present, and future for the good of other living beings. By giving up everything, our minds course toward liberation. Since we will eventually be forced to give up everything anyway, when death comes, it is better to do it for a good cause and of our own free will.

The first thing you must do is develop the right attitude toward the bodhisattva's training: you must want to do it. In other words, you must aspire to being a bodhisattva and doing what bodhisattvas do, always remembering that the key to a bodhisattva's practice lies in the willingness to give to others. You will begin by making mental gifts and training the mind in becoming whatever it is that other beings want and need. The aspirant to bodhisattvahood wishes to become a source of material assistance to those in need, a protector to those who are afraid, a friend to those who are lonely, and so on.

While meditating in this vein, you should also make positive efforts in the real world to promote the mental happiness and physical well-being of others. Become their helper in removing problems, sorrows, and unhappiness, and their generous donor in sharing with them whatever goods you possess. You need not go overboard at the beginning and give away every stitch you own. Train yourself in giving what is commensurate with your ability to give freely, with right intention and right view. Again, the *Bodhicharyāvatara* and other scriptures recommend that the beginner practice giving only to the extent that he is able. Start by making gifts of flowers, vegetables, fruit, and the like.

When you become skilled in making gifts of this kind, you will learn to make larger gifts, until finally you can give away property of any value without hesitation—and you can even give away your husband or wife, children, your own body, or your own life if it will benefit other beings. Of course, when you have attained insight into the nature of ultimate reality, it is not necessary actually to give away your body, but neither would that be any more difficult than it is for us to make offerings of flowers and fruit now. This is so because the bodhisattva is free from all belief in a self and does not distinguish between self and others, or think of either of them as being real. As the *Bodhicharyāvatara* states:

The Buddha, our guide, taught that we should first make gifts of vegetables and the like. Practicing in this way, we will gradually be able to give away even the flesh of our bodies, for when we see that our bodies are no more ours than vegetables are, what difficulty is there in offering them?

Specific Training in the Six Perfections

Here we have three subjects to discuss: (i) the definition of the six perfections, (ii) the way they are to be accomplished, and (iii) the benefit derived from their accomplishment. Let us take up the first of these. The six transcendent virtues, by which we can transcend both saṃsāra and nirvāṇa, both worldly existence and quiescent liberation, are:

1. the perfection of giving, which consists of offering your own material possessions;

2. the perfection of morality, which consists of relinquishing all unwholesome or sinful actions or inclinations that may be harmful to other beings;

3. the perfection of patience, which consists of maintaining an undisturbed, unagitated mind no matter what injury is done to you by others;

4. the perfection of vigor, or diligence; perfection of, which consists of enthusiasm in the performance of virtuous deeds;

5. the perfection of meditation, which consists of single-pointed mental concentration on wholesome objects (not merely an image, but also a virtuous concept, like the thought of love or compassion); and

6. the perfection of wisdom, which is said to be right discrimination among phenomena (i.e., recognizing the components of your existence for what they really are).

With perfect wisdom, you know the five skandhas, the six sense organs, the six sense fields, the eighteen elements of existence, and so forth. You are able to distinguish each one and the functions of each. Through this discrimination, you acquire insight into their interdependent nature and their ultimate nature of voidness. As Nāgārjuna said in the *Precious Garland,* "The perfection of wisdom is the ascertainment of the nature of ultimate reality."

Nāgārjuna summarizes the six perfections in a few short verses, to the effect that giving means to give freely your own possessions; morality consists of accomplishing the benefit of others; patience is giving up anger; vigor is the apprehension of virtue; meditation is the undefiled, single-pointed state of mind; and wisdom is ascertainment of the ultimate nature of reality.

Also, each pāramitā has its particular benefit: giving begets prosperity; morality, well-being; patience, radiance; vigor, splendor; meditation, a tranquil mind; and with wisdom, liberation is gained.

All this relates to the accomplishment of four qualities that are friendly to the six perfections, and the avoidance of seven kinds of attachment that are hostile toward them. These four qualities require (1) a state of mind free of the six negativities of miserliness, immorality, anger, laziness, distraction, and wrong knowledge (i.e., the opposites of the six perfections); (2) that each of the six pāramitās be accomplished with transcendent, nonconceptual wisdom, wherein no gift, giver, recipient, giving, or merit from the action is perceived; (3) that the results of your accomplishment of the six perfections fulfill the needs and wishes of others; and (4) that, through skill in means, your actions bring to spiritual maturity those whom you seek to help through the three vehicles of realization (namely, arhatship, pratyeka-buddhahood, and bodhisattvahood).

The seven hostile forces are also called the seven attachments. They are: (1) attachment to whatever is unfriendly to the training and practice of the bodhisattva; (2) attachment to giving up such things as the bodhisattva career or a good work before they are finished; (3) attachment to easy satisfaction, such as an act of little virtue, a short retreat, or a small donation in situations where more could be done; (4) attachment to rewards—saying, for example, "By doing this now, I'll get a good rebirth, an easy trip through the bardo, or I'll become a great bodhisattva"; (5) attachment to ripening results, these being rewards on the karmic level; (6) attachment to dormant mental impressions even after all outward attachments and defilements seem to have been removed from the mind, so that it still harbors potential for the six negativities (the opposites of the pāramitās); and (7) attachment to distractions, which applies to all six transcendent virtues, each of which must be kept free of all seven attachments.

With regard to the fourth of these, there is the story of a miserly old monk who was so attached to his virtue that when he had recited a hundred million Om mani padme hum mantras, he bragged to his brother monks of his merit and refused to dedicate it to the enlightenment of all beings, as he had been taught to do. Not only all the other monks but his own teacher (and mine), Gatön Ngawang Legpa Rinpoche, told him he was ignorant, yet he would not dedicate the merit that he was clinging to. Stubborn to the last, he did his work and kept the merit, then stayed up late to do a few extra rounds on his mālā, the merit of which he did dedicate to all sentient beings.

37

A PROTECTOR OF THE PROTECTORLESS

FOR ANY WORK to be meaningful, it must produce a desired result. This is especially true of the efforts that a follower of the Great Way must make to achieve his or her spiritual goals. Our own efforts in seeking out Buddhist teachings, reciting verse, meditating, and training in virtuous habits become meaningful only when they are accomplished mindfully. Here mindfulness entails awareness of the three stages in any virtuous or religious action: (1) the mental preparation, (2) the main practice, and (3) the completion of that action.

First, to be mindful of our mental preparations involves approaching study with the right attitude—namely, seeking to learn not out of idle curiosity or lack of something more interesting to do, but because we really intend to take the teachings to heart in order to further our own and all beings' spiritual enlightenment. This is called bodhichitta. From the Mahāyāna point of view, the mental preparation for any action must involve this mindful arousing of right intent, so that we wish, by our actions, to promote the enlightenment of all living beings. A good deed alone, while fine in itself, does not necessarily become fruitful on the Mahāyāna path. Indeed, many do not, for lack of being directed toward buddhahood. Thus the first step in undertaking all actions is to develop and maintain this right attitude.

Second, we should accomplish these efforts with single-pointed attention, without allowing the mind to be distracted elsewhere, all the time we are actually practicing virtue—whether sitting in mediation, studying the Dharma, reading books, listening to a teacher, helping those who are in need, or protecting the lives of the threatened. For example, at the time of study, you should focus your attention on the effort you are making, rather than allowing your thoughts to traipse off in other directions. No matter how earnest you are about making right actions, you must also remember not to fall into the trap of becoming attached to those so-called spiritual efforts, thinking, "I am quite real, this is my real virtuous action, and the result of my actions is real merit." Keep in the back of your mind the recognition that, while on the conventional level these actions do have reality, from the ultimate point of view they are not real. Understand that there is more to the occasion than meets the eye, and that what appears real on the conventional level must not be construed as being truly substantial.

You can at least approximate the right point of view during the main thrust of your meditation or study by actively recalling that things are not what they seem, that they are not real in the way we like to think of them being, and that there is, ultimately, no subject or object. Even on the conventional level of reality, try to think of things as magical illusions or dreams. This little exercise is meant to keep your mind from becoming overly attached to your spiritual efforts.

Third, after you have completed the session of study, meditation, or virtuous action, remember to dedicate all the good that has been accomplished toward your eventual enlightenment and that of all other beings. By doing so, the action is completed in the best possible way, since the good results of your efforts are magnified through mindfulness and through being shared with others. If you take this approach to all three stages of your religious efforts, you can be assured that your actions will be attuned to the way of the bodhisattvas and performed to the best of your ability.

We approach meditation and meditative texts through a twofold categorization: preliminary instructions and practices, and advanced instructions and practices. This systematization is to be found in the Nyingma tradition in the form of its distinction between *trek-chö* (*khregs-chod*, "cutting through resistance") and *tö-gäl* (*thod-rgal*, "all-surpassing realization"),[57] and in the Gelug system as the division between *lam-rim* ("stages of the path") and *ngag-rim* (*sngags-rim*, "stages of mantra"). In the Kagyu tradition, a distinction is made between the Six Doctrines of Nāropa (*Nā-ro chos-drug*) and the mahāmudrā doctrine. In the Sakya school, the *Lam dre* is divided into two systems, known as the three visions (*snang-gsum*) and three continua (*rgyud-gsum*). *The Three Visions* is, of course, the name of the text we are currently studying. It consists of three sets of instructions, which are called visions because they correspond to the three levels of spiritual perception experienced by followers of the Mahāyāna path.

The first level of perception is called the impure vision and happens to describe our own point of view. Unenlightened beings involved in secular affairs, not having had the benefit of meditative and philosophical training, perceive their experience and environment from a subjective point of view that is erroneous and influenced by negative mental states such as desire, attachment, aversion, indifference, and the like. Because it is not an accurate point of view, this perception does not truly relate to actual experience and thus is called impure or clouded. This is the point of view of ordinary human beings.

Once a person has undertaken to follow the Mahāyāna path and to mediate and accomplish the training of a bodhisattva, he will find his point of view undergoing a transformation. Where formerly he saw things as substantial, pure, subjective, and even permanent, he now sees that they are not really substantial but are transient, impermanent, devoid of any inherent nature of their own, and lacking in purity. This change in perception is called the vision of the path or the vision of experience. But this is not the final Buddhist view. It is only an intermediate or transitional stage through which a practitioner must pass.

The final or pure vision occurs when the practitioner has attained spiritual liberation or buddhahood. At this point, his sight is no longer obscured by emotive habits such as attachment and aversion, nor by that ignorance which proceeds from the mistaken belief in subject and object. This state of direct perception of things as they are is called "the nonduality of clarity and voidness" (*gsal-stong zung-'jug*) and is the view of enlightened beings.

To reach the goal of buddhahood, a practitioner has first to know what to expect when he undertakes to follow the Mahāyāna path. Thus far, we have discussed the instructions for beginners, whose level of perception is that of ordinary beings—instructions on impermanence, death, the difficulty of obtaining the opportunity to practice, the law of karma (retribution for good and bad actions, and our responsibility for them), and so forth. All these teachings are intended to turn the mind away from overinvolvement in worldly activities in the present life. When our minds have been reoriented toward a spiritual goal such as the attainment of buddhahood, we have in fact gone beyond the first stage of perception and entered the path of experience, or vision of the path.

Here the problem is not attachment to worldly affairs but attachment to spiritual experiences. The temptation is to cling to those accomplishments as if they, too, were real—in effect, to substitute the spiritual world for the secular, and then develop attachment to it. The practitioner must learn to overcome this kind of attachment by developing a sense of altruism, a spirit devoid of self-interest. This is done by training the mind to perform actions for the good of others rather than oneself. One trains in selflessness, unselfishness, and in developing a universal attitude about the efforts one is making.

Then, through training in the two stages of meditation—concentration (*samatha*) and insight (*vipaśyanā*)—the mind learns not to cling to spiritual efforts and accomplishments as real but to see that they, too, lack any inherent nature of their own. Thus the mind avoids becoming arrested in its spiritual progress by clinging to accomplishments, states of existence, or things as real in a dualistic way (i.e., a way in which a subject and object are thought to be involved).

Finally, through right practice—that is, nondual compassion and emptiness (or compassion and wisdom)—the practitioner does become his ideal: he becomes a great bodhisattva. He enters the stage of buddhahood and there is free from all the constraints of the preceding levels of perception, for he sees things exactly as they are, however many they are. This state of unhindered perception is the pure vision of the enlightened ones.

We have almost completed the instructions for the vision of the path. We have already discussed the bodhichitta of aspiration and are now discussing the bodhichitta of application, or the enlightened attitude as it is manifested on the level of conventional reality through the bodhisattva's training. We have said that, to bring our own minds to spiritual maturity, we should train in the six transcendent virtues of the bodhisattvas: giving, moral conduct, patience, diligence, meditation, and wisdom. But the practitioner's responsibility doesn't end there. To bring others to spiritual maturity, he must also train in the "four social means," a term used to describe how a sincere Mahāyāna practitioner should conduct himself in order to encourage others to gain the benefits of a spiritual life.

The Four Social Means

The four social means are described in one of the *Jātaka Tales*, the stories of the Buddha's past lives. There it says that the bodhisattva should gather others about him "with a wave of giving." As a bodhisattva, you summon others with this gesture of giving and converse with them with pleasant speech. You put them at ease by attuning yourself to their states of mind, development, insight, and their particular areas of interest. Finally, you act in accord with what you preach: you set a good example for others.

The Four Kinds of Gifts. As it is said in the *Jātaka Tales*, the bodhisattva attracts people to become interested in learning more about the Buddha, the Dharma, and the Mahāyāna path by making gifts to them. He does this through four kinds of gifts.

First, to the needy the bodhisattva gives what they need: to the poor he gives property; to the hungry, food; to the thirsty, water. Whatever beings are in need of, he gives it to them. This is considered the lowest of the four kinds of gift.

Second is the gift of fearlessness. To beings who are unhappy, lonely, in need of a friend, in fear for their lives, or helpless, the bodhisattva becomes all that they need. He removes their fears; he rescues them from danger; he befriends them when they are surrounded by enemies, when they are lonely, and so forth. Thus the bodhisattva becomes a protector for beings.

Third is an even higher gift, that of love. Realizing that all beings share the same essential nature and are no different from himself, the bodhisattva is able to empathize with all other beings, no matter what their condition. Recognizing the true nature of beings, he loves them and in no way remains indifferent to them. The bodhisattva does not neglect beings but cares for them all as if each one were his only son. In this way, he provides them with the gift of love.

Fourth is the highest gift that a bodhisattva can make, called the gift of Dharma. This is the gift of the teachings of enlightenment, and it is through this gift that beings become able to help themselves, for they become aware of their condition and of the methods that will enable them to achieve their own liberation from suffering and their own enlightened and highest good. Thus, through many skillful means, the bodhisattva endeavors to provide these teachings. Whether through words, actions, or skill in helping them learn via their own experiences, the bodhisattva helps beings acquire the teachings of the Dharma. This is the highest gift because it enables beings to help themselves.

There are two kinds of gifts for each of these four, because there are two ways of giving: you can make an impure gift or a pure one. An impure gift might be counterproductive, and a bodhisattva would go to great lengths to avoid making such a mistake. What would constitute an impure gift? First, wrong motive would make a gift impure. For example, your motive is impure if you are generous, do good, save lives, and so forth harboring the idea that you will get a very nice reward for all this. To seek a reward for giving is not in the bodhisattva spirit. It is true that, if you make all these kinds of gifts, in this life and in future lives you will experience good results from these actions. But the bodhisattva lets those results come without giving any thought to them at all. It is like planting rice: if the seed is whole, healthy, and planted correctly, then the plant, flower, and fruit will be healthy and abundant. Similarly, the bodhisattva doesn't think about the results of his actions; he just does them and gives up all hope of ever seeing any reward for them.

Second, he avoids making gifts to the wrong recipients. For example, there is not much point in giving money to a rich man or property to a king, and it wouldn't be right for a bodhisattva to pay a prostitute, so he avoids making such donations. He gives money to the truly destitute, protects the lives of those who are in danger, gives food to the hungry, and the like. He doesn't misdirect his acts of giving.

Third, he doesn't give the wrong gifts. For example, if you offer a chicken to a butcher, that would be a wrong gift, and meat and alcohol would only harm the recipient. There are thirty-two kinds of wrong gifts listed in the. By avoiding all wrong gifts—wrong intent, wrong recipient, wrong object, and so forth—you can train in making pure gifts and thereby attract beings to the Buddhist religion.

To add a practical note to these four kinds of giving, we should remember that there are two kinds of bodhisattvas, ascetics and householders. By ascetics we mean those who have taken vows of renunciation; they have become monks, live in monasteries, meditate in caves. They have renounced the ways of the world and are intent upon practice twenty-four hours a day, trying to attain buddhahood as quickly as possible. The householder bodhisattva does not renounce the world or join a monastery but keeps a job, and perhaps marries and has children. Nonetheless, he is motivated by the resolve to attain buddhahood for the benefit of others.

By virtue of their respective callings, environments, and so on, there are some differences between the types of giving that each of these two are called upon to perform. For example, the bodhisattva who has renounced the world has little in the way of property, so he may not be able to make gifts of material goods. Nor may he be called upon to make gifts of fearlessness, for he may not come into contact with beings in fear for their lives. But the gift of Dharma and the gift of love are enjoined for the ascetic bodhisattva. Whether or not he is near beings, in meditative sessions the bodhisattva can and should at all times make this gift of love. He ought always to remember beings, thinking of their welfare and permeating the ten directions with thoughts of love and compassion for them and prayers for their well-being and liberation from suffering. He should also be ready to make gifts of the Dharma whenever possible, teaching others he comes into contact with, whether human or not.

The householder bodhisattva, in contrast, lives among other unenlightened beings and has many opportunities for making gifts of material goods. Beggars will come by; he will run into the poor. He will have many chances to step in and save other beings' lives, and so forth. Thus the householder bodhisattva probably should cultivate the first two kinds of giving. For example, if he happens to be a government official and has any power at all, he can be instrumental in passing laws prohibiting the hunting of animals or in removing laws that allow for their capture. He can make these gifts of fearlessness to beings on a wide scale if he is an official, setting aside game sanctuaries and the like.

Pleasant Speech. The second of the four social means is pleasant speech. When the bodhisattva has satisfied worldly beings by giving them what they need and want, he tries to help them develop spiritual maturity. It is not possible to start talking about the Buddhist conception of ultimate reality, or insight into emptiness, right off the bat with everyone you want to help. You have to use skillful means, gauging the receptivity of each person and making the Dharma available accordingly. With those who are not interested in religion per se, you find out what interests they have and talk about those things, drawing parallels to religious principles. This can help them absorb religious principles, such as how to avoid nonvirtue and practice virtue, responsibility for one's actions, and so on, without introducing them to the Buddhadharma itself.

With those who are more intelligent, and who have an interest in the teachings of Buddhist enlightenment, you teach all that you know, initially through making gifts and through pleasant speech. Pleasant speech is communication that is done skillfully and with consideration for the person you hope to help. You should always speak words that will please the ears rather than turn people away from what you want them to hear. Even though they learn to listen to Buddhist teachings, such persons may not have any enthusiasm for practice. They may agree that the Buddhadharma is a very fine thing and that it is nice that it's available, but they will not necessarily feel any obligation to practice it.

Attuning Yourself to Others. The next step is to help others awaken interest in embarking on practice by encouraging them to relate to it in terms of their own personal situations, and thus to feel at ease with the teachings and principles of Mahāyāna Buddhism. When you identify with a person's situation, so that you have some rapport with him, then, by being like that person but nonetheless finding something of interest in the Dharma, you will naturally encourage him to practice just as you do.

Practicing What You Preach. Attuning yourself to others leads to the fourth of the social means, to act as you preach. To help others decide to undertake virtuous practices, you must be diligent and mindful in your own performance, thereby setting a good example and becoming an inspiration to those you wish to help.

To summarize, we have a quotation from the *Adornment of the Mahāyāna Sūtras*, in which the first social need is called "equanimity in giving":

When one makes a gift, one should not make distinctions among other beings, not think of one person as more worthy than another, dearer than another, and so forth, but regard all beings equally, thinking of them all with a sense of empathy, so that one regards all as being equally as dear as one's parents. Just as you would not hesitate to serve your parents or do them a good turn, so you should regard all other beings as equally dear. This is called the spirit of equanimity in giving. Second is teaching them, communicating with them through well-chosen words, and third is bringing them into harmony with the Dharma by skillfully identifying with their situation. Fourth is setting a good example. These are the Four Social Needs.

You should think:

Also, I have gone for so long without repaying these beings for their many kindnesses to me. For so long I have thought only of my own selfish interest and have nurtured affection only for myself. I have directed envy toward those who are better off than I am, I have directed contempt toward those who are worse off, and I have harbored thoughts of rivalry and competition toward those who are equal. I have acted in this foolish, futile, and hurtful way for so long, and as a result I have moved about, in this life and others, accumulating grief, misery, and mental pain for myself and causing it for others as well.

But from now on, I am going to give up self-centeredness and the habit of thinking only of myself. I resolve to dedicate all the actions of my body, voice, and mind toward the accumulation of merit that will be helpful for those beings whom I have hurt in the past, and I also resolve to train in acting liberally, without niggardliness, for their benefit. For those who are hungry, I shall provide food and drink. I shall supply clothing for those who need clothes, a bed and shelter for those who are in need of them. I shall be a

servant for those who need one. For the ill, I shall become medicine, a physician, a nurse, and for the destitute, I shall become an
inexhaustible treasure house. I shall be a protector of the protectorless, a refuge for those who have no other place to turn. For those
who travel, I shall be a guide. For those who wish to cross over, I
shall be a boat or a bridge. In sum, may I become an inexhaustible
supply to fulfill the various wants and needs of all those beings.

Think in this way and train in this attitude of service to beings. Whenever
you get the opportunity to actually fulfill the wants and needs of any beings,
you should develop a sense of great joy that you now have the chance, at
least on this one occasion and to this slight extent, to help them as you have
been praying to do.

When you rejoice in virtuous actions, that makes them stronger. The
mind likes to feel happy about things, and by praising yourself again and
again and feeling good about giving, it becomes easier to give the second and
third times. This is the way the mind is reinforced in virtuous actions—by
rejoicing in them. Again you should think:

Now I have already given away my own body and wealth, my
virtues, everything I have, and it is definite that I won't take them
back. Just as we don't have any idea of retaining for further use
something that we have presented to others, so I will no longer
think that my sense organs and so forth are to be used for my own
selfish interests, because I have quite literally given them away to
other beings. No matter how these beings might choose to treat
me—whether they kill me, curse me, beat me, bind me, whether
they scoff at or mock me—no matter how they misuse me or to
what extent they mistreat me, I will not return to selfishness or
take back my self from them. Whatever they choose to do with
that self depends on those beings themselves; as far as I am concerned, my body, speech, and mind belong to them.

Just as the buddhas and the bodhisattvas trained in the six transcendental wisdoms in order to achieve the highest good of self and
others, and just as they trained in the four social means in order to
bring others to spiritual maturity, so I will rightly train myself in
those six virtues and four needs. I shall make unblemished material
gifts, assemble about me others who are fit vessels for the Dharma,
and explain to them the holy doctrine in accord with their mental

capacities. I shall help them enter into right understanding and practice of the teachings, and in order to induce them to enter the path to enlightenment, I myself shall make extensive and profound efforts in practice and be enthusiastic in my own efforts.

Think in this way again and again, until it really becomes your foremost intention to practice in this way. Any time you find yourself able to practice any of the perfections or social needs, be glad that you are at last able to practice rather than merely think about such a noble action. Finally, dedicate any merit you may accrue to the enlightenment of all living beings.

This completes our set of instructions concerning conventional bodhichitta. In the next session, we will take up ultimate bodhichitta.

38

SEEING THINGS EXACTLY AS THEY ARE

IN THE COURSE of our lam-dre discussions, you have heard many times that the opportunity for practice afforded by human existence is extremely rare. This can be verified by merely stopping to think about the spiritual status of most beings in the human realm. There are so many people who are devoid of either the impulse or the opportunity to practice religion. Contrast those people with the few who do have a religious inclination and an opportunity to practice and achieve the results thereof. Then you can easily appreciate what is meant by the statement that the opportunity to practice religion is only rarely encountered.

In our own case, we have come into contact with the teachings of Lord Buddha. We have had the good fortune to meet teachers who are willing and able to impart those doctrines and instructions. And, for the most part, we have the leisure to put those teachings into practice. If we also have a Dharma center, however small it may be, we can number ourselves among the truly fortunate beings. But what really determines whether we are among the most fortunate of beings? Not merely the accessibility of teachings, but the willingness to put those teachings to good use once they have been received.

We have received a number of teachings. We have met lamas and attended tantric initiations. But that in itself, while good, is not the essential ingredient that is needed to make us practitioners of Mahāyāna Buddhism. What is crucial is our willingness and effort as individuals—not merely being present when teachings are given, reading books, or satisfying ourselves that we have understood something. It is only when we expend real effort in practicing the principles of the Mahāyāna path that we discern the flavor of Buddhism and gain some insight into what it is all about.

It is much the same as with a fine meal. You can't claim knowledge of the flavor of a meal until you have actually tasted it, which you cannot do through merely imagining a meal or looking at it. In the same way, you can only gain real appreciation of Mahāyāna Buddhism when you have undertaken to practice it. Through that practice, you gain a personal certitude about the validity of its teachings, and certitude also about their results—

and your ability to integrate them into your own life. Practice, then, is the essential factor.

Thus far, we have devoted most of our efforts here to studies in the lamdre system of meditation. This system contains the quintessence of the religion of Lord Buddha, the Enlightened One. It is a comprehensive system in which all the stages of the path to buddhahood are fully laid out. In our studies, we have learned about the meditations that are useful for turning the mind away from worldly involvement and directing it toward a spiritual goal. We have learned the meditations on impermanence, death, and the law of karma. We have studied the meditations on great love, great compassion, and conventional bodhichitta. We have almost completed our studies on *The Three Visions*, the first of the fundamental texts of the *Lam dre*.

We are about to receive the instructions for the stages of meditative practice—namely, the concentration and insight meditations. Once we have finished our theoretical studies in these two topics, nothing could be more seemly than to undertake at once to practice what we have been studying. It is only then that we will acquire more than theoretical knowledge, and it is only through individual efforts that we will ever develop genuine faith in, or certitude about, the truth and value of these teachings.

We will turn our attention to actual practice, in order that the theoretical knowledge we have acquired not be lost through forgetfulness but be realized through our own individual efforts. Recently, His Holiness the Dalai Lama said in a few words something that is very important and of great value: His Holiness said that it is not enough to be a nominal Buddhist. The real test that we should apply to our own individual situations is that there should be observable spiritual progress within our minds from day to day, month to month, and year to year. We should be able to see that we are making progress in developing mindfulness, compassion, nonattachment, remembrance of and reflection on the teachings of impermanence, and so forth. There should be continual growth within our minds of this insight. If we can see that change is taking place, however slowly, then we can be confident that we are making right efforts. But if we honestly can't observe any positive change within ourselves from one year to the next, then our religion is merely nominal, and we are not, in fact, spiritually alive.

These comments by His Holiness are really quite apt, because they point out the responsibility we have, as practitioners, to internalize the teachings that we hear or read about in books. They remind us that it is not enough just to accumulate facts about the Dharma, to be able to quote books or hold them in our hands, or to be present at teachings. What is really required of Buddhists is that these principles be internalized, and that must be done through individual efforts.

We can learn from the buddhas and bodhisattvas themselves in deciding to practice as individuals. We know that the Buddha praised the reflection on impermanence as most helpful for beginners because there is nothing so stimulating to sincere efforts as this reflection. We can easily accept the idea that the Dharma has value and that the opportunity to practice should not be wasted. We can take impermanence to heart as well, by merely reflecting on how truly insecure and fragile our present good fortune is.

To offer a personal example, I have recently had occasion to open a number of letters from friends and monks in India. These brought the news that certain monks had passed away suddenly from one cause or another. I also received a call from the Karma Triyāna Dharmachakra center.[58] Someone there told me that the father of one of the students had died and asked me to say prayers for him. At the same time, I learned that a Kagyu student had been killed in an automobile accident, and that a twenty-year-old nun in Darjeeling had passed away quite suddenly. When news like this comes in, my own remembrance of Lord Buddha's teachings about impermanence, and the importance of not procrastinating in one's practice, comes home to me. After all, many of these people were young. Like all of us, they were intent on making efforts. Many of them had spent years in meditation or had undertaken some practice; others were definitely intending to live religious lives.

Thus we should not indulge in thinking that this opportunity of receiving teachings and having time to realize them will abide. We should be more honest about our personal situation, recognizing that a long life span is not guaranteed to anyone. If we are serious about wanting to get something out of the Dharma, we should start practicing in earnest.

ULTIMATE BODHICHITTA

We have completed our discussion of how to develop conventional bodhichitta, and will now take up what is known as ultimate bodhichitta. The meaning of the word *bodhichitta* and its sense of being ultimate will be explained through this discussion. A more practical description is that ultimate bodhichitta is a state of mind derived through combining, in your meditative practice, the two aspects of mental concentration and insight (i.e., wisdom, or nondualistic perception).

There are three subheadings to our discussion: (1) the explanation of what we mean by ultimate bodhichitta, or ultimate enlightened mind, (2) the methods for awakening a sense of ultimate bodhichitta within your own mental continuum, and (3) the instructions for putting those methods into practice.

What do we mean by ultimate bodhichitta? First, it has to be distinguished from notions of the ultimate that are entertained by other Buddhist and non-Buddhist religious systems. Ultimate bodhichitta is different from the notion of an ultimate self (*ātman*) ascribed to by some non-Buddhists. It is different from the two Hīnayāna systems, which believe that the ultimate consists of the skandhas, dhātus, and āyatanas.[59] These systems maintain that, while ultimately there is no self, or ego, nonetheless the forms, feelings, perceptions, sense organs, and sense fields that become the basis for our notion of a self *are* present ultimately.

Our particular Sakya notion of the ultimate is different from this. It is also different from the notion of the Mind-Only (*Cittamātra*) school of Buddhism, which says that only consciousness exists ultimately. From our point of view, all these ideas of the ultimate are philosophical extremes and are invalid because they are merely conceptualizations.

Ultimate bodhichitta is a state of mind that dwells unceasingly in being away from all conceptual extremes. It is the realization that the ultimate nature of mind is, and always has been, the source of all the phenomena of saṃsāra and nirvāṇa. Thus ultimate bodhichitta is a state of realizing the ultimate nature of mind. On the conventional level, we identify bodhichitta as being active, thinking, for instance, "I'm here, and there is buddhahood to be attained. I must develop the state of mind of aspiring to buddhahood and must undertake practices that will lead to it." But on the ultimate level, bodhichitta is merely a recognition of that ultimate state of mind, not anything more active than that. In support of this definition, Ārya Nāgārjuna wrote:

> The bodhichitta of the Enlightened Ones is the real state of void, which is eternally unobscured by the conceptualizations of a self, of form, or of consciousness.

This refers back to the fact that the ultimate nature of mind is not to be confused with what non-Buddhists call a self, with what Hīnayānists mean when they talk about the skandhas constituting the ultimate, or with the notion of consciousness alone constituting it. Nāgārjuna says further that, since this ultimate nature of mind is really the root of saṃsāra and nirvāṇa, and of all pleasure and pain, it is possible, through knowing its nature, to know the nature of all other phenomena as well. In support of this, Āryadeva wrote in his *Cloud of Jewels* (*Ratnamegha-sūtra*):

> The nature of a single entity is just the nature of every entity. The nature of every entity is just the nature of a single entity. Anyone who perceives the nature of a single entity also perceives the nature of every entity.

The methods whereby ultimate bodhichitta can be achieved consist of two stages of meditative practice: concentration (Skt. *śamatha*; Tib. *zhi-gnas*) and insight meditation (Skt. *vipaśyanā*; Tib. *lhag-mthong*). Concentration is a technique for achieving complete tranquillity of mind, wherein the mind is free from thought processes and remains fixed wherever it is placed. By insight we mean that the mind is free from all dualism, no longer seeing things in terms of subject and object. When such a mind is directed at internal or external phenomena, it is able to perceive their true nature, and perceiving the nature of each dharma, it is unerring and unconfused, seeing all dharmas exactly as they are, however many there are. In the Buddha's own words:

> What is concentration? It is single-pointedness of mind.
> What is insight? It is right discrimination among phenomena.

This is very similar to the words of the *Adornment of the Mahāyāna Sūtras*, where it is written,

> The meditator relies on his skill in concentration to focus the mind on mind itself, and by doing so, he becomes able to perceive rightly the true nature of all internal and external phenomena.

Our third subheading, on practical instructions, will be discussed in reference to three topics: (a) the meditation of concentration, (b) the meditation of insight, and (c) the meditation of these two in combination.

CONCENTRATION

Concerning concentration, we have Shāntideva's verse from the eighth chapter of the *Bodhicharyāvatara*, which advises us,

> Mental afflictions are to be overcome through insight which is well yoked with concentration. Efforts should be made first in

concentration. This is to be achieved through nonattachment to things of the world.

When we talk about concentration, we are not talking about merely being able to stare for a few minutes at a certain spot or keep the mind thinking about one thing for any length of time, but about a state of mind completely free from thought processes. When you have achieved mastery of concentration, it is not difficult to sit for seven days without having a single thought run through your head. This is what we mean by concentration. It is the ability to focus the mind on any object, but there is much more to it than that.

Say you have achieved this state and are completely free from thought processes. While the negative mental states of attachment, aversion, ignorance, pride, and so forth are not overcome through concentration, they are definitely subdued. They become dormant because there is very little for them to feed on, but they are not really uprooted. That happens later, when you enter the stage of insight. To achieve realization of the ultimate, the defilements that ensue from belief in and attachment to a self must be eradicated. This can only be done when you have reached the stage of insight, and you can do that only after achieving mastery of the stage of concentration. Thus you must start with concentration. Until concentration is mastered, you cannot proceed farther.

Concentration arises from three kinds of solitude: solitude of body, voice, and mind. That is why meditators go into retreat in forests, caves, or retreat cells, which accomplishes the first requirement of physical solitude. Solitude of voice means that the meditator no longer indulges in idle conversation or in talk that would misdirect his psychic energies. To accomplish mental solitude, the meditator renounces all active involvement in worldly affairs that would distract from meditation and devotes his mental energies wholeheartedly to practice.

If you wish to develop concentration, you must begin by relinquishing the larger part of worldly activities. This includes business and attachment to the external sense objects, such as forms, sounds, tastes, and so forth. You must also give up attachment to other beings. This renunciation is necessary to disengage the mind from worldly involvements so that the whole of your mental energy can be directed toward training in concentration. In other words, distraction and concentration are opposites. You either have a distracted mind and think about many things, or you have a concentrated mind and think about one thing. If that one thing is to be the ultimate nature of mind, you must narrow the range of your mind's objects.

If you find yourself unwilling to relinquish business and the like, it is helpful to reflect on the disadvantages of attachment to external activities. These are given in one of the sūtras, where the faults of a student who is overly attached to worldly activities are described. There it says that such a person is not happy when his teacher instructs him to practice. Even if he does enter into practice, he doesn't follow the instructions properly. He is the kind of student who will quickly fail in his efforts at good conduct simply because he is not really willing to make the effort; even if he does make the effort, he does so grudgingly and carries it out perversely. All the time such a student is in meditation, he is thinking about household affairs. His mind is always concerned with other worries. As a result, he never achieves meditation or renunciation. All these faults are due to attachment to external activities.

Concerning the faults of attachment to sense objects, it is important to remember that they are not considered to be evil in themselves. However, at this beginner's stage of meditation, in order to train the mind in concentration, there must be a willingness to forego sense objects for a period of time and turn the mind inward, thus attaining a certain degree of tranquillity and freedom from external stimulation. The *Bodhicharyāvatara* says: "Attachments to the objects of desire are the cause of every state of wretchedness in this world and the next."

If you are attached to external sense objects, you automatically become involved in trying to accumulate them. Even if you succeed, which isn't always easy, you then have to protect them, which involves a great deal of preoccupation. Finally, you become involved in the process of losing them, for you must eventually be separated from them, one way or another. Throughout, your energy is wasted. Whether you are seeking such things, getting them, guarding them, or losing them, all you have to show for it is a lot of worries. This kind of mental preoccupation makes it difficult, if not impossible, to develop a meditative state of mind.

The faults of attachment to other people are described in the eighth chapter of Shāntideva's *Bodhicharyāvatara*:

> If a meditator becomes attached to other people, his perception of reality becomes obscured. He loses his sense of sadness for the sufferings of the world, and eventually he himself is burnt by grief and remorse. Through thinking only of that other person, an entire life

passes quickly by. For the sake of a loved one who is transient, even the eternal Dharma is lost.

In other words, you must give up attachment to other people as well. It simply doesn't work to try to meditate and at the same time keep up your romantic involvements; your mind is too preoccupied with thoughts of the other person, which cloud it to such an extent that you cannot maintain any meditative insight you might achieve, or even get on with the meditation. The result is always painful, because in the end you lose both the loved one and the chance you had of attaining the eternal Dharma.

Then, too, there is the fault of remaining attached to friends and companions. Association with childish people will definitely lead to no good, and the only result of talk about ordinary worldly affairs will be that you lose any inclination toward renunciation, practice, and meditation. Since nothing good comes of it, there is no point in clinging to friendships.

39

INSIGHT YOKED WITH CALM

WHEN WE HAVE ACQUIRED human birth and then encounter the teachings of the Buddha, as well as qualified teachers willing and able to help us understand and practice those teachings, plus the leisure in which to do so, this is an extremely fortunate situation laden with possibilities for great results. When we finds ourselves endowed with such an opportunity, it is most seemly that we should become interested in teachings that offer so much. But beyond that, a certain amount of effort is called for; merely inquiring about the Dharma is not enough. The way to develop more than idle curiosity is to reflect on impermanence.

When we fully appreciate how very brief the human life span is, how quickly it passes away and how easily it is lost, we understand the evanescence of all our other interests. No matter how much money a person might accumulate, he will not be able to take a single penny with him: it will all be irretrievably lost. No matter how powerful, prestigious, or influential a man might be on this earth, he is certain to lose that position in the end. Since death makes naught of us all and takes us away from the very things that we strive to accumulate, it really is futile to make things such as money and power our primary objects of interest. Thus we definitely should have an interest in the Dharma.

There ought to be more than a superficial motivation for becoming interested in the Dharma, however. In the context of our spiritual liberation, the Dharma is the only thing with which we should be concerned. And if we want to make serious efforts to learn the Dharma, we must begin with study and reflection. We need to know the principles, doctrines, instructions, stages of meditation, and various practices that the Buddhist path to liberation involves. Finally, we must learn the results of the different stages of practice and the nature of their ultimate result.

We need a clear understanding of all aspects of the path before embarking upon practice; then, of course, there is no reason not to make diligent efforts. When it comes to practice, many approaches are presented to us. For example, there are the meditative systems of the four great orders of Tibet: the Nyingma, Kagyu, Gelug, and Sakya. These are alike in their presentation of the stages of the path and in their view of its ultimate result of buddhahood. We are engaged in one of these four systems, the *Lam dre*, which originated with the great Indian sage Virūpa, and which was transmitted via his disciples to the five great teachers of the Sakya tradition and thence, generation by generation, to the present. The Indian pandits of this lineage, and the Five Great Jetsüns of the Sakya school, are now buddhas as a result of their practice of this very doctrine.

The *Lam dre* is divided into two areas, preliminary instructions and advanced instructions. As the scriptures tell us, there can be no success in the advanced practices unless the requirements of the preliminary practices have been fulfilled. Therefore, it is essential that we devote ourselves to the careful study and understanding of the preliminary instructions, which are found in *The Three Visions.*

We are presently engaged in study of the second of these visions, the vision of experience. This consists primarily of teachings on the development of love, compassion, and bodhichitta, which has two aspects, the conventional and the ultimate. We are studying the methods by which one attains ultimate bodhichitta, namely, concentrative meditation and insight meditation. We resume with a discussion of concentrative meditation.

Concentration, or tranquillity, is a state of mind that is free from distractions. As quoted in the last lesson, Shāntideva tells us, in the eighth chapter of his *Bodhicharyāvatara*:

> Knowing that the defilements of desire, hatred, and delusion are to be overcome through insight yoked with calm, one should seek first to develop a calm or concentrative state of mind. This, too, is to be acquired through nonattachment.

The first requisite for training in any stage of meditation is a state of serenity, tranquillity, and concentration—that is, the opposite of distraction. Thus you need to develop this faculty of concentration.

The first step in the process is to relinquish the gross causes of attachment, or distraction. The two principal objects of distraction for a beginning meditator are (1) attachment to things—possessions, property, money, and affairs that involve these, and (2) attachment to people—friends, family, and the like. The first problems that a beginner faces as he seeks to develop tranquillity are solved by reflecting on the unsatisfactoriness of attachment in these two areas.

કા ⚜ કા

The greatest fault of attachment to the objects of desire is that it causes involvement in suffering, both in this life and the next. You make yourself wretched by striving to acquire sense objects in this life, often becoming frustrated when you don't obtain them and feeling disappointed even when you do. For example, thieves desire others' wealth but suffer when they are caught and deprived of their own freedom, and in the next life their punishment continues, whether in the hell realms or elsewhere. Then, too, for ordinary people who are overly attached to sense objects, there is the great misery of accumulating, guarding, and finally losing those very things which are the objects of their desire.

How many years, how much energy, how many plans go into trying to accumulate sense objects? And when they are obtained, how much energy and time are wasted in guarding them from tax collectors, governments, thieves, friends, enemies, and the like? Eventually, they are lost: they are stolen, destroyed, become obsolete, or their owners die and are forced to separate from them. For these reasons it is said that there is no hope of liberation for those who are overly attached to things.

There are also many faults involved in attachment to other people, as we began to discuss in the last session. As Shāntideva writes in his eighth chapter:

> If you are attached to other beings, your perception of reality becomes obscured, you lose a sense of sadness and commiseration with the suffering of the world, and finally you become burnt by grief and remorse.

Thus you are not only parted from those to whom you are attached but are also separated from the Dharma, which is what really counted all along:

> By thinking of that loved one only, this brief life is wasted, and for the sake of a transient friend, even the eternal Dharma becomes lost.

The *Bodhicharyāvatara* then goes on to describe some of the faults of attachment to friends and acquaintances:

> If you consort with childish folk, you are sure to fall into states of woe. If they only lead you into unhappiness, what is the use of associating with ordinary people?

In one moment they are your friends or lovers, and the next they turn into your enemies. Ordinary people are hard to please. You try to help them live according to the Dharma, and instead of being glad it only enrages them.

The only thing that pleases ordinary people is going along with them in their own bad habits; then they like to associate with you. Otherwise, Shāntideva points out, "If you speak beneficially, they grow angry. They also turn you away from your own benefit."

For example, people try to dissuade you from making efforts to learn the Dharma, practice, and meditate. They create obstacles to your efforts to benefit even yourself. If you don't listen when they try to dissuade you from doing what is right and useful, they grow angry, and as a result of this anger, they fall into unhappy states. Hence they either turn you away from good or grow angry with you, and that anger is a cause of further harm for them. You help neither yourself nor others by associating with this kind of person:

> The ordinary person is childishly envious of his superiors, contemptuous of his inferiors, and competitive toward his peers. If you speak plainly to such a person and tell him what he doesn't want to hear, he grows furious. If you praise him, he becomes puffed up with pride and conceit. Honestly, what good ever comes from a fool?
>
> If you associate with childish folk, what you will get is a lot of self-praise and disparagement of others, a lot of talk that delights in birth, death, and the round of existence. Whatever you get, it's not going to be virtuous.

These descriptions by Shāntideva[60] agree with the writings of Jetsün Dragpa Gyaltsen, who said that, after those stages of meditation which arise through dwelling in solitude are obtained, when and if one does associate with worldly folk, one should meditate on the unsatisfactoriness of clinging to those associations. In this way, one will acquire a sense of solitude and also become free from misconduct.

In other words, to achieve the first stage of meditation, which is serenity, you must disengage the mind from overweening attachment to things and other people. To the extent that you succeed in doing so, your chances of success in meditation are increased.

You will never attain concentrative meditation as long as you harbor attachment to people and thus allow the mind to remain distracted. A personal example can be seen in the life of my own teacher, Gatön Ngawang Legpa Rinpoche, who, though a great and famous teacher, spent most of his life in solitary retreat in the mountains and elsewhere. He never kept servants, teachers, or family around him. Until he was about seventy, he always took care of himself, made his own tea, prepared his own meals, and strongly resisted any suggestion by his disciples that he have someone look after him. Until he was quite old and unable to work, he insisted on doing it himself. Many knew his greatness as a teacher, meditator, and example to others. All this was due in no small measure to his having learned at an early age to live in solitude, devoting himself single-pointedly to the Dharma. The previous Deshung Tulku's nephew, Ajam Rinpoche,[61] also avoided association with other people and went to great lengths to preserve his privacy.

If you wish to attain serenity of mind, you must learn not only to give up attachment to people and things but also to relinquish anger toward other beings. Anger itself is an attachment, a distraction outward, a kind of reverse and negative way of relating to externals. The *Bodhicharyāvatara* says: "If one harbors the stain of anger within one's heart, one's mind cannot possibly experience peace." And because your mind is unable to be glad or to have a sense of well-being when angry, it becomes sleepless, unsteady, and unable to concentrate.

Not only does anger destroy the requisites for mental concentration, it makes trouble for you in ordinary life as well. You cannot hope to attract friends, followers, or servants if you harbor ill will or anger in your heart. Even rich and generous masters have been known to be killed by their servants simply because they couldn't control their own rage. Not only your friends but your relatives become disheartened and depressed if you have an angry disposition. Even if you try to woo them with gifts, they won't like you. In brief, Shāntideva tells us, "There is no happiness or sense of well-being possible for one who harbors anger in his life."

I might mention here that anger directed toward the faults of the self can be good; rightly used, it can impel you to practice harder. But the bitterness or cruelty of anger—the attitude of "Oh, let them suffer"—is bad. Since you haven't really helped beings up until now, try to discard such anger toward others and work even harder toward attaining buddhahood.

Having thus reflected on the faults inherent in attachment to things and people, and in harboring ill will toward others, you should cease thinking about them and go off to an isolated spot—either a monastery or a solitary place, on a mountaintop or deep in the woods—where you can be alone. There devote yourself to the practice of meditation. As the *Bodhicharyāva-tara* continues, "One should dwell alone, in a pleasant and delightful forest, and devote oneself to meditation on bodhichitta."

This is all very true: solitude is essential; one should be in an isolated place. Unfortunately, however, whenever I myself am alone, I become afraid that ghosts will come, that thieves will find me at home alone, or that something else is going to happen. I am quite sure that meditation alone on a mountainside is good, but I am not sure that I could handle it myself. It would be nice to have someone near in case ghosts come around.

40

POURING WATER INTO A VASE WITH A HOLE IN IT

WE ARE NOW ENGAGED in discussing the development of ultimate bodhi-chitta, which is to be accomplished through two stages of meditation: concentration (*samatha*) and insight (*vipasyana*). We said that concentration can be defined by these subtopics: (1) its nature, or the quality of concentration, and (2) methods for developing concentration.

We have given the definition of concentration and described some of the major obstacles to developing it. We stressed that isolation of body and mind is essential if you are to come to grips with removing various kinds of attachment that effectively prevent the development of concentration—for example, attachment to sense objects and to beings.

Now we will discuss the nature of concentration. To review a bit, the meditator must train in discarding all attachment to the various objects of attraction and aversion, and must dwell alone in a place of solitude. In the wilderness, in a mountain valley or a forest, he must discipline his mind in meditation. This is in accord with the *Bodhicharyavatara*, where we are told:

> One should dwell alone, free from all distractions of mind, in a pleasant forest grove. One should develop enthusiasm for such a place of solitude by reflecting on its many virtues. Dwelling alone in such a place, one can easily put an end to discursive thought processes and properly accomplish the meditation of ultimate bodhichitta.

For success in the practice of concentration, we need to know the factors that hinder the concentrative state of mind, the factors that remove those hindrances, and how the mind is kept in a state of concentration. In other words, we need to know (a) the five negative factors that are obstacles to concentration, (b) the eight remedies that remove those five obstacles, and (c) the nine methods for maintaining the state of concentration.[62]

ↁ ✦ ↁ

The Five Obstacles to Concentration

There are five principal obstacles to concentration. The first is laziness, which is described as failure to apply yourself to virtue and as lethargy, or apathy, toward virtuous effort. When you are lazy, you are inclined to procrastinate in your practice and to make only halfhearted efforts when you do practice. This is the first obstacle that must be overcome.

Even if you shake off laziness and apply yourself diligently to the practice of concentration, a second fault may occur, namely, that of forgetting the instructions for practice. Through carelessness, you forget how to recognize the various obstacles as they arise and the guru's instructions for applying the antidotes to those obstacles. This can easily derail your practice even though you are diligent. Hence you must learn to avoid forgetfulness, remain alert, be mindful, and maintain good recall of the instructions received.

Third, even when you don't forget the instructions and are very diligent, you may well encounter the obstacles that arise from the two principal forces adverse to meditation: (i) mental unruliness, and (ii) mental stagnation. What we are calling mental stagnation is characterized by lack of clarity, in which the mind functions in a semiconscious, unclear, lethargic state. The Tibetan word literally means "sinking." The second great foe to meditation is mental unruliness, in which the mind, no matter how you try to focus it, runs after many trains of thought and is completely distracted.

The fourth obstacle, nonapplication of the antidotes, originates when stagnation and unruliness arise within your own experience. Here, even though you recognize these faults for what they are, you somehow fail to apply the appropriate antidotes. In this way your meditative practice is destroyed.

The fifth obstacle, overapplication, occurs when you make the mistake of applying the various remedies with too much diligence, or in an excessive way. As a result, the mind is unable to focus properly, becoming distracted, scattered, and upset because you try too hard.

These are the five progressive faults, or obstacles, that you are very likely to encounter in your practice of concentration. They are also described in Maitreya's *Discrimination of the Middle from the Extremes* (*Madhyānta-vibhaṅga*), where they are listed as (1) lethargy, (2) forgetting of instructions, (3) the two obstacles of mental sinking and unruliness, and the faults incurred by either (4) nonapplication or (5) excessive application of the antidotes.

The Eight Antidotes

Now we have to know the eight antidotes to these five obstacles to concentration. The first of these five, laziness, has four antidotes: (1) zeal, or enthusiasm, (2) diligence, or vigor, (3) confidence, or faith, and (4) lucidity. Zeal is the taking of great joy in meditation and is said to be the causal factor for right meditation. Diligence is the willingness to persevere in your efforts to practice regularly, maintain that practice, and see it through the various stages without giving up. Confidence is said to be the cause of zeal; you have confidence, or faith, that your practice will produce the results you hope to acquire, so you have confidence in the instruction, confidence in the system, and confidence in your own ability to make it happen. Mental lucidity, or pliancy, is said to ensue from diligence. As a result of your practice, you acquire a sense of mental purity and physical lightness; your entire being seems to become light and joyful, alert and at peace. These mental states that result from diligence are also the antidotes for lethargy when it occurs.

Among the four antidotes to mental lethargy, diligence is said to be foremost because it is essential in undertaking any meditation wholeheartedly. You must discard all inclination to be lazy or halfhearted and apply yourself single-mindedly to practice: this, more than anything else, produces results in meditation. As Shāntideva wrote in his *Bodhicharyāvatara*,

> In undertaking the practice of meditation, you should cultivate diligence, for enlightenment itself is the abiding in diligence. Just as no motion occurs without the presence of wind, so spiritual merit does not arise without the presence of diligence.

Further, he asks, "What is the definition of diligence?" And answers, "Diligence is a delight in virtue."

Enthusiasm for virtuous actions *is* diligence, or vigor, the number-one factor in successful meditation. Hence we need to recognize that the principal adversary of diligence is laziness. There are three kinds of laziness that we can distinguish with reference to a meditator who should be diligent in his practice: (a) languor, (b) attachment to vices, and (c) despondency.

Languor is characterized by taking pleasure in remaining idle. You like to spend time eating, chatting, wasting time, and entertaining yourself; you squander your energy in idle activity. This is a form of laziness that prevents you from succeeding in meditation. If you plan to do a retreat and instead spend a lot of time chatting with friends, looking after social affairs, and so forth, this will certainly prevent any progress in your meditation.

When you indulge in pleasures and sense objects merely through habitual carelessness, you are in the state of attachment to vices. Although you know better, you allow yourself to wallow in sense objects and idle behavior, and also indulge in sleep and lethargic states of mind. As a result, you have no real remorse or sadness upon contemplating the sufferings of the world. You neglect beings or become indifferent to them, rather than keeping sharply in mind the suffering of sentient existence.

Despondency is the result of your own self-denigration. You begin thinking that you are not going to succeed in practice, or that you are just not cut out to be a yogi. You think that, although lamas are meant to meditate, it is all beyond your capacity, or you have no aptitude for it. Hence you give it up. In this way you create quite an obstacle to your practice.

To counter these three kinds of laziness, which constitute the first obstacle in the practice of concentrative meditation, you need to apply the four antidotes of zeal, diligence, confidence, and lucidity.

There are three more antidotes: (5) heedfulness, or application, (6) recollection, or remembrance, and (7) mindfulness. Heedfulness is defined as being conversant with the teachings on the faults of meditation and their antidotes. In other words, you have taken the trouble to learn and to discern the states of mind and the internal and external conditions that are either propitious for or harmful to right practice. With this kind of awareness, you are said to be endowed with carefulness, or heedfulness, about the way in which to practice.

Next, you need to maintain recollection of the instructions for right practice. To give specific examples, you need to keep always in the background of your practice a remembrance of the teachings on the faults of worldly existence, the difficulty of obtaining an opportunity to practice, and the teachings on death and impermanence, so that your meditation is guided by these reflections, made meaningful by them, and supported by right diligence.

Finally, you need mindfulness, the repetitive examination of your own mind. When you are practicing concentrative meditation, you need to keep a close watch on what your mind is up to, in order to be aware of when it is tending to become lazy again, when it is running away, and when it is acting in a wholesome or unwholesome way. You need to be conscious of what is going on so that, if these major difficulties arise, you can deal with them promptly and not find your practice suddenly shipwrecked.

To give a graphic illustration of the importance of these three antidotes, we can liken you, as a meditator, to a man who owns a fine horse. Before going about your daily chores inside the house, you would probably tether your horse on the mountainside in a place where grass and water are available. Once back inside the house, you would keep in mind that "I've got this horse outside in the tall grass near the water. I don't want to forget that I've got a horse out there." This corresponds to the practice of heedfulness, for you are aware of what is happening and what you are about.

Then, from time to time, you would look out the window to be sure the horse hadn't broken his tether and run away into the mountains, been attacked by wild animals, or gotten his feet caught in the rope and hurt himself. This kind of checking is likened to training yourself to watch out for your states of mind, making sure that your mind hasn't run away through unruliness or become mired in some kind of mental stagnation.

Finally, the owner of a horse would remember that he has a horse to take care of, repeatedly looking outside so that if problems arise they can be dealt with promptly. In this way he is able to sustain his property, the horse, and go about his own affairs without problems. Similarly, in your meditative practice, you should again and again check to see whether your mind is progressing in a way that is favorable to good meditation or whether it has been overcome by some mental problem or fallen into distracting and harmful circumstances. All this care in bringing the teachings to mind and applying the antidotes when problems arise is your effort at mindfulness. Without heedfulness, recollection, and mindfulness, you cannot hope to go any farther in right meditation or, for that matter, in right reflection and right practice of moral conduct.

The second problem that you will encounter in practice is the failure to remember the antidotes to the five faults. The way to correct this problem is to train yourself to make very pointed efforts to remember the rules for right meditation, consciously recalling the teachings on death and impermanence, the difficulty of attaining human life, etc. Bring all these teachings very explicitly to mind and go over them again and again; then direct your mind single-pointedly toward the object of meditation (in this case, very likely an external physical object). In this way you will consciously counter the problem of forgetfulness and bring these helpful factors to mind. As Shāntideva said:

Study, reflection, and meditation that lack mindfulness are like water poured into a vase with a hole in it. They don't remain within one's mental grasp, nor can one call them to mind effectively.

In other words, all your efforts, no matter how diligent they may be, are doomed to failure if they are not maintained by this kind of mindfulness.

The third obstacle to concentration is not to recognize the two primary foes of the practitioner: (i) mental stagnation, and (ii) mental unruliness. The antidote is mindfulness in recognizing whether or not you have fallen under the control of either of these negative states of mind. You should be able to determine what your mental state is by asking, in effect, "Is my mind submerged in this kind of mental stagnation or is it distracted?"

It is extremely important that you become able to recognize whether your mind is being dominated by either of these two, and that you be prompt in applying the right antidotes to them. Failing to recognize these two should be countered by diligence in searching them out whenever they may be present.

The fourth obstacle is the failure to apply the antidote to stagnation and unruliness even when you know that they have occurred, due to laziness or a refusal to make the right efforts. You might be tempted just to let the mind have its way, rather than to make the considerable efforts required to put it right again. If you fail to make the right efforts, your meditation will, of course, be very badly impaired. Thus the remedy is to remind yourself of what is at stake. If, for whatever reason, you fail to meet the problem with vigor, you will have no chance to attain any of the desired states of meditation or spiritual results, such as concentration and insight (not to mention enlightenment). This is what is at stake, so however tempted you may be to let the issue slide, you should be diligent in applying the right antidote promptly.

Recognition of stagnation and unruliness, or sinking and distraction, is itself the antidote here. Also apply the remembrances of death and impermanence, which are themselves great opponents to your practice. On the most basic and practical level, if you find yourself sinking, gaze at another point, eat less, wear lighter clothing, and literally straighten up. If you become distracted, close the blinds, put on more clothes, and draw inward. My own great teacher, Gatön Ngawang Legpa Rinpoche, would take off his clothes and pour cold water down his back when confronted with the obstacle of sinking. If you experience sleepiness and exhaustion during your sessions of meditation, stop for a while. If you force yourself too much, there is no benefit, and you may even turn your mind against practice.

Finally, there is the fifth obstacle often encountered by meditators, namely, that they apply the antidotes in excess. Here they treat the mind roughly, trying to force it to avoid negative states, or, in their anxiety to counter such states, they go to extremes in applying the remedy. As a result, their meditation is blighted, since it is hard for a mind treated in this rough fashion to be brought to any beneficial meditative state. The antidote is to remember to bring the mind around to mindfulness, concentration, or tranquillity in a gentle fashion. Just as a wise person measures his words, is careful in his speech, and doesn't shoot off his mouth without thinking, so a meditator learns to be measured and mild in his efforts to place his mind in right meditation.

To give another example, in weighing gold you have to use some common sense in balancing the two pans of the scale. You wouldn't overweight one side of the scale if you were trying to balance out a certain measure with some countervalent object. That would negate the whole idea of trying to achieve some balance. Thus, when you see the strength of your problem, try to find the appropriate remedy and use it in the appropriate measure. If you go about your practice in this commonsensical and mindful way, your meditation will be no difficult chore but will be accomplished quite easily.

To summarize, there are five problems likely to confront the practitioner of concentrative meditation—laziness, forgetting of instructions, the two obstacles of mental stagnation and unruliness, and the faults incurred by either nonapplication or overapplication of the antidotes. These are countered by eight remedies, arrived at on the authority of the bodhisattva Maitreya, who stated in the *Discrimination of the Middle from the Extremes*:

> The eight remedies are earnestness, diligence, faith (confidence), mental purity (lucidity), recollection, mindfulness, application, and equanimity (tranquillity continued).

Thus the last antidote is (8) tranquillity. For example, the mind is not always overcome by one or another of the five faults. When you have made the appropriate efforts, often the meditation does come easily. The mind is concentrated, clear, and alert; it is meditating properly. At that time you don't want to agitate it, so there is no point in remembering death, impermanence, and so forth. When the mind is naturally right and in a state of tranquillity, let it alone. Don't apply anything. You must recognize when to apply an antidote and when to leave the mind alone.

A FOUR-PETALED BLUE FLOWER

WE LIKE TO THINK of ourselves as Mahāyānists. If we truly intend to follow the Great Way, then it is worth our while to learn the essentials of Mahāyāna practice. Since the main thrust of Buddhism is the attainment of enlightenment through right effort, it is essential that we learn how to perform virtue effectively. Our virtuous actions do not automatically lead to enlightenment, so we need to know how to ensure that they are directed toward, and do result in, attainment of that goal.

For this purpose, bodhichitta is a prerequisite. We should have the clear intention that, whatever we are doing, our actions and their results will contribute only to the enlightenment of all beings and ourselves. All our primary efforts should be within the context of performing such virtuous actions. This is expressed in the bodhisattva's resolve that we recite:

> For the sake of all living beings, I must attain the state of supreme enlightenment; for that purpose, then, I am performing this virtuous action.

If you wish to follow the Great Way, and wish also that your actions and efforts will have the desired result, you should keep this resolve to attain enlightenment always in mind.

In situations such as the present one, in which you undertake to study the Mahāyāna path, you should also approach virtuous effort in the most effective way. Your efforts will be effective if you develop the right attitude about study, which includes genuine respect for and receptivity toward the teacher and the teaching, plus a clear understanding that you are approaching as a student, requesting assistance, and soliciting a teaching of great value.

You can check your mental attitude against the following example. If you are a patient suffering from a serious disease and approach your doctor, you have a clear concept of yourself as in need of help and of the doctor as being in a position to help you. Similarly, you should first of all think of yourself as seriously afflicted by the grave ailments of desire, hatred, and delusion, and of your teacher as a qualified physician able to give you the help you require. Second, think of the guidance you receive as the medicine that your physician might prescribe for your particular illness. Third, your reliance on those teachings and your putting them into practice are like following the doctor's orders, taking the medicine he prescribes, and feeling the effects of the cure as a result. As you experience a decrease in your own mental poisons, think that you are like a patient in the process of recovering from a serious disease.

If you have something like the attitude suggested in this analogy, you can rest assured that you are approaching the teachings, study, and meditation with a proper attitude. Of course, other elements are required as well: you must attend regularly and listen carefully, not only to the words but to their meaning, incorporating them into your own understanding of the Way.

Practice can be achieved on a higher level, also, if you approach the teacher not as a human being but by visualizing him or her as Shākyamuni Buddha and yourself as the Bodhisattva of Wisdom, Mañjushrī, who is seeking the Dharma for the benefit of all beings. Visualize that rays of light shine forth from the teacher's heart and touch your mind, dispelling all confusion, mental obscurations, and ignorance and increasing your wisdom to the extent that there arises in your mind a clear understanding of ultimate reality (i.e., insight into the nature of your own mind). It is also very helpful to practice on the level of the pure vision, in which all appearances are seen to be illusory and to have a nature of nondual emptiness and appearance. Even on occasions of study, if you can sustain a practice of the pure vision, it is very helpful in increasing your wisdom.

In our course of studies, we have undertaken to learn various instructions for the impure vision, the vision of experience, and the pure vision. We have completed the instructions for the impure vision and are now concluding our studies on the vision of experience, which consists of instructions for the meditations on love, compassion, and bodhichitta. As we have said, there are two aspects of bodhichitta instruction; one corresponds to practice on the conventional level of reality, and the other to the level of ultimate reality. To achieve the state of mind called "ultimate," it is necessary to undertake training in the two stages of meditative practice: concentrative meditation and insight meditation. We are in the process of explaining the first of these two. We will now discuss the stages of concentrative meditation and the nine principal methods for achieving mental stability, or an unwavering state of mind.

The first aim in the practice of concentrative meditation is a state of mind that is not subject to distraction, thought processes, or mutability but that is characterized by single-pointed concentration. The Tibetan word *shi-nay* (*zhi-gnas*) is derived from the literal translation of the Sanskrit word *shamatha* (*śamatha*), which means "peaceful abiding." *Shi-nay* means peace, tranquillity, serenity. Literally, it means the pacification of mental distractions and unstable thought processes: *nay* (*gnas*), from the Sanskrit *sta*, is a cognate of our English word "stay." Thus *shi-nay* implies staying in one place, or peacefully remaining in tranquillity. This means that you achieve a state in which the mind easily remains fixed on one object or point for as long as you wish it to remain there.

Hence the first thing a yogi must accomplish is "placing the mind." This is done by first arranging the body in proper meditative posture and not moving it. It also entails achieving control over your eyes. Since eye sensations are the source of most of our mental distraction and discursive thought processes, it is important to control eye motion from the beginning. In meditation (and particularly in concentrative meditation), this means being able to keep the eyes from roving about by fixing them unblinkingly on the object of meditation. The emphasis here is on not blinking.

With regard to this second requirement, that of unblinking eyelids, my teacher, the great Gatön Ngawang Legpa Rinpoche, said that the beginner can expect a lot of difficulty. We are not used to restraining the eyes, so when we attempt it, the first reaction is a burning sensation, followed by itching; then tears may flow. We may be inclined to massage the eyes, to wipe the tears from them, but we should refrain. No matter how uncomfortable it is, we must merely continue meditating and disregard the discomfort, because during the first few days of meditating to achieve concentration, we will be uncomfortable in just about every part of the body, and particularly in the eyes. It may be bad the first day or so, but if we continue meditating, the problem will go away and we will achieve control over our eyes.

The third requisite is to have a very clear object of meditation. In other words, the object that we make the basis for our meditative practice must be a very specific one. In the lam-dre tradition, a blue flower, or a drawing of a blue flower, is favored, because this was suggested by the great siddha Virūpa. Be seated in the correct meditative posture, facing a drawing of a four-petaled blue flower, and direct your gaze toward it. You can also use other objects, such as an image of the Buddha, but it should be gold, not one that is multi-colored or has so many details that your mind is distracted by it.

Whether you meditate on an image or a flower, your gaze should not be focused on the whole of the flower or the image. If it is, you will be tempted to think, "This is the Buddha's head, this is his smile, this is his hand, there are his robes," and so forth. Rather, fix on a single spot, such as the forehead of the image. If you are meditating on a flower, don't think, "This is the north, south, east, or west; this is one of its petals, this is its center." This just defeats your purpose, which is to cut off all inclination toward discursive thought processes. Fix your gaze single-pointedly on the center of the flower or the forehead of the Buddha, in order to cut off any chance for thought processes about the object of meditation.[63]

A fourth prerequisite for effective practice of concentration is solitude of body, voice, and mind. Physical solitude is achieved by absenting yourself from society for awhile or taking up residence in an unpopulated place, such as a mountainside, deep forest, or any other pleasant spot where solitude can be found. Vocal solitude is achieved by refraining from speaking with others or making sounds. When you talk, your mind is easily distracted simply by the effort you put into directing it toward the topics you are discussing. This is a very easy way to lose equilibrium and tranquillity, so a yogi avoids talk. Mental solitude is achieved by giving up all unnecessary thought processes. Instead of continuing to review in your mind who you are, what you are doing, what you haven't done, and what you will do, drop all unnecessary thoughts while training in concentrations. Just refuse to generate any more of these unnecessary conceptualizations. In this way you will not lose mental energy by allowing your mind to be distracted by various topics.

Another word about the object of meditation. We said that you can meditate either on an image of the Buddha or on a flower. The former is recommended by several sūtras and is favored by most yogis. The suggestion that you meditate on a blue flower seems to have come from Mahāsiddha Virūpa himself and is found in the lam-dre literature more than anywhere else. Virūpa suggests that you can meditate on a drawing of a blue flower or on a simple patch of dark-colored cloth. Although it makes no real difference what object you use in meditation, it is generally thought that you receive a bit of a blessing by focusing on the image of the Buddha. This is confirmed in the *King of Concentrations Sūtra* (*Samādhi-rāja-sūtra*), which says that one who meditates on the Buddha receives a blessing.

There are also a few remarks in the scriptures about maintaining physical stability. According to the *Stages of Meditation* (*Bhāvanā-krama*) by Kamalashīla, whom Tibetans consider an authority on the subject, when you are engaged in concentration, your eyes should neither be wide open nor squeezed shut. With your eyelids about half open, your gaze should be fixed unwaveringly toward the tip of your nose. You should be seated in a very erect, absolutely straight posture. Your mind should not be focused without but rather contained within, and you should know where your mind is—namely, within yourself and not wandering out to different objects. Your shoulders should be squared evenly. Your head should be neither thrown backward nor bent forward but held straight, facing directly forward and bent very slightly forward at the region of the Adam's apple. You should not be leaning to one side or the other; from nose to navel should be an absolutely straight line. Your jaws should be just open, with the tongue slightly curled up and touching the top front teeth.

It is very important that your breath be moderate. Your inhalation and exhalation should be neither noisy, violent, nor irregular. In all circumstances, when in a state of meditation, your breathing should be performed slowly, spontaneously, and regularly. As you inhale, the breath should be silent and gentle all the way down; be mindful of your inhalation. At the point when you are neither inhaling nor have begun to exhale, be aware that this is the point where the breath is arrested. Then be aware of the exhalation. These are the three processes.

You should seated on a comfortable seat, that is, one that is not made of wood, stone, or the bare ground. It must be a seat that really does not hurt you and that in every way maximizes your ability to remain seated for long periods of time.

The eyes are very important. The eyelids should cover the irises halfway, not more or less than that. Your gaze should be fixed firmly, directly, carefully, unwaveringly, and mindfully on the object of your meditation. This object should be placed about an arm's length in front your nose. Heretics gaze up into the sky, Hīnayānists meditate with the gaze turned downward, but your mainstream Mahāyānist, and especially the Vajrayānist, meditates looking straight ahead. There are some Nyingma practices in which one meditates on the sky, sun, or moon, but these are not mainstream meditation practices.

In this ordinary practice of concentration, the object you focus on is external to your mind, but in tantric, or extraordinary, meditations, you don't focus on any external object. For example, in visualizations of tantric deities, you see yourself in the form of the object of meditation and apply concentration when you focus on the nature of mind, but this is done in the two processes of creation and completion. Still, you do use the shi-nay technique. Thus you must first use external objects to achieve mental tranquillity and the ability to fix your mind wherever you place it, for it is really impossible to do tantric visualizations unless you have achieved a degree of concentration.

The practice of concentration is rightly called "the foundation of the path" because it is essential to the accomplishment of so much of what are called the advanced practices. For example, magical powers, clairvoyance, and other wonderful abilities that you hear of yogis possessing are all a direct outcome of this skill of concentration. There were many in Tibet who were skilled in the practice of shi-nay meditation. Some were able to remain seated in unwavering concentration for seven days, which is quite a feat. They were so absorbed that they were unaware of the passage of time; to them, it seemed as if only a few minutes had passed.

To sit for seven days in concentration is to be very close to the first bhūmi. Just by having this ability, all the mental defilements are almost wiped out (though they are not yet eradicated via the realization of emptiness), so that you are no longer influenced by them, even though their propensities are still in your mind. Moreover, since your mind is in such an excellent state, when you apply insight (such as the wisdom of emptiness), you will very quickly proceed from the path of accumulation to that of application, and thence to the path of perception, at which point you enter the first stage. Thus such a great ability to concentrate indicates to the Mahāyānist that he is very, very close to the first stage.

People like ourselves, who do not practice shi-nay, are unable to help others in any very effective way at all. Lacking in concentration, we may think we want to help beings when in actual fact we are in no position even to help ourselves as we would like. If we go out and try to serve others in our present state of mind (when we, like they, are very much under the control of desire, hatred, and illusion), we will only get into all kinds of unfortunate relationships with those whom we intend to help.

Let us compare this with the bodhisattva, who takes the time to train his mind in shi-nay. By doing so, he removes all the obstacles to helping himself and others and goes on, for their sake, to achieve the first bhūmi, the later bhūmis, and all the qualities of an enlightened buddha. He then devotes himself skillfully to helping many beings in the best possible way, for a very long time. It is not that he turns his back on beings by training in concentration, but rather that he undertakes that practice precisely to become able to serve them. Despite their good intentions, most people start out to serve others and wind up in a pickle.

There were two monks, for instance, at my monastery. One of them fell ill, so the other decided to be a bodhisattva and serve his fellow monk. He started by dropping in every few minutes to see how the patient was doing. He would bring food when needed; he would bring tea again and again; he would change the bed, wash the clothes, and open the windows. He was there day and night; in fact, he was there so much that the patient couldn't sleep and therefore couldn't recover. This helpful monk was making him worse: he was worrying him to death. Finally, the ill monk got angry and told him to get out and stay out. The aspiring bodhisattva was hurt and left him alone. Then the monk died because no one looked after him. Thus one has to be realistic about the help one can effectively give.

Another example is that of a man who decided that he was going to serve beings and give them everything they needed. A beggar came by and asked for some food. The man got out some nice golden tsampa, threw in some butter and a little piece of meat, and gave it to the beggar, who was very happy and went on his way. The next day, another beggar came by and the man did the same thing. This went on and on. The beggars told one another about this man, so more and more of them started appearing on his doorstep. The whole town got word that he was playing the bodhisattva and giving away everything he had, so it wasn't long before everyone was at his door with bowls in their hands. By this time, the man was getting a bit vexed by people's taking advantage of his generosity. He scolded them all and drove them away with a stick. They, in turn, were outraged at the way he was treating them. Soon there was quite a riot.

The point is that, even though it is important to wish to help others, you have to know how to do it. Your intention is the main thing, but you must also be realistic and face the fact that you are not yet able to help them effectively. For the present, you resolve to become able to help them; you pray for them, but that is all you can do. For their sake, you make extra efforts to train your mind in the requisite stages of meditation. If you practice in this way, you really will be acting just like the bodhisattvas of the past, who also developed a resolve and then brought it to fruition for the sake of other beings. It is your intention that brings about the great result of bodhisattvahood, which is so very helpful to all beings in all times and places. Thus your initial intention answers the questions, "Am I being selfish by training in meditation?" and "Shouldn't I be serving beings instead?"

However, if you just practice concentration and insight meditation without any recourse to tantric practice, you may become very skilled in these two stages, obtaining a certain very rarified mental state and other abilities, but you will not be able to attain buddhahood for a very long time. As it is said, through the exoteric practices it takes the bodhisattva three aeons to attain buddhahood, whereas if you acquire skill in concentration and insight into the nature of things and then apply that to tantric practices, it is possible to attain buddhahood in a single lifetime, provided you are a superior practitioner. If you are mediocre, you will gain buddhahood in the bardo or in your next life, and if you are really not a meditator at all, you will still gain enlightenment within sixteen lifetimes. That is the advantage of practicing tantra: it is something like the difference between traveling by car and by airplane.

When you begin to practice concentration, don't overdo it. Don't practice for long periods of time. Act very skillfully and practice properly for short periods of time. Then, before you get tired, stop, take a break, and come back to it several times during the day until you get better at it.

42

THE MONKEYS WERE PERPLEXED

WE ARE AMONG THOSE WHO are fortunate enough to have access to the teachings of enlightenment. We should not deceive ourselves about our present condition, even though we have been born in a time and place where the teachings are available. We are able to appreciate those teachings, find teachers willing to teach us, and take the time to practice. But if we take our good fortune for granted and fail to be diligent in practicing the Dharma, then we are truly deceiving ourselves. No matter how good the present opportunity may be, it avails us little if we don't realize any benefit from it.

His Holiness the Dalai Lama has said, "It is not enough merely to subscribe to the Dharma. What really counts is to practice, to apply oneself to the Dharma." If we think for a moment of the basic insecurity of our conditioned existence, we will see the folly of remaining content with theoretical knowledge and minimal practice. This is a common and very grave mistake. If we wish to be more than nominal Buddhists, we must train our minds in diligence.

When we apply ourselves seriously to the path of enlightenment, we should undergo three experiential processes. First, there should be a progressive sense of connectedness about the unhappiness of others, the causes of their unhappiness, the great scale of their unhappiness, and the endlessness of their unhappiness. Through this reflection comes a great sense of sadness for what they must be experiencing and their prospects of experiencing only unhappiness in the future. Through this sadness for the world and for worldlings, there arises within us a sense of renunciation, a willingness to leave off unimportant attachments and activities and instead direct the mind toward things of real value.

Second, when we develop this sense of renunciation, a resolve to do something for other beings will arise spontaneously within our minds. When we start applying ourselves to meditation, to virtues, and to religious practices (either to help beings correctly or to become able to help them), then we have experienced the awakening of bodhichitta, the resolve to achieve the ultimate good of all beings.

Third, when we have developed a resolve to work for others' benefit, a right understanding of the nature of things arises spontaneously from this compassion. We then understand the Dharma clearly: it makes sense, not only in theory but also from a personal, practical point of view. We understand the nature of mind, the nature of our own being; we understand our purpose, the purposes of all beings, and how best to benefit them. This is called the awakening of right insight, or right view.

Every genuine Mahāyāna practitioner should experience these three essentials of (1) a spirit of renunciation, (2) a resolve to work for the highest good of others, and (3) right vision. If you wonder whether you are making advances in your practice, you have only to ask whether you notice any of these three. Do they seem to be influencing your thoughts, actions, and words? If you can recognize the growth of these three qualities in your mind, it is a mark that your practice is effective and progressive.

To help us understand how to develop these qualities and experiences, we have undertaken to study *The Three Visions*, which starts on the level of ordinary experience and perception. On this level, we are asked to understand how the mind is to be weaned away from worldly attachments and develop the spirit of renunciation. In the second section, we are taught how to develop the enlightened qualities of great love, great compassion, and bodhichitta (the resolve to work for others' good). We are also taught how to train the mind in meditation in order to develop the unerring insight of right vision. All these instructions aim at helping us train the mind so that we can develop the three qualities of renunciation, bodhichitta, and right view.

Therefore, the efforts you make here to study these teachings, any efforts you make to build a center where the Dharma can become available to others, and the efforts you make in meditation to develop this right view—all these, no matter how uncomfortable, inconvenient, or difficult they may seem at the moment, are not lacking in importance. As His Holiness the Dalai Lama said, practice is really where it all begins. It is only when we have learned to control the mind, so that these three qualities can begin to manifest themselves within it, that we can recognize them within our own nature. Efforts at gaining that first level of mental stability are essential for the development of these qualities.

We will now continue discussing the two stages of meditation, which are concentration and insight. Concentration is essential so that the senses can be controlled and the mind gain tranquillity and the ability to focus on the object of meditation for an appreciable length of time. After you have gained a certain amount of mastery in concentration, if you then add insight meditation (i.e., examination of the nature of mind and of all phenomena), you will very quickly achieve all the spiritual results just described. As it is said, "The mind that is free from attachment very quickly achieves the results of meditation."

The point is that, at the beginning, there must be a certain degree of disengagement, of giving up attachments. This is very difficult to do. As the sūtras tell us, the ordinary mind is so controlled by the emotive states of attachment, aversion, indifference, and the rest that almost no mental activity is uncolored by one or more of these negative qualities. The sūtras describe such qualities this way:

Anger rages like a great fire. Desire flows like a great flood. Ignorance is like dense, dark night. Pride is like a stony mountain. Jealousy is like a red gale.

These great defilements govern the mind when we are not examining our mental actions and thought processes. We manifest these qualities all the time and take them for granted. They have tremendous power over our minds and our actions. It is only through mastery of concentration that we begin to deal with these passions and master them. Only through success in concentration are they subdued. As the mind is trained in concentration, they become progressively weaker and finally remain only in a dormant state. At this point it becomes necessary to apply wisdom, developing insight into selflessness, the lack of any inherent identity in either external or internal phenomena. Through this realization, the passions and their source, which is the belief in a self, are destroyed from their very roots. They are removed from the mind, never to return.

Through this process, liberation is achieved, and that is the point of these two stages of meditation. Insight is like the light of a flame, which removes darkness. But if the lamp is exposed to wind, it is either snuffed out or flickers so that it is of little use. Just as you cannot place a flame in the open wind, so insight requires that your mind be tranquil, unshaken by the gross passions of desire, hatred, delusion, pride, and so forth. When the mind is calm, the light of insight shines, removing all doubts and ignorance; then intelligence shines through.

Now, let us proceed to concentration itself. The first thing to be said is that posture is important. Buddhist teachers and Buddhist literature alike have always stressed the basic points of right posture. When your body is seated cross-legged with the spine straight, the eyes fixed at the correct angle, and the breathing moderate, then all kinds of good things proceed merely from that right posture. As the great Sakya Pandita said, "By assuming the right posture, one approximates, in an instant, all the right conditions for insight to arise." When you assume the right posture, the psychic channels in the body automatically become aligned. Through their right alignment, the breath becomes moderate, steady, and calm; through calm breath, thought processes become calm; and through this, you achieve lucidity and an ability to understand the nature of mind. Just by assuming the right posture, you automatically approximate the best conditions for insight.

There are other advantages, too. Gatön Ngawang Legpa Rinpoche, my own great teacher, liked to tell the story of five hundred pratyekabuddhas living in a forest. Like good Buddhist meditators, they dwelt in isolation. Each one assumed the right meditative posture, which was so impressive that the monkeys of the forest got into the habit of dropping fruit and berries in their vicinity. Thus the meditators were able to sustain themselves simply because their posture was so authoritative, while the monkeys actually acquired merit by their ignorant actions of wanting to be near such commanding figures. After the five hundred pratyekabuddhas attained liberation and passed away, the forest was empty.

Then came a band of Hindu meditators. These Hindus were given to different postures of meditation. Some, with vows never to be seated, would remain standing; others would twist their bodies into different shapes; still others would turn their eyeballs up and gaze skyward. The monkeys were perplexed, so they didn't make any offerings. The Hindus were also a bit perplexed, as they had heard that the monkeys were very generous and had done right by the pratyekabuddhas. When the Hindus asked a wise man the reason, he told them that the monkeys were impressed only by the correct meditative posture, not by what was being meditated on. The monkeys couldn't know that; they just knew that meditators sit in a certain way.

Hence the Hindus started meditating in the posture the Buddhists had assumed. The monkeys were delighted and started dropping offerings again. And even though the Hindus were meditating on the eternal soul and other Hindu views, by the power of adopting the correct posture, they attained nirvāṇa and became pratyekabuddhas themselves. Plus the monkeys, of course, got a lot of merit. Thus posture is important. It is the basic element in Buddhist meditation.

☙ ❈ ❧

The Nine Stages of Concentration

In the last lesson, we began to discuss the nine methods of concentration. To review, the first is called *application*, or mental placement, and refers to focusing the mind on one particular object. It is achieved when the mind experiences for the first time an instant or two of lucidity. For just a moment, the mind stops thinking and remains clear.

The second stage is called *constant application*. Here you are still training the mind in getting used to the effort of concentration. This is done by limiting your sessions of meditation to many brief periods a day, so that the mind doesn't become exhausted or discouraged. As a result, the mind starts developing a feel for concentration and there is an increase in moments of lucidity.

The third stage is called *patchwork application*. Just as you patch up a torn or frayed garment so that you can continue using it, so at this third stage you run up against five great obstacles to concentration, become aware of mental distraction and any other possible problems, and immediately apply the appropriate antidote(s). For example, when the mind starts wandering off on thought processes and gets carried away from your meditation, recognize what is occurring and bring it back, gently but firmly, to the object of meditation. It is just a matter of patching up: your mind's steadiness is the patching. You are trying to keep a consistent state of mental calm and concentration, so when that breaks down, you simply patch it up and keep on meditating.

The fourth stage is called *close application* because now, whenever you find the mind tending to get away from the object of meditation, you keep bringing it back, focusing the mind by recalling what will happen if you allow it be distracted and by recollecting the instructions for your meditation practice. Constantly alert, you watch the mind closely and don't allow it to wander. Whereas in the preceding stage you really had to struggle to bring the mind back and deal with these problems, now you simply need to keep close watch on the mind, so that any time it starts to wander, you promptly refocus it on the object of meditation.

The fifth stage is called *the taming process*. Here you subdue the two great enemies of mental stagnation and mental unruliness, or sinking and distraction, by prompt application of the antidotes. These are the two greatest foes of the meditator, being paramount among the five great obstacles. Distraction constitutes those moments when the mind, like a wild horse, simply runs away from you: thought processes become agitated and speed away. Sinking is experienced when the mind becomes sluggish; it doesn't rise to the occasion, and you can't get it back to the mindfulness necessary to focus on the object of meditation.

The meditator has to run a course between these two extremes and find the right antidotes to them. When the mind is attacked by distraction accompanied by the passions, it is helpful to stop and reflect on the sufferings of worldly existence and on death and impermanence. These are very stimulating for making renewed efforts in practice. When the mind is overcome by sinking, try to inspire it by reflecting on the qualities of enlightenment and on the great bodhisattvas who have worked very hard on behalf of all beings. There are also methods to avoid sinking in the first place, such as eating less, wearing lighter clothes, and so on.

The sixth stage is called *pacification*. Here you run into a dry period, or a feeling of dislike for meditation; for example, your eyes don't want to focus on the object of meditation or your mind doesn't want to pay attention. Thus you meet resistance to practice. Coupled with this, the mind still yearns for sense objects: the eyes want to look at other forms; the ears want music and words. Here you need to think about what would happen to your meditation if you gave in to these impulses.

Further, reflect on the danger that indulgence in sense objects represents to you. For example, indulging the eye in its craving for forms is, to the meditator, much like being a moth diving into a flame; indulging the ear in its craving for sound is like being a deer listening to a hunter's call, and then to his rifle shot; indulging the nose in its craving for fragrance is like being an insect that falls into a flower and gets trapped inside; indulging the mouth in its craving for taste is like being a fish biting down on a hook; and indulging the body's craving for sensation is like being an elephant diving into a deep lake to escape the summer's heat, and then drowning.[64] Reflect on these things and pull the mind back from any inclination to turn away from meditation.

The seventh stage is called *thought pacification*. At this point, whenever any of the negative mental impulses of anger, aversion, fear, desire, or ignorance arise, you just ignore them. Go right on with the meditation. Usually when these mental poisons arise, we have to apply the antidote: if the mind gets angry, we try to calm it down, make it happy, and so forth. Now we just ignore any negativity that arises and focus the mind on its object of meditation.

The eighth stage is called *single-pointed concentration*. By this time you can remain seated in single-pointed concentration for at least seven days.

You have attained so much mastery that the mind doesn't even want to wander away, but remains focused where you fix it and will stay there as long as you wish.

The ninth stage of experience is called *single-pointedness of the worldly mind.* This is the highest point of consciousness attainable within the realm of worldly existence. Here the mind remains constantly and totally absorbed in single-pointed meditation. It no longer has even the slightest inclination to get involved in desire, hatred, delusion, or any of the other defiled processes. It doesn't have the slightest urge to engage in nonvirtue, nor does it have any desire to be in a nonmeditative or nonconcentrative state. In other words, the mind has given up and is absolutely malleable.

At this stage, your experience of meditation is one of great ease and comfort, without any further hindrances, obstacles, or any of the other problems against which you have struggled for so long. Also, both mind and body are imbued with a great feeling of pure joy. Here you begin to experience the result of your efforts in meditation. Clairvoyance and the other presciences arise; you can perform miracles and so forth. Having reached this stage, you will spontaneously pass over into the first of the meditative absorptions (*dhyāna*). That is why this final stage of concentration is called the highest point of consciousness still within saṃsāra.

43

THE FLAME OF A LAMP IN A WINDLESS PLACE

THIS TEACHING IS GIVEN in the context of a discussion of the two kinds of enlightenment attitude: conventional bodhichitta (meditation on the sameness of self and others, exchange of self and others, etc.), which subdues selfish inclinations and develops the desire to help all beings; and ultimate bodhichitta, which utterly eradicates the roots of self-clinging and which is achieved through concentration and insight meditation. We have completed the discussion of conventional bodhichitta. The previous few lessons have been devoted to the first part of the discourse on ultimate bodhichitta, which describes concentrative meditation.

Concentration is a single-pointed, unwavering state of mind to be achieved through avoiding the five obstacles to correct concentration by relying on the eight antidotes and training the mind in the nine successive stages.[65] The five obstacles and eight antidotes have already been discussed. We will continue our consideration of the nine stages of concentrative meditation. To reinforce these instructions, we have the words of the *Adornment of the Mahāyāna Sūtras*:

> The mind should be constantly and unwaveringly directed toward
> an unmoving object. Whenever the mind becomes distracted, it
> should immediately be redirected toward its original object.

The sūtra goes on to state the importance of correct posture: body erect and unmoving, eyes and mind fixed unwaveringly on the object of meditation (preferably an image of the Buddha or a blue flower), and alertness maintained, to keep the mind from wandering toward distracting objects or trains of thought.

These instructions refer to the first three of the nine stage of concentration: (1) application, (2) constant application, and (3) patchwork application, which repairs the mind and reapplies it to meditation. In addition, (4) the intelligent practitioner should progressively direct his mind inward, away from sense objects; (5) then, perceiving good qualities in his meditation, the mind becomes tamed, permitting the enjoyment of results, since it is no longer unruly and increased insight is gained; (6) next, because he perceives the unsatisfactoriness of distraction, the meditator's attraction toward distraction is pacified, and he automatically dislikes even the thought of it; (7) hence, the mind becomes increasingly spontaneous in its resistance to all thoughts and distractions, particularly the negative mental states of pride, envy, and covetousness, and spontaneously sets aside or shrugs off negativities because they are a source of mental pain; (8) the diligent practitioner then finds that his mind spontaneously assumes the state of meditative absorption, even without willing his mind to do so; and (9) at this point he need make no effort to maintain his mind in one-pointed concentration, but experiences great joy of body and mind.

At this final stage, the "vital airs" in the body have been replaced by subtle new *prajñā* that arises from the force of practice rather than any karma of physical embodiment. Since it is not influenced by any negative mental state, this stage is known as "the peak of worldly consciousness." Of the three realms of existence (those of desire, form, and formlessness), it is only in the realm of desire that beings are governed principally by desire, greed, craving, impulses, and attachment; the other two realms are achieved through meditation wherein the negative states are progressively shed. At this ninth stage of concentration, one has reached the very summit of the realm of desire. If at this point the meditator conjoins his concentration with insight meditation, he will very quickly attain the first of the four stages of meditative absorption, or *dhyāna* meditation, and will in a short while arrive at the first bhūmi. It is also at this ninth stage that the practitioner begins to experience the six extraordinary powers of clairvoyance, etc.

With regard to each of these nine stages of meditation, you must apply appropriate antidotes to avoid the five obstacles, or hindrances. Stay alert and cultivate the ability to recognize the hindrances as they arise, and apply the antidotes at once. The two greatest hindrances are mental stagnation and mental unruliness. You must understand these well in order to recognize them and make quick, direct application of their antidotes. In fact, you should be aware of this entire schema of stages and antidotes before starting your practice; then you will see how valuable these instructions are.

If you find yourself plagued by the two principal hindrances, in addition to applying the antidotes, there are several other means that may be tried in overcoming them. For mental stagnation, or sluggishness, eat lighter and less food, sit in a higher and cooler place, wear lighter clothing, and recite the refuge formula, guru invocation, and prayers in a loud voice. For mental unruliness, or distraction, think of the faults of allowing the mind to be distracted and the damage it will do to your meditation, darken the room, wear thicker clothing, turn up the heat, and increase your food consumption.

You need to counter the hindrances swiftly when they arise, but you must also know when to stop applying the antidotes and other measures. Don't overrestrain the mind once it is no longer racing, or overstimulate it once it is no longer sluggish, but recognize that the antidotes have worked and return to your normal practice. Patience and persistence are essential: you must practice concentrative meditation regularly for months at the very least. In the beginning, meditate for frequent short periods of a few minutes each, gradually increasing the length of each session and decreasing their number.

The Five Moods of Meditation

The first experience the meditator is likely to have is despair. The longer he sits, trying to concentrate, the more difficulties will arise. The mind will seem to have even more thoughts and be even madder than usual. This is called the waterfall experience. Your impulse will be to say, "I'm not a meditator." Not to worry: you are only becoming aware of the normal state of your mind, which is always ready to run away with itself. This is good, not a reason to despair. This first mood of meditation is known as "recognition of the normal state of mind."

Next, you will experience intermittent periods where the mind is concentrated, tranquil, and free from thought processes, but whenever you notice this, the mind will once again become like a waterfall. This second mood, which is characterized by periods of clarity and bursts of unruliness, is likened to a mountain lake that is sometimes placid and sometimes roiled by waves.

The third mood is called the plains lake mood. Here, after diligent meditation, thoughts will just suddenly vanish, as sharply as in a sneeze. This means that thought processes are weakening, so you must be mindful lest this state deteriorate into torpidity. If you find this happening, reapply the mind to meditation, since at this point you must still exert effort, for which you will be rewarded from time to time with periods of concentration and lucidity. Thus this mood is likened to a rushing, turbulent mountain stream that suddenly broadens into a placid lake in the plains due to the presence of a dam.

If you persist, you will find that your meditation is free from thought by and large, but that thoughts still burst forth from time to time and then retreat. This fourth mood is likened to a peaceful ocean where waves arise upon occasion and then subside.

The fifth and final mood occurs when, after great persistence in practice, thought processes no longer arise. The mind remains lucid and single-pointed throughout the meditative session. This mood is called the waveless ocean.[66]

Be aware, however, that you can achieve a false state of concentration where no thoughts seem to arise. This is called "repressed thought processes." When your thoughts have become weakened, it is possible to try so hard to maintain a thoughtless state that they are really only suppressed. This is not the total lucidity that characterizes the true state of concentration.

I am reminded of a student of Gatön Ngawang Legpa Rinpoche who, during meditation, became oblivious to his surroundings and was apparently without thoughts. After a day passed, his teacher said that he had only suppressed his thoughts and had not truly attained the desired state. He prescribed going to a higher elevation and allowing the mind to be spontaneous and expansive. This, he said, could help achieve the true state of single-pointedness. When the student followed these instructions, he experienced the correct lucidity, which led to his developing precognition.

In the final stages of meditation, the mind should be like the flame of a lamp in a windless place, alert and clear but undistracted and unwavering. When you can meditate in this way, you can dispense with external objects and focus the mind on mind itself. If hindrances again arise, you can once more skillfully apply the antidotes. To sum up, concentration is characterized by complete, unwavering mental clarity, free from thought.

If your practice is weak at the beginning of a meditation session but becomes better later on, you need a little more discipline at the outset to focus the mind. If, by tightening up the mind in this way, it becomes taxed or rebellious, you have been too forceful and must loosen the mind a bit. Also, eat as your meditation requires; don't overdo it. Watch the amount and type of food. Moderation is the watchword. Don't sleep during the daytime. Take good care of your body. Maintain your health and apply yourself diligently in practice.

44

A Storm of Thought Processes

Not only are we fortunate in having attained human birth, we have also, against great odds, encountered and gained the friendship of teachers who are willing and able to guide us in the practices that lead to liberation. Finally, we are fortunate to have the leisure to practice and to experience the results of our efforts. Thus it is preeminently sensible that we not waste an opportunity which is so rare.

Among humans in the world today, there are very few who encounter the teachings of enlightenment. Few are even interested in religion in general, and among those who have a general interest in a religious life, there are even fewer who meet with teachings that will enable them to achieve their highest spiritual aims. All religious systems are beneficial to the extent that they teach people what they need to know—the avoidance of unwholesome ways and practice of wholesome ones, etc. But although they promise to deliver one or another form of salvation, whether attainment of the heavens or a temporary form of liberation, only Mahāyāna Buddhism enables a human being to achieve the stage of buddhahood, which is the highest possible spiritual goal. Buddhahood involves complete and perfect liberation from worldly existence and attainment of the highest spiritual insight of which the human mind is capable. When you count yourself among those who have encountered the teachings that lead to a goal such as this, you can surely be called fortunate among the fortunate. If you do consider yourself in this context, it behooves you to appreciate your present opportunities for practice.

Having heard the teachings, you cannot afford to relax and be content with mere temporary success, for there is no guarantee of human life and the leisure in which to practice in the future. Further, it is not really intelligent to relax your efforts before you have truly undertaken to make the best possible use of your opportunities. If a patient is satisfied merely to receive a prescription from a doctor, without bothering take the medicine prescribed, what are the chances of his recovering from his illness? Can a thirsty person quench his thirst by walking to the edge of a freshwater lake but not bothering to drink?

These examples illustrate our present situation, in which we have drawn near to these teachings of enlightenment. They are now available to us; we can receive the instructions that promise the result of enlightenment. Yet there is still much to be done: each of us has the personal responsibility to put these instructions into practice and experience their results for him- or herself.

These instructions for practice and guidelines that enable a practitioner to achieve buddhahood have been communicated through the body of teachings known as the Dharma. In Tibet, these teachings were transmitted by one or another of the four great religious traditions known as the Sakya, Nyingma, Kagyu, and Gelug orders. Nonetheless, there is no difference in the essence of the teachings themselves. All these great traditions are alike both in the nature and content of their teachings *and* in the results obtainable by practice. Whether you study the *Lam rim* of the Gelugpa, the four thoughts that turn the mind of the Nyingmapa and Kagyupa, or the three visions of the Sakyapa, you can rest assured that you will not miss any doctrine contained in any of the other three.

In our particular tradition, the Sakya, we are engaged in the study of the system of meditation known as the *Lam dre*, which originated with the Buddha Vajradhara, was transmitted by the goddess Nairātmyā to the great Indian sage Virūpa, and was then passed down through a succession of Virūpa's students. By relying on the instructions for practice contained in this system, countless meditators in India and Tibet have undergone the experience of the path and attained total enlightenment. Therefore, the *Lam dre* merits our serious attention and consideration.

For convenience, the system itself has been divided into two levels of practice, the preliminary and the advanced. The preliminary level is concerned with preparing your mind for the experiences incurred on the advanced stage of meditation, and consists of the instructions contained in *The Three Visions*. The three visions are the vision of the ordinary worldling, the vision of the path, and the pure vision of the enlightened ones. Briefly put, the instructions that correspond to the first level of perception are intended to turn the mind away from overweening involvement in worldly affairs and from attachment to the things of this life, so that it becomes reoriented toward spiritual goals. This is to be achieved by practices through which the mind becomes imbued with an awareness of impermanence and with renunciation of the futile and insubstantial affairs of this world. The instructions that correspond to the second level of perception are designed to develop a universalist attitude toward one's practice—that is, one learns to include all beings in the scope of one's efforts toward liberation, developing great love, great compassion, and bodhichitta, the firm resolve to include all living beings in the attainment of ultimate liberation.

At present, we are discussing the two kinds of bodhichitta: conventional bodhichitta, the universalist attitude developed through meditations on the sameness of self and others and the exchange of self for others; and ultimate bodhichitta, which is developed through the practice of concentration and insight. At this point, we are concluding our discussion of concentration.

The quintessence of Mahāyāna Buddhism is bodhichitta, the universalist resolve to make efforts for the liberation of all living beings. This is the motive that underlies the training in the six bodhisattva practices engaged in by followers of the Mahāyāna path. These six perfections are developed through practice that is not limited by reference to subject and object. For example, when you undertake generosity—the perfection of giving to others—you are able to accomplish this without thinking of yourself as the giver, some being as the recipient, and the gift as a real object. When you accomplish giving in an ultimate way, you truly perfect it, which results in the attainment of the Buddha's Form Body.[67]

As Ārya Nāgārjuna wrote, through the accumulation of transcendent merit and transcendent wisdom, the two bodies of wisdom are attained. Through the accumulation of merit, one ultimately attains the Body of the Buddha's Form, and through the accumulation of insight, one achieves the Body of the Buddha's Gnosis, or transcendent wisdom. Thus the bodhisattva undertakes training in the six perfections, or transcendent virtues, in order to achieve, for the sake of others, these two bodies of enlightenment. In various Buddhist scriptures, we hear of three, four, or five bodies of enlightenment. These are all valid categorizations; they are just different ways of looking at the ultimate state of enlightenment. For our purposes, following Nāgārjuna's schematization, we will discuss the six spiritual perfections with reference to attainment of the two bodies of buddhahood.

First, the bodhisattva trains in giving, in learning how to share with others. Through training in giving, he opens up to beings. Second, through training in moral conduct, the bodhisattva learns how to use his own being in the service of others. To achieve their well-being, he trains himself to be able to serve them, and to better accomplish this good, he trains in moral discipline. Third, when he has accomplished that, he is also able to put forth efforts in forbearance toward other beings, even those who maliciously or unwittingly cause him injury. When he learns to be tolerant of such beings, he has trained in the perfection of patience.

Having withstood the various hindrances that may have arisen internally and externally in his practice, the bodhisattva also has to develop tremendous energy, or drive, in pursuit of liberation for the sake of others. Vigor, the fourth spiritual perfection, is said to consist of an enthusiasm for virtuous actions that enables him to accumulate merit for the sake of others. As long as there is not this impetus—the strong motivation to act for others—little progress can be made in the fifth stage of practice: meditation. Through the force of his will to accomplish the good of others, the bodhisattva tackles the fifth perfection and undertakes to train his mind in the two stages of meditation: concentration and insight. As a result, he achieves realization of the ultimate nature of phenomena, internal and external. This is the sixth perfection: wisdom.

The first three perfections of giving, moral conduct, and patience, when accomplished without reference to subject and object, constitute the accumulation of transcendent merit. The fifth and sixth perfections, meditation and wisdom, constitute the accumulation of transcendent gnosis. The fourth perfection, vigor or diligence, belongs to both accumulations, for it is part of the practices that result in transcendent merit and of those that result in transcendent gnosis.

Through the accumulation of merit, we said, one achieves the result of the Buddha's form, or what is called the Form Body of Enlightenment, and through the accumulation of transcendent gnosis, one achieves the Enlightenment Body, or Body of Wisdom. The relationship between bodhichitta and the task of training in the six perfections and attaining the two bodies of buddhahood should be well understood.

In the last few lessons, we described the nature of the mental state of concentration, the five obstacles that hinder its development, the eight antidotes by which those obstacles can be removed, and the nine progressive stages of experience in concentrative practice. We will conclude with how to reflect on these instructions as a whole. To develop within your mind an appreciation for the necessity of training yourself in concentration, reflect again and again on the right way to practice concentrative meditation, its benefits, and so on.

How to Reflect on and Practice Concentration

As we have said several times, be seated in a quiet place, on a comfortable seat, and assume the correct meditation posture, as has been described in detail. Precede the following reflections with taking refuge in the Buddha,

Dharma, and Sangha. Also pray to the masters of your spiritual lineage for their blessings and resolve to undertake this practice in order to promote the enlightenment of all living beings. In every session of meditation, these are essential: (1) taking refuge, (2) invoking the blessings of your teachers and lineage, and (3) awakening bodhichitta. Then, seated in that quiet place, proceed to think along these lines:

> Alas! From beginningless time up to the present moment, my mind has been agitated by a storm of thought processes that cause me to think about anything that happens to come to mind, without being able to fix my mind on wholesome topics or virtuous objects even for the length of time it takes to snap my fingers. In this manner I have passed an inconceivably long time.
>
> Even now, I am not able to direct my mind single-pointedly toward virtue for a single instant. As a result, I still haven't much prospect of being able to cross the ocean of worldly existence or develop the ability to rescue others. From now on, however, I shall rely on the instructions of my spiritual friend and achieve mental and physical purity through the practice of meditation. Having trained my mind in single-pointed concentration, I shall attain the great enlightenment of buddhahood.

After you have reflected in this way, becoming serious about the meditation you are about to undertake, focus on your breath. If your breathing is not moderate and even, calm the breath and then count twenty-one cycles of breathing very slowly (one cycle being an inhalation and an exhalation). Through this, the mind and body should become tranquil, which helps dispel the coarser effects of passion, excitement, and ragged breathing.

When the mind has attained a certain amount of equilibrium through this exercise, investigate your thought processes and the state of your subconscious. If, for example, your mind seems to be filled with desire, attachment, lust, and the like, try to counter them by meditating on the appropriate antidote—in this case, the impurities of the human form and so forth. Ordinary people have basic misperceptions about the human body, thinking that it is substantial, permanent, clean, pure, and the source of great pleasure and delight, but a moment's reflection should tell you that this is not true. If you were really to contemplate the composition of your body, you would probably throw up. Hence, if you find your mind filled with lust, pause for a moment and reflect on the contents of the human body or on different stages of decomposition in the human corpse. This will set you right.

If you find, when you sit down, that your mind is angry or irritable, try to counter that negative mental state by meditating on love. You know the instructions for the meditation of great love. First, wish for the well-being and benefit of loved ones, and then extend that to others, even your enemies. In this way your anger will be weakened.

If you find that your mind is overwhelmed by ignorance—that you don't really know what's going on in your mind, or don't care—meditate on the twelve links of dependent origination. Then reflect on the wheel of life. Rehearse this reflection in your mind; this dispels ignorance.

If you find that your mind is filled with jealousy and envy, meditate on the sameness of self and others; if your mind is filled with pride, meditate on the exchange of self for others. We have already discussed the instructions for these meditations. If you are feeling conceited, self-satisfied, and so on, that's no good: meditate on exchanging self for others. You should care for their well-being and be concerned with them, not with your own interests and exaltation.

You can also meditate on the analysis of the constituent elements within your being. For instance, what is the point of harboring egotism or pride in your attainments when "you" consist only of the five senses, the four great elements, and so on? Study your physical body; your eyes, ears, and so forth are quite impersonal. There is really nothing there that you can be proud of, nothing that distinguishes your sense organs from those of any other being. There is no reason for clinging to any idea of inherent superiority about your constituents compared with those of others. Thus you can either take yourself and others at face value and meditate on the exchange of self for others, or you can apply a bit of insight and analyze the grounds for any pride your mind might be harboring.

In these ways, you should prepare your mind for meditation. When you first sit down, before you can really engage in your main practice of single-pointed, nonconceptual concentration, you must go through these coarser states of mind. You have just come off the street, as it were, so your mind is filled with one or another of these negative thought processes, which inevitably color and hinder your efforts to achieve equilibrium at first. Recognize these states, take some time, and apply the antidotes as we have stated them here.

When your mind doesn't have such hindrances, go on to the next stage of meditation, which is to focus the mind on a single object. You will recall that two objects were suggested for this practice—an image of the Buddha or a blue flower. Focus on an appropriate object and strive to achieve single-pointed concentration without the experience of thought processes. If you experience either of the two principal obstacles to right concentration—namely, mental unruliness and mental stagnation—deal with it by applying the appropriate antidote, recalling the instructions we gave in the last lesson.

Remember that if you try to control the mind too much, you run the risk of a mental revolution as the mind tries to break away from its restraint. It is like reining a horse in too much; it will be forced to rebel and throw its rider. Don't provoke the mind to distraction by applying too much control; if you find that you are slipping into applying too much pressure, just relax for a while and let the mind become comfortable again. At the same time, apply mindfulness, recollecting the instructions for practice and the teachings on the importance of training your mind rightly for meditation. By soothing the mind and bringing it back gently to right practice, you can overcome the obstacle of mental unruliness.

However, if you go too easy on the mind and don't apply enough discipline, you run the risk of its becoming lazy and sleepy on you, lacking the ability to focus, and so forth. To firm it up, apply some discipline before it sinks all the way into irretrievable sluggishness. Stimulate the mind to be alert and conscious of all its faculties and all the clarity you can get out of it, so that it will focus on the object of your meditation. In this way you can avoid the extreme of mental stagnation.

By avoiding these two obstacles, your mind should gradually become trained in a state of meditative absorption that consists of single-pointed, nonconceptual concentration. Here the state of mind is one of equilibrium, serenity, and clarity, not characterized by anything else and untroubled by dissonant mental states, ragged breathing, and so forth. Learn to recognize distraction and sluggishness at the first moment in order to achieve this optimum state of mental equilibrium.

When you succeed in avoiding or overcoming the obstacles to single-pointed, nonconceptual meditation, you will progressively experience the various stages of meditation and concentrative absorption. You should know that the true state of concentration is perfect lucidity of mind, total alertness. Not only is the mind free from thought processes, it is also characterized by great clarity and awareness. This state of mental lucidity is the hallmark of right concentrative absorption. But if you allow the mind to be overwhelmed by mental sluggishness or distraction, and then overexert yourself in applying the antidotes or try to rein the mind in too sharply, you can do real damage. You can go crazy simply by applying the antidotes so strongly that the mind cannot function either in meditation or in ordinary life. That is not the point of practice.

Use common sense in recognizing problems when they arise, have a sense of proportion in applying the antidotes, and when they have proven effective, carry on bit by bit, in a sensible way. In the early stages of practice, meditate only for a few minutes but have a large number of brief sessions; when you improve, decrease the number of sessions but increase the length of each one. In this way you will eventually be able to meditate for long periods of time without a break. All this will occur via successful practice.

After you have attained skill in the nine stages of concentrative experience, as already described, you can dispense with external objects and focus internally, on clarity of mind itself. In undertaking the successful practice of mental concentration, don't feel that you have a great project that must be accomplished on schedule. Remain friends with your mind; have a sense of ease about your practice. Through not worrying about the past, not anticipating future problems, not being anxious about your practice, and having a mind that is matter-of-fact about the training, you should succeed in spite of everything. If you should find that your meditative state is occasionally interrupted by good or bad thoughts, or whatever, just diligently apply the antidotes. With a relaxed, businesslike attitude about what you are doing, you will be able to progress and experience the nine different stages of concentrative meditation.

When it is time to end your session, by all means end it, even if you are having a good run and things are going well. When it is time to stop, stop. If you push it, you will have a hard time later on, for it is very likely that you will encounter obstacles like the ones just described and will regret having overtaxed the mind in previous sessions. Once again, just take the bad with the good. When there are obstacles, do what is necessary. When there are none, meditate as long as your session is good, but don't overdo it. I myself have had sessions in which I sat too long, thinking that it was going very well, and it was really very difficult to bring the mind back the next time.

When it is time to arise from your session of meditation, conclude by dedicating any merit you have accomplished by training the mind; then get up and refresh the body and mind. Allow the body to get fresh air and the rest it needs to unwind. This is called, literally, "refreshing the elements." If you are in retreat, maintain solitude during your off-session hours and do not run after distractions. Avoid causes of agitation. It would be well to set yourself the goal of continuing your efforts until a session can last a day and a night. At that point, you will know that you are really meditating. If you really devote yourself to it, you might reach this level after six months of serious practice.

45

TEN MILLION BLIND MEN

SINCE A GREAT DEAL OF EFFORT is required of one who undertakes to follow the Mahāyāna path, much skill is also required. Therefore, it is taught that a practitioner of the Great Way should cultivate three kinds of excellence whenever he or she engages in study or practice of, or reflection on, the Dharma.

The Three Kinds of Excellence

The first of these three kinds of excellence is called "excellence in transformation" (or in reorientation). Briefly put, it involves transforming your perception of yourself and your aims. This entails turning the mind away from its ordinary, worldly preoccupations and redirecting it toward transcendent matters, eschewing self-interest and trying to attain transmundane spiritual goals for the sake of other beings. This redirection of mental energy and cultivation of a new attitude about your purpose in life and your relationship to other beings is, in fact, bodhichitta, that essential element in all Mahāyāna practices.

The second kind of excellence follows the development of bodhichitta in the preliminary stage of a session of practice. In the next stage, when you wholeheartedly engage in the main practice (whether that be meditation, reflection, study of a text, or listening to an explanation of the Dharma), you need to develop a correct apprehension of your setting. At this point you should not cling to subjective notions of yourself and your relationship to the teacher and the teaching (e.g., "I am here, I am getting this teaching, it is for me; I am the one who is making this great effort"). Rather, think of the teacher from whom you are receiving the teaching as none other than Lord Buddha himself, and conceive of yourself not in ordinary terms but as the prototypic Bodhisattva of Wisdom, Mañjushrī, who is seeking this particular teaching for the sake of all living beings. Do not cling to ordinary notions that tend to crystallize and reify the present moment. Instead, think of the teacher, yourself, and the setting as illusionlike, neither existent nor nonexistent, ineffable, and away from all the conceptual extremes that the human mind likes to attribute to reality.

All things, including your own form and the teacher's form, are not solid phenomena but illusory. While clearly apparent, they are not substantial; they are void in nature. For example, a rainbow's form, though clearly visible, nonetheless lacks substance on its own. Similarly, through interdependent origination, the appearances of the present moment should be seen to be illusionlike.

This right view of the factors involved in your practice is called, literally, the "excellence of objectlessness." In other words, throughout your main session of practice, whether of meditation or study, keep in mind that things are not what they appear to be. In your view of the present moment, try to approximate its essential reality and thereby free yourself from overweening attachment to the belief in a self and in the conventional reality of ordinary things. Through this perception of objectlessness, you will avoid the error of substituting one form of worldly attachment to externals for a more rarified attachment to the present moment and your own role in it.

Third, when you have completed this stage of meditation or study, remember to dedicate whatever merit you may have accumulated to the eventual enlightenment of all living beings. This is consistent with the basic motif of all bodhisattvas' practice, namely, that any training on the path be beneficial for all living beings rather than for oneself alone. This final step is called "excellence in dedication." Once done, the dedication of this sort of merit—small as it may be, yet conditioned by an ongoing awareness of the illusionlike nature of yourself as the performer of merit, of all beings as the acquirers of merit, and of merit itself—is heightened and magnified by being in accord with the true nature of reality. It is this kind of dedication that all the sages of the Great Way have described as most excellent.

When you undertake a session of practice or a particular aspect of training with these three excellences in mind, your efforts will assuredly be most effective, which is precisely what you intend in doing the practice or pursuing the training in the first place. If you neglect these three factors of right practice, you cannot be assured of any good result at all. As the great teacher Shāntideva wrote in his *Bodhicharyāvatara,* all austerities, recitations of mantras, and the like, even when performed for very long periods of time, are futile if they are done by one whose mind is distracted. If you attend a teaching but allow your mind to think about all sorts of matters—in particular, your subjective, egocentric perception of your role in the present moment—you really cannot call that practice, because it may very well result in little good. Needless to say, it is very important for serious practitioners to keep these three excellences of right effort in mind whenever they have the opportunity to practice.

Why is the possession of a human body said to be so special? Although there are many humans on this and other planets among the world systems known in Buddhist cosmology, very few are endowed with the conditions that enable them to attain liberation. Among the many modes of existence, humans are the only beings whose mental, physical, and karmic makeup enable them to escape from the round of birth and death.

Yet human existence itself is limited and conditioned. A human being lives about a hundred years at the most. The chances are extremely slim of finding yourself sufficiently free of karmic obscurations to be receptive to the teachings of liberation, and also fortunate enough to live in a time and environment where these teachings are available. Even when these conditions are met, the chances are quite high that you will be prevented from, or interrupted in, the practices that lead to liberation—whether because of apparently external causes, such as disease and war, or internal causes, such as distraction and the like. Human life is fragile and brief.

Moreover, if we cannot bear even slight amounts of pain and discomfort now, nor exercise the least control over our karmic destinies, what are we going to do at death, when we are faced with the possibility of unbearable, extremely long-lasting sufferings in unhappier states of existence? We have nothing but the virtues we have accumulated and the efforts we make in this present moment. We have no other assurance that we will not be faced with terrible and long-lasting sufferings. Therefore, while we have the opportunity to influence our own futures, it is only sensible that we apply ourselves with all seriousness and diligence to the task.

These teachings of enlightenment are available in their entirety from each of the four Tibetan orders of Buddhism (the Nyingma, Sakya, Kagyu, and Gelug), and from the Bönpo—not the black but the white ones.[68] These traditions are repositories of all the authentic teachings of enlightenment, which are recognized as such by virtue of having been spoken by the Buddha, compiled by the arhats, translated by the pandits, and meditated on by the siddhas, Buddhist saints, sages, and others who have attained realizations. No matter how good they may sound, so-called dharmic teachings to which these qualifications cannot be ascribed should be regarded as spurious.

All four Tibetan Buddhist traditions contain these same authoritative communications of the Dharma. With respect to our own Sakya tradition, we have further truth of their validity in that many great masters of the Sakya tradition, such as Dorje Chang,[69] Dragpa Gyaltsen, and their respective disciples, attained enlightenment by relying on these teachings. There is no doubt that they were the equals of the greatest of the Indian Buddhist sages, such as Nāgārjuna. By the examples of their careers, we know that the teachings which we are presently studying are indeed authentic and worthy of our most serious consideration.

In addition, this system of practice that our tradition expounds is not only authentic but also valid for everyone. The key to the attainment of liberation lies in the realization of selflessness, which can be achieved only through diligent efforts. All beings, male and female alike, are endowed with the same quintessential buddha-nature. Anyone, male or female, who applies diligence and fortitude to right efforts can, and will, achieve liberation. This has been demonstrated throughout Buddhist history, in which we can, of course, point to Shākyamuni Buddha, the bodhisattvas Mañjushrī and Avalokiteshvara, and other male teachers. However, we can also point to the goddess Nairātmyā (Non-Self Lady), to whom we owe the lam-dre system of meditation and who is regarded as the very essence of non-self, as her name implies. We can point to the bodhisattvas Tārā, Vijayā, and Sarasvatī as well.

Indeed, whenever we say that there were many male Buddhist teachers—Nāgārjuna, Asanga, and others—we must also point to the many females who contributed to the development of Buddhist thought in India—to the great nuns Niguma and Shrīmatī, to Sucasitā, and others. These women played eminent roles in the development of the Buddhist tradition. No less than their male counterparts, they attained the various stages of compassion and wisdom all the way up to buddhahood, by virtue of their fortitude and diligence in practice.[70]

The same can be said of Tibetan history. It is true that Marpa, Milarepa, and the Five Great Jetsüns, the founding patriarchs of the Sakya order, were male. But these greatest of meditators had their equal in the great Tibetan lady Machig Labdrön, to whom we owe the introduction into Tibet of the esoteric doctrine and practice of the *chod* (*gcod*) system,[71] which to this day exercises great influence over the tantric practice of all four great orders. She was recognized to be of such great achievement that the highest male Tibetan hierarchs came to her for instructions and blessings. From as far away as India, pandits came to debate with her, and, according to Tibetan chronicles, she bested them.

In modern times, we have the example of the great nun Lochema,[72] whose teachings and empowerments were sought by the heads of the Tibetan orders. The Holinesses, the Karmapa, and other heads of the various monasteries and traditions sought teachings and empowerments from her and practiced her instructions because of her superiority in meditative discipline.

Thus spiritual attainment is not a matter of externals, such as gender or rank; it is simply a matter of fortitude and diligence in practice. This is illustrated in the account we have of the great Indian tantric master Shāntipa, who became known as one of the Eighty-Four Mahāsiddhas. Shāntipa was famed for his great learning and advanced stage of spiritual development, and was widely sought after as a teacher. On one occasion, he was traveling to Ceylon at the invitation of the king, who had requested teachings from him. Along the way, he met a humble plowman tilling a field by the side of the road. On a compassionate impulse, Shāntipa paused for a moment and told the man, whose name was Tog-tsepa, that he really should exert himself in the practice of Dharma rather than merely tilling the soil.

Tog-tsepa did just that. He began to practice the instructions for meditation that the lama left with him, and did so with great perseverance for twelve years, during which time he attained the siddhis and became enlightened. He was filled with gratitude, remembering that his sudden change in status from the lowest kind of worldliness to the highest form of saintliness had been due to his brief encounter with Shāntipa, so he decided to seek him out and thank him for his great kindness.

Shāntipa was still teaching at the great monastery in Ceylon; by this time, he had grown old, almost blind, and was on a special diet. There he was, surrounded by his many disciples and attendants. Tog-tsepa obtained an audience with him and started to thank him for his many kindnesses, but Shāntipa asked, "Who are you? Why are you here?"

Tog-tsepa told him, "I was farming by the road and you helped so very much, many years ago. You gave me instructions for practicing a particular meditation, and by your kindness I have now attained enlightenment; I am here to thank you for it."

Shāntipa was amazed and said, "I myself have not attained the siddhis from that practice; I have been so busy that I haven't been able to apply myself to it. Although you call me your guru, I must now seek instructions from you. It is clear that I must begin practicing myself." Then Shāntipa took Tog-tsepa off into a quiet corner, received the teachings and empowerment from his student, and set about practicing in earnest until he, too, experienced the attainments.

In the lam-dre system of meditation, we have discussed the various instructions for the impure, or worldly, vision and are now studying the instructions for the experiential vision of the path. We have completed our look at the instructions for developing concentrative meditation. We will now undertake those concerning the next stage of practice, that of insight meditation.

INSIGHT

Insight, or vipashyanā (*vipaśyanā*), as it is known in Sanskrit, is rightly considered to be the essence of all the teachings of the Buddha, because the thorough truth, or right view of reality, is achieved by insight (which is, in turn, rightly based on concentrative meditation). As Shāntideva wrote in his *Bodhicharyāvatara*,

> All these many aspects of the doctrine were taught by the Buddha
> for the purpose of developing insight. Therefore, one who wishes
> to put an end to all sufferings should definitely develop insight
> within himself.

Insight has been explained as right discernment of all phenomena, whether external or internal, material or spiritual, or what have you. It is also the right perception of personal and phenomenal selflessness. This insight, as we have said earlier, is the key factor in attaining liberation. Thus it is rightly considered to be the quintessence of all the many Buddhist doctrines and practices.

If you aren't endowed with this right insight, meditation on emptiness and training in the pāramitās will not be able to lead you to enlightenment, no matter how diligently you practice them. This is because the six perfections are not free from the subjective perception of a self that is the giver, an object that is the gift, and so forth. Hence you will not necessarily have the right view, or insight into the true nature of reality, while performing these virtuous actions. As the *Perfection of Wisdom Verses* (*Prajñāpāramitā-sañcaya-gāthā*) tells us:

> How would ten million blind men, who do not even know the
> Path, ever be able to find their way to the Golden City? In the

same way, these first five transcendent virtues, of giving through meditation, will never be able to lead one to the Result, the attainment of Buddhahood, so long as they are not guided by insight.

Insight is the guide. Insight, or wisdom, constitutes the spiritual "eyes" that lead the six perfections to the stage of buddhahood. Just as blind men can easily make their way to a city when led by someone who can steer them on the right path, so the transcendent virtues very easily result in the attainment of buddhahood when they are guided by insight.

As long as you lack insight into the true nature of all dharmas, you will continue to flounder about in the ocean of worldly existence. You can attain the liberation of an arhat or pratyekabuddha by relying on the meditation of emptiness alone, but it lacks the extensive methods of love, compassion, and bodhichitta that enable you to attain the full enlightenment of buddhahood. For that very reason, the Buddha taught wisdom. As the *Perfection of Wisdom Verses* puts it, one who lacks wisdom falls down into the state of the shrāvaka, or Hīnayāna disciple. And the *Miracles of Mañjushrī Chapter Sūtra* (*Mañjuśrī-vikurvāna-parivarta-sūtra*) says that if one perceives only emptiness and abandons beings, then one has fallen victim to a deed of Māra.[73]

If you perceive with wisdom but remain attached to thinking of beings as real objects of compassion, then you have also fallen victim to Māra. The great sage Saraha said that we will never attain the highest path of enlightenment if we relinquish compassion and rely on the meditation of emptiness alone, nor will we obtain liberation merely by cultivating compassion. What is required is that we combine nondually the realization of selflessness and great, objectless compassion. The essence of the bodhisattva's career consists in just such a skillful combination; to the extent that either compassion or wisdom is lacking, the bodhisattva will remain unable to attain his goal and liable to backslide from his efforts on the path.

The *King of Concentrations Sūtra* says that, even when worldlings do meditate on emptiness, they remain unable to relinquish their apprehensions of things as real. As a result, desire, hatred, and delusion arise in their minds with even greater force than before.

46

REBIRTH AS A WOODCHUCK

As practitioners of Mahāyāna Buddhism, we should ever be mindful of the three kinds of excellence in practice: (1) excellence in mental preparation for practice, (2) excellence in the stage of actual practice, and (3) excellence in the dedication of merit.

To review this briefly, we said in the last lesson that, for a virtuous action to be most in accord with our aim of attaining enlightenment, we should begin with mindfulness and right intent. Whether we are undertaking a session of study or meditation or an action to benefit others, we should be mindful of our intention to accomplish it in order to promote the eventual enlightenment of all living beings, including ourselves. It is for this reason that each session of meditation begins with taking refuge and resolving to win enlightenment as expressed in the bodhichitta formula. When we sincerely and mindfully perform virtue for the benefit of others, the virtue of that action is greatly enhanced due both to its limitless object and to our having expanded the intent of our actions to include all living beings. Thus, whenever we undertake a session of practice, we should always do so with a sincere wish that, through our efforts, all living beings may ultimately obtain the highest possible benefit.

When actually engaged in study, meditation, or the performance of some virtuous act of body, voice, or mind, we should again be mindful and ensure that our actions are accompanied by the second form of excellence, which consists of the perception of objectlessness. For instance, when we undertake a session of study, we should not cling to the mental supports of ordinary conceptualization, viewing our teacher as simply an elderly gentleman and ourselves as ordinary people fashioned of flesh and blood. Rather, we should conceive of the teacher as none other than Shākyamuni Buddha himself, seated on a jeweled throne, radiant in color, with all the attributes of a fully enlightened buddha, and should think of ourselves as none other than the Bodhisattva of Wisdom, Mañjushrī, who tirelessly seeks out the teachings of enlightenment for the sake of all living beings. Along with these visualizations, we should try to approximate Mañjushrī's attitude of seeking the well-being of all beings by undertaking such actions as study of, and listening to, the Dharma. See yourself doing all this in exactly the way that Mañjushrī would do it.

Now, as to objectlessness: rather than thinking of the teacher, ourselves, and the present environment as being real in the way that ordinary human minds like to think of things, we must shift to a subtler perception of them, one that at least approximates the Enlightened One's view of phenomena. We should see our surroundings, ourselves, and the merit we are accumulating through our efforts as illusionlike. We should see them not as inherently real by their very nature but as nondual emptiness and appearance, like the form of a rainbow or a mirage. We should think of our own form and the present moment as illusionlike; rather than seizing the moment and trying to make it solid and substantial, we should see it as ultimately devoid of subject and object. There is no teacher, student, or teaching that exists from an ultimate point of view. This is not to say that they simply never existed, but that as they happen, they are, by nature, a manifestation of nondual emptiness and appearance.

Gradually, we will learn to accumulate virtue through this perception of objectlessness—the realization that there is no performer, no recipient of an action, and no virtue accumulated through the process. This results in a tremendous amount of good, because our deeds then approximate that measureless accumulation of merit achieved by the enlightened ones, who act for the liberation of beings on the level of ultimate reality.

When our session of study, practice, or performance of good deeds is complete, we should also be mindful of achieving the third and final kind of excellence, the excellence of the dedication of merit. We should never fail to turn over all the merit we have accumulated to the highest possible enlightenment of all living beings.

These three kinds of excellence should attend all our actions, however minor the latter might seem. We should ever be mindful of the excellences, and if they are not already present in our actions, we should be sure to include them. This is extremely important; all teachers of the Dharma have said so. The three excellences enhance the effectiveness of our efforts on the Mahāyāna path; without them, our virtuous actions are often of unsure benefit. Virtuous actions may or may not result in virtue if they are not attended by right intent (*bodhicitta*) and guided by insight into objectlessness, or the real nature of what is going on. And if they are not safely transferred to others through the dedication of merit, actions that seem to be virtuous, or that are performed for the sake of virtue, may have little or no benefit, even though we had hoped for that result. Therefore, it is extremely important that all our actions include these three kinds of excellence.

We are now ready to discuss the last topic in the second section of *The Three Visions*, which concerns the experiential perception incurred by someone who has undertaken Mahāyāna meditation. We have said that insight meditation (*vipaśyanā*) is the practice through which we can develop that state of consciousness which we call ultimate bodhichitta. We have said that insight is essential as a guide to the development and fulfillment of the other transcendent virtues required of the bodhisattva. We have also said that, in the bodhisattva's mind, this insight into the voidness, or true nature, of all phenomena must be conjoined with great compassion for all living beings. It is important for the practitioner on the bodhisattva path to keep both spiritual qualities in mind, thus developing both insight into emptiness and great compassion for living beings.

Āchārya Saraha summarized this point by writing:

> Not by emptiness alone, where compassion has been discarded, can the path supreme be won. And is there any liberation from the worldly round if compassion alone be meditated?

Saraha was one of the great Buddhist sages of India, one of the Eighty-Four Mahāsiddhas, and was also Nāgārjuna's teacher. He said that insight and compassion must be cultivated together, that the meditator cannot afford to separate them or rely on one rather than the other. Though the bodhisattva may, through insight into selflessness (that is, personal non-self and phenomenal non-self),[74] succeed, like the arhat, in getting out of the world, he will never succeed in attaining buddhahood. That Great Way is open only to bodhisattvas who have both insight into emptiness and great compassion for all beings.

Compassion, while an admirable quality—and essential in the attainment of buddhahood—is not by itself enough to enable a bodhisattva to escape from the round of birth and death. To do that, the bodhisattva must realize the emptiness of the whole process of birth and death and become free from it through insight. And to lead him to buddhahood, there must be a perfect merger of liberating insight and great compassion that doesn't abandon beings.

Saraha's point, then, is that wisdom and compassion are essential and must be present *together* for buddhahood to be attained. We shan't be able to transcend worldly existence if our views based on attachment to the notion of a self are not cut off, and these views cannot be cut off either by meditation on emptiness distinct from realization of the two kinds of selflessness (see below) or by mental concentration devoid of discriminating insight. Thus, to attain liberation from saṃsāra, we cannot rely either on meditation on emptiness (*vipaśyanā*) or on concentration practice (*śamatha*) alone.

The insight that is required in conjunction with compassion consists of realization of the two kinds of selflessness: personal non-self and phenomenal non-self. This is the goal of insight meditation (*vipaśyanā*). When true insight into the two kinds of selflessness is conjoined with great compassion, the result is buddhahood.

It is for this reason that the *King of Concentrations Sūtra* tells us,

> Even though he meditates on emptiness, a worldling cannot check
> this grasping at things as real, and so the passions again rise up, just
> as in the case of Udraka's meditation.

This verse refers to the story of the Hindu meditator Udraka, who sat in unceasing meditation for twelve years, the only result being that he was reborn as a cat. The reason was that he relied on concentration alone and hoped that that would lead him to liberation. His mind may never have been blemished by thought processes, distractions, defilements, and so forth, but he did not attain a higher rebirth because he didn't make the right efforts to cut off the passions. Though he was not acting on them, they were still present within his mind. Udraka relied on simply stopping thought processes, checking the mind, and fixing it in single-pointed meditation. He expected that to bring liberation. It didn't, its only result being an inferior rebirth.

I am reminded of a verse from Sakya Pandita's *Jewel Treasure of Wise Sayings* (Skt. *Subhāṣita-ratna-nidhi*; Tib. *Legs bshad snying po*),[75] in which he states that the meditation of fools, who rush into practice without bothering to study the stages of the path with a qualified teacher, is simply a very good method of attaining animalhood:

> Without examining the instructions for practice, fools apply them-
> selves to meditation and thereby greatly increase their ignorance—
> and wind up reborn as woodchucks.

The Tibetans call woodchucks great yogis because they come out in large numbers on the hillsides, fold their hands as if in prayer or meditation, and make sounds as if they are chanting mantras. The popular belief is that woodchucks are reincarnations of humans who meditated ignorantly, just dashing into caves and practicing without learning how to do it properly.

Sakya Pandita also says that uninformed meditation is like climbing a ladder without hands: it is very risky and results in downfall, through attaining either a view that you don't understand or an insight that you are unable to cope with, since neither is supported by right understanding. In other words, it is the sign of a fool to undertake meditation without fore-knowledge about the stages of the path, instructions for following it, and achievement of the right view. When your mind is ready for right medita-tion and your efforts are supported by right understanding and knowledge, practice will be successful. Otherwise, the only result can be poor medita-tion—a result that you did not have in mind.

The important point here is that mindfulness must attend your practice. Merely cutting off thoughts and remaining in single-pointed concentration will not get you where you want to be. You must be mindful of what you are about and well prepared at all times. It is not enough to cut off all thoughts; you must understand why they must be cut off, what you need to experience, what you are experiencing, what it leads to, what you do then, and so forth. As I once pointed out to one of my students, if your medita-tion is attended by mindfulness, then you are indeed meditating, but with-out mindfulness, you aren't.

Mindfulness is what enables us to know whether or not we are integrating within our practice the factors that we need for progress, and whether or not we are avoiding or getting rid of those factors that hinder our progress. Shāntideva teaches us the same thing:

> An arrested mind will again emerge, because it lacks the realization
> of emptiness, as in the case of consciousnessless meditation.
> Therefore, emptiness should be meditated on.

We have already given the example of Udraka, whose meditation led to rebirth as an animal because he relied too much on a single aspect of medi-tation. This is also the case with meditators who train only in the stages of concentration or other types of meditation that lack the insight of object-lessness developed through the realization of emptiness. Such meditators do attain the ability to remain in states of meditative absorption for very long periods of time, even to the point of being reborn in the realm of formlessness. But, as Shāntideva points out, "an arrested mind will again emerge." A mind whose mental processes have simply been checked, whose defilements have been stopped but not purified or eliminated through the realization of their emptiness, can hold those manifestations of egotism for a very long period of time. Sooner or later, they will reemerge in the mind.

Shāntideva gives the example of a particular Hīnayāna meditation called the consciousnessless meditation. In this state, one is free from all mental processes whatsoever, and this meditative absorption can last for very long periods of time. However, a meditator who enters this stage of meditation (or any of the other states of absorption that are not endowed with the realization of non-self) may find that, whenever the mind does emerge from those states of absorption, its old tendency to think in terms of duality immediately goes back into operation.

The meditator usually reacts with great fear, because by this time he has convinced himself that he has attained liberation from all thought processes. When he emerges from meditation and finds that nothing has really changed, he thinks that he has been royally deceived: far from attaining liberation, he has attained nothing from his many years or lifetimes of diligent meditative absorption. As a result of his alarm and grief at being (as he thinks) deceived by the teachings of Buddhism, he usually falls into one of the hells, because he rejects the teachings of liberation altogether, thinking, "I entered into those stages of meditation and didn't win liberation; therefore, there is no liberation."

This is something you should avoid; therefore, you should meditate on emptiness. This is why the realization of non-self, or selflessness, is essential—and it is precisely what those meditators missed. They thought in terms of merely stopping the works, not of seeing through them with insight and realizing that—in all the operation of the thought processes, the ego, and so forth—nothing is really substantial, since things are nondual emptiness and appearance. As our text, *The Three Visions*, continues:

> Thus the attainment of enlightenment requires that all these three factors be present: Wisdom, which is like an arrow; Compassion, which is like a bow; and a person versed in right methods, who is like a skilled archer.

The *Higher Linkage* (*Uttara-tantra*) of the bodhisattva Maitreya also tells us:

> Having dispelled, through wisdom, all craving for self, the Loving One attains no nirvāṇa because of his attachment to living beings.

Thus the Noble One, employing the methods of attaining enlightenment through wisdom and love, neither remains in saṃsāra nor crosses beyond into peace.

The bodhisattva must be skilled in balancing these two essential factors that lead to the attainment of enlightenment. Through wisdom, he gives up all notions of a self, and thereby all clinging to selfish interests on the path. And through giving up all craving for the self, he is free from bondage in saṃsāra, which is a synonym for egotism and all its operations. He is free from saṃsāra because of his insight into selflessness, but because of his selfless attachment to living beings, he does not enter nirvāṇa. He cannot bear to leave all those unenlightened beings in their unenlightened state, so he attains what is called "nonabiding nirvāṇa" and is, as a result, neither in saṃsāra nor out of it. This is in contrast to the static nirvāṇa of an arhat, who really does leave the round of birth and death and experience individual liberation.

As the *Higher Linkage* goes on to tell us, "The bodhisattva has to be skilled in employing the *methods!*" This is the whole point of our discussion of meditation: that to be effective and right, your meditation must be (1) guided by the three excellences, (2) endowed with the two factors of wisdom and compassion, and (3) done with mindfulness. Otherwise, meditation is just a bad idea. In the *Compendium of Trainings*, Shāntideva tell us that, "Through developing a realization of emptiness that has as its essence compassion, one's merit becomes purified." Thus intelligent persons, who are endowed with understanding and a wish to benefit themselves and others, should strive to master the ways of developing the awareness of selflessness, which is the remedy for suffering and its cause, without allowing it to become separated from the methods of great compassion.

This stage of insight meditation consists in part of developing insight into personal and phenomenal non-self. Lack of this insight is said to consist of suffering and to be the cause of suffering. So long as a person believes in a personal self, and that things are as real as they appear to be, he is bound to experience all the deluded sufferings attendant upon a dualistic perception of his experience. Therefore, the awareness of these two kinds of selflessness is said to be the remedy for suffering and its cause.

Intelligent people who really want to do something for themselves will seek to develop this insight into selflessness. And because they wish to avoid the negative results of relying on a single aspect of meditation (such as meditating on emptiness devoid of compassion, or compassion devoid of emptiness), they will take care to combine their development of insight into selflessness with great compassion for living beings. This great compassion is called "methods," or "skillful means" (*upāya*). It consists of the skillful means of accomplishing the benefit of others while not losing your insight into selflessness and the objectlessness of the situation.

As it is further asserted in the *Bodhicharyāvatara*, "Egoism, which is suffering's cause, increases through the delusions of a self. It is checked by the meditation of selflessness." This is a response to those meditators (particularly adherents of the Hindu schools that posit the belief in an eternal self, or *ātman*) who claim that you should meditate on the self in order to gain realization of the self, and that, through gaining some identification with the ultimate self, liberation can be achieved. Shāntideva counters by saying that all this belief in a self, no matter how you perceive it (whether as the finite, individual ego or the immortal and ultimate super-self), is really the cause of suffering. The more you think about a self, the more you reinforce the notions of self, thereby increasing delusions about it. This is the only result of meditating on a self: far from making progress toward attaining liberation, you are actually enhancing the cause of your bondage.

As Shāntideva says, you cannot check these notions of a self by strengthening the belief in a self. It is better to strive for liberation by meditating on selflessness. But if you have doubts about whether it is better to meditate on non-self or self, there are three things you can do: (1) recognize the nature of appearances, (2) place your mind in a state that is away from all extremes, and (3) develop certain knowledge about the nature of that inexpressible state.

This is a challenge to the meditator—to really try meditation exactly as Shāntideva and other Buddhists have laid it down. Will you meditate on non-self? Will you meditate on the non-self of appearances? Recognizing that there is no real ego, or self, within, place the mind in a state of consciousness away from every extreme and develop certain knowledge about this state as the true ultimate. If you can do these three things without clinging to them as real, you will see for yourself whether or not you are liberated. In other words, Shāntideva and others are quite sure that, through meditating on non-self, you will get the result of liberation.

The Three Visions tells us that, with regard to the first of these three, recognition of the nature of appearances, we must understand that all outer and inner dharmas appear only through the power of the mind that manifests them. In reality, not even the slightest entity exists. You might object,

"It is not so that they are nonexistent, because the existence of a self as the agent who creates both happiness and suffering is accepted by non-Buddhists, and the existence of an 'I,' a 'mind,' and the rest are easily proven even in the natural knowledge of ordinary folk." But what the text is saying here is that all these appearances of outer and inner dharmas are only manifestations of mind, and that you need not treat them as if they were really external in themselves. They are projections of mind: in other words, mind is the only thing that counts. Even the mind that manifests these appearances has no real existence as an entity on the level of ultimate reality. In reality, not even the slightest entity exists.

The objections to this view of selflessness usually begin with a defense of duality, along the lines of, "It's not true that a being is devoid of a self, due to the notion, accepted by everybody, about an agent who is responsible for actions that result in pleasure, pain, and so forth. Everyone—except Buddhists—agrees that there really is a self. Even worldly people who aren't trained in philosophy can tell you that there really is a self and that these concepts of 'I' and 'mine' are real. On top of this natural knowledge of, and belief in, a self, there are sophisticated systems of thought based on the premise of a self and buttressed by logic, appeals to experience, and so forth. For all these very weighty reasons, there is no need to accept the argument that there is no subjective self."

Of course, it follows from such a line of thinking that there really is, within this human organism, that which corresponds to our conventional notion of a self. The Buddhists argue that, "If a self exists that is the object of this universal conceptualization, let's see it. Is it name, body, mind, or what? Exactly what is meant by this notion of a self?" The Buddhist argument goes on to say that if you were to mistake a coil of rope for a snake, you might feel quite justified in responding with alarm and taking action based on this notion: indeed, that would seem the appropriate thing to do. However, if someone came along with a light, and you saw that what you had thought was a snake was nothing but an inert piece of rope, you would realize that your reactions had not corresponded to the reality of the situation but had been based on a false premise.

The same can be said of this notion of a self. We all accept the premise that there is a self, and we act selfishly for its sake. We take action based on this notion of a real "I," which in turn justifies the notion of "mine" and the idea of distinguishing others as being not-self. Therefore, we feel justified in acting with attachment to our own side, aversion to all that is not-self, and indifference to that which does not appeal to us.

All those who believe in a self feel that their behavior is justified in this way. The Buddhist challenges them to investigate whether there really is anything that corresponds to their notion of a self, and if not, to recognize the situation for what it is.

We are advised to go about this by inquiring whether the self happens to be the name, body, or mind of a person. Is a person's name the self? Very few people would argue that it is, because to most people it is obvious that name is a mere conventional ascription, not anything that can be established as real, substantial, and tangible. "Name" is obviously empty of any real form or content in itself: "Devoid of name are dharmas all, yet by names are they denoted."

If the name is not self, might it not be "body"? If it were, then if the body were mutilated, we would lose part of ourselves; when the body died and decayed, the self would be lost. Body cannot be what we mean by self because the body is destructible, whereas all concepts of self hold that it is eternal, and hence cannot be destroyed. Indeed, if the body were the self, we would no longer have to concern ourselves with questions about the hereafter.

If the self is not name or body, might it not be "mind"? Here we have a problem, because mind is seen to consist of discrete moments of cognition. One flash of consciousness arises and perishes within an instant, to be succeeded by a second flash of cognition, which is succeeded by a third, and so forth. This is the way mind works: it is of no more than a millisecond's duration. If mind were the self, then the self would last for only a millisecond. This does not coincide with the popular notions already mentioned, so we cannot look to mind to fill the bill.

47

SAMSĀRA FALLS APART LIKE A TATTERED RAG

AS WE HAVE SAID, all attempts to learn the Dharma should be attended by three kinds of excellence. The first is excellence in motivation. In a word, your efforts to master the Dharma must be guided by the intent to learn in order to promote the eventual enlightenment of yourself and all beings— i.e., your efforts must be guided by the spirit of bodhichitta. Next, your effort during the process of learning must itself be guided by excellence in view. That is, your view of yourself and the effort you are making must be in harmony with the Dharma in a philosophical sense. You should seek to see them not in a deluded, unenlightened way (i.e., as substantial and real), but as they really are: without a subjective "I," or agent, without any real effort made, and without any real merit acquired. In other words, try to see what is happening on the level of conventional reality through the vision of ultimate reality. Finally, there should be excellence in the completion of your efforts. Never fail to dedicate all merit acquired through effort and study to the enlightenment of all living beings. When these three kinds of excellence attend your efforts, their efficacy is assured. For this reason, their importance has been stressed.

It is helpful to conceive of study itself as a formal session of meditation. Beginning with the awakening of bodhichitta (the resolve to study in order to further the highest spiritual interests of all beings), you should at least approximate the objectlessness of activities that occurs on the level of ultimate reality. Do not think of this present situation as ordinary and mundane. Rather, think of your teacher as none other than Shākyamuni Buddha and of yourself as the Bodhisattva of Wisdom, Mañjushrī, who seeks out the teachings for the sake of all living beings. Your present environment is that of a celestial mansion. Think that, as you concentrate on the instructions given by the teacher, rays of light shine forth from his heart to touch all beings inhabiting space, removing their obscurations and sufferings. Like you, they find that their obscurations and sufferings are thereby removed and that great wisdom arises within their minds. Their forms, like your own and like all appearances, become illusionlike—clearly apparent but void by nature.

When you have finished your session of study, remember to dedicate from the heart whatever merit you might have acquired in this effort to learn the Dharma. Dedicate that merit to all living beings, that they might attain buddhahood and always experience only happiness and the well-being that ensues from virtue.

The Sakya tradition is a storehouse of many profound doctrines and systems of meditation. Among them, the system of the Path with Its Result has a place of preeminence because of its depth and its vast range of methods. This lam-dre system has two levels, the preliminary and the advanced. We are engaged in the study of *The Three Visions*, which contains the instructions for the preliminary level of practice. We have discussed in detail the instructions for awakening a sense of renunciation through meditation on death, impermanence, the law of karma, and the like. We have discussed developing a sense of unselfishness in practice through the meditations of great love and great compassion. We have also discussed the two kinds of bodhichitta, the conventional and the ultimate. The instructions for the former are contained in the meditations on the sameness of self and others and the exchange of self and others; those on the latter consist of guidance related to the two stages of Mahāyāna meditation, shamatha and vipashyanā (concentration and insight). We have completed our discussion of concentration meditation and have begun the discussion of insight.

Technically speaking, the goal of Mahāyāna practices is the attainment of the three bodies of buddhahood (the *nirmāṇakāya, sambhogakāya,* and *dharmakāya*) and the five kinds of transcendent gnosis that attend total enlightenment.[76] The causes that produce total enlightenment, and hence these three bodies and five wisdoms, lie in the training pursued by the aspirant to buddhahood, the bodhisattva. The bodhisattva trains in what are called the six pāramitās, or transcendent virtues. The product of training in these six perfections is the accumulation of merit and wisdom, which result in the Form Body of Buddhahood and the Knowledge Body of Buddhahood.

More specifically, it is the first four of the transcendent virtues that produce merit: giving, moral conduct, patience, and, according to some teachers, meditation. It is through training in insight or wisdom, the sixth transcendent virtue, that we accumulate insight into objectlessness, or the realization of the two kinds of selflessness, personal and phenomenal, which we began to discuss in the last lesson. Since the fourth transcendent virtue, vigor or diligence, is required in both accumulations, it is included as a factor in both categories. You need vigor in undertaking and accomplishing generosity, patience, and meditation; you also need it in awakening insight. Thus these six virtues are the method whereby merit and wisdom—the direct causes of buddhahood—arise.

Our topic here is insight meditation. The heart of this discussion is the special Buddhist concept of selflessness, how it is developed, and how it leads to the attainment of enlightenment. To summarize the last lesson, we said that the core of the problem of worldly suffering is the erroneous belief in the real existence of a self where there is none. Through this habitual belief in the existence of a self/soul/ego/"I," deluded beings find themselves involved in the process of becoming, which inevitably leads them to one or another painful experience. As long as they subscribe to the false notion of a self, they find themselves undergoing birth, death, and the round of pain. The ignorant mind that mistakenly clings to a notion of a self perceives reality in dualistic terms, discriminating between all that is self and not-self. Based on this false dichotomy, it gives rise to the naturally negative mental states of attachment, aversion, and indifference. Actions that proceed from these three further involve the mind in experiences of mental and physical pain.

If this process is not checked at the very concept of self, the mind will continue, as the Buddhist scriptures put it, to whirl about in the realm of worldly existence. Therefore, it is a cardinal principle with Buddhists that this root cause of suffering—the belief in a self—be exposed as faulty by right investigation, which forms the heart of insight meditation. Insight, in a word, is insight into the nonexistence of that self to which worldlings subscribe. As we have stressed in earlier lessons, this stage of insight meditation must be firmly based on mastery of concentrative meditation. When your mind has become tranquil and steady through training in concentration, you will be able to focus it on mind itself.

In investigating the status of this notion of self, we are interested first in learning what is meant by this notion to which we all subscribe. Accordingly, we try to approach it from three angles. Is a person's self synonymous with his name, with his body, or with his mind? If none of these, then with what? We have progressed to the point of investigating whether a person's name might constitute the notion of a self. By several arguments, that possibility was rejected. We will now investigate whether a person's body might constitute a self.

Name is not self, we said, because it is mere ascription. Nor is the body the self. If you investigate and examine the body analytically, it cannot be found. What do we mean by that? We mean that if you look for the body as a whole, you won't find it; you will only find it in its parts. Aside from the many components of the body (the limbs, atoms, etc. that are required to make up the composite body), there is no body itself, so if you search for it, you cannot locate it. For example, is the hand the body? No, it is only a part of the body. Analyzing each part of the body in turn, none of them can rightly be identified with what is meant by "body"; rather, they are all parts.

Moreover, if a thing doesn't exist in its parts, the mere generalization, or mere whole of its parts, will not make up anything more than the concept of, in this case, "body." To give an example, there is no such entity as "a forest"; there is only an aggregation of individual trees. There are definitely trees that are considered to be parts of the forest, but this tree is not the forest, the next one isn't, and so on, for all the trees under consideration. Hence the concept of forest is simply made up by human minds because it is convenient to think in terms of a whole, albeit a whole that does not exist in its individual parts.

The same is true of the body, and if the body itself does not exist as an entity, or integral whole, then it can hardly constitute something such as a self. This is corroborated by the ninth chapter of the *Bodhicharyāvatara*, which states that "the body is not the feet or shins, nor is it thighs or hips," and so on. Shāntideva then concludes:

> Hence the body does not exist, and only due to being confused about your hands, and other parts that are not the body, does a mind that mistakes them to be body come about, in the same way that, due to the particular way in which a pile of stones is shaped, a mind that apprehends it to be a man comes about.

Thus we turn to the mind, to see whether it might be what we are searching for. This seems more promising, because most people think of the self as conscious, sensible, cognizant; they seem to feel that it has accurate cognition, self-awareness, and so forth. But when mind itself is subjected to an examination, no mind is obtained. As the *Bodhicharyāvatara* explains:

> Mind consciousness dwells not in the organs of sense, nor in form and the rest, nor in between. Mind is to be found neither within nor without, nor in any other place.

When we look for the mind, where do we look for it? What are we looking for? Is it located within the body? Exactly where in the body is it located? If you search there, examining within, can you find it? If it is not inside the body, is it outside it? If so, where? Or is it somewhere in between? Is it a combination of within and without?

Since mind isn't tangible, it is hard to locate. When you look for it, you learn very quickly that it has neither color, shape, size, nor any other quality, except that you know that you do have a mind. But the mind is not a thing. Not only is it not an entity (something that can be pinned down and located), it is also quite ephemeral. Of all things (although we have just said that it is not a thing!), mind changes more than any other. That creates problems when we are trying to isolate and identify as real something that is worth living and dying for, such as the notion of a self, eternal soul, ego, or what have you.

What we *can* say about mind consciousness is that it can't be found. We are aware that there is consciousness manifested in the eyes, ears, nose, tongue, skin, and mental organs (or brain). But when we look for the mind to see if it is located in any one of these, we cannot find it. And if it is not in any one of those locations, it is not going to be in all six together, as if they were a whole.

Nor is the mind in the objects of cognition. It is not in the sense organs, nor is it in the sense objects: not in form, not in feeling, not in sound, not in taste or smell. Nor is it in between the sense organs and sense objects, or in a combination of these. Mind cannot be located inside, outside, or in any other place. No matter where you search for the mind, you will not find any object that corresponds to our notion of it.

This raises the question of how the mind could possibly constitute the so-called self that we are seeking. As the *Bodhicharyāvatara* points out,

> Past and future minds are not the self, for indeed, they do not exist.
> And, supposing the present mind to be self, again no self exists
> when it ceases.

Now, we have said that mind is impermanent: it changes from instant to instant. Mind consists of discrete moments of cognition that immediately pass away, succeeded by other moments of cognition. Hence, when we talk about mind, we are just talking about these brief flashes of cognition.

Is that what we mean by self, when we say mind is the self? Do we mean that self is really only a moment's cognition that is followed by successive selves? The past mind—for example, the thought that you had just five seconds ago—has long since passed. That could not have been the self, nor can the future mind be the self: future moments of cognition cannot constitute a self because they do not exist. Thus past moments of cognition have vanished for good, while future moments have not yet come into existence. And should you like to think that this present moment of cognition might be your self, be prepared for an early death, because the present moment passes very quickly and takes your self with it, if you identify mind with self.

To sum up, we have a verse from the scriptures which tells us:

> Name is no self, for it is mere ascription. Body is no self, for, like some outer wall, its flesh and bones are an aggregation of gross elements. Mind, too, is no self, for it is not an entity.

Through investigating and meditating on name, body, and mind, we come to understand that none of them could possibly constitute the self. When we understand this, we also understand that there is no point in searching in other people for one's self. And since the self cannot be found in name, body, or mind and there is no possibility of finding it elsewhere, the conclusion is that there may well be no self at all.

At first, you must understand this theoretically. Thus you analyze it, going through all the steps of thinking it out: "Is the hand the self?" "Is the finger the self?" "Is the elbow the self?" And so forth. "Or is the name the self?" You run it backward and forward. This kind of discursive analysis is helpful because it intellectually introduces the concept of selflessness to your mind. The next stage is to reflect: "How can this be?" "In what way is it possible that there can be no self?" Finally, when you have gained some degree of acceptance and understanding, meditate and realize directly that there is, indeed, no self to be found.

That realization, which comes through meditation, constitutes the insight into selflessness. Insight into selflessness, we said, is the key principle of Mahāyāna Buddhism. It is this realization that alone provides access to buddhahood. The realization of selflessness comprises the sixth and last of the pāramitās and is called "the perfection of wisdom." It is through this realization that you acquire the accumulation of wisdom essential to buddhahood.

Accumulating merit by training in the other transcendent virtues has been called "the long way to buddhahood," whereas training in the realization of selflessness has been called "the shortcut to buddhahood"; however, the latter is much more difficult than the former. Attaining genuine insight into selflessness requires considerable courage, honesty, diligence, intelligence, and merit. As Āryadeva wrote in his *Four Hundred Verses*:

> They who have little merit will not even begin to wonder whether
> or not there is a self. But for the one who has doubts about the exis-
> tence of a self, the realm of saṃsāra falls apart like a tattered rag.

Here the idea is that ordinary people, who don't have a great store of merit, will never even begin to wonder, "Have I really got a self or not?" They will just take it for granted that they do, because everything in their experience seems to reinforce the notion. Hence it doesn't occur to them to examine whether or not they have a self. But those who have superior merit begin to doubt whether there really is an ego, soul, or self as commonly held. From that moment on, the realm of birth and death begins to fall apart; the bonds of delusion begin to loosen and very quickly drop away. As we said, it is this realization of selflessness that leads, more than any other factor, to the attainment of buddhahood.

At this point you are probably ready to ask, "If there is no self, then what is the basis for this concept of a self that we all have? From birth onward, we all share the same notion, and that can't be without cause. There must be a reason for everyone having this belief, even though, when we search for a self, we can't seem to find anything."

Buddhists answer that this concept of self is nothing more than an irrational notion acquired through the habitual practice of wrongly apprehending a self in the five skandhas, or aggregates (form, feeling, perception, impulse, and consciousness), which are the components of the human organism. Rather than seeing them as aggregates, the ordinary point of view seizes upon them as a whole. For example, rather than seeing a forest as the sum of many trees, the mind forms the generalized concept that "there is one forest here," when in truth there are just many individual trees. In the same way, the human mind seizes upon its component parts, the five skandhas, and assumes that they somehow contain a self. Instead of examining this notion in light of accurate knowledge about a being's component parts, the mind identifies with the five skandhas and develops the notion of a self for purposes of orientation, thinking, in effect, "It is this organism with which I identify."

Hence the mind makes the easy mistake of wrong, or baseless, identification, rather than taking the trouble to find a valid basis for its identification with the skandhas. This is very much like the classic example of mistaking a rope for a snake. You remember this example: in the distance or in gloomy light, you see a rope lying in your path and mistake it for a snake. Without thinking twice, you react with alarm. If you then shine a light on the object and see that it is merely a harmless piece of rope, you realize how very inappropriate your reaction was: it did not correspond to the facts of the matter. In the same way, within the five skandhas, you mistake the real existence of a self.

You have long accepted this unexamined notion of a self as being based in fact. Now it is habitual, simply because the mind has been practicing it for aeons. From beginningless time, the mind has been operating on the basis of this wrong idea, which is very much entrenched by now. But if the light of insight is cast upon this notion, you can very clearly see that there is no basis for apprehending a self within the five skandhas. As in the example of the rope/snake, all your mental and physical actions that are based on this false premise become highly inappropriate. Just as your reaction to the harmless rope lying in your path was seen to be inappropriate, so striving for the aggrandizement of the self and slaving for the concepts of "I" and "mine" now appear that way. All aversion to whatever threatens the so-called interests of the self is also seen to be absurd. Through insight into the true facts of the matter, you become free from the vicious negative states of desire, hatred, and delusion.

We must become absolutely certain that the "self" or "I," which is the object of that false apprehension we are talking about, does not exist. If it should exist, then ordinary worldlings are correct and there is no possibility for Buddhist liberation; indeed, there is nothing further to be said. But if, as Buddhists claim, there is no self, then not only are the actions based on that premise highly inappropriate, but they may also be, as Buddhists hold, the very cause of bondage and suffering. To avoid those states and attain liberation, the realization of non-self will then be as important as Buddhists say it is.

Thus we must become certain (via thoroughly discriminative analysis) that, due to the nonexistence of an "I," "mineness" also does not exist. It is an error to cling to these notions of "I" and "mine," which are the roots of every fault. We have already explained, in considerable detail, how this unexamined notion of the self becomes the core of your concept of the duality of self and non-self. Everything that you identify with—or try to identify with—becomes distinguished from all that is "not I," "not mine." This interaction between self and not-self gives rise to all the problems of coveting what is not-self. There is also the wish to avoid everything that seems to threaten this concept of a self. It is obvious, then, that clinging to these notions is, indeed, the root of every fault.

If you accept this, it follows that you need to practice the method for relinquishing this belief in a self. In his *Introduction to the Madhyamaka* (*Madhyamaka-avatāra*), Chandrakīrti wrote,

> Having understood through discriminative wisdom that all the faults of the passions arise from the view of things as truly substantial, and having realized, too, that the self is the object of that view, the meditator rejects the self.

We explain this to mean that all the faults of worldly existence (desire, hatred, delusion, and all the karmic actions and results that flow from them) are based on the belief in a truly existent self.

Now, there are two kinds of belief in a self: (1) belief in a personal self—namely, that there really is an "I" whose interests should be made paramount, and (2) belief in any number of other selves. The meditator learns how to self-eradicate the belief in a personal self. If he succeeds only in getting rid of the personal-self belief, he is liberated as an arhat or pratyekabuddha. But eradication of belief in a personal self within dharmas of any kind—i.e., realization of phenomenal non-self—yields full enlightenment.

To become certain that neither type of self exists, rely on scripture, reason, and your teachers. There is no external thing that could be the object of a notion of an independently existing entity: things "out there" don't exist, any more than your own personal self does. The Hīnayāna schools get as far as expounding the doctrine of no personal self, but do not go into the nonexistence of external phenomena. Mahāyānists must examine the sūtras, where it is said that the realms of form, formlessness, and desire appear only because the mind makes projections that are the result of defiled and obscured perceptions. This takes us as far as the Mind-Only school.

48

If You Think of Yourself as a Tiger

DESPITE DIFFERENCES IN FORM, faculties, and social and political status, all beings are endowed with the same buddha-nature, due to which each one strives toward enlightenment. Nor is there any difference between the buddha-nature of the Buddha and that of other sentient beings: it is the same. Still, it is not correct to think that, since our buddha-nature is equal to the Buddha's, we don't have to try to achieve buddhahood. Nor is it true that, because all beings have buddha-nature, they will all become enlightened. Animals have buddha-nature but cannot achieve buddhahood. You must be a human being and have all the necessary opportunities and the eighteen requisite conditions. In other realms, such as the hell realms and animal realms, you cannot aim for buddhahood.

While you have such a precious human life, it is necessary to find a teacher who is qualified by his lineage to show others the right path, and who practices himself. When you have found such a teacher, you must have confidence in, and strive to understand, his teachings; when you have understood the teachings he gives you, you must then contemplate them; after that, you must meditate on what you have studied and practiced so as to gain the right experience. If you rightly implement whatever you have learned from your teacher, this will ultimately become a source of purification and merit. When you have gained purification and have enough merit, you will proceed on the path, which ultimately will become the path of the buddhas.

Of the four lineages of Tibetan Buddhism, we are following the Sakya lineage, which has numerous teachings as deep as the ocean. Of these, we have chosen to study the *Lam dre*, which is well known throughout Tibet. It has three parts: introduction, main body, and conclusion. We are now studying the introduction, entitled *The Three Visions*, which discusses the impure vision, the vision of experience, and the pure vision. The buddhas have only pure vision, for they possess no impurities. There are four parts to the impure vision: the nature of saṃsāra, the preciousness of human life, impermanence, and the law of karma. The vision of experience has three parts: great love, great compassion, and bodhichitta. We have already completed the sections on love and compassion and are now studying bodhichitta, which has two parts, the relative and the ultimate. We have completed the former and are currently discussing the latter. In developing bodhichitta, two kinds of meditation are necessary: concentration and insight. We have already discussed the first of these and now proceed with the second.

Insight meditation has a lengthy and profound explanation, much of which we have completed. The purpose is to realize selflessness. There are two different kinds of self, or identity: (1) human beings have a sense of personal self, and (2) dharmas—that is, all existing phenomena—have an identity; every phenomenon has its own self-nature. These are known as "personal self" and "phenomenal self," respectively.

We have such a feeling of self-nature and cherish our "self" so much that even in sleep we think or dream of ourselves, and during the daytime we experience happiness, unhappiness, frustration, and so on. All this is due to the belief in a self. Through the study of insight meditation, we must find out whether or not our "I" exists.

Now, while investigating this, I might assert that my personal name is the real evidence for the existence of an "I," or that my body is the object that I can consider to be the "I." However, I don't really believe that my name stands for my true nature, because when I was born, my parents used to call me "baby"; when I began to walk, I got the name Ngawang Sangpo; when I grew up, I was recognized as an incarnate lama and named Deshung Tulku; and when I moved to the United States, I was given a different name, Kunga Labrang. Thus I have had all these different names and cannot claim that any one of them is the real point on which I can posit my "I." Names were simply created and given to me.

I might claim that my body is the "I," but that is not true either, because when I die, my body may be cremated, buried, or thrown into a river, but I will not die with it: I will continue existing within the realms of the world.

And if you say that my mind is the basis of the "I," that is not true because consciousness is momentary in its duration. The mind that I have right now is not the same as the mind I had this morning. It changes momentarily and is comprised of moments of cognition, of successive thoughts.

Thus in none of these things—name, body, or mind—is an "I" found to exist. Since we can see that it is nonexistent, why do we have such a strong feeling of attachment to it? Why are we so concerned for its welfare? This is due only to the illusion of our mental conception of reality. For instance, if you see a rope in a dark place and someone says, "There's a big snake," you will get frightened, thinking it will bite you. Because of all the stories you've heard, you will not approach that rope but will try to avoid it. But if someone says, "That's not a snake, it's only a rope," you will take his word for it and feel no fear. You will be able to realize that it is only a rope.

Trying to understand the real nature of your self is something like realizing the true nature of the rope. When you create the notion of an "I" and cherish it, you have automatically created the notion of "others" as well. When there is such a sense of "I" and "you," you experience conflicts of all sorts, having to do with friendship, enmity, and the like. Due to all these circumstances, you accumulate karma. Yet if you understand the futility of the "I" and attain the realization of selflessness, there is no reason to commit all these unwholesome deeds.

Realizing your self-nature is the best way to subdue all evil forces, such as jealousy, ignorance, and hatred. And once you have realized your self-nature, you can proceed on the path of the buddhas and ultimately become enlightened. But as a prerequisite, you must understand and realize your own self-nature. This is the antidote to all harmful forces. Although I have already spoken about the "I" and self-nature, I will try to give a summary of the nature of the self so that it can be understood more fully.

Dharmas include everything: what we can see, what we hear, what we think, what the Buddha taught. Their nature is usually felt in three different ways: we all think that whatever we see, such as trees and rocks, is (a) permanent, (b) stable, and (c) real. This is the idea we use to hold them in our minds, and it is known as "attachment to dharmas." We must cut that attachment. The Buddha said that whatever appears is a creation of the mind. Thus, to cut this attachment, we must realize the nonexistence of dharma-nature itself and be able to prove that this nonexistence is something we can believe.

There are four different methods through which we can analyze this. The Buddha said that all phenomena are only mind; thus we use the Buddha's teachings as the first proof. The second proof is our intelligence. The third proof is our implementation, experience, and application of our thoughts. The fourth proof is the lamas' special teachings, which can be used to verify the first three methods of analysis. We have already finished the discussion of the Buddha's teachings. We will now discuss how we can use our intelligence in verifying the facts.

The things that we see are nonexistent in reality, because although we can conceive of something that does not exist, we can also conceive of that which does exist as being nonexistent. For example, a person with jaundice sees everything as yellow. If you put a white conch shell before him, he will see it as yellow; *you* know that it is actually white, but he can't see that: for him, the white conch does not exist, just as for you, the yellow one doesn't.

We also think that a given thing exists as many entities when it is actually one. For instance, take water: to human beings, it is a clear liquid that we bathe in and drink. But to beings in the cold hells, it appears as a great snowy mountain; to those in the hot hells, it appears as molten iron. To hungry ghosts, water appears as blood and pus; to animals, it appears to be a dwelling place or something to drink. To the demigods, it appears to be a huge pile of armaments; to the meditative gods, it seems to be meditation. To those who meditate on everything as infinite, water becomes as infinite as everything else; to those who believe in nothing but the mind, water is all-pervasive mind; and to those who see all things as nothing, it appears as nothing. This is a very difficult subject, very hard to understand, and one that requires a lot of study.

Do beings really exist as described in the six realms? Like the Buddha, the great Indian siddha Asanga, the bodhisattva Shāntideva, and many others have said that everything is the creation of mind. Water, which we took as an example, appears in different ways; no matter how much we think of it as real, it is only the creation of our minds and does not exist in reality. Only because of our misconceptions do we take everything to be existent. For instance, we say that there are all kinds of hell realms with floors of molten iron, sword-covered trees that you are forced to climb, and so on. But who would make such things? They are only the creations of our minds.

To resume, besides seeing one thing as many, we also see many things as one. For example, each of us thinks of our "self" as one person, yet we are made of billions of atoms. The conception that a single entity can be made of countless particles is false. There are many explanations for the combination of atoms in the different Buddhist schools. For instance, some Hīnayāna schools say that the sun's rays are made of seven times more particles than those we see, that these particles, or atoms, are permanent and existent, and that all things are made up of them, so that without them nothing exists. This is a very low order of Buddhist thought.

These schools also maintain that the minds we have now are different from the minds we had this morning. But they hold that, between these changes of mind, there is a very, very clear mind that has no direction and is permanent. That is to say, our thoughts come and go just as time is marked on a watch, and between all these thoughts there is a very clear, permanent mind. This mind lies between the obstruction of the last/past thought and the development of the next/future thought, and is thus an extremely subtle mind. For example, if there are 120 moments within one brief instant, the permanent mind exists for the duration of only one of these moments.

Just as we have the four orders in Tibetan Buddhism, so there were four schools of Buddhist philosophy in India—the Madhyamaka, Chittamātra (Mind-Only), Sautrāntika, and Vaibhāshika. Of these, the Sautrāntikas and the Vaibhāshikas believed in the theory we have just described, i.e., in a minute but permanent particle of mind between all past, present, and future thoughts. These lower groups say that such a minute particle has no direction. But if you get one atom from each direction and add them up to make that particle, it ultimately becomes a big one and does have direction. This nullifies the theory that such particles have no direction, size, or motion.

The defect of not accepting the theory of the dimensions and directions of atoms is that we cannot make any form larger than a single atom. Then, ultimately, nothing can exist. Thus we must accept the theory of the directions and dimensions of atoms argued by the Mind-Only school. If we don't believe in the theory of atoms, whatever we see is nonexistent, even in the realm of form itself.

The theory that all the great siddhas have emphasized is that all phenomena are the creation of your mind. This is illustrated by the story of a very highly accomplished yogi meditating near the Brahmaputra River. He got thirsty one day, so he got up and went to his water pot. He found that his pot was empty, so he went to a small spring, but it was dry. Since he was near the river, he went there, but found that it, too, was completely dry. He crossed the riverbed with his robes on but couldn't find any water, so he left his robes there and went home. He got up the next morning, went to the pot, and found it full of water. He went to the spring and found it full of water. The river was flowing again, and his robes were where he had left them on the other side. He had to get a boatman to take him across the water to retrieve his robes. All this appeared, or seemed to occur, due to the yogi still being in a state of illusion.

Thus we see that nothing exists in reality, even though we see many appearances. Why is this? It is due to our being in illusion, and to the impression of that illusion in our minds; since time immemorial, that illusory impression has been so strong that we cannot separate from it. For instance, when we are asleep, though we are actually wrapped in blankets and lying in bed, we dream that we are as active as in our waking time. There is a sūtra which says that while dreaming we can experience all the things we do while awake, such as eating, wearing clothes, and so on. When we wake up, we see that we were dreaming, but when we are dreaming, we think we are awake. By the same token, what we experience when we are awake is just the same as a dream.

A god's son asked Mañjushrī how we ought to think of, or see, external objects. Mañjushrī advised him that the way we see things is due to the illusory impression we have inherited since time immemorial, and that we should try to stop that impression. The god's son said to Mañjushrī, "No matter how much I try, that is not possible. The impression is too hard."

Mañjushrī said, "Yes, it can be. Once upon a time, there was a yogi in Vārānasī who loved tigers. He always meditated as if he himself were a tiger, and ultimately he turned into a tiger. So that is the truth: the impression of illusion is so strong that, if you think of yourself as a tiger, ultimately you may become one."

49

IT IS "NATURAL" NOT TO BE NATURAL

THE EIGHTY-FOUR THOUSAND TEACHINGS of Lord Buddha can be condensed into Hīnayāna and Mahāyāna groups, the latter of which we are studying. There are three parts to all Mahāyāna teachings and practices: (1) the introduction, (2) the main body of the lesson or meditation, and (3) the dedication of merit. At the outset, we generate the motivation to practice for the benefit of others. When we study or practice, we remain mindful that everything is illusory, like a dream. This contributes to fulfillment of the main body of the practice, which is emptiness. Finally, when we dedicate the merit, we think that, for the benefit of all sentient beings, we will purify ourselves of the two kinds of defilements.

These are not ordinary but special teachings, so we should not think of ourselves as ordinary beings; rather, we should feel ourselves to be superior. Also, we should see our teacher as a real buddha who is teaching us. We should visualize our location as Sukhāvatī itself (i.e., as a heavenly buddha-realm of great bliss), not as an ordinary place, and should imagine light rays emanating from the teacher's heart and purifying our defilements. At the same time, we should feel everything to be illusion.

There are four different schools in Tibet that are preserving and following the teachings. We are following one of them, the Sakyapa. Among these four groups, there is not the slightest difference in terms of how to develop bodhichitta, practice the six perfections, or achieve buddhahood. In terms of the path itself there are some small differences, but by following the paths of the different orders, there have been saints as numerous as the stars.

We are studying the *Lam dre*, the main essence teachings of the Buddha. The great siddha Virūpa analyzed this special lam-dre teaching, based on the Buddha's teachings in the *Kangyur*. It has three different parts, or visions, within the main body of the text. Although different names are given to this essential teaching by each of the four schools of Tibetan Buddhism, in practice they are all the same. The *Lam dre* has special techniques given by Virūpa. It has seven or eight different explanations, but we are following the one given by an abbot of Ewam Chöden known as Könchog Lhündrub. He was a highly accomplished lama both in terms of practice and knowledge, and his explanation is regarded as the best.

The three visions are the vision of impurity, the vision of experience, and the vision of purity. In considering the impure vision, we studied in detail the nature of saṃsāra, impermanence, and cause and effect. At the stage of experience, we have discussed compassion and love. The stage of purity covers the qualifications of the Buddha, his special marks, his names, and his outstanding qualities. We have yet to discuss this pure vision.

We are studying the vision of experience, in which we have already discussed love and compassion; we have yet to complete the discussion of ultimate bodhichitta, though we have finished that of conventional bodhichitta. When you study conventional or relative bodhichitta, try to understand how we exchange, how we share with others, how we develop love and compassion. In terms of ultimate bodhichitta, try to understand the true methods and benefits of concentration and insight meditation. We have already finished our discussion of concentration, and now continue our study of insight meditation.

Due to the force of all the negative aspects of our lives, such as hatred, ignorance, and jealousy, we have to pass through the cycles of misery, or saṃsāra. To subjugate all these harmful elements, we must have strong meditation. If we have stabilized concentrative meditation, that will subdue those negative aspects; if we have accomplished the high standard of insight meditation, that will dissolve even the mere influence of such unwholesome elements. But until we have mastered both, there is no way we can overcome our negative qualities.

To accomplish insight, we must first understand and realize the true nature of all existence. Then we must understand that whatever we see or hear is the creation of our own minds. This is very important, but people usually don't accept it as true. All the Buddha's teachings agree that everything is a creation of the mind, which can also be analyzed intellectually as to whether or not it is true. For example, human beings see water as for drinking or washing in; gods see it as nectar; demigods see it as a weapon; animals find it a place to live; hell beings see it as molten metal; and hungry ghosts see it as pus and blood. To each and every sentient being, it appears in a different way, which is why it is said to be a creation of our own minds. If that were not the case, then water would appear to all beings in the same way that it appears to us.

If everything is a creation of our own minds, how can there be mountains, oceans, and all other appearances? The answer is this: "Life is but a dream."

Things exist in a concrete form that we can see, but they do so because of the illusory impression imprinted on our minds since time immemorial. It is due to our previous experience that we see what we do in this life. For example, in our dreams, we can experience all sorts of things, but when we wake up, we understand that we were dreaming and are no longer attached to them. We dream that everything happens as if in reality, yet when we wake up, nothing has happened. Waking existence is like this, too; indeed, all existence is like this.

Another example, which we mentioned at the end of the last lesson, concerns the god's son who asked Mañjushrī how to view all phenomena in terms of their relationship toward matter and toward other beings. Mañjushrī said that nothing exists externally, that everything we perceive is due to the illusory impression of influences we have felt since time immemorial, and that this impact still continues. The god's son said that he understood this, but that no matter how strong the illusory impression could be, it couldn't produce mountains and so on. Mañjushrī said, "Yes, you can have the illusion of mountains, and I will show you an example." Mañjushrī said that once, in Vārānasī, there was a yogi who used to visualize that he himself was a tiger, and ultimately he became one. Many people saw him and ran away out of fear; this was how strongly he thought of himself as a tiger, and that thinking became a reality.

Sakya Pandita said, in his logical analysis entitled the *Treasure of Knowledge and Reasoning* (*Tshad ma rigs gter*), that everything is a creation of mind, but that those who have a very strong impression of past experience have a more stabilized sense of everything as reality, while those who don't have such a strong impression have some sense that things are an illusion. Even the inferior schools of Buddhist philosophy accept that all phenomena are creations of mind. In one school, it is said that mind creates all. Another school is not as correct; it holds that, although phenomena are reflections of mind, the mind itself is real.

According to Vasubandhu, too, everything is the creation of mind. Thus, if there is nothing ultimately to be attached to, there can be no attachment. If we understand this teaching, we will be less driven by desire and aversion. By not dividing all phenomena into good or bad, we will experience equanimity. But even then, we will create new karma unless we also realize that all phenomena are completely empty.

The nonexistence of phenomena can be further delineated by considering the interdependence of subject and object. If objects don't exist, there can be no consciousness of objects. If consciousness doesn't exist, then objects cannot exist to be cognized. This underscores the ultimate groundlessness of self. Chandrakīrti, expounding on the principles of Nāgārjuna, said:

> If there is no object, there is no subject that can know it. Since subject and object are interdependent, if there is no subject, there can be no object.

This can be understood by considering the nature of all sets of opposites: right and left, top and bottom, mountain and valley, and so on. The two opposites of each pair are mutually dependent: they define each other; without one, the other couldn't exist. It is just like this with subject and object: if the object doesn't exist, then mind doesn't exist; if mind doesn't exist, the object cannot exist. In this context, all phenomena can be seen to be nonexistent. Likewise, the concepts of "I" and "you," like other relative views, can be shown to be nonexistent in absolute reality. This is the reasoning asserted by Nāgārjuna and other Madhyamaka sages.

Since beginningless time, however, we have clung to these dualities of subject and object, self and other, as real. Because of this, the impact of appearances has led us into travail in samsaric existence. But if there is nothing to be attached to, then there is no one to be attached; if there is no "you," there is no "I." In ultimate reality, nothing is existent, nor is there any mind. If you first immerse your mind in equanimity and then meditate on the nature of mind under the guidance of a qualified teacher, you will find the mind to be absolutely clear. This is the so-called nonduality of clarity and emptiness (*gsal-stong zung-'jug*). It cannot really be pointed out or directly shown; it must be realized.

All sentient beings are endowed with basic buddha-nature. There is no difference between a buddha and the lowliest ant in terms of basic nature; if there were such a difference, we could not hope to achieve buddhahood. Because of the ultimate sameness of all beings, we can in fact reach the same status as the buddhas. The only difference between ourselves and the enlightened ones is that we are clouded with mental impurities and karmic contaminations.

After meditating on Maitreya for twelve years, the pandit Asanga was ushered by that bodhisattva into the pure land called Tushita, where he was given many teachings. He spent the equivalent of fifty human years in Tushita, although only a few of our hours passed before he returned to this world. After this, he became, along with Nāgārjuna, one of the excellent holders of the Buddha's teaching.

Asanga, like the Buddha and others, stated that everything is the creation of mind. But what of mind itself? If objects don't exist, then mind cannot exist. Thus separated from all attachment, the true nature and clarity of mind become manifest. In this light, mind itself is none other than the *dharmadhātu*;[77] mind in its true nature is the basis of all existence. If we realize this, we can then realize the dharmakāya and have all the outstanding qualities of a buddha, but if we remain ignorant of the true nature of mind, we will continue to wander in saṃsāra. It is also mentioned in one of the Sakya texts that mind is the basis of all phenomena, and that if we realize this, we can reach the state of the dharmakāya.

The true nature of mind is clear. It has been likened to a cleaned glass, and is referred to as the "clear light" in the six yoga teachings of the Kagyu order. In one text, it says that there is no mind but only this clear light, and that when we are able to understand this nature of mind, we will likewise understand the nature of saṃsāra. In another text, it is said that to attain buddhahood we must first understand emptiness; thus realization of emptiness is a prerequisite to enlightenment. Yet another text holds that every phenomenon is perceived by mind: the clearer the mind, the more clearly we will perceive phenomena. And Saraha said that the nature of mind is the real wish-fulfilling gem. Knowledge of the mind's ultimate nature will bring us to real liberation from the sufferings of saṃsāra. Until now, we have been misguided due to ignorance of the true nature of mind, but when we do realize it, that will be sufficient.

We must try to understand who we are. Meditate as follows: sit in the correct meditation posture and be as natural as possible. Remain in the present, focusing on neither past nor future. Sitting like this, you will see that it is "natural" not to be natural. Thoughts arise. The point is not to be victimized by these thoughts—simply let them pass and visualize the clear aspect of mind. In this way, you will eventually obtain unabstractible insight; subsequently, you will develop this insight in a stable fashion and will maintain it even when engaged in other activities. At that point, the sense of the emptiness of phenomena will always be with you.

50

PAYING THE TAX OF COMPULSIVENESS

A LAMA WAS REQUESTED TO GIVE a teaching on the nature of the mind, so he asked three people to go into different rooms to sleep, and in the morning to return with an explanation of the mind. The next morning, two came earlier than the third. The first said, "Yes, mind is white." The second said, "No, mind is black."

Then the third appeared, crying, "Oh, Lama, I didn't sleep all night, trying to find out how the mind works. But I failed completely. These other two were very fortunate because they were able to find a result to tell you. I'm an unlucky fellow; I haven't been able to find out where the mind is or how it works."

The lama said, "Yes, these are two great liars. You are very good. Mind is something that even the Buddha was not able to find out." Later, the third man became a great disciple.

We have said that there are three different feelings, or perceptions: those of impurity, experience, and purity. We have concluded the teachings on impurity and are proceeding with the teachings on bodhichitta from the viewpoint of meditative experience. Remember that there are two kinds of bodhichitta, relative and ultimate. We have already discussed relative bodhichitta. Ultimate bodhichitta also has two parts, concentration and insight. We have finished the teachings about the former; on the latter, we have discussed the idea that mind creates all phenomena, asserting that since nothing has ultimate reality, everything must be a creation of our minds. To see whether or not this is true, we have consulted the Buddha's teachings, analyzing them and applying our understanding and knowledge. We have also finished this aspect of the teaching.

We have come to the heart of our subject. To gain buddhahood, we must realize our true nature, which is, in reality, nonexistence. By acquiring such a knowledge through concentration and insight, we can gain buddhahood and, ultimately, the dharmakāya. To understand and practice insight meditation, we must first understand the nature of our own minds.

❧ ❧ ❧

First, you must understand the different acts of the six senses: taste, touch, smell, sight, hearing, and mental consciousness. Mental consciousness is the real focal point for understanding the nature of mind, since the senses are all generated by the mind itself. When we see objects through our eyes, we must know that they are motivated by the mind. When we apprehend a beautiful appearance, we have a sense of attachment; when we see something ugly, we have a sense of disgust and rejection, not because of how the object looks but because of what the mind says. We must understand the true nature of our consciousness, which acts in these five ways. After realizing this, we will come to the conclusion that the five senses are prompted by mental consciousness.

The five senses are known as noncognizable consciousness, whereas mental consciousness is cognizable. That is, the five different senses have no independence; it is mental consciousness that uses and directs them as the mind wishes. Say you have a big house with five windows and one monkey inside who looks from them. From outside, it may look like there are five different monkeys, but in reality there is only one. The nature of the mind is like that. Hence, when you meditate, try to have a posture like a stone. Do not look outside; if you open your senses and look outward, you will not be meditating. Try to look in on the mind that directs these senses.

When different thoughts are constantly being generated due to hatred and attachment, you will be unable to attain concentration or insight. Hence you need to recognize all these thoughts, how they are developed, and whether or not they change. After this recognition, do not reflect on what you have been doing or anticipate what you will be doing, but have no thoughts. Try to see yourself and the nature of your mind as very lucid, full of airiness, and as clear as the sky—so spacious you cannot measure it, so empty you cannot point at anything that can be called mind. Whether your meditation is concentration or insight, you should come upon this point of lucidity and spaciousness—for it is believed that the mind is that union of emptiness and crystal clarity—and on that point you should meditate.

Briefly, when you have a mood without any thoughts, a sense of calm that lasts for a while, you are approaching concentration; when you understand that the mind is empty and clear, that you cannot point it out or understand its color or shape, you are nearing insight. Once you understand the mind without looking back or ahead and can concentrate on your meditation without being disturbed by thoughts, that can be called concentration. When you understand yourself as nonexistent of true nature in reality and see yourself as infinite and yet very clear, that is the significance of insight meditation.

From now on, it is important that, when meditating, you gaze not outward but inward, using your mind to understand your mind. A simile may help bring this point home. When there are no clouds, the sky is very spacious, very clear, and so vast that it cannot be measured. But suppose there is never a time when it is unclouded: the ordinary mind is something like that. It never has any freedom when it is clouded by constant thoughts, and when a patch of blue does appear, perhaps due to meditation, it is soon covered over again.

This teaching has taken some time, and I don't know how beneficial it has been for you, but to recapitulate the important points: try to understand (1) the focal point, which is mind, and (2) how to meditate, as well as what to meditate on. If you came here merely to pay the tax of compulsiveness, it won't benefit you to the extent of really understanding the teachings, even though hearing such teachings does have merit and can bring fruit. To reiterate, all the external measures of phenomena are the creations of our mind, but mind itself is empty, baseless. Though it is full of clarity, still it is empty. Hence meditation is needed.

When every external matter is the creation of mind, and mind is empty, that nullifies the misconception of duality and indicates that every phenomenon is nonexistent: we are nonexistent, objects and subjects are nonexistent. In Chittamātrin (Mind-Only) philosophy, all external matter is impermanent but mind itself is permanent, existent in reality. Chittamātrins describe mind as a self-realizing mirror that can understand itself. But if that is the case, why is it that a knife, no matter how sharp, cannot cut itself? A finger cannot touch itself, and a lamp, however brightly it can light up the darkness, cannot illuminate itself. Similarly, the mind is such that it cannot see itself. Chittamātrins do not give the true explanation of the nature of mind.

Shāntideva and Madhyamaka teachings counter the Chittamātrin belief, which is not acceptable in terms of Mahāyāna teaching. They try to prove that the true nature of mind is nonexistent in reality and in substance. As a watch ticks away minute by minute and second by second, so the flow of our thoughts is unstoppable, and as they vanish, all our thoughts die. Hence mind cannot observe itself. If the mind is true, then we must know its size, shape, and color. This no one has understood so far. Where, then, does mind exist? Inside the body or outside? From all aspects, it is nonexistent.

Buddha said that mind has no color, shape, or size, that it is abstract. He gave a full explanation in the *Kangyur* volumes of the Tibetan Buddhist canon. Vajrapāni said that the nature of mind is such that no past, present, or future buddha has understood or will understand it and be able to speak about it so that ordinary human beings can understand it. The Buddha told Vajrapāni that the mind is not of any color or any shape, not short or long, not like daylight or darkness, and not like any of the sexes, male, female, or neuter; it is not the body of desire, nor is it of the world of form. It is none of these. It does not lie outside or inside our bodies, and it does not stay anywhere.

This is also said in the *Mahākāshyapa Chapter Sūtra*. Kāshyapa was one of the main disciples of the Buddha; he requested the Buddha to teach on the nature of mind and then composed a book which states that mind lies neither inside nor outside nor in between and that it cannot, indeed, be found. The Buddha said that if you don't find anything when you look for the mind, then there is nothing to imagine, meditate on, or aim at it.

A god's son asked the Buddha to teach him, and the Buddha said that all phenomena are a creation of the mind, but that mind is not something you can point out, because it is unabstractible and formless. You won't be able to discover the nature of mind even if you try. Your own mind cannot see the nature of mind; if it could, you wouldn't be able to have your own mind. Thus, since mind itself is such, everything is nonexistent in ultimate reality.

Hearing this, the god's son asked, "Why is the mind such a hard thing to discover?"

The Buddha replied, "Because it does not have to take any birth, or origin, like other sentient beings. As it does not have any origination, it is so baseless, so pointless, that we cannot point it out no matter how much we look for it."

Why doesn't mind have any origination? The Buddha said that if it had an origin, it would have form or color. If you want to know who came first, the Buddha or sentient beings, you won't be able to find out, just as you can't know which came first, the chicken or the egg.

Similarly, all phenomena are very hard to explain. For instance, if we touch fire we get burned. Why? Though the nature of fire is heat, why should it burn? The nature of fire is heat; that is all the explanation we can give. No one knows how or where that heat is started. Thus fire has no origin; likewise, the mind has no origin.

If we say mind has a seed or substance, we must then prove how this is developed. For instance, when we sow rice, it sprouts, shoots come out of the ground, and then there is a rice plant. But the rice is in some sense distorted, and mind cannot come from such a process. Without distorting or changing the seed, there cannot be a fruit; it is impossible for seed and fruit to exist simultaneously.

Therefore, you will not be able to find a place of origin or abidance for the mind, nor the ultimate place where mind is abstracted: the mind is like the sky. Jetsün Dragpa Gyaltsen supports the Buddha's statement that the mind is as empty as the sky, but cautions that one should not therefore think that the mind is baseless or mere nonsense. This would be an emotional, negative thought.

How should you think of mind? You should not shape it; let it remain as natural as possible; don't try to change the course of thought. This is the true and correct way of meditating. If you think that mind is originless and so on, you will be creating yet another kind of thought, which will be detrimental to your practice.

Next, the god's son asked the Buddha, "Is it your philosophy that mind is nonexistent? Isn't it terminated at a certain time?"

The Buddha answered that he didn't deny the existence of the mind itself: "That is another kind of extreme. We have to be at the border, without saying yes or no." He wanted to be in the middle; that is why he started teaching the Madhyamaka philosophy.

Shāntideva, too, said that we must remain on the Middle Way without confining ourselves to yes or no. The mind is such that it is neither existence nor nonexistence, not a combination of both, and not something different from these three. You simply cannot prove the true nature of mind from any of these four directions, because it is something in the middle of them all. In the *Kangyur* it says that mind is not something understood by any buddha, yet it is the basis on which the wheel of saṃsāra is turned. In spite of this, it is not something the Buddha understood or clarified.

Whatever we do in practice, we must fulfill three main points: (1) hearing and understanding the different teachings, (2) meditating on these teachings, and (3) from meditation, gaining certain experiences. Through repeated meditation, we can develop a sense of knowledge and clear realization. Right now, we don't have any of these qualities, so we are beginning with hearing and need to listen carefully to what our teachers have to say.

An understanding of the teachings is not sufficient unless you implement what you understand. Through the knowledge you gain from hearing, understanding, and then meditating, you will be able to understand the true teachings of concentration and insight. The fruit of insight will come from inside rather than from outside. You will not manifest the practice of concentration or that of insight in concrete form; through repeated efforts you may have good insight and concentration, but this won't happen without meditation. Understanding alone will not help; otherwise, there would be many siddhas and bodhisattvas among us, because many people devote a lot of time to study these days. But to gain enlightenment, you must have experience as well as knowledge—i.e., you must practice as well as understand.

51

AWAKENING CERTITUDE

THE LAM-DRE SYSTEM OF MEDITATION includes the most profound and effective methods for attaining the perfection of buddhahood. It originated with the primordial Buddha himself and was transmitted via the great Indian sage Virūpa and many generations of enlightened masters to the present. We should approach this profound teaching with the pure intention of taking to heart its instructions, which, if followed, result in nothing less than the realization of true reality.

These instructions, as you know, concern the preliminary and advanced stages of practice. We are learning the instructions for the preliminary level, which have been codified in the three progressive stages described in *The Three Visions*. The first stage, or vision, which is intended to develop a sense of renunciation, includes meditations on death and impermanence, the faults of worldly existence, and so forth. Once these have been achieved, the meditator is encouraged to go on to the second stage and develop a universalist attitude toward his spiritual goal by cultivating love, compassion, and the right view of emptiness. We have completed the instructions for these first two stages of practice, except for the very last topic in the second stage, namely, the development of bodhichitta.

As you recall, there are two kinds of bodhichitta. The first is the conventional, which is to be developed through meditations on the sameness of self and others and the exchange of self and others, whereby egotistical impulses are modified and subdued. The second type, ultimate bodhichitta, is realized by means of the two stages of meditation, concentration and insight. Through these, the false beliefs in a real, personal self and in the reality of phenomena in general are eradicated. Through realization of these two kinds of non-self, the meditator attains the experience of ultimate bodhichitta. We have concluded our teachings on concentration and have been discussing insight. It is at this point that we resume our studies.

A Mahāyānist earnestly aims to achieve total enlightenment. He or she makes efforts directed solely toward the attainment of buddhahood, in order to accomplish the highest good of all living beings, bar none. The methods on which such a person must rely have been described as the six transcendent virtues: giving, moral conduct, patience, vigor, meditation, and wisdom. Through mastering them, enlightenment is obtained. The first five are instrumental in the accumulation of merit, not wisdom, for they are accomplished with reference to an object, and hence are what is known as "object-endowed practices": we make gifts to a recipient, practice patience toward an enemy, and so forth. Through their practice we do indeed perform virtue, and the result of virtuous actions is merit. But it is the sixth pāramitā that produces wisdom, the second essential factor needed to attain the goal of buddhahood.

The sixth pāramitā produces not merit but wisdom because it has no object. Wisdom that courses in objectlessness is the most important of the six perfections because it is insight into the selflessness, or true nature, of internal and external phenomena that truly liberates the human mind from what is known as "bondage." It is also this insight that guides the mind in performing the other five perfections, so that they become truly conducive to enlightenment rather than mere virtuous actions accomplished at random and for odd purposes. Indeed, merit becomes transcendent only when informed by wisdom. Thus wisdom is often praised in the sūtras as the eye, or guide, to the five "blind" pāramitās. Just as a whole train of blind men stumbling along the road will not be able to reach the city on their own, so the first five pāramitās alone can never bring one to buddhahood. But taken in hand by the sixth pāramitā, the other five are easily led to the City of Enlightenment. For this reason, wisdom is extolled as the highest and most important of the six perfections. And since wisdom is none other than the meditation of insight that we are discussing, all this is by way of introduction to what I am going to say next.

I could say a great deal about this profound view of insight, which we are referring to as transcendent wisdom, insight meditation, or the realization of ultimate reality, but will, instead, attempt only the briefest explanation possible. Much as one might extract only the butter from a hundred gallons of milk, I will extract only the most essential points of this doctrine for our discussion.

Just as the Nyingmapas have their highest doctrine of dzog-chen, and the Kagyupas speak of mahāmudrā, so we Sakyapas have a term for this view of ultimate reality, namely, "the nonduality of clarity and voidness" (*gsal-stong zung-'jug*). This view, which is also known as "the nondifferentiation of saṃsāra and nirvāṇa" (*'khor-'das-dbyer-med*), is the quintessential doctrine of the Sakya tradition. If you understand this view, you are a Sakyapa. Everybody in Tibet knew that this view was identified with the Sakya tradition, and that only a Sakyapa would be able to understand and perceive it.

If you suspect that you haven't quite attained this view, I suggest that you pray very earnestly to the great Sakya Pandita that he bless you with the awakening of this insight by the power of his own buddhahood. This can be helped along by taking the trouble to sit from time to time, with your mind clear and at ease, and—after invoking Sakya Pandita's blessings—by observing your own mind and trying to see its nature. Through this practice, reinforced by virtuous deeds of body, voice, and mind, you will gradually begin to experience the awakening of this very rare view. It is difficult to achieve, but it is achievable. It is rare in the world, but it can be attained by those who have sincere hearts and who use the right methods. As the rarest thing in the world, it is certainly worth seeking.

There are three essential steps in the attainment of this exalted view of the nonduality of voidness and clarity. The first is "recognition of clarity" (*gsal-ba-ngo-bzung*), that is, recognition of the true nature of mind. It is implicit in this recognition that all appearances are expressions of mind alone: all that you experience is merely a manifestation of your own individual consciousness. As Jetsün Dragpa Gyaltsen stressed, the view that there are no phenomena outside mind is essential to the process of Mahāyāna meditation.

Although all appearances do indeed appear to be external to mind, they are no more so than are the various appearances perceived in the dream state. Just as those dream appearances are nothing more than projections of the mind that perceives them, so when you awaken to enlightenment, you realize that all appearances and experiences of this world are dreamlike, illusionlike, and in themselves quite unreal. With this knowledge, you seek to understand the nature of that mind which is the source of all these appearances. Through introspection, you focus mind on mind and come to the conclusion that mind cannot be isolated as an existent entity. There is no entity there of which it can be said, "This is the mind" or "That is mind." This brings about a realization of the void nature of mind, as well as the understanding that, though the mind is not existent as we like to think of entities existing, nonetheless, it is also not "nonexistent."

Mind is not merely the absence of anything. It is not simply a "no thing," a nothing. Through its power of cognition, mind does have the attribute of consciousness, and you can't distinguish between the two any more than you can separate heat from flame. You can't say, "This is the flame and this is the heat." When you touch the flame and feel pain from the heat, you cannot blame the burn that you feel on either the heat or the flame alone. They are simply nondual by nature, and so it is with mind. Its nature consists of its nonduality of voidness and cognition, or voidness and clarity.

This insight leads you to understand that you cannot view the mind as existent (as a thing) or as nonexistent (as something that simply doesn't exist). Nor is it a combination of thing and nothing, nor is it neither of these. The true nature of mind is away from the conceptual "tetralemma" that it either (1) is, (2) is not, (3) is and is not, or (4) neither is nor is not. Here you need to forget about theory. I want you to see for yourself the nondual nature of your mind. I want you to be able to tell me what it is like.

The second step needed to realize the nonduality of clarity and voidness is "absorption of the mind in extremelessness" (*mtha'-brel*), that is, realization that the nature of mind is away from the four extremes just noted. None of these four is adequate to describe the truth; none correlates with the mind's true nature. Although this sounds like mere theory, let us not underestimate the exalted nature of this view. It is difficult to attain but it is attainable. It is rarely attained because even extremely learned men, who quote sūtras and know complicated doctrines, may yet be ignorant of this "entering of the mind into extremelessness," in which case they don't know the heart of Mahāyāna Buddhism. Moreover, a person ignorant of learning may yet attain this insight and be enlightened by it via "the liberation of knowing all things through knowing one thing." That is, once you know this one thing, you know everything, whereas others may know many things but fail in insight into this single essential perspective.

The third step is called "awakening certitude about the ineffable" (*brjod-brel-la nges-shes-skye-ba*). Now, if you are thinking that insight into the nature of mind as away from all extremes is the true nature of mind, it is not. There is no such thing as a state that is away from all extremes, although each of the four possible extremes has been negated. But that state of ultimate mind which does not correspond to any of these four is not something in itself that we can then point to and say, "It wasn't this extreme, it wasn't that one, nor the third possibility, nor the fourth, but it is something else, which we will call the Madhyamaka ultimate view. There is something left, and whatever it is, we will call it the ultimate point of view and say, 'This is it.'"

The state of mind away from all extremes is therefore called ineffable, inexpressible, and indescribable. It is inconceivable; it is beyond the possibility of expression through words or concepts. The human mind cannot possibly grasp it in the terms in which that mind functions. It is simply an experience of ultimate reality, of insight, in which all these concepts and possible modes of being are inadequate.

As we said, modes of being—existence, nonexistence, both of them, neither of them—in no case apply to the ultimate nature of mind. They are all inadequate. Therefore, the *King of Concentrations Sūtra* says that existence and nonexistence, pure and impure, are merely extremes. The sage relinquishes both extremes but does not dwell in the middle, either. The minute you apprehend that particular view and say, "This is the one that's away from all four extremes, and I've got it," you haven't got it. Some foolish people will say that there is, then, no Middle Way—no Buddha and no path. This is called the extreme of nihilism. Others will say, "If the mind is not nonexistent, it's got to be existent. If it's not nothing, it's got to be something." Such people fall into the extreme of eternalism.

The wise man avoids eternalism and nihilism and at the same time does not take his stand on the middle ground between these two. Yet this avoidance of extremes *is* another position. That is why this "ultimate point of view" is inexpressible—because it's inconceivable to the ordinary human mind, whether we use words, concepts, or any other mental functions. Nonetheless, it is an authentic experience of a real, enlightened point of view. As Jetsün Dragpa Gyaltsen wrote in one of his songs, "That state which is away from extremes is not an object of expression."

Hence "the Middle Way," "Mind-Only," and so on are merely terms for ultimate reality, the state of inexpressible extremelessness. These words and concepts in no way correspond to the experience of that ultimate state. If a meditator does not attain direct perception of the ultimate state of mind and meditate according to the instructions for nongrasping, he will inevitably fall into the mistake of trying to apprehend the ultimate, however he conceives of it. Although he may think he is avoiding doing so, even by that much effort he falls into the mistake of apprehension.

The only thing you must do at this stage of practice is realize that this ineffable state is beyond the possibility of apprehension, that you can't seize on it as being this, that, or any other thing. You can't call it anything in Buddhist or non-Buddhist vocabulary, and you cannot possibly capture it by any mental effort. Just realize that its nature is one of nondual clarity and voidness, which do not in any way differ from each other or obstruct each other. This direct experience is all that matters, but it is not something that anyone can apprehend, cling to, dwell in, communicate, or anything else. It is beyond the possibility of all of these.

Please remember that, although the ultimate point of view, or state of mind, may sound quite abstract, I am discussing a real experience at the very heart of all that Mahāyāna Buddhism is about. Go and meditate on the nondual clarity and emptiness of your own mind, with which all other beings are also endowed.

52

TASTING SUGARCANE FOR THE FIRST TIME

LET US KEEP IN MIND the three requisite factors for successful study on the Mahāyāna path: (1) excellence in attitude as we undertake to study the Dharma; (2) excellence in insight, i.e., keeping in mind the essential nature of reality while studying the various stages of the path; and (3) excellence in dedication of merit, i.e., wholeheartedly turning over to all beings the benefits derived from study. These correspond to the three stages of practice: (a) the preliminary stage, when we lay the foundation for meditation or study; (b) the main practice, when we actually meditate or study our main topic; and (c) the conclusion, when we turn over all accumulated merit to other beings, that our efforts may have the maximum beneficial effect.

Let us also recall the three quintessential factors whose presence makes Mahāyānist practices successful and whose absence makes it questionable whether or not we are following the Mahāyāna path: (i) ensuring that our intent is pure, i.e., directed toward the eventual attainment of buddhahood, in order to become able to remove the sufferings of all living beings; (ii) listening to the teachings single-pointedly, trying to retain the words and their meaning within our minds, and remembering the ultimate nature of dharmas (here we should try to think of the present situation as a dream that is empty of any inherent nature of its own, thus freeing ourselves from concepts of teacher, student, and lesson, and approximating, at least to some degree, the ultimate nature of all things, which are devoid of any real nature of their own); and (iii) being mindful, from the heart, to offer whatever merit we have acquired in our efforts to listen to the Dharma to the true happiness and benefit of all other beings.

To understand the significance of our efforts to learn the Dharma, let us consider the significance of the present situation. The great bodhisattva Shāntideva wrote in his *Bodhicharyāvatara* that the purpose of human existence is attainment of the rare opportunity to realize the holy teachings of enlightenment. If this opportunity is wasted, how will it ever be regained? We have been so fortunate as to obtain human birth and come into contact with the teachings of enlightenment. Further, we have had the good fortune to meet spiritual friends and teachers who are willing and able to explain those teachings and guide us in their practice and realization. Finally, we have the leisure to put those teachings into practice and experience for ourselves the Great Way and the perfection of buddhahood.

Is it not the height of self-deception to squander such an opportunity through carelessness, laziness, distraction, or a lack of appreciation of its true value? Having lost such a chance, where is the guarantee that we will ever regain it? From what source will we again enjoy this auspicious conjuncture of human existence, sufficient merit to find the teachings and teachers, and leisure to practice?

The gods who inhabit the realms of the devas are endowed with long lives. They may dwell at ease for what seem to us to be incalculable periods of time. Even those humans who are born in the northern world system, known as the continent of Uttarakuru, have a fixed life span of a thousand years, and there are other species who live for what seem to us to be very long periods of time. But human beings are not like that; their life span is very brief. Even a so-called long human life is only rarely achieved in this world. People die at all stages of life. The number that attains even seven to ten decades is quite small, so we haven't any guarantee of long life, or even of reaching old age.

Not only is human life limited by its nature of impermanence, it is brief, and the causes of death are many, while the causes of life are few. Human existence is also conditioned by karma, the operation of the law of cause and effect. It is our karmic actions of body, voice, and mind that have brought us this far. If we are honest we will recognize that, for the most part, our deeds are not really motivated by, and do not really produce, virtue, but are rooted in the defiled states of mind—selfishness, desire, ignorance, anger, and the like. Hence they will only result in a further accumulation of unwholesome karma, which is the very thing that binds us here. The negative mental states have kept us wandering about in worldly existence from beginningless time, and this same pattern of action and result is still going on.

To take stock of our present situation, we have to consider our karmic destiny in light of our present opportunity to practice the Dharma. Could we really bear to experience the animal and hell realms? Could we stand, even for a moment, just a small part of the intense tortures that those beings endure? Consider the extreme mental darkness, ignorance, confusion, and fear experienced by animals, and the various other kinds of suffering that make samsaric existence painful by nature for all beings. In human existence, we are subject to the pains of birth, disease, old age, death, meeting with what we dislike, parting from what we like, and being forced to do what we would not. Even the long-lived gods are subject to the terrible mental agony of falling into the lower realms; their existence, too, is limited by the law of karma, and they suffer unbearably through having to undergo the sudden loss of happiness.

Even in the "happy" realms of humans and gods, there are three kinds of generalized suffering that no one can avoid: (1) the suffering of pain per se (mental and physical pain of one kind or another, birth, death, and so forth), (2) the pain of change (in our fortune or circumstances, in our physical or mental well-being, and being forced to part with what we love and to encounter what we dislike), and (3) the suffering inherent in conditioned existence (human existence arises from ignorance, desire, aversion, and the misapprehension of reality; rooted as it is in these basically erroneous causes, human life is caught up in the suffering of conditioned existence).

Having taken stock of our situation, our next logical consideration should be what to do about it. This has been answered succinctly in two lines from the *Abhidharmakosha*, by the great Indian sage Vasubandhu: "One who abides in moral conduct and applies himself to study and reflection should then become assiduous in the practice of meditation."

Let us take this as a guideline for what to do about being human, and hence both beset by problems and blessed with opportunities for liberation. The Enlightened One and all the authentic great teachers throughout the centuries have taught that, to be a genuine follower of Mahāyāna Buddhism, you should awaken within yourself an enlightened attitude. Through love and compassion for all living beings, you will develop the unshakable, sincere resolve to strive for their highest good. Since that can only be achieved by your own attainment of buddhahood, this resolve shapes and guides your efforts on the spiritual path. One who has this intent at heart will not wish to deceive beings by failing to help them through right practice. Hence the sincere Mahāyānist will train in the six perfections not because they are nice, but because their accomplishment is a natural outflow and expression of bodhichitta, the resolve to win enlightenment for the sake of others.

The bodhisattva, or follower of the Mahāyāna path, understands that, to fulfill his resolve, he needs both merit and wisdom. He must acquire merit to purify former accumulations of unwholesome karma and to attune the mind to the stages of holiness, while wisdom is required to see things as they really are and to escape the various forms of bondage. Hence the six perfections are a natural expression of the bodhisattva's resolve. His or her training in giving, patience, and moral conduct are the methods whereby merit is accumulated. According to most teachers, the fifth pāramitā, meditation, is also included in the accumulation of merit, while the sixth, wisdom, constitutes the bodhisattva's accumulation of wisdom itself. Since the fourth pāramitā—diligence, or vigor—is required in the development of both merit and wisdom, it belongs to both categories. It is through diligence alone that you will succeed in accumulating merit through the first four pāramitās, and likewise through diligence alone that you develop the insight whereby you acquire transcendent gnosis, or wisdom.

Thus, as the sūtras all agree, it is through the bodhisattva's training in the six pāramitās that he acquires the two essential elements that constitute enlightenment, namely, transcendent merit and transcendent wisdom. Wisdom is paramount because it guides a person in the other perfections of giving, patience, morality, diligence, and meditation. Wisdom prevents his getting caught up in them and treating them as real, or as ends in themselves.

Informed by transcendent wisdom, which has no object, the first five virtues go beyond merely producing good fortune and happiness in relation to their objects (e.g., the giver, gift, and recipient) and become truly meritorious: they, too, become transcendent, and their merit then results only in the attainment of total liberation. It is transcendent wisdom alone that enables them to move beyond the limitations of worldly virtue.

Just as a great bird flying through space requires two wings to remain aloft, so the bodhisattva requires both merit and wisdom to keep him spiritually aloft, free from bondage in saṃsāra yet eschewing nirvāṇa out of his compassion for beings. The bodhisattva remains spiritually alive and active through his accumulation of these two transcendent factors. The direct result is, as the sūtras tell us, attainment of the bodies of buddhahood. These include the two Form Bodies—the nirmāṇakāya, or Illusory Body, and the sambhogakāya, or Communication Body—and the dharmakāya, or Body of Reality (also called the Body of Transcendent Gnosis). The Form Bodies result from the accumulation of transcendent merit, while the Body of Reality is the result of the bodhisattva's accumulation of insight.

As you train in these six pāramitās, with the resolve to attain buddhahood and the intent to devote yourself to the practice of meditation, seek out learned teachers of the Dharma for explanations of the stages and doctrines of the path, and for instructions on how to practice. Also try to receive tantric empowerments from qualified teachers, thereby gaining the direct blessings of the bodhisattvas, Buddhist deities, and lineage of enlightened masters. All these influences help to strengthen your efforts to practice steadily in the face of distractions, defilements, and obstacles, within and without. You will be able to obtain experience of the Path with Its Result much more quickly if you rely on spiritual friends and spiritual factors.

We should think again and again about what we have learned from these teachers, trying to employ their advice in our spiritual efforts, both in daily life and in meditative sessions. Besides making the best efforts we can in study, reflection, and meditation, we must be mindful to observe the vows and precepts we have taken upon ourselves, starting with the refuge vow. That is where it all begins, when we take the refuge vow to become a Buddhist, so we must always observe the refuge precepts. Then, as we undertake to follow the Mahāyāna path of training in the pāramitās, we take the bodhisattva vows, and on the tantric level of meditation, we assume tantric vows.

We must be mindful of our pledges to remain within the ambits of the path by not neglecting those vows. If, to the best of our ability, we observe the precepts we have taken on and train in the pāramitās and in the development of tantric meditations, then we can feel some surety about attaining the results of our efforts. Just as suffering is the result of erroneous views and unwholesome actions, so the experience of happiness, all the way up to the attainment of total liberation, is nothing more or less than the result of right actions guided by right vision.

All these factors mentioned as essential to the attainment of enlightenment are elucidated in the lam-dre system of meditation. This system is the direct communication of the Buddha in his tantric aspect of Vajradhara, in which he expounded the *Hevajra Tantra*. In the process, two secondary tantras of explication evolved, called the *Vajra Tent of the Ḍākiṇī* and the *Saṃputa*. Based on these, the great Indian siddha Virūpa expounded, in the form of a commentary, the *Lam dre* as we have it today, codifying the essential elements in his *Vajra Verses*. He transmitted this teaching to his own disciples, who, after attaining enlightenment, transmitted it to their successors. The *Lam dre* continued to be passed down, through a series of enlightened masters, until it reached the great sage Gayādhara, who brought it to Tibet and transmitted it directly to the first patriarch of the Sakya order.

We have received the uninterrupted transmission of this lam-dre teaching. Through the spiritual work of great teachers of the Sakya order, such as Tsarchen Lösal Gyatso,[78] the lam-dre literature has been enriched, over the centuries, with many commentaries and instructional texts. Everything the ordinary, practical Sakya meditator needs to know can be found in two lam-dre volumes, *The Three Visions* and *The Three Continua*. The former is the text we are studying. We have already covered most of it and are now discussing insight, or wisdom, which we have already considered in some detail. We will add a little bit more now.

In the preceding lessons, we talked at some length about (1) realization of the two kinds of selflessness, personal and phenomenal, (2) recognition of the true nature of one's mind, and (3) the essential nature of mind being one of nondual voidness and clarity, or cognition. Let's be a bit more practical and talk about how to undertake insight meditation.

We have said that the *Lam dre* is the special system of the Sakya tradition of Tibetan Buddhism. The quintessence of that system is also quite special—it is the view called "the nonduality of clarity and voidness," also known as "the nondifferentiation of saṃsāra and nirvāṇa." The other schools have their own names for their perception of the ultimate: the Great Perfection or *dzogpa chenbo* of the Nyingmapas, the *chagya chenbo* of the Kagyupas, and the *uma chenbo* of the Gelugpas. The Sakya view, and methods for attaining that view, differ slightly; they are, in essence, the Madhyamaka view of ultimate reality. The instructions for the attainment of the view of ultimate reality, no matter what it is called, do vary slightly from school to school.

The Sakya order differs from the other three schools of Tibetan Buddhism in its insistence that you must first recognize that all appearances, or phenomena, are projections of mind itself. This is essential for Sakya meditation. Through investigation, you come to recognize that all phenomena that appear to be external and real are, like those that you see in dreams, only manifestations of mind and not real in themselves. Then you can proceed to the next stage of examining the nature of mind itself.[79] Thus the very first stage is "recognition of appearances to the mind" (*snang-sems*; *snang* is appearance, *sems* is mind).

It is easy for us to approach this rather new concept by way of examples that are familiar to us. When the great Indian pandit Atīsha was on his way to Tibet, he considered how he would teach the Dharma to Tibetans, who were not familiar with Indian Buddhist literature. He wanted to teach the

Mind-Only doctrine, so he inquired whether Tibetans believed in magic and was told that they had no magic and no sense of it.

In India there are many magicians who go from village to village, setting up shows and doing magic tricks—sleight of hand, illusions, and so forth. Indian Buddhists relied on examples from these presentations, for Buddhists always try to communicate in terms of examples that are familiar to their audiences or somehow similar to the point they are trying to convey. For example, to explain to Indian townspeople that things are empty by nature and that appearances have no reality in themselves, teachers say that worldly phenomena are like those in a magic show, where a magician shows a lady being sawed in half, and so forth: what you see is not the reality, but only a misperception of mind that makes you think it to be real. Indians could grasp that example very easily.

Thus, when Atisha learned that Tibetans didn't have traveling magicians, he asked whether Tibetans dream. Learning that they do, he decided to use the simile of dreams. Everyone who has had a dream can understand how, during that state, we are conscious of the appearance of many things that seem to be very real. This is so much the case that we react to them with all kinds of emotions, treating them as though they were external and as though our own existence were somehow dependent on interaction with them. We dream of a tiger coming after us and respond with fear and a desire to escape, but when we awake, we realize that the tiger never had a speck of true reality, being nothing more than a projection of mind. Our responses to such appearances are altogether erroneous; the mind simply doesn't recognize their true reality of being, for example, merely dream tigers projected by the mind itself.

One who meditates must learn to see all waking appearances as very much like dream appearances. Although waking phenomena appear to be external and real to the nonmeditative, unenlightened mind, to the meditator's mind they have no more reality than dreams. He clearly recognizes them as manifestations of his own mind and proceeds to the next stage. Thus we are left with mind as the source of all our conscious experience of everything, and can understand the importance of recognizing its true nature.

The three progressive stages of insight meditation are: (1) recognition of the nature of mind (literally, recognition of the clarity of mind), (2) placing the mind in a state of extremelessness, and (3) attaining certainty about the nature of the ineffable state of enlightenment.[80] How do you go about these three stages, practically speaking?

First, sit down in the proper posture of meditation. Your back should be very straight, and you should be in a pleasant, quiet place, away from distractions. As always, begin with taking refuge and awakening the enlightenment thought. Next, undertake your main practice, which here begins with recognition of the clarity of mind. Start with the considerations: "Are things external?" "Are external things real, or are they projections of mind?" What you need to do is recognize that things/dharmas/phenomena are not as they appear, external and real, but rather are, like the images in dreams, merely projections of mind.

When you buy that one, you can proceed to the next consideration, namely, that there is nothing but mind, that the sum total of your experience as an individual being—whatever you are at this stage—is just mind. But is mind, then, the sole reality? Is it real? The second step in recognizing the mind's clarity is to examine the mind as the source of all appearances. Is it real? Does it have a location? Does it have size, shape, or color?

Focus your mind on mind itself. Put aside all external distractions, all thought of anything else. After sustained training in the first stage of meditation, concentration, you will have attained steadiness and clarity; undisturbed by unruly thought processes and emotional obscurations, you will be able to focus on the mind itself. What you should be looking for is the true nature of mind: that it is not really a thing. Mind is no thing. It has no size, shape, location, or other qualities that would constitute it as something that is real in itself. It is not something that comes from anywhere, stays anywhere, or goes anywhere. It is void of all such attributes of existence. Therefore, we say that mind is empty by its nature.

But does this mean that the mind is empty like space, which is the absence of substance and form? Is mind just the absence of anything, and hence nothing? Do we mean that mind is just nothingness? No, because mind, although empty, nonetheless is endowed with cognition, with the fact that it is consciousness. To express the fact that it is not any "thing" that can be isolated and called an inherently existing entity, we say that it is empty. But when we say that, we mean that it nonetheless has the nature of cognition: despite its emptiness, there is clarity of mind.

Now, when you see the mind unobscured by thought processes, unsullied by the emotional states of desire, hatred, and delusion—when you see it in a state of unwavering concentrative meditation—then the mind appears as it really is. It is pure by its nature. It is luminous, very bright, very clear. That is what you will see: that it is empty. At the same time, it also has this nature of luminosity, or clarity. You cannot separate its voidness, or emptiness, from its clarity, any more than you can separate fire from heat. You cannot say that the mind's clarity is invalidated or negated through its emptiness, that it is through its clarity that mind is also empty, or the like. This is just the nature of mind: nondual emptiness and clarity. This is what you see when recognizing the mind's clarity; then you go on.

The second stage is seeing that this true nature of mind is absolutely away from all extremes. Here you realize that you can no longer understand mind adequately or accurately in terms of human concepts such as "it is," "it is not," "it both is and is not," and "it neither is nor is not." Mind is not something that can be conceptualized. You cannot seize it and say, "This is the ultimate nature of mind." Yet you see it very, very clearly, with no mistake about it. It is not something that eludes you; rather, you simply see that human concepts are not adequate to describe it accurately. You cannot say that it either is or isn't. This state of mind is also called the ultimate view of the Madhyamaka school, and is characterized as "great iextremelessness," meaning that the ultimate nature of mind is away from all extremes.

Philosophically, we have progressed from the conventional level, where we accepted mind-only as really existent (the Mind-Only, or Chittamātra, school was one of the lower schools of Buddhist doctrine), and have graduated to the Madhyamaka school, which says that mind is away from all extremes and cannot be clung to as a really existent thing. Through meditating on this repeatedly, your mind becomes purer and purer and your insight into this true nature becomes deeper, more profound, more certain. In this way, you develop great certitude that this is truly the realization that had to be attained; it is truly realization of the ultimate nature of mind, and hence of reality.

You can attain buddhahood by means of this realization, and yet it can't be communicated in words. It is something that is so beyond the limits of ordinary human consciousness that it cannot be communicated in signs to those who do not experience it directly and immediately for themselves. This is the third stage of insight meditation, that of attaining certainty about the ineffable nature of enlightenment.

It is as if someone who had never learned words to describe his experiences were to taste sugarcane for the first time. He would be very sure that he was experiencing this new flavor, yet he would have no way of communicating to someone else that it tasted sweet. His experience would be very real for him; he just wouldn't have the means of communicating it. Similarly, one who enters into meditative absorption accepts that there is no way for someone who hasn't experienced it to really know what he is talking about.

This is why the teachings of ultimate reality are taught on the level of conventional reality, by way of similes and worldly examples. Through symbols, ordinary humans can get some idea of what teachers are talking about when they say there is an ineffable state of enlightenment, a state away from all extremes that constitutes the true nature of mind. Yet these are only words that point toward a direct experience of this ultimate perception of reality, which is, as we have said, the very heart of the Sakya tradition.

If you have not meditated enough to have had at least some glimpse of this ineffable, extremeless state of mind, some warmth of that experience yourself, you are not yet a true Sakya practitioner. When you have attained through meditation at least some personal insight, some glimpse of this inexpressible clarity of mind, then you are a true Sakyapa.

With this we conclude our explanation of insight meditation, which leads to realization of the ultimate nature of mind, and thereby to the attainment of buddhahood, our goal.

I wonder whether any good will come of all this. I have a confession to make: I am not particularly fond of teaching. I don't care to teach simply for the sake of teaching; what interests me are its benefits. If you become inspired to apply yourself to meditation and gain some real, direct, immediate, personal insight into the nature of the mind—the nondual emptiness and clarity of mind, its extremelessness and ineffability—then all my teachings will have been worthwhile. But if the teachings remain simply so many words, so much time spent, so much work for the sake of work, then the benefit is hard to see.

Yet you may indeed benefit from all this. For example, there is a very good monk who lives in Darjeeling, Jamyang Gyaltsen by name. Many years ago, when I first escaped from Tibet and was briefly in exile in Darjeeling, this monk, who was then quite young, approached me and said, "Would you explain to me the Sakya doctrine of the nondual clarity and voidness of mind? I have never understood that."

While I was in India for those months, I taught that young monk according to the text we ourselves have been studying. I never heard anything from him; that was twenty years ago.

Recently, I got a letter from Jamyang Gyaltsen, thanking me for those few months of teaching and saying that they had come at the critical period when he had just fled for his life from his homeland. He could have left off religious practice, as so many monks did at that time, but decided to remain a monk because he could see the benefit of the lam-dre system of practice, in which he did persevere.

Another example concerns His Holiness Chobgyay Trichen Rinpoche, a Sakya lineage holder who established a meditation retreat in Lumbini, the birthplace of Lord Buddha, and did several years of meditation there. He wrote from Lumbini that, as he meditates now, my teachings from twenty years ago come back and help him, so that he is experiencing something in his meditation. He is grateful after all these years for the teaching on the nature of mind, so I think that in that case, too, there may have been some benefit in teaching.

There is still a bit more in *The Three Visions* that wraps up this section and that you might care to know. After having first developed your mind adequately through study and reflection, cutting off all doubts, confusion, and misunderstandings about the doctrine and the practice, meditate as we have just described and develop recognition of the nature of mind in these three stages. Then, when you enter into the state of meditative absorption, you will notice that, even though the clear cognition of your mind is not negated in any way, the nature of that mind is completely away from all extremes of existence or nonexistence.

Also, you won't be able to say that it is "this" or "that," or "my experience is this or that," or one thing or the other. You cannot say that the state of meditative absorption is effable, or even that it is ineffable; you cannot say even that much about it. Even the word "ineffable" cannot describe how really inadequate concepts are for this state of experience.

On this level of meditation, there is nothing to express, there is nothing to negate, there is no negation, or anything to be negated. There is no relinquishing or anything to be relinquished. There is no reliance on antidotes at this stage. There is no renunciation of worldly existence. There are no hopes of receiving help from the Buddha. There is no fear of Māra's tricks.

Thus you see things very clearly. Notions of relinquishing or negating reality, or of achieving true reality; hopes for liberation, fears of bondage, and the like; concepts of existent and nonexistent, real and unreal, ideas of empty and nonempty—all these are just thought-constructions. They are mere words, conventions that have no substance in themselves; they are insubstantial, substanceless. From the very beginning they are absolutely pure, absolutely empty. They are not objects of any form of expression, conception, or communication. There is really nothing to them at all.

You become very sure about this. At this point, you can afford to meditate in the manner of one for whom there is nothing to cling to: no existence or nonexistence, no meditator, and no meditation to be performed. If, here, absolutely no nature of mind is obtained, then how can there be any recognition of the nature of mind? There can be such recognition because the true nature of mind transcends expression; it is not an object that can be described in words, since there is, here, nothing at all to tell.

53

A Chamberpot, an Offering Bowl, a Buddha

SHARING AN INTEREST in the teachings of enlightenment, you should generate bodhichitta and develop a sense of devotion and respect for these teachings, which are the source of present and future joys as well as ultimate liberation. Further, you should listen to these teachings in accordance with the
instructions of the Mahāyāna path, which enjoin that, on occasions of
study, you relinquish all attachment to ordinary conceptualizations of yourself and the present moment.

Accordingly, think of this not as an ordinary situation but as an event
taking place on a dharmic level. Think that you are surrounded not by ordinary walls and furnishings but by a celestial mansion, in the center of which
is seated not your human teacher but your teacher in the form of Shākyamuni Buddha. Visualize that he is in fact the Buddha, and that as he teaches rays of light shine forth from his heart, touching you, all beings who are
present, and all beings throughout space, removing all obscurations and
awakening great compassion and insight in their minds as well as in your
own. Think of yourself not as an ordinary person but as none other than
the great Bodhisattva of Wisdom, Mañjushrī, who is here to listen to the
most profound Dharma for the benefit of all living beings.

Beyond this, keep in mind the nature of ultimate reality. Think of
appearances—your own form and other apparent forms—as having a delu-
sion-like nature (not the substantial, solid nature we are wont to attribute
to them). See them as the images and forms that appear to you when you
dream. These many appearances have no inherent, substantial nature of
their own; they are merely projections of mind. Think, too, that the mind
that projects them has as its ultimate nature nondual emptiness/voidness
and clarity/cognition.

When you approximate the ultimate nature of the present moment in
this manner, your efforts to study and listen to the Dharma become more
efficacious, forceful, and authentic. Through these visualizations, recollections, and so forth, you will at least simulate the true reality of the present
moment.

જી ૐ જી

After you have thus prepared yourself, you should know something about the teaching you are about to receive. You should be assured that it is, indeed, an authentic teaching and not a waste of time. Now, our course of study is a series of descriptions of the lam-dre system of meditation, which originated with the Buddha Vajradhara and was transmitted by the goddess Nairātmyā to the great Indian sage Virūpa. After Virūpa had attained enlightenment through his own practice, he transmitted it to his foremost disciples, who handed it down through the centuries until it was introduced to the founder of the Sakya order by the great Indian yogi Gayādhara. As a result of the spiritual activity of the Five Great Jetsüns, the founders of the Sakya tradition, we have an unbroken lineage for transmission of this precious teaching. Through their work, a vast number of commentaries and guides has been provided for the tantras, empowerments, and root texts that make up the lam-dre system proper. Through their kindness, the teaching in its entirety has been successfully transmitted down to the present time for our benefit.

The lam-dre system has been expounded in a number of ways, most conveniently by a division into two easy texts that correspond to the meditator's experience of (1) the beginning stages of the path, and (2) the more advanced stages of tantric practice (and to *The Three Visions* and *The Three Continua*, respectively). We are studying the first of these two texts. As we have said many times, *The Three Visions* consists of instructions that correspond to three levels of spiritual perception: the worldling's impure vision, the meditator's vision of experience, and the pure vision of the enlightened ones. We have completed our discussion of the first vision and all the topics about the second vision through the two stages of meditation, concentration and insight.

We left off with a discussion of the ultimate nature of mind, that is, with the doctrine of the nonduality of clarity and voidness, which is the very heart of the entire Sakya tradition. I have a few things more to say on this topic.

THE NONDUAL COMBINATION OF CONCENTRATION AND INSIGHT

The sūtras agree that the doctrine of the two levels of reality, conventional and ultimate, may be said to consist of appearance and emptiness. That is to say, on the level of conventional reality, things are treated as they appear, while on the level of ultimate reality, the emptiness of those appearances is treated. When the Buddha discussed things on a conventional level of reality, he accepted them as apparent, existent, and just what they appear to be.

Here there are virtue and vice, beings and saints, and all the rest. But on the level of ultimate reality, the discourses of the Buddha do not accept the real existence of those very same things. Here we are talking very simplistically about the two truths, or levels of reality, and are trying to relate them to the two aspects of the ultimate nature of the mind, namely, nondual clarity and voidness. Since conventional reality can be said, for our purposes, to relate to the clear aspect of mind, the emptiness aspect of mind then corresponds to ultimate reality.

We said that, in the beginning, you train the mind in the techniques of concentration. When concentration has been mastered, you develop insight into the real nature of things, including your own mind. We said also that there is a third stage in which these two meditations are brought together nondually. At this point, you are not practicing just concentration or just insight meditation; rather, you combine the two. The insight attained at this third stage is essential for realizing that nondual clarity and emptiness of mind which we have just described as the quintessence of the Sakya tradition.

Now, if you are wondering why we must go through all this, let me remind you again that the nature of unenlightened existence is one of suffering. What is at the root of all that suffering and delusion? What is the source, or cause, of all that pain? Underneath all suffering, at the very center of endless unhappiness, is precisely the erroneous belief in a self. It is this basic error that causes all beings, ourselves included, to whirl about on the round of birth and death. To free the mind from this erroneous perception, it is necessary to realize the emptiness of all phenomena, especially that of the mind which holds to this erroneous belief. It is only through realization of emptiness that the false belief in a self can be eradicated.

The practice of all other kinds of meditation, such as concentration, can purify the mind of emotional negativity to one degree or another, subduing the force of the manifestations of egocentricity so that the mind no longer seems to operate under the delusion of a self. But the seeds of this wrong view—and of future attachment to a self, to existence, and to things that are the outcome of this deluded view—can be eradicated once and for all only through the realization of emptiness. That is why it is necessary to go through these various stages of meditation. After realizing how things are empty, and how even the mind is empty of any independent reality of its own, it is necessary to proceed to an authentic perception of things as they really are—i.e., of the mind as it really is.

❧ ☀ ❧

This brings us to the ultimate view of the Sakya tradition, which we call "the nondifferentiation of saṃsāra and nirvāṇa" ('khor-'das-dbyer-med): that is, that the ultimate nature of the mind is away from all extremes. This highest view of the Sakya tradition has its counterparts among the other orders of Tibetan Buddhism: the Great Perfection of the Nyingmapas, the Great Symbol of the Kagyupas, and the Middle Way view of the Gelugpas. In the early history of Tibetan philosophical schools, the names that the schools gave to this ultimate view were three: *dzogpa chenbo* (Great Perfection), *chagya chenbo* (Mahāmudrā, or Great Symbol), and *uma chenbo* (Mahā-madhyamaka, or Great Middle Way).[81] The Sakya view partakes of all of these. It is identical to the first two and, historically, at least, is most identified with the third view, which was the first expression in Tibet of the Madhyamaka philosophical school. Technically, the Sakya view can be said to be an expression of the *uma chenbo*, although within the Sakya school itself it is known as *khorde yerme*.

So much for the theory. What is required of you in relation to this exalted perception of the ultimate is that you realize this view. You must attain this perception of the ultimate in order to become a true follower of the Sakya school. Anything less might earn you the name "Sakyapa," but it would be merely a nominal achievement, for until you have achieved this view of the ultimate, you can be a Sakyapa in name but not in fact.

It behooves you, then, to undertake the task of attaining this quintessential view of the Sakya order by doing just what you are doing: listening, learning, studying, and questioning. What is this doctrine of the nature of the mind? What is the clear aspect of the mind? What is the empty aspect? What are the stages of meditation? Through rehearsing and repeating what you have learned and comprehending it correctly, you will attain a clear understanding of the doctrine and the instructions for practice. This is the first step, which you are now taking.

The second stage is experience, when you begin to meditate: you undertake daily sessions of practice and regular sessions of retreat; you progress from mere intellectual understanding to personal experience. You experience the first stage of meditation, the second, what is meant by the clear aspect of mind, what is meant by the empty aspect, and so forth. You recognize within your own experience what the various teachings are expressing and how they actually refer to insights gained in your own private practice.

The third stage is that of realization. Through your experience of the various stages and insights, you gain a direct perception of the states in meditation, including the highest one, which is away from all extremes—that is, the perception of the ultimate. This is your own immediate, direct, nondual, ineffable experience of ultimate reality, and constitutes the third stage of your own personal path, namely, realization.

Through this process of (1) understanding, (2) experience, and (3) realization, you will become a genuine Sakyapa. What are most needed on your part are sincerity and diligence. Having determined to practice, you see it through with regularity, mindfulness, and recollection, bringing to bear all those factors which are favorable to successful meditation. You know what factors help you most in your own practice and in furthering your insights and realizations, and act accordingly. You also come to know the factors that hinder you most, and act so that they can be avoided. In this way, you become your own best friend in your meditation practice. This is what is required on the part of a meditator who undertakes these three stages.

Are you really sitting and honestly looking at your mind? I have been stressing that this ultimate view of reality is exalted, quintessential, and necessary. I have been asking you to experience it for yourself. Most Sakya teachers do not teach the ultimate nature of mind at this stage; they save it for much later or reserve it for the most spiritually mature among their disciples, those who are destined to become lamas and the like. Perhaps I am mistaken in explaining it to you in such detail. Perhaps it only incurs demerit to talk about such exalted doctrines, which are very difficult to understand and which few people can become inspired to attain.

However, on the chance that you are interested, I have gone on for a considerable length of time, thinking that some benefit may result. I want to see that benefit. I want to see you turning within, becoming introspective, studying your own mind, giving up distractions and overinvolvement in external attachments, becoming used to the idea of trying to recognize the nature of your mind because it is there.

This is at the heart of what we are trying to do. If you plan to receive the lam-dre teachings from His Holiness Sakya Trizin in the future, do you know what is at the heart of the full teaching and the Hevajra empowerment? It is precisely this insight into your own nature of mind. That is why I decided to lay it out before you again, hoping that you will take it to heart and turn within, focusing your mind on mind itself and trying to see its nondual clarity and voidness.

☙ ❈ ❧

To begin with, there are three things that you should be trying to experience. The first line in this part of *The Three Visions* says that luminosity is the characteristic of the mind. Are there words in English that can adequately translate this idea? What does it mean to you when I say that luminosity, clarity, translucence is the essential characteristic of mind, of consciousness? When we use the term *selwa* (*gsal-ba*) in Tibetan, we mean that there is some clear aspect of mind that can somehow be distinguished from its void aspect.

The second line says that emptiness, or voidness, is the mind's nature. Clarity or luminosity is the mind's essential characteristic; oneness is its nature. You have succeeded in practice when you can actually turn the mind within, focus mind on mind itself, and recognize within your own mind this attribute of clarity, or luminosity, that I use many adjectives to describe. The term for this is *sel sing-ewa* (*gsal-sing-nge-ba*), which means "luminous/clear/radiant/translucent light." This aspect can't be recognized as long as thought processes are going on, as long as you are making efforts at meditation. Apparently, it requires a great deal of relaxation.

The third line in this instruction says that the true nature of the mind is without artifice. That is, it is something that just is. After you have realized the clarity of mind, you examine mind and see that (even though there is this cognitive or radiant, luminous aspect of mind) when you search for its location, size, shape, color, and so forth, you can't find it. The mind just isn't an entity in the sense that we humans like to think of such things: phenomena have to have something, they have to be something, but the mind doesn't and isn't. In this sense, it is said to be void—void from the beginning. Mind is not something that comes from somewhere, gets here, and then goes away; it is just something that is, from the very beginning, empty by its own nature.

You cannot separate these two. You can't say, "This is the clarity of mind, this is its voidness," just as when you burn your hand, you can't separate the flame and the heat. The flame is the heat and the heat is the flame; they are one and the same, not dual. This is the second thing you have to recognize: that there is this luminosity of cognition, but that, when you search for it, mind is void of any independent existence as an entity. It isn't anything we can conceptualize.

Then you enter into the state of meditation that perceives the real nature of mind and is away from all extremes. Mind is none of these human concepts of existence, nonexistence, both, or neither. None of these possibilities is adequate to describe what this ultimate nature of mind is.

Yet it is something that you directly perceive; it is a direct, nondual realization. That is why this view is absolutely authentic; it is something that either is "right on" or isn't. It is not something that you can grasp and say, "This is the view," "This isn't the view," or "I've got to make the view."

The true nature of mind is without artifice. You cannot manufacture it, you cannot seize upon it, you cannot do anything to bring it about. All you can do is enter into meditation in a very relaxed way, without making efforts to produce the result of this insight. You just have to perceive that there is this ultimate nature of your own mind which is there to be perceived. That is why I have expounded this at considerable length, perhaps more than I should. If I have erred in this, I will recite the hundred-syllable mantra of Vajrasattva, but, thinking that there might be benefit for some of you, I nevertheless want you to sit and look within to the true nature of mind.

You may remember, from a preceding lesson,[82] the words of Sakya Pandita on the nature of ultimate reality. He said that there is nothing to attain because, by virtue of realizing the emptiness of all things, you cannot rightly expect, at that level of enlightenment, to find anything that is there to be attained. There are no things. Even though these concepts and words may be difficult to understand, you should ponder them, to keep them in mind, and consider them again and again. In that way, when you do undertake practice, some blessing will ensue through your own insight, by virtue of having made the effort to understand them, and because they are the words of the enlightened ones.

Thus you should apply yourself to gaining a right understanding of these concepts. This is why we have repeated these teachings again and again, and why you must repeat the effort to study and learn them. It pays off in right understanding, experience, and realization.

I want to talk more about the nature of this ultimate reality as it is described in various Buddhist scriptures. For example, in the *Meeting of Parent and Child Sūtra* (*Pitāputra-samāgama-sūtra*), Lord Buddha tells his spiritual children, the bodhisattvas, that in ultimate reality there are no dharmas whatsoever that are perceived. Therefore, in ultimate reality, there is no ascription whatsoever. Now, by "ascription" we mean that it is the nature of the mind to label things: in the first instant, mind has an immediate, raw impression of an appearance or external object; in the second instant, it goes to work and says, "I recognize that from before, and it's called so-and-so"; and from that point, you go on and treat it familiarly.

This is the way the mind ordinarily functions.

But this doesn't work on the level of ultimate reality, because there is nothing that can be an object. As Sakya Pandita said, there is nothing to be attained there, nothing to be grasped and seized upon; there are no objects. Therefore there is nothing to call the level of ultimate reality; there is no nature of ultimate reality—or, ultimately, of dharmas, or things. And everything else, no matter what it is, is merely nominality. You are involved in mere mental elaborations that say, "Yes, there is an object," "Yes, it's called so-and-so," and "Yes, everybody agrees with me." You talk about it, write books about it; it goes on and on. This is called elaboration, or saṃsāra, whereas in the Sakya school the technical word for the ultimate is "elaborationlessness." Elaboration means carrying on and on about something. Your starting point is the premise that you are real and the object is real, and from that you construct saṃsāra.

Hence, everything other than this ultimate-reality-of-things-as-they-are is nominality, words, conventions, mere chitchat; it is merely ascription, nothing more, whereas in ultimate reality everything is unperceived. These are the words of the Buddha. In the *Bodhisattva Collection* (*Bodhisattva-piṭaka-sūtra*), it is written that, "When one neither apprehends all dharmas nor relinquishes all dharmas, then, indeed, one does not abide in dharmas." That is to say, you are not involved or caught up in, nor do you dwell in, phenomena.

For example, when you are still unenlightened, you feel that buddhahood can only be acquired by making strenuous right efforts. This makes a lot of sense, from the viewpoint of the practitioner, until the goal of buddhahood is attained. But once there, there is absolutely nothing to attain. Who is going to attain it? There is no one there who has attained, nothing to be attained, and no such thing as buddhahood as something that's attainable. You no longer perceive yourself as existing in the way you originally thought you existed, and so forth.

Here we are talking about that rarified level of enlightenment at which you don't try to apprehend dharmas. You are not seeking anything. You no longer perceive buddhahood as an object to be attained, nor do you try to relinquish wrong views, saṃsāra, suffering, or anything else, because by realizing the true nature of phenomena, you see that these are merely thought-constructions, ascriptions, and so forth. You are no longer caught up in the network of mental constructions but see true reality.

The *Bodhisattva Collection* goes on: "When one does not abide in all dharmas, one does not arrive and one does not perish." The usual idea is that things arrive, they abide for awhile, and then they perish, just as humans come, stay awhile, and then go. But a person who doesn't perceive any dharmas undergoing this process does not himself abide in dharmas. He doesn't become involved in dharmas because he doesn't perceive any, and if he doesn't perceive any dharmas, he doesn't dwell in dharmas. He doesn't depend on dharmas; therefore, he doesn't undergo the process of arising and passing on, so he is totally liberated from birth, old age, disease, death, and sorrow. He is thus totally free of grief and outcries, weeping and pain, mental unhappiness, agitation, anger, and so forth.

Tathāgatagarbha [83] is the doctrine which states that all beings contain buddha-nature, whether or not they know it. What I am telling you now about the quintessential nonduality of the mind's clarity and voidness is nothing more or less than this doctrine. I wonder whether you know, for example, that there is no Vajrapāni, that Vajrapāni is nothing more than the nature of your mind. One of my students spent forty days and nights in a retreat on Vajrapāni. He recited the mantra all that time. He was using a technique for coming to recognize the nondual clarity and voidness of his own mind. That recognition, when achieved, is the attainment of Vajrapāni's stage. You are Vajrapāni: that is the Vajrapāni you are meditating on. Thus, for example, when a student does her Vajrayogini retreat and recites the mantra, she is not meditating devotedly on some wonderful deity but simply on a recognition of Vajrayogini within, who is nothing more or less than the nondual clarity and voidness of her own mind.

You have heard of the Body of Reality, or dharmakāya. It can be seen in three aspects: (1) causal dharmakāya, (2) the dharmakāya of the path, and (3) resultant dharmakāya. What leads you from the causal stage to the resultant stage is the path. Now, on the causal stage, you already have the dharmakāya. Your own mind, if you but knew it, *is* dharmakāya: dharmakāya is your own consciousness, nothing more than your own mind, which consists of this nonduality of clarity and voidness. Even in its raw state, in the stage of deepest delusion, your mind is still the causal dharmakāya. If that were recognized, even that raw state would be seen as dharmakāya, the transcendent gnosis of the enlightened ones. On the path, also, as you are undergoing purification and training, your mind is still what is called "the path dharmakāya," even though it may not be recognized as such. Finally, through meditation and making efforts on the path, you see your buddha-nature very clearly, recognize this ultimate nature of mind, and therefore become a buddha.

To make this a little more meaningful, we have an example offered by my own great teacher, Gatön Ngawang Legpa Rinpoche. He said, suppose you have some metal, perhaps a chunk of brass. You can use this metal to make a chamberpot, and people will think it is very unclean. They will use it in the john and that's about it; they will always think of it as being very filthy and untouchable. But take that chamberpot, smelt it down, and refashion the same metal into a nice, shiny offering bowl, and the same people will say, "What a lovely bowl! Why, we can't use this in the kitchen, let's use it on the shrine to give offerings to the deities." You can take that same metal, smelt it again, and turn it into an image of the Buddha, and people will be on their faces prostrating, saying that it represents the highest possible good, and showing great devotion. All this can occur with regard to this very same piece of material.

Now, take the ordinary human mind. What, really, do the buddhas have in common with the wretched people you might see staggering in the gutters? What could be more dissimilar? Where is the buddha-nature within those beings? These are beings whose buddha-nature is not recognized; as in the case of the chamberpot, the material or potential for buddhahood is not obvious and clear. Yet a worldly wretch, who may be in the most pitiful plight, still has buddha-nature, regardless of whether he or anyone else recognizes it. He is like the first example of the use of metal as a chamberpot. Take that same wretch, teach him the Dharma, show him how to meditate, how to avoid nonvirtue and accumulate merit, and after a while he will turn into a bodhisattva, because if he keeps trying to act like a bodhisattva, eventually he will succeed. Now he is like the metal that has been turned into an ornamental vessel worthy of being used in worship. And that bodhisattva, if he perseveres, will eventually become a fully enlightened one. This corresponds to the third stage in our example, when the metal was turned into an image of the Buddha.

In all three cases, the same material is used, namely, the basic nature of mind, or buddha-nature. It is this which links the glorious buddhas with the lowliest of unenlightened beings, all the way down to insects. All have this buddha-nature within; it is only a matter of recognition and purification.

Beings are buddhas, only they don't yet know it. Their minds are obscured by adventitious defilements (*kleśa*)—i.e., the negative emotional states of desire, hatred, and delusion, which include this basic ignorance about the nature of mind and the mistaken belief in the self. This is the only difference between buddhas and ordinary beings. If all of us were not endowed with the inherent potential to become buddhas, there would be no point in meditating or train-ing in the Dharma. But by virtue of the existence of buddha-nature within each being's mind, no matter how wretched, there is the possibility of attain-ing enlightenment. That is the meaning of buddha-nature.

The buddhas have purified the adventitious defilements. For example, smoke obscures the sky so that our vision is blocked. That smoke is adven-titious: it is not inherent in the sky. It has just appeared extraneously, sud-denly. However, this haziness can pass, it can be purified, and then we can see that the sky is not obscured in its own nature. In the same way, negative defilements obscure the pure, clear nature of mind so that we don't recog-nize it. In the same way, these kleshas don't inherently belong to mind and thus can be purified. If they couldn't be purified, there would be no point in practicing to get rid of them.

Buddha-nature is nothing more than the nondual clarity and voidness of your own mind. What do we mean by the deities, whether Shākyamuni Buddha, the bodhisattva Avalokiteshvara, Sakya Pandita, or any of the oth-ers? We mean nothing more than the nature of your own mind. When you realize that, you will have attained buddhahood. You will know who the Buddha is, you'll know Sakya Pandita, Avalokiteshvara, and all the rest. This is the goal.

The *Perfection of Wisdom Sūtras* (*Prajñāpāramitā-sūtra*) say that it is through thought-constructs that we roam about in the realms of desire, form, and formlessness, and that it is through non-thought-construction that we do not get involved in these. Further, they say that because a bodhisattva perceives no object, a so-called bodhisattva is just a word; because a buddha perceives no object, a buddha is simply a word. Thus the omniscient, all-knowing, perfectly enlightened Buddha has no nature, and that which has no nature is inexpressible.

How can we achieve the welfare of living beings if "bodhisattva" and "buddha" are mere names? If, in ultimate reality, beings do not exist, what is there to be achieved in terms of beings' welfare, or of anyone being their benefactor? It is difficult to translate these texts thoroughly. Here, to make the point that we have to get beyond thought-constructions, we are saying that you must no longer think in worldly terms, regarding beings, bud-dhas, and so forth as independent entities. In their ultimate reality, you cannot use these concepts or constructs, which are only good for conven-tional reality, where they are very useful (indeed, Buddhists make full use of them on that level). But on the stage of awakening, concepts are no longer appropriate; there you can't talk about achieving the welfare of beings, because the person who is enlightened no longer perceives beings or has a concept of himself as a benefactor of beings. Still, a beginner or a bodhisattva might actually think in those terms.

We also have the *Question of Purna Sūtra* (*Pūrṇa-paripṛcchā-sūtra*), in which Shākyamuni Buddha tells the arhat Purna:

> Having seated myself in the heart of enlightenment,[84] I was perfectly awakened to the incomparable full and perfect total enlightenment. At that time, I did not perceive any beings. What's more, I did not perceive even the name of beings.

In other words, there was not even any thought-construction of beings. Again, quoting from the *Perfection of Wisdom Sūtras*, the Buddha speaks to the bodhisattva Subhūti:

> Subhūti, I did not perceive any beings. But beings perceive— beings form the conceptualization of an existing entity where there is no existing entity. That construction of theirs is merely a worldly convention. In ultimate reality, it does not exist.

Upon realizing this, you cannot even cling to the state of extremelessness. Meditating on the mental impression of emptiness checks you from thinking in terms of really existing entities, while the "not anything at all" meditation gets rid of thinking of the nonexistence of entities. At last you will be rid of both extremes.

54

THE DREAMING MIND DELUDES ITSELF

IN UNDERTAKING ANY SESSION of Dharma study, it is of the utmost importance to begin with the right attitude, which consists, in a word, of bodhichitta, the genuine resolve to strive for buddhahood in order to remove the sufferings of all living beings. With the thought that, through these efforts, you will draw closer to that spiritual goal, listen attentively and single-pointedly to these authentic teachings, which originate from the enlightened mind of Lord Buddha himself and have been faithfully transmitted down to the present. Further, think of your own teacher as none other than the Buddha himself; visualize him complete with rays of light emanating from his form and shining from his heart to touch you and all beings, thereby removing all ignorance and the emotive and cognitive obscurations. Think, too, that as you listen to, and understand intellectually, the various points of discourse, right insight and realization arise within your mind. In other words, promote the arising of insight and nonintellectual understanding by thinking that you have, indeed, achieved realization.

Then visualize yourself not as an ordinary human being but as none other than the golden-formed Bodhisattva of Wisdom, Mañjushrī, who seeks out the Dharma on behalf of ignorant beings. Your form as Mañjushrī should not be thought of as solid and tangible but as having the nature of nondual emptiness and appearance—i.e., while it is clearly apparent, it is not to be thought of as substantial, but more like the mental forms that appear in dreams or magic shows. Your own form and all appearances also have this nature of nondual appearance and voidness through interdependent origination. Keeping in mind this true nature of phenomena, bring your insight, too, into at least some approximation of ultimate reality. Through practicing these visualizations and conceptualizations while listening to the Dharma, your understanding, merit, and concentration may be magnified and thereby rendered more effective.

We are concerned with those instructions which originated with the Primordial Buddha Vajradhara himself, and which were transmitted by the great Indian sage Virūpa through a succession of great masters in India and Tibet down to the present time, in keeping with the path of enlightenment, which, if followed properly, leads us from the very first step to the fulfillment of our spiritual aim. These teachings are, for the sake of convenience, divided into two stages of practice: preliminary and advanced. Our own studies are concerned with a set of two volumes, which correspond to these two stages of practice. We are completing our studies in the first volume, known as *The Three Visions*. We have progressed to consideration of the doctrine of voidness (*śūnyatā*), which is rightly considered to be the very heart of the Buddhist religion. Most certainly it is the quintessential element in the lam-dre system of meditation on which we have embarked. It is essential because without the realization of this state of voidness, there can be no Buddhist liberation. Therefore, it is the sine qua non of Mahāyāna Buddhism.

It is very easy for scholars, students, and meditators to use the term "voidness," but its realization is only seldom attained, for it is a profound perception achievable only by persistent effort, great compassion, and purity of heart. The attainment of this view of emptiness, which is called "the door to liberation," presupposes that the meditator has all these qualities as well as a sufficient accumulation of merit.

As we apply ourselves to the study of this concept, we must understand that the realization of voidness is essential. It is not something that can be sidestepped or neglected. You must be prepared to make all necessary efforts to achieve it, including practical efforts through a succession of stages of practice. Before you can expect to achieve a direct, gnostic insight into what is meant by voidness, you must acquire right understanding through diligent study. Through the study of Buddhist literature, relying on learned teachers, making repeated inquiries, and attentive listening and reflection, you should painstakingly acquire an intellectual, theoretical understanding of what Buddhist sages are talking about when they speak of voidness, or emptiness. Then you must apply yourself to persistent, repeated efforts in right meditation for as long as you have not attained the realization you seek.

There is a right way to meditate on voidness. There is a right way to achieve, as an individual, this profound insight. Though it rarely happens, the view of voidness can be attained if the needed conditions are met. Therefore, after you have learned all you can, apply yourself diligently and regularly to meditation and pray often to your teacher that, through his or her added blessings, right understanding and right realization of voidness may arise within your own mind.

You recall that we have mentioned a threefold succession of insight into the nature of ultimate reality: (1) on a practical level, the meditator must first attain a recognition of the clear nature of mind; (2) he must place his mind in a state that is away from all extremes; and (3) finally, he must develop certainty about the ineffability of that experience. Without repeating our discussion of these three stages, let us apply the following instructions for right meditation on voidness on an individual level.

After you have achieved theoretical and meditative insight into these three stages, you must be mindful, while engaged in meditative absorption, not to cling to realization of the nondual clarity and voidness of your own mind. That is to say, even though you perceive it, you must not apprehend it. Remember the fourth line of the *Parting from the Four Attachments* teaching: "If grasping ensues, you haven't the view."

If you grasp at this ultimate view, trying to apprehend it and rely on that realization, you will automatically lose it. Hence, while engaged in meditation, don't cling to this view of nondual clarity and voidness, and when going about your daily affairs—walking, sitting, eating, etc.—also maintain an intense feeling of great compassion for all worldlings whose minds are bound by attachment to reality, who do engage in grasping reality, and who thereby inflict upon themselves great suffering through ignorance of true reality. Practice rightly in these two ways and be wholeheartedly intent on attaining omniscience after you have purified your mind of the two kinds of obscurations (emotive and cognitive), together with their mental impressions; apply all your energies diligently to insight meditation into the nature of voidness. This accords with the great Shāntideva, who wrote:

> Emptiness, or voidness, is the antidote to the darkness of the emotive and cognitive obscurations. Why, then, should anyone who aspires quickly to attain omniscience not meditate on this doctrine of voidness?

If you are sincerely intent on attaining this realization of emptiness, you must also be prepared to make diligent efforts in accumulating a vast store of merit. This is to be done through the four foundational meditations, or preliminary practices: the hundred thousand refuges, prostrations, mandala offerings, and performances of guru yoga. Thus, in addition to meditating on emptiness to accumulate wisdom, or insight, you should train equally in the accumulation of merit. Otherwise, it will be extremely difficult to achieve the realization of voidness, and even if you do manage to acquire some level of realization, you will fall into the Hīnayāna perception of the truth of cessation.

To elaborate, it is a cardinal teaching of the Mahāyāna path that the bodhisattva must develop method and wisdom in equal measure. If he fails to do this, he will attain a spiritual result on the Hīnayāna level of realization. Through his realization of emptiness, he may acquire freedom from the round of worldly existence, but if he hasn't developed sufficient merit and compassion, he will not be able to attain the bodhisattva stages and the stage of perfect enlightenment. He will indeed be liberated, but on a much lower level, which is something to be avoided. As the *Perfection of Wisdom Verses* (*Prajñāpāramitā-sañcaya-gāthā*) also warn us: "So long as merit has not been made sufficient, so long will one remain unable to realize the truth of voidness."

Sakya Pandita wrote that even shrāvakas, the Hīnayāna disciples, meditate on voidness; as a result, they achieve the realization, or truth, of cessation, which is the third of the Four Noble Truths. The point is that, even at this advanced stage of insight meditation, you must never lose sight of the core element of practice that makes it peculiarly Mahāyānist—namely, the non-separation of method and wisdom. When you develop insight, you must always be careful to develop compassion as well; when you develop compassion, you need to develop emptiness as well. Youe don't separate the two or allow the mind to become weak in either one. Practice that never separates method and wisdom is what the sūtras call the heart of the Mahāyāna path.

Our next topic is how to practice this meditation of voidness. *The Three Visions* says that you should first find a suitable place of solitude and there begin by taking refuge in the masters of your lineal tradition and in the Three Jewels. Also invoke their blessings, praying to them for assistance in attaining this realization. Then, through intense compassion, meditate for a very long time on bodhichitta, the resolve to win enlightenment for the sake of all sentient beings.

Next, meditate on a suitable object to achieve single-pointedness of mind, that is, practice concentrative meditation until the mind becomes tranquil and focused. After achieving this desirable state of mind, reflect on these lines:

> From the beginning, we beings have had as our real nature this ultimate clarity, and from the beginning, we have dwelt in the nonduality of clarity and voidness that is free of distinctions and

partisanship, since the mind doesn't identify with either itself or its circle of friends but is completely nonattached. However, because we don't realize it, we rely instead on the belief in an ego, and consequently roam about endlessly in saṃsāra. There we take to be real these appearances of nonexistent entities that have arisen from our own mental impressions. They appear to exist, and so are taken to exist and believed in as real and substantial. Yet, by their own nature, they really do not exist as they appear.

For example, a person who has an eye disease might perceive two moons or a falling star where none exists, or might have some very clear mental impression of the appearance of something that does not exist at all and that would not be perceived by someone whose eyes were not afflicted. In the same way, unenlightened beings have very clear mental impressions of things appearing to be real. They take them to be real, whereas the Enlightened One, whose perception is pure and accurate, does not at all perceive those very things as existing.

Those appearances are insubstantial, devoid of substance, yet through our apprehension of them we have, like madmen, become wealthy only in errors and constantly made wretched by suffering. But now, through relying on the instructions of my holy teacher, I am going to attain an insight into this incomparable and most profound secret of the mind, this realization of voidness, which is the true import of all the teachings and which is what all the buddhas of the three times were talking about in their eighty-four thousand articles of doctrine. Thus I must deport myself so as not to come under the sway of "the belief in things as real."

Reflect in this way for some time. Then take up the proper posture of meditation and think also:

By having acted with self-indulgence all this while, I have erred in forming the notions of "I" and "mine," based on these five grasping skandhas.

This is the literal translation. The ordinary happy man, whose main motive in life is the accumulation of pleasure, takes as his base this false belief in a real person, or self. He believes there is somebody who is going to experience pleasure and gain the results of his efforts in seeking it. As a result of believing that there is such a personal self within his five empty skandhas, he develops the concepts of "I" and "mine" and proceeds to experience suffering on the basis of these delusions. This is, of course, a rehashing of the refutation of a personal non-self (as you will recall, there are the two kinds of non-self, personal and phenomenal).

At this first stage in your meditation, then, turn your attention to this refutation of personal non-self, and think, "Why is it an error to apprehend 'I' and 'mine' with relation to the skandhas?"

If there were an inherently, really existing self as the object to which all these concepts, notions, and actions refers, then there would be no way to get rid of the self. But when we search for it, we find that the so-called self can be only one of three things within the skandhas: (1) name, (2) form, or (3) mind. It is hardly a person's name, though the "I," or ego, identifies with the name. Yet name is not the self, because it is nothing more than a chance ascription; it is just a label that you acquire, and has no characteristic other than being an adventitious label, so it can hardly be what we mean by "self." The body is also not the self, because it is simply a composite of many components, such as flesh, blood, and bone, none of which, either alone or taken together, constitutes what we think of when we use the concept "self." Thus, even if you search for the self from the top of your head down to the soles of your feet, inside and out, you will not find it.

Finally, the mind is not the self we are searching for, since the mind of the past (i.e., of the preceding moment and all other preceding moments of cognition) is extinct, future moments of cognition have not yet come into existence, and the present moment of cognition (this present mind, or flash of cognition) is just that: momentary, arising and being extinguished within a millisecond. If these present moments constituted a self, you would have an endless series of discrete, momentary selves, which does not correspond to people's notion of the ego. The upshot is to fix within your mind the clear understanding that the notion of a self that we all have individually is without foundation; it is, in fact, nothing more than an error.

Once more I must stress my plea that you meditate and examine the nature of your own mind. What is your mind? Try to turn and see exactly what it is. Search within until you have gained a true recognition of the true nature of the mind. Without that recognition, there is no way you will attain any kind of liberation. I urge you to look within.

To return to our text, after having undertaken an examination of name, body, and mind in order to ascertain the true state of affairs with regard to the personal non-self, investigate all phenomena in order to realize the non-self (or voidness of self) within all phenomena. By "all phenomena" we mean all things—internal, external, animate, inanimate, you name it. Whatever they are, all dharmas have voidness of self as their true nature. Therefore, a good Buddhist does not attribute the existence of these phenomena, internal and external, to the creation of some deity, whether Īshvara (Skt. Īśvara),[85] Chah (Tib. Phyva, a Bönpo deity), or whomever. Nor does a good Buddhist attribute their existence to a concatenation of, or random encounter among, atoms.

You must understand that your mind has the nature of nondual clarity and voidness. If you recognize this, there is hope for you, and you will be a Sakyapa. If you do not recognize this nondual clarity and voidness of your own mind, you are not a Sakyapa. We are at a point in this system of meditation where you should start to recognize this nondual clarity and voidness of your own mind. The reason I am urging you to recognize this aspect of the mind is that there is immeasurably great benefit to be gained if you will only see it.

A Buddhist will not attribute the existence of phenomena to atoms or deities, creators or gods, or what have you, but he will say that all of them owe their existence merely to false appearance: that is, they appear to be real, while in reality they are nonexistent. He will further say that this false appearance of theirs comes about as a result of one's own mind having been stained by worldly mental impressions. For example, say you are having a dream and see a city, horses, elephants. During the dream state, you think all these appearances are quite real, just as they appear. Upon awakening, however, you realize that they had no existence of their own from the very beginning; they were merely projections of your own mind. Worldly appearances have a similar nature. You should think of this again and again, until you have awakened within your mind intense certitude about its veracity.

Now, just as the objects of your sense apprehension are similar to appearances in dreams, so your own consciousness is very much like the subjective mind that has those dream experiences. The dreaming mind deludes itself, thinking there are real objects, tigers, cities, etc., and hence experiences a flow of perceptions, cognitions, actions, and emotions based on those nonexistent appearances. Thus it is a mind going along on false premises and is absolutely deluded. If it weren't for its perception of the objects it is projecting, the dreaming mind wouldn't arise at all; it wouldn't be having these moments of cognition, these subjective experiences.

Our waking experience here in this realm is very similar. The mind is quite deluded; ultimately, it can in no way be established as valid. When you examine it, you can't find the mind to be anywhere in its own right. What you should understand, then, is that all phenomena are deceptive; this is true of all phenomena that can be found anywhere. Everything that is either a subject or an object, whether it is one or the other or both, is a delusion and a deception.

Having understood this, turn the mind inward; become introspective. Focus not on the mind as subject and object, or as a subject with an object, but just on the nature of the mind itself. Simply look within. See mind as it is, free from the obscurations of subject and object; see its own nature of naked clarity, and remain in this recognition for a long time. When you recognize this true nature of mind, you will see that since it is not a thing as we think of it, it is not an existent entity in itself, because of its nature of emptiness.

We have already explained how mind is not simply blank space, since it nonetheless has the condition of consciousness/cognition/clarity. But because it is not something that has an existent nature, it has, from the beginning, no cause. It is not something that is produced or arisen, that comes from somewhere; from the beginning, it has no coming into existence. Look at the mind to see that you can't find any cause for it to come into existence, for without a cause, it cannot come into existence. Therefore, it is birthless, unarisen.

Now look at the mind to see where that mind is located. Look inside the body and outside the body, or somewhere in between, and learn that the mind doesn't reside in any of those places. Not only that, it has neither color nor shape, etc., and no matter how you may search for it, you will never find it. Therefore, it is not only birthless but it is without location.

Finally, look to see where the mind goes when consciousness disappears and thoughts and cognition cease. Since the mind itself is not a thing, it is in no way ever checked or imbued with a cause to cease. The true nature of mind never ceases; it is cessationless.

In this way, you will gain insight into the birthlessness, the abidingless-ness, and the cessationlessness of your own mind. In this way, you examine the mind from the point of view of cause and result and see that it is quite free from all the ordinary characteristics of cause and effect. And since it is nowhere to be established as a real thing, its nature is just one of naked voidness.

✂ ❧ ✂

One who has a direct experience of the emptiness of mind does not necessarily experience the cessation of the cognitive, clear, or conscious aspect of mind. Even when you pinpoint the clarity of mind, you cannot seize upon mind and say, "Aha! It is clear, it has cognition. Therefore it is real; it does exist." And even when you perceive the emptiness of mind, you cannot seize upon that and say, "Aha, the mind is only void. It has no clarity." The correct approach is said to be *sel-tong sung-jug* (*gsal-stong zung-'jug*), the nonapprehension of, or nonclinging to, clarity and emptiness. That is, you don't try to divide and seize upon either or both of these two aspects of mind.

The true nature of mind is away from extremes; it is nonpartisan. It is ineffable. It is a state beyond mind. It is naked. It is inexpressible. When you are in this state of meditation, don't elaborate on, or follow after, the train of your thoughts but apply yourself to remaining in this state of nongrasping. In other words, don't let the mind start grasping and running off when thoughts arise. Keep it on an even keel in this state of nongrasping, once you have attained it.

At first you should, by applying the right method, be very strict with the mind, very firm in controlling it. Then, in the middle of your meditation, let the mind relax once you have obtained the desired state. Just allow it to abide in ease. Finally, let the mind be absolutely free from all fears and hopes. Don't have any expectations about your meditation; don't hope to experience something better than what you are experiencing, something good, something joyful. Have no anticipation at all about your meditation and have no apprehension that perhaps you won't be able to maintain it or that something will go wrong. Without any fear or hope, just let the mind remain in the state of nongrasping. The mind should never waver from this perception of the nondual clarity and voidness of mind itself.

Apply your mind to meditation without any sense of effort; just place the mind into meditation without any conception at all of an object of meditation. At this point, you want effortlessness and ease. And since you will have already realized that there is no such thing as an object of meditation or a meditator, begin by meditating very briefly—frequently, but briefly. Don't overdo it. As Milarepa said, don't meditate for long periods of time until you're able.

When you are engaged in the state of meditative absorption, your perception (if you practice as just described) will be that the ultimate nature of all phenomena is away from all extremes. All dharmas are without attachment. They are inexpressible. They are beyond the limits of the mind. They are not objects of the mind. They are without a substratum, without a base. They are without any foundation. They are like space itself. Think also:

> Through failing to realize this, all beings are bound by the fetters of belief in a self and in a subject or object. These same beings, who are like my own mother to me, experience only deluded, false appearances. For their sake I shall attain the stage of omniscience, or perfect enlightenment, which consists of the great extremeless-ness of mind itself.

When not engaged in formal meditation, you should nevertheless be diligent in perceiving all phenomena as devoid of any substantial existence of their own, but rather as having an appearance similar to magical illusions. Maintaining that perception, strive diligently to accomplish the spiritual good of living beings.

55

TUNING THE VIOLIN OF MEDITATION

WE ARE ENGAGED IN A STUDY of *The Three Visions*. We have completed the instructions for the first two visions, with the exception of those on the three stages of meditation. The first two stages, concentration and insight, we have fully discussed. We will conclude the second vision by elaborating on the third stage of meditation, which is the nondual combination of concentration and insight. In essence, it is that meditative state which recognizes an extremeless state of one's own mind, ineffable and inexpressible.

In the first stage of meditation, concentration, we are concerned to eradicate all thought processes. Through success in that effort, our minds become free of conceptualizations, thought-constructions, and other types of grosser mental activity.

In the second stage of meditation, insight, we develop what is called unerring insight, or wisdom into the nature of our own minds and external dharmas. Through this direct insight, we become free from all doubts, developing certitude about the true nature of things. We see that there is no mental activity to be engaged in, that there is no subject, no object. There is nothing to be done about it. There is no longer any thought, as in concentration, of getting rid of conceptualizations; at the stage of insight, we see that there is no point to mental conceptualization, and find nothing to serve as a source of mental constructs.

In the third stage, we have what is called "meditation on nothing at all." This meditation consists in the nondual fusing of the two earlier stages of meditation. As the *Adornment of the Mahāyāna Sūtras* says, "One should know that the various meditations are all brought together in this path of nondual combination."

The instructions for this practice are very similar to those for the two preceding types of meditation. However, at this stage your meditation is free from (1) the concept of any meditative state to be attained or meditated on as an object or goal, (2) any concept of any methodology, such as a system of meditation or the effort of meditation itself, and (3) the notion of a person who is meditating.

Through your insight, you see that these three are, by their very nature, not to be attained as existing entities. Through that realization, you apply your practice of concentration by focusing single-pointedly on the clear, luminous aspect of mind. This is cognition—unobstructed, unchecked cognition. Whereas thought-constructions and conceptualizations have been left behind, cognition itself—luminosity of mind—is not checked.

Through insight, you see that mere appearance, the mere luminosity of mind that is manifested, is nonetheless unproduced, unborn. It is not something that has ever come about or that will ever cease to be. While manifest and apparent, mind nevertheless has this nature of voidness. This insight into the nature of your mind is, at this stage, a manifestation of your previous training in insight meditation. You nondually combine single-pointed focus and this insight into the nature of mind, effortlessly abiding in meditation that perceives the luminosity of mind.

Detours or Downfalls

Now, it may happen that you overdo this meditation—try too hard or focus too long. The mind may become clouded in reaction to the strain, and you may find yourself sinking into sleepiness, delusions, and lethargy. If you experience this cloudiness, you should make efforts to develop what is called "discriminating awareness." To cultivate this, you go back to the beginning and start over. Examine the mind: Does it exist within or without? If it is within, what is it? Has it size, shape, color, location? Remind yourself about the real nature of mind. That will dispel this clouded state.

Alternatively, if you apply too much wisdom, analysis, and discriminating awareness, thus getting your mind all keyed up into really glaring insight, it will react by again beginning to scatter. It will not remain in that state of meditation but will become skittish. In earlier stages of meditation, this would have been a gross form of distraction; now, the mind simply refuses to stay and face up to this state of meditation, because you're applying too much wisdom.

The method for avoiding these two rarefied extremes is to take it easy. Enter the meditation and maintain it with skill and ease. Keep a sense of balance, not applying too much pressure to the state of meditation. To give a few examples, if you're trying to drop stones in a case, you can't very well succeed if you're trying to do it from a great distance or if you're up too close. When braiding strands to make a rope, if the braiding is too loose, the rope will unravel; it must be done with just the right consistency.

One sūtra tells the story of one of Lord Buddha's disciples, a monk who had been a musician before he renounced worldliness to become a member of the Sangha. He had been experiencing problems in his meditation. Sometimes it would go well, but other times he would find himself overcome with lethargy or dullness of mind, and sometimes his mind would be too distracted. When he would try to rectify matters by easing up, the mind would turn wild and become uncontrollable. Hence he went to the Buddha and asked him for guidance. Lord Buddha said, "Tell me, when you were a musician, did you tune your violin very tightly?" The monk answered, "No, because then it would be impossible to play." Then Lord Buddha said, "Tell me, how did you tune your violin?" The monk told him, "I tuned it neither too tightly nor too loosely, but just right." So the Buddha said, "Tune your meditation in the same way." The monk practiced accordingly, and in a very short time achieved arhatship.

The message is that, even at this rarefied stage of meditation, you must keep a sense of balance in applying insight and concentration. When the two are brought together in equal measure and made nondual, you will avoid all the lapses, downfalls, and detours that can occur. Too much of one or the other results not in buddhahood but in entry into one of the four stages of meditative absorption (*dhyāna*), which we will discuss next. That is the most you can expect from all your efforts, even though you think you are meditating on ultimate reality.

For example, if you apply too much insight, no matter how profound that insight may be, the most you can expect is rebirth in one of the four states of formlessness. In the formless realm, the deities meditate on one or another aspect of formlessness, such as "nothing at all." These are rightly called lapses, or detours, because your meditation is taking you away from your goal of total liberation and into these other experiences, which, however rarefied they may be, are not the goal that you are seeking. Thus it is very important to be aware of these possible detours, their causes, and how to avoid them. The latter is especially important.

When you arise from the state of absorption and go about your daily affairs, you should not allow the mind to become distracted and deluded again. Rather, through the application of mindfulness, remain aware of what you know about mind and what is required to maintain the state of optimum meditation. Go about your activities while remaining mindful, and apply yourself to the best of your ability to accomplishing the good of other living beings.

This completes our instructions on the exoteric level for the bodhisattva's practices.

The Four Meditative Absorptions

Let us discuss these four types of meditative absorption, called the four dhyānas. As you know, in the Buddhist worldview, the various states of existence are categorized as belonging to (1) the realm of desire, (2) the realm of form, or (3) the formless realm. These are viewed progressively, the lowest being our own realm of desire. When a meditator practices concentrative meditation, his mind becomes purified of the gross emotive defilements that cause rebirth in the realm of desire. If he relies strictly on his efforts in concentrative practice, he may eventually be reborn in the realm of form, the next highest realm of existence, whereas if he relies primarily on insight meditation, he may be reborn in the formless realm, the highest of these three realms of existence.

In both these states, or realms, beings derive nourishment from the force of their meditative power and remain in meditative absorption for very long periods of time. In the realm of form, they have what might be called subtle meditative bodies. In the formless realm, they have no form at all, and their experience of existence is based, for example, on the meditation of boundless space, the meditation of boundless consciousness, the meditation of nothing and of nothingness, and the meditation of neither consciousness nor nonconsciousness. This will give you some idea of the nature of beings in the formless realm.

These beings have not attained liberation, even though they have attained rarefied states of mental existence. They are still within the realm of saṃsāra and will continue to be so. That is why it is considered a lapse, even a downfall, for a yogi who has made it to this third state of meditation (the nondual combination of concentration and insight) to fall into one of these two extremes rather than attain the liberation he seeks, which can be done by maintaining the right balance in both insight and concentration.

You may be wondering whether or not an arhat's liberation can be attained through rebirth in the realm of form or in the formless realm. Through his practice of meditation, the arhat does eradicate the first of the two principal causes for continued rebirth within the three realms of existence, in that he purifies the negative mental states of desire, hatred, and delusion through his realization of personal non-self. He also, for the most part, rids himself of belief in things as real, but his insight into phenomenal non-self—namely, that internal and external dharmas have no inherent nature of their own—is not complete. Hence his partial realization of phenomenal non-self, in combination with his realization of personal non-self, keeps him from rebirth in the three realms, although it does not bring about the perfect liberation of buddhahood. Buddhas, in contrast, have completely discarded both types of obscurations, emotive and cognitive alike.

The arhat does not rely only on concentration or only on insight. He does maintain a balance, and in this respect he practices rightly, but he is limited because of his motive. He doesn't cultivate bodhichitta or aim for total buddhahood, as a Mahāyānist does. Instead, he strives for and attains arhatship, a type of Buddhist liberation that is the result of cultivating insight into selflessness and so forth. Concentration and insight are simply skillfully used to guide that insight into liberation from rebirth.

Throughout, we have explained these instructions for the vision of experience from the standpoint of exoteric practice. But just as there is a whole system of exoteric meditations that lead to the realization of this third stage of meditation, so there is an equivalent tantric practice that leads to the same realization. Remember, we are dealing with two sets of teachings. The first book is *The Three Visions*; the second, *The Three Continua*, gives all the details of the practice of a tantric adept. Even though I will not go into any detail about *The Three Continua* here, it is worth remembering the saying of the first Sakya patriarch: "For the ordinary meditator, you give ordinary meditations. For the extraordinary meditator, you should provide the extraordinary meditations."

Who is the extraordinary meditator? He is the person who is a tantric practitioner, as described in *The Three Continua*. What is meant by extraordinary meditations? Those meditations are described in that second volume. What is the extraordinary vision? It is that body of experiences which will arise when we rely on the instructions in that esoteric book.

These experiences are quite inconceivable, beyond the powers of mind to fathom; still, they can be discussed. They can be categorized in terms of fifteen factors. The first three are called the three paths: (1) the path of entrance, (2) the cutting off of attachment, and (3) the great enlightenment. It's quite right that these are not explained in any detail; they cannot be elaborated upon to people who have not received the appropriate initiations— the Hevajra, for example. When you have been properly initiated, it is appropriate to expound them fully, as is done in *The Three Continua*. At this point, you are merely being given a sort of table of contents, so you know there is this other way of looking at it. That is all you need to know for now.

The next category is called the three moods: (4) the physical mood, (5) the mental mood, and (6) the dream mood. To give an example, in meditation, your body feels absolutely exhilarated and light through your conviction of the truth of the Dharma and your devotion to its fulfillment. You feel this sense of devotion and conviction so intensely that your body can hardly endure it. You feel that you cannot do enough; you feel devotion in the very marrow of your bones. This gives you an idea of the mental intensity of devotion and conviction that you feel. Your mind is so purified that the Buddha appears in dreams and teaches you, you have auspicious dreams of turtles and the like, you dream that you see the sun and the moon, that you take a bath, that you color white cloths, and so forth.

The next category is the three warmths: (7) the warmth of foregoing conceptualizations, (8) the warmth of the coming together of the nine elements, and (9) the warmth of the *bindu*.[86] The warmth of the bindu arises when it blazes and then comes together. That is the third kind of warmth we are talking about.

The next category is the three kinds of interdependent origination: (10) the reversal of vital airs, (11) the interdependence of visible appearances, and (12) the interdependent origination of dreams.

The final category is called the three kinds of meditative absorption, or meditation: (13) the meditation of diverse natures, or meditation of the variety of natures, or characteristics, (14) the meditation of the nature of voidness, and (15) the meditation of the ultimate nature of nonduality.

These fifteen can be brought together under the simple topic of pure meditation. These are the same meditations that we earlier described from the exoteric point of view. Here, as tantric meditations, they are provided in fifteen tantric categories. They make sense only when you have received the instructions in detail.

Now we have instructions on how to meditate in order to develop certitude about the validity of these practices. First, we refer to the guidance given by Jetsün Dragpa Gyaltsen in one of his aphorisms:

> In one's meditative sessions, one should diligently practice devotion and service to the Three Jewels, the reading of sūtras, and the two kinds of bodhichitta.

These two kinds of bodhichitta are the conventional, or relative, and the ultimate, or absolute. Our discussion of ultimate reality comes under the latter heading.

The meditator who has first purified his mind by meditating according to the exoteric sets of meditation outlined in *The Three Visions*, and who has accomplished those preliminary meditations, will experience the spontaneous arising of intense great compassion. Even with a small, trifling amount of these two kinds of bodhichitta, insights into the nature of ultimate reality will arise within his mind. In other words, even through the exoteric practices he will begin to get glimpses of ultimate reality, and it is then natural that tremendous compassion for beings arises in the mind. This serves to motivate the practitioner, lending greater impetus to his aspiration to attain buddhahood for the sake of others.

By this time, through his insight into the nature of things and devotion to beings, the meditator may think, "It is really not too much to ask of me that I struggle on for three countless aeons if, by doing so, I attain enlightenment and thereby become able to help all beings." But because the Buddha is extremely skilled and compassionate in imparting his Dharma to beings, it is possible for us to attain enlightenment even sooner. It was taught in the sūtras, in the Buddha's words on right view and right insight, that the Vajrayāna is a path of practice that appears as the result of training in the six pāramitās. After turning the Wheel of Dharma, the Buddha taught that in a future time a shortcut to enlightenment would appear. This is the Vajrayāna, or adamantine vehicle. It can also be thought of as the "result vehicle," because it appears as a result of the causal path of the six perfections.

Here is the proper manner in which to meditate on tantric Vajrayāna practice:

> If I have gained realization through the six pāramitās, then it is sure that Vajrayāna practice will provide even greater results. I will recognize good and bad experiences for what they are and not be agitated by fears, apprehensions, anxieties, obstacles, attainments, and the like. Vajrayāna leads to direct perception of Buddha himself. Other auspicious phenomena will also arise. When attacked by māras and evil spirits, I will be able to deal with them for what they are—concatenations and operations of various factors in the body, such as psychic channels, letters and elements, mandalas and airs. All these operate in the worldling to produce experiences of the internal and external world where things appear. I know that this is true in my case as well. When these phenomena appear, I will see them, with tantric insight, as energies to lead me to enlightenment.

In the times when you are not in a state of meditative absorption, you should not allow the mind to wander too far away, but always retain a kind of mindful recognition of what you know to be the nature of ultimate reality. In that state of mindful awareness, go about accomplishing the good of other beings, doing whatever you have to do for them.

56

THE SHARPNESS OF A THORN,
THE ROUNDNESS OF A PEA

NO ONE EVER SAID THAT PRACTICE of the Buddhadharma would be easy. What we have been assured of is that, practiced correctly, it will be effective. The results that have been described are ensured through right efforts. That is why it is in our own best interests to undertake every virtuous action with the three kinds of excellence in effort: excellence in resolve, excellence in practice, and excellence in dedication.

First, whenever you set about to study, reflect, meditate, or do good deeds, you should approach that task with the right attitude—i.e., the resolve that, through your present effort, all beings might share in the attainment of perfect enlightenment. Only when you have this universalist resolve within your heart do your actions become attuned to the Great Way of the bodhisattvas.

Second, there must be present in your mind excellence in perspective, or vision—i.e., while acting, you should keep in mind that, in ultimate reality, all phenomena are away from all extremes and devoid of any inherent nature of their own. Through this voidness of inherent nature, you, your actions, the beneficiary of your actions, and the result of your actions are ultimately identical in nature. Remembering this even as you engage in virtuous actions is an approximation of ultimate reality that both magnifies the intensity of your efforts and increases the benefits that result from them.

Further, keep in mind that even in conventional reality (reality as it appears to unenlightened beings such as ourselves), all phenomena, all actions, virtuous and nonvirtuous, and all beings, yourself included, are like dreams and illusions. Through maintaining this perspective on yourself, your actions, and their results, you will be freed from the temptation to seize upon them as real, thus making them a source of bondage rather than liberation. Moreover, your virtue will be purified, made more effective, and will become a cause of attaining buddhahood.

Ordinary virtuous actions may be a source of merit, leading to future happiness and rebirth in better states, but they are no guarantee of ultimate buddhahood. If you intend to attain enlightenment for the sake of others, you will naturally want your virtuous actions to bring you closer to that goal, rather than merely accumulating merit for merit's sake. Excellence in perspective ensures that your virtue will result in buddhahood and not in any other attainment. Always try to remember, to the best of your ability, this problem with regard to the two levels of reality.

Third, upon the completion of your task, whatever it may be, you should not forget to dedicate the merit by offering an unfeigned prayer that, by virtue of your merits accumulated through study, reflection, and practice, all beings might become liberated from the round of birth and death and attain perfect enlightenment. This is a hallmark of the Great Way of the bodhisattvas. One doesn't cling to one's actions or to their results, but turns them over immediately to promote the well-being and enlightenment of all living beings.

The recollection in practice of these three kinds of excellence should never be forgotten by those who undertake to perform virtue according to the Mahāyāna path. It is also helpful if, while receiving the teachings of the Dharma, you conceive of the teacher not as a human teacher but as Lord Buddha himself, in person, who is seated before you on a lion throne. As he expounds to you the principles of the Buddhadharma, visualize that rays of light shine forth from his entire form—and from his heart into your own body and consciousness—dispelling the darkness of ignorance, delusions, obstructions, and obscurations and awakening within you an unerring certainty about these teachings and their true sense. Think of yourself not as an ordinary person but as the golden-hued bodhisattva of wisdom, Mañjushrī, who is tireless in seeking out all the teachings of the Dharma on behalf of living beings. Maintaining this visualization, listen with an attentive, unwavering, and receptive mind to the words of the teaching you are receiving.

In our studies in the lam-dre system of meditation, we have discussed the first two of the three visions of spiritual perception. Each set of instructions was presented with a specific purpose in mind. Those concerning the first level of perception, the impure vision, were intended to awaken within our minds renunciation of worldly aims. The second set of instructions, relating to the vision of the path, or the experiential level of perception, was intended to develop a sense of magnanimity about our efforts, helping us overcome both the temptation to cling to the experiences of the path and attachment to worldly matters in general. Through those instructions we have developed a sense of unselfish striving for the sake of others. We will now discuss the third level of perception, the pure vision.

THE PURE VISION

The purpose of discussing the third vision is to awaken within our minds a better understanding and clearer appreciation of the Mahāyāna practitioner's spiritual goal, thus heightening our enthusiasm for its attainment. In the last lesson, we said that after you have trained in concentration, insight, and so on, you should enter into tantric practice in order to achieve buddhahood more quickly. Thus you might be wondering, "If we are supposed to make efforts on the tantric path after all this training and preliminary practice, what was the point of those previous practices?"

The answer is that they are necessary to attain a level of enlightened pure vision, the stage of sugatahood, endowed with inexhaustible qualities of body, voice, and mind. The preliminary practices are the cause of these qualities and, as such, have a direct relationship with their result: namely, perfect enlightenment, or buddhahood. The epithet "Well Gone" (Sugata) is a synonym for Lord Buddha, or for any being who has attained the stage of perfect, total enlightenment. It carries with it the sense of one who has traversed with ease the path of the two accumulations of merit and wisdom and gone on to the stage of the four bodies of enlightenment.[87]

We will next describe certain of the Buddha's qualities that we should should be aware of. These are, in brief, the inexhaustible qualities of his body, voice, and mind.

THE ENLIGHTENED BODY

The inexhaustible qualities of the Buddha's body, or form, refer to two aspects: (1) the inconceivable scope of his body of enlightenment, and (2) the totality of his form. The inconceivable scope of his form means that unenlightened beings cannot possibly apprehend properly the whole of the Buddha's body. It is so vast in scope that, no matter who they may be or how they may perceive him, they can never fathom the true extent of the Buddha's body.

For example, in the *Great Castle of Jewels Sūtra* (*Mahāratnakūṭa- sūtra*), we have the account of a bodhisattva who once had a desire to appraise the size of the Buddha's cranial protuberance (*uṣṇīṣa*).[88] But no matter how he tried to perceive its extent, he couldn't do it. Through his miraculous power as a bodhisattva, he ascended Mount Sumeru and gazed at the Buddha's *ushnisha*, but still it rose out of sight beyond him. From there he ascended to the top of the heavens of the thirty-three thousand gods' worlds, and there, too, he couldn't get a glimpse of the top of it. From there he went in desperation to the realm of Brahmā, and then proceeded farther and farther up through the realms, through a billion world systems.

From each vantage point, he tried to see just where the Buddha's ushnisha would end. He reached the very peak of those billion world systems, Padmāvatī ("The Lotus One"), but still couldn't see the top. He went to the palace of King Padmashrīgarbha ("Seed of the Glorious Lotus") but still couldn't see the top of the Buddha's ushnisha, so he finally gave up trying. The point is that the form of the Buddha is really inconceivable. The vastness of the ushnisha, which symbolizes the Buddha's perfect enlightenment as well as his omniscience, indicates that there is no way for lesser beings to fathom the true extent of a buddha's form. Similarly, all the qualities of buddhahood are unfathomable and inconceivable for lesser beings.

The second aspect to the Buddha's form, its totality, means that in his nirmāṇakāya aspect, his illusory form, he has the power to manifest himself in whatever form he wishes in order to demonstrate the way to enlightenment and accomplish his aims for the benefit of living beings. As we know from Buddhist history, the Buddha appeared as the historic Shākyamuni Buddha and as a hare, tiger, lion, boat, bridge, etc. He appeared in any form that was necessary to help beings, expound the Dharma, and accomplish his aims for the sake of those beings. Therefore we say that his forms are similarly comprehensive, that there is no fixed limit to the manner of his appearance. He can appear in any form.

THE ENLIGHTENED VOICE

Next, there are two aspects of the Buddha's voice: (1) its inconceivable scope, and (2) its comprehensiveness. Under the first heading, the Enlightened One's voice is perfect. Whether you listen to it from near or far, its sound is always perfectly clear and comprehensible, never muffled or misunderstood: if you listen to the Buddha's speech from very near, his voice is never loud, and if you listen from miles away, his voice is never too faint. It is said that when Lord Buddha teaches the Dharma in the human world on this planet, his voice and teachings are heard as far away as the buddha-realm of Sukhāvatī in the West; indeed, a billion world systems beyond that, in the world system known as "The Radiant One," his perfectly modulated voice is clearly understood. Even if you go to the buddha-realm of the Tathāgata, the Buddha's speech will not grow faint.

The comprehensiveness of the Buddha's voice means that it is not limited to one manner or mode of utterance; rather, in sounding the principles and the path of liberation, the range of his voice is truly limitless. To the gods, he speaks the language of the gods; to humans, he speaks the language of humans; among the demons (*yakṣa*), he speaks in the language of demons; among the serpent spirits (*nāga*), he speaks the language of serpent spirits; among animals, he speaks so that they, too, understand. Whatever beings the Buddha encounters, he expounds the Dharma to them in their own language. Thus the qualities of the Buddha's voice are not limited in scope or in application.

The Enlightened Mind

The two characteristics of the Buddha's mind are (1) its inconceivable scope, and (2) its comprehensiveness. The enlightened mind of the Buddha is unlimited: it is in every respect free from limitations. We know from the Buddha's own words and from the testimony of the sūtras that the historical Buddha was able, through his omniscience, to perceive and know that which others were unable to perceive or to know. He saw things exactly as they are in their true nature, and could perceive them also in the particulars of their mode of being. This the other holy men were unable to do.

For example, the great Buddhist arhat Maudgalyāyana was noted for his miraculous powers and expertise in all the stages accomplished through profound meditation. In short, he was a miracle worker among the early Buddhist saints, but even he had limits. His pure perception, for example, was limited by distance. He could see through other realms of existence to a certain extent, but he couldn't see what was going on quite far away. When his own mother died, he was curious to know where she had been reborn, because he wanted to make sure she had had a good rebirth. He searched for her in heaven, in the human realm, the nāga realm, and so forth, but couldn't find where his mother had been born. Finally, he asked Lord Buddha if he could tell him. The Buddha was able to see that she had been born in the Radiant Buddha-Realm.

The historical Buddha was also able to fathom the past and future course of the karma of beings, which others could not do. Others might be able to remember something of their past lives, perceive the past for a certain number of lifetimes, or look ahead into the future for a limited period. But Lord Buddha had unchecked vision of the past course of other beings' karma. For example, the assembly of arhats was trying to decide whether a certain householder named Splendorborn had the slightest amount of merit that might possibly ripen into eventual liberation. Though they searched very hard, they could not find an iota of merit within him that could be cultivated and help him attain enlightenment. They then consulted the Buddha, who was able to discern that seven lifetimes before Splendorborn had been a dog, and that a pig had chased him around a stūpa a number of times. Through that slight amount of merit, Splendorborn had accumulated some karmic connection with the Dharma that could, with cultivation, enable him to attain enlightenment.

The Buddha is endowed with transcendent gnosis. In his omniscience he is fully able to perceive things, however many they are, exactly as they are. In other words, his omniscience is unlimited. This means that, for all dharmas, whatever they are, he perceives unerringly their true nature and their true mode of being as it is on all levels of reality. He sees things as they are in all aspects, on all levels. He has unerring knowledge of all things. And no matter how many they are, his knowledge comprehends the nature of all things. He can perceive even the most minute phenomenon exactly as it is in the particulars of its own mode of being. He knows all there is to know about it, even on the level of conventional reality. He can see each thing without blurring or generalizing about it.

For example, he can perceive the interdependent origination of cause and effect in its totality, with regard to all phenomena, even down to the sharpness of a thorn, the roundness of a pea, or the squareness of a stone. He can perceive the interdependent origination of cause and effect even in the characteristics of very mundane, trivial, prosaic things, as it causes them to assume that mode of existence. He does this without being the least bit less than particular in his knowledge. He perceives each item without any restriction as to his comprehension of it. In other words, he sees things as they are, the particulars of their existence on whatever level, all simultaneously. In his omniscience, he can perceive each thing accurately.

Another characteristic of the Buddha is that he is adorned with majesty, grandeur, and splendor. He is beautiful because, by being endowed with the triune form of a buddha, he is able spontaneously and effortlessly to accomplish his own and others' aims. He has attained the *dharmakāya*, the Body of Reality; to help others, and spontaneously manifests both his radiant, majestic form (*sambhogakāya*), in which he appears to saints, and his various illusory forms (*nirmāṇakāya*), in which he appears to ordinary beings on their level, as Shākyamuni and so forth. This enables him to accomplish their liberation, and because he is able to do this, his form is one of majesty.

Since the Buddha first attained enlightenment and turned the Wheel of Dharma for the unenlightened, there have been a million billion beings whom he has caused to attain enlightenment. Each one of these has then been able to cause a similar number to attain enlightenment. Hence another attribute is that, from the time he first attained enlightenment until the worlds of existence are completely unpopulated, the Buddha's spiritual work of revealing the Dharma will never cease.

Yet another attribute of an enlightened one is his pure vision. His mode of perception is flawlessly pure. Through his transcendent gnosis, he perceives all phenomena, whether in saṃsāra or nirvāṇa, as they really are. He does not look upon saṃsāra as negative and therefore to be relinquished, renounced, or abandoned, nor does he look upon nirvāṇa as positive and therefore to be attained. He perceives them both as having a single nature; in his purity of vision, he sees them as identical. This is the quintessential view of the Sakya order—the nondifferentiation of saṃsāra and nirvāṇa (*'khor-'das-dbyer-med*)—and this is his pure vision.

Through the strength of having trained himself on the path while he was still an ordinary being, and thereby having attained buddhahood, the Buddha perceives that buddhahood and beings are of one continuity, that there is no disjuncture between them. Formerly, while he was on the path of yoga and was a meditator, he experienced the path becoming absorbed into the result, or becoming one with the result. Therefore he perceives that the path and the result have a single flavor, that they are identical.

By virtue of having trained himself to regard conceptualizations and thought-constructions as something to be relinquished, and by having experienced how all conceptualizations merge into ultimate reality, he now perceives that that which is to be abandoned and its antidote also have a single flavor. Whereas formerly he trained in getting rid of thought-constructs through concentration and insight, seeing them as hindrances to meditation and the like, when attaining enlightenment he saw that, in their nature, they were also nothing more than, and not different from, suchness, or ultimate reality.

Therefore, the Buddha sees that there is no difference between thought-constructions and their antidotes, no difference between virtuous phenomena that should be acquired and nonvirtuous phenomena that should be relinquished, no difference between what one accepts and what one gets rid of, no difference between relinquishment and attainment. He sees that saṃsāra and nirvāṇa, the world and liberation, have an identical nature and are of a single continuity.

These are all qualities of his inconceivable pure vision.

CONCLUSION

Now that we have finished our studies on *The Three Visions*, it should be a cause of great happiness for you, as it is for me, that we have seen it through and have accomplished a not inconsiderable dharmic work. In the teaching I see great benefit, and in your listening I also see great benefit.

The third of the three excellences discussed earlier consists of dedicating merit to the enlightenment of all living beings. To accomplish this dedication upon the completion of our course of study, you can light a few extra candles on the altar and recite the prayer of Samantabhadra, the bodhisattva of good actions. During the recitation, offer sincere and heartfelt prayers that, through your own efforts to learn this teaching, all beings might share with you in the attainment of perfect enlightenment.

The concluding topic of our text is how to regard the qualities of buddhahood that we have just discussed. Reflect on the various qualities and attributes of an enlightened one, and think:

> As a result of these preliminary practices, conjoined with future Vajrayāna practices, I myself will attain just such qualities and attributes of buddhahood: the inconceivable qualities of body, voice, and mind. Unceasingly and spontaneously, I will accomplish the benefit of these beings.

In this way you should arouse within yourself a feeling of great enthusiasm and zeal in practice, in order quickly to attain these qualities and attributes for the sake of others.

You should reflect on the various topics we have discussed here. Go into solitary retreat and perform a certain number of meditative sessions each day. If you are good, you will do four sessions a day; if you are mediocre, three; and if you are the lowest kind of meditator, you will do two sessions a day. How long should you continue meditating on these topics? You should not quit until you have developed within yourself these various meditative experiences. Meditate on insight until you yourself have attained that state; don't quit until you have within yourself those qualities that you are meditating on.

How do you perform your meditations? In each session, begin by taking refuge, followed by invoking the blessings of the enlightened ones and the gurus of your spiritual lineage. During your meditation proper, train in whatever topic you have before you. Always dedicate the merit to the enlightenment of others. In your nonsessional periods, constantly keep mindfulness and recollection. These basic stages of practice apply to each of the topics discussed in this entire text.

For the ordinary type of meditator, the lam-dre teachings help develop the aspiration to buddhahood in order to accomplish the benefit of others through training in the vision of experience. Extraordinary meditators, through use of this same text, develop a sense of zeal and enthusiasm for obtaining the tantric teachings, through which the extraordinary vision of experience is gained.

Enthusiasm for the results of the path of experience is what leads to the attainment of buddhahood. Those who learn, meditate, and teach others with great zeal bring their students step by step to spiritual maturity, omitting nothing and enabling those students to become worthy vessels for tantric empowerment. In this way, all the compassionate masters of the past have led their disciples from ignorance to the path of experience, and thence to the attainment of pure vision.

This completes the text of *The Three Visions*. There are two notes concerning the text itself, which I will very briefly give to you.

There are several verses that describe *The Three Visions* as the best method of practice for those who are endowed with faith, and as the cause for attaining the three levels of spiritual perception. Ngorchen Könchog Lhündrub says, in essence, that this teaching is meant for the student who has just undertaken the Mahāyāna path, and that it is also a manual for masters who are trying to help their students progress along that path. *The Three Visions* was specially designed for those people and was written at the specific request of Kunga Samdup and Tashi Gyaltsen Päl Zangpo. It was written exactly according to the oral and written instructions that Ngorchen Könchog Lhündrub received from his own three great lamas, Könchog Pelwa (Ratnavardha), Sangay Rinchen, and Jamyang Kunga Sönam Dragpa Gyaltsen Päl Zangpo.

If there are any omissions or errors whatsoever, the author prays that his teachers will compassionately forgive his failure. He identifies himself as the Buddhist monk Könchog Lhündrub; actually, he is being very modest. He was one of the greatest of the Sakya masters, the grand abbot of Ngor Monastery, and probably unequaled by other Tibetan lamas of his day. A great scholar and meditator, he wrote on just about every aspect of sutric and tantric practice, and was particularly interested in giving guidance for practice. Much of the Hevajra and lam-dre literature was written by him, including *The Three Continua.*

Ngorchen Könchog Lhündrub then gives the date and place where he wrote *The Three Visions* and the name of the scribe who copied it, Lungrik Maway Gonpo Rinchen. He closes with the injunction that teachers expound this text according to the capacity of their students to understand it fully.

In our case, we have received the teaching in its entirety. I feel that it was a work well done, and like you, I am very happy that we have accomplished this good work of teaching and studying for the benefit of all.

Outline of the Text

Note: The numbers in parentheses are the pages on which the topics begin.

THE PRELIMINARIES

I. Prefatory Remarks   *(3)*
  A. The three stages of practice   *(5)*
  B. The authenticity of the teachings   *(6)*
  C. Qualifications of the teacher   *(8)*
  D. Qualifications of the student   *(8)*
  E. The three stages of the path   *(9)*
  F. The origin of the *Nang Sum*   *(12)*
  G. The preliminary verses   *(13)*
  H. The eleven special features of the *Lam dre*   *(26)*
  I. The four kinds of valid authority   *(28)*

II. Faith   *(33)*
  A. The three kinds of faith   *(36)*
  B. The four causes of abandoning the path   *(38)*
  C. How to cultivate faith   *(45)*

III. The Requisites for Meditation   *(46)*

IV. Refuge   *(47)*
  A. The refuge prayer   *(53)*
  B. The objects of refuge   *(54)*
  C. Invoking blessings   *(57)*
  D. Heedfulness, recollection, and mindfulness   *(61)*
  E. The benefits of taking refuge   *(63)*

THE MAIN TEACHING

I. The Impure Vision   *(69)*
  A. The unsatisfactory nature of worldly existence   *(69)*
    1. The three kinds of suffering   *(72)*

2. The suffering of suffering in the three lower realms   *(75)*
  a. The sufferings of the hell realms   *(77)*
    1) The eight cold hells   *(77)*
    2) The eight hot hells   *(83)*
    3) The neighboring hells   *(87)*
    4) The temporary hells   *(93)*
  b. The sufferings of the preta realm   *(96)*
  c. The sufferings of the animal realm   *(101)*
3. The suffering of change in the three higher realms   *(105)*
  a. General aspects of the suffering of change   *(105)*
  b. The sufferings of the human realm   *(110)*
    1) Birth, old age, disease, and death   *(111)*
    2) Other sufferings of the human realm   *(117)*
  c. The sufferings of the asura realm   *(119)*
  d. The sufferings of the gods' realm   *(120)*
    1) Gods of the desire realm   *(120)*
    2) Gods of the form and formless realms   *(122)*
4. The suffering of conditioned existence   *(128)*
  a. Ceaseless human activities   *(129)*
  b. Never being satisfied by the objects of desire   *(131)*
  c. The inability to renounce the round of existence   *(137)*
B. The difficulty of obtaining the opportunity to practice Dharma   *(144)*
  1. The rarity of human birth   *(145)*
  2. The eighteen favorable conditions for practice   *(147)*
  a. Freedom from the eight negative conditions   *(147)*
  b. The ten auspicious conditions   *(148)*
  3. The benefits of human birth and right practice   *(152)*
  4. Death and impermanence   *(161)*
  a. Reflections on death and impermanence   *(161)*
  b. The certainty of death   *(165)*
    1) Death is the fate of all conditioned phenomena   *(165)*
    2) Death is certain since the human body is insubstantial   *(166)*
    3) Death is certain because human life is impermanent   *(168)*
  c. The uncertainty of the time of death   *(178)*
C. The law of karma   *(186)*
  1. Why virtue is the only help when death comes   *(191)*
  2. Illusory appearance and karmic appearance   *(198)*

3. How our deeds follow us into death   *(199)*

4. Unwholesome karma   *(200)*

  a. The ten kinds of unwholesome action   *(201)*

  b. The results of the ten unwholesome actions   *(204)*

  c. Renunciation of unwholesome action   *(207)*

5. Wholesome karma   *(211)*

  a. The ten kinds of wholesome action   *(212)*

  b. The results of the ten wholesome actions   *(212)*

  c. Cultivation of wholesome action   *(214)*

6. Neutral karma   *(223)*

7. The problem of evil and the law of karma   *(230)*

II. The Vision of Experience   *(233)*

  A. Great love   *(240)*

    1. Recognition of your mother   *(240)*

    2. Recognition of your mother's kindness   *(241)*

    3. Recognition of the need to repay your mother's kindness   *(243)*

    4. Meditation on repaying your mother's kindness   *(244)*

  B. Great compassion   *(264)*

    1. Compassion toward beings   *(266)*

    2. Compassion toward phenomena   *(270)*

    3. Objectless compassion   *(271)*

    4. Meditation on great compassion   *(272)*

  C. Conventional bodhichitta   *(277)*

    1. The benefits of awakening bodhichitta   *(281)*

    2. Special characteristics of bodhichitta   *(282)*

    3. The bodhichitta of aspiration   *(286)*

    4. The bodhichitta of application   *(289)*

      a. The sameness of self and others   *(296)*

      b. The exchange of self and others   *(303)*

    5. The six pāramitās   *(322)*

      a. General training in bodhisattva conduct   *(323)*

      b. Specific training in the six perfections   *(324)*

      c. The four social means   *(330)*

        1) The four kinds of gifts   *(330)*

        2) Pleasant speech   *(333)*

        3) Attuning yourself to others   *(333)*

        4) Practicing what you preach   *(333)*

D. Ultimate bodhichitta   *(339)*
   1. Concentration   *(341)*
     a. The five obstacles to concentration   *(352)*
     b. The eight antidotes   *(353)*
     c. The nine stages of concentration   *(371)*
     d. The five moods of meditation   *(377)*
     e. How to reflect on and practice concentration   *(382)*
     f. The three kinds of excellence   *(389)*
   2. Insight   *(394)*
   3. The nondual combination of concentration and insight   *(454)*
     a. Detours or downfalls   *(476)*
     b. The four meditative absorptions   *(478)*

III. The Pure Vision   *(485)*
   A. The enlightened body   *(485)*
   B. The enlightened voice   *(486)*
   C. The enlightened mind   *(487)*

IV. Conclusion   *(490)*

NOTES

Note: The works referred to in short form below (i.e., by author, title, and translator alone) are cited in full in the bibliography to this volume. However, those cited in full in the notes are not repeated in the bibliography, either because they are specific to the note in which they appear or because they are not generally available and are not being actively prepared for (re)publication as far as is now known.

1. The introduction as a whole was vastly improved by the inclusion of many substantive details provided through correspondence with David Jackson, and by frequent reference to the April 1994 draft of his "Biography of Dezhung Rinpoche," cited in the bibliography at the end of this volume. This first section of the introduction is based on several short works by Jared Rhoton, including the introduction to *A Gift of the Dharma to Kublai Khan* by Chögyal Phagpa (see bibliography); *The Mañjushrī Tradition* (India, 1967; out of print); and "The Sakya Order of Tibetan Buddhism" (unpublished ms., n.d.). "The Five Founding Masters of the Sakya School" by Judy Robertson, a longtime student of Deshung Rinpoche, was also consulted (see bibliography).

2. See Tsepon W. D. Shakabpa, *Tibet: A Political History*, p. 61.

3. This section is based on "The Sakya Order and the Lam-dre Tradition," a six-page unpublished essay compiled by Lama Pema Wangdak from Tibetan sources, and on several short works by Jared Rhoton (see note 1 above).

4. For definitions of this and other Sanskrit, Tibetan, or English terms that may be unfamiliar, see *The Encyclopedia of Eastern Philosophy and Religion* and *A Handbook of Tibetan Culture*.

5. For the text of the *Nang Sum* itself, see Ngorchen Könchog Lhündrub, *The Beautiful Ornament of the Three Visions*, translated by Lobsang Dagpa, Ngawang Samten Chophel [Jay Goldberg], and Jared Rhoton. A second volume of lam-dre teachings by Ngorchen Könchog Lhündrub, the *Gyu Sum* (*Three Continua*), has not yet been published in English. See also the section entitled "The Origin of the *Nang Sum*" in chapter 2 below.

6. Deshung Rinpoche discusses "the nondifferentiation of saṃsāra and nirvāṇa" (*'khor-'das-dbyer-med*) and "the union of luminosity and emptiness" or "nonduality of clarity and voidness" (*gsal-stong-zung-'jug*) in chapters 51–54 below.

7. This brief biography is derived mainly from the memory of Deshung Rinpoche's brother, Dr. Kunsang Nyima. Handwritten notes were made by Jared Rhoton when he and Dr. Nyima talked not long after Deshung Rinpoche died. They were helped by Geshe Jamyang Tsultrim. These notes were later typed up by Carolyn Cather; both the original and the typed versions were consulted here. Information has been added from a variety of sources—notably David Jackson's draft "Biography of Dezhung Rinpoche"—to identify teachers, practices, and so forth.

8. According to Jared Rhoton's handwritten notes made while talking with Dr. Nyima (see note 7), the name of this disciple of Deshung Rinpoche II was "Drupthob Sangye Kaplen." The transliteration given here, as well as the phoneticization in the glossary, are courtesy of David Jackson (personal communication, August 1994).

9. Dagmo Kusho is the wife of His Holiness Jigdal Dagchen Rinpoche, Head Lama of Sakya Tegchen Chöling Monastery in Seattle, Washington. For her life story, see Jamyang Sakya [Dagmo Kusho] and Julie Emery, *Princess in the Land of the Snows*.

10. For a bit more on Jamyang Khyentse Wangpo Rinpoche (1820–1892), see the next section of the introduction, entitled "Gatön Ngawang Legpa Rinpoche."

11. Lama Gedün was the brother of Lama Jamyang Gyaltsen, mentioned below.

12. For a translation of the *Bodhicharyāvatara*, see Shāntideva, *A Guide to the Bodhisattva's Way of Life*, translated by Stephen Batchelor. For commentaries, see Tenzin Gyatso, the Dalai Lama of Tibet, *Transcendent Wisdom*, translated, edited, and annotated by B. Alan Wallace; idem, *A Flash of Lightning in the Dark of Night*, translated by the Padmakara Translation Group; and Geshe Kelsang Gyatso, *Meaningful to Behold*, translated by Tenzin Norbu, edited by Jonathan Landaw. The *Bodhicharyāvatara* is quoted frequently in the main body of *The Three Levels of Spiritual Perception*, as well as in *The Three Visions* itself.

13. For more on Khenchen Samten Lodro, the eleventh Pälpung Situ Rinpoche, and the text that Khenchen taught to Deshung Rinpoche, see David Jackson, "A Biography of Dezhung Rinpoche," chapter 4.

14. See David Jackson, "A Biography of Dezhung Rinpoche," part 2, p. 6 for more detail.

15. There were two Jamyang Gyaltsens in Deshung Rinpoche's family. The other was his maternal uncle already mentioned.

16. *Vajrakīlaya* was the earliest of the tantras given to the Sakya lamas by Padmasambhava, and hence a specialty of theirs; every generation, the Sakya Trizin would bestow it upon the reigning Dalai Lama.

17. Death pills, an Indian custom, are pills said to be offered by ḍākinīs to adepts who then bless them. A virtuous state of mind at the moment of death is considered more important than all the virtuous deeds done during one's life. The power of the pill itself, even apart from its blessing, is thought to help ensure this.

18. See Thubten Jigme Norbu and Robert B. Ekvall, *The Younger Brother Don Yod*; C. W. Cassinelli and Robert B. Ekvall, *A Tibetan Principality: The Political System of Sa-skya*; and Ekvall's *Fields on the Hoof* and *Religious Observances in Tibet*.

19. Deshung Rinpoche's Seattle teachings included an in-depth account of the life history of Sachen and the other four founders of the Sakya tradition, as well as discourses on the *Heart Sūtra*, the *Four Thoughts that Turn the Mind*, the *Parting from the Four Attachments* (see note 20 below), Atīsha's *Seven Points of Mind Training*, the six perfections, dream yoga, and many other topics. He also gave numerous initiations (often *dbang*, *lung*, and *khrid*) in Seattle, several of which he bestowed on more than one occasion (Judy Robertson, personal communication, September 1992).

20. See the first section of the introduction for more on Jetsün Dragpa Gyaltsen, one of the founders of the Sakya school. Deshung Rinpoche quotes Dragpa Gyaltsen's *Parting from the Four Attachments* (*Zhen pa bzhi bral*) several times in *The Three Levels of Spiritual Perception*. See also Sakya Trizin, His Holiness, and Ngawang Samten Chophel [Jay Goldberg], translators, *A Collection of Instructions on Parting from the Four Attachments*.

21. In note 383 of his April 1994 manuscript, "A Biography of Dezhung Rinpoche," David Jackson identifies Maksorma as the protective goddess Pārvatī. It may seem anomalous that, after first dreaming of her, Deshung Rinpoche "met difficulty in traveling," but this is how Jared Rhoton's handwritten notes read. This reading is supported by Deshung Rinpoche's preceding statement that dreaming of her is "usually" a good sign—and also, perhaps, by the fact that he did successfully escape Tibet.

22. Vis-à-vis *The Instruction of the Gnosis-Guru* (*Khrid yig ye shes bla ma*), in note 397 of "A Biography of Dezhung Rinpoche," David Jackson says that "this rDzogs-chen introduction to the nature of mind composed by 'Jigs-med gling-pa is often given to those about to die."

23. See note 20 above.

24. See note 4 above.

25. On the three bodies of buddhahood, see *trikāya* in *The Encyclopedia of Eastern Philosophy and Religion*, as well as references to the *dharmakāya*, *sambhogakāya*, and *nirmāṇakāya* in *A Handbook of Tibetan Culture* and in the index to *The Three Levels of Spiritual Perception* itself. The four and five bodies of a buddha are not discussed further in *The Three Levels*, but see under *rūpakāya* and "form body" in *A Handbook* for a bit more information.

26. See note 25. The five transcendental wisdoms are not discussed further in *The Three Levels of Spiritual Perception*, except briefly in the section of chapter 5 entitled "The Objects of Refuge."

27. Despite the fact that Deshung Rinpoche here states that both *The Three Visions* (*Nang Sum*) and *The Three Continua* (*Gyu Sum*) "will be the basis for our discussions throughout this course of study," his commentary per se only goes up through the end of *The Three Visions* itself. He does, however, include "a sort of table of contents" of *The Three Continua* in chapter 55, and discusses the special philosophical view of the Sakya school at some length in the last few chapters as well (see note 6 above). See also note 44 below.

28. The thirteenth-century tangka reproduced on the front cover depicts this story of "Virūpa Arresting the Sun."

29. An asterisk preceding a Sanskrit title, such as the *Mārga-phala vajra-*

gāthā (*Vajra Verses on the Path with Its Result*), indicates that it has been reconstructed from the Tibetan and that the text, while extant in Tibetan, no longer exists in the original Sanskrit. (In this case, one reason there was no official title in Sanskrit is that the work was never written down in that language but was only transmitted orally; David Jackson, personal communication, August 1994.) This root text by Virūpa is known as the *Vajra Verses,* or *Dorje Tshigkang* (*Rdo rje tshig rkang*), for short. Its full title is *gSung.ngag Rin.po.che Lam 'Bras.bu Dang bcas.pa'i gZhung rDo.rje'i Tshig rKang Zhes Bya.ba bZhugs.so,* according to note 3 to the preface of Ngorchen Könchog Lhündrub, *The Beautiful Ornament of the Three Visions.*

30. The Tibetan title of the *Vajra Tent of the Ḍākiṇī Tantra* (*Ḍākiṇī- vajra-pañjarā-tantra*) is *Mkha' 'gro ma rdo rje gur,* or *Dorje Gur* (*Rdo rje gur)* for short. See the bibliography and glossary of Tibetan names and terms below.

31. See note 26 above.

32. For more on Shāntideva's *Bodhicharyāvatara,* see note 12 above.

33. The names of some of the hot, cold, and neighboring hells that follow are onomatopoeic. The Sanskrit is from Mark Tatz and Jody Kent, *Rebirth: A Tibetan Game of Liberation*; the Tibetan is from the original transcript of *The Three Levels of Spiritual Perception* (see the acknowledgments and the note to the reader above).

34. Kāmadevas are celestials who inhabit the realm of desire. See also the section in chapter 8 entitled "The Unsatisfactory Nature of Worldly Existence."

35. The name "Heaven of the Thirty-Three" (Trāyātriṁśa) refers to either thirty-three gods or thirty-three regions (Mark Tatz, personal communication, July 1994). For more on this and other realms mentioned in the next few chapters, see Tatz and Kent, *Rebirth*, and Patrul Rinpoche, *The Words of My Perfect Teacher*, translated by the Padmakara Translation Group.

36. The name "Heaven of Ruling the Creations of Others" (Paranirmita-vaśavartin) refers to how its gods have merely to think of what they want to have it appear, whereas those in lower heavens obtain enjoyments only through some effort. See Tatz and Kent, *Rebirth*, p. 103.

37. Here Deshung Rinpoche added, in answer to a question at the end of the session, that "Jambudvīpa means 'rose-apple continent.' Videha gives the sense of *deha*, meaning body. Usually *videha* means 'bodiless,' but here it has something to do with the type of body that is in the east. Godanīya means 'the continent of cattle,' where the people are red-faced and enjoy great herds of cattle, something like thundering herds of buffalo. Uttarakuru means 'the continent of raucous noises.' It has unpleasant sounds, whistling winds, and the like. These four continents surround the great Mount Sumeru, the axis mundi. The space around Sumeru is not the place where the animals get lost. They're stuck in between these different continents, where there are oceans and oceans of space." For more on these continents, see Tatz and Kent, *Rebirth*.

38. For more on and by Patrul Rinpoche (1808–1887), see *Enlightened Living*, translated by Tulku Thondup; Patrul Rinpoche, with commentary by Dilgo Khyentse, *The Heart Treasure of the Enlightened Ones*; and Patrul Rinpoche, *The Words of My Perfect Teacher*.

39. See the section in chapter 8 entitled "The Unsatisfactory Nature of Worldly Existence."

40. See note 38 above.

41. For more on Gatön Ngawang Legpa Rinpoche (1864–1941), see the introduction, especially the section that bears his name, and also the section in chapter 19 entitled "Reflections on Death and Impermanence."

42. See the introduction for more on Gatön Ngawang Legpa Rinpoche and his relation to Deshung Rinpoche.

43. This is the third example; the second example, that of a prisoner being led to the place of execution, is not further described.

44. In other words, the full instructions concerning the third level of perception (the pure vision of enlightened beings) appear not in *The Three Visions* but in its sequel, *The Three Continua*. See the note to the reader in the front matter of this volume for more on Deshung Rinpoche's convictions about the relation of the foundational instructions to advanced practices; see also note 27 above.

45. *Mani* wheels are prayer wheels containing many copies of the words *Om mani padme hum*, the six-syllable mantra of the Bodhisattva of

Compassion, Chenresi (Avalokiteśvara). Turning rows of large mani wheels, or spinning a small, hand-held prayer wheel, is thought to accumulate much spiritual merit for the sake of all beings.

46. This is chapter 7, verse 30 of Shāntideva's *Bodhicharyāvatara*. In a draft translation by Lozang Jamspal and Ngawang Sonam Tenzin (Jared Rhoton), made from autumn 1966 to winter 1970, in Varanasi, India, it reads as follows: "Therefore, having mounted the steed of the enlightenment thought which removes all sadness and fatigue, one will move on from happiness to happiness—who that is thoughtful would become downcast?"

47. This is chapter 5, verses 13 and 14 of the *Bodhicharyāvatara*. In his 1966–70 draft translation (see note 46 above), Jared Rhoton rendered these verses as follows: "How can all these lands be covered over with leather? Yet by simply covering the sole of the shoe with leather, all the earth is as if covered. Thus, I cannot restrain outer objects, but by restraining my own mind, what need (have I) to restrain others?"

48. As mentioned in the note to the reader, there was a fifteen-month gap in the teachings at this point. Deshung Rinpoche began his commentary on September 7, 1977 (chapter 1), and continued weekly through April 26, 1978 (chapter 27); he then taught elsewhere and returned to his home in Seattle to welcome His Holiness Sakya Trizin (see introduction). The teachings resumed on July 10, 1979 (chapter 28), and concluded on February 26, 1980 (chapter 56).

49. For a bit more on Sakya Pandita (1182–1251), see the introduction. See also David Jackson, *The Entrance Gate for the Wise*; Nagarjuna and Sakya Pandit, *Elegant Sayings*; and Sakya Pandita, *Illuminations: A Guide to Essential Buddhist Practices*, translated by Geshe Wangyal and Brian Cutillo. Several other works by Sapan will appear in English for the first time with the publication of [Sakya Pandita or] Jamgon Sapan, Kunga Gyalts'an Pal Zangpo, *Three Works by Sapan: The Three Codes of Buddhist Conduct, Eight Epistles, and A Jewel Treasure of Wise Sayings, including Gorampa's "Life of Sapan,"* translated and annotated by Jared Rhoton, edited by Victoria Scott (press not yet determined) .

50. See note 49 above.

51. This is chapter 1, verse 9 of the *Bodhicharyāvatara*. In his 1966–70 draft translation (see note 46 above), Jared Rhoton put it thus: "Even a

wretch, a prisoner bound by existence, becomes acknowledged as a Son of the Sugata at the moment of his producing the enlightenment thought, and worthy of salutation by the worlds of gods and men."

52. This is chapter 8, verses 93 and 94 of the *Bodhicharyāvatara*, according to Jared Rhoton's 1966–70 draft translation (see note 46 above), in which it appears as follows: "When both myself and others are alike in wishing happiness, what distinguishes my own self that I strive for its happiness alone? When to both myself and others fear and pain are hateful, what distinguishes my own self that I protect it and not the others?" Jared also worked on a more polished (and as yet unpublished) translation of chapter 8, supplied to the Sapan Fund by James Sarzotti and Michal Bigger. In this second draft translation, from the 1980s, these two verses are numbered 95 and 96 but are almost identical in wording to the earlier version just quoted. Jared characteristically attributed this later translation to others first—in this case, to the Tibetan Classics Translators' Guild of New York, which he had helped to found.

53. See the first part of note 29 above.

54. In Tibetan, the word translated here as "alas" is *kyihud*, derived from a Sanskrit exclamation which is a cry or sound of pity, commiseration, or compassion (see the subsection entitled "The Eight Cold Hells" in chapter 9 above, where the fourth cold hell is called the "ky-hoot" hell; Skt. *hahava*, Tib. *kyihud serba*). Sometimes it is used in the sense of shame or embarrassment, but in this case, of course, it is a cry of pity.

55. For more detail, see the introduction and the story of Virūpa in chapter 2 above.

56. *Kena* is a Sanskrit expression of compassion.

57. The translations of *khregs-chod* as "cutting through resistance" and *thod-rgal* as "all-surpassing realization" are from *A Handbook of Tibetan Culture*, p. 303 (under the entry for *dzogchen*), where it is added that these two meditative techniques "lead respectively to the manifest realisation of the Dharmakaya and the Rupakaya." See also note 25 above. For more detail, see Dudjom Rinpoche, Jikdrel Yeshe Dorje, *The Nyingma School of Tibetan Buddhism: Its Fundamentals and History*, 2 vols., translated and edited by Gyurme Dorje with the collaboration of Matthew Kapstein (Boston: Wisdom, 1991).

58. According to *A Handbook of Tibetan Culture*, the Karma Triyāna

Dharmachakra center in Woodstock, New York, was founded in 1978 by H. H. Gyalwa Karmapa.

59. For definitions of *ātman, skandha, dhātu,* and *āyatana,* see *The Encyclopedia of Eastern Philosophy and Religion.*

60. See the end of chapter 38 for another on-the-spot interpretation of some of these extracts from the eighth chapter of the *Bodhicharyāvatara.* In a later, polished translation of Shāntideva's eighth chapter (see note 52 above), Jared Rhoton and the Tibetan Classics Translators' Guild of New York rendered verses 4 through 14 as follows:

> Knowing that defilements are overcome
> by discriminative insight well yoked with calm,
> one should seek tranquillity first;
> that, too, is easily gained by detachment from the world.
>
> Should a person who is transient himself
> become attached to the transient?
> For, even in thousands of lifetimes,
> he will not again see that one he loves so.
> One grows joyless, not seeing the beloved,
> and dwells in meditation no longer;
> yet, even having seen, one is still discontent
> and vexed, as before, by craving.
> Reality becomes completely obscured
> through one's longing to meet the beloved
> and, fallen because of that disquiet,
> at last one is burnt by grief.
> Through thinking of that one only,
> this brief life uselessly passes away;
> for the sake of a transient friend
> even the eternal Doctrine is lost.
>
> Through participation in the behavior of fools,
> one will surely go to realms of ill.
> What is the use, then, of fools' company
> if it leads one to such misfortune?
> Though friends at one moment,
> they change into foes in a second.
> Angered at one where they should be glad,
> ordinary folk are hard to please.
>
> They grow enraged if one speaks helpfully

and turn one also away from good.
If no one pays heed to their counsel,
they go to evil realms because of their wrath.

Since he is envious of his superiors,
hostile toward equals and proud toward the lowly,
conceited by praise and enraged by blame,
when does good ever appear from the fool?
Praise for self and censure for others,
talk that delights in the world and the like:
some non-virute is sure to rise out of folly
if one consorts with a fool.
And so only wretchedness results
from his companionship—
alone shall I dwell,
happy and untroubled in mind.

Cf. Ngorchen Konchog Lhundrub, *The Beautiful Ornament of the Three Visions*, pp. 159–60, and Shantideva, *A Guide to the Bodhisattva's Way of Life*, translated by Stephen Batchelor, pp. 97–99.

61. For more on Deshung Ajam Kunga Gyaltsen Rinpoche, see the introduction to this volume.

62. For another detailed exposition on these five obstacles to concentration, eight remedies or antidotes, nine methods for maintaining concentration, and for much more on concentration and insight meditation as a whole, see Takpo Tashi Namgyal, *Mahāmudrā*, translated and annotated by Lobsang P. Lhalungpa. In the preface, p. xviii, Lobsang Lhalungpa writes, "I here also express my deep respect and appreciation to the Venerable Dezhung Rinpoche, a great eclectic Lama and a teacher of the Sakyapa Order, for his advice and explanations of the difficult passages found in this text and in the many other texts I read."

63. In another exposition on concentration (Skt. *śamatha*; Tib. *zhi-gnas*), "A Light for the Path to Liberation: A Way to Cultivate a Profound Absorption of Tranquil Abiding and Penetrative Insight," translated by Richard Barron (1985, unpublished ms.), Deshung Rinpoche describes four factors needed to place or settle the mind (which is the first of the nine stages of concentration, described in chapter 42 below): (1) an unwavering focus of attention, (2) an unmoving body, (3) unblinking eyelids, and (4) a clear image of the focus.

64. The source of these examples is Patrul Rinpoche. See the subsection of chapter 15 entitled "Never Being Satisfied with the Objects of Desire," and note 38 above.

65. For the names of these nine stages of concentration, enumerated below, see chapter 42. For the five obstacles to concentration and their eight antidotes, see chapter 40. See also note 62 above.

66. In "A Lamp for the Path to Liberation," translated by Richard Barron (see note 63 above), Deshung Rinpoche describes these five experiences a meditator has as he or she passes through the nine stages of concentration as: (1) movement, like a cascade of water down a cliff-face; (2) attainment, like a torrent in a deep ravine; (3) familiarization, like a meandering river; (4) stability, like an ocean free of waves; and (5) consummation, like a mountain.

67. See note 25 above.

68. For a bit more on Bön, see *The Encyclopedia of Eastern Philosophy and Religion* and Tatz and Kent, *Rebirth*, p. 90. For more detail, see Tenzin Wangyal, *Wonders of the Natural Mind: The Essence of Dzogchen in the Native Bon Tradition of Tibet*, foreword by H. H. the Dalai Lama (New York: Station Hill, 1993), and Shardza Tashi Gyaltsen, translation and commentary by Lopon Tenzin Namdak, edited by Richard Dixey, *Heart Drops of Dharmakaya: Dzogchen Practice of the Bon Tradition* (Ithaca, N.Y.: Snow Lion, 1993).

69. Dorje Chang (literally, "holder of the scepter") is Tibetan for Vajradhara, the mystical form of the Buddha. Here it would seem to refer to Deshung Rinpoche's own teacher Gatön Ngawang Legpa Rinpoche (according to David Jackson, personal communication, August 1994), although time did not permit checking this against Deshung Rinpche's own words on the original cassette tape of this teaching session.

70. For more on Niguma, see *Selected Works of the Dalai Lama II: The Tantric Yogas of Sister Niguma*, compiled, edited, and translated by Glenn H. Mullin (Ithaca, N.Y.: Snow Lion, 1985). For more on the historical and contemporary roles of women in Buddhism, see *Women & Buddhism*, a special issue of Spring Wind–Buddhist Cultural Forum, vol. 6, nos. 1, 2, & 3 (Toronto and Ann Arbor: Zen Lotus Society, 1986); *Feminine Ground: Essays on Women and Tibet*, edited by Janice D. Willis (Ithaca, N.Y.: Snow Lion, 1987); *Sakyadhītā: Daughters of the*

Buddha, edited by Karma Lekshe Tsomo (Ithaca, N.Y.: Snow Lion, 1988); and Susan Murcott, *The First Buddhist Women: Translations and Commentary on the Therigatha* (Berkeley, Calif.: Parallax, 1991). Also of interest are Keith Dowman, *Sky Dancer: The Secret Life and Songs of the Lady Yeshe Tsogyel* and Tsultrim Allione, *Women of Wisdom,* foreword by Chögyam Trungpa, both (London: Routledge & Kegan Paul, 1984); Sandy Boucher, *Turning the Wheel: American Women Creating the New Buddhism* (San Francisco: Harper & Row, 1988); and Miranda Shaw, *Passionate Enlightenment: Women in Tantric Buddhism* (Princeton, N.J.: Princeton University Press, 1994).

71. *A Handbook of Tibetan Culture,* p. 292, says that the practice of *chod* (*gcod*) seeks "to overcome both a self-cherishing attitude and the apprehension of an inherently existing self-identity, which two kinds of obscurations lie at the root of all our delusions and suffering. These obscurations in the form of the yogin's body are symbolically turned into an 'object of cutting' and compassionately offered as a feast-offering to unfortunate spirits, often in the awesome surroundings of a charnel ground." For more, see Jerome Edou, *Machig Labdrön and the Practice of Chöd,* translated from the French by Hubert Decleer (Ithaca, N.Y.: Snow Lion, 1995).

72. Lochema (b. 1853 or 1865) was also called Shugseb Lochen Rinpoche and was a great practitioner of *chod* (David Jackson, personal communication, August 1994). In *Tibet, the Sacred Realm: Photographs 1880–1950,* preface by Tenzin Gyatso, His Holiness the Dalai Lama, chronicle by Lobsang P. Lhalungpa (An Aperture Book, published in association with the Philadelphia Museum of Art, 1983), p. 33, Lobsang Lhalungpa describes meeting Lochema in the early or mid-1940s in Tibet:

> Not long after that I went to visit a holy woman mystic named Jetsun Lochen at her nunnery in the Juniper Forest, thirty miles from Lhasa, in order to receive from her the highest esoteric teachings and initiations of the Nyingmapa order, known as Atiyoga. Her religious center was situated on the high slope of Mount Gangri Thokar (Whitehead Mountain), one of the most sacred places in Tibet. The only daughter of poor parents, Jetsun Lochen had shaped her own destiny in childhood. Showing intense interest in religious songs and studies, she had risen to the eminence of a revered lama. Long before I went to her, my family had been among her ardent followers. Some of

my close relatives were nuns at the nunnery.

During my first two-week visit I met with Jetsun Lochen for several hours a day, sometimes in the company of her main disciples. She was an extraordinary woman, small in stature, with a serene face radiating compassion and sensitivity. Only her white hair betrayed her age: she died a few years later at the age of one hundred thirteen. In her presence we felt an awesome power that permeated our whole stream-being. Her teachings and blessings have given me inner strength and inspiration ever since. To me she was the personification of the great woman [*sic*] teachers of Tibet.

Endorsing my eclectic attitude, she said to me: "I always looked upon every Buddhist order as being a different vehicle capable of transporting fortunate seekers across the great ocean of Samsara."

See also H. Havnevik, *Tibetan Buddhist Nuns* (Oslo: Norwegian University Press, c. 1991), p. 76.

73. Māra is the Buddhist personification of evil, that is, of all the forces that are hostile to enlightenment.

74. Personal non-self and phenomenal non-self are discussed in some detail in the next untitled subsection, as well as later in this chapter.

75. In this case, the existence of a Sanskrit title for *A Jewel Treasure of Wise Sayings* (*Legs bshad snying po*) is due in part to the fact that its author, Sakya Pandita, was a Sanskrit scholar (see note 49 above). As David Jackson puts it, "It was a custom for learned Tibetans to give Sanskrit titles to otherwise Tibetan works. An elegant touch, in a way. But in this particular case Sapan adapted some of the verses from Sanskrit originals, or used some Tibetan verses that had already been so adapted" (personal communication, August 1994).

76. See note 26 above.

77. *Dharmadhātu* means, literally, "realm of dharma," according to *The Encyclopedia of Eastern Philosophy and Religion*, p. 88, which adds that, "in the Mahāyāna, it developed into the notion of a true nature that permeates and encompasses phenomena." *A Handbook of Tibetan Culture*, p. 299, says that "as the 'expanse' of reality, dharmadhatu refers to the emptiness which is the dimension of the Dharmakaya."

78. As mentioned in the section of the introduction entitled "The Lam-dre Teachings," Tsarchen Lösal Gyatso (1502–1556) was the founder of the Tsar school of the Sakya order.

79. The stage of examining the nature of mind itself is called "recognition of the nature of mind (literally, recognition of the clarity of mind)" in the next untitled subsection, which gives practical instructions for how to go about attaining it. This "'recognition of clarity' (*gsal-ba-ngo-bzung*), that is, recognition of the true nature of mind," is discussed in chapter 51 as well.

80. For more detail and the Tibetan names for these three progressive stages of insight meditation, see chapter 51.

81. For more on *mahāmadhyamaka*, see *A Handbook of Tibetan Culture*, pp. 380–81, under the entry for *shentong*. The *Handbook* contains entries for *dzogchen* and *mahāmudrā* as well.

82. See chapter 49.

83. *A Handbook of Tibetan Culture*, p. 393, says that "the 'nucleus of the tathagata' (tathagatagarbha) refers to the seed of Buddhahood or buddha-nature, present but uncultivated in the mental continuum of all sentient beings, and without which the attainment of enlightenment or buddhahood would be impossible."

84. When the Buddha says that he seated himself "in the heart of enlightenment," he is referring to sitting under the bodhi tree, where he finally attained ultimate enlightenment.

85. *The Encyclopedia of Eastern Philosophy and Religion*, p. 157, says that Īshvara means, literally, "lord of the universe," and identifies him with "the concept of a personal god as creator of the world."

86. *Bindu* translates literally as "particle, dot, spot," according to *The Encyclopedia of Eastern Philosophy and Religion*, p. 37, and is "a symbol for the universe in its unmanifest form." The *Encyclopedia* adds that "in Tantra, the term refers to the male semen, out of which new forms and new life emerge." See also *A Handbook of Tibetan Culture*.

87. See note 25 above.

88. The *ushnisha* (*uṣṇīṣa*) is the bump or protuberance on top of the Buddha's head, which is one of the major marks of an enlightened being.

BIBLIOGRAPHY

Note: Works are cited by title rather than author. Not all sources have been identified. Sanskrit and Tibetan texts do not include those mentioned in the introduction, unless they are referred to in the text itself as well. A few well-known titles are cited in Sanskrit both here and in the text itself; in all other cases, the English title appears first, followed by the Sanskrit and Tibetan when available. Only complete translations into English are noted.

SANSKRIT AND TIBETAN TEXTS CITED

Abhidharmakosha (*Treasury of Advanced Doctrines*)
  Abhidharma-kośa
  Chos mngon mdzod
  Author: Vasubandhu (third–fourth centuries)
  Translated by Leo M. Pruden, from the French translation by Louis de la Vallée Poussin, as *Abhidarmakośabhāsyam*, in 3 volumes (Berkeley: Asian Humanities Press, 1988)

Adornment of the Mahāyāna Sūtras
  Mahāyānasūtra-ālaṅkāra
  Mdo sde rgyan
  Author: Maitreya (third–fourth centuries)

Advice to a King Sūtra
  Rāja-avavādaka-sūtra
  Rgyal po la gdams pa

Array of Stalks Sūtra
  Gaṇḍavyūha-sūtra
  Sdong po bkod pa
  Translated by Thomas Cleary as Volume 3 of *The Flower Ornament Scripture* (Boston: Shambhala, 1987)

Bodhicharyāvatara (*Guide to the Bodhisattva's Way of Life*)
  Bodhisattvacāryāvatāra
  Byang chub sems dpa'i spyod pa la 'jug pa
  Author: Śāntideva (eighth century)
  Translated from the Sanskrit by M. L. Matics as *Entering the Path of*

Enlightenment (London: Macmillan, 1970)
Translated from the Tibetan by Stephen Batchelor as *A Guide to the Bodhisattva's Way of Life* (Dharamsala: Library of Tibetan Works and Archives, 1979)

Bodhisattva Collection Sūtra
Bodhisattva-piṭaka-sūtra
Byang chub sems dpa'i sde snod

Cloud of Jewels Sūtra
Ratnamegha-sūtra
Dkon mchog sprin

Compendium of Doctrines Sūtra
Dharmasaṁgīti-sūtra
Chos yang dag par bsdud pa

Compendium of Trainings
Śikṣāsamuccaya
Bslab pa kun las btus pa
Author: Śāntideva (eighth century)
Translated from the Sanskrit by C. Bendall and W. H. D. Rouse as *Śikṣā-samuccaya: A Compendium of Buddhist Doctrine* (2nd ed., Delhi: Motilal Banarsidass, 1971)

Dhammapada
Translated by Max Müller as *Sacred Books of the East,* Vol. X, Part 1 (Oxford, 1881)

Discrimination of the Middle from the Extremes
Madhyānta-vibhaṅga
Dbu dang mtha' rab tu 'byed pa
Author: Maitreya (third–fourth centuries)

Dispelling Sorrow
Śoka-vinodana
Mya ngan bsal ba
Author: Aśvaghoṣa (dates unknown)

Exalted Utterance
Udāna-varga
Ched du brjod pa'i tshoms
Translated by Raghavan Iyer in *The Dhammapada with the Udāna-varga* (London: Concord Grove Press, 1986)

Exhortation to Higher Aspiration Sūtra
    Adhyāśaya-saṃcodana-sūtra
    Lhag pa'i bsam pa skul pa

Extended Play Sūtra
    Lalitavistara-sūtra
    Rgya cher rol pa

Four Hundred Verses
    Catuḥśataka
    Bzhi brgya pa
    Author: Āryadeva (second century)
    Translated in *Yogic Deeds of Bodhisattvas: Gyeltsap on Aryadeva's Four Hundred*, commentary by Geshe Sonam Rinchen, translated and edited by Ruth Sonam (Ithaca, N.Y.: Snow Lion, 1994)

Great Castle of Jewels Sūtra
    Mahāratnakūṭa-sūtra
    Dkon mchog brtsegs pa chen po

Heart Sūtra
    Prajñāpāramitā-hṛdaya-sūtra
    Translated by Edward Conze in *Buddhist Wisdom Books* (London: Allen & Unwin, 1958)

Hevajra Tantra
    Hevajra-tantra
    Kye'i rdo rje rgyud
    Translated by David L. Snellgrove as *The Hevajra Tantra*, Part I (London: Oxford University Press, 1959)

Higher Linkage
    Uttara-tantra
    Rgyud bla ma
    Author: Maitreya (third–fourth centuries)

Hundred Verses on Karma
    Karmaśataka
    Las brgya tham pa

Introduction to the Madhyamaka[a]
    Madhyamaka-avatāra

---

[a] Or *Supplement to [Nāgārjuna's] "Treatise on the Middle Way."*

Dbu ma la 'jug pa
Author: Chandrakīrti (seventh century)
Translated by C. W. Huntington, Jr., with Geshe Namgyal Wangchen, in *The Emptiness of Emptiness* (Honolulu: University of Hawaii, 1989)

Jātaka Tales (Garland of Past-Life Tales)
Jātaka-mālā
Skyes rabs phreng ba
Author: Āryasūra (dates unknown)
Translated by W. Speyer (Pali Text Society, 1895)

Jewel Treasure of Wise Sayings
*Subhāṣita-ratna-nidhi [b]
Legs bshad snying po
Author: Sa-skya Paṇḍita (1182–1251)
Translated by James Bosson as *A Treasury of Aphoristic Jewels* (Bloomington: Indiana University Publications, Uralic and Altaic Series, vol. 92, 1969)

Jeweled Lamp Sūtra
*Ratnapradīpa-sūtra
Dkon mchog sgron ma

King of Concentrations Sūtra
Samādhi-rāja-sūtra
Ting nge 'dzin gyi rgyal po

Letter from a Friend
Suhṛllekha
Bshes pa'i spring yig
Author: Nāgārjuna (first–second centuries)
Translated by Geshe L. Tharchin and A. B. Engle as *Nāgārjuna's Letter* (Dharamsala: Library of Tibetan Works and Archives, 1979)

Letter to a Student
Śiṣkyalekha
Slob spring
Author: Chandragomin (seventh century)

Mahākāshyapa Chapter Sūtra
Mahākāśyapa-parivarta-sūtra
'Od srugs kyi le'u

---

[b] For the meaning of the asterisks preceding Sanskrit titles, see notes 29 and 75.

Meeting of Parent and Child Sūtra
  Pitaputra-samāgama-sūtra
  Yab sras mjal ba

Miracles of Mañjushrī Chapter Sūtra
  Mañjuśrī-vikurvāna-parivarta-sūtra
  'Jam dpal rnam par 'phrul pa'i le'u

Ordination of Nanda Sūtra
  Nanda-pravrajyā-sūtra
  Dga' bo rab tu 'byung ba'i mdo

Parting from the Four Attachments
  Zhen pa bzhi bral
  Author: Grags-pa-rgyal-mtshan (1147–1216)

Perfection of Wisdom Sūtras
  Prajñāpāramitā-sūtra
  Shes rab kyi pha rol du phyin pa'i mdo
  See, for example, Edward Conze, *The Perfection of Wisdom in Eight
    Thousand Lines and Its Verse Summary* (reprinted Bolinas, Calif.:
    Four Seasons Foundation, 1973)

Perfection of Wisdom Verses
  Prajñāpāramitā-sañcaya-gāthā
  Shes rab kyi pha rol tu phyin pa sdud pa tshigs su bcad pa
  Translated by Edward Conze in *The Perfection of Wisdom in Eight
    Thousand Lines and Its Verse Summary* (reprinted Bolinas, Calif.:
    Four Seasons Foundation, 1973)

Precious Garland
  Ratnāvalī
  Rin po che'i phreng pa
  Author: Nāgārjuna (first–second centuries)
  Translated by Jeffrey Hopkins in *The Buddhism of Tibet* (Ithaca, N.Y.:
    Snow Lion, 1987)

Question of Purna Sūtra
  Pūrna-pariprcchā-sūtra
  Gang pos zhus pa

Question of the Sage Vyasa Sūtra
  Rsivyasa-pariprcchā-sūtra
  Drang srong rgyas pas zhus pa

Saṁpuṭa Tantra
Saṁpuṭa-tantra
Yang dag par sbyor ba'i rgyud

Stages of Meditation
Bhāvanā-krama
Bsgom rim
Author: Kamalaśila (eighth century)

Stations of Mindfulness of the True Dharma Sūtra
Saddharma-smṛti-upasthāna-sūtra
Dam pa'i chos dran pa nye bar bzhag pa

Summary of the Path with Its Result
Lam 'bras don bsdus ma
Author: Sa-chen Kung-dga'-snying-po (1092–1158)

Tales of the Wise and the Foolish
*Damamūka-sūtra
Mdzangs blun mdo
Translated from the Mongolian by Stanley Frye as *The Sūtra of the Wise and the Foolish* (Dharamsala: Library of Tibetan Works and Archives, 1980)

Three Continua
Rgyud gsum mdzes rgyan
Author: Ngorchen Könchog Lhündrub (1497–1557)

Three Visions
Snang gsum mdzes rgyan
Author: Ngorchen Könchog Lhündrub (1497–1557)

Treatise on Valid Sources of Knowledge
Pramāṇa-vārttika
Tshad ma rnam 'grel
Author: Dharmakīrti (sixth century)

Treasure of Knowledge and Reasoning
Tshad ma rigs gter
Author: Sa-skya Paṇḍita (1182–1251)

Vajra Flag Sūtra
Vajradhvaja-sūtra
(not in Tibetan canon)

Vajra Tent of the Ḍākiṇī Tantra
  Ḍākiṇī-vajrapañjarā-tantra
  Mkha' 'gro ma rdo rje gur

Vajra Verses on the Path with Its Result
  *Mārga-phala vajra-gāthā
  Lam 'bras rdo rje tshig rkang
  Author: Virūpa (seventh century)

Vinaya (Discipline Scripture)
  Vinaya-āgama (or -sūtra)
  'Dul ba'i lung (or mdo)

ENGLISH WORKS CITED AND FURTHER READING

Amipa, Lama Sherab Gyaltsen, *The Opening of the Lotus: Developing Kindness and Clarity,* foreword by His Holiness Sakya Trizin (London: Wisdom, 1987).

Beyer, Stephan, *The Cult of Tārā: Magic and Ritual in Tibet* (Berkeley: University of California Press, 1973).

Candragomin, *Difficult Beginnings: Three Works on the Bodhisattva Path,* translated with commentary by Mark Tatz (Boston and London: Shambhala, 1985).

Cassinelli, C. W., and Robert B. Ekvall, *A Tibetan Principality: The Political System of Sa-skya* (Ithaca, N.Y.: Cornell University Press, 1969).

Chang, Garma C. C. *The Hundred Thousand Songs of Milarepa,* in 2 volumes (New Hyde Park: University Books, 1962).

Chattopadhyaya, Alaka, *Atīśa and Tibet* (Calcutta: Indian Studies Past and Present, 1967).

Chogay Trichen Rinpoche, *The History of the Sakya Tradition: A Feast for the Minds of the Fortunate,* translated by Jennifer Stott, introduced and annotated by David Stott (Bristol: Ganesha, 1983).

Dezhung Rinpoche, "A Light for the Path to Liberation: A Way to Cultivate a Profound Absorption of Tranquil Abiding and Penetrative Insight," translated by Richard Barron, unpublished ms., 1985.

Dowman, Keith, *Masters of Mahāmudrā: Songs and Histories of the Eighty-Four Buddhist Siddhas* (Albany: State University of New York Press, 1985).

Ekvall, Robert B., *Fields on the Hoof* (New York: Holt, Rinehart and Winston, 1968).

Ekvall, Robert B., *Religious Observances in Tibet: Patterns and Function* (Chicago and London: University of Chicago Press, 1964).

Encyclopedia of Eastern Philosophy and Religion: Buddhism, Taoism, Zen, Hinduism, edited by Stephan Shuhmacher and Gert Woerner (Boston: Shambhala, 1994); a shorter, earlier version is the *Shambhala Dictionary of Buddhism and Zen* (Boston, 1991).

Gyatso, Geshe Kelsang, *Meaningful to Behold: View, Meditation, and Action in Mahayana Buddhism; An Oral Commentary to Shantideva's "A Guide to the Bodhisattva's Way of Life" (Bodhisattvacharyavatara)*, translated by Tenzin Norbu, edited by Jonathan Landaw (London: Tharpa Publications).

Handbook of Tibetan Culture: A Guide to Tibetan Centres and Resources throughout the World, compiled by the Orient Foundation, edited by Graham Coleman (Boston: Shambhala, 1994).

Jackson, David Paul, "A Biography of Dezhung Rinpoche: Humble Nonsectarian Tibetan Saint of the Twentieth Cen,tury," unpublished ms., Part I, 110 pp.; Part II, 168 pp., April 1994 draft (publication forthcoming).

Jackson, David Paul, *The Entrance Gate for the Wise (Section III): Sa-skya Paṇḍita on Indian and Tibetan Traditions of Pramāṇa and Philosophical Debate* (Vienna: Arbeitskreis für Tibetische und Buddhistische Studien, Universität Wein, 1987).

Kunga Rinpoche, Lama [Tartse Kunga Rinpoche], and Brian Cutillo, translators, *Drinking the Mountain Stream: Further Stories and Songs of Milarepa, Yogin, Poet, and Teacher of Tibet; Eighteen Selections from the Rare Collection, "Stories and Songs from the Oral Tradition of Jetsun Milarepa"* (New York: Lotsawa, 1978).

Kunga Rimpoche, Lama, and Brian Cutillo, translators, *Miraculous Journey: Further Stories and Songs of Milarepa, Yogin, Poet, and Teacher of Tibet; Thirty-seven Selections from the Rare Collection, "Stories and Songs from the Oral Tradition of Jetsun Milarepa"* (Novato, Calif.: Lotsawa, 1986).

Lhundrub, Ngorchen Konchog, *The Beautiful Ornament of the Three Visions: An Exposition of the Preliminary Practices of the Path Which Extensively Explains the Instructions of the "Path Including Its Result" in Accordance with the Root Treatise of the Vajra Verses of Virūpa*, translated by Lobsang Dagpa, Ngawang Samten Chophel [Jay Goldberg], and Jared Rhoton (Singapore: Golden Vase, 1987; rpt., Ithaca, N.Y.: Snow Lion, 1991).

Nagarjuna and Sakya Pandit, *Elegant Sayings* (Berkeley, Calif.: Dharma, 1977).

Nagarjuna and the Seventh Dalai Lama, *The Precious Garland and the Songs of the Four Mindfulnesses*, The Wisdom of Tibet Series, vol. 2, foreword by His Holiness the Fourteenth Dalai Lama, translated and edited by Jeffrey Hopkins and Lati Rinpoche, with Anne Klein (London: George Allen and Unwin, 1975).

Norbu, Thubten, and Robert B. Ekvall, *The Younger Brother Don Yod* (Bloomington: Indiana University Press, 1969).

Patrul Rinpoche, with commentary by Dilgo Khyentse, *The Heart Treasure of the Enlightened Ones: The Practice of View, Meditation, and Action*, translated from the Tibetan by the Padmākara Translation Group (Boston & London: Shambhala, 1992).

Patrul Rinpoche, *The Words of My Perfect Teacher (Kunzang lama'i shelung): A Complete Translation of a Classic Introduction to Tibetan Buddhism*, translated by the Padmakara Translation Group, foreword by H. H. the Dalai Lama (San Francisco: Harper, 1994).

Phagpa, Chögyal, seventh patriarch of Sakya, *A Gift of the Dharma to Kublai Khan*, translated by Āchārya Lobsang Jamspal and Āchārya Mañjusiddhārtha [Jared Rhoton], with an introduction by the latter (Victoria, B.C.: Victoria Buddhist Dharma Society, 1976).

Rinchen, Geshe Sonam, *Yogic Deeds of Bodhisattvas: Gyeltsap on Aryadeva's Four Hundred*, translated and edited by Ruth Sonam (Ithaca, N.Y.: Snow Lion, 1994).

Robertson, Judy, "The Five Founding Masters of the Sakya School," *The Varjadhatu Sun*, December 1983–January 1984.

Sakya, Jamyang [Dagmo Kusho], and Julie Emery, *Princess in the Land of Snows: The Life of Jamyang Sakya in Tibet*, foreword by the Dalai Lama, introduction by B. Alan Wallace (Boston & Shaftesbury:

Shambhala, 1990).

Sakya Pandita, *Illuminations: A Guide to Essential Buddhist Practices*, translated by Geshe Wangyal and Brian Cutillo (Novato, Calif.: Lotsawa, 1988).

[Sakya Pandita or] Jamgon Sapan, Kunga Gyalts'an Pal Zangpo, *Three Works by Sapan: The Three Codes of Buddhist Conduct, Eight Epistles, and A Jewel Treasure of Wise Sayings, including Gorampa's "Life of Sapan,"* translated and annotated by Jared Rhoton, edited by Victoria Scott, unpublished ms., 1994 (publication forthcoming).

Sakya Dragpa Gyaltsen, *Chandragomin's Twenty Verses on the Bodhisattva Vow and Its Commentary*, translated with an introduction by Mark Tatz (Dharamsala: Library of Tibetan Works and Archives, 1982).

Sakya Trizin Rinpoche, Kyabgon, "Parting from the Four Clingings," in [Tibet House], *Essence of Buddhism: Teachings at Tibet House* (New Delhi: Tibet House, 1986).

Sakya Trizin, His Holiness, and Ngawang Samten Chophel [Jay Goldberg], translators, *A Collection of Instructions on Parting from the Four Attachments: The Basic Mind Training Teaching of the Sakya Tradition* (Singapore: Singapore Buddha Sasana Society, 1982).

Shakabpa, Tsepon W. D., *Tibet: A Political History* (New York: Potala Publications, 1988).

Shantideva, *A Guide to the Bodhisattva's Way of Life*, translated by Stephen Batchelor (Dharamsala: Library of Tibetan Works and Archives, 1979).

Shantideva, *Śikṣā-samuccaya: A Compendium of Buddhist Doctrine, Compiled by Śāntideva Chiefly from Earlier Mahāyāna Sūtras*, translated from the Sanskrit by Cecil Bendall and W. H. D. Rouse (1st ed., London, 1922; 2nd ed., Delhi: Motilal Banarsidass, 1971, rpt., 1981).

Takpo Tashi Namgyal, *Mahāmudrā: The Quintessence of Mind and Meditation*, translated and annotated by Lobsang P. Lhalungpa, foreword by Chögyam Trungpa (Boston & London: Shambhala, 1986).

Tate, John [Ngawang Phuntsok], *An Interview with His Holiness Sakya Trizin: A Buddhist Essence Teaching* (Cambridge, Mass.: Palden Sakya, 1981).

Tatz, Mark, and Jody Kent, *Rebirth: The Tibetan Game of Liberation* (New York: Anchor/Doubleday, 1977).

Tenzin Gyatso, the Dalai Lama of Tibet, *Transcendent Wisdom: A Teaching on the Wisdom Section of Shāntideva's "Guide to the Bodhisattva's Way of Life,"* translated, edited, and annotated by B. Alan Wallace (Ithaca, N.Y.: Snow Lion, 1988; rpt. 1994).

Tenzin Gyatso, the Fourteenth Dalai Lama, *A Flash of Lightning in the Dark of Night: A Guide to the Bodhisattva's Way of Life,* translated by the Padmakara Translation Group, foreword by Tulku Pema Wangyal (Boston & London: Shambhala, 1994).

Thondup, Tulku, translator, *Enlightened Living: Teachings of Tibetan Buddhist Masters,* edited by Harold Talbott (Boston & London: Shambala, 1990).

Thrangu Rinpoche, Khenchen, *Buddha Nature: Ten Teachings on the Uttara Tantra Shastra,* translated by Eric Pema Kunsang, edited by S. Lhamo (Kathmandu: Rangjung Yeshe, 1988; rpt. 1993).

Thrangu Rinpoche, Khenchen, *The Uttara Tantra: A Treatise on Buddha Nature, A Commentary on the Uttara Tantra Śāstra of Asaṅga,* translated by Ken and Katia Holmes (Delhi: Sri Satguru Publications, a division of Indian Book Centre, 1994).

Glossary of Tibetan Names and Terms

Note: Works cited in the main body of *The Three Levels of Spiritual Perception* appear in the bibliography and are not included here unless they are cited in the introduction as well. However, a few phoneticizations of important titles and terms are included here because they appear only in translation, followed by the Tibetan transliteration, in the introduction and/or main body of the text.

English phoneticization	*Tibetan transliteration*
Ajam Kunga Gyaltsen	A-jam Kun-dga'-rgyal-mtshan
Ani Chimey Drolma	A-ne 'Chi-med-sgrol-ma
chagya chenbo	phyag-rgya-chen-po
Changchub Nyima	Byang-chub-nyi-ma
Chapa Chökyi Sengay	Phya-pa Cho-kyi-seng-ge
Chijönsum	*Spyi ljon (brtag) gsum*
Chobgyay Trichen Rinpoche	Bco-brgyad-khri-chen Rin-po-che
chod	gcod
Chögyal Phagpa	Chos-rgyal 'Phags-pa
Chökyi Gawa	Chos-kyi-dga'-ba
Dagchen Rinpoche	Bdag-chen Rin-po-che
Dagmo Kusho	Bdag-mo Sku-zhabs
Dawa	Zla-ba
Denma	Ldan-ma
Derge	Sde-dge
Deshung Chöphel	Sde-gzhung Chos-'phel
Deshung Rinpoche, Kunga Tenpay Nyima	Sde-gzhung Rin-po-che, Kun-dga' bstan-pa'i nyi-ma
Dilgo Khyentse Rinpoche	Dil-mgo-mkhyen-brtse Rin-po-che
Dorje Chang	Rdo-rje-'chang
Dorje Gur	*Rdo rje gur*[a]
Dorje Pagmo	Rdo-rje-phag-mo
Dorje Tshigkang	*Rdo rje tshig rkang*[b]
Dragpa Gyaltsen	Grags-pa-rgyal-mtshan
Dragshul Trinlay Rinchen	Drag-shul Phrin-las-rin-chen

---

[a] See the bibliography, under *Vajra Tent of the Ḍākinī Tantra.*
[b] See the bibliography, under *Vajra Verses on the Path with Its Result.*

English phoneticization	*Tibetan transliteration*
Drolma	Sgrol-ma
Drigung	'Bri-khung
Drogmi Shākya Yeshe	'Brog-mi Śākya-ye-shes
Dropu Lotsawa Jampay Päl	Khro-phu lo-tsā-ba Byams-pa-dpal
Drugpa Kunleg	'Brug-pa-kun-legs
Drupthab Kuntü	*Sgrub thabs kun btus*
Drupthon Sangye Khaplen	Grub-thob Sangs-rgyas-khab-len
Dsongsar	Rdzong-gsar
Dsongsar Jamyang Khyentse Rinpoche	Rdzong-gsar 'Jam-dbyangs-mkhyen-brtse Rin-po-che
dzog-chen	rdzogs-chen
Dzogchen Shenga	Rdzogs-chen Gzhan-dga'
dzogpa chenbo	rdzogs-pa-chen-po
dzog-rim	rdzogs-rim
Ga	Sga
Ga Rabjampa Kunga Yeshe	Sga rab-'byams-pa Kun-dga'-ye-shes
gedun	dge 'dun
Geleg Rinpoche	Dge-legs Rin-po-che
Gelugpa	Dge-lugs-pa
Geshe Jamyang Tsultrim	Dge-bshes 'Jam-dbyangs-tshul-khrims
Gonpo Drocu	Mgon-po khro-bo-bcu
Gorampa Sönam Sengay	Go-rams-pa Bsod-nams-seng-ge
Goshung	Go-shung
Gyalpo Pehar	Rgyal-po Pe-har
Gyu Sum	*Rgyud gsum*[c]
Horkog	Hor-khog
Jamgon Kontrul Lodro Taye	'Jam-mgon Kong-sprul Blo-gros-mtha'-yas
Jampa Namkha Kunzang Tenpay Gyaltsen	Byams-pa Nam-mkha'-kun-bzang-bstan-pa'i-rgyal-mtshan
Jamyang Gyaltsen	'Jam-dbyangs-rgyal-mtshan
Jamyang Khyentse Chökyi Lodro	'Jam-dbyangs Mkhyen-brtse-chos-kyi-blo-gros
Jamyang Khyentse Wangchuk	'Jam-dbyangs Mkhyen-brtse-dbang-phyug

---

[c] See the bibliography, under *Three Continua.*

English phoneticization	*Tibetan transliteration*
Jamyang Khyentse Wangpo	'Jam-dbyangs Mkhyen-brtse-dbang-po
Jamyang Kunga Sönam Dragpa Gyaltsen Päl Zangpo	'Jam-dbyangs-kung-dga'-bsod-nams Grags-pa-rgyal-mtshan-dpal-bzang-po
Jamyang Rinchen Dorje	'Jam-dbyangs Rin-chen-rdo-rje
Je Khenpo	Rje Mkhan-po
Jetsün Chimey Luding	Rje-btsun 'Chi-med Klu-sdings
Jetsünma Pema Trinlay	Rje-btsun-ma Padma-phrin-las
joedrel la ngeshe kyewa	brjod-brel-la nges-shes-skya-ba
Kadampa	Bka'-gdams-pa
Kagyupa	Bka'-brgyud-pa
Kälsang Gyaltsen	Bskal-bzang-rgyal-mtshan
Kalu Rinpoche	Ka-lu Rin-po-che
Kangkar Karma Drupgyüd Chökyi Sengay	Gangs-dkar Karma-sgrub-brgyud-chos-kyi-seng-ge
Kangyur	*Bka' 'gyur*
Kham	Khams
Kha'u Dagdzong	Kha'u Brag-rdzong
Khaypay Shellung	*Mkhas pa'i zhal lung*
Khenchen Samten Lodro	Mkhan-chen Bsam-gtan-blo-gros
Khenpo Appey	Mkhan-po A-pad
Khenpo Jamyang Sherab	Mkhan-po 'Jam-dbyangs-shes-rab
Khön	'Khon
khorde yerme	'khor-'das-dbyer-med
Könchog Gyalpo	Dkon-mchog-rgyal-po
Könchog Lhündrub	Dkon-mchog-lhun-grub
Könchog Pelwa	Dkon-mchog-dpal-ba
Kunga Gyaltsen Päl Zangpo	Kun-dga'-rgyal-mtshan-dpal-bzang-po
Kunga Labrang	Kun-dga' bla-brang
Kunga Samdup	Kun-dga'-bsam-grub
Kunga Tenpay Nyima	Kun-dga'-bstan-pa'i-nyi-ma
Kunga Yeshe	Kun-dga'-ye-shes
Kunsang Nyima	Kun-bzang-nyi-ma
Kunu Lama Tenzin Gyaltsen	Khu-nu-bla-ma Bstan-'dzin-rgyal-mtshan
Kyegu	Skye-rgu
kye-rim	bskyed-rim
Kyirong	Skyid-grong

English phoneticization	*Tibetan transliteration*
Lama Gedün	Bla-ma Dge-'dun
Lama Josay Jamyang Gyaltsen	Bla-ma Jo-sras 'Jam-dbyangs-rgyal-mtshan
Lama Lodu	Bla-ma Blo-gros
Lama Thubten Yeshe	Bla-ma Thub-bstan-ye-she
lam-dre	lam-'bras
lam-rim	lam-rim
Langdarma	Glang-dar-ma
lhag-tong	lhag-mthong
Lhündrub Gyatso	Lhun-grub-rgya-mtsho
Lithang	Li-thang
Lobsang Lhalungpa	Blo-bzang Lha-lung-pa
lob-she	slob-bshad
Lodrag	Lho-brag
Losar	lo-gsar
Lü Wangpo Sungwa	Klu'i-dbang-po-bsrung-ba
Luding Khen Rinpoche	Klu-sding-mkhan Rin-po-che
Lungrik Maway Gonpo Rinchen	Lung-rigs smra-ba'i Dgon-po Rin-chen
Lungrik Nyima	Lung-rigs-nyi-ma
Machig Labdrön	Ma-gcig Lab-sgron
Maksorma	Dmag-zor-ma
Marpa Lotsawa	Mar-pa Lo-tsa-ba
Mayla Karchung	Me-la-dkar-chung
Milarepa	Mi-la-ras-pa
Mi-nyak	Mi-nyag
Muchen Sempa Chenbo	Mus-chen-sems-dpa'-chen-po
Namgyal Dorje	Rnam-rgyal-rdo-rje
nang sem	snang-sems
Nang Sum	*Snang gsum* [d]
Nangdzin Wangmo	Nang-'dzin-dbang-mo
Naro-chö-drug	Nā-ro chos-drug
ngag-rim	sngags-rim
Ngawang Kunga Rinchen	Ngag-dbang Kun-dga'-rin-chen
Ngawang Kunga Tegchen Chökyi Lodro	Ngag-dbang Kun-dga'-theg-chen Chos-kyi-blo-gros
Ngawang Lodro Nyingpo	Ngag-dbang Blo-gros-snying-po

---

[d] See the bibliography, under *Three Visions*.

English phoneticization	Tibetan transliteration
Ngawang Nyima	Ngag-dbang Nyi-ma
Ngawang Thutop Wangchuk	Ngag-dbang Mthu-stabs-dbang-phyug
ngön-dro	sngon-'gro
Ngorchen Könchog Lhündrub	Ngor-chen Dkon-mchog-lhun-grub
Ngorchen Kunga Zangpo	Ngor-chen Kun-dga'-bzang-po
Ngorpa	ngor-pa
Nyingmapa	Rnying-ma-pa
Nyugulung	Myu-gu-lung
Ösel Lari Gang	'Od-gsal La-ri-sgang
Palyul Lama Sherab Ozer	Dpal-yul-bla-ma Shes-rab-'od-zer
Patrul Rinpoche	Dpal-sprul Rin-po-che
Pema Chözom	Padma-chos-'dzom
Pema Wangchok Gyalpo	Padma-dbang-mchog-rgyal-po
Pema Wangdak	Padma-dbang-grags
phowa	'pho-ba
Puntsog	Phun-tshogs
Puntsog Drolma	Phun-tshogs-sgrol-ma
Pönpori	Dpon-po-ri
rimay	ris-med
Rinchen Chungden	*Rin chen 'byung ldan*
Rinchen Tsering	Rin-chen-tshe-ring
Sachen Kunga Nyingpo	Sa-chen Kun-dga'-snying-po
Sakyapa	Sa-skya-pa
Sakya Pandita	Sa-skya Paṇḍita
Samye	Bsam-yas
sel-tong sung-jug	gsal-stong zung-'jug
selwa	gsal-ba
selwa ngo-sung	gsal-ba-ngo-bzung
sel sing-ewa	gsal-sing-nge-ba
Sakya Kabum	*Sa skya bka' 'bum*
Sangay Rinchen	Sangs-rgyas-rin-chen
Sangpu	Gsang-phu
Shejama	*Shes bya ma*
Shenpa Shidrel	*Zhen pa bzhi bral* [e]
sherab	shes-rab

---

[e] See the bibliography, under *Parting from the Four Attachments*.

English phoneticization	*Tibetan transliteration*
shi-nay	zhi-gnas
Sönam Tenzin (Jared Rhoton)	Bsod-nams-bstan-'dzin
Sönam Tsemo	Bsod-nams-rtse-mo
Sönam Wangdu	Bsod-nams-dbang-'dus
Surkhang	Zur-khang
tadrel	mtha'-brel
Taklung	Stag-lung
tangka	thang-ka
Tangtong Gyalpo	Thang-stong-rgyal-po
Tarik Tulku	Tra-ruk Sprul-sku
Tarlam	Thar-lam (originally: Thag-lung)
Tartse Kunga Rinpoche	Thar-rtse Kun-dga' Rin-po-che
Tartse Shabdrung	Thar-rtse Zhabs-drung
Tarthang Tulku	Dar-thang Sprul-sku
Tashi Gyaltsen Päl Zangpo	Bkra-shis-rgyal-mtshan-dpal-bzang-po
Tashilhunpo	Bkra-shis-lhun-po
Tenzin Choepel Lama	Bstan-'dzin Chos-'phel Bla-ma
tö-gäl	thod-rgal
Tratön	Pra-ston
trek-chö	khregs-chod
Triyi Yeshe Lama	*Khrid yig ye shes bla ma*
Tsang	Gtsang
Tsarchen Losäl Gyatso	Tshar-chen Blo-gsal-rgya-mtsho
Tsarpa	tshar-pa
Tsechu Rinpoche	Tshes-bcu Rin-po-che
Tsemay Rigter	*Tshad ma rigs gter* [f]
tsog	tshogs
tsog-she	tshogs-bshad
tulku	sprul-sku
Tupa Gongsel	*Thub pa'i dgongs gsal*
uma chenbo	dbu-ma-chen-po
Yuthog	Gyu-thog

---

[f] See the bibliography, under *Treasure of Knowledge and Reasoning.*

INDEX

Note: See the glossary of Tibetan names and terms for transliterations of the English phoneti-cizations below. See the outline of the text for the page on which each major topic and subtopic begins.

A-Mye Shab 12
Abhidharma xxix, xxxiii, 6, 36, 46
  counters ignorance 55
Abhidharmakosha 79, 86, 88, 98, 102–
  103, 128, 179, 198, 217, 443
Abrams, Michal liv
Absorption of the mind in extremeless-
  ness 404, 438, 447, 467. *See also*
  Extremelessness; Nondual clarity
  and emptiness/voidness, three steps
  in attaining
Accumulations, two. *See under* Merit;
  Wisdom
Achala xxxiii
Actions, karmic strength of
  how to reinforce 335
  seven determining factors
    intention 216–218, 220–221, 300,
      365, 397
    monastic status 219–220
    number of doers 218
    object 217
    occasion 218
    place 218
    time 215
  three steps in committing any deed
    216
Adornment of the Mahāyāna Sūtras 39, 46,
  71, 192, 265, 334, 341, 375, 475
Advanced meditations/practices, defined
  32. *See also Lam dre,* two levels of;
  Tantra(s); *The Three Continua*
Advice to a King Sūtra 177, 199
Aggregates. *See* Five aggregates
Ajam Rinpoche. *See* Deshung Ajam
  Kunga Gyaltsen Rinpoche
Ajātasatru 210
Akshobhya 54

Ambits of the path 32, 445
Amitābha li, 54, 114
Amoghasiddhi 55
Analogies
  of faith to a seed 33, 45
  of faith to hands or feet 36
  of guru as doctor, student as patient
    259, 359–360
  of human bodies to plantain trees
    167, 271
  of human life to a waterfall, etc. 170
  of insight to a flame 369, 378
  of mistaking a rope for a snake 271,
    279, 311, 317, 405, 414, 419
  of plantain tree to good deeds and wish-
    fulfilling tree to bodhichitta 282
  of the mind to a fine horse 62–63, 355
  of *Three Visions* to a house and *Three
    Continua* to its inhabitants 61
Analysis
  applying too much 476
  discriminative 414
  discursive 412
  four methods of 419
  logical 425
  of the causes of suffering 143
Ānanda 210
Anecdotes
  of "Rockefeller of Sakya" 183–184
  of Droshi Kai and the crocodile 94
  of Drugpa Kunleg, crazy lama of
    Tibet 35
  of fisherman feeding his baby some
    fish 110
  of frog accidentally killed by monk
    259
  of geshe and the red- and black-hat
    hells 89

Anecdotes (*cont'd.*)
of miserly monk attached to his accumulated merit/spiritual efforts 325
of monk who died rather than abandon the Dharma 40
of monk with black and white pebbles 224–225
of nun who got angry 207
of Patrul Rinpoche and the old man reborn in Tushita 107–108
Anger. *See also* Mental poisons
as cause of abandoning the Dharma 39
countering of 55, 349
directed toward faults 252, 349
residues of 252
results of 95, 207–208, 220, 246, 348–349
your greatest enemy 252–253
Angulimāla 210
Ani Chimey Drolma xxxv, xlvi, xlix–li, lx, lxvi
Animal realm
Buddhist attitude toward 103
cause of rebirth in 104
how to meditate on 104–105
life spans in 103–104
three categories in 101–103
Anthology of Tantric Practices xxxvi, xli, xlv, xlviii
Antidotes
eight, to obstacles to concentration 351, 353–357, 376, 506
how to apply 371–372, 376
to mental poisons 383
when to stop applying 358, 377, 386
Appearance, illusory and karmic 198–199
Appearances 407, 422, 424, 426, 447–448, 454, 465, 469. *See also* Phenomena, conditioned; Recognition of clarity/mind/appearances
as projections of mind alone 405, 437, 446, 453. *See also under* Mind
dream 437, 447, 471
false 471, 474
illusory 360, 390

interdependence of 480
non-self of 404
waking/worldly 447, 471
Apprehension, two senses of (perception and anxiety) 69
Arhat(s) 110, 159, 166, 261
liberation of 153, 210, 237, 282, 290, 307, 395, 399, 403, 415, 478
three reasons not to seek 239
limited motive of 238, 479
motives for taking refuge 50
training of 236
Array of Stalks Sūtra 42
Āryadeva 129, 182, 240, 341, 413
Asanga 7, 392, 420, 426–427
Ascription 410, 412, 460, 470
defined 459
Ashvaghosha 166
Aspiration to attain enlightenment. *See* Bodhichitta
Asura realm 119
cause of rebirth in 120
Atīsha xxviii, 40, 64, 446, 499
Attachment. *See also* Mental poisons; Renunciation
countering of 55, 425
how to loosen 191, 369
to activity/work 129–130, 186, 343
to dharmas 419
to other beings 133, 342–344, 346–348, 351
selfless 403
to our bodies 168
to sense objects 131–132, 343, 346–347, 351. *See also* Desire, object(s) of
to spiritual efforts 325, 327, 329–330
Attachments, four xxviii. *See also* *Parting from the Four Attachments*
Attachments, seven. *See under* Six perfections
Attainments. *See* Realizations.
Auspicious conditions. *See* Ten auspicious conditions
Authenticities, four xxxiii. *See also* Valid authority, four kinds of; Teaching(s), spiritual, authenticity of

Avadhūtipa xxxii
Aversion. *See* Mental poisons
Avīci Hell 41, 70, 85, 106, 122
Awakening certitude about the ineffable
    (*joedrel la ngeshe kyewa*) 404, 438,
    447, 449, 467. *See also* Certitude;
    Doubt(s); Nondual clarity and
    emptiness/voidness, three steps in
    attaining

Bedi, Freda lvi
Bhūmi. *See* Bodhisattva(s), ten levels of
Bindu 480, 510
Black Mañjushrī lii
Blessings, invoking 57–59
    on your mother's behalf 255, 267
Bodhgaya xxxi, 149
Bodhicharyāvatara xli, 36, 41, 62, 208,
    221, 271, 278, 286, 294–295, 298,
    306–308, 311, 319, 323, 390, 498,
    503
    eighth chapter 297, 341, 343,
        346–347, 504–506
    fifth chapter 253
    first chapter 281
    ninth chapter lii, 156, 410–411
    on anger 39, 95, 349
    on attachment 129, 133, 187, 343
    on bodhichitta 281, 350–351
    on death 179–181, 188, 190
    on defilements 41, 170
    on diligence 139, 353
    on eighteen favorable conditions 145
    on erroneous belief in a self 404
    on exchange of self and others 314
    on hell realms 84
    on insight 394
    on mindfulness 61
    on moral conduct 145
    on rarity of human birth 154, 441
    on unwholesome karma 207
    on wholesome karma 214
    seventh chapter 192
    tenth chapter liii
Bodhichitta 143, 214, 236, 321, 367–
    368, 389, 397, 407, 443, 468. *See
    also* Enlightenment thought;
    Resolve to attain enlightenment

as right attitude/intent 327
benefits of awakening 281
best possible refuge 282
conventional 248, 280, 283, 285,
    318, 340
    bodhichitta of application 283,
        289–290, 293, 330
    defined 293
    how to meditate on 291
    bodhichitta of aspiration 283,
        286, 293–294
    benefits of 286, 288
    defined 286
    rarity of 289
    defined 234
defined 277, 381
four stages of 283
impetus for 248
naturally follows great love and com-
    passion 277
other ways to categorize 283–285
special characteristics of 282
two kinds of (conventional and ulti-
    mate) 58, 375, 381, 435, 480
two ways to awaken (formally and
    spontaneously) 283, 285
ultimate 249, 280, 283, 286, 318,
    339, 399
    defined 235, 340
    how to awaken 341
    how to meditate on 341
Bodhisattva Collection 460
Bodhisattva(s)
    deeds of 248. *See also* Six perfections
    defined 55–56
    five paths of 262, 364
    just a word 463
    motive of great compassion 5, 50,
        136, 297–298
    path of 4, 36, 395
    qualities of 39, 307, 323, 403
    story of Beloved Daughter 287–288
    ten levels of (*bhūmi*) xxxiii, 19, 51,
        107, 160, 261–262, 269, 283,
        322, 364, 376
    training of 16, 55, 236, 283, 329
        in four social means 322
        in giving 238, 323–324, 330, 335

Bodhisattva(s), training of (*cont'd.*)
  in six perfections 322, 324–325,
    408, 443–444
  two kinds of (householders and
    ascetics/renunciates) 332–333
  vows of 63, 219, 283
    preserving 42, 445
Body of Illusion. *See under*
  Buddhahood, bodies of
Body of Reality/Wisdom/the Buddha's
  Gnosis. *See under* Buddhahood,
  bodies of
Body of the Buddha's Form. *See under*
  Buddhahood, bodies of
Body, voice/speech, and mind. *See also*
  Three Doors *and under* Devotion;
  Solitude
  actions of 8, 36, 83, 107, 116, 186,
    201, 223, 228, 230, 255, 299.
    See also Karma
  blessings of xxxvii
  representations of xliv, lix, 54
  use of in practice 5–6, 335
Bön 391, 507
Brahmā 106, 124, 149, 289
Breath
  calm 370
  focusing on 383
  use of 5–6, 363
Buddha(s). *See also* Shākyamuni; Three
  Jewels
  cannot convey true nature of mind
    432–433
  completely discard obscurations 479
  just a word 463
  liberation of 282
  only difference from ordinary beings
    426, 462
  pure vision of 17, 417
  true nature of 461
Buddhadharma. *See* Dharma
Buddha-nature 128, 135, 283
  all beings endowed with 127, 239–
    240, 392, 417, 426, 461–462, 510
  meaning of 151, 463
Buddhahood. *See also* Enlightenment
  bodies of 6, 9, 12, 32, 69, 262, 408,
    485, 500
  Body of Bliss/Communication/
    Buddhahood (*sambhogakāya*)
    144, 304, 444, 488
  Body of Illusion/Manifestation/
    Transformation (*nirmāṇakāya*)
    xl, 51, 59, 144, 291, 444, 486,
    488
  Body of Reality/Wisdom/
    Transcendent Gnosis (*dharma-
    kāya*) 21, 51, 59, 144, 226, 247,
    285, 291, 381–382, 408, 427,
    429, 444, 488
    three aspects of 461
  Form Body/Bodies (*rūpakāya*) 226,
    381–382, 408, 444
  causes of 22, 25, 58, 400, 409, 413,
    444, 463, 483
  defined 151, 379
  five faculties essential for attaining 46
  in a single lifetime 259, 366
  no such thing as 460
  nothing better than 153
  shortcut to 412, 481. *See also*
    Tantra(s), methods of, compared
    to sūtras

Cather, Carolyn 498
Causal stage 5, 26, 263, 461
Certitude 449, 471, 475. *See also*
  Awakening certitude about the
  ineffable *and under* Meditation
Chah 471
Chakrasamvara 19
Chandragomin 78, 97, 112, 114, 137,
  153–154
Chandrakīrti 266, 415, 426
Channels, psychic 5–6, 370, 481
Chapa Chökyi Sengay xxix
Chenresi (Avalokiteśvara) xxxiii, lii, 26,
  264, 392, 463, 503
Chijönsum xliii
Chobgyay Trichen Rinpoche xxxii, liii,
  lvii, lix–lx, 451
Chod 392, 508
Chögyal Phagpa xxx, 497
Chögyam Trungpa Rinpoche lv, lviii

Chökyi Gawa xxxvi
Clarity. *See* Luminosity
Cloud of Jewels 341
Cognition 410, 437, 451, 472–473,
    476. *See also* Consciousness; Mind
    moments of 406, 411–412, 418,
        470–471
    objects of 411
    or clarity 151, 438, 446, 448, 453,
        458, 472
Compassion. *See* Great compassion
Compendium of Doctrines Sūtra 264
Compendium of Trainings 43, 46, 403
Completion stage (*dzog-rim*) 32, 314
Concentration (*śamatha*) lx, 9, 235, 478.
    See also Equanimity; Tranquillity
    arises from solitude 342, 348, 351
    defined 50, 143, 341–342, 346, 351,
        375, 378
    false state of 378
    first aim of 360
    five obstacles to 352–353, 355–357,
        371, 376, 506
    how to practice 384, 430
    how to reflect on 382
    must precede insight 342, 364, 409,
        448
    nine stages of 351, 360, 371–373,
        375–376, 386, 506
    perfection of 324
    posture for 361–363, 369–370, 375
    purpose of 475
    requires renunciation 342–344
    single-pointed 372, 376, 384–385,
        401, 468
    subdues mental poisons 342, 369,
        424, 455
    translation of term 361
Conjuncture of the eighteen auspicious
    conditions. *See* Eighteen favorable/
    requisite conditions
Consciousness 399, 404, 413, 418, 437,
    448–449, 458, 472, 484. *See also*
    Mind *and under* Self, search for
    boundless 478
    cognizable (mental) and noncogniz-
        able (five senses) 411, 430

highest attainable in saṃsāra 373, 376
    individual 437, 461, 471
    mental 410–411, 430
    of objects 426
Conventional reality 248, 272, 293,
    327–328, 330, 407, 463, 488. *See
    also* Ultimate reality
    clear aspect of mind and 455
    defined 235, 483
Conze, Edward lii
Cosmology, Buddhist, four continents in
    102. *See also individual continents*
Cranial protuberance (*uṣṇīṣa*) 485
Creation stage (*kye-rim*) 32, 314

Dagchen Rinpoche xxxii, xlvii–xlviii,
    l–lv, lviii, lx, lxiii, lxvi, lxviii, 498
Dagmo Kusho xxxv, xlvii–xlviii, l–liii,
    lviii, lx, lxvi, 498
Dalai Lama, fourteenth (Tenzin Gyatso)
    xlviii, li, lvi, 338, 367–368
Dāmarūpa xxxii
Dawa (Deshung Rinpoche III's atten-
    dant) lx
Dawa Drolma Lama, Carolyn lxiii
Death
    certainty of 165, 171, 190, 195, 345
        due to impermanence of human
            life 168
        due to insubstantiality of human
            bodies 167
        how to meditate on 176–177
        how to recollect in daily life 177–178
    how to meditate on 193–195
    reflection on
        benefits of 196
        deeds follow us into 189
        eloquence useless at time of 189–190
        friends useless at time of 188
        property useless at time of 187
        virtue only help at time of 188,
            191–193
    uncertainty of time of 165
        because causes of uninterrupted
            life are few 182
        because human life span has no
            fixed limit 178–179

Death, uncertainty of time of (*cont'd*.)
  because its causes are many
    180–182
  how to meditate on 182–183
Death and impermanence 170, 177,
    184–185, 356
Defiled defilements 96
Defiled pleasure 120
Defilements 17, 21, 41, 167, 402. *See
    also* Mental poisons
  adventitious 462–463
  how to overcome 346
  mental/emotional 104, 172, 257,
    364, 369, 478
  purification of 423
  three kinds of 96
Delusion 413, 461, 472. *See also*
    Ignorance; Mental poisons
  about the self 404
  defined 144
  greatest possible 156
  opposite of 224
Demigods. *See* Asura realm
Derge xl, xlii–xliii, xlv
Deshung Ajam Kunga Gyaltsen
    Rinpoche xxxviii–xxxix, xlii–xliii,
    xlv, liii, 349
Deshung Chöphel xxxix
Deshung Monastery xxxiii–xxxv, xlii, xlv
Deshung Rinpoche. *See* Deshung
    Rinpoche III
Deshung Rinpoche I (Changchub
    Nyima) xxxiii
Deshung Rinpoche II (Lungrik Nyima)
    xxxiv–xxxv, xxxviii–xxxix, xlvii
Deshung Rinpoche III (Kunga Tenpay
    Nyima) xxvii, xxxii, xxxiv, xxxvii,
    lxvi, lxviii–lxx
  childhood of xxxiv–xxxvi
    first meeting with Gatön Rinpoche
      xxxvi
    five-year retreat during xxxv
    siblings xxxv
    studies during xxxv
  daily practice of lii–liii
  death of lxii
  emigration to USA li–liii
  escape from Kham xlix–li

full monastic ordination of xlii
further study and practice xl–xliii
knee injury of xliii, lii
last words lxii
long life prayer of xl
mother of xlvi–xlvii. *See also* Pema
    Chözom
pilgrimage to Sakya xlv–xlvii
recognition as Gatön Rinpoche's suc-
    cessor xliv–xlv
recognition as tulku xxxiv, xxxviii–
    xxxix
reestablishment of Tarlam lvi–lviii
return to Nepal lviii
root gurus of xxxiv, xlvi
Sanskrit grammar and xl–xlii, lix
teachings in America liv–lvi
willingness to follow guru's advice
    xxxviii, lix
Deshung Rinpoche IV (Ngawang
    Kunga Tegchen Chökyi Nyima)
    lxiii, lxxi
Desire. *See also* Mental poisons; Realm
    of desire
  as cause of abandoning the Dharma
    38
  object(s) of 105, 131–132
  or attachment 55
  sexual 134
    antidote to 383
  weariness of indulging in 132
Desire realm. *See* Realm of desire
Detachment. *See* Renunciation
Detours or downfalls 476–478
Devotion 453, 462, 480
  bodhichitta acquired through 283
  expression of (bodily, vocally, and
    mentally) 54, 56–57
  merit and 103
  root of 34–35
  signs of 480
  toward all beings 239, 481
Dhammapada 166
Dharma. *See also* Listening to Dharma;
    Teaching(s), spiritual; Three
    Jewels
  as an object of refuge 51
  defined 313

Dharma (*cont'd.*)
  difficulty of obtaining the opportunity
    to practice 4, 11, 31, 45, 75, 93,
    109, 144, 156–157, 169, 185, 442
  four causes of abandoning (desire,
    anger, fear, and ignorance)
    38–42, 45
  protectors of liii, 29, 63
  two aspects of (scriptures and realiza-
    tions) 51, 56
Dharma wheel (*dharmacakra*) 149, 481,
    488
Dharmadhātu 427, 509
Dharmakāya. *See under* Buddhahood,
    bodies of
Dharmakīrti xxix, 271
Dharmas (phenomena) 51, 214, 269,
    341, 395, 404, 415, 418, 441,
    459, 488. *See also* Phenomena,
    conditioned
  defined 419, 473
  not abiding in 460–461
Dignāga xxix
Dilgo Khyentse Rinpoche xxvii, xlviii,
    liii, lv, lvii, lix–lxii
Diligence 70, 104, 135, 152, 196, 233,
    356
  as antidote to laziness 353
  defined 353
  examples of 163
  excessive 352
  how to awaken 150, 197
  key to success in spiritual practice 9,
    176, 393
  need for 138–139, 367, 457
  perfection of 324, 382, 408, 444
  requires reflection on impermanence
    176
  results in buddhahood 143, 392
Discipline. *See* Vinaya
Discriminating awareness 476
*Discrimination of the Middle from the
    Extremes* 352, 357
Dispelling Sorrow 166–167
Distraction. *See* Mental unruliness
Dorje Pagmo 1
Doubt(s). *See also* Certitude *and under*
    Faith

about existence of a self 413
about Mahāyāna path 238
about meditating on non-self or self
    404
about possibility of enlightenment
    45, 258
gods and 122
removal of 8, 32, 46, 369, 451, 475
Dr. Nyima. *See* Kunsang Nyima
Dragpa Gyaltsen xxix, lvii, 4, 32, 70,
    76, 106, 109, 137, 165, 186, 237,
    348, 392, 433, 437, 439, 480,
    499. *See also Parting from the Four
    Attachments*
Dream(s)
  Atīsha's simile of 447
  auspicious 480
  Deshung Rinpoche II and xxxiv
  Deshung Rinpoche III and xl, li, lvii,
    lxi
  Dragpa Gyaltsen and xxix
  everything is illusory like a 271, 423,
    448, 453, 483
  inauspicious 18
  inner biography and xxvii
  interdependent origination of 480
  life is but a 17, 72, 107, 422, 425, 441
  of ourselves 418
  Sakya Pandita and xxix
  Virūpa and 18
Drogmi Shākya Yeshe xxviii, xxxi–xxxii,
    160, 313
Drogön Sakya Centre lviii
Dropu Lotsawa Jampay Päl 192
Drupthon Sangye Khaplen xxxiv
Dsongsar Jamyang Khyentse Rinpoche
    lvii, lx
Dsongsar Khyentse Rinpoche II
    (Jamyang Chökyi Lodro) xli–xliii,
    xlv, xlviii, l–li, liv, lvii, lx, lxvii
Dsongsar Monastery xxxvii, xl–xlii,
    xlviii, li, liv
Dsongsar seminary xxxix, xli
Dudjom Rinpoche lvii
Dzog-chen 12, 300, 436, 500. *See also*
    Nyingma tradition
Dzogchen Shenga xxxvii

Ego. *See* Self
Eight negative conditions/restless states 145, 147–148
Eighteen favorable/requisite conditions 145, 147, 152–154, 156–157, 417
Eighty-Four Mahāsiddhas 12, 393, 399
Eighty-four thousand teachings. *See under* Shākyamuni
Ekvall, Robert B. lii
Elaborationlessness 460. *See also* Ultimate reality
Elimination of Bad Rebirths xxxix
Emptiness. *See* Realization of emptiness; Nondual clarity and emptiness/voidness; *and under* Meditation; Mind
Enlightened body 485–486
Enlightened mind 487
Enlightened ones. *See* Buddha(s)
Enlightened voice 486–487
Enlightenment. *See also* Buddhahood
  causes of (compassion, wisdom, and merit) 22, 395, 402–403
  defined 353
  depends on exchange of self and others 304
  foundation of 135
  most important thing of all 65
  occurs through mental actions 301
  omniscience and 17, 474, 486
  path to 37, 48, 56, 63, 249, 291, 336
    eight negative conditions and 147
  perfect 21, 69, 135, 214, 247, 261, 468
    defined 144, 282
  possibility of 40, 463. *See also* Buddha-nature
  requires bodhichitta 278, 359
  transforming delusions into 27
  two essential elements of (transcendent merit and wisdom) 403, 436, 444
  ultimate bodhichitta and 58
Enlightenment Body. *See* Buddhahood, bodies of, Body of Reality
Enlightenment thought 57, 104, 192, 240, 281, 283, 448. *See also* Bodhichitta

Enthusiasm 139, 309, 324, 353, 490–491. *See also* Diligence *and under* Pure vision
Equanimity 357, 425–426. *See also* Concentration
Esoteric presentation (*slob-bshad*) xxxii
Eternalism 439
Exalted Utterance 166, 179
Excellence, three kinds of 389–391, 397–399, 403, 407, 441, 483–484, 490
Exchange of self and others 280, 296
  ability develops gradually 307–308
  as antidote to erroneous belief in a self 307
  as antidote to pride 384
  benefits of 308
  essential to enlightenment 303, 305, 307
  how to extend to all beings 310, 315–316, 318
  how to meditate on 309–312, 314–318
  how to visualize 304
  taking and sending 318
Exhortation to Higher Aspiration Sūtra 130
Existence, worldly/conditioned. *See also* Saṃsāra
  five modes/six realms of 70–72
  impermanence of 73, 161
  interaction between realms 106–107
  root cause of 144
  three realms of (desire, form, and formlessness) 70, 376
  unsatisfactory nature of 69–72, 110, 128, 137–138, 185
Extended Play Sūtra 105, 112, 131–132
Extremelessness (*tadrel*) 439, 449–450, 464, 474. *See also* Absorption of the mind in extremelessness

Faith
  as antidote to laziness 353
  as first requirement of a spiritual path 9, 33–34
  as motive for taking refuge 48, 50

Faith (cont'd.)
  blind 36
  how to cultivate 45–46
  lack of 33, 258
  of aspiration/desire 37, 46, 50
  of clear appreciation/belief 38, 50
  of confidence 50
    in the Four Noble Truths 37
    in the law of karma 36
    in the Three Jewels 37
  removes doubts 34
  steady 38, 40, 42, 46
  three kinds of (confidence, aspiration,
    and clear appreciation) 36, 38, 50
Fathers. See also Mothers
  all beings as 237
  how to visualize 245
Fear
  as a result of attachment 188
  as cause of abandoning the Dharma
    40–41
  as motive for taking refuge 48–49
Field of elders 217
Field of mercy 217
Field of virtues 217
Five aggregates (skandha) 73, 128, 166,
    199, 266, 271–272, 278, 306,
    324, 340, 413–414, 469–470
Five buddha races/families 54
Five Great Jetsüns 57, 160, 346, 392, 454
Five transcendental wisdoms 12, 32,
    55, 262, 408, 500
Form and formless realms. See Realm of
    form; Realm of formlessness
Form Body/Bodies. See under
    Buddhahood, bodies of
Foundational meditations/practices. See
    Fundamental meditations/practices
Four extremes 438. See also
    Extremelessness
Four Hundred Verses 129, 182, 413
Four Noble Truths 37, 236, 468
  essence of Buddhist teachings 315
Four Profound Dharmas of Sakya xxxii
Four reflections for turning the mind
    169, 380
Four social means. See also under
    Bodhisattva(s)

attuning yourself to others 333
four kinds of gifts 332
  gift of Dharma 331
  gift of fearlessness 331
  gift of love 331
  to the needy what they need 330–331
how to meditate on 334–336
pleasant speech 333
practicing what you preach 333–334
summarized 334
Fundamental meditations/practices,
    defined 31. See also Lam dre, two
    levels of; The Three Visions

Ga Rabjampa Kunga Yeshe xxxix
Garuda(s) 102, 154
Gatön Ngawang Legpa Rinpoche xxxiv,
    xxxvi–xliv, xlviii, lxv, 325, 349, 356,
    361, 370, 378, 462, 507
  death of xlv
  Deshung Rinpoche III's opinion of
    xxxviii
  emphasis on preliminary practices 164
  fifteen-year retreat of xxxvii, 150, 163
  Lam dre his special practice xxxvii
  realizations of 164
Gayādhara xxxii, 12, 28, 262, 313, 445, 454
Geleg Rinpoche lx
Gelug tradition 313
  distinction between lam-rim and
    ngag-rim 328
General presentation (tshogs-bshad) xxxii
Geshe Jamyang Tsultrim lxi, 498
Gifts, pure and impure 331–332
Giving. See also under Bodhisattva(s)
  commensurate with your ability 323
  equanimity in 334
  perfection of 324, 381
  results of 323, 331
Gnosis. See Wisdom
Godan Khan xxix
Godanīya 102, 502
Gods' realm
  how to meditate on 123–124
  life span in 442
  realm of desire 120–122
  realms of form and formlessness
    122–123

Gods' realm (*cont'd.*)
    sufferings greatest in 120
Gonpo Namgyal xxxviii
Good Destiny Sūtra xxxix
Gorampa Sönam Sengay lv
Graded/graduated path to enlighten-
    ment 12, 169. *See also Lam rim*
Great Castle of Jewels Sūtra 485
Great compassion 15, 58, 91, 236,
    315, 381, 403
    as foundation of Mahāyāna path 265
    as motive for taking refuge 48, 50
    connection to bodhichitta 293
    defined 234, 248, 264
    essence of 266
    for your enemies 250, 268, 274
    for your mother 266, 273
    how to extend to all beings 250–251,
        267–268, 273–274
    how to mediate on 272–274
    source of 481
    three types of
        directed toward beings 265–267
        directed toward dharmas 265–266,
            269–271
            defined 270
        objectless 266, 271, 395
            purpose of 272
    transforms fear into happiness 265
Great love 58, 236, 381
    as antidote to anger 384
    benefits of 253
    defined 234
    first prerequisite for Mahāyāna path
        240
    four subtopics of
        meditation on repaying your
            mother's kindness 244–246,
            255
        recognition of need to repay your
            mother's kindness 243–244,
            254
        recognition of your mother
            240–241
        recognition of your mother's kind-
            ness to you 241–243
    how to extend to all beings 245,
        249–250, 252, 254

leads naturally to great compassion 248
obstacles to 252–253
overcomes mental poisons 251
three stages of (wish, formalization,
    and prayer) 255
Guru(s). *See also* Teacher(s), spiritual
    lineal 56
    root xxxiv, xxxix, xlii, 56
    translation of term 15
Gyalpo Pehar xxxviii
Gyatso, Janet liv
Gyu Sum. See The Three Continua

Hadrungpa l
Happiness
    appearance of 124
    cause of 131, 445
    futile to seek for yourself alone
        305–306. *See also* Arhat(s)
    not to be expected in worldly exis-
        tence 71, 105
    relative 127, 212
    source of 240
    temporary 312
    ultimate 127, 312
Harinanda xxix
Heart Sūtra 4
Heedfulness 61–62, 197
    defined 354
Hell realms
    eight cold 77–80
        how to meditate on 80–81
        life spans in 79–80
    eight hot 83–85
        how to meditate on 87
        life spans in 86–87
    eighteen 76
    how to meditate on 90, 95
    meaning of teachings on 87, 89, 95,
        420
    renunciates' actions leading to 219–220
    six neighboring 87–90
    temporary 93–94
        cause of rebirth in 95
        in the human realm 94
Hevajra lii, lxii, 492
    empowerment xlvi–xlvii, 110, 314,
        322, 457, 479

Hevajra Root Tantra xxxi, xxxiii
Hevajra Tantra xxix, xxxi, lix, 6–7, 28, 32, 445
  meant for everyone 26
  three Sakya texts on xliii
Higher Linkage 402–403
Hinduism xxix, 370, 400, 404
Human birth
  benefits of 152–157
  essence of 159
  goal of 153
  rarity of 145–147, 156–157
Human realm
  as motive for practicing Dharma now 116, 118, 442–443
  birth 111–112
  cause of rebirth in 145
  death 115–116
  disease 114–115
  how to meditate on 156–157
  life span in 442
  most fortunate of all realms 154
  old age 112–114
  other sufferings in 117–118
Hundred Verses on Karma 199
Hungry ghosts. *See* Preta realm
Hīnayāna path 11, 321, 340
  can lead to realm of formlessness 71
  on nature of mind 420–421
  on personal non-self 415
  truth of cessation and 468

Ignorance. *See also* Delusion; Mental poisons
  as cause of abandoning the Dharma 41
  as cause of suffering 49
  countering of 55
  root of 259, 271, 274
Illusory appearance 198–199. *See also* Subject-object dichotomy
Impermanence
  how to meditate on 171–173
  reflection on 161–165
    benefits of 161–162, 175, 339
    crucial in awakening diligence 176
    crucial in awakening renunciation 161, 176
Impure vision 14, 185, 328

defined 197–198
  major topics in 9, 152, 175, 185, 329, 417
  renunciation and 69, 175, 263
Indra 124
Insight (*vipaśyanā*) 9, 15, 235, 467, 478. *See also* Wisdom
  awakening of 368
  benefits of 265
  defined 143, 341, 369, 394, 409
  goal of 400
  how to accomplish 424
  how to practice 427, 430–431, 439, 446, 448, 490
  into selflessness 369, 399, 403, 409, 412–413, 418, 436, 479
  lack of 395, 403
  leads to buddhahood 450
  other terms for 436
  purpose of 475
  requires tranquillity 369
  three progressive stages of 404, 447, 467. *See also* Nondual clarity and emptiness/voidness, three steps in attaining
Instruction for the Wise lii
Instruction of the Gnosis-Guru lxii
Instruction on the Path with Its Result xxxi. *See also* Lam dre
Intention. *See* Right intention *and under* Actions, karmic strength of
Interdependent origination 236, 390, 465, 480, 488
  as antidote to ignorance 384
Intermediate state (*bardo*) 75, 111, 146, 179
Introduction to the Madhyamaka 415
Īshvara 471, 510

Jackson, David lvi, 497–498, 500, 509
Jambhala xxxiv, liii
Jambudvīpa 102, 502
Jamgon Kongtrul Lodro Taye Rinpoche xxxvii
Jampa Namkha Kunzang Tenpay Gyaltsen xliv
Jamyang Gyaltsen 499
Jamyang Khyentse Wangchuk 12

Jamyang Khyentse Wangpo Rinpoche
    xxxvi–xxxvii, xli, xlviii, 498
Jamyang Kunga Sönam Dragpa
    Gyaltsen Päl Zangpo 491
Jamyang Rinchen Dorje 163
Jātaka Tales 166, 189, 220, 330
Je Khenpo lix
Jetsün Chimey Luding liii, lviii
Jetsün Sakya Centre lv–lvi, lviii
Jetsünma Pema Trinlay xlvii
Jewel Treasure of Wise Sayings 400, 509
Jeweled Lamp Sūtra 33, 46
Jñānagarbha 7
Jyekundo Monastery xxxvii, xlviii

Kadam tradition 313
Kagyu tradition 313
    distinction between Six Doctrines of
        Nāropa and mahāmudrā 328
    on true nature of mind 427
Kalu Rinpoche xxvii, liii–lviii
Kamalashīla 362
Kāmarūpa 309
Kangkar Karma Drupgyüd Chökyi
    Sengay xlv
Kangyur xxxvi, 423, 432–433
Karma. *See also* Actions, karmic
        strength of; Appearance, illusory
        and karmic
    collective 167, 179, 198
    defined 70
    gist of 186, 231
    how our deeds follow us into death
        199–200
    how to meditate on 226–229
    individual 198–199
    law of 104, 147, 185
        defined 329
        problem of evil and 230–231
    neutral 200
        defined 223, 225
        transforming into wholesome
            225–226
    ripening of 104, 219, 230–231, 309
    unwholesome/bad 83, 88, 419, 442.
        See also Ten unwholesome
        actions
    defined 186, 200–201, 223

wholesome/good 107, 135. *See also*
        Ten wholesome actions
    defined 186, 211–212, 223
Karmapa, sixteenth xlv, l, lvii
Karmic appearance 198–199
Kāshyapa 432
Katyāyana 94
Kham province xxx, xxxix, xli, l
    Deshung region xxxiii, xxxix
    Ga district xxxvii, xlix, lx, 163
    Lithang district xxxiii, xlii, xliv
Khenchen Samten Lodro xliii, 499
Khenpo Appey Rinpoche xxxix
Khenpo Jamyang Sherab lxii
Khön family xxvii–xxviii, xlvii
    two palaces (Drolma and Puntsog)
        xxx, xlvi
Khorde yerme. *See* Nondifferentiation
        of saṃsāra and nirvāṇa
Khyentse Rinpoche. *See* Dsongsar
        Khyentse Rinpoche II
Khyentse Wangchuk xxxii
King of Concentrations Sūtra 362, 395,
        400, 439
Knowledge Body. *See* Buddhahood,
        bodies of, Body of Reality
Könchog Gyalpo xxviii
Könchog Pelwa (Ratnavardha) 491
Krishnapāda 160
Kublai Khan xxx
Kukuripa 7
Kunga Samdup 491
Kunga Sönam 12
Kunga Yeshe 186
Kunrig xxxix, lxii
Kunsang Nyima xxxv, xliv, xlvi, xlviii–l,
        lvi, lx, lxiii, lxvi, 498

Lam dre. See also Path with Its Result
    as quintessence of Buddha's teachings
        25, 261, 338, 423
    authenticity of 144, 262, 454
    combines exoteric and esoteric xxxiii,
        5, 11, 26, 163, 314
    derived from *Hevajra Tantra* xxxiii, 7
    Deshung Rinpoche III and xlii–xliii,
        xlviii
    eleven special features of 26, 263

Lam dre (cont'd.)
eminent masters of xxxii
lines of transmission xxxii, 28, 445
origin of xxxi–xxxii, 262, 313, 380
profound view of xxxiii, 32. *See also*
Nondifferentiation of saṃsāra
and nirvāṇa
special doctrine of path as result
263, 489
three stages of (three visions/founda-
tional practices, three continua/
advanced practices, and buddha-
hood/the result) 6, 12, 152
translation of term 262
two levels of (fundamental/prelimi-
nary and advanced) 21, 32,
109–110, 185, 269, 322, 346,
380, 408, 454, 466
Lam rim 12, 380. *See also* Gelug tradition
Lama Ganga lvi
Lama Gedün xxxvii, 498
Lama Jamyang Gyaltsen xlii, xlv, 498
Lama Josay Jamyang Gyaltsen xliii
Lama Kälsang Gyaltsen lx, lxii
Lama Kunga. *See* Tartse Kunga
Rinpoche
Lama Lodu lvi
Lama Pema Wangdak lx–lxii, 497
Lama Thubten Yeshe lvi
Langdarma xxxi
Lay precepts, preserving 42
Laziness
as obstacle to concentration 352
four antidotes to 353–354
three kinds of 353–354
Letter from a Friend 84, 89, 94, 96, 98,
101, 106, 119–120, 123, 137–138,
147, 167–168, 180, 210–211
Letter to a Student 97, 112, 114, 137,
153–154
Lhatsa Kargyal 183
Lhündrub Gyatso xxxii, 12
Lineages of Tibetan Buddhism xxx, 6,
28, 56, 159, 313. *See also* Tibetan
Buddhist orders, four
Listening to Dharma
how to strengthen 453, 465

need for 433, 441, 465, 484
not sufficient in itself 139, 150, 333,
339, 360, 379, 431, 450
Living beings
all wish happiness and to avoid pain
237, 296
benefits of recognizing as your parents 307. *See also* Mothers
crucial to attaining enlightenment
238–239, 304
defined 151
Lobsang Lhalungpa liv
Lochema 393, 508–509
Lord Buddha. *See* Shākyamuni
Lord of Death. *See* Yama
Love. *See* Great love
Lozang Jamspal 503
Lü Wangpo Sungwa xxviii
Luding Khen Rinpoche xxxii, liii, lvii
Luminosity (*selwa*) 449, 458, 476. *See*
also Union of luminosity and
emptiness
Lungrik Maway Gonpo Rinchen 492

Machig Labdrön 392, 508
Madhyamaka philosophy xli, 32, 421,
426, 431, 433, 438, 446, 449, 456
Mahākāla xliii–xlv, 165
Mahākāla Tantra 8
Mahākāshyapa Chapter Sūtra 116, 432
Mahāmudrā 12, 261, 328, 436, 456.
See also Kagyu tradition
Mahāsiddha(s). *See* Eighty-Four
Mahāsiddhas; Virūpa
Mahāyāna path 11, 321, 327–328,
337, 484
deep secret of 294
easiest path of all 238–239
esoteric 5, 169, 479
essentials of 359
exoteric 5–6, 169, 249, 477, 479
goal of 408
heart of 468
root of 256
three essentials on (renunciation,
bodhichitta, and insight)
367–368
unique feature of 50

Mahāyāna path (*cont'd.*)
  what to expect on 329
Mahāyāna teachings, three parts of 423
Maitreya xxxiii, 39, 46, 71, 107, 286,
    294, 352, 357, 402, 426
Maitripa 7
Maksorma lxi, 500
Manifestation Body. *See under* Buddha-
    hood, bodies of
Mañjushrī xxviii, xli, 7, 164, 261, 392,
    422, 425
  regarding yourself as 269, 321, 360,
    389, 397, 407, 453, 465, 484
Māra 395, 451, 509
Marpa Lotsawa xxxii, xxxv, 392
Maudgalyāyana 487
McDonald, Sandy and Ariane li
Meditation. *See also* Practice, spiritual
  auspicious place for 47
  consciousnessless 402
  expectations about 473
  five moods of 377–378
  how to accomplish rightly 42, 366,
    378, 386, 403, 457, 473, 476,
    490
  linked to bodhichitta 244
  linked to intention 244
  obstacles to (attachment to inanimate
    objects and other beings) 133
  on emptiness 56, 214, 394, 466–470
  on nothing at all 475
  perfection of 324, 382
  requisites for 46–47
  seven points of correct posture for 47
  tantric 26, 480. *See also* Tantra(s);
    Vajrayāna path
  three levels of (concentration, insight,
    and nondual combination of
    the two) 143
  to develop certitude 480
  two stages of (concentration and
    insight) 235, 249, 280, 329,
    338, 351, 365, 368–369, 382,
    408
Meditative absorption(s) (*dhyāna*) 71,
    122–123, 149, 373, 376, 385, 402,
    450–451, 467, 473, 477–478, 480
Meeting of Parent and Child Sūtra 459

Mental lucidity 353, 371
Mental poisons 58, 111, 127, 185, 223,
    280, 360, 372. *See also* Defilements;
    Obscurations; Passions; *and under*
    individual poisons
  countering of 55
  purification of 229
Mental stagnation (sinking) 352, 356,
    371–372, 376, 385
Mental unruliness (distraction) 352,
    356, 371, 376, 385
Merit
  accumulation of 15, 36, 104, 144,
    214, 249, 304, 334, 381–382,
    408, 412–413, 436, 444, 467,
    484, 503
  purpose of 443
  dedication of 58, 81, 214, 328, 390,
    407–408, 484, 490
  destroyed by anger 40
  sending to others 317–318, 323
  transcendent 214, 381–382, 436, 444
Methods. *See* Skillful means
Mi-nyak xliv–xlv
Milarepa xxxii, xlvi, 150, 392, 473
Mind
  guarding of 62, 221
  how it works 406
  how to meditate on 433, 459
  location of 411, 432–433, 448, 472
  most important to train 300, 307, 368
  no different from dharmakāya 461
  projections/creations of 415, 419–420,
    424, 427, 447–448, 471. *See also*
    Appearances
  search for 472, 476. *See also under* Self
  true nature of xxxiii, 34, 143, 151,
    278–280, 300, 306, 340,
    427, 429–432, 438–439, 446,
    452, 458–459, 470, 472–476.
    See also Recognition of clarity/
    mind/appearances; Ultimate
    reality
  defined 448
  two aspects of (clear and empty) 448,
    455–456, 458, 472–473, 476.
    See also Nondual clarity and
    emptiness/voidness

Mind-Only (Cittamātra) school 340, 415, 421, 431, 439, 447, 449
Mindfulness 61–63, 81, 186, 196, 233, 397, 403, 457, 477, 491
  as antidote to mental stagnation and unruliness 356, 372, 385
  benefits of 306
  defined 354, 401
  reinforces refuge 58
  three stages of 327–328
Miracles of Mañjushrī Chapter Sūtra 395
Monastic discipline. *See* Vīnaya
Moral conduct 8, 56, 148, 157, 219, 355, 443
  defined 307
  perfection of 324, 381–382
  requisite for human birth 146
Mothers. *See also* Great love, four subtopics of
  all beings as 137, 237, 272, 295, 304, 474
  how to help 245, 252, 267, 310–311, 316–317
  how to visualize 240, 250–251, 254, 309, 311–312, 315–318
  kindness of xlvi, 240, 250–251, 267, 273, 304, 309
  responsibility toward xlvii, 267, 315
  seeing your enemies as 246, 268, 274
Mount Sumeru 137, 172, 485, 502
Muchen Sempa Chenbo xxxii

Nāga(s) 102–103, 154, 487
Nāgārjuna 7, 13, 32, 58, 85, 98–99, 103, 110, 123, 205, 209, 298, 340, 381, 392, 399, 426. *See also Letter from a Friend; Precious Garland*
Nairātmyā. *See* Vajranairātmyā
Nālandā Monastery xxxiii, l
Nālandā University xxxiii, 12, 18–19, 40, 160, 259
Namgyal Dorje xxxiv
Nang Sum. See The Three Visions
Nangdzin Wangmo xxxv
Nāropa 7. *See also under* Kagyu tradition
Negativities, six 325
Ngawang Kunga Rinchen xxx, xlvi–xlvii

Ngawang Lodro Nyingpo 163
Ngawang Nyima xxxv–xxxvi, xlvii, liii
  death of xlvii
  Deshung Rinpoche III's first teacher xxxv
  lifelong retreat of xxxv
Ngor Monastery xlvi, liv, 163
Ngorchen Könchog Lhündrub xxxii, xxxv, 13–16, 21, 29, 53, 57–58, 297, 423, 491
Ngorchen Kunga Zangpo xxxii, xxxviii, 4, 32, 57
Niguma 392, 507
Nihilism 439
Nirmāṇakāya. *See under* Buddhahood, bodies of
Nirvāṇa 37, 166, 324, 370, 444
  nonabiding 282, 403
  static 236
Nominality 460
Non-self. *See also* Selflessness
  essence of 392
  meditating on 404
  realization of 402, 414
  two kinds of (personal and phenomenal) 435
Nonapprehension of/nonclinging to clarity and emptiness. *See* Nondual clarity and emptiness/voidness
Nondifferentiation of saṃsāra and nirvāṇa (*khorde yerme*) xxxiii, 12, 32, 322, 436, 446, 456, 489, 498
Nondual appearance and voidness. *See* Nondual emptiness/voidness and appearance
Nondual clarity and emptiness/voidness (*sel-tong sung-jug*) 58, 151, 329, 426, 436, 446, 453–455, 457–458, 463, 467–468, 471, 473, 498
  no different from tathāgatagarbha 461
  three steps in attaining 437–440, 449–451. *See also* Insight, three progressive stages of
Nondual combination of concentration and insight 400, 476–479
  defined 455, 475
Nondual compassion and wisdom 330, 395, 399–400

Nondual emptiness/voidness and appearance 321, 360, 398, 402, 465. *See also* Nondual clarity and emptiness/voidness

Nonexistence of phenomena. *See* Phenomena, conditioned, true nature of

Nonsectarian movement (*rimay*) xxvii, xxx, xxxvii, xli, xlviii, liii, lvi, lxvii

Nonseparation of method and wisdom 468. *See also* Nondual compassion and wisdom

Not-self 200, 279, 405, 409, 414

Nyingma tradition 300, 313, 363
distinction between trek-chö and tö-gäl 328, 504
early relation to Sakya xxviii, xxxiii

Nyugulung xxxii

Object-endowed practices 436

Objectless compassion. *See under* Great compassion

Objectlessness 390, 397–398, 404, 407, 436
defined 408

Obscurations (emotive and cognitive) 465, 467, 479. *See also* Mental poisons
antidote to 467

Obstacles on the path. *See also under* Concentration; Great love; Meditation
creating 220
defined 27
dispelling 32, 49, 63
six 257–258
transforming into attainments 27, 263

Ordination of Nanda Sūtra 146

Padmasambhava xxviii, liii, 37, 499

Palyul Lama Sherab Ozer xli

Pāramitā. *See* Six perfections

Parents. *See* Mothers

Parting from the Four Attachments xxviii, 75, 106, 111, 136–137, 155, 162, 237, 467

Passions 14, 16, 34, 37, 120, 137, 157, 280, 400, 415. *See also* Mental poisons
source of 369

Path of activity 318

Path with Its Result 5, 313, 408, 445. *See also Lam dre*

Patience
as antidote to anger 39
perfection of 324, 381–382

Patrul Rinpoche 107, 131, 502, 507

Pema Chözom xxxiv, xxxviii. *See also* Deshung Rinpoche III, mother of

Perfection of Wisdom Sūtras 463–464

Perfection of Wisdom Verses 394, 468

Perfections. *See* Six perfections

Personal self 415, 418, 435

Personal selflessness/non-self 394, 399–400, 403, 470, 478

Phenomena, conditioned
as creations of mind 421, 425, 429, 431–432, 446
defined 165, 471
impermanence of 105, 161, 168
nonexistence of 425
source of 340
true nature of 17, 25, 75, 151, 235, 249, 382, 460, 465, 483

Phenomena, internal and external. *See* Phenomena, conditioned

Phenomenal self 418, 435

Phenomenal selflessness/non-self 394, 399–400, 403, 415, 471, 478

Posture. *See* Right posture *and under* Meditation

Practice, spiritual. *See also* Meditation
benefits of 337
essential to faith and insight 338
how to strengthen 445
mere semblance of 155, 229–230, 338, 367
nonsessional/in daily life 64, 81, 177–178, 195, 229, 256, 259, 274, 318, 445, 467, 474, 477, 482, 491
procrastination in 170, 172, 178, 228, 339, 352
resistance to 372
three personal stages of (understanding, experience, and realization) 456–457, 459
three reasons for 187

Practice, spiritual (*cont'd.*)
three stages of (preliminary, actual, and concluding) 5, 91
Lam dre stages correspond to 6, 12, 152
Mahāyāna teachings' parts correspond to 423
mindfulness stages correspond to 327–328
refuge stages correspond to 48
steps in committing any deed correspond to 216
three kinds of excellence correspond to 389, 397, 441
three visions correspond to 6
Practitioner(s), spiritual. *See also* Student(s), spiritual
three efforts of (moral conduct, meditation, and insight) 62
three faults that impair 257
three types of 135–136, 153, 162, 169, 192, 261, 366, 490
Prajñāpāramitā xxxi, liii, 11
Pratyekabuddha(s) 208, 370
liberation of 307, 395, 415
motives for taking refuge 50
training of 236
Preceptor(s), defined 14. *See also* Guru(s)
Precious Garland 42, 81, 200, 202–204, 206, 212–213, 324
Preliminary/preparatory meditations or stages of practice. *See* Fundamental meditations/practices
Preliminary practices (*ngön-dro*) xxxv, liv–lv, 28, 163–164, 467
necessary for enlightenment 485
Preta realm
cause of rebirth in 96, 99
how to meditate on 99
life span in 98
three categories in 96–98
Pride 34–35, 190, 217, 257
Progress, spiritual 32
defined 338
how to recognize 368
unique opportunity for 233
Puntsog Drolma xxxv, xlvi

Pupalo 315
Pure vision 14, 17, 185, 329–330, 360, 502
enthusiasm and 69, 175, 264, 485
major topics in 9, 424
of Shākyamuni 489
purpose of 485
Purification 215, 219–220, 403, 417, 449, 461–463. *See also under* Mental poisons; Ten unwholesome actions; Virtue
Purusha 153

Question of Purna Sūtra 464
Question of the Sage Vyasa Sūtra 121

Ratnasambhava 54
Realization of emptiness 15, 22, 25, 51, 162, 214, 342, 364, 401, 403, 467–468. *See also* Wisdom
eradicates erroneous belief in a self 455
prerequisite to enlightenment 427, 466
requires great compassion 26, 399
Realizations (attainments/results/*siddhi*) xlvii, 5, 12, 27, 160, 163–165, 225, 263, 391, 393–394
Realm of desire (*kāmadhātu*) 70, 120, 122, 376, 415, 463, 478, 501
Realm of form (*rūpadhātu*) 71, 122, 415, 421, 463, 478
Realm of formlessness (*arūpadhātu*) 71, 122, 415, 463, 477–478
Rebirth
avoidance of 138, 236, 399, 479
causes of 155, 214, 236, 272, 483
five modes of 112
Recognition of clarity/nature of mind/nature of appearances (*selwa ngo-sung/nang sem*) 58, 404, 437, 446–447, 467. *See also* Nondual clarity and emptiness/voidness, three steps in attaining
Recollection 61–63, 81, 175, 457, 484, 491
defined 354
Reflection. *See* Study *and under* Concentration; Death; Impermanence

Refuge
   benefits of 48, 63–65
   five main features of (motive, object,
      manner, benefits, and instruc-
      tions) 48–49
   four-part formula 52–54, 57
   instructions for taking 49
   manner of taking 48
   object of (Three Jewels) 48, 51
   objects of (guru and Three Jewels)
      54–57
   prayer 53–54
   rejoicing in 63
   sincerity in taking 50, 52–53, 61, 63
   three motives for taking (fear, faith,
      and great compassion) 48, 50
   three stages of 48
   three ways to protect (heedfulness,
      recollection, and mindfulness) 61
   three-part formula 22, 50
   vows of, preserving 445
Renunciation xxviii, 152, 247, 380. See
      Attachment *and under* Impure
      vision
   how to awaken 83, 128, 150, 161, 367
   how to meditate on 139–140
   transcending 451
Resolve to attain enlightenment (*bodhi-
      citta*) xxviii, xxxiii, 9, 141, 156,
      255, 359. See also Bodhichitta
Result stage 5, 26, 263, 461
Results, spiritual. *See* Realizations
Reynolds, John liv
Rhoton, Jared lv, lxix, 497–498, 500,
      503–504
Ri-khu xlv
Right actions 255, 294, 327, 445
Right antidotes 356, 372
Right attitude 110, 144, 152, 233, 307,
      323, 359. See also Bodhichitta
   defined 327, 465, 483
Right concentration 385
Right diligence 354
Right discernment 394
Right discrimination 324, 341
Right efforts 151, 153, 157, 159, 161–
      162, 197, 211, 233, 248, 285, 289,
      338, 356, 392, 400, 460, 483. See

also Practice, spiritual
Right experience 417
Right insight 368, 394, 465, 481
Right intention 323, 327, 397–398.
      See also Bodhichitta
Right investigation 409
Right livelihood 81
Right meditation 42, 353, 355, 357,
      401, 466–467. *See also* Meditation,
      how to accomplish rightly
Right methods 210, 402, 437, 473. *See
      also* Skillful means
Right motivation 42, 93. *See also* Great
      compassion *and under* Bodhisattva(s)
Right perception 394
Right posture 369–370
Right practice 25, 48, 107, 116, 118,
      143, 150, 152, 154, 161, 169,
      330, 354–355, 385, 390, 443
Right realization 466
Right reflection 355
Right understanding 45, 104, 336,
      401, 459, 466
   defined 368
Right view 323, 328, 368, 390, 394,
      401, 435, 481
Right vision 368, 445
Rinchen Tsering xlix, lx–lxi
Robertson, Judy 499
Root of saṃsāra and nirvāṇa xxxiii, 340.
      See also Mind, true nature of; Non-
      dual clarity and emptiness/voidness
Rūpakāya. *See under* Buddhahood,
      bodies of

Sachen Kunga Nyingpo xxviii–xxix, xxxii,
      3, 22, 31, 57, 499
Sage's Intent lviii
Sakya
   canon xxviii, xlii, lv, 7
   authenticity of 8
   first patriarch, quoted 479
   history of xxvii–xxxi
   Monastery xxviii
   Ngor school of xxxviii, lvii, 313
   practitioner, defined 437, 450, 456–
      457, 471
   principality of xxx

tradition of 313
 distinction between three visions
  and three continua 328
 Lam dre preeminent in 408
 view of the ultimate 340, 437,
  446, 456. *See also* Nondifferentiation of saṃsāra and
  nirvāṇa; Ultimate reality
Tsar school of xxxii, xlviii, lvii, 313
Sakya Kabum lv, lvii
Sakya Pandita xxix–xxx, xxxvii–xxxviii,
 xlv, liii, lviii, 164–165, 258, 370,
 400–401, 437, 463, 468, 503
 great compassion of 275
 no different from Shākyamuni lxii
 on ultimate reality 425, 459–460
Sakya Tegchen Chöling liv, lvi, lviii, lxiii
Sakya Trizin, fortieth (Ngawang Thutop
 Wangchuk) xxx, xlvi
Sakya Trizin, forty-first (Ngawang Kunga)
 xxx, xxxii, xlvi, liii, lv, lvii, lxiii,
 lxx, 457
Sakya Trizin, thirty-ninth (Dragshul
 Trinlay Rinchen) xxxviii, xlvii
Sakya, Minzu li, lviii
Samādhi xlvii, lxii
Samantabhadra lix, lxii, 490
Sambhogakāya. *See under* Buddhahood,
 bodies of
Sameness of self and others 296
 as antidote to jealousy 384
 how to justify 297–298
 how to meditate on 299–300
Saṃputa Tantra 28, 445
Saṃsāra 229–230, 252, 283, 315, 403,
 413, 478. *See also* Existence,
 worldly/conditioned
 defined 424
 liberation from 324, 400, 427, 444
 or elaboration 460
 reason for 319, 427
 suffering of 49, 279–280, 305
 wheel of 64, 433
Saṃvara Tantra xxxi
Samye xxviii, l
Sangay Rinchen 491
Sangha 477. *See also* Three Jewels
 as an object of refuge 51, 55

Sapan. *See* Sakya Pandita
Saraha 395, 399, 427
Sarasvatī 392
Sarasvatī Grammar lix
Sautrāntika school 421
Sel sing-ewa (luminous/clear light) 458
Sel-tong sung-jug. *See* Nondual clarity
 and emptiness/voidness
Self
 and other, dichotomy of 279–280,
  306, 409, 419. *See also* Subject-
  object dichotomy
 erroneous belief in 16, 235, 259,
  265–266, 271–274, 278–280,
  296, 317, 342, 369, 414, 418,
  462, 469–470
 causes rebirth 272
 how to uproot 281, 415
 root of all suffering 278–280, 295,
  306, 311, 404, 409, 455
 two kinds of (personal and phenomenal) 415
 search for 405, 409, 412–413, 470
 not a person's name 311, 406,
  409, 418
 not consciousness 311, 406, 410–
  412, 418
 not the body 311, 406, 410, 418
 ultimate (*ātman*) 340, 404
Self-centeredness 253, 278, 296–297,
 305, 311, 334
Self-cherishing attitude 49
Self-deception 157, 179, 442
Self-doubt. *See* Doubt(s), of gods
Self-indulgence 469
Self-liberation. *See* Arhat(s), liberation of
Self-nature 418–419
Selfishness 265, 285, 296, 335
 leads to rebirth in lower realms 305
 results only in suffering 294–295,
  306
 three steps in transforming 296
Selflessness 123, 257, 329. *See also*
 Non-self *and under* Insight
 concept of 412
 leads to rebirth in higher realms 305
 meditating on 404
 objections to 405

Selflessness (cont'd.)
  realization of 392, 395, 419
  remedy for suffering 403
  two kinds of (personal and phenome-
    nal) 400, 408
Sentient beings. See Living beings
Serenity 346, 348–349, 361
Shakra 105–106
Shākyamuni (the historical Buddha)
    xxxiii, xxxviii, 3, 7, 14, 392, 463
  answers refuge prayers 64
  as an object of refuge liii, 51
  body of 167
  death of 166
  definitions of concentration and
    insight 341
  diligence of 35
  earlier lives 220, 309
  eighty-four thousand teachings and
    55, 321, 423
  enlightenment of 11, 149
  Four Noble Truths and 37, 49
  life of 39
  on death 191, 199
  on desire 131
  on how to meditate 477
  on impermanence 105, 161
  on life spans in hell realms 79
  on monastic status 219
  on phenomena as creations of mind
    419
  on rarity of human birth 146
  on sufferings of human realm 112,
    116
  on true nature of mind 431, 433
  on ultimate reality 459, 464
  on worldly existence 72
  qualities of 38, 51, 56, 59, 148, 290,
    308, 485–489
  regarding your teacher as 269, 321,
    360, 389, 397, 407, 453, 465,
    484
  source of Lam dre 144
  taught tantras as well as sūtras xxxi,
    14, 21, 25
  true nature of 463
Shākyashrī xxix
Shamatha (śamatha). See Concentration

Shāntarakshita xxviii
Shāntibhadra (Shāntipa) xxxi, 393–394
Shāntideva 43, 46, 133, 153, 155–156,
    168, 187, 193, 209, 214, 240, 272,
    296, 303, 305, 323, 348–349, 355,
    401, 403–404, 420, 431, 433, 467.
    See also Bodhicharyāvatara
Shejama xxxvii, 164
Shi-nay. See Concentration
Shigatse xlvi–xlvii
Shrāvaka(s) 395, 468
Shrī Sambhava 41, 46
Shrīmatī 41, 46, 392
Siddhi. See Realizations
Sincerity
  inspiration for 161, 178
  need for 176, 457
Sinking. See Mental stagnation.
Situ Rinpoche, eleventh Pälpung (Pema
    Wangchok Gyalpo) xliii, xlv, 499
Six perfections (pāramitā) 5, 18, 34,
    143–144, 169, 234, 236, 308,
    314, 330, 335, 381–382, 394,
    412, 436. See also individual per-
    fections and under Bodhisattva(s)
  defined 324
  foundation for tantric practices 322,
    481
  four qualities friendly to 325
  individual benefits of each 325
  seven attachments hostile to 325
Six realms of existence. See under
    Existence, worldly/conditioned
Skillful means (upāya) 290, 296, 325,
    331, 333, 403–404
Smith, Gene liv
Sogyal Rinpoche lx
Solitude
  needed for concentration 348, 351,
    362
  needed for meditation on emptiness
    468
  three kinds of (body, voice, and mind)
    342, 362
Sönam Tsemo xxviii
Song of the Names of Mañjushrī xli
Songs of Milarepa xxxv
Source of Jewels xliii

Spiritual maturity 192, 322, 457
  bringing others to 16, 323, 325, 330,
      333, 335, 491. *See also* Skillful
      means
  bringing yourself to 323, 330
Stages of Meditation 362
Stations of Mindfulness of the True Dharma
      Sūtra 70, 96, 122, 134
Sthiramati 259
Student(s), spiritual. *See also* Practitioner(s),
      spiritual
  defined 57
  qualifications of 8–9
  responsibilities of 29, 41, 228, 338, 380
Study
  benefits of 321, 345–346
  defined 307
  need for 466
  not sufficient in itself 434, 466
  right attitude toward 359–360
Subhūti 464
Subject–object dichotomy 14, 17, 151,
      198, 425–426, 472. *See also* Self,
      and other, dichotomy of
Sucasitā 392
Suchness. *See* Ultimate reality
Sudhana 41
Suffering. *See also* Four Noble Truths;
      Unhappiness; *and under* Saṃsāra
  antidote to 162
  extrication from 132
  of the hells, hard to credit 71, 116
  source of 204, 208, 274
  three kinds of 72–73, 75, 127, 137,
      270, 443
    suffering of change/impermanence
        72, 105–106
    suffering of conditioned existence 73,
        128
      due to ceaseless human activities
          129–130
      due to inability to renounce birth
          and death 137–141
      due to never being satisfied by
          objects of desire 131–134
      three manifestations of 129
    suffering of suffering/sheer pain
        72, 75–76, 105

Sugatahood 485
Sukhāvatī li, 165, 423, 486
Summary of the Path with Its Result 31
Sūtra(s) xxxiii, 6. *See also individual titles*
  authenticity of 21
  counter hatred 55
  on conventional and ultimate reality
      454
  on death 190–191
  on defilements 369
  on dreaming and waking 422
  on hell realms 84
  on repaying your mother's kindness 255
  on search for self 412
  on wisdom 436, 444
  quoted/cited 33, 208, 362, 415, 468,
      476–477, 487

Tales of the Wise and the Foolish 309
Tangtong Gyalpo xlvii
Tantra(s). *See also* Causal stage; Result
      stage; Meditation, tantric; Vajra-
      yāna path; *and under individual*
      titles
  anuttarayoga xxxii
  authenticity of 21
  counter mental poisons 55
  history of in Tibet xxviii
  kinds of xxxi
  location of mind and 300
  major xxxi, 8
  methods of, compared to sūtras 5, 11,
      363, 365–366, 479, 485
  secret 28
  triple xxxi–xxxii
  twin processes of 32
  Virūpa's practice of 18
  vows of, preserving 42, 445
Tārā xxxiii, xl, xlviii, liii, 392
Tarik Tulku lvii, lix–lx, lxii
Tarlam Monastery xxxiv–xxxvii, xxxix–xl,
      xliii–xlv, xlvii–xlviii
  reestablished in Nepal xxxv, lvi–lvii,
      lix, lxiii
Tarthang Tulku liv
Tartse Kunga Rinpoche liii–liv, lvi, lviii
Tartse Shabdrung Rinpoche xliv
Tashi Gyaltsen Päl Zangpo 491

Tathāgatagarbha 461, 510
Teacher(s), spiritual. *See also* Guru(s)
  as embodiment of Three Jewels 51–
    52, 54–55
  qualifications of 8
  responsibilities of 29
  three ways to show respect for 3, 61
Teaching(s), spiritual. *See also* Dharma
  authenticity of 6–8, 28, 159, 261
  purpose of 156
Ten auspicious conditions 148. *See also*
    Eighteen favorable/requisite condi-
    tions
Ten Tathāgatas 54
Ten unwholesome actions 37, 145,
    201–204. *See also* Karma
  how to meditate on 209–210
  purification of 210
  renunciation of 207–210
  results of, threefold
    fully ripened result 204
    owner's result 206–207
    results similar to their causes
      204–206
Ten wholesome actions 62, 145, 212. *See
    also* Karma
  cultivation of 214–221
  results of, threefold
    fully ripened result 212–213
    owner's result 213–214
    results similar to their causes 213
Tenzin Choepel Lama lxiii
The Three Continua (*Gyu Sum*) 13, 314,
    446, 492
  corresponds to advanced practices 6,
    21, 61, 110, 269, 479
  table of contents of 479–480
The Three Visions (*Nang Sum*) xxxii, xxxv,
    9, 368, 399, 446, 451, 468, 481
  as a whole 247–249
  as introduction to *Lam dre* 417
  corresponds to fundamental practices
    6, 21, 61, 109, 160, 263, 269,
    313, 346, 380, 408, 435, 479
  Deshung Rinpoche III's teaching of
    lv–lvi
  designed for beginners and masters 491
  how traditionally studied 3–4

on recognition of clarity/mind/
    appearances 404
  origin of 12–13
  part of tantric system 51
  preliminary verses 13–16, 18–21, 23
  quoted 402, 458
Thirteen Golden Dharmas xlviii
Thought-constructions 451, 460, 463,
    475–476, 489. *See also* Mind
Thousand-Armed Chenresi liv
Three Doors (body, speech, and mind)
    62, 318–319
Three faults. *See under* Practitioner(s),
    spiritual
Three higher realms 105. *See also* Human
    realm; Asura realm; Gods' realm
  how to meditate on 124
Three Jewels 22, 48, 53, 148, 203
  as the object of refuge 51
  how to show respect for 64
  reliance on 64
  why so called 37
Three levels/stages of spiritual perception.
    See Three visions
Three lower realms 76, 204. *See also* Hell
    realms; Preta realm; Animal realm
Three poisons. *See* Mental poisons
Three visions 6, 14, 69, 314, 380. *See
    also* Impure vision; Vision of expe-
    rience/the path; Pure vision; *The
    Three Visions*
  all other Buddhist teachings can be
    related to 249
Thubten Jigme Norbu lii
Tibetan Buddhist orders, four xxxi,
    xxxvii, xli, xlv, lii, 391. *See also
    individual traditions*
  alike in all essential respects 136, 143–
    144, 169, 249, 261, 313, 345,
    380, 423
  all equally profound 32, 159–160,
    170, 346, 392
  differences among 313, 446
  Indian teachers venerated by 7
  names for buddhahood 12
  names for fundamental and advanced
    practices 328
  names for ultimate reality 446, 456

Titans. *See* Asura realm

Tog-tsepa 393–394

Trabin, Tom liv

Tranquillity 343, 346, 357–358, 361, 368. *See also* Concentration
defined 133
how to attain 134

Transcendent gnosis. *See* Wisdom, transcendent

Transcendent merit. *See under* Merit

Transcendent virtues. *See* Six perfections

Transference of consciousness (*phowa*) xxxi, xlvii, 108

Transformation Body. *See under* Buddhahood, bodies of

Treasure of Knowledge and Reasoning xxxvii, 425

Treatise on Valid Sources of Knowledge 280

Triple Gem. *See* Three Jewels

Truths, two (conventional and ultimate) 160, 455

Tsang province xxviii

Tsarchen Lösal Gyatso xxxii, 446, 510

Tsechu Rinpoche lix

Tushita xxxiv, 86, 107–108, 288, 426

Udraka 400–401

Ultimate reality. *See also* Realization of emptiness; Nondual clarity and emptiness/voidness; Conventional reality
approximation of 390, 398, 407, 441, 453, 465, 483
attuning yourself to 321
cognition of 143
defined 198, 235, 249, 360
empty aspect of mind and 455
experience of 439, 457
hindrances not different from 489
nature of 459–460, 467, 481–482
no beings exist in 266, 271–272, 328, 405, 426, 432, 463
other terms for 439
perfection of wisdom and 324
pure vision and 14
realization of emptiness and 25
taught on conventional level 450
view of 32, 327, 436

Unhappiness. *See also* Suffering
childish folk and 347
endless 367, 455
examples of 72
how to end 46
in the future, how to avoid 208–209
in the present, appreciating 231
source of in wrong views 204, 271, 306
wish to remove for all beings 234, 236, 248. *See also* Great compassion

Union of luminosity and emptiness xxxiii. *See also* Nondual clarity and emptiness/voidness

Ushnisha. *See* Cranial protuberance

Uttarakuru 102, 442, 502

Vaibhāshika school 421

Vairochana 47, 54

Vajra Flag Sūtra 215

Vajra Tent of the Ḍākiṇī Tantra 28, 445, 501

Vajra Verses on the Path with Its Result 28, 70, 144, 501

Vajradhara 144, 160, 380, 445, 454, 465, 507

Vajrakīlaya xlvi–xlvii, 499

Vajranairātmyā 7, 19, 262, 269, 322, 380, 392, 454
no different from Hevajra 313

Vajrapāṇi 7, 261, 432, 461

Vajrasattva liii, 459

Vajrayāna path 5, 11, 169, 314, 322
how to meditate on 481

Vajrayoginī xlvii, lii, lxii, 461

Vajrayoginī Tantra 7

Valid authority, four kinds of 28. *See also* Authenticities, four

Vārānasī (Benares) 20

Vararuchi 8

Vasubandhu xxix, 198, 259, 425, 443

Videha 102, 502

View of the ultimate, including the result 32. *See also under* Sakya, tradition of

Vigor. *See* Diligence

Vijayā 392

Vikramashīla Monastery xxxi

Vimalakīrti 7
Vinaya xxxi, xxxvii, 18, 200, 209, 215
  counters attachment 55
Vipashyanā (*vipaśyanā*). *See* Insight
Vīravajra xxxi
Virūpa xxxi, 3, 7, 12, 15, 22, 70, 144,
    165, 346, 361–362, 423, 465
  Lam dre and 25, 31, 144, 160, 262,
      269, 313, 322, 380, 445, 454
  life of 18–20
  tantric teachings and 28, 501
Virtue 353, 359, 367, 398, 436. *See
    also* Merit
  accumulation of 62, 107, 131, 188,
      398
  karmic results of 228
  purification of 483
Virtues, transcendent. *See* Six perfections
Vision of experience/the path 14, 16,
    185, 233, 329–330
  bodhichitta and 69, 175, 263
  major topics in 9, 234, 248, 417
Vision of the buddhas. *See* Pure vision
Vital airs 376, 480
Voidness (*śūnyatā*) 466. *See also*
  Emptiness

Wei Chi Huang, Dr. lviii
White Tārā xliv–xlv, xlvii, lii
Wisdom. *See also* Insight
  accumulation of 15, 144, 381, 408,
      412, 444, 467
    purpose of 444
  applying too much 476–477
  defined 436
  how to increase 360
  perfection of 324, 382, 412, 436, 444
  transcendent xl, 15, 21, 53, 57–58,
      144, 325, 381–382, 444, 461,
      488–489. *See also* Buddhahood,
      bodies of
Women eminent in Buddhism xlvii, liii,
    392–393, 507–509
Wrong views 16, 123, 147–148, 163,
    203–205, 216, 220, 455. *See also*
    Self, erroneous belief in
Wylie, Turrell li–lii

Yaksha(s) 154, 487
Yama (Lord of Death) 115, 166
Yamāntaka xliii
Yidam(s) 64. *See also* Maksorma

Zeal. *See* Enthusiasm

THE VIKRAMAŚĪLA FOUNDATION

THE VIKRAMAŚĪLA FOUNDATION is a non-profit organization for religious, educational, and scientific purposes. Under the patronage of His Holiness Sakya Trizin, the head of the Sakya order of Tibetan Buddhism, the Foundation was founded in 1989 in New York City and Fair Lawn, New Jersey, by the Venerable Lama Pema Wangdak.

Based on the teachings of the Sakya school, the Foundation seeks to provide the wisdom of the East here in the West through Buddhist and educational centers, meetings and conventions, special religious and social services, literary publications, and introductory and higher Tibetan Buddhist studies and meditative practices.

The affiliates of Vikramaśīla Foundation are the Palden Sakya centers of Woodstock, Buffalo, and New York City, New York. The Foundation can be contacted at:

13-04 EASTERN DRIVE
FAIR LAWN, NEW JERSEY 07410-2302

or

P. O. BOX 1603 CATHEDRAL STATION
NEW YORK, NEW YORK 10025-1603

THE SAPAN FUND

THE SAPAN FUND was founded in 1991 to further the publication of Tibetan Buddhist texts in translation, particularly of the Sakya Tradition. The Sapan Fund is a special project of the Melia Foundation, a non-profit organization that promotes the cross-fertilization of different psychological schools.

Our aim is to help preserve important Buddhist texts and teachings by publishing the works of heretofore neglected scholars and practitioners whom the Tibetans themselves hold in high esteem, such as Sakya Pandita, Gorampa Sönam Sengay, the Venerable Deshung Rinpoche, and Hiroshi Sonami (Sönam Gyatso).

For more information about our archiving and publishing projects, please contact:

Michael Roche
2305B Prince Street
Berkeley, California 94705

Thank you very much.

WISDOM PUBLICATIONS

WISDOM PUBLICATIONS is a non-profit publisher of books on Buddhism, Tibet, and related East-West themes. Our titles are published in appreciation of Buddhism as a living philosophy and with the special commitment to preserve and transmit important works from all the major Buddhist traditions.

If you would like more information, or a copy of our mail order catalogue, and to keep informed about our future publications, please write or call us.

WISDOM PUBLICATIONS
361 Newbury Street
Boston, Massachusetts, 02115
USA
Telephone: (617) 536-3358. Fax: (617) 536-1897.

THE WISDOM TRUST

As a non-profit publisher, Wisdom is dedicated to the publication of fine Dharma books for the benefit of all sentient beings. We depend upon sponsors in order to publish books like the one you are holding in your hand.

If you would like to make a donation to the Wisdom Trust Fund to help us continue our Dharma work, or to receive information about opportunities for planned giving, please write to our Boston office.

Thank you so much.

Wisdom is a non-profit, charitable 501(c)(3) organization and a part of the Foundation for the Preservation of the Mahayana Tradition (FPMT).

CARE OF DHARMA BOOKS

DHARMA BOOKS CONTAIN the teachings of the Buddha; they have the power to protect against lower rebirth and to point the way to liberation. Therefore, they should be treated with respect—kept off the floor and places where people sit or walk—and not stepped over. They should be covered or protected for transporting and kept in a high, clean place separate from more "mundane" materials. Other objects should not be placed on top of Dharma books and materials. Licking the fingers to turn pages is considered bad form (and negative karma). If it is necessary to dispose of Dharma materials, they should be burned rather than thrown in the trash. When burning Dharma texts, it is considered skillful to first recite a prayer or mantra, such as OM, AH, HUNG. Then, you can visualize the letters of the texts (to be burned) absorbing into the AH, and the AH absorbing into you. After that, you can burn the texts.

These considerations may also be kept in mind for Dharma artwork, as well as the written teachings and artwork of other religions.